Principles and Applications of Business Intelligence Research

Richard G. Herschel
Saint Joseph's University, USA

BUSINESS SCIENCE
Reference

Managing Director:	Lindsay Johnston
Editorial Director:	Joel Gamon
Book Production Manager:	Jennifer Romanchak
Publishing Systems Analyst:	Adrienne Freeland
Assistant Acquisitions Editor:	Kayla Wolfe
Typesetter:	Nicole Sparano
Cover Design:	Nick Newcomer

Published in the United States of America by
Business Science Reference (an imprint of IGI Global)
701 E. Chocolate Avenue
Hershey PA 17033
Tel: 717-533-8845
Fax: 717-533-8661
E-mail: cust@igi-global.com
Web site: http://www.igi-global.com

Library of Congress Cataloging-in-Publication Data

Principles and applications of business intelligence research / Richard Herschel, editor.
    p. cm.
  Includes bibliographical references and index.
  Summary: "This book provides the latest ideas and research on advancing the understanding and implementation of business intelligence within organizations"--Provided by publisher.
  ISBN 978-1-4666-2650-8 (hbk.) -- ISBN 978-1-4666-2681-2 (ebook) -- ISBN 978-1-4666-2712-3 (print & perpetual access)
1. Business intelligence. I. Herschel, Richard T.
 HD38.7.P745 2013
 658.4'72--dc23
                        2012029158

British Cataloguing in Publication Data
A Cataloguing in Publication record for this book is available from the British Library.

The views expressed in this book are those of the authors, but not necessarily of the publisher.

Table of Contents

Section 1
Organizational Issues

W. O. Dale Amburgey, Saint Joseph's University, USA
John C. Yi, Saint Joseph's University, USA

Françoise Bousquet, ZFIB Conseil, France
Vladislav V. Fomin, Vytautas Magnus University, Lithuania; Turiba School of Business
*   Administration, Latvia*
Dominique Drillon, La Rochelle Business School, France

Irina Dymarsky, Purdue Pharma, USA

Joseph Morabito, Stevens Institute of Technology, USA
Edward A. Stohr, Stevens Institute of Technology, USA
Yegin Genc, Stevens Institute of Technology, USA

Daniel O'Neill, Avon Products Inc., USA

**Section 3
Technology Issues**

Detailed Table of Contents

Section 1
Organizational Issues

Chapter 1

W. O. Dale Amburgey, Saint Joseph's University, USA
John C. Yi, Saint Joseph's University, USA

Higher education often lags behind industry in the adoption of new or emerging technologies. As competition increases among colleges and universities for a diminishing supply of prospective students, the need to adopt the principles of business intelligence becomes increasingly more important. Data from first-year enrolling students for the 2006-2008 fall terms at a private, master's-level institution in the northeastern United States was analyzed for the purpose of developing predictive models. A decision tree analysis, a neural network analysis, and a multiple regression analysis were conducted to predict each student's grade point average (GPA) at the end of the first year of academic study. Numerous geodemographic variables were analyzed to develop the models to predict the target variable. The overall performance of the models developed in the analysis was evaluated by using the average square error (ASE). The three models had similar ASE values, which indicated that any of the models could be used for the intended purpose. Suggestions for future analysis include expansion of the scope of the study to include more student-centric variables and to evaluate GPA at other student levels.

Chapter 2

Françoise Bousquet, ZFIB Conseil, France
Vladislav V. Fomin, Vytautas Magnus University, Lithuania; Turiba School of Business
*   Administration, Latvia*
Dominique Drillon, La Rochelle Business School, France

More and more companies operate today in a worldwide market under conditions of globalization, increased complexity, and competition. In such an environment, business decisions need to be made quickly yet intelligent, substantiated by the most salient and relevant information available. Under the global competition, with a diligent and measured manner, many companies are increasingly treating business like an economic war. Enterprises are methodically monitoring and investigating their competitors, while deploying all the resources they have at their disposal in order to beat their current or future rivals. Competitive Intelligence (CI) has become the 'latest weapon in the world war of economics'. This paper contributes to the growing body of literature on competitive intelligence by synthesizing knowledge stemming from many years of experience in the standardization arena. The authors aim to show how, in the economic war, engaging in committee-based standards development may be used for winning the competition battle.

Although Gartner's EXP 2006 CIO Survey ranked Business Intelligence (BI) as the top technology priority, BI projects face tough competition from other projects in IT portfolios promising more tangible financial returns (Wu & Weitzman, 2006) Two major hurdles that prevent BI projects from shining in portfolios are vague requirements and weak benefits calculations. Both can be addressed by examining and learning from a number of case studies that prove tangible ROI on BI solutions when scoped and designed with a focus on specific, measurable, achievable, results-oriented, and time bound SMART business goals. In order for BI projects to compete in IT portfolios based on financial measures, like ROI, BI champions need to approach BI requirements gathering with the goal of addressing a specific business problem as well as employ standard ways of calculating BI benefits post project go live. By examining common failures with BI requirements and case studies which demonstrate how successful BI implementations translate into tangible benefits for the organization, BI champions develop a toolkit of tips, tricks, and lessons learned for successful requirements gathering, design, implementation, and measure of business results on BI initiatives.

This paper examines the key issues associated with current and future implementations of business intelligence (BI). The authors review the literature and discover both the growing importance and emerging issues associated with BI. The issues are further examined with an exploratory, but detailed, case study of organizations from a variety of industries, yielding a series of lessons learned. The authors find that organizations are rapidly moving to an enterprise perspective on BI, but in an unsystematic way. The authors present a prescription for the future of BI called "enterprise intelligence" (EI). EI is described in a framework that combines elements of hierarchy theory, organization modeling, and intellectual capital.

Enterprises today continue to invest in business intelligence (BI) initiatives with the hope of providing a strategic advantage to their organizations. Many of these initiatives are supporting the tactical goals of individual business units and not the strategic goals of the enterprise. Although this decentralized approach provides short term gains, it creates an environment where information silos develop and the enterprise as a whole struggles to develop a single version of the truth when it comes to providing strategic information. Enterprises are turning toward a centralized approach to BI which aligns with their overall strategic goals. At the core of the centralized approach is the business intelligence competency center (BICC). This paper details why the centralized BICC approach should be considered an essential component of all enterprise BI initiatives. Examining case studies of BICC implementations details the benefits realized by real world companies who have taken this approach. It is also important to provide analysis of the two BI approaches in the areas of BI process and BI technology/data and people relations. The findings indicate the benefits of the centralized BICC outweigh the deficiencies of the decentralized approach.

This paper addresses where BI developers have failed to create applications suited for the common end-user and provide a conceptual roadmap to address these shortfalls. It is argued that BI's impact on analyses and decision-making depends on the development of less complex applications. Research conducted for this paper finds that BI lacks a commo n definition and standard, that BI tools are too complex for the common user, and that a shortage of analytical literacy relevant to BI among business professionals is a barrier to BI adoption. The paper suggests that until BI analysis tools become more "human-centric, design-oriented" and less from a "technology-centric, engineering-oriented perspective", BI will continue to fail in its objective to routinely improve business decision-making.

The online word-of-mouth behavior that exists today in the Web represents new and measurable sources of information. The automated discovery or mining of consumer opinions from these sources is of great importance for marketing intelligence and product benchmarking. Techniques are now being developed to effectively and easily mine the consumer opinions from the Web data and to timely deliver them to companies and individual consumers. This study investigates this emerging field named 'opinion mining' in terms of what it is, what it can do, and how it could be used effectively for business intelligence (BI). A rigorous review of the research literature on opinion mining is conducted to explore its current state, issues and challenges for its use in developing business applications for competitive advantage. The study aims to assist business managers to better understand the current opportunities and challenges in using opinion mining for deriving BI. Future research directions for further development of the field are also identified.

The world's largest aircraft manufacturers like Boeing and Airbus have traditionally been dominant in the commercial aerospace industry, but due to the rise of several smaller commercial aircraft companies and in spite of air travel increasing each year, it will be paramount for Boeing and Airbus to thoroughly understand past and current market conditions and be able to combine their understanding with the proper analytical tools to anticipate the market demands of the future if they are to remain the world leaders in their industry. This paper presents a discussion of industry factors such as airline routes, past passenger demands in different regions of the world and the sizes and types of aircraft that were required to support those demands, and more importantly, how analysis of that information is integral to the projection of future demands within the commercial aerospace market which will facilitate Boeing and Airbus positioning themselves to provide their airline customers with the right product at the right time.

Performance management is tied to external forces and stakeholders whose assessment of performance is more focused on societal outcomes than purely financial outcomes. Government, corporate, and even personal performance measurement should take into account societal indicators that link these disparate yet intertwined spheres of influence. New initiatives in both government and commercial sectors are bringing greater understanding of how societal indicators can measure performance. This paper highlights how societal indicators are used to measure performance in corporate and government sectors. Corporate societal indicators are explored primarily though literary research. Government societal indicators are explored through an examination of the EPA and Superfund program. The paper demonstrates that there is synergy between corporate, government, and personal government performance measures and how business intelligence tools are making these relationships more transparent.

The implementation of BI into the business strategy and culture is laden with many potential points that could result in failure of the initiative, leaving BI to be underdeveloped and a source of wasted resources for the company. Due to the unique nature of BI in the business space, properly setting up BI within the organizational structure from the onset of integration minimizes the impact of the most common hurdles to BI implementation. Many companies choose to mitigate these problems by using a centralized approach by building a Center of Excellence, but their place in the company's organizational structure needs to be well-defined and properly empowered to be effective. This paper also reviews how the concept of centralization is defined, how it relates to the implementation of BI, and how it can effectively in overcome the common implementation hurdles.

During the recent recession the number of jobs lost has been widely publicized. However, lurking among this obvious and simple metric of how human capital is involved in the workforce, there is the need to analyze and predict future talent. As economic conditions are slow to improve, decisions to simply cut the traditional costs, benefits, compensation and headcount are no longer enough. Companies have already started using business intelligence (BI) to transform and maximize the potential of their human capital. The use of human capital based business intelligence (BI) has increasingly become one of the vital strategic components for world-class companies. This paper will focus on why companies should use analytics (a subset of Business Intelligence (BI)) to transform and maximize the potential of their human capital.

Section 2
Analytic Issues

Chapter 12

Lakshmi S. Iyer, The University of North Carolina at Greensboro, USA

Rajeshwari M. Raman, Market America, USA

Organizations use web analytic tools and technologies to measure, collect, analyze, and report web usage data to help optimize websites. Traditionally, most of this data tends to be non-transactional and non-identifiable. In this regard, there has not been much integration with transactional data that is collected, stored, analyzed, and reported through Business Intelligence (BI). Emerging trends in web analytics provide organizations the ability to aggregate and analyze web analytics data with transactional data to provide valuable insights for building better customer relationship strategies. In this paper, the authors give an overview of web analytics tools, key players, new technology trends and capabilities to integrate web analytics with BI so organizations can leverage intelligent analytics for new marketing initiatives. While the benefits are significant, there are some challenges associated with the integration and a few possible solutions to address.

Chapter 13

José Antonio Robles-Flores, ESAN University, Peru

Gregory Schymik, Arizona State University, USA

Julie Smith-David, Arizona State University, USA

Robert St. Louis, Arizona State University, USA

Web search engines typically retrieve a large number of web pages and overload business analysts with irrelevant information. One approach that has been proposed for overcoming some of these problems is automated Question Answering (QA). This paper describes a case study that was designed to determine the efficacy of QA systems for generating answers to original, fusion, list questions (questions that have not previously been asked and answered, questions for which the answer cannot be found on a single web site, and questions for which the answer is a list of items). Results indicate that QA algorithms are not very good at producing complete answer lists and that searchers are not very good at constructing answer lists from snippets. These findings indicate a need for QA research to focus on crowd sourcing answer lists and improving output format.

Section 3
Technology Issues

Chapter 14

Sam Schutte, Unstoppable Software, Inc., USA

Thilini Ariyachandra, Xavier University, USA

Mark Frolick, Xavier University, USA

Test-driven development is a software development methodology that has recently gained a great deal of traction in the software development community. It focuses on creating software-based test cases that define the business requirements of an application before beginning the coding of the application itself.

This paper proposes that test-driven development could be a useful methodology for data warehouse projects, in that it could help team members avoid some of the major pitfalls of data warehousing, and result in a higher-quality end product.

Nenad Jukic, Loyola University Chicago, USA

Svetlozar Nestorov, University of Chicago, USA

Miguel Velasco, University of Minnesota, USA

Jami Eddington, Oklahoma State University, USA

Association rules mining is one of the most successfully applied data mining methods in today's business settings (e.g. Amazon or Netflix recommendations to customers). Qualified association rules mining is an extension of the association rules data mining method, that uncovers previously unknown correlations that only manifest themselves under certain circumstances (e.g. on a particular day of the week), with the goal of improving action results, e.g. turning an underperforming campaign (spread too thin over the entire audience) into a highly targeted campaign that delivers results. Such correlations have not been easily reachable using standard data mining tools so far. This paper describes the method for straightforward discovery of qualified association rules and demonstrates the use of qualified association rules mining on an actual corporate data set. The data set is a subset of a corporate data warehouse for Sam's Club, a division of Wal-Mart Stores, INC. The experiments described in this paper illustrate how qualified association rules supplement standard association rules data mining methods and provide additional information which can be used to better target corporate actions.

Adam Hill, The Nielsen Company, USA

Thilini Ariyachandra, Xavier University, USA

Mark Frolick, Xavier University, USA

Demand for business intelligence solutions continues to grow in the industry at record rates to combat competitive pressures and to attain business agility. Still organizations continue to struggle on how to implement successful business intelligence solutions. Despite its growing popularity and maturity as a field, it appears that organizations follow key guidelines that ensure the failure of their business intelligence implementation. This paper highlights ten major principles that organizations follow to ensure the failure of their BI solution and in so doing describes how to avoid BI failure in terms of strategy and design, implementation management and communication, and technology and resource investment for BI solutions.

Fletcher H. Glancy, Lindenwood University, USA

Surya B. Yadav, Texas Tech University, USA

A business intelligence conceptual model (BISCOM) is proposed as a process-focused design theory for developing, understanding, and evaluating business intelligence (BI) systems. Previous work has concentrated on subsets of the BI systems, use of BI tools, and specific business functional area requirements. BISCOM provides a unified and comprehensive design theory that integrates and synthesizes existing research. It extends existing research by proposing functionality that does not currently exist in BI systems. The BISCOM is validated through descriptive methods that demonstrate the model utility and through prototype creation to demonstrate the need for BISCOM.

Business Intelligence (BI) has often been described as the tools and systems that play an essential role in the strategic planning process of a corporation. The application of BI is most commonly associated with the analysis of sales and stock trends, pricing and customer behavior to inform business decision-making. There is a growing trend in utilizing the tools and processes used in the analysis of data and applying them to security event management. Security Information and Event Management (SIEM) has emerged within the last 10 years providing a centralized source to enable both real-time and deep level analysis of historical event data to drive security standards and align IT resources in a more efficient manner.

While the potential benefits from BI are vast, organizations have struggled to successfully deploy it. BI applies myriad advanced techniques, performed by the firm's Information Technology (IT) group, to fulfill the reporting, analysis, and decision-support needs of the Lines of Business. Two of the greatest challenges in BI are accurately and continuously communicating requirements from the business to IT and quickly yet affordably delivering the requested functionality from IT to the business. Companies can overcome these challenges by embracing a prescribed set of Agile development methodologies for BI. This paper examines the history of selected systems development approaches, weighs the advantages and disadvantages of prevailing practices, and ultimately recommends a path forward to succeeding in BI through the application of Agile methodologies.

Traditional data warehouse projects follow a waterfall development model in which the project goes through distinct phases such as requirements gathering, design, development, testing, deployment, and stabilization. However, both business requirements and technology are complex in nature and the waterfall model can take six to nine months to fully implement a solution; by then business as well as technology has often changed considerably. The result is disappointed stakeholders and frustrated development teams. Agile development implements projects in an iterative fashion. Also known as the sixty percent solution, the agile approach seeks to deliver more than half of the user requirements in the initial release, with refinements coming in a series of subsequent releases which are scheduled at regular intervals. An agile data warehousing approach greatly increases the likelihood of successful implementation on time and within budget. This article discusses agile development methodologies in data warehousing and business intelligence, implications of the agile methodology, managing changes in data warehouses given frequent change in business intelligence (BI) requirements, and demonstrates the impact of agility on the business.

Preface

INTRODUCTION

This book examines many issues that concern the field of business intelligence (BI). BI remains an emerging field, but it is one is rapidly maturing. The field has multiple facets as it is comprised of several disciplines. BI is the application of data, technology, and analytics in the pursuit of insights and knowledge that enables decisions and actions that yield value for a firm. BI creates value by providing evidence that organizations can use to make informed decisions about people, processes, products, and services.

Figure 1 presents a vision of BI as an integrative application of technologies, models, techniques, and practices. In Miori and Klimberg's (2010) framework, each of the three circles of the Venn diagram represent applications that have previously been considered quite distinct: (1) information systems and technology, (2) statistics, and (3) operation research/management science. This structure serves to encapsulate a broad definition of BI, where BI is characterized from each of three viewpoints, which consist of (1) business information intelligence (BII), (2) business statistical intelligence (BSI) and (3) business modeling intelligence (BMI). Each of these three viewpoints has particular business aspects

Figure 1. Business intelligence/business analytics breakdown (Klimberg & Miori, 2010)

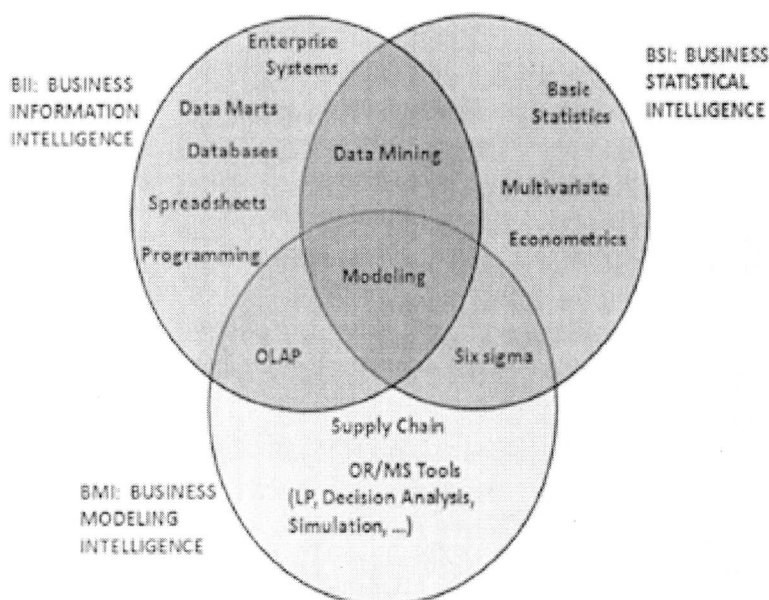

that are independent of the other viewpoints. Conversely, each viewpoint can work together or utilize techniques/skills from one or possibly two of the other disciplines. For example, data mining, which requires a high level of statistical knowledge as well as the availability of necessary data, may require significant IT skills and/or knowledge. Further, if data mining analysis demands a systematic process of analysis, modeling skills may be required. Within the context of this framework, data is secured by technology and then is subjected to statistics and modeling analytics to derive understanding of the data to facilitate evidence-based decision-making.

This book acknowledges the complexity of business intelligence and its papers explore the diversity of topics and issues that BI faces. For example, papers in this volume explore such concerns as the application of BI in college admissions, long range planning in the aerospace industry, organizational talent acquisition, the importance of BI in examining Web-based information, and BI application development techniques.

To facilitate the exploration of the various BI topics presented in this book, I have organized the papers presented in this volume into three groups: organizational issues, analytic issues, and technology issues. In doing so, the volume is consistent with the themes I routinely see as Editor of the *International Journal of Business Intelligence Research*. I think you will find the papers included in this collection informing while also helping to advance this important field.

ORGANIZATIONAL ISSUES

In their paper, *Using Business Intelligence in College Admissions: A Strategic Approach*, Dale Amburgey and John Yu note that higher education often lags behind industry in the adoption of new or emerging technologies. They state that competition increases among colleges and universities for a diminishing supply of prospective students, the need to adopt the principles of business intelligence becomes increasingly more important. They analyzed data from first-year enrolling students for the 2006-2008 fall terms at a private, master's-level institution in the northeastern United States for the purpose of developing predictive models. A decision tree analysis, a neural network analysis, and a multiple regression analysis were conducted to predict each student's grade point average (GPA) at the end of the first year of academic study. Numerous geodemographic variables were analyzed to develop the models to predict the target variable and the overall performance of the models developed in the analysis was evaluated by using the average square error (ASE). The authors find that three models had similar ASE values that indicated that any of the models could be used for the intended purpose. Amburgey and Yi make suggestions for future analysis include expansion of the scope of the study to include more student-centric variables and to evaluate GPA at other student levels.

Anticipatory Standards Development and Competitive Intelligence is a paper by Françoise Bousquet, Vladislav V. Fomin, and Dominique Drillon who state that more and more companies operate today in a worldwide market under conditions of globalization, increased complexity, and competition. In such an environment, they assert that business decisions need to be made quickly yet intelligent, substantiated by the most salient and relevant information available. Under the global competition, with a diligent and measured manner, many companies are increasingly treating business like an economic war. The authors report that enterprises are methodically monitoring and investigating their competitors, while deploying all the resources they have at their disposal in order to beat their current or future rivals.

Hence, Competitive Intelligence (CI) has become the 'latest weapon in the world war of economics'. This paper contributes to the growing body of literature on competitive intelligence by synthesizing knowledge stemming from many years of experience in the standardization arena. The authors aim to show how, in the economic war, engaging in committee-based standards development may be used for winning the competition battle.

In *Champion for Business Intelligence: SMART Goals For Business Focused and Financially Backed Results,* Irina Dymarsky notes that although Gartner's EXP 2006 CIO Survey ranked Business Intelligence (BI) as the top technology priority, BI projects face tough competition from other projects in IT portfolios promising more tangible financial returns (Wu & Weitzman, 2006) Irina states that two major hurdles that prevent BI projects from shining in portfolios are vague requirements and weak benefits calculations. However, she asserts that these hurdles can be addressed. This is accomplished by examining and learning from a number of case studies that prove tangible ROI on BI solutions that have been scoped and designed with a focus on specific, measurable, achievable, results-oriented, and time bound SMART business goals. In order for BI projects to compete in IT portfolios based on financial measures, like ROI, Dymarsky declares that BI champions need to approach BI requirements gathering with the goal of addressing a specific business problem as well as employ standard ways of calculating BI benefits post project go live. She says that by examining common failures with BI requirements and case studies which demonstrate how successful BI implementations translate into tangible benefits for the organization, BI champions develop a toolkit of tips, tricks, and lessons learned for successful requirements gathering, design, implementation, and measure of business results on BI initiatives.

Joseph Morabito, Edward A. Stohr, and Yegin Genc examine the key issues associated with current and future implementations of business intelligence (BI) in their paper *Enterprise Intelligence: A Case Study and the Future of Business Intelligence.* The authors review the literature and discover both the growing importance and emerging issues associated with BI. The issues are further examined with an exploratory, but detailed, case study of organizations from a variety of industries, yielding a series of lessons learned. The authors find that organizations are rapidly moving to an enterprise perspective on BI, but in an unsystematic way. Morabito, Stohr, and Genc then present a prescription for the future of BI called "enterprise intelligence" (EI). EI is described in a framework that combines elements of hierarchy theory, organization modeling, and intellectual capital. The authors note that organizations are emphasizing tools and technology sub-systems to detriment of the other, necessary, interacting structural sub-systems. In fact, they assert, *each* sub-system must be designed and managed to realize the full potential of EI.

In *Business Intelligence Competency Centers: Centralizing an Enterprise Business Intelligence Strategy,* Daniel O'Neill states that enterprises today continue to invest in business intelligence (BI) initiatives with the hope of providing a strategic advantage to their organizations. He asserts that many of these initiatives are supporting the tactical goals of individual business units and not the strategic goals of the enterprise. Although this decentralized approach provides short term gains, it he says creates an environment where information silos develop and the enterprise as a whole struggles to develop a single version of the truth when it comes to providing strategic information. Hence, he notes that enterprises are turning toward a centralized approach to BI that aligns with their overall strategic goals. At the core of this centralized approach is the business intelligence competency center (BICC). This paper details why the centralized BICC approach should be considered an essential component of all enterprise BI initiatives. He demonstrates that examining case studies of BICC implementations details the benefits realized by real world companies who have taken this approach. O'Neill states that it is also important to provide analysis of the two BI approaches in the areas of BI process and BI technology/data and people relations. O'Neill's findings indicate the benefits of the centralized BICC outweigh the deficiencies of the decentralized approach.

Robert Sawyer's paper, *BI's Impact on Analyses and Decision Making Depends on the Development of Less Complex Applications*, examines why BI developers have failed to create applications suited for the common end-user and it provides a conceptual roadmap to address these shortfalls. He argues that BI's impact on analyses and decision-making depends on the development of less complex applications. Research conducted for his paper finds that BI lacks a common definition and standard, that BI tools are too complex for the common user, and that a shortage of analytical literacy relevant to BI among business professionals is a barrier to BI adoption. Sawyer suggests that until BI analysis tools become more "human-centric, design-oriented" and less from a "technology-centric, engineering-oriented perspective," BI will continue to fail in its objective to routinely improve business decision-making.

In *Discovering Business Intelligence from the Subjective Web Data*, Ranjit Bose states that the online word-of-mouth behavior that exists today in the Web represents new and measurable sources of information. He declares that automated discovery or mining of consumer opinions from these sources is of great importance for marketing intelligence and product benchmarking. This is because techniques are now being developed to effectively and easily mine the consumer opinions from the Web data and to timely deliver them to companies and individual consumers. His study investigates this emerging field named 'opinion mining' in terms of what it is, what it can do, and how it could be used effectively for business intelligence (BI). He provides a rigorous review of the research literature on opinion mining to explore its current state, issues and challenges for its use in developing business applications for competitive advantage. This study aims to assist business managers to better understand the current opportunities and challenges in using opinion mining for deriving BI. Future research directions for further development of the field are also identified. Bose believes that the key to the future success of opinion mining is integrating the strengths of two worlds – creating technology that combines a human's linguistic capabilities with the speed and accuracy of a computer. He posits that advances in natural language processing research are beginning to close the gap between the human and computer language processing capabilities and he asserts that the research community has come to a conclusion that machine learning based approaches with the help of natural language processing is the most promising way to go for future developments. However, he is optimistic that there will be novel automated techniques coming out in the next few years to make opinion-mining technology practical for large-scale applications.

David Ellis examines *Business Intelligence Enhances Strategic, Long-Range Planning in the Commercial Aerospace Industry*. David notes that the world's largest aircraft manufacturers like Boeing and Airbus have traditionally been dominant in the commercial aerospace industry, but due to the rise of several smaller commercial aircraft companies and in spite of air travel increasing each year, he argues that it will be paramount for Boeing and Airbus to thoroughly understand past and current market conditions and be able to combine their understanding with the proper analytical tools to anticipate the market demands of the future if they are to remain the world leaders in their industry. His paper presents a discussion of industry factors such as airline routes, past passenger demands in different regions of the world and the sizes and types of aircraft that were required to support those demands, and more importantly, how analysis of that information is integral to the projection of future demands within the commercial aerospace market which will facilitate Boeing and Airbus positioning themselves to provide their airline customers with the right product at the right time. He finds that due to the complexity of the required data analysis for forecasting, the utilization of business intelligence methodologies such as regression and correlation analysis greatly enhance long-range, strategic planning in the commercial aerospace industry.

In *Performance Management through Societal Performance Indicators*, Joe White states that performance management is tied to external forces and stakeholders whose assessment of performance is more focused on societal outcomes than purely financial outcomes. He declares that government, corporate, and even personal performance measurement should take into account societal indicators that link these disparate yet intertwined spheres of influence. White says that new initiatives in both government and commercial sectors are bringing greater understanding of how societal indicators can measure performance. His paper highlights how societal indicators are used to measure performance in corporate and government sectors. Corporate societal indicators are explored primarily though literary research. Government societal indicators are then further explored through an examination of both the EPA and Superfund program. White's research demonstrates that there is synergy between corporate, government, and personal government performance measures and he shows how business intelligence tools are making these relationships more transparent.

In his paper, *Business Intelligence Should Be Centralized*, Brian Johnson argues just that. His paper also reviews how the concept of centralization is defined, how it relates to the implementation of BI, and how it can effectively in overcome the common implementation hurdles. Johnson maintains that the implementation of BI into the business strategy and culture is laden with many potential points that could result in failure of the initiative, leaving BI to be underdeveloped and a source of wasted resources for the company. Due to the unique nature of BI in the business space, he believes that properly setting up BI within the organizational structure from the onset of integration minimizes the impact of the most common hurdles to BI implementation. His analysis finds that many companies choose to mitigate these problems by using a centralized approach by building a Center of Excellence. However, Johnson argues that when doing this their place in the company's organizational structure needs to be well defined and properly empowered to be effective. He states that Core BI functions must be centralized, but consumerist functions like analytical processing can be farmed out to business units, or be housed in a central analytical unit as works best with the company's culture.

In a paper entitled, *The Future Talent Shortage Will Force Global Companies to Use HR Analytics to Help Manage and Predict Future Human Capital Needs*, Carey Worth examines exactly that issue. Her paper focuses on why companies should use analytics (a subset of Business Intelligence (BI)) to transform and maximize the potential of their human capital. During the recent recession the number of jobs lost has been widely publicized. However, Carey states that lurking among this obvious and simple metric of how human capital is involved in the workforce, there is also a need to analyze and predict future talent. She emphasizes that, as economic conditions are slow to improve, decisions to simply cut the traditional costs, benefits, compensation and headcount are no longer enough. She notes that companies have already started using business intelligence (BI) to transform and maximize the potential of their human capital and that the use of human capital based business intelligence (BI) has increasingly become one of the vital strategic components for world-class companies. By using HR analytics, Carey asserts that organizations become more effective in managing and improving the performance of human capital and in the process become more competitive and profitable. HR analytics helps an organization improve its profitability through more effective workforce cost control, balancing the lowest effective headcount while ensuring satisfactory service delivery. Managers can analyze top and bottom-performing employees to better develop and retain key talent pools addressing any retention trouble spots or looming gaps in needed competencies. Both executives and managers alike can better understand, she says, the causal effect of workforce investment on operational results.

ANALYTIC ISSUES

Lakshmi Iyer and Rajeshwari Raman present a paper entitled, *Intelligent Analytics: Integrating Business Intelligence and Web Analytics*. They state that web analytics is an evolving area that presents companies with myriad opportunities to enhance their online presence. In this paper, they make a case for organizations to find ways to integrate web analytics with traditional BI to be proactive in the competitive market place by exploring new growth strategies. Iyer and Raman first identify growing trends in web analytics that pave the way for integration and they then discuss the capabilities that organization must consider in looking at possible solutions to adopt. The authors suggest that if organizations find possible ways to accomplish the integration, the ability to track and market to existing or new consumer needs can give firms a sizable competitive advantage. The challenge, they note, though is the constant innovation of online technologies to track user behavior. They assert therefore that it is therefore important that as the BI field grows, structure and standards be implemented to balance stakeholders' concerns such as data rights management, accuracy, and privacy. They urge more research into developing standards for data representation, development of methods to analyze complex data such as audio or video, identifying appropriate metrics for measurement, examining organizations and governance issues, and assessing the impact of text analysis of social media data.

In *Strategies for Improving the Efficacy of Fusion Question Answering Systems*, José Antonio Robles-Flores, Gregory Schymik, Julie Smith-David, and Robert St. Louis state that web search engines typically retrieve a large number of web pages and overload business analysts with irrelevant information. One approach that has been proposed for overcoming some of these problems is automated Question Answering (QA). This paper describes a case study that was designed to determine the efficacy of QA systems for generating answers to original, fusion, list questions (questions that have not previously been asked and answered, questions for which the answer cannot be found on a single web site, and questions for which the answer is a list of items). Results indicate that QA algorithms are not very good at producing complete answer lists and that searchers are not very good at constructing answer lists from snippets. These findings indicate a need for QA research to focus on crowd sourcing answer lists and improving output format. The authors also assert that precise, timely, and factual answers are especially important when communication channels are limited. The point out that a growing number of Internet users rely on mobile devices such as internet-enabled cell phones, which do not have the luxury of a large screen space. Moreover, military personnel, first-responders, and security specialists frequently are under such tight time constraints that every additional second spent browsing through search results put human lives at risk. A high priority for BI researchers should be additional research to determine the extent to which QA algorithms can get the right information to the right person at the right time and in the right format to make the right decision.

TECHNOLOGY ISSUES

Sam Schutte, Thilini Ariyachandra, and Mark Frolick present a paper entitled *Test-Driven Development of Data Warehouses*. They introduce their topic by stating that over the course of the last decade, the business of software development has gone through rapid changes due to the introduction of new lightweight methodologies. These methodologies - such as Extreme Programming, Agile Development, and SCRUM - emphasize a focus on frequent inspection and adaptation of business requirements and technical architectural structure, and introduce new programming methods such as peer programming and stand-up meetings that help reduce re-work and improve quality. One of the newer methods used by Agile development teams, they note, is test-driven development, which is a software development technique that uses short development iterations based on pre-written test cases that define desired improvements or new functions. The authors state that the overall result of the introduction of these new methodologies has been a measurable improvement in the quality, time-to-market, and productivity of software development teams. The authors note that at the completion of a test-driven data warehouse project, the end result would be a provably correct system. Additionally, any future changes to this system that "break" the rules of the requirements would quickly be visible because a test case would begin to fail. The authors conclude by asserting that with the vast amount of data that resides in data warehouses, the only way to have such a provably correct system is through the use of automated tests. By using test-driven development they believe that data warehouse implementation project teams can better strive towards implementing a provably correct warehousing solution.

Uncovering Actionable Knowledge in Corporate Data with Qualified Association Rules is a paper by Nenad Jukic, Svetlozar Nestorov, Miguel Velasco, and Jami Eddington. The authors first note that Association rules mining is one of the most successfully applied data mining methods in today's business settings (e.g. Amazon or Netflix recommendations to customers). They then note that qualified association rules mining is an extension of the association rules data mining method, that uncovers previously unknown correlations that only manifest themselves under certain circumstances (e.g. on a particular day of the week), with the goal of improving action results, e.g. turning an underperforming campaign (spread too thin over the entire audience) into a highly targeted campaign that delivers results. They add that such correlations have not been easily reachable using standard data mining tools so far. Their paper describes the method for straightforward discovery of qualified association rules and demonstrates the use of qualified association rules mining on an actual corporate data set. The data set used by the authors is a subset of a corporate data warehouse for Sam's Club, a division of Wal-Mart Stores, INC. The experiments described in this paper illustrate how qualified association rules supplement standard association rules data mining methods and provide additional information that can be used to better target corporate actions. They conclude by stating that by utilizing qualified association rules, organizations can add an inexpensive, and yet very practical and fruitful method of analyzing data that can quickly discover a layer of knowledge that was previously unknown. Moreover, they say, once this additional knowledge is discovered, its potential to affect and improve corporate performance is immediately apparent.

Adam Hill, Thilini Ariyachandra, and Mark Frolick present a paper entitled, *10 Principles to Ensure Your Data Warehouse Implementation is a Failure*. The authors begin by acknowledging that the demand for business intelligence solutions continues to grow in the industry at record rates to combat competitive pressures and to attain business agility. Despite this fact, the authors find that many organizations continue to struggle on how to implement successful business intelligence solutions. Despite BI's growing popularity and maturity as a field, the authors believe that it appears that organizations follow key guidelines that ensure the failure of their business intelligence implementation. Their paper highlights ten major principles that organizations follow to ensure the failure of their BI solution and in so doing they describe how to avoid BI failure in terms of strategy and design, implementation management and communication, and technology and resource investment for BI solutions. They conclude by asserting that if a company is clear on what it intends to achieve with the project, allocates sufficient thought to design, ETL processes, and resource and technology investments, and benchmarks its progress, providing regular communication to all key stakeholders, it will have a much greater chance at achieving success in their data warehouse implementation.

Business Intelligence Conceptual Model is a paper by Fletcher Glancy and Surya Yadav. In this paper, a business intelligence conceptual model (BISCOM) is proposed as a process-focused design theory for developing, understanding, and evaluating business intelligence (BI) systems. The authors allege that previous research has concentrated on subsets of the BI systems, use of BI tools, and specific business functional area requirements. BISCOM, however, provides a unified and comprehensive design theory that integrates and synthesizes existing research. The authors say that BISCOM extends existing research by proposing functionality that does not currently exist in BI systems. The authors validate BISCOM through descriptive methods that they claim demonstrates the model utility. Moreover, through prototype creation, they avow they can demonstrate the need for BISCOM.

Kenneth Lozito notes that business intelligence has often been described as the tools and systems that play an essential role in the strategic planning process of a corporation. In his paper, *Mitigating Risk: Analysis of Security Information and Event Management*, he notes that the application of BI is most commonly associated with the analysis of sales and stock trends, pricing and customer behavior to inform business decision-making. However, Lozito proclaims that there is a growing trend in utilizing the tools and processes used in the analysis of data and applying them to security event management. He states that Security Information and Event Management (SIEM) has emerged within the last 10 years and it provides a centralized source for enabling both real-time and deep level analyses of historical event data to drive security standards and align IT resources in a more efficient manner. Lozito states that SIEM is a solution that requires cooperation and planning from within an organization. The benefits of compliance and gaining a centralized view of a security infrastructure as a whole gives distinct advantages over other organizations that do not implement this type of solution. Another key benefit of SIEM is the ability to perform deep threat analysis to drive security policy initiatives that will reduce the risk of exposure overall.

In *IT and Business Can Succeed in BI by Embracing Agile Methodologies*, Alex Gann contends that while the potential benefits from BI are potentially substantial, organizations have struggled to successfully deploy it. He notes that BI applies myriad advanced techniques, performed by the firm's Information Technology (IT) group, to fulfill the reporting, analysis, and decision-support needs of the Lines of Business. Gann suggests that two of the greatest challenges in BI are accurately and continuously communicating requirements from the business to IT and quickly yet affordably delivering the requested functionality from IT to the business. He argues that companies can overcome these challenges by embracing a prescribed set of Agile development methodologies for BI. This paper examines the history of selected systems development approaches, weighs the advantages and disadvantages of prevailing practices, and ultimately recommends a path forward to succeeding in BI through the application of Agile methodologies.

The final paper entitled *Agile Development in Data Warehousing* is also focused on Agile development. Here Nayem Rahman, Dale Rutz, and Shameem Akhter state that traditional data warehouse projects follow a waterfall development model in which the project goes through distinct phases. Each phase must complete before the next one can commence. These phases include requirements gathering, design, development, testing, deployment and stabilization. The issue is that both business requirements and technology are complex in nature. The waterfall development model can easily take six to nine months or longer to fully implement a solution, and by then business as well as technology has often changed considerably. The result is usually disappointed stakeholders and frustrated development teams. The authors detail the agile development approach that implements projects in an iterative fashion. Also known as the sixty percent solution, the agile approach seeks to deliver more than half of the user requirements in the initial release, with refinements coming in a series of subsequent releases that are scheduled at regular intervals. The authors assert that the agile data warehousing approach greatly increases the likelihood of successful implementation on time and within budget. This article discusses agile development methodologies in data warehousing and business intelligence, implications of the agile methodology, managing changes in data warehouses given frequent change in business intelligence (BI) requirements, and demonstrates the impact of agility on the business.

REFERENCES

Klimberg, R., & Miori, V. (2010). Back in business. *OR/MS Today, 37*(5). Retrieved from http://www.informs.org/ORMS-Today/Public- Articles/October-Volume-37-Number5/Back-in-Business

Section 1
Organizational Issues

Chapter 1
Using Business Intelligence in College Admissions:
A Strategic Approach

W. O. Dale Amburgey
Saint Joseph's University, USA

John C. Yi
Saint Joseph's University, USA

ABSTRACT

Higher education often lags behind industry in the adoption of new or emerging technologies. As competition increases among colleges and universities for a diminishing supply of prospective students, the need to adopt the principles of business intelligence becomes increasingly more important. Data from first-year enrolling students for the 2006-2008 fall terms at a private, master's-level institution in the northeastern United States was analyzed for the purpose of developing predictive models. A decision tree analysis, a neural network analysis, and a multiple regression analysis were conducted to predict each student's grade point average (GPA) at the end of the first year of academic study. Numerous geodemographic variables were analyzed to develop the models to predict the target variable. The overall performance of the models developed in the analysis was evaluated by using the average square error (ASE). The three models had similar ASE values, which indicated that any of the models could be used for the intended purpose. Suggestions for future analysis include expansion of the scope of the study to include more student-centric variables and to evaluate GPA at other student levels.

DOI: 10.4018/978-1-4666-2650-8.ch001

INTRODUCTION

Higher education has long been rich in data but slow in converting that data into useful information. In institutions ranging from large public research universities to small liberal arts colleges, vast amounts of data are collected by every internal entity. Some of the largest amounts of data are captured within universities' enrollment management divisions. Admissions offices are inundated with geodemographic data on prospective students. Financial aid offices constantly collect data points relating to the personal or family financial situations of prospective and current students. Retention offices collect data to help identify students that may be at risk of dropping out. Enrollment management divisions are among the largest data collectors in higher education; however, they tend to lag behind the corporate world in conversion of data into usable information.

With the voluminous amounts of data collected within enrollment management divisions, only within the past decade has there been a concerted effort to use that data to develop predictive models. Consulting groups have added enrollment management services to capitalize on the popular cultural shift to use of historical data to develop predictive analytics.

One of the most common uses of predictive analytics in enrollment management is for forecasting future first-year student enrollments. Many institutions, especially private colleges and universities, are tuition dependent, with most of their net revenues generated by student tuition. Being able to accurately forecast the number of entering students each year enables them to better plan and strategize improved benefits and services for all members of the college or university community.

PURPOSE OF THE STUDY

The purpose of this study is to develop a predictive model to assist undergraduate admissions officers in determining the likelihood of academic success for entering first-year students.

Incorporating into the admissions process a predictive model to identify the potential for success can be very advantageous. University admissions offices are seeing an increasing percentage of the applicant pool fall into a marginal category. Marginal applicants are loosely defined as those who are not definite admits or definite denials. These students' academic credentials are not as sound as those of the upper-tier applicants but significantly better than those of unsuccessful applicants. Using a predictive model to determine applicants' potential to have a strong grade point average (GPA) at the end of the first year should help alleviate most of the conjecture currently applied to making admissions decisions about marginal applicants.

As pertinent data is collected during the initial inquiry stage, these predictive models may be used to shape recruitment strategies and to target a specific message to the many audiences in the inquiry pool. For example, marketing messages relating to tutoring services or student success programs may be directed to applicants identified as having a low likelihood of earning a high end-of-first-year GPA.

Admissions counselors may also use predictive models to better counsel prospective students during their college search. Admissions representatives can counsel prospective students who display characteristics known to indicate academic distress about the possibility of future success. These discussions can help prospective students determine whether the rigor of the institution's academic environment is suitable to their skills and abilities.

STUDY DESIGN AND METHODOLOGY

The primary methodology of the study consists of analysis of historical student data to determine the best-fit model to predict applicants' end-of-first-year GPA. Three types of analytical models will be developed, and comparison testing will be conducted to determine the model displaying the lowest error.

Data stewards of the institution representing the Office of the Registrar, the Office of Financial Assistance, and the Director of Enrollment Analysis conferred to develop standards of acceptable use of the historical data. All agreed that the potential results of the study were significant enough to justify use of the data and that the study had to strive to protect the anonymity of the student data.

DATA COLLECTION AND ANALYSIS

Data was collected for entering first-year students at a midsized private university in the northeastern United States. The data was collected for first-year students beginning studies in the fall academic terms from 2006 through 2008. The data was collected from numerous sources within the enrollment management division and in other divisions of the university. The Common Application, the university application, the College Board, and the Free Application for Federal Student Aid (FAFSA) were some of the sources for collection of applicant data.

To assure the individual students' anonymity, unique identification numbers were generated to replace any identifiable student identification numbers in the data set. Three types of predictive models—a decision tree analysis, a neural network analysis, and a multiple regression analysis—were developed for comparison of predictability as determined by the average square error (ASE).

SIGNIFICANCE AND LIMITATIONS

Several limitations were encountered during the study. An initial limitation is that data was collected only from entering first-year students at the participating institution. Data from applicants who had not completed the application process or who had been admitted but had chosen to attend another institution was not considered.

Another limitation is that all data is assumed to be truthful and accurate. The data collection took place by manual data entry and electronic uploads. It is assumed that there were no significant data entry errors and that all electronic upload processes were functioning correctly.

Since data from the FAFSA was used, the possibility of a large number of missing variables is present because entering students are not required to complete the form. At the participating institution, it is assumed that approximately 40% of entering first-year students will complete the FAFSA.

The FAFSA data also represents the most recent financial aid data available for entering students. An entering student may have submitted several iterations of the FAFSA, and the potential for numerous changes within the data variables is possible.

LITERATURE REVIEW

Use of data to aid decision making has long been accepted in the corporate world but has been slower to gain momentum in higher education. Some higher education professionals anecdotally state that it is not unusual for the lag time for adopting corporate best practices in an academic setting can be as long as a decade. This statement, if accurate, describes a process that could be a mixed blessing for those in the academic world. Practices and procedures tend to undergo several revisions until they become best practices, and higher education may benefit from this delay by not having to be concerned about establishing a practice until the revision cycle is complete. If anything, higher education is not an area where constant change is embraced.

A shift in the mindset of enrollment management professionals must take place if the true potential of using business intelligence to aid in achieving goals and objectives is to be realized. It is imperative to gain an overview of enrollment management to better understand the historical philosophies of the practice and the motivations behind the implementation of those philosophies.

Overview of Enrollment Management

Approximately four decades ago, the need to develop more structured marketing communications and the benefits of developing relationships between prospective students and the institution were identified. During the early 1970s, the term *enrollment management* was first used in conjunction with student recruitment and retention. During the 1980s, institutions began developing and adhering to detailed enrollment plans. These plans coupled the use of integrated marketing communication plans with the strategic use of financial aid packages (Merante, 2009, p. 5).

As funding for higher education fluctuated in the late 1980s and certain demographics began to shift, the enrollment plans became more aggressive to overcome obstacles in the marketplace. The enrollment plans during this period became more vigorous, and the use of direct mail and targeted marketing campaigns became established practices at many institutions (Fiske, 2008; Merante, 2009, pp. 5-6).

By the middle of the 1990s, enrollment management continued to develop and incorporated a more strategic nature than had been used previously. During this period, the multitude of departments that represented functions of enrollment management was collectively grouped to form a unique division. Also during this period, the marketplace became better informed and began to display the desire for institutional data. Prospective students and their families began asking questions about placement rates, graduation rates, and descriptive academic statistics as had never been seen previously (Fiske, 2008; Merante, 2009, p. 6).

The new millennium has brought developments in enrollment management that could not have been foreseen a decade earlier. The college view book was at one time the most visible and significant piece of marketing that an institution's admissions office could produce. Now, view books have become much smaller as the focus has switched toward use of websites and social media to promote the institution to prospective students. The pace of technological innovation is ensuring that the future of recruitment and retention activities has the possibility of being personalized and delivered in a format that recipients choose and at any time they want (Fiske, 2008; Merante, 2009, p. 6).

Enrollment management is a term that may seem understandable in theory but proves difficult to define in practice. Sutton (2007) defines *enrollment management* as "simply a name that has been given to the evaluation of data and implementation of planning that will result in a more efficient academic institution" (p. 1). This definition seems rather broad, but it does incorporate all the activities that may fall under the enrollment management umbrella. Stewart (2004) states that "as a process, enrollment management helps institutions: develop a keener awareness of their purpose and character in relation to the student marketplace, improve ties to prospective client groups, and attract students into and through the institution" (p. 21). This description of enrollment management begins to encompass the "whole life" nature of the process, beginning with the initial inquiry and concluding with the transformation from a graduated student to an active alumnus.

In some institutions, *enrollment management* is used interchangeably with *the undergraduate admissions office*. Often, this is perpetuated by the massive infusion of new revenue to the institution that results from the enrollment of each new undergraduate entering class. This is especially relevant at private institutions, where tuition revenue is especially vital to funding institutional operations (Antons & Maltz, 2006, p. 69).

The two most critical components of the fiscal nature of enrollment management are the yield rate of admitted students and the tuition discount rate. The yield rate is calculated by estimating the percentage of admitted students who will matriculate at the institution. Fluctuations in the yield percentage can have significant effects on net tuition revenue. The discount rate "is the projected financial aid to be allocated to students as a percentage of tuition" (Antons & Maltz, 2006, p. 69). The ability to offer financial assistance to students is an important component of prospective student recruitment and current student retention. A discount rate that is too high can result in the institution's overspending its financial aid budget and placing considerable strain on its other institutional resources. One that is too low can lead to its under-achieving its enrollment goals and drastically reducing its net tuition revenue (Antons & Maltz, 2006).

The composition of enrollment management divisions lacks complete consistency but it does have a few root components. As mentioned earlier, some see enrollment management as being synonymous with undergraduate admissions. This is usually because undergraduate admissions are the largest and most visible component of the enrollment management division. The financial aid office is another important component of the enrollment management division that has a presence throughout the entire student life cycle. This office is instrumental in the student recruitment process by making the institution affordable to entering students. It also plays a crucial role in

student retention by assisting current students with the financial obligations they have undertaken.

Although many may not see the connection, the future of university admissions and the strategic use of financial aid are built on the foundations of business intelligence. As technological advances permit more prospective student data to be captured for analysis, the number of data-mining professionals housed institutionally and of external consulting groups offering predictive analytical services is poised for tremendous growth.

Developing predictive models to assist in the marketing, recruitment, and admission of prospective students holds the potential to leverage an institution's history in making the best strategic decisions not only for the organization, but for the prospective student as well. The scarcity of fiscal resources, in concert with the increasing number of educational alternatives, will necessitate the use of business intelligence to compete in the higher education marketplace.

Use of Predictive Analytics to Determine Educational Outcomes

Some have embraced the use of business intelligence principles within higher education. The primary goal of data mining should be to analyze data and convert it to useful information on which informed decisions can be made. The vast amount of data collected at colleges and universities provides a ripe environment to yield the benefits of business intelligence.

One of the most important uses of data within enrollment management, and especially within a university admissions office, is its use in predicting outcomes. The ability to analyze variables to determine the individual's potential for success should be an important component of decision making and strategic planning in an admissions office.

There are numerous examples where predictive analytics have been used to forecast educational outcomes. The art and science of making college admissions decisions can greatly benefit from the use of business intelligence and predictive analytics. Some variables used in the admissions decision process are standardized while a great number may be unique to an individual high school.

Tam and Sukhatme (2004) evaluated the potential for a student's college academic success on a newly constructed high school percentile rank variable (p. 12). The researchers used data collected from the enrolling freshmen cohort at the University of Illinois at Chicago (UIC) for fall term 1994. The academic progress of the cohort was tracked over a six-year period with the definition of success being graduation from the institution within that time window (p. 13).

Historically, the institution arrived at freshman admissions decisions by calculating a selection index determined by the ACT score and the percentile class rank. Since the ACT is a standardized test, all students had an equal chance of achieving a high test score. However, earning a higher-percentile class rank proved more difficult because it would be more difficult for a student to achieve a higher class rank in a more academically challenging high school. This motivated the researchers to measure the academic quality of the participants' high schools. However, they were faced with a multitude of variables that could be considered when defining high school quality (Tam & Sukhatme, 2004, pp. 12-14).

The researchers decided to use a high school's average ACT score for all students as the means of defining academic quality. They made this choice primarily because of the availability of data for analysis. In evaluating the admissions decisions made over the six-year period, Tam and Sukhatme found that much better admissions decisions could have been made by using the high school academic quality indicator. The results led to the generation of a new variable called *the modified student high school percentile rank* to be incorporated into the UIC admissions decision criteria. Including the new criterion in the selection process proved to yield much better admissions decisions as measured by student success (Tam & Sukhatme, 2004, pp. 12-14).

Predictive analytics are beneficial to more areas than just undergraduate admissions. Making decisions at the graduate level sometimes proves to be as difficult as or even more difficult than at the undergraduate level. Naik and Ragothaman (2004) evaluated ways to improve prediction of MBA (Master of Business Administration) students' performance by using predictive analytics to assist with admissions decision making.

In their research, Naik and Ragothaman compared the outcomes of using neural networks, logit, and probit models to make MBA admissions decisions. They incorporated 10 explanatory variables into their research, encompassing areas such as campus location, undergraduate major, GMAT (Graduate Management Admission Test) scores, and undergraduate institution. The applicants were divided into successful and marginal groups based on many of the explanatory variables defined (Naik & Ragothaman, 2004, pp. 143-144).

The purpose of Naik and Ragothaman's research was to determine whether neural networks could be used in the MBA admissions decision-making process with the same level of effectiveness as the more traditional statistical models such as probit and logit models. The outcomes proved that the neural network performed as well as the probit and logit models in predicting MBA student performance. Their final recommendation was that the incorporation of neural networks into the MBA decision-making process could assist MBA directors and business school deans in making better admissions decisions on which applicants to accept in their respective programs (Naik & Ragothaman, 2004, pp. 146-147).

Often, those charged with making admissions decisions at any level do not think of incorporating any method of business intelligence into the process. The innate instinct is to try to evaluate the applicant based on the academic and professional credentials contained in his or her record. However, the potential to make even better decisions using statistical data while relying less on the proverbial "gut instinct" lies with employing business intelligence principles.

Another interesting study, conducted by Johnson (2008), examined the relationship of the type of high school a student attended to enrollment, persistence, and graduation rates at a public university. The study attempted to build on previous studies relating to college choice and persistence by incorporating the effects of high school–related and individual student variables on academic success (p. 777).

The research questions guiding the study centered on the characteristics of high schools that had a higher probability of graduating students who would enroll in and succeed at the university, along with the effect of student attrition rates, depending on the type of high school attended. The research was conducted at a doctoral/research university with an enrollment of approximately 12,000 students. It focused on the traits of in-state students at the institution, who composed almost 80% of the 2,000 entering first-year students enrolling directly from high schools. Data was collected from students over the course of the fall 2001-2005 entering cohorts. Some of the high school attributes examined related to academic quality, poverty levels, and ethnic composition. Data collection used internal, institution-specific data, along with external sources, such as a U.S. Department of Education database (Johnson, 2008, p. 779).

The data analysis included development of a matriculation model, a persistence model, and a graduation model to estimate the desired effects. The matriculation model was used to estimate the effects on the odds of a student's enrolling in the institution. The persistence model evaluated the odds of an enrolled student's being retained after the first year. Finally, the graduation model evaluated the likelihood of an enrolled student's graduation from the institution within five years (Johnson, 2008, p. 793).

The results of Johnson's (2008) research with the three independent models indicated that the type of high school did matter when evaluating the dependent variables of enrollment, persistence, and graduation. Understanding how the individual-related and high school–related variables can be evaluated to provide the odds of the dependent variables can be critical to enrollment managers and admissions officials. The models used in this study can have strong implications on planning recruitment and enrollment strategies because they can effect decisions ranging from marketing messages to enrollment decisions.

Allen and Robbins (2008) conducted a large-scale research project to develop a predictive model that would assess the probability of a first-year student's persisting in his or her chosen major area of study. They used three hypotheses to guide the purpose of their study: The first was that "major persistence is predicted by interest-major fit" (p. 65). The second stated "that students with higher first-year GPA are more likely to persist in their entering major" (p. 65). The final hypothesis was "that indicators of pre-collegiate academic preparation (high school GPA and ACT Composite score) are related to major persistence, but are mediated by high school GPA" (p. 65). For the purpose of their research, major persistence was determined to have occurred if the student remained in his or her initial major in the third year.

The initial sample population included almost 88,000 first-time entering students from 25 four-year colleges and universities. The outcome of concern for the researchers was the third-year major. To remain in the sample, a student had to be enrolled in a major during his or her third year of study, and his or her initial major program of study selection had to be known. Applying this parameter to the sample reduced the sample size to just over 48,000. This sample size allowed for the sample to be split into an Estimation group and a Validation group. The analysis led to the development of a regression equation generated from the Estimation group that was tested against the Validation group (Allen & Robbins, 2008, p. 65).

The research supported the claims that interest-major fit and the academic performance at the end of the first year were both instrumental in predicting whether or not a student remained in his or her major of choice. Understanding this relationship can be extremely beneficial to academic advisors at colleges and universities as they assist and counsel students early in their college career. The predictive model that was developed could aid students in finding a major closely aligned with their interest and abilities, while providing the framework to improve the quality of their college experience as a whole (Allen & Robbins, 2008).

Use of Predictive Analytics to Determine Potential Enrollment

Business intelligence has tremendous potential to help admissions and enrollment management professionals make decisions in areas other than the applicants' potential success. The voluminous amounts of data that filter through an enrollment management division may be analyzed to determine the potential enrollments of prospective students. The benefits of using business intelligence go well beyond predicting the number of enrolling students. Decisions about recruitment strategies and budget expenditures can be affected by the same predictive models that forecast enrollments.

Chen (2008) examined ways predictive modeling could be used to determine enrollments at a university in the Midwest. What makes Chen's discussion interesting is that the research was truly a longitudinal study that analyzed enrollment data from 1962 to 2004. The research evaluated the predictive nature of 15 variables and incorporated individual student indicators, along with economic indicators. These variables were used to develop two predictive models for comparison in predictability (p. 1).

An autoregressive integrated moving average (ARIMA) model and a linear regression model were developed to predict institutional enrollments. When comparing the two models, the ARIMA model yielded an r-squared value of 0.96 and a mean absolute percentage error (MAPE) of 2.11%. The linear regression model had an r-squared value of 0.97, just slightly better than the ARIMA model. The MAPE of the linear regression model was 1.62%, which was almost half a percentage point less than the ARIMA model. The high r-squared values indicate that well over 95% of the variability in the data set is accounted for by the variables contained within the respective model. Also, the state high school graduate variable and the one-year lagged institution enrollment variables emerged as primary enrollment functions of the institution in both models (Chen, 2008).

The research of Goenner and Pauls (2006) involved the development of predictive analytics to aid in the marketing efforts an institution made in response to enrollment inquiries. The researchers hoped to prove that analysis of the inquiring student's behaviors could be used to positively affect the institution's marketing efforts. The interesting approach to the research was that the analysis focused on the initial inquiry and the inquirers' eventual enrollment decision rather than on those who had applied or been accepted to the institution (p. 936).

Because the manner by which a prospective student inquires often results in limited amounts of data, the researchers also built in geodemographic data to aid in developing the model. A sample of almost 16,000 inquiring students was used to develop the predictive model, with the dependent variable being a calculated binary variable associated with enrolling. Given the presence of the binary variable, a logistic regression model was used for the analysis (Goenner & Pauls, 2006, pp. 946-947).

The results of the analysis yielded a model that predicted enrollment behavior almost 90% of the time. The model had a sensitivity, or the ability to predict the number of students who eventually enrolled, of 36%. Conversely, the model had a specificity, or the ability to predict the number of inquirers who would not enroll, of 97%. Using the model allowed the institution to better segment marketing campaigns to prospective students. The predictive model had been used to score ZIP codes so that marketing campaigns could be directed to a more concentrated area, where the potential for enrollment truly lay (Goenner & Pauls, 2006, p. 953).

Chang (2006) also evaluated the use of business intelligence to predict admissions yield through a case study at a large state university. One of the questions that Chang's research attempted to answer was whether applicants enrolled randomly or in identifiable patterns. Also, the presence of enrollment trends within specific groups and the accuracy of enrollment forecasts were questions that guided the study (p. 54).

The data set of the research contained nearly 3,000 admitted first-year, transfer, and nondegree students at a large state university. Data was analyzed, and an enrollment status indicator variable was added for purposes of modeling. The study contained C&RT (classification and regression trees), neural networks, and logistic regressions as the predictive models for analysis. The data set was divided into a Training group, to be used for model development, and a Testing group, to be used for model validation. All the models used generated predictions at the individual student level (Chang, 2006, pp. 62-63).

The research concluded that use of a data-mining approach to predictive modeling yielded better results than use of traditional statistical forecasting tools such as logistic regression. The data-mining models provided outcomes that could be considered extremely actionable and preferable because of the potential to be connected to a live database. Modeling on live data offers a tremendous opportunity to make enrollment decisions in the moment and to amend strategies and goals in a more immediate manner (Chang, 2006, p. 68).

Summary

Enrollment management is an extremely dynamic component of higher education where the advantages of business intelligence could aid in the process of decision making on a multitude of issues. Though the structure of an enrollment management division may be unique to an institution, the vast amounts of data collected remain consistent. Also consistent is the general lack of motivation to mine the data to determine potential use of the information that may be present. As population demographics continue to shift in the future, the necessity to apply business intelligence practices to higher education will become critically important.

Research has shown that there are instances where predictive analytics have been used to successfully address issues within higher education. The most common themes present in those instances are the ability to predict applicants' future academic success or to forecast the size and composition of an entering class. The potential benefits that lie with having accurate predictive models can only aid enrollment managers as they are forced to become more competitive in recruitment of prospective students and increasing retention of current students.

Demographic shifts occurring in some regions of the United States may force institutions to adopt the use of predictive analytics in enrollment and marketing strategies. As the number of high school graduates trends downward in some areas, higher education institutions must look to predictive analytics to maximize the yield from a potentially smaller pool of inquirers and applicants. Conversely, as demographic trends track upward in other areas, predictive analytics become an integral component in enrollment planning. A growing inquiry and applicant pool has implications for institutional selectivity and increases the potential for over enrollment. Applying business intelligence principles to these situations will provide institutional leadership with the road map needed to achieve goals while maximizing net tuition revenue.

DATA ANALYSIS

In the present study, the data for analysis was retrieved from a private, midsized university in the northeastern United States. The data represented first-year students enrolling for the institution's fall academic term from 2006 through 2008. The data set included 3,576 student records, and it contained 40 variables that represented an array of academic and demographic data. The dependent variable for this analysis was the interval data value End-of-First-Year GPA. This variable represented the GPA at the end of the spring semester and was the focus of prediction for this study. All variables used in analysis are found in Table 1.

Data was collected in cooperation with the various data stewards at the participating institution, and necessary precautions to maintain student anonymity were enacted. This included generat-

Table 1. Variables used for decision tree, neural network, and multiple regression analysis

Variable	Role	Level
End-of-First-Year GPA	Target	Interval
Citizenship Type	Input	Nominal
Gender Description	Input	Nominal
High School Quality Index	Input	Interval
Institutional Characteristic Description	Input	Nominal
Major Description	Input	Nominal
Religion Description	Input	Nominal
SAT Mathematics Score	Input	Interval
SAT Verbal Score	Input	Interval
SAT Writing Score	Input	Interval
SAT Total Score	Input	Interval
Secondary School GPA	Input	Interval
State_Province	Input	Interval

ing a dummy identification variable to prevent personally identifiable features within the data set from being used for identification purposes. Data was also analyzed to identify any erroneous variables. The data is considered to be truthful and representative of the demographics of the study sample.

The data analysis represented two methods pertaining to data mining and a traditional statistical analysis method. The decision tree and neural network analyses are more closely associated with data mining and predictive analytics, while the multiple regression analysis is more rooted in the realm of traditional statistical analysis. Comparing the results of the three analyses allows for the selection of a model that will most accurately predict the level of success a student may experience during his or her first year of college academic study. The resulting model may then be used in a variety of ways to make an enrollment management decision, especially in the undergraduate admissions office.

Decision Tree Analysis

Decision tree analysis is a data-mining tool used to reduce a large number of data records into smaller and smaller collections by applying a series of decision rules. Decision trees are based on use of a series of "if-then" statements that sequentially divides the data into smaller, more homogenous groups. The eventual outcome is to arrive at a decision tree that will identify numerous target groups in relation to the numerous variables input into the model. Decision trees also have an interactive nature that permits the ability to prune the tree in numerous ways (Berry & Linoff, 2004, Matignon, 2007).

In this study, the data set was partitioned into a Training group and a Validation group for the purpose of conducting a decision tree analysis. The End-of-First-Year GPA was used as the target variable, and the remaining variables were defined (see Table 1) as input variables. The basis for measuring the overall performance for the model was the ASE of the validation population.

The decision tree analysis yielded an ASE of 0.331 for the Training group and of 0.379 for the Validation group. The assessment plot indicated that the ASE was the smallest with a decision tree containing 12 leaves. However, using the ASE of the Validation group, the decision tree could be trimmed to three leaves and increase the ASE by only 0.009. This is represented in Figure 1, where a noticeable flattening of the ASE values for the Validation group occurs after Leaf 3.

The decision tree analysis output also generated a ranking of the importance of the variables. This value was based on the number of occasions when a variable was used in splits within the model. The Secondary School GPA was the variable of most importance, with a value of 1.00. The High School Quality Index, with a value of 0.425, was the only other variable with an importance value greater than 0.40.

Choosing to use the 3-leaf tree versus the 12-leaf tree proves to be an interesting outcome. Ideally, a decision tree with fewer leaves would be preferred. However, an enrollment manager may want to see how the remaining variables contribute to model performance. One of the advantages of decision tree analysis is the ability to allow the researcher to make determinations about the inclusion and exclusion of the leaf variables.

Multiple Regression Analysis

Regression is one of the statistical procedures more commonly used to predict an outcome. Multiple linear regression analysis is used to forecast a target variable that contains interval-level data. Multiple regression models may contain numerous input variables that span both categorical and continuous data types. A multiple regression model is also used to explain the variability of the predicted value in relation to the input variables contained within the model. Ideally, the best regression model is one that provides the least error and has the fewest parameters (Matignon, 2007).

A stepwise multiple regression analysis was conducted to determine a predictive model for the target variable End-of-First-Year GPA. The data was portioned into a Training group and a

Figure 1. Average square error for the decision tree analysis

Average square error

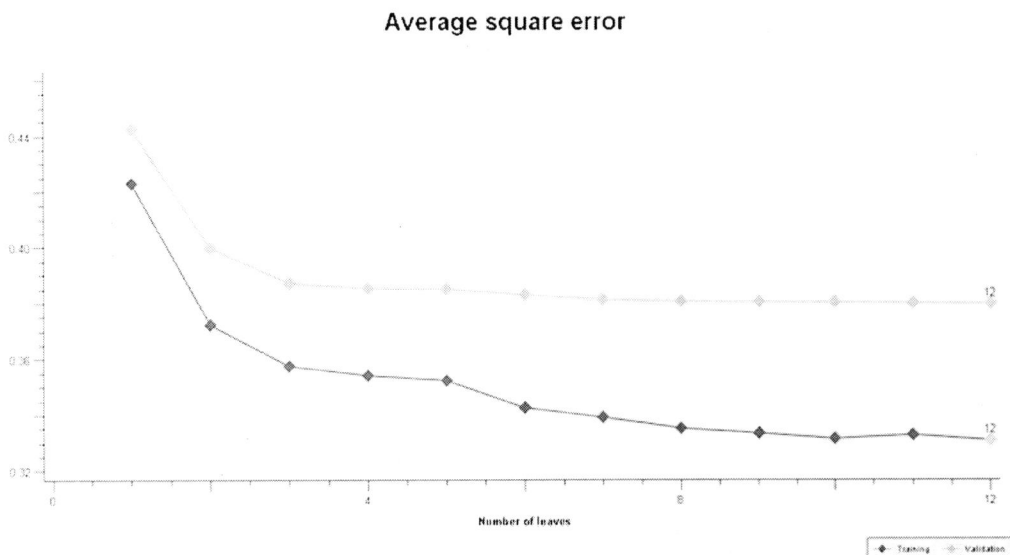

Validation group for purposes of analysis. The Training group was used to develop the model, and the Validation group was applied to measure performance. The ASE was the basis of model performance for the multiple regression analysis.

The stepwise multiple regression model yielded an ASE of 0.347 for the Training group and of 0.382 for the Validation group. The selected model occurred during step 8 and used the following effects: Gender Description; High School Quality Index; Institutional Characteristic Description; Major Description; SAT Mathematics Score; SAT Writing Score; Secondary School GPA; and State_Province. Figure 2 both provides a visual display of the ASE leveling off at step 8 and shows the variability between the ASE values for the Training and Validation groups. The selected model had an *r*-squared value of 0.4647, which indicates that almost 47% of the variance in End-of-First-Year GPA could be attributed to the variables in the model.

Neural Network Analysis

The neural network is a popular tool in business intelligence because of past successes in use of numerous data-mining and decision-making analysis applications. Neural networks are composed of basic structures that attempt to imitate the human brain. Three basic structures compose a neural network: the input layer, which represents the variables to be input; the hidden layer, which may contain one or many levels; and the output level, which represents the predicted value of target variables (Berry & Linoff, 2004; Matignon, 2007).

In this study, a neural network analysis was completed to create a predictive model to estimate the target variable End-of-Year GPA. As in the prior completed analyses, the data set was split into a Training group and a Validation group. The performance of the model was determined by the ASE of the Validation group.

The neural network analysis yielded an ASE of 0.359 for the Training group and of 0.373 for the Validation group. The neural network was a large model, as indicated by the model degrees of freedom value of 247.

Figure 2. Average square error for the multiple regression analysis

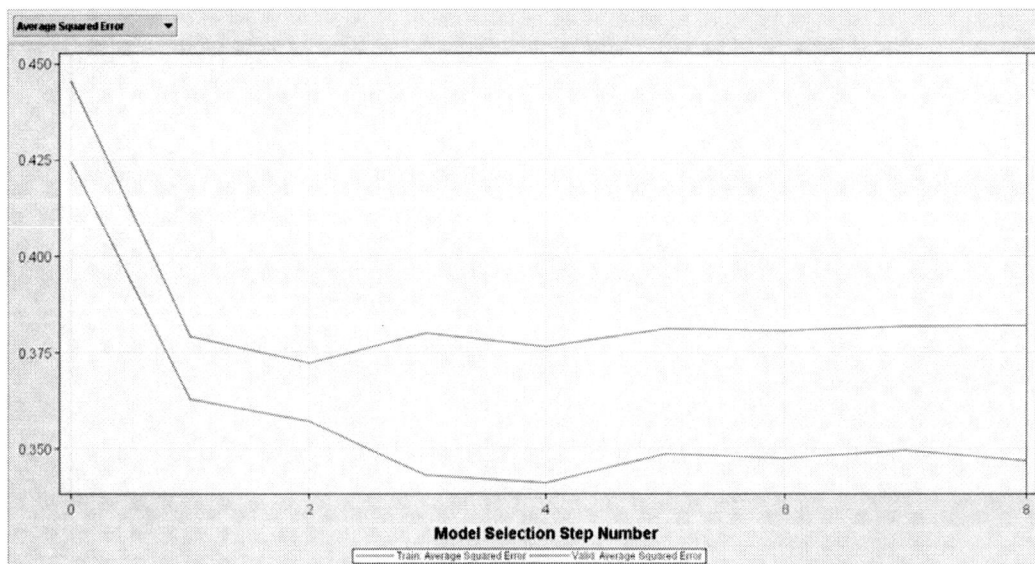

Figure 3 contains a visual representation of the ASE yielded from the neural network analysis. A large divergence in the ASE values for the Training and Validation groups occurs at training iteration 3. Primarily, this type of occurrence takes results from a large number of weights in the fitted neural network model. The effect of this phenomenon may be lessened by

reducing the number of inputs in the neural network model. This reduction of inputs would lead to a smaller number of model weights and perhaps have a positive impact on model performance.

Comparison of Model Performance

The purpose of this study was to create a predictive model that may be used by undergraduate admissions officers to help them arrive at admissions decisions for applicants, especially whose academic credentials may be marginal. Further, the predictive nature of the model may also be used to assist in marketing and recruitment strategies.

Three models were created to forecast the GPA that an applicant could be expected to attain at the end of the first year of academic study at the institution. The decision tree analysis and neural network analysis are closely associated with business intelligence and have not been incorporated to a significant degree within higher education analysis. The multiple regression analysis can be considered more traditional because it is firmly rooted in traditional statistical analysis and has been more widely used in higher education analysis.

Numerous methods may be used to determine the performance of a predictive model. The usefulness of the models developed in this study was determined by the calculated average square error for each model, as determined by the Validation group. Comparing the three models developed in this analysis showed that the neural network model yielded the lowest ASE value (0.373); the decision tree model yielded the next-lowest ASE value (0.379); and the multiple regression model yielded the highest ASE value (0.382).

Figure 3. Average square error for the neural network analysis

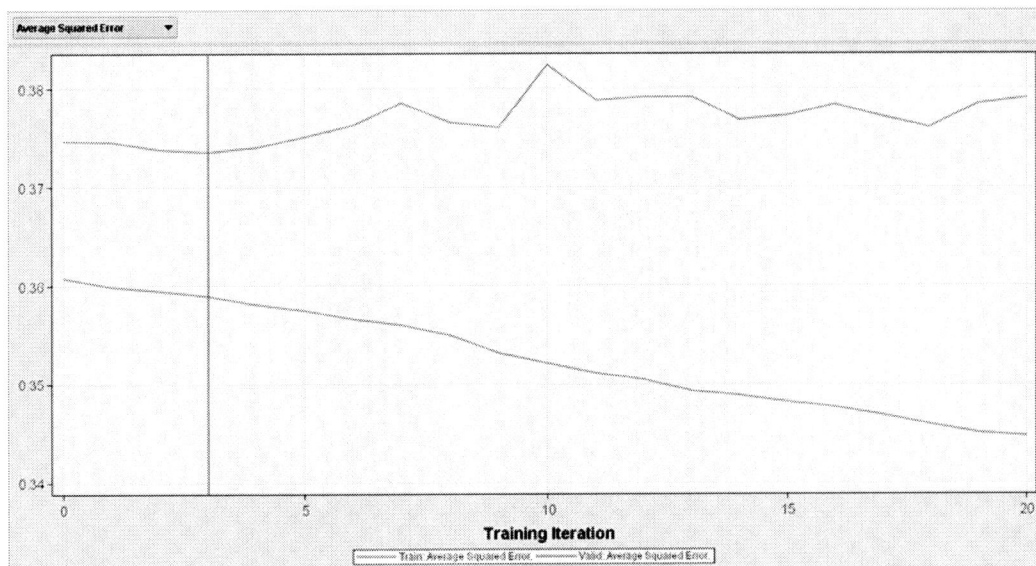

Based on the calculated ASE values, the neural network would be the model of choice. However, because the ASE values of all three models were similar, an argument could be made that any of the models could be used to forecast an applicant's End-of-First-Year GPA. Each model contained a variety of data variables, and some may be more appealing to admissions officers than others. Situations like this are prime examples of the intersection of the science and art of data analysis.

SUMMARY AND CONCLUSION

The decision-making environment of the corporate world uses business intelligence principles on a daily basis. Mining the vast quantities of quantitative and qualitative data gathered has led to the creation of business intelligence units within organizations to manage such analyses. Higher education historically trails the corporate world in embracing principles that could improve performance and lead to more certain decision outcomes. Using predictive analytics in a grander scheme could allow educational institutions to operate with higher levels of efficiency and effectiveness.

Implications for Enrollment Management Leadership

The changing demographics of the educational marketplace are almost forcing the need for educational institutions to embrace business intelligence principles. Incorporating the models developed in this study could be of great assistance to any enrollment management division in many ways.

First, understanding the potential academic success of an applicant can help eliminate much of the guesswork in the evaluation of applicants with marginal credentials. On many campuses, such decisions are currently made by admissions committees representing a variety of areas. These decisions often include anecdotal analysis comparing the marginal applicant to similar past applicants. This methodology is far from scientific and relies heavily on individuals' recalling specific details and circumstances of past applicants. A more consistent, equitable approach would be to use a predictive model to generate a forecasted level of academic success and combine that outcome with other mitigating circumstances, such as the type of high school curriculum the applicant had pursued.

Predictive models may also be incorporated earlier in the admissions funnel than the applicant stage. Understanding how inquirers may perform academically could lead to a more targeted marketing campaign earlier in the admissions process. Inquiries forecast to be not so academically successful may be sent promotional materials about academic, mentoring, and student success resources to raise their awareness of ways these services can aid in the transition from secondary academics to a college curriculum. Further, students who have excelled in their secondary school studies and are forecast to excel in a college curriculum may receive targeted communications regarding honor societies and academic research opportunities.

These predictive models would provide enrollment managers a tool that could be applied consistently across all inquirers or applicants and reduce dependence on some of the historical methods of making decisions. Using an institution's historical data for decision making would appear to be more reliable than using arbitrary values of standardized test scores and secondary school GPAs.

Suggestions for Future Study

This study's methodology focused on enrolling first-year students at the participating institution over a three-year period. However, enrolling students compose a small facet of the overall admissions funnel. Opportunities exist for future study, using the same parameters contained in the current study and expanding the number of years' worth of data used for analysis. The current study used three years' worth of data, but future analysis might use as many years' worth of data as have been collected. Conducting a true longitudinal study may yield a specific type of model that may be more accurate.

Another aspect to be considered for future study would be incorporation of more student-centric variables during the first year of study. While the current study used few descriptive variables of the first-year student environment, incorporating variables to the analysis such as the number of credit hours a student attempts, the number of hours a student studies each week, and whether or not a student holds some sort of employment could make the model more robust.

Finally, it is recommended that the scope of analysis be expanded to increase the predictive nature of the study from the end of the students' first year of study to include other level classifications. Understanding the relationship between the first-year GPA and future GPAs can allow academic advisors the opportunity to better serve their students and possibly be alerted to potential academic deficiencies much earlier. Early detection of any academic weakness is critical in determining a course of action to modify the behavior that may lead to the academic deficiency.

Most important, higher education institutions must embrace business intelligence techniques to remain competitive in the academic marketplace. The projected shrinkage in the number of high school graduates in certain regions means that colleges and universities need to use every tool within their grasp to achieve institutional goals. Business intelligence principles contain the pathway to organizational success only if higher education chooses to embrace them.

REFERENCES

Allen, J., & Robbins, S. B. (2008). Prediction of college major persistence based on vocational interests, academic preparation, and first-year academic performance. *Research in Higher Education, 49*(1), 62–79. doi:10.1007/s11162-007-9064-5

Antons, C. M., & Maltz, E. N. (2006). Expanding the role of institutional research at small private universities: A case study in enrollment management using data mining. *New Directions for Institutional Research, 131*, 69–81. doi:10.1002/ir.188

Berry, M. J. A., & Linoff, G. S. (2004). *Data mining techniques* (2nd ed.). New York: Wiley.

Chang, L. (2006). Applying data mining to predict college admissions yield: A case study. *New Directions for Institutional Research, 131*, 53–68. doi:10.1002/ir.187

Chen, C.-K. (2008). An integrated enrollment forecast model. *IR Applications, 15*, 1–17.

Fiske, E. B. (2008). How college admissions came to be hawked in the marketplace. *The Chronicle of Higher Education, 55*(5), A112.

Goenner, C. F., & Pauls, K. (2006). A predictive model of inquiry to enrollment. *Research in Higher Education, 47*(8), 935–956. doi:10.1007/s11162-006-9021-8

Johnson, I. (2008). Enrollment, persistence and graduation rate of in-state students at a public research university: Does high school matter? *Research in Higher Education, 49*(8), 776–793. doi:10.1007/s11162-008-9105-8

Matignon, R. (2007). *Data mining using SAS enterprise miner*. New York: Wiley. doi:10.1002/9780470171431

Merante, J. A. (2009). *The digital frontier: The implications of evolving technology on strategic enrollment management.* Retrieved March 30, 2010, from http://www.blackboard.com

Naik, B., & Ragothaman, S. (2004). Using neural networks to predict MBA student success. *College Student Journal, 38*(1), 143–149.

Stewart, G. (2004). Defining the enrollment manager: Visionary, facilitator, and collaborator. *Journal of College Admission, 183*, 21–25.

Sutton, P. (2007). A brief history of the enrollment management industry. *Innovation Ads*, 1-2.

This work was previously published in the International Journal of Business Intelligence Research, Volume 2, Issue 1, edited by Richard Herschel, pp. 1-15, copyright 2011 by IGI Publishing (an imprint of IGI Global).

Chapter 2
Anticipatory Standards Development and Competitive Intelligence

Françoise Bousquet
ZFIB Conseil, France

Vladislav V. Fomin
Vytautas Magnus University, Lithuania; Turiba School of Business Administration, Latvia

Dominique Drillon
La Rochelle Business School, France

ABSTRACT

More and more companies operate today in a worldwide market under conditions of globalization, increased complexity, and competition. In such an environment, business decisions need to be made quickly yet intelligent, substantiated by the most salient and relevant information available. Under the global competition, with a diligent and measured manner, many companies are increasingly treating business like an economic war. Enterprises are methodically monitoring and investigating their competitors, while deploying all the resources they have at their disposal in order to beat their current or future rivals. Competitive Intelligence (CI) has become the 'latest weapon in the world war of economics'. This paper contributes to the growing body of literature on competitive intelligence by synthesizing knowledge stemming from many years of experience in the standardization arena. The authors aim to show how, in the economic war, engaging in committee-based standards development may be used for winning the competition battle.

DOI: 10.4018/978-1-4666-2650-8.ch002

INTRODUCTION

Standardization is one of the best sources of competitive intelligence available. (Purcell, 2007)

Competitive intelligence (CI) is "the process of ethically collecting, analyzing and disseminating accurate, relevant, specific, timely, foresighted and actionable intelligence regarding the implications of the business environment, competitors and the organization itself".[1] CI is an emerging discipline, which has only become increasingly important in the business arena since the early 1980s, notably following the publication of Michael Porter (1980) on the technique of competitive intelligence to analyze industries and competitors (Du Toit, 2003, p. 113).

In the contemporary changing global political and social environment, with the increasing pace of business, increased global competition, and rapid technological changes, the growing number of companies are treating business like an economic war: "with ever-increasing vehemence, … enterprises are methodically monitoring and investigating their competitors, while deploying all the resources they have at their disposal in order to beat their current or future rivals" (Du Toit, 2003, p. 113). While it is argued that CI has become the "latest weapon in the world war of economics" (Kahaner, 1996, p. 25), in this paper we will argue that it is rather standardization than competitive intelligence, which deserves the title of a "weapon". Competitive intelligence, as the term unambiguously suggests, is first and foremost the process of intelligence, i.e., inward-oriented process of gathering information for making strategy decisions. Standardization, on the other hand, *utilizes* the CI processes to develop *products* or *services* to be offered to the market. Thus, standardization gives a company the possibility to change the way the competitors "fight" in the market, where the "standardizer"[2] keeps control on the market development trajectories.

Akin to competitive intelligence, standardization has only recently begun receiving wide attention in business affairs. Yet it has already become a cornerstone issue for companies engaged in virtually any business operation, from new products or processes design (King et al., 1994), to responding to customer requirements (Fomin, King, Lyytinen, & McGann, 2005, p.569), to outsourcing or devising globalization strategies (Lovelock & Yip, 1996; Swaminathan, 2001).

While the role of *existing* standards in the global markets received substantial attention among scholars (Farrell & Saloner, 1985; Funk, 2002), to this date, with few notable exceptions (de Vries, 1999; Mattli, 2001) hardly any systematic studies exists to guide company's involvement in the *process of developing* formal or consortia standard, i.e., *anticipatory standardization process*. Anticipatory standards define future capabilities of products or services *ex ante* in contrast to *ex post* standardizing existing practices or capabilities through de facto standardization in the market. The lack of scholarly attention to anticipatory standards development may be attributed to the fact that this subject matter isn't granted its own theory. Another reason may be in the complex organizational nature of the international standardization arena, which entails innovation system, market place, and regulatory regime (Lyytinen & King, 2002, p. 98).

In this paper we wish to contribute to the growing body of knowledge in two distinct, yet intricately linked domains – these of competitive intelligence and standardization. As science often progresses from a practical knowledge of how to do something, to a deeper knowledge of why this something works the way it does (Stokes, 1997)[3], our contribution draws on years of personal experience of the first author in the field of standardization. This paper contributes to empirical domain of knowledge by explaining how company's competitive intelligence practice can utilize specific tasks of standardization process.

Standardization and Competitive Intelligence

To discuss how standardization can become a major tool of competitive intelligence (CI) and the "weapon" for competition battles, the concepts we operate with have to be first defined.

Intelligence system in general terms can be defined as a communication facility serving the conduct of business (Luhn, 1958, p. 314). A typical CI process can be defined to consist of a series of business activities that involve identifying, gathering, developing, analyzing and disseminating publicly available information (Chen, Chau, & Zeng, 2002, p. 2) on direct and indirect competitors in a range of fields: general business activity, business development, strategy and tactics, market penetration, patent registration, etc. (Rouach & Santi, 2001, p. 552).

Standardization in general terms can be defined as a process of making a standard. A standard is a document that establishes uniform engineering or technical specifications, criteria, methods, processes, or practices, becomes a "tool for an easy dialogue between buyers and suppliers" (Bousquet, 2003a, p. 51). The aim of standardization is establishing a necessary consensus for a common solution to interoperability and portability. Standards therefore form the common reference for the dialogue between suppliers and customers, act as the tools to ensure exchange of goods and services in anonymous (global) markets (Bousquet, 2003a; Pedersen, Fomin, & Vries, 2009).

In this article we focus on anticipatory standards development, leaving market-driven de-facto standardization out of discussion. Anticipatory standards development, conducted either through formal standards development organization (SDO) or standardization consortia, is a collaborative process of (technology) design, during which relevant stakeholders interact to build a common specification (Fomin & Vries, 2009). Although substantially more risky and costly (West, 2006), anticipatory standardization can be carried out also

by any market player in isolation. In either case, the standard's developer(s) will have to gather information on trends and strategies of different relevant stakeholders to develop their own standardization strategy. Thus, standardization is akin to competitive intelligence, in that it entails such processes as gathering information (requirements discovery), analyzing what would be desirable and feasible (technology) design solutions (Lyytinen, Keil, & Fomin, 2008), devising strategy for establishing the desired (technology) standard (Gao, 2005), and developing the standard (Keil, 2002).

In this article we argue that there are more similarities than differences between the CI and standardization (see Figure 1). Standards professionals working for a firm must be able to turn raw information into usable intelligence to help strategic decision making for the firm. The entailing tasks are akin to those of CI, which is concerned with "collecting, processing and storing information to be made available to people at all levels of the firm to help shape its future and protect it against current competitive threat" (Rouach & Santi, 2001, p. 553). Recognition of the importance of CI as a management practice is growing (Rouach & Santi, 2001, p. 552). Many major companies, such as Ernst & Young and General Motors, have formal and well-organized CI units that enable managers to make informed decisions about critical business matters such as investment, marketing, and strategic planning (Chen et al., 2002, p. 1). Standardization-related intelligence processes, on the other hand, are rare in the management practice, despite the growing importance of standards.

Companies, which recognized the importance of CI, are ready to use the tools CI offers to gain advantage in the economic battle: create or increase market share, promote own technology, block technology of the others if it is convenient, etc. In this paper we demonstrate how standardization becomes one of these tools. In military practice, to win a battle, it is *essential* to have a really good strategy, good weapons, well prepared soldiers,

Figure 1. The scope of standardization and competitive intelligence processes

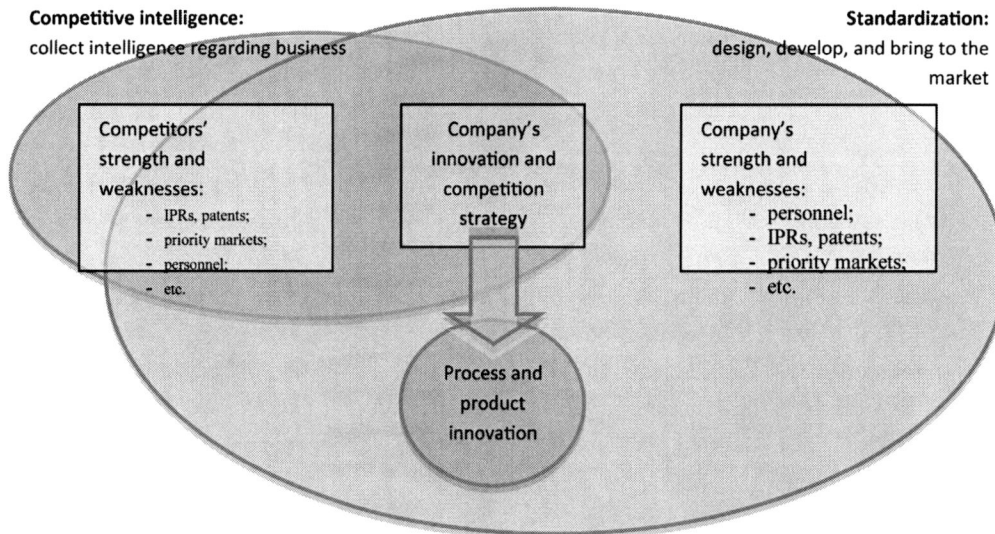

good knowledge of the battlefield and of the enemies' strengths and weaknesses. While the former two "essentials" directly pertain to the domain of intelligence, in the following sections we argue that in the competitive "war", all the aforementioned "essentials" can be attained through standardization process. What follows is a professional wisdom of the first author drawn from many years of professional experience in standardization. The presented observations and insider knowledge on standardization-as-intelligence process can help a company chart a better development strategy through securing the vital "essentials" for the "economic war".

Choosing the Involvement Strategy

In its competitive strategy formulation, a company's attitude vis-à-vis standardization may be twofold depending on their risk analysis. The company can take an active role in promoting own technology through standardization. Establishing a world-wide *de facto* standard and having all the rents from the standard is a "paradise" for

any market player (West, 2006), which can be enjoyed only by few.[4] Therefore, most companies resort to collaborative standards development, or a *laissez-faire* position – monitoring the environment and conducting a normative watch aimed to minimize the risk of being thrown out of business by a surprise.

If company chooses an active role in standards development, it must get involved in standardization process, organize strategic alliances with others to have a possibility to anticipate the future and to influence the final choices for new technology architecture.

Even if company adopts a passive attitude and only organizes standardization monitoring and watch, leaving it to the others to fight, the company still can gain a competitive advantage through spotting the best moment for entering the market with a compatible and/or competing product.

Whatever attitude has been chosen, to be passive and only organize a normative watch or, to be proactive and participate in the standardization process, a company has to define a strategy for standardization according to its business strategy, then set up the corresponding organization (hopefully, a team of full time standardizers at the highest level possible, and standardization experts coming from the different business units to participate, where it is necessary in the process). At this point, knowledge about the standardization environment will be the first gift.

The Organization of International Standards Development

A substantial number of the couple of hundred thousand standards (Schepel, 2005; Toth, 1997; WTO, 2005, p. xxv) in use today is set by formal international standards development organizations (SDOs). The most important and largest collections are those of International Standards Organization (ISO), International Electrotechnical Commission (IEC), and the International Telecommunication Union (ITU).

There are also hundreds of consortia developing international standards, some of the most known ones being World Wide Web Consortium (W3C) overseeing development of Web standards, 3rd Generation Partnership Project (3GPP) overseeing strategic coordination of mobile telecommunications standards bodies, and Internet Engineering Task Force (IETF), which oversees development of technical standards for the Internet.

The differences between different SDOs and Standards consortia are found in the rules for and fees of membership, technology domain, the status of produced standards, among other. To a large extent, these differences stem from and at the same time determine the organizational setup of standards organizations.

To give the reader a better understanding of what company's involvement in standardization process implies, we present here an brief overview of organizational structures of two formal SDOs – ISO and IEC – which can serve as a proxy to most standards development organizations.

Hierarchical Organization of the International Standardization

At such international SDOs as ISO and IEC, standards are developed in Technical Committees (TCs), each of which may have several Subcommittees (SCs) and Working Groups (WGs) (Figure 2).

TCs and SCs have a status of *permanent* units, responsible for overseeing a certain business or technology domain, which normally includes a large number of standards. SCs have a narrower scope than TCs, and can be seen as "support units" for TCs. WGs are set up on a *temporary* basis, to deal with only a few standards: WGs have the responsibility to draft standard on the basis of the *technical expertise* (knowledge about the content of the standard) of its members.

At each level of hierarchy (TC, SC, and WG), there is *a chairman* and *a secretariat* attached to the committee. The function of the secretariat is to coordinate and document the work of the respective unit, including editorial work. In general, an

Figure 2. Hierarchical organization of the international standardization

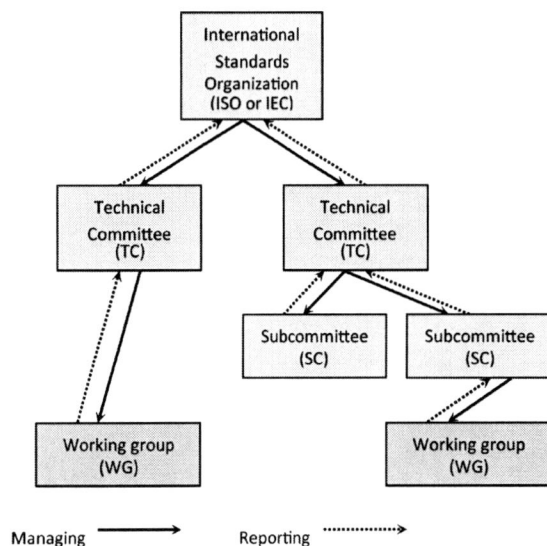

international standards development organization does not provide the secretarial support to their TCs–this activity is left to their national members. In most cases, the chairman is from industry or an important other stakeholder, and the secretary is a technical officer of a national standards organization. Chairman offices and secretariats are scattered across different countries. This holds for the different technology domains (different TCs), and, in most cases, also for the different SCs and WGs of the same Technical Committee (TC).

An important organizational character of international formal standards development is that National Standardization Organizations (NSOs) that are members of ISO and/or IEC, to a large extent contribute to the development of international standards, both in terms of content and in terms of administrative support. ISO has 157 national members, for IEC the figure is 72. In most countries, this contribution is prepared in committees of the NSO itself. In the United States the situation is different, in the sense that American National Standardization Institute (ANSI) being the national standards organization for the United States, has accredited more than 250 standards organizations, which do the major part of the work.

NSOs rely on the input of national stakeholders, which opens the doors for company interests' representation in the standardization process at the national level. However, international standards are developed at the international level, where neither the committees' nor working groups' members can represent interests of any particular national stakeholder (Figure 3). So the national stakeholders' interests become "lost in translation" from the national to the international level (see Figure 4): NSOs usually mirror the international organization of a standards development, and nominate TC and SC members to ISO/IEC to represent their *country interests* in standardization decision-making, and WGs members to act in their *personal capacity* in standard's specifications' development.

The complex national-international setup of the process makes identification of the influence possibilities for any particular company blur at best: to understand how the company's interests can be promoted is not a trivial task, which requires a substantial "homework" to be done in further scrutinizing the process of standards development. The knowledge we share in this article can spare a company a good deal of time in doing the homework.

Figure 3. The process flow in the development of international standards

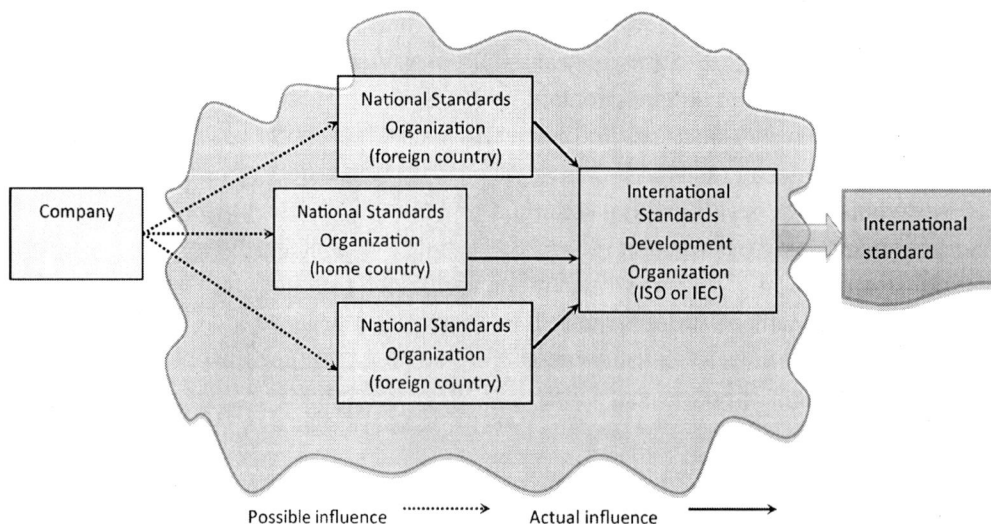

Figure 4. Influencing standardization outcomes

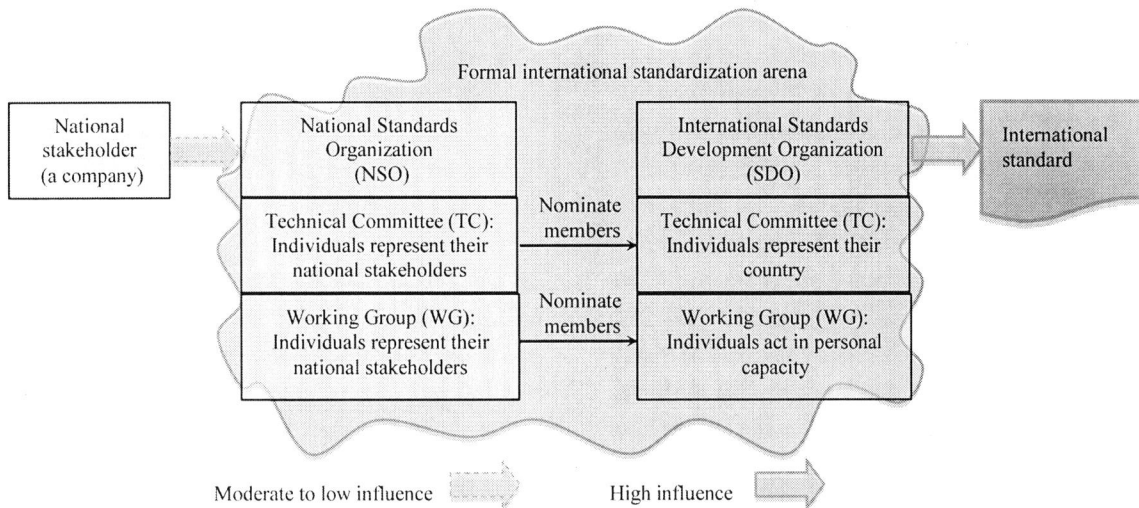

Getting Involved in Standardization Process

Decision to engage in standardization may be prompted not only by company's need for a specific standard, or a need to promote its own technology (internationally), or a need to prevent the risk of emergence of a new standard, but also by the need for a better intelligence of its environment (competition, technology trends etc.). The first question a company has to respond to when deciding to adopt an active standardization attitude, is: how to participate, where and at which level? Good standards require good infrastructure, i.e., good people serving as technical officers, committee secretaries, etc. It therefore becomes necessary to identify an appropriate SDO to join in order to get the best service.

Which SDO to Join?

The choice of the standards setting organizations to join (to be able to evaluate their services as far as training, lobby, influence, secretariat, service to the members etc., against the cost of membership)

is a key question. The standardizers have to know standards bodies relevant to their professional domain and benchmark their specific and different practices. The standardizer should also know in which ones the "future" is. Finding answers to these questions is a part of the intelligence job, which, if done well, can help a company establish a lead in the competitive battle (joining a group may be forcing other companies to do the same, thus preventing the others to choose a disadvantageous to your company solution).

At Which Level of SDO to Act?

Another point in choosing the standards organization is to know at which level you can participate in the standardization process (Fomin & Vries, 2009). As different standardization organizations have different rules for membership, some are only accessible by country representatives (national body, as is the case of ISO and IEC), for instance. Many multinational companies know the price to pay for being actively involved in the process. They have to pay the membership fee in several national bodies' organizations and their level of influence has to be maintained in each country. It is worth noting that most of the international official organizations dealing with standards in the Information and Communication Technologies (ICT) field have understood the issue and are now proposing specific structures based on a workshop principle which allow for direct participation by companies. While the documents elaborated in these structures are not recognized as official standards, they represent a real and significant consensus of industry stakeholders and could then be proposed as background working document for a future standard in the concerned field. It is the case for ISO and IEC, which have allowed the creation of specific workshops, with direct access for companies and producing IWA (International Workshop Agreement) or ITA (Industrial Industry Agreement). In the same way, in Europe, the CEN/ISSS[5] has set up workshops producing CWA: CEN Workshop Agreement, prepared in meetings where companies may be represented directly.

Play by the Rules, Play with the Rules!

One should also know the voting rules of the different organizations. It is a precious fruit of competitive intelligence to know the fact that in ISO and IEC there is one vote per national body which gives Europe a phenomenal advantage and strength if its member countries agree on a solution that, for instance, USA would not favor.

In other structures standardizers may have more voices for the vote if they pay more (it is the case in ETSI – The European Telecommunications Standards Institute). In some countries and for some standardization bodies, only professional organizations of companies have the membership right. A company can therefore be represented by a professional organization, and not directly by a standardizer, which decreases the company's level of influence. Such is the case, for instance,

for the British Standard Institute (BSI) for almost all standardization domains (except for ICT).

Furthermore, some standard setting organizations, e.g., IETF[6] and IEEE – The Institute of Electrical and Electronics Engineers[7] – accept individuals as members. In that case, a company may encourage (and pay for the corresponding expenses) their employee to participate if the issue concerned is of interest for them. Companies have to choose which channel they will benefit the more. They will have to evaluate the different possibilities, choosing to join the structure where the services rendered are the best, where the future stands, where the influence over the public administration is the most efficient, etc.

When participating in standardization process, choosing which standards organization to join, a company must take into account the chosen organization's IPR policy. Different standards bodies have different IPR rules and policy. The knowledge of these rules and policy determines the choice and the strategy related to the patents that therefore must be a part of the company's standard development process. Would the company's IPR included in the standard be royalty free, or treated on RAND (Reasonable And Non Discriminatory) principle?

DOING THE INTELLIGENCE WORK

Gathering Information

Being involved in standardization process opens venues for competitive intelligence activities. The company's standards professionals – the "standardizers" – can learn about the stakeholders' interests and trends, their roles and positions in the committees, the level of the consensus reached, if any (international standard, technical report, else), and much more, as afforded by their participation in the process.

As mundane artifact as a list of attendees at a meeting, for example, could indicate the particular interest of a competitor for the concerned subject if several of their experts participate in the discussion, or the contrary. The agenda of a meeting can tell what are the fields of interest. The contributions, the issues they deal with, their number and origin also carry information relevant for competitive intelligence. The meeting report and minutes provide a standardizer with information about the level of consensus, the reactions and positions of the different participants (competitors or allies) and also the resolutions adopted, as well as the endeavors of some, who would like to seize the influential positions (chairmanship, secretariat) in the process.

All the aforementioned sources provide a standardization participant with a wealth of important indications on the issues and concerns for the future technology development, the trends and the involvement of the other stakeholders (competitors, collaborators) and competing/alternative standardization bodies (for best practices in standard setting organizations see Bousquet, 2003b). It will be then the responsibility of the standardizer to evaluate the information, to report to the management of the Standardization cell, which will be then in a position to link with others in the Competitive Intelligence (CI) structure of the company.

Developing a Foresight

Through participation in the process, the standardizer acquires a better sense of the probable timing within which things happen: publication of a standard, vote on a standard at different stages, consolidation of comments etc. This means that the company will have the possibility, if informed by its standardizers, to adapt its strategy to better meet the arrival of the future standard – for example, to foresee the date from which it will be

necessary to comply with a standard. Knowledge of standardization rules can be used to the benefit of the company, depending on the strategy adopted (slowing down the process, blocking the process, accelerating the process, etc.). Another thing that also may be anticipated is the reaction and behavior of the different members of the stakeholders' community according to the experience they have, their culture and possible language difficulties. In general, being equipped with a good knowledge of the process and watching it, or participating in the process – both options offer a standardizer the means to have a foresight on the future market (technology, competition, etc.).

Working Head-To-Head With Competitors

If a company possesses a capacity to gather the necessary data on competitors and allies, to get to understand the characteristics of the "battle field", to anticipate the future, then the company won't be taken by surprise – knowledge on the competitors and allies will protect the company from unexpected market developments.

That knowledge on competitors comes from one of the major advantages of standardization-as-competitive-intelligence: the standardizer has the legitimate right to meet the competitor, to talk and discuss with the competitor, to eventually be welcomed on the competitor's premises for a meeting. The confidential information that would be otherwise inaccessible through CI activity, can be obtained by a standardizer in a legitimate way. One can say: "this is a war, however, my soldiers in this fight will negotiate with yours". That also shows the limits of the exercise: own "soldiers" should absolutely know what are the limits of the *status quo*. They should have good negotiation skills, good technical knowledge, and be well instructed by their management on the limits of what they are permitted to discuss.

Influencing

The standardization arena is certainly one of the best places to influence the choice of the future dominant standards and best practices (see Figure 4), as long as the standardizers know the process (rules and procedures) (Fomin & Vries, 2009), as long as they have the necessary qualities of lobbyist and diplomat, as long as they have understood the cultural and linguistic differences of the stakeholders and, obviously, as long as they are fully aware of the strategy of their company.

Let us describe, for instance, the strength one gets from knowledge of the process. Knowing when is the right moment to intervene, knowing the right rules to gain the possibility to modify the rules (procedures and processes), to make them more favorable for one's interests. If a standardizer is familiar enough with the standards setting organizations to choose the best one for one's interest, to exactly know the steps of the standard development and how and when one can play the game and influence the outcome. If company management acquires this knowledge thanks to its standardizers, they become masters of the game – they can delay or block other's choices and push their own and at the end, make the standard to contain the company's intellectual property rights, or else its preferred technological solution.

Obviously, one may also have the needed knowledge on the process and decide not to participate. One can also influence the process by being in the right positions for that: being the chairman of a committee, the secretary, the editor – all positions which, according to the type of organization, may give a company the power to slow down a process if it is in its interests, to promote own solutions etc.

Risks and Solutions

Standardization is a collective process. In principle, all participating to standardization process stakeholders have identified a need for a common solution to a specific problem and look for a consensus on how to reach that solution. On the other hand, each participating party may also count to gather intelligence on its competitors through the involvement in the standards development process. The risk for the company is, then, that participation in standard setting reveals similar competitive intelligence about the gatherer as is gathered on competitors[8], i.e., for each of the participating parties there is a risk of revealing their own strategy and business secrets.

The solution to the risk of "mutual orientation" of the competitive intelligence in standardization is that first of all, the standardizer representing his company's interests should perfectly know what s/he may say and reveal, what may be used as a business intelligence weapon, developing an obfuscation strategy, for instance.

DISCUSSION AND CONCLUSION

In this paper we used the metaphors of "economic war" and "weapon" to refer to global competition and tools and methods for successfully operating in the global competitive environment. By drawing a parallel between competitive intelligence (CI) and standardization, we reported on a number of ways how a company can obtain crucial for its business strategy data – information related to its competitors and collaborators, the process – all together constituting the "weapons" of competitive battle, the tools for formulating strategies for winning these battles.

We have argued here that standardization contributes to CI in many important ways (see Table 1 for the summary) – through involvement in standardization process standardizers will obtain a good knowledge of the "battlefield", which will allow the company to execute crucial strategy decisions – where to intervene and push, when to preach for status quo, when to try to delay the process, etc. Indeed, standardizer's skills and knowledge are of the same nature and at the

Table 1. Complementarities and differences between standardization and competitive intelligence. Pertinence of one domain to the other is indicated with arrows

	Standardization essentials		Competitive Intelligence essentials
The benefits	Knowledge of the environment	←→	Knowledge of the environment
	Knowledge of the competition	←→	Knowledge of the competition
	Increasing capacity of influencing and anticipating	←→	Increasing capacity of influencing and anticipating
	Better offer of products and services		
	Common references for trade relationship		
	Scale economies		
	Better competitive position		
Required organizational support	Positioning standardization in the company (a strategic function?)		Positioning CI in the company (a strategic function?)
	Definition of the standardization attitude (a strategic choice)		
	Coordination of standardization efforts		Coordination of CI efforts
	Choice of the Standardization organizations	←→	Choice of networks and sources
	Allocation of resources (membership fees, travels, time)		Allocation of resources (membership fees, travels, time)
	Positioning in the different organizations (chairmanship, secretary, etc)	→	
The tools	Face to face meetings	←	Software tools, web, meetings, conferences
	Networks	←	Networks
	ICT tools		ICT tools
	Standardization organizations services		
	Knowledge of processes and procedures		
	Use of Competitive Intelligence techniques and organization	→	Participation in standardization
Required skills	Diplomacy		Diplomacy
	Charisma		Charisma
	Understanding linguistic and cultural differences		Understanding linguistic and cultural differences
	Expertise in their field		
	Understanding and knowledge of the Company strategy		Understanding and knowledge of the Company strategy
	Expertise in standardization processes and procedures		
Difficulties and issues	Awareness and culture of the management		Awareness and culture of the management
	Positioning of the function		Positioning of the function
	Getting resources		Getting resources
	Demonstrating the ROI		Demonstrating the ROI
	Long term results		Long term results
	Personnel carriers and training		Personnel carries and training

same level as the ones of experts in competitive intelligence. Both company structures should work together for a mutual benefit. Expertise in CI implies experience, charisma and requires recognition by peers, as well as skills for lobbying and negotiation. The same holds for the standardizers – they are ambassadors of their company, of their country and as diplomats they must be able to know when to give and to take, where win-win solutions are possible (Isaak, 2006, p. 7).

Besides the illumination of processes and informational sources relevant to competitive intelligence, this paper contributes to standardization studies by presenting empirical knowledge on the possible risks associated with the "weapons" used in the battle. So, norms and standards may represent an important risk to the company's engagement, if not properly understood or managed. During the standardization process, the company representatives collect important and sensitive information on competitors and (future) markets, and therefore behavioral, cultural and linguistic issues come to play an important role in the process of information gathering. Besides, the success of standardizers will hinge on their abilities and skills to negotiate, lobby, know when to take and to give, and their diplomatic attitude.

As an ironic remark, one must note that the difficulties to set up inside a company the two functions (standardization and CI) and corresponding structures are also similar. For instance, the difficulty to convince the management on the utility of such structures, to have the management understanding the value brought to the company as far as information related to its environment is concerned, to have the management understanding the possibility of influencing and foreseeing the market developments. Also to be noted, for both functions the results are of a long-term nature, and that the return on investment is difficult to prove.

We believe that empirical knowledge presented in this paper can contribute to both promoting the importance of competitive intelligence and standardization in companies, and the develop-

ment of the academic field by enlisting a number of "issues", which can be further studied to better understand the role of standardization in the global business environment and how it contributes to competitive intelligence process.

ACKNOWLEDGMENT

Vladislav Fomin is thankful to Dr. Henk J. de Vries from Rotterdam School of Management for his kind and patient explanations on the organization of and the influence mechanisms in the international standardization work. The section "Hierarchical organization of the international standardization" in this article is partially based on earlier collaborative work with Dr. de Vries.

Vladislav Fomin acknowledges support from the European Community's Seventh Framework Programme (FP7), under the grant agreement No. SSH7-CT-2008-217457, "China EU Information Technology Standard Research Partnership" project.

REFERENCES

Bousquet, F. (2003a). *Dealing with standardization: do you need a guru? Paradoxes and tricks of standardization management.* In T. Egyedi (Ed.), *The 3rd International Conference on Standardisation and Innovation in Information Technology (SIIT)*, Delft, The Netherlands (pp. 51-57).

Bousquet, F. (2003b). *Role and best practices of "technical officers" in standards setting organizations.* Paper presented at the The European Academy for Standardization 9th EURAS Workshop on Standardization, Paris.

Chen, H., Chau, M., & Zeng, D. (2002). CI Spider: a tool for competitive intelligence on the Web. *Decision Support Systems, 34*(1), 1–17. doi:10.1016/S0167-9236(02)00002-7

Chesbrough, H. W., & Appleyard, M. M. (2007). Open Innovation and Strategy. *California Management Review, 50*(1), 57–76.

de Vries, H. (1999). *Standards for the Nation. Analysis of National Standardization Organizations.* Unpublished Doctoral Dissertation, Erasmus University Rotterdam, Rotterdam, The Netherlands.

Du Toit, A. S. A. (2003). Competitive intelligence in the knowledge economy: what is in it for South African manufacturing enterprises? *International Journal of Information Management, 23*(2), 111–120. doi:10.1016/S0268-4012(02)00103-2

Farrell, J., & Saloner, G. (1985). Standardization, compatibility, and innovation. *The Rand Journal of Economics, 16*(1), 70–83. doi:10.2307/2555589

Fomin, V. V., King, J. L., Lyytinen, K., & McGann, S. (2005). Diffusion and Impacts of E-Commerce In the United States of America: Results from an Industry Survey. [CAIS]. *Communications of the Association for Information Systems, 16*(31), 559–603.

Fomin, V. V., & Vries, H. J. d. (2009). *How balanced is balanced enough? Case studies of stakeholders' (under-) representation in standardization process.* In T. Morioka (Ed.), *Proceedings of the 6th biennial Standardisation and Innovation in Information Technology (SIIT) conference,* Kogakuin University, Tokyo, Japan (pp. 99-112).

Funk, J. L. (2002). *Global Competition Between and Within Standards. The Case of Mobile Phones.* New York: Palgrave.

Gao, P. (2005). Using actor-network theory to analyse strategy formulation. *Information Systems Journal, 15*(3), 255–275. doi:10.1111/j.1365-2575.2005.00197.x

Isaak, J. (2006). The Role of Individuals and Social Capital in POSIX Standardization. *International Journal of IT Standards and Standardization Research, 4*(1), 1–23.

Kahaner, L. (1996). *Competitive intelligence: From black ops to boardrooms: How businesses gather, analyze, and use information to succeed in the global marketplace.* New York: Simon & Schuster.

Keil, T. (2002). De-facto standardization through alliances - lessons from Bluetooth. *Telecommunications Policy, 26*(3-4), 205–220. doi:10.1016/S0308-5961(02)00010-1

King, J. L., Gurbaxani, V., Kraemer, K. L., McFarlan, F. W., Raman, K. S., & Yap, C. S. (1994). Institutional Factors in Information Technology Innovation. *Information Systems Research, 5*(2), 139–169. doi:10.1287/isre.5.2.139

Lovelock, C. H., & Yip, G. S. (1996). Developing global strategies for service businesses. *California Management Review, 38*(2), 64–86.

Luhn, H. P. (1958). A business intelligence system. *IBM Journal of Research and Development, 2*(4), 314–319. doi:10.1147/rd.24.0314

Lyytinen, K., & King, J. L. (2002). Around the cradle of the wireless revolution: the emergece and evolution of cellular telephony. *Telecommunications Policy, 26*(3-4), 97–100. doi:10.1016/S0308-5961(02)00002-2

Lyytinen, K. J., Keil, T., & Fomin, V. V. (2008). A framework to build process theories of anticipatory Information and Communication Technology (ICT) Standardizing. *International Journal of IT Standards and Standardization Research, 6*(1), 1–38.

Mattli, W. (2001). The politics and economics of international institutional standards setting: an introduction. *Journal of European Public Policy, 8*(3), 328–344. doi:10.1080/13501760110056004

Pedersen, M. K., Fomin, V. V., & Vries, H. J. d. (2009). The Open Standards and Government Policy. In Jakobs, K. (Ed.), *ICT Standardization for E-Business Sectors: Integrating Supply and Demand Factors* (pp. 188–199). Hershey, PA: IGI Global.

Porter, M. E. (1980). *Competitive strategy: techniques for analyzing industries and competitors.* Toronto: Maxwell Macmillan Canada.

Purcell, D. E. (2007). *Presentation on course for Strategic Standardization at the School of Engineering, Catholic University of America.* Delft, The Netherlands: Delft University of Technology.

Rouach, D., & Santi, P. (2001). Competitive intelligence adds value: five intelligence attitudes. *European Management Journal, 19*(5), 552–559. doi:10.1016/S0263-2373(01)00069-X

Schepel, H. (2005). The Constitution Of Private Governance: Product Standards. In *The Regulation Of Integrating Markets* (*Vol. 4*). Oxford, UK: Hart Publishing.

Stokes, D. E. (1997). *Pasteur's Quadrant: Basic Science and Technological Innovation.* Washington, DC: Brookings Institution Press.

Swaminathan, J. M. (2001). Enabling customization using standardized operations. *California Management Review, 43*(3), 125–135.

Toth, R. B. (1997). *Profiles of National Standards-Related Activities.* NIST.

West, J. (2006). The Economic Realities of Open Standards: Black, White and Many shades of Gray. In Greenstein, S., & Stango, V. (Eds.), *Standards and Public Policy.* Cambridge, UK: Cambridge University Press. doi:10.1017/CBO9780511493249.004

WTO. (2005). *World Trade Report 2005: Exploring the Links between Trade, Standards and the WTO.* Geneva, Switzerland: World Trade Organization (WTO).

ENDNOTES

[1] As defined by the Society of Competitive Intelligence Professionals, http://www.scip.org.

[2] Here and further in the text we call a "standardizer" a company representative(s) involved in standardization process.

[3] As cited in (Chesbrough & Appleyard, 2007, p.60).

[4] E.g., the Microsoft's Windows operating system or document formats, or Apple's iPod music player with its proprietary digital rights management (DRM) standard for digital music.

[5] CEN/ISSS does not exist anymore. It was a structure serving as a single entry point in CEN for the whole ICT Standardization. CEN/ISSS has developed the concept of workshops and their products – CWAs – today are used in all domains.

[6] The Internet Engineering Task Force.

[7] The Institute of Electrical and Electronics Engineers, Inc. Today, the organization's scope of interest has expanded into so many related fields, that it is simply referred to by the letters I-E-E-E.

[8] We are thankful to anonymous reviewer for pointing this out.

This work was previously published in the International Journal of Business Intelligence Research, Volume 2, Issue 1, edited by Richard Herschel, pp. 16-30, copyright 2011 by IGI Publishing (an imprint of IGI Global).

Chapter 3
Champion for Business Intelligence:
SMART Goals for Business Focused and Financially Backed Results

Irina Dymarsky
Purdue Pharma, USA

ABSTRACT

Although Gartner's EXP 2006 CIO Survey ranked Business Intelligence (BI) as the top technology priority, BI projects face tough competition from other projects in IT portfolios promising more tangible financial returns (Wu & Weitzman, 2006) Two major hurdles that prevent BI projects from shining in portfolios are vague requirements and weak benefits calculations. Both can be addressed by examining and learning from a number of case studies that prove tangible ROI on BI solutions when scoped and designed with a focus on specific, measurable, achievable, results-oriented, and time bound SMART business goals. In order for BI projects to compete in IT portfolios based on financial measures, like ROI, BI champions need to approach BI requirements gathering with the goal of addressing a specific business problem as well as employ standard ways of calculating BI benefits post project go live. By examining common failures with BI requirements and case studies which demonstrate how successful BI implementations translate into tangible benefits for the organization, BI champions develop a toolkit of tips, tricks, and lessons learned for successful requirements gathering, design, implementation, and measure of business results on BI initiatives.

DOI: 10.4018/978-1-4666-2650-8.ch003

INTRODUCTION

What?

A major initiative in 2010 for IT Leadership has been the widespread adoption of portfolio management. More scrutiny is applied to projects which make it through the selection phase to get funded and staffed. Project Managers (PM) and Business Relationship Managers (BRM) are tasked with collecting numerous details; from start and end dates, to capital returns, to intangible benefits all in an effort to select only those projects which offer the highest financial return on the proposed investment.

Selections become purely mathematical based on comparisons of costs, planned value, rate of return, and total return on investment. Infrastructure deployment, consolidation of support, and system upgrades all have very clear financial benefits. Business Intelligence (BI) typically depends on intangible benefits such as better decision making from reporting and metrics to drive the case for the project. Because of this, BI is often considered less valuable than funding and resourcing operational projects. Without a good way of documenting benefits, BI projects will be thrown out in the earliest phases of portfolio trimming. BI professionals need to get proficient at measuring tangible results from BI projects, become champions of BI initiatives in their environments, and work to change the perception of BI.

Despite promising competitive advantages organizations can gain by effectively using their data, they cannot get anything out of their BI implementations unless more time and effort is invested into BI focused requirements gathering. Requirements for BI are often documented at a very high summary level which repeatedly produces solutions that are not tailored to solving any business problem.

Furthermore, BI leaders must adopt a standard methodology for conveying measurable benefits of BI solutions rather than focusing on intangible benefits which cannot compete with dollars saved or goods sold.

Now and Then

Since the 1800s management theories, developed by the likes of Frederick Winslow Taylor, aim to increase efficiency through data analysis. This limited mindset is responsible for the fact that many organizations today still view BI as a reporting tool for examination of historical information and do not take advantage of the full potential of BI solutions to enable predictive analytics (Rollings, 2010).

Even in many mature corporations, BI is in its infant state. Analysis of one large pharmaceutical company demonstrate that current reports only focus on addressing "what happened" and "why did it happen" questions and are not yet sophisticated enough to predict what will happen, real-time what is happening or enabling action. The only way for BI implementation to deliver mature results, is for BI champions to become more proficient in collecting more complex business requirements and build up the financial case for larger BI investments which will produce more sophisticated reports to enable the business to truly respond to the information ahead of the trend.

How?

This paper addresses ways for BI leaders to exert greater business impact and increase effectiveness of the organization's current BI initiatives. This is not an easy task and requires most significant changes in the first and last steps of a BI initiative: requirements gathering and measure of value post go live.

- Requirements Gathering

If BI requirements are approached in the same way as an operational system's functional specification, the project will deliver limited results, encouraging management to believe that BI can only deliver limited value. BI requirements need to focus on larger patterns in the data in order to deliver a truly robust solution for long term analysis.

• Value Post Go-live

Learning from successful BI implementation case studies, BI champions need to practice working with their business partners to quantify the benefits of the BI solution. This type of information can be collected through informal interviews of the BI user community and by engaging the users; they become invested in articulating the true value of the solution. Even cost savings that may seem insignificant on their own, such as eliminated cost of paper and ink used in producing physical copies of legacy reports can be aggregated for an impactful total. The benefits presentation is further enhanced when access to the BI solution is not restricted and saving of a few minutes, few pages, few dollars, etc., can be multiplied by the large number of employees (Evans, 2010).

RESEARCH SECTION: GATHERING REQUIREMENTS AND CALCULATING BENEFITS

Gathering Requirements

This section identifies two main reasons for failures in BI requirements gathering:

1. The needs of BI end users are not considered.
2. User and functional requirements are not specific to a business problem.
    a. Generic BI Requirements
    b. Data Element List(s)
    c. Generic Functional Requirements
    d. The needs of BI end users are not considered.

Ad hoc query tools, as powerful as they are, can be understood and used effectively only by a small percentage of the potential data warehouse business user population. (Ralph & Ross, 2002)

In the world of competing priorities, the BI portion of large system implementations, such as SAP's ERP suites, is given less consideration than the actual transactional system. Often, there is no separate BI requirements gathering initiative and BI requirements are derived from the transactional system requirements. Although, no project manager would ever design a transactional system that does "a lot of stuff that users can figure out for themselves," that is exactly what happens when the BI requirement becomes "all the data that exists in the transactional system," and users are expected to drag-and-drop the elements they need for their reports (Quinn, 2007).

'Self-service BI,' in which business users create reports using graphical interfaces connected to back-end tables and/or data warehouse, is a myth, and is more likely to wreck havoc than achieve any results. The sheer quantity of facts and figures can make any attempt at analysis overwhelming, but another more concrete danger in this scenario is users selecting too many data elements which are not logically related, creating complex queries that slow down processing for any other application using the data. In a world of instant gratification, long processing time frustrates users causing them to give up on their information search and ultimately on BI. In reality, users typically need only a small percentage of the elements they unnecessarily include in their queries (Eckerson, 2007).

Not understanding how many concurrent users the systems will have or how the users will be interacting with the data can be truly disastrous from an infrastructure and system architecture perspective. In the case of Plano Independent School District, their BI implementation had to be postponed for six months, until school officials along with their vendor could reengineer the infrastructure, which failed within 15 seconds of a test deployment, to handle the expected production system usage (Kelly, 2009).

Those who do not understand BI, assume that the value of BI software is "general purpose analysis." That is simply not true. A business user faced with a blank screen of an ad-hoc reporting tool and a list of hundreds of tables each containing hundreds columns of data is overwhelmed and confused. Even when training is provided, it is typically not extensive enough to overcome the initial shock of not knowing where to begin and the immediate reaction that this exercise is not worth the time and effort (Quinn, 2007). *Refer to Analysis section on Interactive Reports for recommended solution.*

Although the principle of simplicity applies not only to BI implementations, a question every BI project manager must ask is: when "does too much of a good thing become more overwhelming than beneficial?" Focus on what is necessary, be selective, and simplify the user experience (Fielding, n.d.).

USER AND FUNCTIONAL REQUIREMENTS ARE NOT SPECIFIC TO A BUSINESS PROBLEM

Generic BI Requirements

Experienced BI professionals, like Jayanthi Ranjan (from the Institute of Management Technology, Ghaziabad, India), know, and experiences at several corporations show, that historically the BI need in organizations is not planned in conjunction with new business application deployments, but rather delivered afterward via a large data transfer into the data warehouse. The data itself and its formatting are not defined based on business requirements but often match the design of the transactional source system (Ranjan, 2008).

The starting point for creating a BI solution, like any other IT system, should always be a specific

problem identified in the organization. The only way any BI implementation is going to succeed is by having a very specific business objective from the beginning.

Instead, time after time BI projects come up with very broad, generic BI requirements:

- "…produce enhanced organizational capabilities to manage data and information as organizational assets."
- "…provide a single version of the truth."
- "…enable consistent and reliable access to accurate corporate-wide data."
- "…provide more sophisticated reporting and analysis, faster turnaround, improved accessibility and enhanced quality."
- "…a single touch point where detailed financial transaction information can be filtered on user-entered selection criteria, viewed online, downloaded in standard file formats and used to generate real time reports" (Williams, 2008).

These statements are hard to prove and measure post implementation and will not translate into an ROI calculation because they cannot be tied to any financial gains.

Data Element List

Another common pitfall of BI requirements is to create a list of data elements that the business users will be able to use in their ad-hoc reporting. Although a catalog of all data elements is in fact a positive asset for the development team, as a basis for requirements it does not provide any information about how the user may want to use these data elements or how they need to be integrated with other organizational information (Williams, 2008).

Even in well established, mature organizations such as Johnson & Johnson analytics groups still request lists of required fields for their daily analysis instead of focusing on functionality they need to achieve from the data set. In one case, the project team discovered during testing that some of the mappings were done incorrectly because there was no process to tie the requests to, and transactional systems like SAP often use a single data element in multiple contexts.

Generic Functional Requirements

Examples of non-specific functional requirements:

- The system shall provide the ability to drill down, drill across, and slice-and dice.
- The system shall provide the ability to specify organizational hierarchies and display performance scorecards for each organizational unit.
- The system shall enable role-based access to information.
- The system shall provide capabilities to route alerts to business users according to user-defined parameters.
- The system shall enable integration of data from multiple disparate sources (Williams, 2008).

Functional requirements such as those listed above are necessary for custom IT development, but for commercially available BI tools they are all standard features and do not add any value to addressing the business data need. Unlike other IT initiatives, the challenge of a successful BI implementation is not technology, but rather the greater demands on solid process, broad skill set, and business focus (Howson, 2006).

Ultimately, the use of inappropriate methods for gathering BI business requirements leads to failed implementation and generates the belief that BI investments are ineffective business tools and are not a practical financial investment (Williams, 2008).

CALCULATING BENEFITS

As discussed in the section above, purchasing a BI solution for "general purpose reporting and analytics" is not only un-impactful for the business users, but is also the largest expenses and the smallest ROI (Quinn, 2007).

As reported in a 2003 IDC study, "The Financial Impact of Business Analytics," well planned BI implementations can have realized returns ranging from 17 percent to more than 2,000 percent with a median Return on Investment (ROI) of 112 percent. "According to the study, analytics implementations generate an average five-year ROI of 431 percent with 63 percent of the companies having a payback period of two years or less" (Sutcliff, 2004).

The sections below will cover different types of profit measures and summarize the most common categories for realizing benefits from BI implementations.

FINANCIAL MEASURES

Return on Investment (ROI)

In finance, ROI, is the ratio of money gained or lost on a business venture or a project relative to the amount of money invested and is the most commonly accepted financial measure for evaluating benefits (Wikipedia, n.d.).

ROI = ((NPV of Savings) / (Initial Investment)) * 100 (Sutcliff,2004)

Net Present Value (NPV)

NPV compares the value of the investment today to the value of investment in future monetary measures based on inflation and returns (Investopedia)

$$NPV = I_0 + \frac{I_1}{1+r} + \frac{I_2}{(1+r)^2} + ... + \frac{I_n}{(1+r)^n}$$

- I = yearly income amount
- Subscripts and exponents in the denominators = year numbers with zero denoting current year.
- R = discount rate (constant in this example)
- N = number of years the investment lasts (Baker, 2000)

Internal Rate of Return (IRR)

IRR is the rate of growth a project is expected to generate (Investopedia, n.d.). The payback period determines the number of years for the project to break even.

Payback Period = (Initial Investment) /

(NPV of Gains / Total Number of Years in the Planning Horizon) (Sutcliff, 2004).

Profit Measure

The profit measure alone cannot defend a project in a portfolio, but combined with ROI, it gives an easier to understand perspective of the value gained from the implementation.

Profit = ($ Contribution to Profit) - ($ Cost of the BI system) (Hoberman, 2006)

BENEFITS REALIZATION CATEGORIES

Many organizations rely on ROI measures; however, there is no sure way to prove that a revenue increase of 10 percent is 100 percent directly attributable to the BI project. Other factors such as market fluctuations, level of employee

training or new competition may influence the revenue change (Howson, 2006). The difficulty in quantifying BI benefits is that a BI solution itself does not provide financial returns. This is a major difference between BI implementation and other IT projects and must be clearly articulated to executive sponsors. BI projects typically do not make possible server retirements, saved electricity costs, but they can contribute to increased revenue or decreased costs from new processes that the BI solution makes possible or existing processes that it enhances (Sutcliff, 2004). Although a BI system that analyzes data from data center operations, can provide insight into inefficiencies in the facility's operations, leading to changes that do in fact provide savings from better use of resources.

Two examples below from Evan Levy (n. d.), partner and co-founder of Baseline Consulting, offer insight into translating 'soft' or 'intangible' improvements into financial results:

- Higher staff involvement has been shown to decrease staff turnover, resulting in decreased costs. With a calculated cost of $100,000 per customer service representative, reducing employee turnover by 5 percent equals $1.25 million annually in saved hiring and training costs.
- By providing on-demand reports to salespeople in the field, the sales staff was able to double their acquisition rates for new accounts. In the first year, this represented an additional $23 million in sales revenues (Levy, n.d.).

Direct benefits of BI implementations are decreasing costs and increasing revenue (Sutcliff, 2004). One way of decreasing costs is by increasing efficiencies. In Case Study 3, the US Coast Guard reduced cost of holding inventory through better visibility into the true needs and more accurate forecasting. The Blue Mountains Resorts case study also claims increased efficiencies in their processes for monitor reservation volumes and guest activity, adjusting room rates, and assigning workers to different resort areas.

Another way to decrease costs is to eliminate redundant systems. Again, the US Coast Guard was able to reduced system downtime by combining two legacy systems into one for reporting.

In Case Study 1, Harrah's Entertainment claimed increased revenue by successfully tying in the acquisition of more customers and an increase in current customer spending to its new BI system.

Cost avoidance such as reducing employee turnover, or customers lost to competitors is an additional way to consider increased revenue. In Case Study 2, Martin's Point Health Care, avoided the cost of hiring extra headcount due to the increased efficiency of its current group.

Indirect benefits are hours saved (translated into dollars) of staff time spent on analytical and interpretive knowledge work rather than transactional and routine tasks such as data mining or report creation. Case Studies 1 (Harrah's Entertainment), 2 (Martin's Point Health Care), and 3 (US Coast Guard) all pointed to increased productivity of their current analytics groups as indirect benefits of their BI implementations. Furthermore, a 2007 Congressional study found that on average, analytics contracting costs for are almost twice what the same work would cost if performed in-house (Stiens & Turley, 2010).

Most importantly, to claim success the BI solution must not only have strong financials, but all benefits must be tied to business strategies; specific solutions to business problems.

CASE STUDIES

A successful BI initiative should always tie directly to business strategies. To illustrate value of the project in relation to business strategies is a key win for BI champions (Sankaran, 2002). The following section is a review of four case studies of BI investments with a strong focus on business strategy and positive ROI calculations.

Each case contains a short summary and business strategy sections explaining the business driver for the initiative, as well as investments and returns supported by graphs. The results section of each case study ties back to the direct and indirect benefits categories defined above.

CASE STUDY 1: HARRAH'S ENTERTAINMENT (NUCLEUS RESEARCH, INC., 2004)

ROI: 389% Payback: 4 months

Summary

Harrah's Entertainment, Inc. turned to a BI solution to help improve one of the company's goals of building lasting relationship with its customers. The company used BI to track customer interactions across all the properties instead of just one and implemented a Total Rewards Program based on its new findings.

Business Strategy

The development of Harrah's BI tool was driven by the business strategy to analyze customer relationships across properties with the goal of driving additional revenues. The solution was considered a success for its support of holistic analysis and reporting of customer trends.

Investment(s)

Biggest investment for Harrah's Entertainment, Inc. is personnel (42 percent) - reliance on internal IT department and consulting work. Software was the second largest investment (36 percent) spent on data warehouse, reporting and querying tools (Figure 1).

Figure 1. Costs and benefits for Harrah's Entertainment, Inc

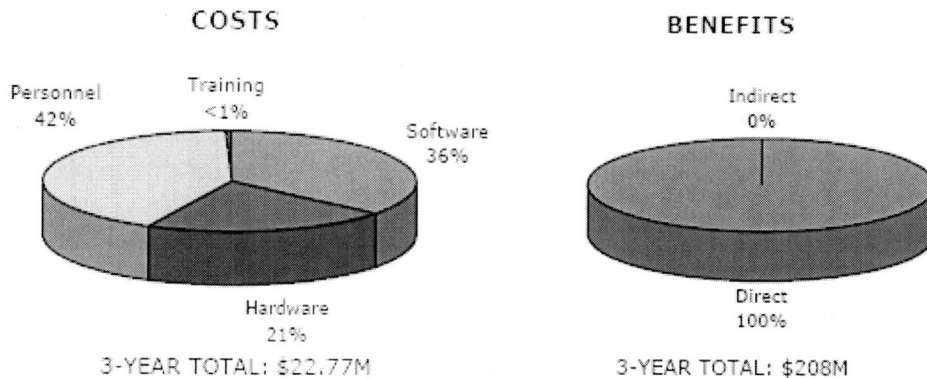

COSTS

Personnel 42%
Training <1%
Software 36%
Hardware 21%
3-YEAR TOTAL: $22.77M

BENEFITS

Indirect 0%
Direct 100%
3-YEAR TOTAL: $208M

Return(s)

Increased revenue generated from the rewards program is a direct benefit towards the ROI calculation for the BI investment. Harrah's Entertainment, Inc. found that current employees could now spend significantly more time analyzing data rather than collecting it and factored the saving of not hiring extra resources (annual fully loaded cost of employees) as another direct benefit toward the ROI calculation (Figure 1).

CASE STUDY 2: MARTIN'S POINT HEALTH CARE (NUCLEUS RESEARCH, INC., 2009)

ROI: 1,185% Payback: 1 Month (Average Annual Benefit: $335,250)

Summary

By realigning its Information Technology and Analytics department, Martin's Point Health Care created a functionally specialized group solely for analytics. The group was able to move away from ad-hoc / custom report creation to instead enabling users to interact with their data by truly understanding the requirements.

Business Strategy

The informatics team defined three specific obstacles that limited their ability to help end users access information and make decisions. These challenges we defined as: data diversity, report volumes, iterative analyses.

Investment(s)

The main investment was the time spent by members of the informatics department to strategize the new roadmap for the team, scope deliverables, write up new job description, and perform other administrative tasks associated with the new direction of the group (Figure 2).

Return(s)

Martin's Point Health Care considered both direct and indirect benefits in its ROI calculation. The main direct benefit was the avoided headcount to achieve the new higher level of analysis. The indirect benefit was the increased productivity of the end users via the new tools (Figure 2).

Figure 2. Costs and benefits for Martin's point health care

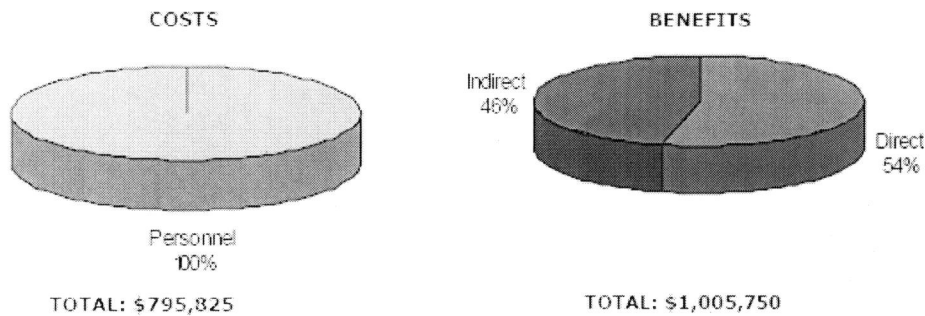

COSTS

Personnel
100%

TOTAL: $795,825

BENEFITS

Indirect
46%

Direct
54%

TOTAL: $1,005,750

CASE STUDY 3: US COAST GUARD (NUCLEUS RESEARCH INC., 2005)

ROI: 102% Payback: 8 months

Summary

Flight itineraries, aircraft status, maintenance, and supplier information were stored in two legacy systems making it difficult to track inventory purchases and duplicating data entry. By implementing a BI solution the US Coast Guard was able to combine the data for analysis.

Business Strategy

US Coast Guard included BI requirements as part of a larger project to consolidate flight operations data into a single system. The team focused on data requirements to eliminate duplicate entry and creating a consolidated view of data previously split across systems, while delivering a web based reporting tool with zero footprint on the desktop.

Investment(s)

As with previous examples (Case 1 and 2) the personnel investment is the largest with 61 percent of total project cost. This total includes development and ongoing maintenance of the system.

The analysis of costs was conducted over three years (Figure 3).

Return(s)

The US Coast Guard quantified ROI by considering both direct and indirect benefits (Figure 3).
The direct factors are:

- Reduced system downtime by combining two legacy systems into one for reporting.
- Reduced inventory through better visibility into the true needs.

The indirect factors are:

- Reduced requisition reorders (their costs contribute to ROI as cost avoidance) though expanded user access to the information.
- Improved forecasts for parts demand.
- Workforce productivity gains by the improved ability to retrieve/access flight log entries.

Figure 3. Costs and benefits for US Coast Guard

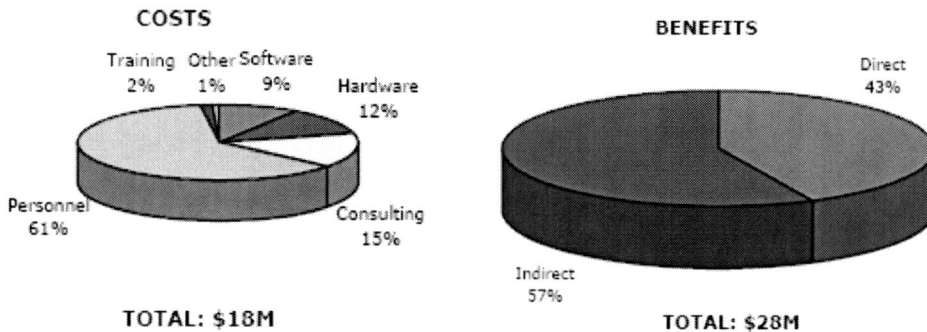

COSTS

Training 2% Other 1% Software 9% Hardware 12%

Personnel 61%

Consulting 15%

TOTAL: $18M

BENEFITS

Direct 43%

Indirect 57%

TOTAL: $28M

CASE STUDY 4: BLUE MOUNTAIN RESORTS (NUCLEUS RESEARCH INC., 2008)

ROI: 1,822% Payback: 1 month

Summary

Becoming a publicly-held company Blue Mountain Resorts needed a different level of reporting on its profitability as required by the public markets. The company needed to consolidate analysis across its numerous business lines.

Business Strategy

The switch from a private to a public-held company created new operational visibility need to deliver profitability reporting as required by the public markets.

Investment(s)

Software and personnel are the top expense categories. Training includes cost of instruction delivered from the vendor (Figure 4).

Return(s)

Direct benefits include cost avoidance for administrator headcount to monitor reservation volumes

and guest activity, adjust room rates, and assign workers to different resort areas. All of this information is now being generated in automated reports which allow the current administrators to take on expanded responsibilities. Blue Mountain Resorts also observed a reduction in excessive labor costs and inventory levels with the help to better forecasting ability (Figure 4).

ANALYSIS SECTION

This section is a combination of best practices, recommendations and methodologies found in the industry. When implemented, the toolkit's precise focus on up front planning, requirements gathering, and business alignment is a sure way to achieve success on BI projects in any industry. The section contains:

- SMART Business Goals
- Three Step Toolkit for BI Requirements Gathering
- User Interview
- Interactive Report

SMART BUSINESS GOALS

A summary of all the aspects discussed in the Gathering Requirements Research Section comes down

Figure 4. Costs and benefits for Blue Mountain Resorts

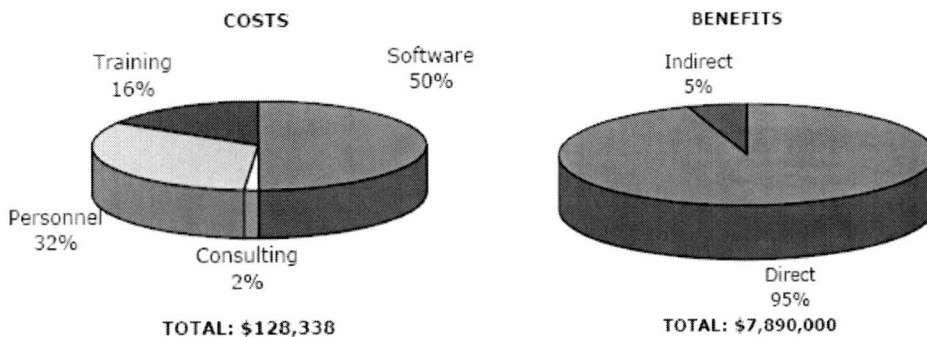

COSTS

Training 16%
Software 50%
Personnel 32%
Consulting 2%

TOTAL: $128,338

BENEFITS

Indirect 5%
Direct 95%

TOTAL: $7,890,000

to a focus on a specific, measurable, achievable, results-oriented, time bound SMART business goal. The acronym SMART, which for the purposes of this paper stands for Specific, Measurable, Achievable, Results-oriented, and Time-bound, is not specific to BI. The term first appeared in the November 1981 issue of Management Review by George T. Doran and has since been widely used in project management and employee performance management (Doran, 1981).

Whether building a BI competency center as Aiman Zeid describes in his article or championing a single BI initiative SMART goals are the key to success (Zeid, 2006).

- **Specific (S):** Identify top business priorities and objectives as a basis for determining scope, structure, and required skills.
- **Measurable (M):** Monitoring user interactions with the BI system and making sure all agreed policies and procedures are being followed will ensure that any concerns are addressed before they develop into a negative stereotype about the capabilities of the system or an unwarranted judgment about the capabilities of the analytics group.
- **Achievable (A):** An extensive BI implementation, especially for large organizations with a large number of data elements and processes is a slow process. Defining

goals for multiple iterations ensures that development targets the greatest benefits first and that advanced features evolve as the users get more comfortable with the system.

- **Results-Oriented (R):** The only way to know if the project is staying on course or if post deployment is trending to the anticipated benefits is to collect and publishing performance metrics as soon as there is sufficient information.
- **Time-Bound (T):** Similarly to the incremental development plan, benefits should be measured using multiple time scales. Defining short and long term performance metrics will enable benefit calculations and communications stay relevant and current.

THREE STEP TOOLKIT FOR BI REQUIREMENTS GATHERING

The first step to building a strong business case for a BI solution is to be able to articulate, in business terms, the specific improvement to business results (Figure 5).

After creating the business case, explicitly link business intelligence and one or more targeted business processes. Center of Figure 6 depicts an example of well defined BI-driven business im-

Figure 5. Business-driven BI requirements development process (sub-process 1.1 – BI opportunity analysis) (© 2008 DecisionPath Consulting – Used with permission)

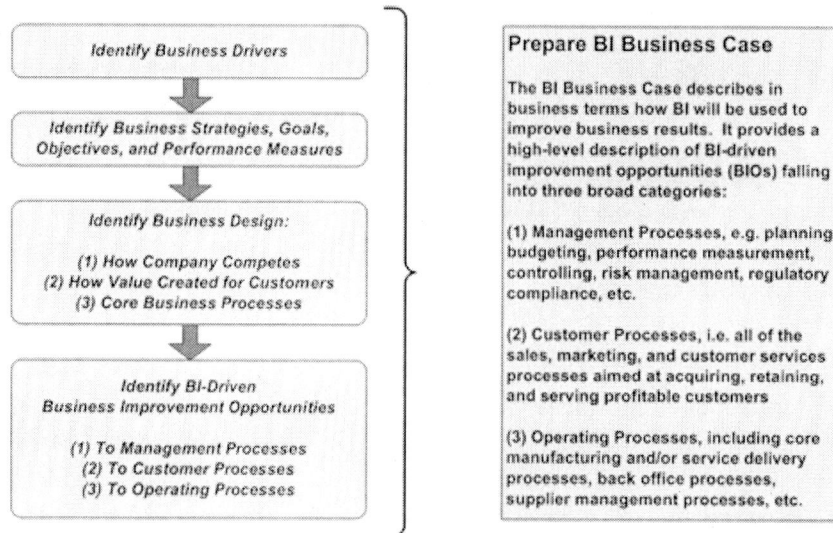

Figure 6. Business-driven BI requirements development process (sub-process 1.2 – BI portfolio definition) (© 2008 DecisionPath Consulting – Used with permission)

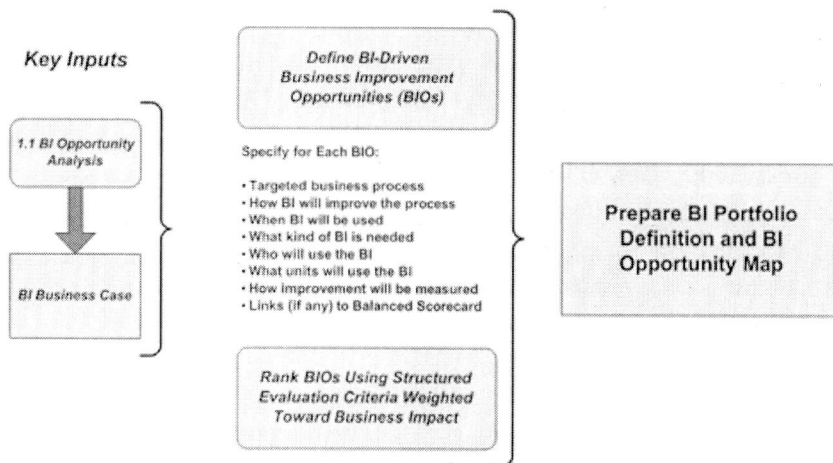

provement opportunities (BIOs) each used to improve a targeted business results.

This is a necessary but often difficult step, as even well established organizations "often do not have easily accessible or well-articulated strategic business goals statements" (Ranjan, 2008).

The last step in forming strong business-focused BI requirements right is to concentrate on the details in the areas of (Figure 7):

A. Business Information
    Example: Established and recognized metrics and Key Performance Indicators (KPIs).

Figure 7. Business-driven BI requirements development process (sub-process 1.3 – BI requirements definition) (© 2008 DecisionPath Consulting – Used with permission)

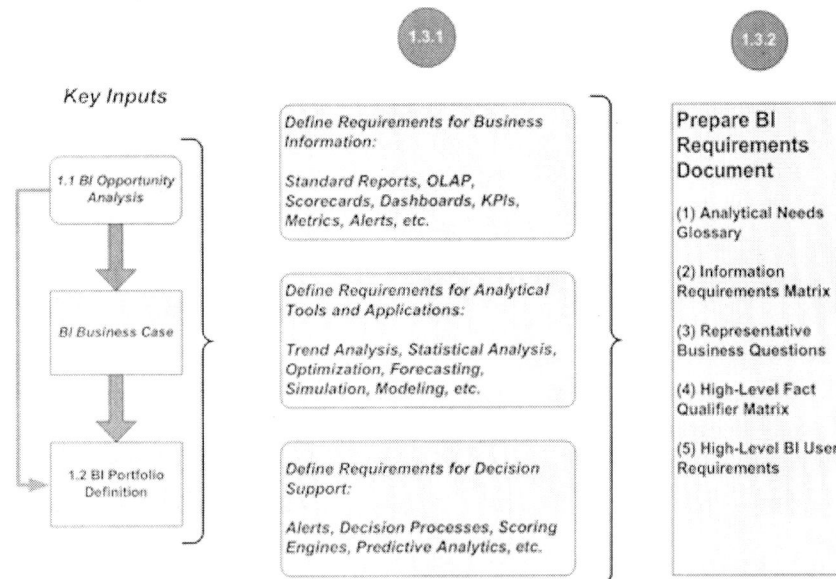

B.   Analytical Tools and Applications
     Example: Use of filtering or prompts to enable user data mining.
C.   Decision Support
     Example: Email alert to management.

Common challenges faced in this step are (Ranjan, 2008):

1.   Defining KPIs that align with business objectives. *Refer to section on User Interviews for facilitation instructions.*
2.   Extending usage of those KPIs across all functional areas and hierarchy levels in the organization. This will enable a common language when using analysis results of the BI tool.
3.   Integrating results with current operational activities and financial outcomes so that executives can hone in on the impact on the set strategic goals.

Without proper definitions around *what* will be measured through BI and *how* the measurements are defined, the lack of consistent answers to business questions will earn the BI tool a reputation for being unreliable and worthless. In reality, the true cause of inconsistency is the lack of key metrics, accounts, and terms for the usage of the tool. Specific pre-defined and well communicated definitions and calculations are the key to getting to a harmonious view of business activity and enabling executives to make critical decisions based on the information (Eckerson, 2007).

USER INTERVIEWS

In preparation for interviews, users should prepare samples of the reports they currently produce or use for analysis. Results of interviews can be recorded into a Business Requirements Document (BRD) which also contains objective, purpose and scope of the BI initiative and the data requirements (McKnight, 2003).

User interviews question set:

- What are your business objectives?
- How do you interpret data set results?
- How should the data you work with be organized?
  - Should it be organized by customer, product, geography and time?
  - Should it be organized by account, salesperson, distribution channel and month?
- What are the hierarchies, rollups or aggregations used with these dimensions?
  - Do customers roll up to geographies that roll up to total?
  - Do products roll up to product groups?
  - Do salespeople roll up to districts that roll up to regions?
- What types of summary reports do you work with?
- What are the measures or facts you work with?
  - Examples: revenues, expenses, balances, variances, percent growth, percent of total?
  - How are they defined?
- Do you "filter" the data?
  - Do you need data only at the top and bottom accounts?
  - Do you review the performance of only certain types of products?
  - Do you segment the data based on demographics?
- How often do you obtain refreshes of the data?
  - Do you obtain them daily, weekly, monthly or quarterly?
  - Do you need it this often?
- What tools do you use to interact with the data?
- Is the data clean?
- Do you receive the data in a timely fashion?

- Do the tools you use support your requirements?
- What types of things would you like to do that you can't do today?
- What is your tool functionality?
- What is your data availability?
- Do you spend most of your time on analysis or preparation for analysis?

INTERACTIVE REPORTS

To combat the issue of overwhelming table names and data elements users encounter in do-it-yourself ad-hoc reporting environments is to use the interview results to build a set of reports that users can interact with in a pre-defined and limited manner. According to Wayne Eckerson (2007), a well defined dashboard or scorecard containing filters can replace dozens, if not hundreds, of existing reports. He recommends that the dashboard focus on a specific domain, but still allow users enough flexibility to create their own personalized view. It is the best of both worlds, users feel that they have enough ad-hoc power to customize their analysis, but every option is pre-defined and tested during development (Eckerson, 2007).

CONCLUSION

The future success of BI projects is dependent on alignment to business strategy and mathematically based payback calculations.

Addressed in both the Requirements Gathering and Benefits Calculation sections is the focus on the needs of BI end users. Traditionally, IT groups have been tasked with calculating ROI for technology investments. However, it is imperative to involve business stakeholders in project justification discussions. Business sponsors need to define the benefits of the BI solution and articulate how increased functionality or better data support their strategic goals. Once the project is associated with solving a business problem any realized improvements must be converted to financial metrics (like revenue, cost, and profit) (Levy, n.d.).

Using the requirements gathering and business case methodology proposed in the Analysis section along with the financial metrics presented in the Calculating Benefits section, BI champions can deliver on all the SMART goals of current BI solutions and create enticing proposals for expanded BI initiatives to enable organizations to harness the full power of data for trend analysis and forecasting.

REFERENCES

Baker, S. L. (2000). *Economics interactive tutorial: Perils of the internal rate of return*. Retrieved from http://hadm.sph.sc.edu/courses/econ/invest/invest.html

Doran, G. T. (1981). There's a S.M.A.R.T. way to write management's goals and objectives. *Management Review, 70*(11).

Dyché, J. (2010). *How to make the case for a BI center of excellence*. Retrieved from http://www.information-management.com/issues/20_1/center_of_excellence_bi_business_intelligence-10016936-1.html

Eckerson, W. W. (2007). *The myth of self-service BI*. Retrieved from http://tdwi.org/articles/2007/10/18/the-myth-of-selfservice-bi.aspx

Evans, P. (2010). *Business intelligence is a growing field*. Retrieved from http://www.databasejournal.com/sqletc/article.php/3878566/Business-Intelligence-is-a-Growing-Field.htm

Fielding, R. L. (n.d.). *The CEO's guide to the top 5 issues that misguide business intelligence decisions*. Retrieved from http://www.advancingwomen.com/mobile%20cell%20phone/the_ceos_guide_to_the_top_5_issues_that_misguide_business_intelligence_decisions.php

Hoberman, S. (2006). *What is the enterprise data model ROI?* Retrieved from http://www.information-management.com/issues/20060501/1053415-1.html

Howson, C. (2006). Seven pillars of BI success - BI tools are getting better, but technology is only part of the story. *Intelligent Enterprise, 9*(9), 33.

Investopedia. (n. d.). *Investopedia*. Retrieved from http://www.investopedia.com

Kelly, J. (2009). *School district overcomes 'catastrophic' business intelligence deployment failure*. Retrieved from http://searchbusinessanalytics.techtarget.com/news/1507086/School-district-overcomes-catastrophic-business-intelligence-deployment-failure

Levy, E. (n. d.). *Ten mistakes to avoid when estimating ROI for business intelligence*. Retrieved from http://www.bi-bestpractices.com/view-articles/4781

McKnight, W. (2003). Business intelligence requirements analysis, part 1. *DM Review, 13*(11), 50.

Nucleus Research Inc. (2004). *ROI Case Study: Teradata Harrah's Entertainment, E65*. Retrieved from http://nucleusresearch.com/research/roi-case-studies/roi-case-study-teradata-harrahs-entertainment/

Nucleus Research Inc. (2005). *ROI case study: Cognos United States Coast Guard, F66*. Retrieved from http://nucleusresearch.com/research/roi-case-studies/roi-case-study-cognos-united-states-coast-guard/

Nucleus Research Inc. (2008). *ROI Case Study: IBM Cognos TM1 Blue Mountain Resorts, I65*. Retrieved from http://nucleusresearch.com/research/roi-case-studies/roi-case-study-cognos-blue-mountain-resorts/

Nucleus Research Inc. (2009). ROI case study: IBM Cognos BI Competency Center Martin's Point. *Health Care, J40*, Retrieved from http://nucleusresearch.com/research/roi-case-studies/roi-case-study-ibm-cognos-bicc-martins-point-health-care/.

Phillips, N. (2010). *Achieve business intelligence project success with executive sponsorship.* Retrieved from https://community.altiusconsulting.com/blogs/noelphillips/archive/2010/03/05/achieve-business-intelligence-project-success-with-executive-sponsorship.aspx

Quinn, K. R. (2007). *Worst practices in business intelligence: Why BI applications succeed where BI tools fail.* Retrieved from http://www.b-eye-network.com/files/2007%20Information%20Builders%20Worst%20Practices%20in%20BI%20WP.pdf

Ralph, K., & Ross, M. (2002). *The data warehouse toolkit: The complete guide to dimensional modeling* (2nd ed.). New York, NY: John Wiley & Sons.

Ranjan, J. (2008). Business justification with business intelligence. *Vine, 38*(4), 461–475. doi:10.1108/03055720810917714

Rollings, M. (2010). *Too much automation, not enough insight -- the redefinition of BI.* Retrieved from http://blogs.computerworlduk.com/computerworld-archive/2010/03/too-much-automation-not-enough-insight--the-redefinition-of-bi/index.htm

Sankaran, V. (2002). *Justifying your BI project in these times of need.* Retrieved from http://www.gantthead.com/article.cfm?ID=93697

Stiens, K. P., & Turley, S. L. (2010). Uncontracting: The move back to performing in-house. *The Air Force Law Review, 65,* 145–186.

Sutcliff, M. (2004). Beyond ROI: Justifying a business intelligence initiative. *DM Review, 14*(1), 44.

Wikipedia. (n. d.). *Rate of return.* Retrieved from http://en.wikipedia.org/wiki/Rate_of_return

Williams, S. (2008). *BeyeNETWORK: Business intelligence business requirements and the BI portfolio.* Retrieved from http://www.b-eye-network.com/view/6887

Wu, J., & Weitzman, N. (2006). *Information management.* Retrieved from http://www.information-management.com/issues/20060801/1060142-1.html?pg=1

Zeid, A. (2006). Your BI competency center: A blueprint for successful deployment. *Business Intelligence Journal, 11*(3), 14–20.

This work was previously published in the International Journal of Business Intelligence Research, Volume 2, Issue 2, edited by Richard Herschel, pp. 22-36, copyright 2011 by IGI Publishing (an imprint of IGI Global).

Chapter 4
Enterprise Intelligence:
A Case Study and the Future of Business Intelligence

Joseph Morabito
Stevens Institute of Technology, USA

Edward A. Stohr
Stevens Institute of Technology, USA

Yegin Genc
Stevens Institute of Technology, USA

ABSTRACT

This paper examines the key issues associated with current and future implementations of business intelligence (BI). The authors review the literature and discover both the growing importance and emerging issues associated with BI. The issues are further examined with an exploratory, but detailed, case study of organizations from a variety of industries, yielding a series of lessons learned. The authors find that organizations are rapidly moving to an enterprise perspective on BI, but in an unsystematic way. The authors present a prescription for the future of BI called "enterprise intelligence" (EI). EI is described in a framework that combines elements of hierarchy theory, organization modeling, and intellectual capital.

INTRODUCTION

The origins of this research began somewhat informally and anecdotally with comments from our students in Stevens' process innovation, knowledge management, and data warehouse and business intelligence courses. Also, we were receiving comments from experts in consulting firms and companies about business intelligence (BI) concerns and trends that we found intriguing from both an academic and practical perspective. Initially, the concerns were centered on centralized versus decentralized BI (Whiting, 2004). However, as we reviewed the literature on BI issues and trends, we saw immediately that a more comprehensive approach was called for.

DOI: 10.4018/978-1-4666-2650-8.ch004

From our preliminary investigation there emerged two primary research questions:

1. How are major companies organizing their BI approach to meet the demands of their environment?
2. What are the relative roles of IT and the business units in BI?

According to a survey of business technology professionals in 2009, their number one goal is to "plan to train in-house BI experts and power users on analytical tools" (Henschen, 2009). Similarly, the 2010 IBM survey of global CEOs highlighted the usage of "intelligence and analytics to create foresight" to create advantage out of complexity (IBM, 2010). In contrast to this optimism, the Gartner Group describes a consistent gap between "theory" and "practice"; most notably, an over reliance on tools and reporting, unclear responsibility and governance lines, data quality and modeling issues, disconnected project portfolios, and so on (Bitterer, 2010).

In a Financial Times Special Report, "Managing Intelligence: How to make sense of the pieces," a series of six articles describes both the promise and challenge of BI (Financial Times, 2009). Selected titles reveal those promises and concerns: "The final frontier of business advantage", "Finding a home for all that data", "Search goes on for a 'single version of the truth'", Lighting up the road ahead", "IT aims to overcome the blind spots", and "Historians asked to become forecasters". Embodied in the titles are the same advantages and concerns found in the IT literature, but from a business perspective, including everything from managing data to city-center redesign.

In general, our reading of both the trade and academic literature highlights a technology-centric approach to BI. Whether we are speaking about "promises" or "realities", the questions and answers are typically framed as IT problems. In contrast, we approach BI as an *organizational design* problem, where, quite often, the same

technology issues discussed in the trade press are considered from an organizational perspective.

To investigate these research questions, we decided on an initial but detailed exploratory case study of a small number of selected organizations from a wide variety of industries that we identified as data intensive and technically mature. The combination of a small number of carefully selected organizations with a detailed analysis covering a large number of BI topics allowed us to "initialize" our research and adopt a comprehensive approach, necessary we believe, to better understand both the conceptual and practical issues of BI. The case study and its results are described.

We believe that there are three transformative trends in IT: business intelligence, social networking, and mobile technology for ubiquitous IT. BI must support and guide the other two major trends and be seamlessly integrated with the hundreds, if not thousands of processes that exist both within the firm and between the firm and its partners. For BI to fulfill the promise of a transformative discipline, it must be *systematically* expansive and deep. Accordingly, we have developed a framework – *enterprise intelligence* – that synthesizes several viewpoints that we believe are necessary for a transformative approach to business intelligence: systems thinking, intellectual capital, and management perspectives. This paper builds on the case study research and describes our prescription for business intelligence, which entails a more comprehensive view that we call "enterprise intelligence."

CASE STUDY METHODOLOGY

To the best of our knowledge, there has been no comprehensive study of the issues raised by our two research questions. Thus, the current state of BI in organizations with regard to governance and usage issues remains largely unknown despite the large number of articles in the trade literature as briefly summarized above. We therefore elected

Table 1. Sample companies and interviewees

Industry	Interviewee Title/Function
Financial services	Senior vice president; Director
Pharmaceutical services	Senior architect
Healthcare services	Physician-researcher
Legal services	Director
Telecommunications	Director

to use an exploratory case study approach (Yin, 2003). On the other hand, though exploratory, the case study questions are fairly detailed and address the nitty-gritty of architecture and operations that BI managers confront daily.

The case study included a structured interview of 25 questions (Appendix), followed by one round of Delphi question and answer. The interviewees were all senior level people with responsibility for business intelligence in their respective organizations (Table 1.) All of the respondents were intimately familiar with most, if not all, aspects of BI in their respective organizations. All the organizations were large and represented a variety of industries, including financial services, pharmaceutical, healthcare, legal services, and telecommunications.

Most interviewees were given the questionnaire several days before the interview. The questions were sufficiently detailed that a certain amount of preparation was necessary for in-depth answers. The key parameter of the interview was that the answers are unstructured and free form; each interviewee was encouraged to either select a choice and elaborate or simply answer as he or she saw fit. The results were summarized and submitted to the interviewees for additional commentary.

Business intelligence is "large" in every sense of the word. Even though our questions narrow the focus of our research to issues of BI organization and locus of BI use, the questions included in the interviews necessarily covered a variety of overlapping areas or dimensions. These dimensions are based on the general concerns described above in the trade press, and include, for example, the question of governance, the "single version of the truth" issue, etc. Also included are the more scholarly issues raised by Davenport (2010) and others; for example, the apparent fact that line knowledge workers are the least served BI community (Aberdeen Group, 2009). (Note: this is verified in our research results.) But if key knowledge workers are not being served, who is? This brings us full circle to one of the author's experience as a senior BI manager: it is easier to sell and implement BI as an improved reporting tool rather than a transformative organizational system (Also verified in our research results).

Accordingly, drawing on both the literature and extensive BI experience, we first developed a series of premises that have been identified in the literature (e.g., single version of the truth, etc.) or that we believe represent the managerial problems of BI managers or vice presidents (e.g., enterprise vs. local data, economies of scale, etc.). This is shown in Table 2. This was followed by the development of our research dimensions and possible choices (see Table 3 for selected dimensions) from which we categorized the questions. See the Appendix for the specific questions. Both the premises and the dimensions and their corresponding questions were communicated to the respondents prior to each interview.

The authors relied on both their academic and business experience in BI to guide the interviews. This expertise proved invaluable in understanding and integrating the nuanced comments of the interviewees. Also, in our discussion of the case study results, we have tried to use the words and phrases of the respondents to maintain the color and intent of their answers.

Table 2. Premise of research

In general, the questions were framed with the following ideas in mind:
  1. Seeing "the right data at the right time". This encompasses a variety of issues including data sourcing, data quality, meta-data, master data management, and the "single version of truth". In this case study, data quality is defined as user confidence in data sources, accuracy, completeness, ease-of-access, and timeliness (Strong et al. 1999).
  2. Breadth and depth of BI penetration, including process and organizational integration. This includes the pervasiveness of BI in the organization (Aberdeen Group 2009).
  3. Centralized vs. decentralized BI
  4. Governance and leadership
  5. Scale in moving and processing data (e.g., cleansing), including the usage of tools
  6. Enterprise vs. local data
  7. Development of actionable knowledge
  8. Development of analysts

Table 3. Selected research dimensions

Dimension	Range of Choice
Distribution of BI	Departmental vs. organizational
Functions supported	Executives, managers, business analysts, operational workers, knowledge workers
BI utility	Reports, scorecards & dashboards, data manipulation (e.g., OLAP, data mining)
User sophistication	PhD, SME training, casual (e.g., report reader)
Process-BI binding	Uncoupled, informal, formal
Data quality, distribution, and type	Accuracy, user confidence in source, ease-of-access, completeness, timeliness; Enterprise vs. local data; Historical vs. real-time (or near real-time)
Meta-data utility & form	Enterprise repository, DBMS, tool-specific, none
Architectural configuration	Data-centric, user-centric, composite architecture
Data warehouse integration	Isolated, conformed dimensions, consolidated
Alignment between classical BI and analytics (mining)	Formal, informal, separated
Governance - management	BI environments managed separately; centralized mgt
Governance - functional	Centralized, decentralized, federated
Toolset	Standardized across the organization, partial, none
Scale – ETL & cleansing	Integrated tools, separate tools, no processing tools
Cloud BI	Yes, no, under consideration

CASE STUDY RESULTS AND COMMENTARY

Below we present the results of our case study. Given the complexity of BI we also include a commentary on selected details where appropriate to promote understanding. Later in the paper we provide our general observations of the case results.

Distribution of Business Intelligence

The key issue in this section concerns the deployment of BI across departments and the job roles that utilize BI. There are two principle findings with respect to the distribution of BI.

A.   The first is that virtually all the organizations we interviewed are making BI more available throughout their departments and divisions, at all levels, and in all job roles.

Current distribution ranges from implementation in a single department (i.e., marketing) to full organizational deployment. For example, a large pharmaceutical organization currently in transition is using successive BI deployments as learning environments to establish their architecture and standards. This company has marketing users with plans to rollout BI into a supply chain management initiative; this will be used as the platform for pharmaceutical implementation, to be followed by global rollouts.

B.   BI is most commonly used by executives and analysts, as well as operational workers.

There is a push to rollout to managers. However, *BI in knowledge work is rare*. This latter observation is seen in another observation discussed below – BI is used primarily as a reporting rather than a knowledging tool. Clearly, this represents an opportunity for improvement with significant benefit to the competitiveness of the organization. A knowledging tool extends value to business analysts (who currently use BI) as well as knowledge workers.

User Profile and Access

We structured our analysis of users around the interrelated dimensions of user skill and utility, access frequency, and business process binding (i.e., connectedness).

A.   In our sample, BI is used primarily as a reporting tool, including associated activities such as drilling.

Increasingly, there is a push for dashboard use, but this remains comparatively small. Analytics, both OLAP and data mining (particularly the latter) is very small; the exception, of course, is when the BI system is specifically used as a research tool, as we found with the healthcare organization. Also, the legal services firm was an exception, as many as 20% of its users manipulate data through spreadsheets, OLAP, or mining. This is in contrast to the other companies where the percentage was about 5%. In general, it appears as if BI is being used as an integrated and improved replacement for OLTP reporting instances rather than a platform for high-end analytics and knowledge discovery.

B.   This latter observation is further seen in the type of training provided – point-and-click navigation, report, and dashboard use. High-end analytical training is minimal.

If a PhD is hired he or she is expected to have the necessary skills. However, our organizations sometimes train subject matter experts (SME) on specific analytical tasks to use OLAP or particular statistical tools tailored to those tasks. Only the pharmaceutical company makes extensive use of PhDs; the healthcare organization uses interdisciplinary teams of physicians, pharmacists, and statisticians; the legal services firm uses no PhDs or statisticians.

C.   Access varied from daily to periodic (i.e., daily or monthly) with occasional on-demand usage, depending on the job role of the user. In all of the companies, there is a large month-end spike in use.

Marketing users, for example, access BI every day while higher managers access BI monthly. Also, daily access users are sometimes being steered to interactive dashboard use.

D.   For most of our organizations, BI is closely coupled with business processes, particularly core operational processes.

People engaged in specific tasks require BI to do their job; furthermore, this dependency extends to virtual and organizational groups. Functional teams use BI to provide valuable monthly information to middle and executive management. Multiple performance measures require access to the data found in BI systems. This result is not surprising since the industries represented in the case study are information-intensive. On the other hand, the association between BI and business processes does not appear to be formal; rather, BI supplies "data" for performance management and other month-end activities. A formal – i.e., design driven – connection is required if BI is to support the knowledging tasks of the organization

DATA

The key issues in this section include the quality of data, meta-data and its effect on reuse and productivity, and the role of local data in BI.

A. Data quality – defined in this case study as user confidence in data sources, accuracy, completeness, ease-of-access, and timeliness – varied from moderate to very high.

Of primary concern is the quality of source systems. Organizations are responding by using the BI development process to identify quality issues in the source systems, which are then recycled back to the originating applications for enhancement. Also, customer data was cited as the one dimension in most need of improvement.

B. All organizations have locally generated and controlled, department- or facility-specific data.

Local data allows for subunit flexibility and most companies plan to do little to change. However, one organization plans to migrate local data to central control, while currently providing roadmaps to local data. Only one company currently requires all local data to go through a centralized

data warehouse, and interestingly, this is the one organization that has a single data warehouse for the entire organization (see architecture discussion below).

C. There is low to moderate use of meta-data.

Most meta-data resides in simple data dictionaries or is tool-specific. One organization uses a data dictionary in combination with SharePoint for Q&A among users to share definitions. Still another organization did not use meta-data at all, even though it plans to do so. In all these cases, meta-data is used in what we would describe as a descriptive mode to inform an interested party. One organization, which custom codes its ETL process, embeds reuse in code modules with algorithms in reference tables. Only one organization actively and *formally* uses meta-data to promote reuse. Our organizations recognize this weakness and several have plans to promote reuse and improve data quality (particularly customer data) through meta-data and master data management techniques. Meta-data appears to be an area in need of improvement, particularly with respect to reuse and productivity. A solid meta-data initiative may also be used to logically identify and integrate local and centralized data.

ARCHITECTURE

This section is the most extensive and includes several aspects of architecture, such as logical architecture, data design approach, data alignment between traditional BI and analytics, among others.

A. Most organizations in our study employ what we have termed "early BI architectures"; that is, isolated warehouses or marts. Figure 1 depicts the evolution of BI architectures over time.

Figure 1. Evolution of BI architectures

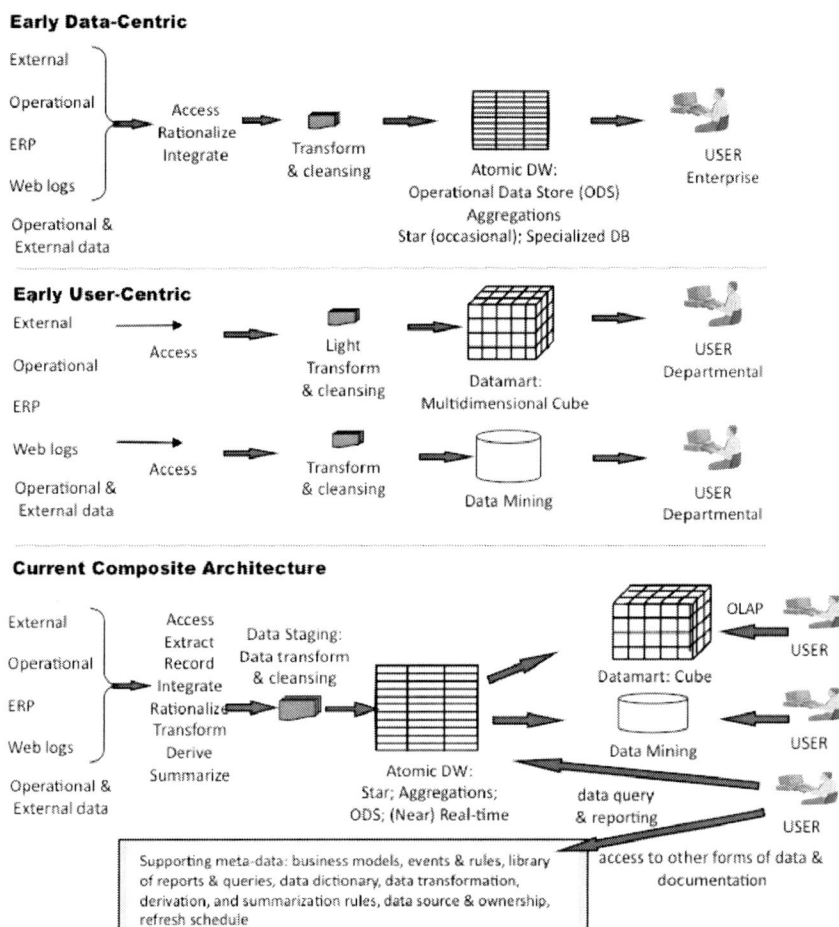

An isolated data warehouse can be thought of as an "atomic" data warehouse (Inmon, 1996) while a data mart is a small departmental data store made popular by OLAP vendors. The first arrangement supports simple data analysis while the second produces a collection of stores with data of varying quality (i.e., definitions, cleansing algorithms, etc). In contrast, a "current BI architecture" is a composite of both types of early architectures – an atomic data warehouse with corresponding data marts and OLAP cubes (Morabito et al., 2009). The organizations were divided between "early" and "current" configura-

tions. The "early" organizations consider the "current" to be their "target" design.

B. Another finding concerned the data design philosophy itself. Several organizations use operational data stores (ODS) as either stand-alone data warehouses or in combination with data marts.

An ODS is a fully normalized, integrated data store that is typically used as part of a data staging environment or as the principle atomic data warehouse itself. When used as a data staging store the ODS is invaluable in maintaining data integrity; however, as a data warehouse an ODS is more suitable for integrated OLTP queries rather than analytical OLAP queries that often retrieve millions of data records. This too was somewhat surprising: we had expected either star schemas or a combination of ODSs (as a data staging component) with stars. It is likely that organizations with ODSs used as principle atomic data warehouses make extensive use of aggregation tables. This is an area for future research.

C.   Interestingly, one organization (a telecommunication company) uses a single, organization-wide ODS in combination with OLAP cubes.

In this case, we suspect the architects consider the reports, dashboards, and OLAP cubes generated from the organizational ODS to be the analytical "deliverable" while the ODS itself is reserved for IT-use or OLTP queries. Not surprisingly, this organization maintains a fully centralized (e.g., no local data) environment within IT. This too is an area for future investigation.

D.   Another organization envisions the creation of a single, organization-wide data warehouse with corresponding marts, but is unclear on the data design philosophy. Unlike the organization discussed in the previous paragraph, this organization has more local data than any we investigated and is likely to remain largely decentralized.

This too is an interesting, if curious finding: a goal of a single data warehouse in the midst of facility-specific data under local control. This is yet another area for future research.

E.   At the other end of the spectrum, one financial services organization with a large number of mature BI environments is seeking to consolidate into 11 environments.

When complete, the 11 environments will be a mix of all architectural configurations and data design philosophies. Also, the consolidated "authoritative" 11 environments will employ both logical and physical conformed dimensions in an enterprise architecture embracing all BI environments.

F.   In general, we found a large variety and combination of architectures between and sometimes within organizations: atomic data warehouses, departmental data marts, and combinations of data warehouses and marts ("current architecture"). The same may be said of the detailed data design approach, which ranged from ODSs, star schemas, to OLAP cubes.

G.   Of the organizations with several BI environments, there is little formal integration between warehouses or marts.

However, there is a recognized need to align, logically or physically, through conformed dimensions or warehouse consolidation. The pharmaceutical organization mentioned above will be using its successive deployment strategy as a vehicle to identify its conformed dimensions. The legal services firm is concerned about the quality of its customer dimension.

H.   Another finding is that not all access to data goes through a BI environment – there remains selected access to source OLTP systems, but this is being reduced.

I.   There is relatively little near- or real-time data available through BI.

This suggests limited operational utility for BI, and represents a possible contradiction to the answer above that current users include operational workers.

J.   All organizations use relational and multidimensional data stores.

K.   For most organizations, the data used for mining is usually but not always requested from BI.

That is, there is an informal association between traditional BI and data mining areas. However, in the case of the telecommunication company mentioned above, if raw data is needed for mining, it is the IT department that gets the data; this is in keeping with its highly centralized architecture and governance structure. In the pharmaceutical organization only the mature BI environments have a close association with data mining; most environments have informal connections with pockets of complete separation.

Data Mining

All organizations have a goal for a formal connection between BI and data mining. This finding may have historical roots. Data mining has often existed in the business units outside of IT control. However, as organizations pursue the goal of being an "analytical competitor" (Davenport, 2004) there is developing a centralizing paradigm (supported by this research) that makes such isolation between the business units and IT less desirable. The result is that data mining is moving closer to traditional BI. Interestingly, the OLAP cube that is part of BI is also an analytical tool used with mining (Davenport et al., 2010); thus, architecturally speaking, tying together the functions of BI and mining.

Governance

This section concerns two primary areas: the management of multiple BI environments and the functional management of BI activities such as data transformation, report development, and data mining.

A.   Other than the telecommunication company that manages a single BI environment, dif-ferent BI environments within the same organization are each managed by separate groups.

However, our organizations recognize the necessity of centralized governance and have adopted innovative structures to manage in a federated fashion. For example, the financial services company has implemented cross-sector and cross-regional governing bodies that set direction and use policy. The governing units consist of representatives from the business units and IT and control such functions as data modeling and report design. On the other hand, there is a single technical unit responsible for the "plumbing" of the target 11 environments. The healthcare organization has national policies, but each BI environment is managed separately with local rules. The pharmaceutical organization has separately managed environments, but is moving toward a centralized BI group for governance and strategy; furthermore, they are planning a BI management office for development, similar to but different than a project management office. Finally, the legal service firm simply manages their environments separately. Note that centralized or federated governance is particular important in an organization that has not yet consolidated their data warehouses nor implemented conformed dimensions. In fact, a federate governance structure facilitates and is complementary to consolidation or conformed design.

B.   Most BI functions reside in separate groups, or sub-groups that either tree-up to a group manager or are tied together through a virtual governing group.

The one exception is the telecommunications company that manages a single environment; however, its marketing group is separate but closely coupled with IT. One financial services organization uses its cross-sector governing units – made up of key stakeholders across all business lines and geographies – as virtual governance groups to manage the separate BI functions (e.g., extract, transform, data design, report development, etc.). In the healthcare organization the environment architecture, technology, and access to data are managed by IT, while all other functions (e.g., mining for research and mining for planning) are entirely local. The pharmaceutical company plans to put all functions within its new centralized BI group. Lastly, the legal services firm has mostly functional separation, but is moving toward centralization to leverage its resources.

Observe that all the organizations studied recognize a need to bring analytics under the control of BI. However, currently there is generally a loose association (architecture and governance) between BI and data mining.

Toolset

This section concerns the type of tools used by organizations, the division of authority between BI and user groups, and whether organizations are gaining scale through reuse of their ETL and cleansing tools.

A. All organizations in the case study use a wide variety of tools and include, for example, ETL, OLAP, and statistical and mining tools.

However, the telecommunication company does not use an ETL tool; rather it uses its development staff to program the ETL functions as well as to promote reuse (described in *Data*, section c above)

B. BI tools are generally under the control of a centralized BI or technology group.

In one organization, user groups are either given tools or they select from a predefined list. If a user group wants to use an unapproved tool it will either be rejected or not supported.

C. Perhaps most importantly, there is little scale and reuse in the use of data churning tools (i.e. ETL, data cleansing). This is additionally seen in the limited, formal use of meta-data.

Cloud BI

A. Organizations are investigating cloud BI and none of our respondents have found it appropriate for BI.

The reasons stated include maturity of technology, data security, and the necessity to cultivate an internal data and analytical competency. One organization stated that they use an "external cloud" for operational data and statistics (e.g., outages, changes, service-level data); however, this is part of a finished SAS solution. It is not likely their other BI environments will follow.

B. There may also be a legal issue: both the healthcare and pharmaceutical organizations cited HIPPA as an obstacle.
C. In general, there is little interest in cloud BI at this time, or as one director stated: "definitely not".

Future Plans

A. All of our organizations plan to grow their BI initiatives and implement the data, architecture, and governance structures discussed above.

However, there is variation in degree: the telecommunication company will expand and grow without appreciable structural change; other organizations (e.g., legal services) will centralize and improve data quality (i.e., customer data); yet others (e.g., pharmaceutical) will promote systems and functional integration, process interconnectivity, improved data quality (master data management), while growing organizational breadth and depth.

KEY OBSERVATIONS FROM THE CASE STUDY

The most important finding is that organizations are making a strong move to centralize BI through both architecture and governance structures. This is more than an attempt by IT to control data, but rather an initiative by organizations to use their data to promote consistent and fact-based decision-making on an organization-wide basis. However, the results also indicate an unsystematic, bottom-up approach that fails to address several issues and opportunities revealed in our case study; in particular, an over-emphasis on reporting and performance management and little BI support for analytics or knowledge work.

BI is most commonly used as a reporting tool and as a dashboard to communicate key performance indicators (KPI) and other performance metrics. Executives and analysts are the most common users. Operational workers also use BI, but the relatively low volume of near- or real-time data suggests addition investigation is required. One possibility is that operational workers are accessing local data, outside the control of BI.

For significant parts of the organization, BI is embedded, formally or informally, in the processes of the organization. Both individuals and groups (real or virtual) use BI to do their jobs and to produce information, particularly at month end, for senior managers and executives. In accordance with a model of BI and organizational decisions advanced by Davenport (2010), our findings suggest that most organizations straddle the loosely-coupled and structured-human relationships. BI is more of a secondary structure rather than an integral element in process design. This is seen in the type and utility of BI integration – reports and scorecards for executives and analysts. The value-adding activities of the organization appear to be largely neglected and represent an opportunity to integrate BI into the knowledging activities and processes of organizations.

BI is rarely used by knowledge workers and represents a significant opportunity for improvement. This is not to say that knowledge workers do not use analytics, but based on the results of this research, it would, for most organizations, be outside the control of BI. To move to an enterprise intelligence perspective, knowledge (K) itself, K-work and K-processes, and K-workers will have to be addressed.

Our organizations have a moderately high level of data quality. However, all recognize a need to improve, particularly their customer data. Master data and meta-data management techniques have been cited as vehicles to improve both data quality and to facilitate the coordinated design and management of multiple BI environments.

Organizations have local data. While one organization drives local data through its centralized data warehouse, in effect removing local data from the company, the others appear to be doing little. However, one organization is migrating its local data to central control, more through governance rather than centralized storage. The management of local data remains a largely unaddressed issue.

An outstanding issue remains the integration of BI with high-end analytics. There is the natural conflict between the economies of scale of centralized BI and the flexibility required in local business units. Federated design and the virtual governance units used in one of the financial services organizations in this case study may be one solution to this dilemma. A BI management office (as in the pharmaceutical company) is also a possible solution.

There is a need to consolidate or conform existing BI environments. As BI technology and design techniques have improved and organizations have learned, early adopters are faced with a need to align their existing environments, through consolidation or conforming dimensions. Here too, good meta- and master-data management would be beneficial.

Significant opportunities exist to promote scale and reuse, of both data and knowledge. This requires a long-term commitment, but the value to organizations is potentially large.

Our organizations are using innovative techniques to govern and manage across departments, including a BI management office and virtual governance groups. The organizations are not blindly consolidating, but striving to realize the benefits of both centralization and decentralization, and in effect, to develop a federated approach to BI.

As we look at the results as a whole, there is a strong effort by the organizations to push data to all parts of the organization, at all levels. However, it is largely targeted to the "bottom line" as opposed to the "top-line"; hence, the reliance on reports for executives and managers as a principle BI product. A move to an enterprise intelligence perspective requires embedding BI into the knowledging areas of the organization, all within the context of current BI technologies and organizational structures. This is the thrust of our prescription for the future of business intelligence.

ENTERPRISE INTELLIGENCE AND THE FUTURE OF BUSINESS INTELLIGENCE

Emergence of Enterprise Intelligence

This research indicates an emerging enterprise intelligence paradigm. This most evident example is seen in the centralizing activities organizations are using to design and deploy BI systems. An enterprise approach has started to appear in the literature, though most papers concern tools and technologies rather than a new paradigm. For example, the term "enterprise intelligence" has been used to refer to next generation BI reporting tools (Kosambia et al., 2008), or integrated platforms and analytics (SAS, 2010). Similarly, "enterprise intelligence" appears in the title of a presentation concerning Web 2.0 while the author's corresponding web site makes reference to aligning queries and data to establish enterprise context (Jonas,

2006). In contrast to these technical approaches, Tom Davenport has developed an organization-wide framework that he calls "DELTA": data, enterprise orientation, leadership, targets, and analysts; however, "DELTA" concerns enterprise analytics rather than an integrated BI-analytics approach (Davenport et al., 2010).

In contrast to a technology or single-threaded focus, both the results of this case study and the authors' experience strongly suggest a multi-faceted approach. Accordingly, we draw on an umbrella, educational framework of business and IT developed by Dhar and Sundararajan (2007). The top part of Figure 2 shows their framework while the bottom part illustrates our application to EI.

There are several key ideas that we draw from Figure 2. For example, modularization as used by Dhar and Sundararajan (2007) indicate modularized programming. We may extend this idea for BI and assert that modularization leads to the idea of data nuggets (e.g., meta-data), which in turn, promotes understanding and what we term "thinking with data." When we "think with data" we uncover patterns of interest, or knowledge (K) nuggets. To continue further, an EI system pushes K-nuggets into other organizational systems, including strategy development, process innovation, and culture.

A working definition of a knowledge nugget is a pattern of interest to the organization that is both actionable and "well-formed"; for example, a non-instantiated query or database view that provides actionable information in a specific context for a specific purpose. By "well-formed" we mean a K-nugget with clearly defined boundary conditions – necessary for capture, storage, reuse, and assembly into more complex nuggets. We must separate what is generally known as meta-data from K-nuggets. Meta-data is descriptive and typically used for informing, such as communicating something about the structure of a data element to a database administrator or a definition to a business user. In contrast, a K-

Figure 2. Overarching framework for enterprise intelligence

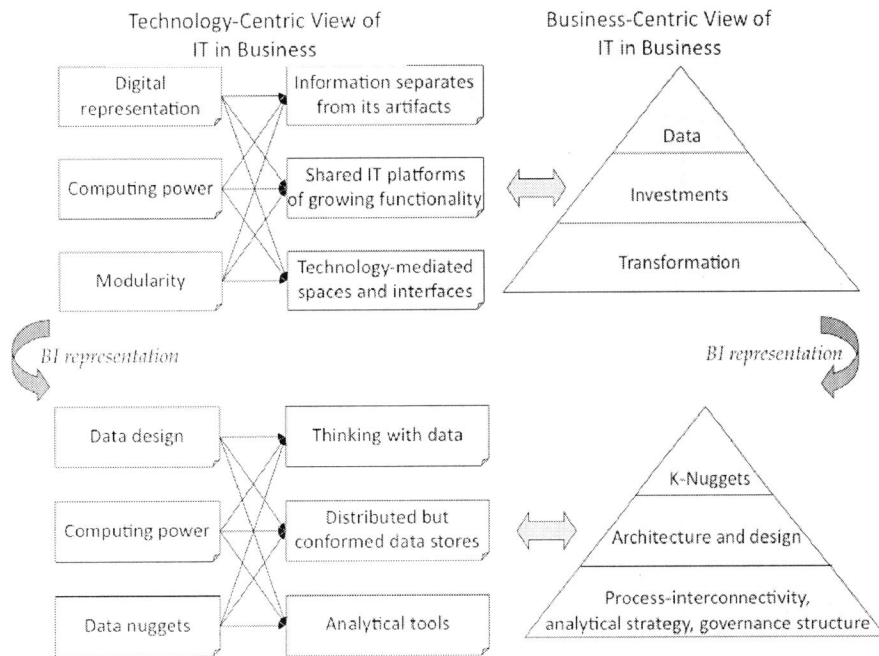

nugget is simultaneously insightful and actionable and may have commercial value. However, not all K-nuggets need be commercial; for example, a complex data cleansing algorithm is a K-nugget for internal use.

Enterprise Intelligence

We define enterprise intelligence (EI) as an *organizational system of intelligence*. We characterize EI by synthesizing the concepts associated with open systems from classical organization theory (Robbins, 1990) and those of the knowledge organization (Nonaka et al., 1995). In general, *an organizational system of intelligence is a set of artifacts and activities that systematically promote knowledge and knowledging and that are embedded in the strategies, processes, culture, and technologies of the organization.* As with all systems, EI is comprised of differentiated and specialized components that operate as a synchronized whole.

In fact, in our framework EI is a special kind of system known as a *hierarchy* – a system with a set of interacting sub-systems that implement the higher-level system and from which unique properties emerge (Simon, 1973). We may additionally refine hierarchical intelligence with the notion of an organization molecule (Morabito et al., 1999). An organization molecule is a representation of an organizational system (e.g., strategy, process, culture, etc.) following the rules associated with both object-oriented analysis (Morabito et al., 1993) as well as hierarchy theory. Naturally, each sub-system, in turn, is itself a hierarchy that is implemented with *its* corresponding set of interacting sub-systems, and so on. We may further describe an EI system using language associated with the literature on intellectual capital. In particular, we have synthesized the work of the Konrad Group and Roos et al. in their model of the Intellectual Capital Index (Andriessen, 2004). This composite framework – *an enterprise intelligence molecule* – is illustrated in Figure 3.

Figure 3 illustrates an *enterprise intelligence molecule*: a set of three interacting, "intangible" sub-systems that implement and give rise to the higher-level EI system, which additionally exhibits emergent characteristics. Also, by "intangible" we refer to assets or resources, without physical or monetary substance, that are based on intellectual capabilities and activities that, in combination, are able to produce future benefits for an organization (Andriessen, 2004).

The first sub-system is *human capital*. Its primary constituents (i.e., sub-systems specific to human capital) include individual competence and intellectual agility. Individual competence refers to the knowledge (tacit and explicit) and skills of individual people while intellectual agility includes personal innovation, adaptation, and the ability to use knowledge from one context in another (adapted from the Intellectual Capital Index). For example "education level" is one measure of individual competence. Recall from our case study that PhDs were rare, but were compensated for by specialized training to SMEs.

Structural capital is a hierarchy of four interacting sub-systems. Perhaps the most important is

represented by the pair-wise, mutually interacting data and knowledge sub-systems. Patterns discovered in data may be defined as meta-data and lead to knowledge nuggets, or meta-knowledge. K-nuggets, in turn, should follow strict object- and systems-principles that allow for their formal definition, storage, distribution, and assembly into more complex nuggets. Organization contexts refer to the other organizational systems that both comprise and interact with EI. We list three contexts that were of importance to the respondents in our case study, but other systems may be included. Of critical importance is that they concern knowledge and knowing; for example, a knowledge process would include drug discovery but not data entry. The last structural sub-system is tools and technologies and may be considered optional – it has physical substance and is thus not an "intangible". There is an issue in the literature as to whether infrastructure is part of the structural capital of the firm. Sullivan (1998) includes it as a complementary tangible asset to commercializing intellectual assets, but most researchers do not include tangibles. From a practical management perspective, however,

Figure 3. Enterprise intelligence molecule

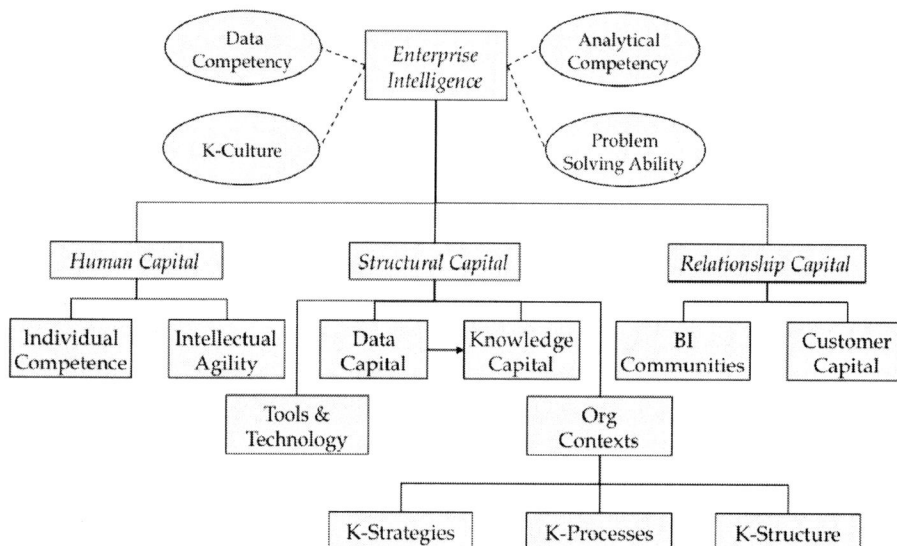

we believe tools and technologies to be a critical interacting sub-system provided it is confined to knowledging. For example, a multi-dimensional database would be included, as would a data and knowledge repository. As another example, the case study revealed one organization that did not use an ETL tool (i.e., a structural sub-system); this would thus affect the overall data churning and reuse capability of the organization.

The last EI sub-system is *relationship capital*. Its primary constituents include customer capital, but by extension may include suppliers, alliance partners, shareholders, and other stakeholders (re IC-index). However, we draw special attention to customer – in our case study the customer dimension was in most need of improvement. Finally, BI communities include communities of people, both within and without the organization, that develop and transfer knowledge. In this sense, a BI community is similar to a community of practice, but one focused on the activities of BI, from data transformation, multi-dimensional database design, and data mining, and so on.

Finally, the *emergent properties* of an EI system include, for example, data and analytical competence and the ability to solve problems. The ability to solve problems would naturally extend to customers and alliance partners as well as to internal clients. Ultimately, a knowledge culture emerges which, at once, embraces and facilitates knowledge creation, discovery, capture, codification, storage, dissemination, and sharing; in fact, activities associated with knowledge management as well as analytics and BI.

In conclusion, it is important to realize that the representation of EI as a molecule means that we are elevating BI to an organizational system comprised of other interacting systems or sub-systems. *The properties of EI in a given organization will be determined by the instantiation, quality, and management of each of its sub-systems.* For example, recall that the Gartner Group identified over reliance on tools as an issue; using the EI molecule as an analytical tool, we would say

that organizations are emphasizing the tools and technology sub-system to detriment of the other, necessary, interacting structural sub-systems. In fact, *each* sub-system must be designed and managed to realize the full potential of EI.

CONCLUSION AND FUTURE RESEARCH

We consider the current research to be Phase 1 of an on-going research project in BI. The breadth of the current research suggests more questions and even recommendations. Perhaps the most striking lesson and opportunity identified in our study is the observed disconnect between BI and knowledge workers.

Future research will include a full explication of each sub-system in the EI molecule. Based on the results of this case study, we believe that it is necessary to strengthen those sub-systems required to promote knowledge work. In particular, we will concentrate on the following:

- Developing a library of reusable knowledge nuggets;
- Improving the quality of data using master data management;
- Integrating data and BI within organizations using conformed dimensions;
- Embedding knowledge into the business processes of the organization.

REFERENCES

Aberdeen Group. (2009). *The business value of pervasive BI*. Boston, MA: Aberdeen Group.

Andriessen, D. (2004). *Making sense of intellectual capital: Designing a method for the valuation of intangibles*. Maryland Heights, MO: Elsevier Butterworth-Heinemann.

Bitterer, A. (2010). *The BI(G) discrepancy: Theory and practice of business intelligence.* Stamford, CT: Gartner Research.

Davenport, T. H. (2004). Competing on analytics. *Harvard Business Review.*

Davenport, T. H. (2010). Business intelligence and organizational decisions. *International Journal of Business Intelligence Research, 1*(1). doi:10.4018/jbir.2010071701

Davenport, T. H., Harris, J. G., & Morison, R. (2010). *Analytics at work.* Boston, MA: Harvard Business Press.

Dhar, V., & Sundararajan, A. (2007). Information technologies in business: A blueprint for education and research. *Information Systems Research, 18*(2). doi:10.1287/isre.1070.0126

Financial Times. (2009, November 27). Digital digest managing intelligence: How to make sense of the pieces. *Financial Times.*

Henschen, D. (2009). *4 technologies that are reshaping business intelligence.* Retrieved from http://www.informationweek.com/news/business_intelligence/analytics/showArticle.jhtml?articleID=219500363

IBM. (2010). *The enterprise of the future.* Armonk, NY: IBM.

Inmon, W. H. (1996). *Building the data warehouse* (2nd ed.). Hoboken, NJ: John Wiley & Sons.

Jonas, J. (2006). *Enterprise intelligence – my presentation at the third annual Web 2.0 summit.* Retrieved from http://jeffjonas.typepad.com/jeff_jonas/2006/11/enterprise_inte.html

Kosambia, S., & Mandhana, S. (2008). *Enterprise intelligence everywhere.* BI Review Online.

Morabito, J., Sack, I., & Bhate, A. (1999). *Organization modeling: Innovative architectures for the 21st century.* Upper Saddle River, NJ: Prentice Hall.

Morabito, J., & Singh, M. (1993). A new approach to object-oriented analysis and design. In *Proceedings of the 11th International Conference of Object-Oriented Languages and Systems,* Santa Barbara, CA (pp. 45-55).

Morabito, J., & Stohr, E. (2009). Online analytical processing. In Hossein, B. (Ed.), *The handbook of technology management.* New York, NY: John Wiley & Sons.

Nonaka, I., & Takeuchi, H. (1995). *The knowledge-creating company.* New York, NY: Oxford University Press.

Robbins, S. P. (1990). *Organization theory: Structure, design, and applications.* Upper Saddle River, NJ: Prentice Hall.

SAS. (2010). *Technologies/enterprise intelligence platforms.* Retrieved from http://findaccountingsoftware.com/directory/sas-institute/sas-financial-intelligence/sas-enterprise-intelligence-platform/

Simon, H. A. (1973). The organization of complex systems. In Pattee, H. H. (Ed.), *Hierarchy theory: The challenge of complex systems.* New York, NY: George Braziller.

Strong, D. M., Lee, Y. W., & Wang, R. Y. (1997). Data quality in context. *Communications of the ACM, 40*(5). doi:10.1145/253769.253804

Sullivan, P. H. (1998). Basic definitions and concepts. In Sullivan, P. H. (Ed.), *Profiting from intellectual capital: Extracting value from innovation.* New York, NY: John Wiley & Sons.

Whiting, R. (2004). *Centralized intelligence at work.* Information Week.

Yin, R. K. (2003). *Case study research: Design and methods* (3rd ed., pp. 5–7). Thousand Oaks, CA: Sage.

APPENDIX

Questionnaire

Each question is open-ended and you may answer as you see fit. However, we provide possible choices for several questions to guide your response. Please provide your detailed answer in the comments section provided for each question.

Distribution of BI

1. How is BI distributed in the organization?
    a. Most BI usage is confined to specific departments such as R&D or marketing?
    b. There is a fairly widespread distribution of BI

COMMENTS:

2. If BI is not widely distributed, is there any demand for more BI "pervasiveness"? (Select one answer.)
    a. Yes, there is a big demand for more pervasive BI.
    b. Yes, there is some demand but it is not highly prioritized.
    c. No, there is not any demand for more pervasive BI

COMMENTS:

3. What are the functions of BI in your organization? (Select all that apply.)
    a. Executive support
    b. Managerial support
    c. Business Analysis support
    d. Operational support
    e. Knowledge work

COMMENTS:

User Profile

In BI, the three determinants of a user profile are Binding with Process, Frequency of Access and Skill Level. The following section is to gather information about these determinants.

4. What are the different types of users and their percentage distribution based on their skill levels in your organization? (Select all that apply.)
    a. Users who strictly read and drill reports
    b. Users who utilize dashboards (i.e., accesses multiple displays in a single window) regularly.
    c. Users who actually *manipulate* data through spreadsheets, OLAP, or data mining.

COMMENTS:

5. Of the people who manipulate data (i.e., mining), what proportion have a background in statistics or have a PhD (i.e., this question concerns the degree of user sophistication)?
    COMMENTS:
6. What is the level of frequency and percentage distribution for BI activities? (Select all that apply.)
    a. Frequent access, mostly daily.
    b. Periodically but not daily (e.g., monthly)
    c. On-demand (e.g., only when needed)

COMMENTS:

7. Please describe the level of binding in BI activities. By binding we mean the degree to which access to BI is integrated into processes of the organization; i.e., BI is a formal part of the process specification – access, use, and display (e.g., dashboard) are formally defined by a job role within a process.

COMMENTS:

8. How sufficiently are your users trained in BI? (Select all that apply.)
    a. They are trained in reporting and dashboard features. (e.g. drill)
    b. They are trained in full OLAP capabilities
    c. They are trained in data mining

COMMENTS:

Data

9. How would you describe the quality of your data? By quality, we mean user confidence in the data source, ease-of-access, timeliness, and completeness.

COMMENTS:

10. Do departments in your organization use "local" data or must all data go through a centralized data warehouse? By "local" we mean data that is specific to a given department. For example, a marketing survey after a new product launch is specific to the marketing department and does not go beyond the boundaries of that department.

COMMENTS:

11. Do you use meta-data and in what form?
    a.   Enterprise repository
    b.   Tool-specific (meta-data resides in a collection of tools; e.g., DBMS catalog, modeling, ETL, and query tools)
    c.   We do not rely on meta-data

COMMENTS:

Architecture

12. How would you describe your architecture? (Select all that apply.)
    a.   Data warehouse stores only.
    b.   Isolated, departmental data marts.
    c.   Data warehouse stores, each with a set of corresponding data marts.

COMMENTS:

13. How would you describe the integration of data warehouses?
    a.   Separate and isolated data warehouses.
    b.   Separate but conformed data warehouses.

COMMENTS:

14. How would you describe access to data?
    a.   All data access goes through a BI environment.
    b.   Data access goes through both a BI environment and OLTP reporting environments.

COMMENTS:

15. Is real-time or near real-time data available to users through the BI environment? (Select one answer.)
    a.   Yes, there is real time availability.
    b.   Yes, there is near-real time availability.
    c.   No, there is neither real nor near-real time availability

COMMENTS:

16. Is there a need to consolidate separate data warehouses (i.e., data warehouses built without conformed dimensions)? (Select one answer.)
    a. Yes, there is a need to consolidate them into a single data warehouse environment.
    b. Yes, there is a need to consolidate them into separate but integrated through conformed dimensions warehouses.
    c. No, there is no need for consolidation.

COMMENTS:

17. Do you use a combination of relational and multi-dimensional data structures?
    a. Yes.
    b. No.

COMMENTS:

18. What is the level of connection between BI and data mining? (Select one answer.)
    a. Formal connection: all data used for mining goes through the BI architecture.
    b. Informal connection: data used in mining is usually but not always requested from BI.
    c. Separate: data used in mining is usually obtained separately from BI (note: mining sometimes requires raw data)

COMMENTS:

Governance

19. Is there an architectural separation for governance? More specifically; if your organization has more than one data warehouse, are they managed in a single group (department) or is each data warehouse managed separately?
    a. Yes, data warehouse environments are managed separately
    b. No, data warehouse environments are managed in a single group

COMMENTS:

20. Is there a functional separation for governance? More specifically; for each data warehouse environment, are the data warehousing (including ETL and data warehouse design and population), data mart (including data mart design and population (OLAP), and report and dashboard design), and data mining separate groups?
    a. Yes, data warehouse, mart/OLAP, and mining are separate organizational groups
    b. No, data warehouse, mart/OLAP, and mining reside in a single organizational group

COMMENTS:

Toolset

21. What kind of tools does your organization use and how are they distributed?

COMMENTS:

22. What is the decision process for BI tool selection?
     Are departments permitted to select their own tools?
     Is tool selection mediated by a centralized BI group?

COMMENTS:

23. Do you use ETL and data cleansing tools?
     a. Yes and they are integrated to gain scale.
     b. Yes but separate warehouse groups manage their own tools.
     c. No we don't utilize such tools.

COMMENTS:

24. Are you using or considering "cloud BI"; that is, using BI as a service where, for example, the data or analytical tools may reside outside of the organization?

COMMENTS:

Future Plans

25. What are your immediate and long-term plans for BI?

COMMENTS:

This work was previously published in the International Journal of Business Intelligence Research, Volume 2, Issue 3, edited by Richard Herschel, pp. 1-20, copyright 2011 by IGI Publishing (an imprint of IGI Global).

Chapter 5
Business Intelligence Competency Centers:
Centralizing an Enterprise Business Intelligence Strategy

Daniel O'Neill
Avon Products Inc., USA

ABSTRACT

Enterprises today continue to invest in business intelligence (BI) initiatives with the hope of providing a strategic advantage to their organizations. Many of these initiatives are supporting the tactical goals of individual business units and not the strategic goals of the enterprise. Although this decentralized approach provides short term gains, it creates an environment where information silos develop and the enterprise as a whole struggles to develop a single version of the truth when it comes to providing strategic information. Enterprises are turning toward a centralized approach to BI which aligns with their overall strategic goals. At the core of the centralized approach is the business intelligence competency center (BICC). This paper details why the centralized BICC approach should be considered an essential component of all enterprise BI initiatives. Examining case studies of BICC implementations details the benefits realized by real world companies who have taken this approach. It is also important to provide analysis of the two BI approaches in the areas of BI process and BI technology/data and people relations. The findings indicate the benefits of the centralized BICC outweigh the deficiencies of the decentralized approach.

DOI: 10.4018/978-1-4666-2650-8.ch005

INTRODUCTION

According to Gartner's latest CIO survey, Business Intelligence (BI) remains one of the top 5 CIO priorities in 2010 (Gartner, 2010). Enterprises today are looking to gain a competitive advantage by investing in BI initiatives. Many of these initiatives are developed to support the goals of individual business units or departments and eventually provide a short term return on their investments. As these BI silos begin to develop within the enterprise, the long term value of the BI investments begin to decrease due to issues such as data quality, data availability and application redundancy. To avoid some of these pitfalls and to begin to align BI investments with the overarching corporate strategy, enterprises are turning toward an approach of implementing a centralized business intelligence competency center (BICC). "The BICC is designed for organizations that consider business intelligence to be a priority, but are struggling due to its uneven adoption across the organization, misunderstood uses or underutilization of business intelligence tools, or increasing numbers of "spreadmarts" or spreadsheets built on disparate data silos" (Teradata, 2010). These issues are the reason the transformation of the BI strategy needs to reach across the enterprise and the underlying business units who see value in leveraging BI but have issues using information efficiently. The BICC centralizes the people, systems, and standard processes needed to support a single enterprise BI strategy.

This paper will provide definitive evidence that the BICC should be an essential part of an enterprise BI strategy because it has proven to maximize an enterprise's BI investment. It is important to define the BICC to be able to understand the value it provides to an enterprise BI strategy and to understand the weight of executive sponsorship as the foundation of the BICC. Also at the core of the BICC are the people from within the enterprise who possess the skills related to technology, business as well as analytics. This paper will then examine the unique blend of skills and people which make-up the BICC.

The majority of the research section will define the importance of the BICC's scope. The scope of the BICC reaches across IT and other areas of the enterprise. The BICC assumes a number of different areas of responsibility that can be considered as necessities of most BI initiatives. Integrating these areas into the BICC is what makes the centralized BI approach so beneficial to the enterprise BI strategy. The scope of the BICC can be generalized in the following items.

It is from the BICC scope (Table 1) that individual roles are defined within the BICC. The roles performed by the BICC and its members will be discussed.

While defining the BICC's scope and roles provides insight in to the value of the BICC, the best evidence is found in real world case studies of enterprises that have taken the approach of implementing a BICC. Including these findings reinforces the value found from enterprises that have taken this approach to their BI strategy.

Table 1. BICC scope (Ciric, 2009)

BICC Scope
Data Models Standardization
Process Standardization
Best practice
Support Services
Documentation
Infrastructure Development
Technology/Infrastructure
Data Governance
License management
People Relations
Promotion
Training

Research reviewed for this paper serves as the basis for the ensuing analysis section that will compare the alternative approach to the centralized BICC which is a decentralized model for a BI strategy. The intent will be to prove that the centralized BICC approach to the enterprise BI strategy is far more valuable than a decentralized approach. The long term value of the BICC will far outweigh the short term gains of a decentralized, tactical approach to the BI strategy. Based upon the scope of the BICC, specific areas of the decentralized model can be identified as areas which are deficient to the organization's BI strategy.

Research: Defining the BICC, BICC Scope and Real World Results

The purpose of this section is to define the value the BICC provides to the enterprise and the overall BI strategy. In this section the definition of BICC and its roles and scope are explored. This includes examining the importance of executive sponsorship as well as identifying the people, needs and responsibilities necessary to make the BICC functionally effective. This section will conclude with two real world case studies which review the value provided by integrating the centralized BICC approach.

Defining the BICC and the BICC Roles

The BICC should not be looked at as a technical group but as a cross functional center that is governed by both the business and technology groups. "The BICC is part of and contains members of the business. It should not be a technology organization, but a functional/technical organization within the business, run by the business and working for the business" (Hewlett Packard, 2009, p. 15). The effective implementation of the BICC begins with the alignment and prioritization of business intelligence initiatives within the enterprise. Alignment with the strategic goals of the enterprise is

one of the main reasons executive sponsorship is needed when designing and integrating a BICC into an enterprise. An executive sponsor is also needed to communicate the value of the BICC across senior management. "Support needs to come from the top down in order to propagate the objectives of the BICC effectively throughout the organization. Obtaining senior level support is critical to the business accepting the BICC. The business members of the BICC team play a large role in the process"(Hewlett Packard, 2009, p. 13). Without an executive sponsor, the value of the BICC can get lost because the message is not being communicated from executive management down throughout the business.

From a staffing standpoint, the BICC consists of individuals from not only information technology (IT) but business workers as well. Having representation from both the business and IT within the same team enhances the communication between both sides of the enterprise when it comes to BI strategy and decision making. Also, having representation from across the business can help market the value of the BICC and its resources back to the individual business groups represented in the BICC. Bringing together business and IT workers integrates a unique blend of skill sets into the BICC. "BICC should comprise a mix of business skills, analytic skills, IT skills and program-management skills. The idea is to help the technologists understand what's vital to the business while business people and analysts get a sounding board to know what's technically possible and realistic" (Henschen, 2008).

In the illustration (Figure 1), the skill sets for business, analytics and IT converge within the BICC. The result is a center of BI excellence which is focused on the goals of the enterprise's strategy and performs each of the following roles:

- **Manages BI Programs:** All BI projects would be managed within the BICC. The BICC would be responsible for managing

Figure 1. Skill sets for business, analytics and IT (Hostmann, 2007)

and prioritizing the projects in the overall enterprise BI portfolio.

- **Defines the BI Vision:** The BI vision would clearly communicate the enterprise BI strategy across all areas of the business and would be aligned with the overall enterprise goals.
- **Control BI Funding:** The BICC would make the decision for funding those strategic BI initiatives which are determined to provide the most value to the enterprise.
- **Establishes BI Standards:** In alignment with the BI vision, the BICC would create the BI standards for the enterprise. For example, BI standards can be created for the data sourcing and modeling process, technology selection and the management of BI projects in the enterprise.
- **Build BI Technology Blueprint:** The BICC would establish the technology standards needed to support the enterprise's BI strategy. This includes defining the BI applications which would be used to deliver the information to end users as well as the

database and data warehouse investments needed to support the BI infrastructure.

- **Organize BI Methodology:** The BICC organizes the BI methodology so that BI projects are more strategic focused as opposed to tactical. Following a standard methodology means that the processes can be leveraged and shared amongst current and future BI initiatives within the enterprise. This shortens the BI project lifecycle.
- **Develop Users Skills:** The BICC would be responsible for training and educating users on the BI tools available to them, the data which they can access as well as the benefits of adopting the BI strategy.

It is the diverse skill set of the members of the BICC which allows the group to support the different roles which are part of the centralized BI model. The roles supported by the BICC tie directly in to the scope of the BICC. The scope would be considered the functional areas of the BI strategy which are supported by the centralized model.

BICC Scope/Structure

This section will review the structure and function of the BICC (scope). As defined earlier, these areas include Data Models Standardization, Process Standardization, Infrastructure Development and People Relations.

BICC Scope: Data Models Standardization

"Data issues typically are the leading cause of failure and most costly element of BI implementations" (Miller, Brautman, & Gerlach, 2006, p. 7). Within an enterprise, data can come from many sources. If there is no way to align this disparate data, users can end up providing different answers to the same business questions. This can lead to credibility issues with the data and those who are responsible for maintaining it. This can also create a lack of trust from end users and subsequently can have an impact on adoption of BI technologies. By standardizing the data models within the enterprise, the BICC can improve the accuracy of data and improve data availability. In the 2005 BetterManagement survey, companies were asked to name the top three changes BI users would benefit from most. The top answer, identified by 56% of the respondents, was "Improved quality of information available to them" (Miller, Brautman, & Gerlach, 2006, p. 26). Centralizing the management of data and creating standards on modeling of the data is the focus of the BICC.

"In 2007, the Gartner BI User Survey revealed that organizations which have a BI competency center are less likely to have data that is highly inconsistent or fragmented across systems and departments" (Hostmann, 2007). As part of the standardization of data models, the BICC assumes the role of the data steward within the enterprise. As the data steward, the BICC takes on the role of managing, consolidating and standardizing the information from the different source systems within the enterprise. This begins with the align-ment of data definitions between IT and the end business users.

When the data is centralized, for example, into a data warehouse, the definition or metadata needs to be reviewed and approved by both IT and the end business users. This could mean that data changes may need to be made either on the source operational systems feeding information to the data warehouse or changes would need to be made to the data within the warehouse itself. Having BICC members from across the business can assist in this process. The members of the BICC can layout the data and create standard definitions to be used in all BI initiatives within the enterprise, no matter which department needs to use the information. This approach provides a single version of the truth within the enterprise, which means end users can spend less time trying to validate numbers between different reports from different sources. Using a standard, predefined set of data models to support all aspects of the enterprise can eliminate many of the issues encountered with data quality prior to the integration of the BICC. Once the data structure has been standardized, the processes which support the existing BI strategy would need to be standardized to support a repeatable approach to implementing and successfully launching BI initiatives which align with the overall enterprise strategy.

BICC Scope: Process Standardization

"The BICC helps establish processes for more consistent and organized enablement that ultimately results in increased end user adoption, higher success rates, and efficiency of the BI solution" (MacMillan, 2008). The standardization of the BI processes across the enterprise is a key factor for a successful BICC and BI strategy. The BICC takes responsibility for controlling all projects and processes related to BI within the enterprise. This enables the BICC to create repeatable processes which "Lead to BI deployments that have higher success and deliver more value, at less cost, in less time" (Ciric, 2009).

Process standardization is where much of the true value of the BICC is achieved. When the BICC drives the process across the business there is a framework by which all BI initiatives follow. "Often BI projects start in isolation. They are not in sync with other BI projects occurring elsewhere in the organization. There, the result is a lot of overlap, redundancy, and information silos that do not allow the organization to connect different sources of information"(Miller, Brautman, & Gerlach, 2006, p. 10). Reduced redundancy and overlap can lead the business to achieve a lower TCO (Total cost of ownership= Acquisition cost + Operating cost) because the enterprise will be responsible for maintaining fewer BI applications and will not need to try to integrate different data sources to support one strategic goal.

Process standardization in the BICC is achieved through the development of best practices, the development of support services for end users and documentation to support repeatable actions for each new BI initiative. As each BI initiative is completed, the BICC develops more efficient ways to produce tangible results from their projects. The BICC maintains the best practices developed through their past BI initiatives. The best practices can be used to enhance the process standards which would be applied to future BI projects. Providing support services is another way to communicate the process standards from the BICC and throughout the organization. The BICC is frequently interacting and communicating with end users and this channel should be used to promote the BI standards developed by the BICC which have proven to be successful for other users or on other projects. This information must also be documented and maintained by the BICC. Documenting the BI process standards and best practices is an ongoing and dynamic process. As business needs change and the strategic direction changes, the BICC will need to update their process standards to align with the direction of the

business. When standardizing the BI processes, the correct infrastructure should be in place to support the BICC approach. The infrastructure needs to use a standard set of applications and hardware which is the same for most BI initiatives. This helps support a repeatable approach to BI initiatives. Infrastructure development, the next area of the BI scope covered in this paper, is the backbone of the enterprise BI strategy and should be focused on reducing the application and hardware redundancy seen in many decentralized BI organizations.

BICC Scope: Infrastructure Development

The BICC is responsible for the infrastructure development needed to support the enterprise BI strategy. Infrastructure needs to be clearly defined as it can be interpreted as hardware only. "Infrastructure refers to the hardware, software, networking tools, and technologies that create, manage, store, disseminate, and apply information"(Miller, Brautman, & Gerlach, 2006, p. 121). The infrastructure needs to be scalable so it can grow with the BI strategy. It also needs to be flexible so it supports the needs of numerous business units and end users. Most of all, the infrastructure needs to be dependable and meet the performance expectations of the end users. Creating an infrastructure defined by service level agreements (SLAs) means the back-end BI hardware will need to be available to provide timely data and reporting for end users. Users will need to know their BI services can be provided on a consistent basis with minimal interruption. Users also need to know how frequently their data is updated. If data is refreshed nightly or weekly, this must be communicated across the enterprise. Having the technology and infrastructure in place to support the BI strategy is important to the success and adoption of an enterprise BI strategy.

"One of the aims of the BICC is to provide the business with solutions that fit their requirements and support them (the business) in using them (the solutions) appropriately" (Miller, Brautman, & Gerlach, 2006, p. 10). The BICC focus, from an application standpoint, is to develop and maintain the BI technology blueprint for the enterprise. The BICC should aim to deliver a common BI platform which can be leveraged across all business units. "Rather than a best of breed approach (for the enterprise BI architecture), which often leads to a patchwork of various tools and products that are impossible to get to work with each other, the preferred way for building an enterprise BI architecture is to go for a suite of components that can be integrated with each other and share a common metadata layer" (Miller, Brautman, & Gerlach, 2006, p. 127). Taking this approach reduces any integration work which would be needed to bring together different solutions, from different vendors, supporting different business units. Having the BICC manage a common BI platform has many benefits which can be reflected throughout the enterprise. "A lack of tool standards limits collaboration and portability of applications, and it also increases training and software licensing costs" (Henschen, 2009). Taking the BI suite approach provides different flavors of functionality to end users from ad-hoc and OLAP reporting to data mining. Sharing a common metadata layer across each of these functions provides the enterprise with the single version of the truth no matter what type of reporting is being performed.

Using a common suite of BI applications also means users need to register for access and their usage of the BI reports can be monitored. This gives the BICC the capability to monitor end user adoption of the BI resources made available as part of the enterprise BI strategy. "Use governance systems to track and review the operation and success of the BICC. Respond and adapt to new and changing business requirements. Research new approaches and technologies before the business ask for them" (Hostmann, 2010). Tracking usage patterns can provide the BICC with information which would allow them to be proactive in pro-

viding BI solutions before they are approached by a business user with a request.

Another key component of the BICC's infrastructure development is data governance. Data governance is the management of data that occurs after the initial data model standardization takes place. Data governance consists of monitoring data quality, standardizing data policy, and data management. The data governance role of the BICC is tasked with delivering consistent data, of the highest quality to the end users of the BI applications and to prevent the common data issue referred to as "garbage in, garbage out". "With the business focus and the commitment that a well-formed BICC can provide, a company can give end users the necessary level of access to information, achieve semantic consistency in that information, and ensure that the information is high-quality" (Hostmann, 2007). When developing the infrastructure to support data quality and data management, the BICC needs to integrate solutions which can automate these processes. "It is better to use an integrated approach where data quality routines are constantly applied than to make sporadic efforts to maintain data quality" (Miller, Brautman, & Gerlach, 2006, p. 122). This approach will allow the BICC to stay ahead of any data quality issues as well as freeing up resources to focus on other functions within the BICC group.

The final component of infrastructure development is license management. License management is important because the BI infrastructure has the potential to touch a number of different vendors whose hardware and applications are being used throughout an enterprise. The goal of the BICC is to first, when possible, minimize the number of vendors they are working with to support the BI infrastructure. "It is desirable to keep the total number of vendors to a minimum --- ideally down to a single vendor" (Miller, Brautman, & Gerlach, 2006, p. 125). Trying to minimize the number of vendors can be a difficult task because the vendor needs to offer the capabilities necessary to support the BI needs of the enterprise. Finding a one-size fits all suite is possible, but certainly not normal. The BICC should balance the approach of using vendors with quality offerings that can integrate their products with other systems which will be needed to support the overall BI strategy.

The license management function not only works to define the vendors who will be used to provide the infrastructure but they also need to define their customer service offerings as well. "Experts agree that customer service is just as important as the product itself in gauging a BI vendor"(Miller, Brautman, & Gerlach, 2006, p. 159). Services such as training and consulting are highly valued as BI infrastructures are put into place and post production support is needed from the vendor. Having these vendor resources in place will help to provide a positive initial experience for users which will hopefully drive other users to see the value in adopting such technologies.

Defining the technology which will support the BI strategy can be difficult but it can provide savings in the areas of integration cost and the cost of maintaining redundant BI applications, which is often seen in a decentralized BI model. This work can be for naught though if the users do not understand and leverage the technologies appropriately. The scope of the BICC reaches the area of people (user) relations and provides the users with the opportunities to learn the effective ways to use the BI tools available to the enterprise as well as the best practices and successes of other users within the enterprise. The purpose of the BICC's people relations is outlined in the next section and it is at the core of assisting with user adoption of the BI strategy.

BICC Scope: People Relations

The purpose of the BICC is to expose the right people, to the right resources to allow them to make educated decisions at a moment's notice. For the BICC to achieve this, they need to promote the benefits of adopting the BI strategy and also

provide training to the users of their applications. "To continue to receive funding for initiatives, and to improve user adoption and acceptance of them, BI competency centers should devote around 85 percent (plus or minus 10 percent) of their time to work that is not technologically intensive -- for example, training users; promoting the adoption of practices, methodologies, tools, and applications; and marketing their efforts, progress, and impact via management update reports, user-oriented newsletters, and cross-organizational user groups" (Hostmann, 2007). Effectively communicating the successes of the BICC and training users on the BI application so they are using them effectively is key to growing the support for the BICC which will strengthen support for future BI initiatives as well.

The BICC should have the capability to clearly communicate the value being provided to the enterprise. After communicating "what the BICC is and what the BICC is not", "the second most-important communication goal is creating a sense of community and celebrating successes that are shared by business and IT. That gets people talking and inquiring whether they can join the success" (Henschen, 2008). The hope is that the value of the BICC can become almost "viral" within an enterprise. Getting the message to the users, across all levels of the business, is essential. There are different avenues which can be used to successfully promote the BICC. "Newsletters, intranet sites, portal pages and presentations are the typical outlets for success stories. Be sure to detail the technologies used, the deployment timeline and the key contributors on both the business and IT sides (particularly if they serve on the BICC)" (Henschen, 2008). Providing these particulars can be very beneficial to the adoption of the overall BI strategy.

The second area of focus for people relations is training on the BI processes and applications being enabled through the BICC. "When users are not properly trained, they often find alternative methods to analyze and report information"

(Hewlett Packard, 2009, p. 7). Training should not be viewed solely as applications training. Users need to understand the process used to capture the data they will be using, the data quality filters which are in place, as well as the frequency that their information is updated. This will help with the interpretation of the information being provided to the user's audience. Users will also be trained on the applications available to them through the BICC. "To ensure the "buy in" of the project by the user community it is very important to train the correct audience and to explain exactly what they can expect from the newly deployed application"(Cabrera, 2009). Application training should not only be introduced during the roll-out period but it should be a continuing process which adapts to the changes of the business needs and the BI strategy. Some users will use the application on an "as needed basis" and will need to be retrained to refresh their skills more often than power users. The BICC sees training as a way to confirm that the end user makes the most of the tools available to them. Proper training can lead to a better user experience which will lead to better adoption. Training provides the most exposure of the BICC to its end users and it should be an experience tailored to the specific user group or department being engaged. This will enhance the perception of the BICC as a trusted business partner who provides a considerable amount of value to the enterprise.

BICC Research: Case Studies

As part of the research of the BICC, it is important to illustrate the benefits the centralized BICC approach has provided in real world applications. In the first case study, MassHousing needed to consolidate their data sources and their BI applications in an attempt to centralize their BI strategy. In the second case study, Martin's Point Health Care needed to redesign their process for supporting their end user reporting requests which had grown to a point of being unmanageable. Implementing

a BICC allowed them to realign their resources and standardize a reporting structure which was dynamic enough to reduce the need for custom reporting. It is important to understand the benefits these two BICC approaches provided to each of these companies.

CASE STUDY 1: MASSHOUSING (COGNOS, 2008) AND (MACMILLAN, 2008)

Issue Overview

MassHousing, a provider of affordable housing across the state of Massachusetts, established a BICC after consolidating their reporting systems which were located in six different business units. MassHousing had difficulty providing a single version of the truth due to their conflicting data sources.

BI and BICC Strategy

MassHousing's Executive Information System group began by consolidating the information from the six different databases which would include standardizing a holistic data model. Reports would no longer be provided from the individual business unit databases. MassHousing implemented the Cognos 8 BI business suite across their enterprise. This suite was able to support the BI reporting needs across all of their business units. Next, a portal was implemented to allow end users to access the reporting capabilities as well as other internal systems through an internal web site. MassHousing uses their intranet portal as the channel for BI reporting. Reports are sent to executives and are directly accessed through this portal. The portal is the central point of reporting within their enterprise.

The BICC at MassHousing recruited users from the individual business units to help establish the direction of the BI strategy. This open line of communication between the business and the BICC helped to develop a more customized experience for the users. The BICC also worked with the application vendor to provide standard training across the business units on the new BI suite.

Benefits Realized

By centralizing their BI functions and integrating a BICC, MassHousing has seen increased efficiency in their reporting as well as shorter design times for report development. The business users now have the "single version of the truth" which wasn't available under the decentralized BI approach. This single version of the truth is accessible on a single platform and the data has been standardized and consolidated. The BICC can provide repeatable results for future BI initiatives at MassHousing due to this new centralized and standardized approach to their BI strategy.

CASE STUDY 2: MARTIN'S POINT HEALTH CARE (NUCLEUS RESEARCH, 2009)

Issue Overview

Martin's Point Health Care is a non-profit health care provider which operates in New York and Northern New England. The internal reporting support team at Martin's Point Healthcare Care, informatics, was encountering issues with their BI support because they did not have a unified approach to supporting report requests being sourced from their data warehouse. The data warehouse integrated data coming from seven enterprise applications and 20 databases spread across 13 business units. There were also issues maintaining the report catalogue which had grown to more than 300 reports. These reports were not very dynamic so resources were spending a considerable amount of time creating custom reports. Martin's Point needed the capability to

service their users' reporting needs without these issues standing in the way.

BI and BICC Strategy

Martin's Point decided to create a BICC which would divide the informatics team into three different groups: BI tool administration, reporting and data architecture. A process was then implemented that would only allow reports to be designed by the team if the functionality was not available to build the report on the end user side of the application. This would free up resources to focus on other BICC tasks. The group then took the initiative to design reports and dashboards which gave end users a standard, aligned view of all of the organization's data. The BICC then communicated the changes to executive management, reeducated them on the BI resources available and how the end users could leverage them most effectively.

Benefits Realized

Martin's Point benefitted from reduced reporting costs as a result of their process changes. Specifically, they now try to leverage existing reports to support requests for custom, ad-hoc reports. If the BICC receives a custom report request for a report which is available in the application, the BICC team member will reach out to the user and educate them on how to extract the information they had requested. This along with high user adoption and effective deployment of end user BI functionality reduced the team's report building cost by 20 percent.

End user productivity improved because the BICC was able to independently create reports that could be manipulated by the end users. Providing reports which can be manipulated enables the end users to adjust the information available instead of having to locate static reports which would provide information which is generally the same but may have been filtered in a slightly different manor. There is no need for the user to have to cross validate multiple reports if one dynamic report can be manipulated to support the needs of many static reports.

The BICC integration within Martin's Point was an immediate success. It was determined that the ROI within the first year was 1185% and that the project paid for itself in only one month. This clearly shows how the proper implementation of the centralized BICC, with centralized skills and standardized processes for supporting the business, can produce an increased return to the business and justify the BI investment.

Analysis Section

The purpose of the analysis section is to argue that the centralized BICC approach to a BI strategy is far more valuable than the decentralized approach (No BICC). This will be illustrated by comparing the process, technology/data and people components of each approach.

Centralized BICC vs. Decentralized BI Strategy

When defining the scope of the BICC in the research section the benefits could be seen in three areas: process, technology/data and people. It is in these three areas where the decentralized approach is deficient. Comparing the two approaches to the BI strategy in these three sections will clearly show why the BICC is a better approach. Recommendations are then provided on how to approach the BI strategy and integration of the BICC within an enterprise. The recommendations will be provided for the areas of executive sponsorship, data consolidation and standardization, infrastructure, process and people relations.

BI Process Comparison

The decentralized approach to BI strategy supports a model which allows BI initiatives to be defined by the needs and goals of an individual department or business unit(s). This means that the individual initiatives will implement processes which are specific to the users being supported and the data being used for the specific initiative. Because these initiatives are focused on an individual department or business unit, there is no shared or standardized process which is put into place which can be used to support future BI projects in other areas of the business. This translates into longer project lifecycles for each BI initiative the enterprise allows their departments to begin on their own. The BICC approach supports the sharing of processes across their catalogue of BI initiatives. Having a repeatable, standardized process for releasing and supporting BI initiatives can increase the return on investment because in the centralized approach, each BI initiative isn't treated as brand new. Instead the initiatives in the centralized approach leverage best practices from prior initiatives. The BI collaboration across processes is not as strong in the decentralized approach and amounts to increased costs as a result of the extended project timelines.

Technology/Data

Technology and data, for the purposes of this analysis, are grouped together because of their interdependencies. The decentralized model encounters two major issues when it comes to data and technology: the data sources are specific to the area where the project is taking place (data silos) and individual applications are used to support each BI initiative.

In the decentralized approach, there is little to no integration of the departmental data with any other data coming from other business units within the enterprise. This information is very tactical and can only provide value to the individual department. The BICC takes the approach of standardizing and consolidating data so it can align with the strategic goals of the enterprise. The decentralized model has no version of the "single truth". The data cannot be aligned with any other sources within the enterprise because it does not share the same metadata definitions. For example, a metric or measurement in one department can have the same name or description as a metric in another department but both metrics could have two fundamentally different purposes and underlying business logic. This is an issue for senior management because resources need to be used to validate the information coming from each of the individual silos. This is not an issue with the centralized approach because the data has been consolidated and all of the business units leverage the same consolidated data source (usually a data warehouse) to support their tactical and strategic goals. The centralized data follows the same metadata definitions and standards and the data is also refreshed consistently across all of the departmental data sources feeding the main data repository.

The decentralized BI strategy not only promotes data silos but it can support the use of disparate BI technologies. As a BI initiative is developed for an individual business unit or department, there is usually an infrastructure which is unique to that individual area of an enterprise. "Since individual departments historically have been run like separate businesses, often each has been free to pursue its own IT infrastructure."(Miller, Brautman, & Gerlach, 2006, p. 7)As additional departments or units adopt their own BI strategy, more complexity is introduced into the enterprise. Eventually resources within the IT group are tasked with providing support across the different infrastructures. This is why the decentralized approach increases the TCO of a BI infrastructure. IT is tasked with supporting different BI applications, for different users, across the enterprise. The centralized approach reduces the redundancy in the infrastructure as well as in the different BI applications used to produce the information for the end users. As MassHousing demonstrated in their centralized approach, the decision to use one single instance of a BI suite can increase the return on investment (ROI) exponentially. The

decentralized approach fails to recognize this and uses the approach of creating short term ROI gains instead of gauging the impact of BI technology investments on the enterprise as a whole.

People

Having to deal with different technologies and data sources in the decentralized model can have a negative impact on the users of the BI tools. From an end-user standpoint, the complex web of databases and BI reporting tools involved with the decentralized approach can be overwhelming. Users have to run reports from different systems, in different business units or departments, and then integrate and validate the data to confirm its accuracy. This is a taxing process which in many cases will result in the loss of user adoption. There also is no standard process in place to train users on all of the different applications which provide the requested information. The training, in the decentralized model, would be specific to each area of the business that owns its specific BI tools or applications. The BICC, with the introduction of a consolidated, centralized BI strategy, educates the users on the preferred applications and resources which will meet their needs. The BICC would also be staffed by members who would have been imbedded as power users in a decentralized model. In the BICC, these subject matter experts from the business units would be able to provide business requirements directly to their teammates within the BICC and increase the development time for reporting. This centralized model of IT and BI team members working together would provide much more value than the isolated power users who are distributed among the individual business units in the decentralized model. The BICC approach means that all of the business user's best interests are represented in the adoption and implementation of the BI strategy by the BICC. From an end user standpoint, the centralized BICC approach provides a better user experience which is standard and can be adopted across the different areas of the enterprise.

As illustrated above, there is clear evidence based upon the research section that the centralized BICC approach is the approach with the highest return on investment. The BICC offers standards for process, technology, data quality, and user experience. The decentralized model can be very costly to an enterprise and the longer the decentralized approach is taken, the more costly it can become to change. Implementing a BICC can be large undertaking which needs to begin with sponsorship from senior leadership. Once in place, the centralized BI strategy, with the BICC at its core, can move BI from being a departmental tactical resource to a catalyst of strategic advantage across the enterprise. The recommendations in the following section highlight those actions which should be taken when considering the centralized BICC approach.

Recommendations

This paper highlighted how disconnected a BI initiative can become without following companywide standards related to data, technology, process and people relations. Many of the standards are developed to align the BI strategy with the overall strategy of the enterprise. Having a blend of business and technical users maintaining and supporting these standards is important to the adoption throughout the enterprise. It should be clear, based on the arguments provided herein that implementing the centralized BICC approach to BI strategy is the preferred strategy. The BICC plays the role of BI champion, promoting the value and standards throughout the enterprise. To realize this role within the organization, the following areas of recommendation should be considered for a centralized, enterprise BI strategy, which leverages a BICC.

- **Executive Sponsorship:** A project like a BICC deployment should begin with the sponsorship of a C-level executive. The recommendation is to have the sponsorship of the COO or CFO. The COO or CFO would be in a better position to align the BICC strategy with the strategy of enterprise. The CIO, although an executive sponsor, is not recommended as the sponsor of the BICC unless absolutely necessary. The BICC needs to be driven by the direction and goals of the business and not the capabilities of the technology group. This makes the COO or CFO a better sponsor.

- **Data Consolidation and Standardization:** Data sources from the business units and departments within the enterprise need to be consolidated, integrated and standardized. A data warehouse approach would be recommended in this instance. The BICC would assume the data management role after the data has been integrated. This data, for the data warehouse, would be made available throughout the enterprise. Reports would no longer be pulled from departmental production databases for reporting purposes.

- **Infrastructure:** The enterprise should investment in an efficient infrastructure which can meet service level agreements set with the business. The enterprise should choose a BI platform which offers a suite of products from a single established vendor. This vendor should also offer a comprehensive support program for end users during the development and post production stages of the BI initiative.

- **Process:** The BICC must be tasked with standardizing and documenting the BI processes within the enterprise. These process standards, as well as best practices, can be applied to all future BI initiatives assigned to the BICC reducing the lifecycle of the BI projects within the enterprise.

- **People Relations:** The BICC must establish strong relations with the business users as well as the management within the enterprise. If possible, the BICC should align its members with individual business units. This will provide the business units with a direct point of contact in the BICC who is familiar with all aspects of their processes and their unit's direction. The BICC must provide training on the enterprise applications on an as needed basis. The BICC must also promote successes to their end user constituency in an attempt to support adoption of the BI applications within the enterprise.

CONCLUSION

As this paper has documented, developing business intelligence standards is at the core of building a centralized business intelligence strategy which is anchored by the BICC. The centralized BICC is responsible for maintaining, communicating and implementing these standards across the enterprise. The BI strategy standards are being maintained by BICC team members who are versed in BI technology, possess analytical skills and members who at once were the end users of the data being provided by the BI infrastructure. These three skill groups collaborate and make sure the standards being enforced can be supported by the infrastructure, align with the business needs and will be adopted by end users. The blends of skills possessed by the members of this team are unique because they cross so many departmental boundaries within the business.

It is important to remember that the BICC is not a technology group. The requirements of the business and senior management steer the focus of this group. Aligning the BI initiatives across all level of management and departments is a requirement of the BICC and the centralized strategy. The BICC will be tasked with difficult decisions on priority and funding of requested BI initiatives. The most important factor which will support their decision is the alignment to enterprise strategy and the value the requested project will provide to the overall enterprise strategy. This will determine the priority of the initiatives in the BI portfolio. This approach will cut costs, as has been shown in the research and analysis, and focus funds and resources toward those initiatives that provide the biggest return to the enterprise for the investment. It is in the best interest of the BICC to communicate these decisions to senior management and the sponsor so the BICC can show the value being provided back to the business. This is the point when the value of the BICC will be truly understood by the business and the management who promoted the development and use of the BICC.

REFERENCES

Cabrera, C. (2009). *BI projects or BICC: Building the dream team.* Retrieved from http://www.element61.be/e/resourc-detail.asp?ResourceId=53

Ciric, B. (2009). *Business intelligence competence center – the essential need of strategic deployment of BI.* Retrieved from http://www.globaldata-consulting.net/articles/best-practice/business-intelligence-competence-center-%E2%80%93-essential-need-strategic-deployment

Cognos. (2008). *Customer success in the public sector.* Retrieved from http://public.dhe.ibm.com/software/data/sw-library/cognos/pdfs/cas-estudies/ss_bundle_customer_success_in_government.pdf

Gartner. (2010). *Gartner EXP worldwide survey of nearly 1,600 CIOs shows IT budgets in 2010 to be at 2005 levels.* Retrieved from http://www.gartner.com/it/page.jsp?id=1283413

Henschen, D. (2008). *Seven steps to successful BI competency centers.* Retrieved from http://intelligent-enterprise.informationweek.com/

Henschen, D. (2009). *Readers weigh in on biggest obstacles to business success.* Retrieved from http://www.informationweek.com/news/business_intelligence/analytics/showArticle.jhtml?articleID=215901169&queryText=BICC

Hewlett Packard. (2009). *Building the business intelligence competency center: Business white paper.* Retrieved from http://h20195.www2.hp.com/v2/GetPDF.aspx/4AA2-7082ENW.pdf

Hostmann, B. (2007). *BI competency centers: Bringing intelligence to the business.* Retrieved from http://bpmmag.net/mag/bi_competency_centers_intelligence_1107/index1.html

Hostmann, B. (2010). *Business intelligence competency center key initiative overview.* Stamford, CT: Gartner.

MacMillan, L. (2008). *Strategies for building a successful business intelligence competency center (BICC).* Retrieved from http://www.dbta.com/Articles/Editorial/Trends-and-Applications/Strategies-for-Building-a-Successful-Business-Intelligence-Competency-Center-%28BICC%29-52022.aspx

Miller, G. J., Brautman, D., & Gerlach, S. (2006). *Business intelligence competency centers: A team approach to maximizing competitive advantage.* Hoboken, NJ: John Wiley & Sons.

Nucleus Research. (2009, June). *ROI case study: IBM Cognos BI competency center: Martin's Point Health Care.* Retrieved from http://nucleusresearch.com/research/roi-case-studies/roi-case-study-ibm-cognos-bicc-martins-point-health-care/

Teradata. (2010). *Teradata professional services helps to establish business intelligence competency center.* Retrieved from http://www.rfpconnect.com/news/2010/9/8/teradata-professional-services-helps-to-establish-business-intelligence-competency-center

This work was previously published in the International Journal of Business Intelligence Research, Volume 2, Issue 3, edited by Richard Herschel, pp. 21-35, copyright 2011 by IGI Publishing (an imprint of IGI Global).

Chapter 6

BI's Impact on Analyses and Decision Making Depends on the Development of Less Complex Applications

Robert Sawyer
I.B.I.S. Inc., USA

ABSTRACT

This paper addresses where BI developers have failed to create applications suited for the common end-user and provide a conceptual roadmap to address these shortfalls. It is argued that BI's impact on analyses and decision-making depends on the development of less complex applications. Research conducted for this paper finds that BI lacks a commo n definition and standard, that BI tools are too complex for the common user, and that a shortage of analytical literacy relevant to BI among business professionals is a barrier to BI adoption. The paper suggests that until BI analysis tools become more "human-centric, design-oriented" and less from a "technology-centric, engineering-oriented perspective", BI will continue to fail in its objective to routinely improve business decision-making.

INTRODUCTION

This paper examines the commonality in defining BI has led to the development of BI applications that have failed to appropriately consider the types of people performing the analysis. Analysis tools are critical for employees from all levels of an organization. However, analytical efforts are often hindered by BI tools that are "too complex for wide-spread use" (Harris, 2010). The scarcity of business analysts combined with the lack of training and skill set of most common users impedes businesses from being able to take advantage of the available sophisticated BI tools (Kelly, 2009).

DOI: 10.4018/978-1-4666-2650-8.ch006

According to recent estimates, 20% of BI end-users can be classified as power users which typically have both the academic training and experience to maximize the analytical tools of most BI applications. For the other 80%, which range from the most senior level to the most junior, not only do they lack the experience but also the knowledge to merely interface with the tools. Additionally, the various layers of complexity additionally frustrate users to the point of creating their own impromptu analysis tools which often leads to more than one version of the truth. Having multiple versions of the truth further denigrates the propensity for an enterprise to harness the potential of both its human and asset capital (Harris, 2010).

Maximizing the full potential of BI begins with first defining BI then designing applications that are equivalent to that definition. By incorporating a uniformed characterization of BI, "discussions… could be made more consistent and constructive [focusing]…on what matters – outcomes" (Herschel, 2010). This would help to concentrate application design efforts towards outcomes rather than building the infrastructure of data that falls short on engaging the "human-computer interaction that possesses intelligence: the human half" (Few, 2006, p. 1).

Due to BI not having a standardized definition, various interpretations from academia to IT contributes to a general misunderstanding of not only what BI is but also what it is supposed to be when it is simply about "using data and data analysis to understand and manage your business" (Davenport, 2010). Variations of defining BI has led to designing complex applications that "are some of the most difficult to use relative to a variety of technologies" (Howson, 2010, p. 1). The complexities in these applications have made it even more challenging to find a qualified work force suited to use BI for analysis.

As companies have discovered, having powerful, analytical BI applications means nothing without the kinds of people that have the "patience, aptitude, or interest to become proficient in BI

software, learn how data is structured, or how to do statistical analyses" (Lucker, 2010). Training is a critical need for end-users to maximize the value of "sophisticated applications…that essentially the users are not taking advantage of [owing to a lack of training]" (Kelly, 2009).

One of the biggest issues that hinder end-users from using BI to impact analyses and decision making is because "BI tools are considered hard to difficult to use, with largely unappealing interfaces" (Howson, 2010, p. 1). Research confirms that the design of BI applications is preventing a wider adoption of BI despite the critical role it can play in discovering new opportunities and supporting more of a scientific approach to decisions (Howson, 2010, p. 3).

RESEARCH

Why Does BI Lack a Common Definition?

In 1958, the term Business Intelligence was first used by Hans Pete Luhn in an IBM Journal and defined as "the ability to apprehend the interrelationships of presented facts in such a way as to guide actions towards a desired goal"(Luhn, 1958). However, it wasn't until Howard Dresner, a Gartner fellow, defined BI in 1989 as "concepts and methods to improve business decision making using fact-based support systems" that it started to become a more commonplace term (Martens, 2006; Few, 2010). Herschel (2010) argued that BI was often losing sight of its ultimate objective. He defined BI as "the application of data, technology, and analytics to gain insight and knowledge that enables decisions about people, processes, products, and services that yield positive economic outcomes for the firm."

Standardizing a definition of BI is an important first step in eliminating misunderstanding of BI. However, attempts to more distinctly classify BI vary with individual interpretations that "[seem] to depend heavily upon your particular perspective or training" (Klimberg & Miori, 2010, p. 2).

In the early 1990s, the data warehousing industry began to use the term BI to "breathe new life into the data warehousing industry" and promote its products while regenerating interest in the technology. However, rather than developing methodologies and applications to bring Dresner's vision to fruition, the focus remained on building infrastructure instead of "activities that actually made sense of information and use it to support better decisions" (Few, 2010). As a result of BI emerging from the data warehousing industry, early initiatives were often costly resulting in "large unused data warehouses that represented significant wasted investment" (Kaufman, 2007).

Software vendors also contribute to a general misunderstanding of BI by developing their own definitions based on their suite of applications for sale and using a universal solutions approach without custom tailoring according to the needs of the common user. As Dresner notes, the definition of BI varies and has been "perverted over time by vendors trying to find new ways to market their products" (Kotadia, 2010). Examples range from CRM (customer relationship management) applications and ERP (enterprise resource planning) to decision support systems, OLAP (online analytical processing), knowledge management, and web personalization. As Nicole Engelbert, senior analyst, public sector technology at Datamonitor notes "Everyone and their uncle is calling their solution business intelligence" (Angelo, 2008). Defining BI is not just a problem with the IT industry; it is also a subject of debate among universities.

Currently, academia also struggles with BI. This is reflected by the variability in where BI-related courses and programs are housed. As Klimberg and Miori (2010) note:

Organizations, both corporate and academic, have been rushing to the table with their own BI groups and programs. University level courses *and curriculum in business intelligence / business analytics (BI/BA) may appear in Business Arts and Sciences or Engineering schools, in mathematics, computer science or statistics department, and in undergraduate or graduate programs. (Klimberg & Miori, 2010, p. 6).*

WHY IS BI UNNECESSARILY COMPLEX FOR THE COMMON USER?

Since December 2007, the economy has been in a recession losing more than 1.2 million jobs in just the first 10 months alone according to the National Bureau of Economic Research (Isidore, 2010). This has resulted in an increasing demand for workers to make more tactical decisions while "[accomplishing] more with less...and [leveraging] organizational experience" to influence greater impact on the bottom line (Lucker, 2010). Although companies realize the need to progress beyond individual spreadsheets in order to "provide more sophisticated...BI solutions to more end-user decision makers" (McKendrick, 2010), there is still a struggle to develop an efficient enterprise solution. As Klimberg and Miori (2010) state, "Firms are drowning in data but starving for knowledge. Organizations... [can] make themselves more intelligent through knowledge intensive decision support methods."

In response, BI developers have attempted to add even more functionality but "often unneeded capabilities [resulting] in much more complex products that require more and more BI training so that people can become proficient in them". Additionally, the ensuing environment has resulted into "too many features chasing a diminishing group of users who care about them" (Sherman, 2010). According to Englebert however, much of the confusion could be eliminated if "the vendor community [would] do a better job of communicating and provide better examples of how BI is used" (Angelo, 2010).

For the common user, "less than 20% of employees with BI tools can actually use them – and those who can are typically the analysts hired for such a purpose" (Eckerson, 2010). The remaining 80% of the workforce fail to "gain insights that can help drive a business – no doubt effecting efficiency and the bottom line" (Harris, 2008). When designed properly, BI tools can allow the user to be "submerged in thoughts about data [not] the hoops you must jump through to reach insight" (Few, 2006, p. 1). Unfortunately, the BI industry has lost sight that BI tools "[will be] only as effective as its ability to support human intelligence… and extend our cognitive abilities" (Few, 2006, p. 1). Without a clear vision, BI tools can become more of a hindrance "too often…in the way…interrupting and undermining the thinking process rather than complementing and extending it" (Few, 2006, p. 1).

According to a recent survey conducted by TWDI consisting of 255 companies, BI tools are considered both difficult to comprehend and use. Alternatively, ease of use is also difficult to quantify, "highly subjective and not well understood" (Howson, 2010, p. 2). The survey responses varied greatly with gender, age, training, and job role with only 23% of respondents considering their BI tool as easy to use. Ease of use is also influenced by familiarity with the tool and professional experience. While training does have an influence on perception, it does not necessarily equate to equivalent change in opinion that a BI tool now becomes easy to use when it was once thought difficult.

As Figure 1 illustrates, only transaction systems that are primarily used to monitor inventory or track sales data are ranked more difficult to use.

Developing less complex BI tools oriented to the common end-user of which too often has not been academically trained will greatly enhance efforts to spend more time analyzing data and less time searching for it. Businesses should take not also that ease of use perceptions regarding BI tools also pose as a significant barrier to business adoption (Howson, 2010, pp. 5-8).

Barriers to BI Adoption

BI has hit a proverbial wall in business adoption. The BI industry is more concerned about ETL than, "the activities that actually make sense of information and use it to support better decisions [and] have remained behind a wall that they've failed to scale and have never seriously tried to scale" (Few, 2010).

Figure 1. Response to survey question-How easy do you find the following tools to learn and use?

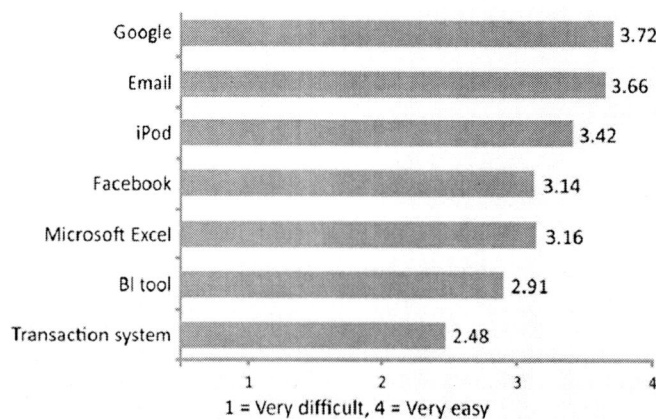

1 = Very difficult, 4 = Very easy

Note: From "Ease of Use and Interface Appeal in Business Intelligence Tools" by C. Howson, p.5 (2010)

As Few illustrates in Figure 2, the left side of the wall is where most developers remain because of their technology-centric, engineering oriented approach to developing BI tools that serve as inhibitors to enterprise wide adoption of BI. The right side of the wall is where the industry should be in terms of what end-users need.

Despite continuing hype about how BI's impact on business is a game changer that makes the difference in decisions, Cindi Howson, founder of BIScorecard, notes "for more than a decade… BI penetration still lags…[and] has been mostly unchanged" (Swoyer, 2010). Since first being tracked, BI adoption "hasn't budged since we first began assessing this point in 2005." Additionally, Howson's research reveals that contrary to popular belief BI usage has actually decreased and that "the percentage of employees using BI in 2007 was 25 percent and was 24 percent in 2009" (Swoyer, 2010).

According to Howson's survey, companies' perceptions about their experiences with BI have also slipped. From 24% in 2007 of companies rating their experience with BI as "very successful" to only 21% in 2009, it appears that BI is losing valuable momentum moving forward (Swoyer, 2010). Despite these changes, it is important to consider how the impact of reduced IT budgets has also influenced buyers to expect even greater impact from BI adoption. As Howson notes, "while there is a strong correlation between BI success rates and BI's contribution to business performance, it is not exact" (Swoyer, 2010).

A company's perception of BI also affects who within an organization will be granted access. Some organizations are convinced that not all users need BI. However, as Howson notes "a bigger challenge is that BI is rarely considered, asked for, or made relevant beyond information workers" (Swoyer, 2010). Beyond perception, there is also an internal struggle among business users and the IT department. According to Leah MacMillan, Vice President of Product Marketing at Cognos:

Business Intelligence epitomizes the classic struggle between IT and business: Business users will not embrace BI until they can get it on their own terms. They protest that they can't wait for IT and need direct access to information. Yet they say they need to see things their own way, which may lead them to say BI is too hard to use, and they prefer a different interface. (MacMillan, 2010).

In order to create a more collaborative environment among departments and extract the greatest ROI on their BI investment, companies must be involved with managing expectations of end-users

Figure 2. Few's illustration of BI inhibitors

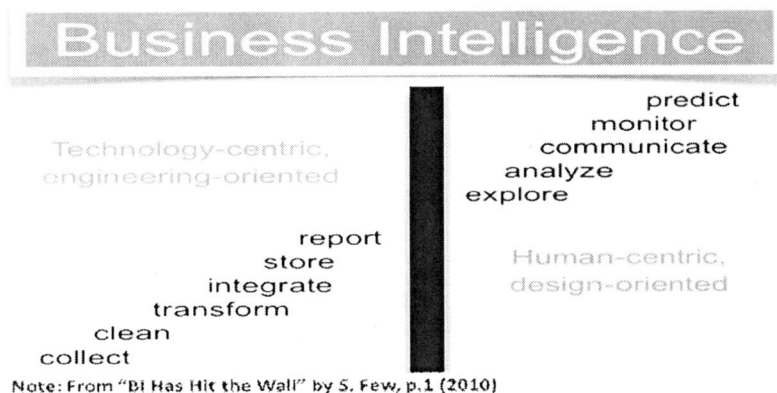

Note: From "BI Has Hit the Wall" by S. Few, p.1 (2010)

to ensure that they understand how BI can have a positive impact on their performance.

Managing Expectations of End-Users

From the beginning, it is important to manage the expectations of end-users by utilizing relevant descriptive words that a common user can understand and therefore begin to visualize how it will impact their performance.

What we need to work on with business intelligence [is to] find a way to describe it so that it yields positive imagery. That is words to create an image that elicits a positive impression of business intelligence in others. (Herschel, 2010).

Articulating an image that empowers users to view BI as a "difference maker" would assist in drawing the types of talent needed much like the same type of trait that "attracts people to medical care" (Herschel, 2010). Transforming the industry will greatly depend on recruiting the right kinds of people that has the intellectual curiosity of an engineer combined with the communication skills of a sales executive.

Managing expectations is also an important part of developing a culture to maximize the value of BI. According to Gartner analysts Kurt Schlegel and John E. Van Decker, the five main reasons that prevent organizations from discovering the full potential of BI are:

- A lack of coordination between IT and the business – viewing users as customers rather than partners;
- A lack of connection between BI tools and corporate strategy – department level projects are often not integrated with corporate level strategy;
- A lack of connection between BI and business processes – BI must become an integral part of business processes not separate;

- A lack of BI governance or, in some cases, too much governance – Excessive departmental control causes BI bottlenecks;
- A lack of skills in business users – users lack sufficient training to take full advantage of BI tools. (Kelly, 2009)

A common theme among all these points is the importance of coordination. Regardless of the level coordinating efforts, a lack of technical analytical skills among business users will hinder any efforts and overwhelm the trained professionals that are employed (Harris, 2008).

A Shortage of Trained Professionals

Trained professionals are often overwhelmed by ad-hoc requests for information not because a problem cannot be defined or needing assistance to determine what information is needed but because "BI tools [are so] complex…business users aren't able to take that next step on their own" (Harris, 2008). Large sized companies have traditionally assigned analysts to develop dashboards and scorecards to track key performance indicators (KPI) as part of the BI tools used to monitor business performance real time. However, when management attempts to build reports that require additional information beyond what these BI tools can provide, quite often they do not have the skill set to address what may be a simple fix.

Analysts quite often are being tasked to respond to ad hoc requests that consist of either "frequently misinterpreted or poorly articulated specifications" further compounding the problem that they are already overburdened with other duties and cannot keep up with demand (Harris, 2008). When analysts are constantly redirected to fulfill ad hoc reporting requests in what typically is an inefficient, arbitrary process, they are not able to "give their full attention to interrogating underlying business data and uncovering opportunities" (Harris, 2008). In order for analysts to have the kind of culture where their efforts are oriented towards a more strategic focus, management must reevaluate their approach to decision making and determine the root cause behind their lack of faith in their corporate data.

Senior Management, BI, and Buy-In

Organizational "buy-in" needs to come from the top yet out of all respondents from a survey conducted by the Aberdeen Group one third (33%) cite lack of top-management commitment to projects (Hatch, 2008). According to research by Cambridge University, good decision making is as a critical factor that can improve the average performance of a company by more than five percent of which makes BI all the more critical to "separate market leaders from the rest of the pack" (Cruickshank, 2010).

Senior Management is also at times both skeptical of BI and distrusting of its own corporate data often questioning whether "the reports, charts, and analytic tools in use today represent the truth" (Hatch, 2008). In a recent Accenture survey, some of the reasons for this skepticism and mistrust are:

- Managers waste two hours a day searching for information;
- More than 50 percent of managers use the wrong information at least once a week;
- More than 50 percent of the information that managers receive is perceived as having no value. (MacMillan, 2010)

Beyond the results of this survey, there are other underlying issues that also contribute to senior management's lacking confidence in using data as a fundamental component of decision making.

One of the overall purposes of BI is to "improve decision-making by providing business leaders with rich valuable insights into their business and a holistic view of their actual performance"

(Cruickshank, 2010). Despite BI being established for more than 15 years, many senior executives do not have positive views of the technology and have experienced "BI initiatives ultimately fail to deliver any real value" (Cruickshank, 2010). Research by Cambridge University also confirms that 9 out of 10 of all executives interviewed "admitted that their BI capabilities were not living up to their expectations" (Cruickshank, 2010). In addition to these findings, senior management may also be heavily influenced by their exposure to computers as Howson notes "a...work force that has grown up with computers...may have a different view of BI than workers who once relied on paper and colored pencils" (2010, p. 2).

Senior management is also expected to be the principal drivers of executing corporate strategy and aligning goals supporting the CEO's vision that makes it "politically difficult for people to say I need help making decisions. They get paid the big bucks and they think they should be good at decision making" (Davenport, 2010). It is not a zero sum game when it comes to employing wisdom gained from years of working experience as a basis for decision making as "creative judgment and expertise will always play a vital role...but the balance between art and science is shifting" (Davenport & Harris, 2009).

With many CEOs, their previous work experience also does not necessarily equate to experience in analytically based decision making although enterprises are actively collecting more data from 150 Exabytes (150bn Gigabytes) in 2005 to a current estimate 1,200 Exabytes. As Davenport (2010) observes:

There's a big, big gap between the most analytical and the least analytical. American business has a fair number of CEOs with engineering backgrounds, and they tend to be relatively analytical. At the same time, an awful lot have sales backgrounds, and they're not analytical at all. Clearly you could do a lot of analytical with sales, but people don't generally go into sales because they like numbers. (Davenport, 2010).

Data driven decision making is not just a problem with senior level management. Despite many in the work force growing up with computers, the college major appears to also have a significant influence. As Klimberg and Miori (2010) note:

The skills of analyzing problem situations and building models are already fundamental skills to most scientists and engineers. However, these problems are severely lacking in and must also become fundamental skills for other disciplines, such as business managers, educators, and healthcare providers. (Klimberg & Miori, 2010, p.7).

As important as it is to recognize the need for developing relevant analytical skills in order to extract the greatest value from BI, it is also important for senior management to understand that "[BI] is not a substitutes for decision making nor [does it]…provide automatic, infallible answers" (Davenport & Harris, 2009, p. 30). Even workers with an analytical skill set must not solely rely on numbers when analyzing a business. Many aspects of a business are "unstructured… [and] not well suited to the highly structured data requirements of a database application (Herschel, 2008). According to some estimates "up to 80% of business information is not quantitative or structured in a way that can be captured in a relational database" (Herschel, 2008). Additionally, simply having an analytical skill set is often not enough because "even if they had…the skills, time and inclination, they would still need to know where to find the data" (Harris, 2008).

Simplify Data Access

The amount of data organizations track, store, and retain is growing exponentially. This data is often stored in "numerous locations often in different formats and isolated silos" which means the data is not a part of a collaborative approach to analysis because it is not shared and can result in multiple versions of the truth (MacMillan, 2010). The key is managing the data both efficiently and effectively so that it can be transformed into valuable information that "enables people at all levels of an organization to gain a clear understanding of how they are performing" (Macmillan, 2010). Currently, accessing this type of information is not as simple as asking a question in plain language. Even when the information needed is clearly defined, most BI software requires knowledge of a query language, usually SQL, to extract the information from a database which usually requires the assistance of an analyst.

Redefining the BI Acquisition Process

Each year, new BI software is released where "vendors add more and more features…yet a typical business worker uses only a small percentage of the available features…chasing a diminishing group of users who care about them" (Sherman, 2010). This is typically the result of BI purchases decided by the IT department or BI teams which are driven by power users to evaluate the products and develop selection criteria where "the more features the better" (Sherman, 2010). A CEO's views about technology can also "[affect] the nature of a firms technology adoption decisions" (Herschel, 2008).

Business users should play a critical role in the acquisition process. Despite business users ultimately being the consumers, they "are almost an afterthought [which results in] purchasing a large number of licenses for BI software that… "becomes expensive shelfware"…and business users go back to using the Excel spreadsheets" (Sherman, 2010).

Figure 3. Defining user groups

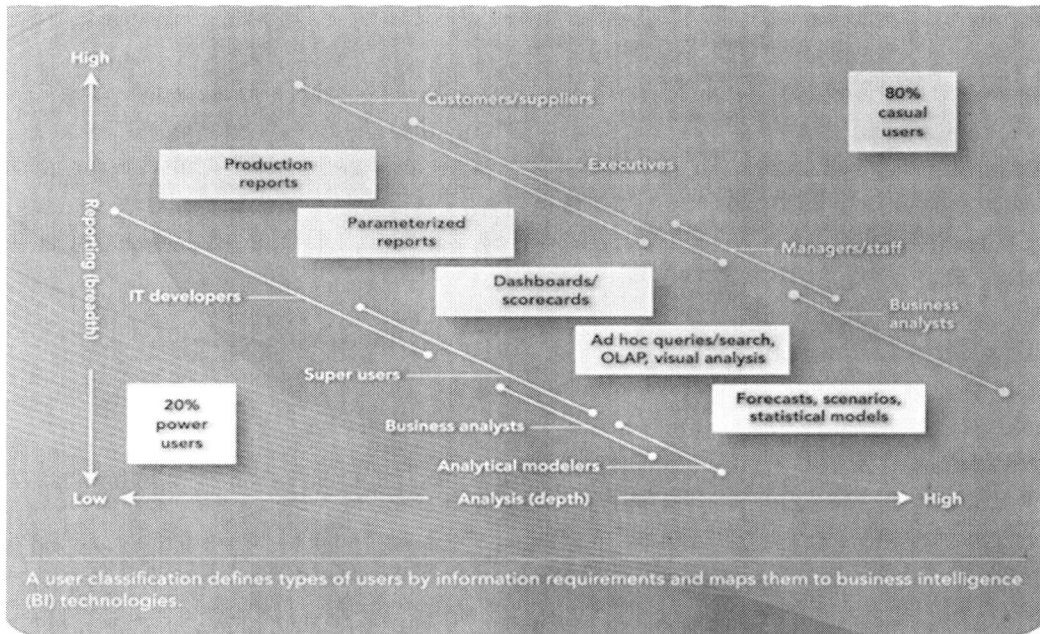

ANALYSIS

Identify Groups by Usage Level

Attempting to provide a universal BI solution to end-users is not an efficient way to manage both human capital and IT resources especially when only 20% of users are classified as power users. With varying levels of academic backgrounds, professional experience levels, and analytical skills, BI teams must be formed to navigate the work force from the current operating procedures to a more analytical, optimal BI environment (Eckerson, 2009). Although senior level management could at times use BI tools that will perform analysis on all levels of a business, "most won't… [neither will] other types of users" (Eckerson, 2009). Steps to implement a more optimal BI environment should include the following:

- Distinguish between casual users and power users. Casual users and power users have different needs when it comes to in-formation. Providing casual users with BI tools that are too complex and power users with tools that are not sufficient to analyze data at the highest level of granularity will result in infrequent to little use of the tools.

- Understand the nuances of self-service BI. This will allow casual users to navigate through defined data paths using prompts or drop down selections for various ad hoc needs and power users will have the ability to create reports and dashboards.

- Classify users. Users should be grouped according to skill sets and their information needs whether it is from an information consumption or producing standpoint.

- Fit BI tools to the categories. Match users in accordance with their needs to the right BI tools to avoid over fitting. These tools should also be standardized so that any analysis can be validated and to minimize multiple versions of the truth from being generated.

In Figure 3, Eckerson presents an alternative by grouping users into two main groups: information users or casual users and information consumers or power users. By defining BI users and grouping them accordingly, BI resources can be appropriately matched to the kinds of BI technologies suited for their needs and "customized to people's roles and personalized according to their tastes" (Eckerson, 2009).

Industry Standard is Lacking

Due to the BI industry lacking any definitive standard, expectations of BI also varies wildly. Despite these conditions, BI remains a "top technology spending priority in today's organizations" due to BI projects:

- Leverage existing information investments
- Deliver proven high return on investment (Business Objects, n.d.)

A pragmatic solution to more efficiently manage an organization's BI assets is to implement a standardized approach even in the absence of an industry standard to essentially accomplish the following:

- **Lower Costs:** Coordinated purchasing of BI software contracts, vendors, and tools will lowers support, administration, and training while delivering a faster ROI
- **More Control and Fewer Data Inconsistencies:** Provides more reliable data, reduces multiple versions of the truth by controlling the source making comparisons of data across departments reliable, and makes sharing information across departments straightforward
- **Better Alignment with Business Users:** Reducing friction between business users and IT, provides more timely answers, and increases competitive advantage by bet-

ter leveraging enterprise data/ information (Business Objects, n. d.)

The opportunities in standardizing BI for an organization provide an opportunity to fully exploit the benefits of BI while further increasing the competitive advantage that BI provides even in a less efficient state ((Business Objects, n. d.).

BI AND THE END-USER

For BI to deliver the greatest value, it will have to be employed in all facets of an organization. However, the varying skill set of the end-user which may range from "a doctorate in mathematics to an associate degree from the local community college" may hinder such an initiative (Marion, 2010). The varying skill set of the end-user should also directly influence the purchase of BI software ensuring that the "user interface, graphics and what-if query capabilities... [are] intuitive (Marion, 2010). Although a different industry, Apple was faced with similar challenges in developing their products.

Apple realized that in order to reach a broad base of users, it had to sell beyond niche users of IT and early adopters resisting the temptation to add more features while ensuring their devices are "easy to learn and can be self taught regardless of technical expertise" (Sherman, 2010). BI developers could learn by taking a similar approach. If fewer features are developed but more suited according to end-users' greatest needs which also constitutes the largest group, the base of BI users would increase and organizations would become more efficient in managing their resources.

CONCLUSION AND RECOMMENDATIONS

BI has the potential to greatly impact an organization from increasing operational efficiency to discovering hidden opportunities through trend analysis. However, when end-users are forced into using a technology that they have been minimally trained to use or the work force overall lacks the skill set to properly employ BI, productivity can suffer. Research and analysis presented through this paper confirms that BI's impact on analyses and decision making depends on the development of less complex applications. Evidence also confirms that until BI is customized according to the majority of end-users' needs and skill sets, the full potential of BI's impact on analyses and decision making will be minimized.

Apple Methodologies for Future BI Development

Apple did not invent the MP3 player, the computer, or cell phone but in each of these categories it did revolutionize the product by masking the complexities of its functionality and included a set of features that are most wanted while transforming a utility device into a must have. Apple's products were designed with simplicity in mind without sacrificing style and are easy to learn regardless of how tech savvy the user is. Even for power users, advanced features are also available. If BI developers could create tools specifically customized to the other 80% of end-users that are either not academically trained or lacking analytical skills relevant to BI, the potential for ROI in BI initiatives are significant.

Natural Language Ad Hoc Query and Web Search Technologies

Learning query language can be an unwelcome challenge to learn especially when the primary interest is obtaining data to transform into information for analysis not the methodology or complexities on how it is obtained. If natural language and web search technologies were combined, using something as simple as a search box for enterprise search could allow users to search for and find information using a business language and would require no additional training. Like Google, prior search history could be stored and used to obtain information routine information quicker without submitting an ad hoc request to an analyst.

BI on Demand

Creating a BI framework where users can access information rapidly and build ad hoc reports using a natural language methodology will provide an opportunity for all needing information a way to make better decisions with real-time information. BI on demand provided a way for the end-user to get an immediate view of things of the want they to see, the way they want to see it, and when they want to see it without requiring the assistance of an analyst.

REFERENCES

Angelo, J. (2008). *Business intelligence: A new technology can analyze data at amazing speeds. So why is higher ed slow to adopt?* Retrieved from http://www.universitybusiness.com/viewarticle. aspx?articleid=659

Business Objects. (n. d.). *Business intelligence standardization.* Retrieved from http://www. kleere.com/docs/white_paper_bi_standardization.pdf

Cruickshank, B. (2010). *Making business intelligence work.* Retrieved from http://proquest. umi.com.argo.library.okstate.edu/pqdlink?did= 2155971561&Fmt=3&clientld+4653&RQT+30 9&VName+PQD

Davenport, T. H. (2010). Are you ready to reengineer your decision making? *MIT Sloan Management Review*, 2-7.

Davenport, T. H., & Harris, J. G. (2009). What people want (and how to predict it). *MIT Sloan Management Review*, 23-31.

Eckerson, W. (2009). *One size does not fit all.* Retrieved from http://www.teradatamagazine. com/v09n04/Features/One-size-does-not-fit-all/

Few, S. (2006). *BizViz: The power of visual business intelligence.* Retrieved from http://www. perceptualedge.com/articles/b-eye/visual_business_intelligence.pdf

Few, S. (2010). *BI has hit the wall.* Retrieved from http://www.perceptualedge.com/blog/?p=820

Hall, M. (2010). *A solution for IT.* Retrieved from http://global.factiva.com.argo.library.okstate.edu/ga/default.aspx

Harris, L. (2008). *Delivering useful BI tools for the masses.* Retrieved from http://www.busmanagement.com/article/Delivering-Useful-BI-Tools-for-the-Masses/

Hatch, D. (2008). *BI: Is one version of the truth still out there?* Retrieved from http://www.ecommerce-times.com/rssstory.65359.html?wlc-1288713846

Herschel, R. (2010). *Marketing business intelligence.* Retrieved from http://www.b-eye-network. com/print/12563

Herschel, R. (2010). *What is business intelligence?* Retrieved from http://www.b-eye-network.com/print/13768

Howson, C. (2010). *Ease of use and interface appeal in business intelligence tools.* Retrieved from http://www.beyeresearch.com/study/13006

Isidore, C. (2008). *It's official: Recession since Dec. '07.* Retrieved from http://money.cnn. com/2008/12/01/news/economy/recession/index. htm

Kanaracus, C. (2010). *Professors cite challenges in teaching BI.* Retrieved from http://www.pc-world.com/businesscenter/article/192138/professors_cite_challenges_in_teaching_bi.html

Kaufnabb, M. (2007). *Common business intelligence (BI) mistakes.* Retrieved from http:// searchbusinessanaltytics.techtarget.com/tip/ Common-business-intelligence-BI-mistakes

Kelly, J. (2009). *Business intelligence not all it can be at most organizations, according to Gartner.* Retrieved from http://searchbusinessanalytics. techtarget.com/news/1507079/Business-intelligence-not-all-it-can-be-at-most-organizations-according-to-Gartner

Klimberg, R. K., & Miori, V. (2010). Back in business. *ORMS, 37*(5).

Kotadia, M. (2006). *Business intelligence lies beyond IT: Dresner.* Retrieved from http://www. zdnet.com.au/business-intelligence-lies-beyond-it-dresner-139240318.htm

Lucker, J. (2010). *The BI and analytics treadmill.* Retrieved from http://techdecisions.com/ Issues/2010/March/Pages/The-BI-and-Analytics-Treadmill.aspx

Luhn, H. (1958). A business intelligence system. *IBM Journal of Research and Development, 2*(4), 314. doi:10.1147/rd.24.0314

MacMillan, L. (2010). *The full promise of business intelligence.* Retrieved from http://www. information-management.com/newsletters/

Marion, L. (2010). *Business intelligence software: 10 common mistakes.* Retrieved from http:// itmanagement.earthweb.com/entdev/article. php/3776376/Business-Intelligence-Software-10-Common-Mistakes.htm

Martens, C. (2006). *Business intelligence at age 17.* Retrieved from http://www.computerworld. com/s/article/266298/BI_at_age_17

McKendrick, J. (2009). *Business intelligence comes to the masses.* Retrieved from http://www.dbta.com/Articles/Editorial/Trends-and-Applications/Business-Intelligence-Comes-to-the-Masses--54648.aspx

Nash, K. (2010). Analyzing the future: When business intelligence is used to inform business process changes, companies find new ways to save money and connect more closely with customers. *CIO, 23*(14).

Sherman, R. (2010). *Business intelligence vendors, BI buyers could do more with less.* Retrieved from http://searchbusinessanalytics.techtarget.com/news/2240022985/Business-intelligence-vendors-BI-buyers-could-do-more-with-less

Swoyer, S. (2010). *Pervasive business intelligence: Still not a vision, not reality.* Retrieved from http://tdwi.org/articles/2010/01/20/pervasive-bi-still-a-vision-not-reality.aspx

This work was previously published in the International Journal of Business Intelligence Research, Volume 2, Issue 3, edited by Richard Herschel, pp. 52-63, copyright 2011 by IGI Publishing (an imprint of IGI Global).

Chapter 7
Discovering Business Intelligence from the Subjective Web Data

Ranjit Bose
University of New Mexico, USA

ABSTRACT

The online word-of-mouth behavior that exists today in the Web represents new and measurable sources of information. The automated discovery or mining of consumer opinions from these sources is of great importance for marketing intelligence and product benchmarking. Techniques are now being developed to effectively and easily mine the consumer opinions from the Web data and to timely deliver them to companies and individual consumers. This study investigates this emerging field named 'opinion mining' in terms of what it is, what it can do, and how it could be used effectively for business intelligence (BI). A rigorous review of the research literature on opinion mining is conducted to explore its current state, issues and challenges for its use in developing business applications for competitive advantage. The study aims to assist business managers to better understand the current opportunities and challenges in using opinion mining for deriving BI. Future research directions for further development of the field are also identified.

1. INTRODUCTION

Consumer opinions used to be very difficult to obtain before the Web was widely available to and used by every day citizens. To find consumer opinions about their products and those of their competitors, companies usually conducted consumer surveys or engaged external consultants.

Getting consumer feedback meant asking them to participate in filling out survey instruments. This cumbersome approach had many problems such as making a survey for each product or feature; the format, distribution and timing of the survey (asking to send a form right after purchase might not be very informative); and the reliance on the goodwill of consumers to take the survey. Addi-

DOI: 10.4018/978-1-4666-2650-8.ch007

tionally, consumers shared their views primarily through spoken word of mouth. Thus, irrespective of how the consumer opinions were collected, they lead to a long period of latency before a brand's weakness or strengths were known to all – the producers and consumers.

With the rapid expansion of e-commerce in recent years, more and more products are being sold on the Web, thus more and more consumers are buying products online. In recent years, the Web has dramatically changed the way consumers express opinions on products that they have purchased and used, or on services that they have received from various companies. Opinions and reviews are easily posted on the Web, such as in merchant sites, review portals, blogs, internet forums, and social networking sites (Wang *et al.*, 2009). These data are commonly referred to as user-generated content or user-generated media. Both the product manufacturers as well as the potential customers find this online "word of mouth" very useful (Chen *et al.*, 2008). The product manufacturers receive information on their customers' likes and dislikes, as well as the positive and negative comments on their products whenever available, giving them better knowledge of their products' limitations and advantages over their competitors. The potential customers on the other hand receive useful and "first hand" information on the products and/or services which assist them in their future purchase decision making process.

As more and more common users are becoming comfortable with the Web, an increasing number of them are writing reviews. Consequently, the number of reviews that a product receives is growing rapidly. Popular products can get hundreds or even thousands of reviews at some large merchant sites. Many of these reviews are long and have only a few sentences containing opinions on the product. This makes it hard for a potential customer to read them all to make an informed decision on whether to purchase the product. If the potential customer only reads a few reviews, they may get a biased view. Similarly,

the large number of reviews also makes it hard for product manufacturers to keep track of customer opinions of their products. Moreover, the product manufacturer face additional difficulties since many merchant sites may sell the same product and the manufacturer normally produces many kinds of products.

The online word-of-mouth behavior that exists today in the Web represents new and measurable sources of information. Mining these consumer opinions is of great importance for marketing intelligence and product benchmarking. Techniques are now being developed to effectively and easily mine the consumer opinions from these sources and to timely deliver them to companies and individual consumers. In the past few years many researchers have been actively involved in developing this nascent and highly potent field of study, which is called *opinion mining* or *sentiment analysis* (Pang *et al.*, 2008b; Liu, 2010).

Opinion mining is a very new field of study that attempts to develop automatic systems to determine human opinion from text written in natural language. It is a discipline at the crossroads of information retrieval and computational linguistics. The task of opinion mining is technically challenging because it requires natural language processing, which itself is a tedious job (Kao *et al.*, 2007). The research and development that has taken place and is currently taking place in this field have been performed by the computer science and computational linguistics communities. Consequently, the published results are not friendly to or are easily understood by business professionals unless they are technically trained. The purpose and contribution of this research is twofold. First, it summarizes and presents the state of the art in opinion mining in a way that is easily comprehensible by business professionals encompassing a wide range of backgrounds or expertise. Second, it categorizes the existing literature into a classification framework that is intended to help management information systems researchers to study this field in further details for future business benefits.

The textual information that is found in the Web is broadly classified into two main categories, *facts* and *opinions*. Facts are objective statements about entities and events in the world. Opinions are subjective statements that reflect peoples' sentiments or perceptions about the entities and events. Much of the existing research on text information processing has been, almost exclusively, focused on mining and retrieval of factual information, e.g., information retrieval, Web search, and many other text mining and natural language processing tasks. Until only recently, work has begun on the processing of opinions. Yet, opinions are so important that whenever one needs to make a decision one wants to hear others' opinions. This is not only true for individual consumers but also true for organizations. Good sentiment detection tools, for blogs and other social media, tailored to businesses and individuals can be highly useful in today's society (Das *et al.*, 2007).

To illustrate the research contributions, this paper is structured to accomplish the following objectives. First is to bring together and present some of the latest developments and results in the field of opinion mining. Second, to help business managers better understand the challenges and opportunities that exist today in using opinion mining for business intelligence. Third is to identify future research directions in opinion mining for further enhancement of the field.

2. THE UNDERPINNINGS OF OPINION MINING

Monitoring relevant Web information sources and summarizing the newly discovered customer opinions are important for companies to improve their services, for them to market their products, and for customers to purchase their objects. Web opinion mining aims to extract, summarize, and track various aspects of opinionated or subjective information on the Web (Ku *et al.*, 2007). These tasks are different from traditional information retrieval and extraction. Conventional information retrieval only identifies which document is relevant to a given topic; it does not identify whether it is positive, negative, or neutral about the topic. In addition, conventional information extraction only recognizes the major components such as named entities and their relationships; it does not report the supportive and the non-supportive evidence. Opinion extraction identifies opinion holders, extracts the relevant opinion sentences, and decides their polarities. Opinion summarization recognizes the major events embedded in documents and summarizes the supportive and the non-supportive evidence. Opinion tracking captures subjective information from various genres and monitors the developments of opinions from spatial and temporal dimensions. Figure 1 displays these goals.

2.1 Enrichment of Business Intelligence

Business intelligence (BI) aims to support business decision-making for competitive advantage by using technologies, processes, and applications to analyze mostly internal, structured data and business processes. The management view of BI is getting the right information to the right people at the right time so they can make decisions that ultimately improve enterprise performance. The technical view of BI typically centers on the process of, or applications and technologies for, gathering, storing, analyzing and providing access to data to help make better business decisions.

The field of BI – which has rapidly developed and matured over the years – has been engaged in the widespread adoption of advanced analytics such as data mining and text mining technologies to drive better decision management (Wang *et al.*, 2008). Increasingly, BI practitioners and vendors are recognizing the contributions of these technologies to the delivery of high-value, decision-oriented functionality such as forecasting and prediction (Froelic *et al.*, 2005). Here we con-

Figure 1. Goals of web opinion mining (adapted from Ku et al., 2007)

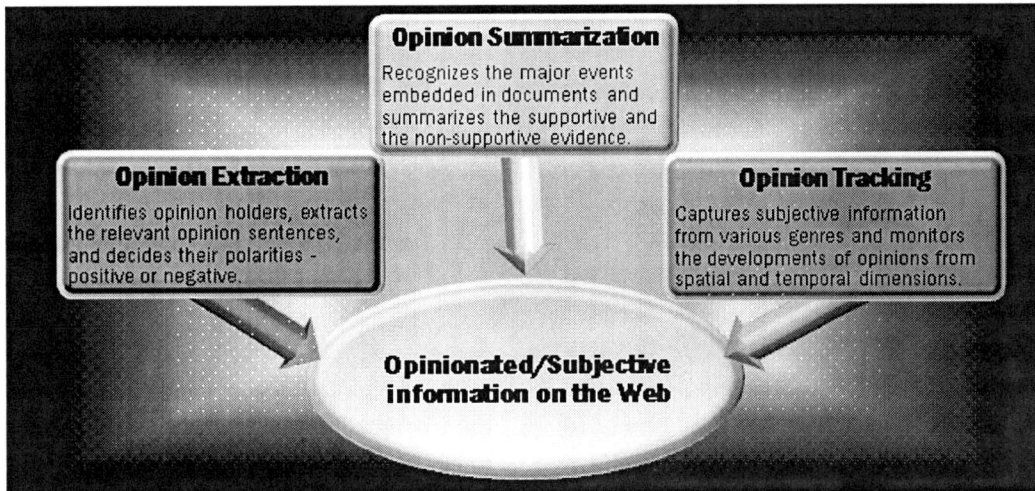

tend that opinion mining technologies extend and further enrich the current capabilities of BI. The Figure 2 shows the progression and enrichment of BI in recent years through the incorporation of data mining, followed by text mining, and now opinion mining technologies.

The data mining technology is powerful for the automatic extraction of patterns, associations, changes, anomalies and significant structures from structured data, such as data from corporate data warehouses. The uncovered patterns from warehouse data play a critical role in decision making because they reveal areas for process improvement. Most of the value of data mining comes from using data mining technology to improve predictive modeling. Subsequent advances have led to a newer trend in data mining – which is called text mining. Applying text mining to unstructured data adds a richness and depth to the patterns already uncovered through the company's data mining efforts (Miller, 2005). Text mining applies the same analytical functions of data mining to the domain of textual information, relying on sophisticated, text analysis techniques that distill information from free-text documents. Data and text mining along with natural language processing technologies are the key contributors

to making opinion mining possible. Opinion mining is concerned with mining Web opinion sources to obtain BI (Dey *et al.*, 2009). Comments made in blogosphere can help a company reposition its products against the competition, highlighting strengths and overcoming weaknesses through an appropriate blend of advertising,

Figure 2. The progression and enrichment of business intelligence in recent years

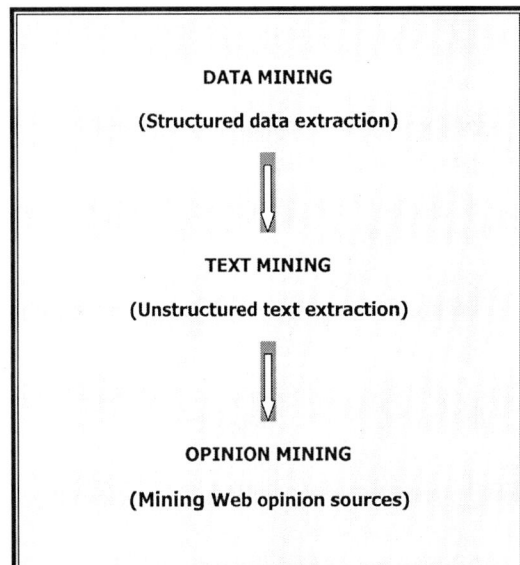

marketing and product engineering. Thus the ability of a company to perform real time opinion mining of the blogosphere – with high level of accuracy enables it to quickly identify trends in opinions about their brands, which in turn enables managers to take appropriate actions quickly and timely.

The social media that we know today describes the online technologies and practices that individual users use to share opinions, insights, experiences, and perspectives with one another (Jansen *et al.*, 2009). Social business intelligence system, which would take the user-generated content from the social media as input, can thus be potentially developed which could possibly have one or more of the following features or capabilities.

- Discover what people think of a company's brand or products;
- Monitor what is being said about a company and its products, across blogs, and forums;
- Provide discussion boards and news sites to the customers;
- Discover the sentiment and opinions of these people;
- View the main influencers of a company's brand;
- View bloggers mood trends over days, weeks, months and years;
- Setup alerts to email managers when bad press events occur;
- Alert customer service for very dissatisfied customers; and
- Gain intelligence to develop more targeted marketing, improve products and gain even more customers.

2.2 Related Technologies

Due to the heterogeneity and lack of structure of the Web data, automated mining of customer opinion is a challenging task. It calls for novel methods that draw from a wide range of fields spanning data mining, machine learning, natural language processing, statistics, databases, and information retrieval. In particular natural language processing, data mining, and text mining technologies are briefly summarized below within the context of opinion mining.

2.2.1 Natural Language Processing

Natural language processing (NLP) is concerned with the interactions between computers and human (natural) languages. Technological advances have begun to close the gap between human and computer languages. The field of natural language processing has produced technologies that teach computers natural language, enabling them to analyze, understand, and even generate text (Kao *et al.*, 2007). NLP has significant overlap with the field of computational linguistics, which deals with the application of computers to the processing of natural language.

2.2.2 Data Mining

The business value of data mining comes from using data mining technology to improve predictive modeling. Data mining is used by executives belonging to all three levels of management. Strategic managers use data mining for competitive intelligence, identifying market opportunities, product launch decisions and product positioning. Managers responsible for tactical decision make use of data mining for sales forecasting, direct marketing, customer acquisition, retention and extension purposes and marketing campaign analysis. Finally, operational managers can use for decisions such as the choice of sub-prime borrowers or supply chain management.

While data mining successfully helps find the gold (business intelligence) hidden in a company's data, it addresses only a very limited part of a company's total data assets: the *structured* information available in databases. Probably more than 90% of a company's data are never being tapped or looked at: letters from customers, email, correspondence, recording of phone calls with customers, contracts, technical documentation, patents, and so on. Since the prices of digital storage are becoming increasingly affordable, coupled with their increasing speed and capacity, companies are collecting more and more of such data online. The emergent text mining tools help dig out the hidden gold from the different format of textual information mentioned above.

2.2.3 Text Mining

Text mining applies the same analytical functions of data mining to the domain of textual information which is unstructured or semi-structured, relying on sophisticated, text analysis techniques that distill information from free-text documents (Feldman *et al.*, 2007). Text mining software operates on the digitized form of organizational textual data to provide the capability of pattern identification, visualization support to aid pattern identification, modeling support to identify or confirm relationships, and drill-down query tools to enable analysts to focus on key problem areas. Report generation tools also aid the text mining process.

3. WEB OPINION MINING CLASSIFICATION

This section intends to bring together and present some of the latest developments and results in the field of opinion mining or sentiment analysis.

3.1 Prelude to Classification

Technically opinion mining and sentiment analysis have slightly different notions nevertheless, these two terms are similar in their essence and fall under the umbrella of analysis of subjective or opinionated information found on the Web.

Opinion mining was coined by the researchers focused in information retrieval research. Sentiment analysis was coined by the researchers within the artificial intelligence group focused on NLP research. Opinion mining aims at extracting and further processing users' opinions on different subjects or entities. Sentiment analysis aims at retrieval of sentiments expressed in texts. Both attempt to provide an in-depth view of the emotions expressed in subjective text, and enable the further processing of the data, in order to aggregate or summarize the opinions, or identify contradicting opinions. Opinion mining nevertheless is an important and challenging problem for the researchers to deal with because the quality of the results obtained from the opinion mining process is critical for the success of all subsequent tasks these results are used in.

During the last few years, the business community witnessed an increasing interest in the processing and analysis of unstructured data, with a special focus on web text data. The wealth of information on the Web makes this endeavor not only rewarding in terms of newly produced knowledge, but also necessary, in order to leverage all this available information. Table 1 captures a range of application cases of opinion mining in different domains to illustrate the recognition and usefulness of opinion mining across the society.

However, performing opinion mining or sentiment analysis is quite challenging and difficult. Much of the current research in this field is devoted to sentiment classification: determining whether a particular document or portion thereof is subjective or not, and/or determining whether the opinion it expresses is positive or negative.

In general, the research community has adopted one of two approaches to meeting the challenges that opinion mining or sentiment analysis presents. Many groups are working to directly improve the selection and interpretation of indicators through the *incorporation of linguistic knowledge*; given the subtleties of natural language, such efforts are critical to building operational systems. Others

Table 1. A snapshot of web opinion mining application cases

APPLICATION CASES	BRIEF DESCRIPTION
Product review	Reviews of products such as hotel and restaurant found in review websites such as *epinions* and *tripadvisor* are mined to determine the sentiment, attitude or opinion to advice new users to help them with their travel plans.
Movie review	Online reviews for movies found in the internet movie database (IMDB) are mined for the movie goers to guide them when they are unsure about which movies to watch (Zhao *et al.*, 2009).
News review	Several news monitoring systems are available on the internet providing various functionalities such as breaking news alerting. Systems for mining opinions from quotations (reported speech) in newspaper articles have been proposed.
Politics review	Using OM election candidates have become more knowledgeable about specifics of the opinion poll which helped identify where their strengths and weaknesses lie according to their electorate.
Tweets	Tweets or micro-blogging, as a form of electronic word of mouth, for sharing consumer opinions concerning brands have been mined.
Analyzing YouTube Comments	Analysis of the social video sharing platform YouTube revealed a high amount of community feedback through comments for published videos as well as through meta ratings of these comments
Multilingual	Opinion mining in multiple languages has been conducted. These languages include Arabic, Chinese, Dutch, English and Spanish.
Financial Domain	Opinion mining system to automatically determine the sentiment of financial bloggers towards companies and their stocks.
Evaluation of opinions within on-line communities	Evaluation of review helpfulness of the Amazon.com website reviews using opinion mining. The problem statement was not "What did Y think of X?" but rather "What did Z think of Y's opinion on X?"
Competitor mining	Mining competitors from the Web automatically – to not only know which companies are primary competitors but also in which domain the company's rivals compete with itself and what its competitor's strength is in a specific competitive domain.

have been pursuing a different track: *employing learning algorithms* that can automatically infer from text samples what indicators are useful. These learning-based systems are found to be more cost-effective, more easily ported to other domains and languages, and more robust to grammatical mistakes. Nevertheless, research indicates that incorporating deep knowledge about language will be absolutely crucial to developing systems capable of high-quality (as opposed to merely high-throughput) sentiment analysis. Both the linguistic and the learning approach have considerable merits; the research community has, as one would expect, moved towards finding ways to combine their advantages to increase the quality of sentiment analysis.

Summarizing existing research, we identified that the process of opinion mining or sentiment analysis comprises of three main tasks: (a) development of linguistic resources, (b) sentiment classification, and (c) opinion summarization. Table 2 captures them and it also provides the different approaches researchers have taken to perform these tasks. A brief description of these approaches is presented below.

The linguistics knowledge resources have been developed using the following four approaches: (a) conjunction method; (b) PMI method; (c) WordNet (Miller *et al.*, 1990) exploring method; and (d) Gloss classification method. The conjunction method relies on an analysis of textual corpora that correlates linguistic features or indicators with semantic orientation. This method demon-

Table 2. Main tasks for opinion mining and the different approaches for doing them

	TASKS	APPROACHES
OPINION MINING	DEVELOPMENT OF LINGUISTIC RESOURCES	Conjunction Method
		PMI Method
		WordNet Exploring Method
		Gloss Classification Method
	SENTIMENT CLASSIFICATION	PMI Method
		Machine Learning Method
		NLP Combined Method
	OPINION SUMMARIZATION	

strated that conjunctions between adjectives explicitly indicate the relationship between adjacent sentences. Point-wise Mutual Information (PMI) is a measure of association used in information theory and statistics. Web search using AltaVista search engine has been used to estimate PMI between a seed set of indicators of known polarity (positive or negative) and any phrase to determine semantic orientation (Yu *et al.*, 2008). Adjective synonym set and antonym set in WordNet (an online lexical database of English) have been used to predict semantic orientation of adjectives. WordNet is used to anchor different types of semantic knowledge. It groups nouns, verbs, adjectives and adverbs into sets of synonyms (called synsets), each expressing a distinct concept. Linguistic resources have been developed by using a method for determining the orientation of a term based on the classification of its glosses.

Sentiment classification is the task of determining the sentiment of a textual corpus or document. The output of the task is binary – positive or negative. The three approaches reported in the research literature for sentiment classification are:

(a) PMI method; (b) Machine learning method; and (c) NLP combined method. A process has been used to classify sentiments where phrases containing adjectives or adverbs were extracted and the semantic orientation of each phrases were estimated using the PMI method. "Excellent" and "poor" were used as the base terms calculating the PMI. Reviews were then classified based on the average semantic orientation. The machine learning method is the most commonly used method. It could be either a supervised or unsupervised method. The supervised method entails the use of a labeled training corpus (which is created using techniques such as Support Vector Machines, Naïve Bayes Multinomial, and Maximum Entropy) to learn a certain classification function. The trained corpus is then used to carry out the sentiment classification of a document. The unsupervised method can label a corpus, which is later used for supervised learning (especially semantic orientation is helpful for this). With the PMI or machine learning method, it is not easy to get appropriate contextual polarity from texts. Currently, accurate sentiment classification that takes into account contextual meaning is being developed by combining the natural language processing (NLP) techniques. The NLP combined method has been used to recognize contextual polarity at the phrase level. This method requires a lexicon where lemmas are labeled with prior polarity. Contextual polarity classification is done as a two-step process that employs machine learning on a variety of features.

The last task, opinion summarization, aims to give the overall sentiment of a large amount of reviews or other form of opinion resources at various granularities. This task combines fine-grained opinion information to form a summary representation in which expressions of opinions from the same source/target (source denotes the opinion holder, and target denotes the entity toward which the opinion is directed) are grouped together, multiple opinions from a source toward the same target are accumulated into an aggregated opinion, and cumulative statistics are computed for each source/target.

Currently, within the research community, there exists a growing interest in capturing interactions between subjectivity and subject — that is, we not only need to know what an author's opinion is, but what that opinion is about. For example, while in a broad sense a review of a particular smartphone (say iPhone 4) is only about one topic (the smartphone itself), it almost surely discusses various specific aspects of the phone. One would ideally like a sentiment analysis system to reveal whether there are particular features that the review's author disapproves of even if his or her overall impression was positive.

3.2 Classification Framework

The state-of-the-art theories and models related to opinion mining from the existing literature are reviewed and classified into six categories as shown in Table 3. These categories cover the different techniques used to mine opinions, classify sentiment of mined items and features, as well as the strength of the sentiment. The ultimate goal of opinion mining is to extract customer opinions (sentiments) on products and present the information in the most effective way that serves the chosen objectives of its end user (Kobayashi *et al.*, 2007; Tang *et al.*, 2009). This means that the necessary steps and techniques used for opinion mining can be different depending on how the summarized information is needed to be presented to the end user – thus the six categories.

The sentiment or opinion extracted from an evaluative document or corpus provides useful indicators for many different purposes. These sentiments can be categorized into two categories: positive and negative; or into an n-point scale, e.g., very good, good, satisfactory, bad, and very bad. In this respect, a sentiment analysis or opinion mining task can be interpreted as a classification task where each category represents a sentiment or opinion (Pang *et al.*, 2008a).

Classifying an evaluative text at the document level or the sentence level does not tell what the opinion holder likes and dislikes (Ding *et al.*, 2007). A positive document on an object does not mean that the opinion holder has positive opinions on all aspects or features of the object. Likewise, a negative document does not mean that the opinion holder dislikes everything about the object. In an evaluative document such as a customer review of a product, the opinion holder typically writes both positive and negative aspects of the object, although the general sentiment on the object may be positive or negative. To obtain such detailed aspects, feature-based opinion mining has been proposed in the literature to summarize the overall opinion.

In feature-based opinion mining, features broadly mean product features or attributes or functions. The main tasks in this technique are: (a) identifying product features that have been commented on, (b) decide whether the comments are positive or negative, and (c) summarizing the discovered information. In the feature-based opinion summarization method, for each product class, at first it automatically extracts general features, then specific features or attributes and then assigns polarity to each of these feature or attribute (Balahur *et al.*, 2008).

Determining the degree to which a sentiment is positive, negative or neutral for the entire evaluative content or a segment of the content is described to be an important aspect of opinion mining.

Mining opinions in comparative sentences are performed to determine either which entities in a comparison are preferred by its author or which feature(s) of an entity in a comparison are preferred by its author (Murthy *et al.*, 2008). An entity is the name of a person, a product, a company, a location, etc. under comparison in a comparative sentence. A feature is a part or attribute of the entity that is being compared.

Table 3. Opinion mining or sentiment classification framework

ACTIVITY GOAL	DESCRIPTION	EXAMPLE
Item Extraction (a.k.a. Opinion Extraction)	The process of extracting the subject matter (a.k.a. a situation or a product) where opinions have been expressed on in customer reviews.	Extracting the subject matter or product such as Apple's iPhone 4 from the reviews where customers have expressed their opinions on
Feature Extraction	The identification of features (or attributes or functions) of products which customers have expressed their opinions on their reviews and feedbacks.	Extracting the features of Apple's iPhone 4 such as screen sharpness, video camera, and camera flash from the reviews.
Sentiment Classification on Item	The determination of whether a given text has a positive or negative connotation on its subject matter (situation or product) only.	The type of opinions (positive or negative) expressed by the customers on Apple's iPhone 4.
Sentiment Classification on Features	The determination of whether a given text has a positive or negative opinion on its subject features (attributes or functions).	The type of opinions (positive or negative) expressed on each extracted feature of Apple's iPhone 4.
Strength of Sentiments	The process of determining whether a positive opinion expressed by a text on its subject matter is weakly positive, mildly positive, or strongly positive, and/or whether a negative opinion expressed is weakly negative, mildly negative, or strongly negative.	The degree of positivity or negativity of the opinions that were expressed on Apple's iPhone 4 in the reviews.
Comparison of Items and Features	The process of comparing products in the same product groups mentioned in customer reviews in terms of their features.	Comparison between (a) Apple's iPhone 4 and (b) Sprint's HTC EVO 4G, both are smart phones. For example: battery life of a is much longer than battery life of b, or I like the screen sharpness of a but prefer the battery life of b.

4. BUSINESS IMPLICATIONS OF OPINION MINING

4.1 Application Opportunities

As online opinions increase their popularity day by day, they represent a wealth of information which can be beneficial for the industries as well as consumers. Today there exists plenty of opportunities for businesses to make use of the opinion mining technology to increase their performance effectiveness and/or improve their competitive advantage amongst their competitors. They can be applied to various industries and domains. For consumers, decision support systems can be developed to help them do comparison shopping over the web. Recommender systems are being used by an increasing number of e-commerce sites to help consumers find products to purchase.

Practically, every business function can potentially develop opinion mining applications. The examples presented below are not intended to be exhaustive but simply a snap shot of possibilities. The competitive intelligence area is fertile for opinion mining application (Bao *et al.*, 2008). Competitive intelligence is broadly conceptualized as the action of defining, gathering, analyzing, and distributing intelligence about products, customers, competitors and any aspect of the environment needed to support executives and managers in making strategic decisions for an organization. Therefore, the need to organize and modify their strategies according to demands and to the opportunities that the market present requires that companies collect information about themselves, the market and their competitors, and to manage enormous amount of data, and analyzing them to make plans for action. Opinion mining could directly contribute to this effort by helping define relevancy and the type of analysis needed.

Opinion mining technologies could potentially be applied to manage human resources of an organization strategically, mainly with applications aiming at analyzing staff opinions, monitoring the level of employee satisfaction and motivation, as well as reading and analyzing curriculum vitae and cover letters for the selection of best new personnel based on the requirements of the job/ projects (Bolasco *et al.*, 2005).

In the customer relationship management domain the most widespread applications are related to the management of the contents of clients' messages. This kind of analysis often aims at automatically rerouting specific requests to the appropriate service or at supplying immediate answers to the most frequently asked questions. Customer opinion analysis on virtual communities such as email and newsgroups is a natural application of opinion mining for needed customer care (Bolasco *et al.*, 2005).

Prominent market research companies such as A.C. Nielsen and Information Resources in USA, GfK and Infratest Burke in Europe apply opinion mining tools to the user-generated web data. These companies collect data on special markets, analyze the collected data and sell data and analyses to their clients. Many financial analysis applications can use the intelligence derived from opinion mining as input to the execution of predictive modeling techniques, such as statistical regression or neural networks, for tasks like portfolio creation and optimization and trading model creation.

Opinion mining can enhance natural language processing systems. For example, in the construction of websites that supports questioning in natural language. Research literature indicates that there have been developments of some opinion mining systems which are multilingual and can read and analyze documents that might prove difficult for a given group of human analysts (Abbasi *et al.*, 2008; Ku *et al.*, 2009; Su *et al.*, 2008; Subrahmanian, 2009).

The number of blogs in the legal domain is growing at a rapid pace therefore many potential applications for opinion detection and monitoring are arising as a result. Opinion mining of legal blogs, also known as blawgs, is currently a hot application domain (Conrad *et al.*, 2007). Potential applications of opinion mining in legal blogs include: (a) profiling – analyzing reactions to high-level court decisions, (b) alerting – subscribers to unfavorable news and disclosures that may impact a firm's clients, (c) monitoring – for example, what communities are saying about commercial legal research services, (d) tracking – reputations of law firms based on client feedback over time, and (e) hosting and surveying – blog space for practitioners to comment on legal topics and decisions that can subsequently be mined for trends.

Table 4 presents a few popular opinion mining tools that are currently being used by business application developers.

4.2 Challenges to Overcome

The business information systems research and development community faces a few current challenges to deal with.

Finding opinion sources and monitoring them on the Web is still a formidable task because there are a large number of diverse sources, and each source may also have a huge volume of opinionated text. Thus, the need for developing automated opinion mining and summarization systems. Opinion mining is a challenging natural language processing problem. Thus far the research studies have primarily taken a structured approach to exploring the problem. Meaning, natural language documents are regarded as unstructured data, while the data in relational databases are referred to as structured data. One of the current challenges facing the researchers and developers is converting the unstructured text into an equivalent structured text for processing. The structured approach requires the unstructured text to be converted to structured data, which enables traditional data management

Table 4. Popular opinion mining or sentiment analysis software tools

PRODUCT/TOOL NAME	COMPANY'S WEBSITE	COMMENTS
SAS Social Media Analytics	www.sas.com	Integrates, analyzes and enables organizations to act on intelligence discovered from online conversations occurring across professional and consumer-generated media sites. It enables organizations to attribute online conversations to specific parts of their business, allowing an accelerated response to shifts in the marketplace.
WebFountain	www.ibm.com	An Internet analytics engine for the study of unstructured data on the web. It collects stores and analyzes massive amounts of unstructured and semi-structured text that enables the discovery of trends, patterns and relationships from data.
Lexalytics	www.lexalytics.com	Provides entity extraction, sentiment analysis, document summarization and thematic extraction from user-generated web content
SinoBuzz 2.5	www.sinotechgroup.com.cn	Provides online reputation management analytics, brand competitor analytics, and social media marketing analytics
Attensity360	www.attensity.com	Continuously monitors and analyzes social media conversations and their impact on businesses
ScoutLabs	www.scoutlabs.com	Powerful web-based application that tracks social media data to help build better products and strong customer relationships
Radian6	www.radian6.com	Provides a software platform to listen, measure and engage in conversations across the social web

tools to be applied to slice, dice, and visualize the results in many ways. This is extremely important for applications because it allows the user to gain insights through both qualitative and quantitative analysis. It is a fast-growing research area, in which progress has been made in recent years.

Another challenge is to fully convince people that opinion mining can actually replace traditional sources of opinion collection and analysis such as surveys or panels. Currently the researchers mostly deal with content on the Web without understanding credibility, intent or source. They look at sentiment analysis to filter out blatant attempts at misrepresentation. Additionally, the length of comments from the happy customers in the future must balance out with that of unhappy customers. Currently, people who are unhappy are commenting in much greater detail than the research community initially thought. Thus at this time, opinion mining and survey research are seen as highly complementary instead of them being mutually exclusive.

Finally, it has been noted that B2B brands and small consumer brands aren't discussed in significant volume on the Web, so currently there is not much opinion to mine for them. Many companies also complaint that the Web discussions don't address questions that they need answers to from their customers.

5. IMPLICATIONS FOR RESEARCH AND PRACTICE

Organizations increasingly need to study and use their consumers' opinions on their products and services in their operational and strategic decision-making processes. However, the identification of opinion sources, extraction of important topic features, summarization of relevant opinions, and effective prediction of the polarity of an opinion are all very challenging tasks. These are open research problems.

The focus of opinion mining is to summarize and classify opinionated expressions. Opinion mining research as opposed to the conventional fact-based text analysis research, tries to address the new problems and opportunities related to the identification and analysis of opinions about some topics or facts. Opinion mining techniques are applied to predict the polarity (or inclination) of an opinionated expression related to a topic (i.e., an opinion holder). They are also applied to consolidate and summarize the likely contradictory opinions from a large set of electronic documents such as blogs, online news, consumer comments that contain opinionated expressions. The current research areas in opinion mining include the retrieval of opinionated expressions, identification of opinion holders or the specific features of the opinion holders, classification of the polarities of sentiments related to some opinion holders, and application of opinion analysis to real-world problem solving or decision making. Therefore information systems researchers face many opportunities and challenges for conducting extensive business research in the field of opinion mining.

The most prominent implications for practice follow. For product research and development, product reviews can be used by manufacturing companies to improve features and provide a platform for innovation. For example, Web based applications could offer platforms for customers to design products and submit the designs to the manufacturing companies.

For marketing, companies can make savings on marketing expenses by requesting for reviews on their websites and peer review websites. This eliminates the need for business consultants to conduct surveys as companies can now have all the data they need online. Marketing intelligence could also be obtained through automated opinion mining. Marketing intelligence is the information gathered and analyzed for the purpose of formulating marketing strategies. It is particularly relevant to customer needs, preferences, attitudes, behaviors, and potential changes in the business environment. Traditional market research methods often require arduous human efforts in collecting and analyzing a large amount of consumer data. The social web now is the driving force of a new wave of marketing intelligence, leading to the opinion mining-based approach. Future development in this area should include defining a set of opinion mining problems specifically essential to deriving marketing intelligence and formulating marketing strategies. This vision will help organizations introduce a new wave of marketing intelligence, a new approach of studying consumer behavior, a new connection between marketing and IT, and a new conceptual framework for opinion mining.

6. FUTURE RESEARCH DIRECTIONS

Good sentiment detection tools, for blogs and other social media, specifically tailored to the business world are invaluable. Recently published reports suggest that worldwide 1.3 billion people are online, with 50,000 new Internet users coming online each day. And due to the easy access to social media tools, every Web user has a voice he or she can use to share, seek, recommend and complain. Businesses have come to the realization that social media is a means to an end, not a solution (Thelwall *et al.*, 2010). The act of being social requires businesses to give first and expect nothing in return. Social media can put relationships on a steroid program – relationships, good or bad will be amplified in social media communities. And most importantly, technology is an enabler, not the solution or substitute for relationships. A recent study has indicated that social media is not just for marketing (Xiaowen *et al.*, 2009). Companies like Dell and Starbucks have successfully used it for R&D, gathering customer insights as input for innovation. Social media can support sales, customer service and operations as well.

For good sentiment detection tools, the main challenge is still improving the accuracy of sentiment prediction and solving the associated problems. It is important to note that sentiment analysis is not just a single problem. It encompasses many specific technical problems. Different combinations of them may have different applications. Commercial companies already have some basic tools to support various types of analysis and applications, which is the main progress of the field.

The key to the future success of opinion mining is integrating the strengths of two worlds – creating technology that combines a human's linguistic capabilities with the speed and accuracy of a computer. Advances in natural language processing research are, however, beginning to close the gap between the human and computer language processing capabilities. The research community has come to a conclusion that machine learning based approaches with the help of natural language processing is the most promising way to go for future developments. The community is optimistic that there will be novel automated techniques coming out in the next few years to make opinion mining technology practical for large scale applications.

Although there are currently many research results available in this area, the industry standards and efficient algorithms for the opinion mining are still desirable. Future work may include but not limited to the development of a method to extend the list of product-dependent features and feature-attributes, new methodologies for polarity assignment, a system that could verify the quality of the extracted feature and assigned polarity, and improve the performance of text sentiment orientation analysis among others.

7. CONCLUSION

Opinion mining tools allow businesses to capture consumer sentiments and opinions on a large scale. With the rapid growth of the user-generated subjective content on the Web represented by blogs, wikis and internet forums, opinion mining technologies and methods are opening a promising new door to analyze the Web data for deriving BI. In the last few years the information systems research community has witnessed opinion mining becoming an increasingly popular topic to many of its researchers.

Opinion mining will contribute to the sophistication of search engines. Opinion mining can improve the search experience of users by showing more insights about a topic because the traditional document retrieval can now be combined with such things as consumer ratings, opinion trends and representative opinions on the topic. This in turn will help enrich search engine's user satisfaction. Product marketing and positioning effectiveness will also increase considerable since opinion summarization over product reviews will now reveal the customers' attitude to a product and its features along different dimensions, such as time, geographical location, and experience. Furthermore, businesses can now identify interesting trends and patterns for their decision-making purposes by using opinion mining to track how opinions or discussions evolve over time.

This study reviewed and presented to the business management and research communities the development of sentiment analysis and opinion mining during the last few years, and also provided a classification framework based on the recent advances in opinion mining reported in the research literature. Implications of opinion mining for research and practice have been discussed and an attempt has been made to layout the future research directions in the field.

REFERENCES

Abbasi, A., Chen, H., & Salem, A. (2008). Sentiment analysis in multiple languages: Feature selection for opinion classification in web forums. *ACM Transactions on Information Systems, 26*(3).

Balahur, A., & Montoyo, A. (2008). A feature dependent method for opinion mining and classification. In *Proceedings of the International Conference on Natural Language Processing and Knowledge Engineering*.

Bao, S., Li, R., Yu, Y., & Cao, Y. (2008). Competitor mining with the web. *IEEE Transactions on Knowledge and Data Engineering, 20*(10), 1297–1310. doi:10.1109/TKDE.2008.98

Bolasco, S., Canzonetti, A., Capo, F. M., Ratta-Rinaldi, F., & Singh, B. K. (2005). Understanding text mining: A pragmatic approach. *Studies in Fuzziness and Soft Computing, 185*, 31–50. doi:10.1007/3-540-32394-5_4

Chen, Y., & Xie, J. (2008). Online consumer review: Word-of-mouth as a new element of marketing communication mix. *Management Science, 54*, 477–491. doi:10.1287/mnsc.1070.0810

Conrad, J. G., & Schilde, F. (2007). Opinion mining in legal blogs. In *Proceedings of the International Conference on Artificial Intelligence and Law* (pp. 231-236).

Das, S. R., & Chen, M. Y. (2007). Yahoo! for Amazon: Sentiment extraction from small talk on the web. *Management Science, 53*, 1375–1388. doi:10.1287/mnsc.1070.0704

Dey, L., & Haque, M. (2009). Opinion mining from noisy text data. *International Journal of Document Analysis and Recognition, 12*(3), 205–226. doi:10.1007/s10032-009-0090-z

Ding, X., & Liu, B. (2007). The utility of linguistic rules in opinion mining. In *Proceedings of the 30th Annual International ACM SIGIR Conference on Research and Development in Information Retrieval* (pp. 811-812).

Feldman, R., & Sanger, J. (2007). *The text mining handbook advanced approaches in analyzing unstructured data*. Cambridge, UK: Cambridge University Press.

Froelich, J., Ananyan, S., & Olson, D. L. (2005). Business intelligence through text mining. *Business Intelligence Journal*, 43-50.

Jansen, B. J., Zhang, M., Sobel, K., & Chowdury, A. (2009). Twitter power: Tweets as electronic word of mouth. *Journal of the American Society for Information Science and Technology, 60*(11), 2169–2188. doi:10.1002/asi.21149

Kao, A., & Poteet, S. (Eds.). (2007). *Natural language processing and text mining*. London, UK: Springer. doi:10.1007/978-1-84628-754-1

Kobayashi, N., Inui, K., & Matsumoto, Y. (2007). Opinion mining from web documents: extraction and structurization. *Information and Media Technologies, 2*(1), 326–337.

Ku, L. W., & Chen, H. H. (2007). Mining opinions from the web: Beyond relevance retrieval. *Journal of the American Society for Information Science and Technology, 58*(12), 1838–1850. doi:10.1002/asi.20630

Ku, L. W., Huang, T. H., & Chen, H. H. (2009). Using morphological and syntactic structures for Chinese opinion analysis. In *Proceedings of the Conference on Empirical Methods in Natural Language Processing* (pp. 1260-1269).

Liu, B. (2010). Sentiment analysis and subjectivity. In Indurkhya, N., & Damerau, F. J. (Eds.), *Handbook of natural language processing* (2nd ed.). New York, NY: ACM Press.

Miller, G., Beckwith, R., Fellbaum, C., Gross, D., & Miler, K. (1990). Introduction to WordNet: An on-line lexical database. *International Journal of Lexicography*, *3*(4), 235–312. doi:10.1093/ijl/3.4.235

Miller, T. (2005). *Data and text mining: A business applications approach*. Upper Saddle River, NJ: Pearson.

Murthy, G., & Bing, L. (2008). Mining opinions in comparative sentences. In *Proceedings of the 22nd International Conference on Computational Linguistics* (pp. 18-22).

Pang, B., & Lee, L. (2008a). *Opinion mining and sentiment analysis*. Boston, MA: Boston Publishers.

Pang, B., & Lee, L. (2008b). Opinion mining and sentiment analysis. *Foundations and Trends in Information Retrieval*, *2*(1-2), 1–135. doi:10.1561/1500000011

Su, Q., Xu, X., Guo, H., Guo, Z., Wu, X., Zhang, X., et al. (2008). Hidden sentiment association in Chinese web opinion mining. In *Proceedings of the International World Wide Web Conference* (pp. 959-968).

Subrahmanian, V. S. (2009). Mining online opinions. *Computer*, *42*(7), 88–90. doi:10.1109/MC.2009.229

Tang, H., Tan, S., & Cheng, X. (2009). A survey on sentiment detection of reviews. *Expert Systems with Applications*, *36*, 10760–10773. doi:10.1016/j.eswa.2009.02.063

Thelwall, M., Wilkinson, D., & Uppal, S. (2010). Data mining emotion in social network communication: Gender differences in MySpace. *Journal of the American Society for Information Science and Technology*, *61*(1), 190–199.

Wang, H., & Wang, S. (2008). A knowledge management approach to data mining process for business intelligence. *Industrial Management & Data Systems*, *108*(5), 622–634. doi:10.1108/02635570810876750

Wang, W., & Zhou, Y. (2009). E-business websites evaluation based on opinion mining. In *Proceedings of the International Conference on Electronic Commerce and Business Intelligence* (pp. 87-90).

Xiaowen, D., Bing, L., & Lei, Z. (2009). Entity discovery and assignment for opinion mining applications. In *Proceedings of the ACM International Conference on Knowledge Discovery and Data Mining*, Paris, France.

Yu, L., Ma, J., Tsuchiya, S., & Ren, F. (2008). Opinion mining: A study on semantic orientation analysis for online document. In *Proceedings of the 7th World Congress on Intelligent Control and Automation*.

Zhao, L., & Li, C. (2009). Ontology based opinion mining for movie review. In D. Karagiannis & Z. Jin (Eds.), *Proceedings of the Third International Conference on Knowledge Science, Engineering, and Management* (LNCS 5914, pp. 204-214).

This work was previously published in the International Journal of Business Intelligence Research, Volume 2, Issue 4, edited by Richard Herschel, pp. 1-16, copyright 2011 by IGI Publishing (an imprint of IGI Global).

Chapter 8

Business Intelligence Enhances Strategic, Long-Range Planning in the Commercial Aerospace Industry

David Ellis
Boeing, USA

ABSTRACT

The world's largest aircraft manufacturers like Boeing and Airbus have traditionally been dominant in the commercial aerospace industry, but due to the rise of several smaller commercial aircraft companies and in spite of air travel increasing each year, it will be paramount for Boeing and Airbus to thoroughly understand past and current market conditions and be able to combine their understanding with the proper analytical tools to anticipate the market demands of the future if they are to remain the world leaders in their industry. This paper presents a discussion of industry factors such as airline routes, past passenger demands in different regions of the world and the sizes and types of aircraft that were required to support those demands, and more importantly, how analysis of that information is integral to the projection of future demands within the commercial aerospace market which will facilitate Boeing and Airbus positioning themselves to provide their airline customers with the right product at the right time.

INTRODUCTION

Boeing and Airbus have been the world's leading commercial aircraft manufacturers for decades and the future may indeed look bright to their leaderships given the increase in air travel that appears almost certain to occur in the future; however, with increased competition from manufacturers in Canada, Brazil, Russia and China, it will be increasingly difficult for Boeing and Airbus to preserve their dominance as the commercial aerospace industry expands.

DOI: 10.4018/978-1-4666-2650-8.ch008

As all of the manufacturers attempt to best position themselves to acquire the largest possible share of new aircraft orders resulting from the anticipated increases in air travel, they will not only have to understand past and current market demands, but more importantly, will have to be able to use that knowledge to accurately project future market demands and offer airline customers the correct aircraft at the correct time at the correct price. Historically, Boeing and Airbus have performed quite well in providing the airlines with the sizes and types of aircraft they have needed to meet demand, and in doing so, they have established themselves as leaders in the industry. However, considering the ever-changing landscape of the air travel market and the fact that it takes 7+ years to design, build, certify and deliver a completely new aircraft design, preserving market share in the future may be a challenge. It will be the manufacturer, employing business intelligence tools to develop accurate market forecasts upon which to base long-range planning, that is in the best position to offer airlines the right product at the right time and consequently, to be the industry leader.

1. RESEARCH

A recent report prepared by The Boeing Company indicated the total number of commercial aircraft in the world's airline fleet in 2009 was 18,890 and was expected to grow to 36,300 by 2029. The estimated market value (in 2009 USD) of the increase which was based on several factors including, expected aircraft retirements, freighter conversions, and new aircraft deliveries will be $3.59 trillion (Boeing, 2010).

A similar report released by Airbus Industries considering the same factors projected the size of the world fleet in 2029 to be 36,303. It may seem remarkable that competing companies could independently formulate 20 year industry forecasts with almost identical results, but the explanation for the similarity is quite simple: similar approaches are employed in the data analysis to develop strategic forecasting. Business intelligence tools such as correlation analysis and econometric modeling are used to perform in-depth studies of past market conditions and then use the results of those studies to develop a better understanding of current market conditions, forecast future market demands and develop strategic plans for the future (Airbus, 2009).

Generally speaking, forecasting is an extremely important activity. According to Thomas J. Gallagher, Managing Director of CIBC World Markets Global Aerospace, no endeavor has a greater impact, for good or bad, on the overall success of a corporation than the practice of forecasting. When successful, forecasting integrates the abilities, decisions, and informed perspectives of the entire corporation and converts them into a comprehensive view of the future and a cohesive set of expectations. A successful forecast illuminates, while just below the surface it provides an accurate description of the complexity and intricacy of the reality it attempts to portray. Poor forecasting overwhelms its victims by numbing them with large data arrays of indeterminate relevance, ill-considered assumptions, and undisciplined clumps of emotion. A poor forecast offers confusion, misdirection, and disappointment to those whom its developers were seeking to enlighten. Good forecasting on the other hand achieves lasting value, credibility, and more importantly, clarity and transparency. Furthermore, all of these attributes can be acquired with a good forecast methodology without compromising accuracy (Gallagher, 1998).

Forecasting is particularly critical in the commercial aerospace industry because of the lead time required to bring a new product to the market. For example, if a manufacturer's projection does not extend beyond 5 to 6 years into the future, it would have little value since it would be almost impossible for the manufacturer to design, build and certify a new aircraft within the projected time period should a new model be required. For this reason, most aircraft manufacturers look at least 20 years into the future with market forecasting in order for the result to be of value (Greer & Liao, 1986).

The Market Outlook reports released by Boeing and Airbus indicate that over 17,400 new aircraft are expected to be added to the world fleet over the next 20 years to handle the increase in air travel throughout the world. One may think this figure alone could be quite useful for strategic planning purposes, but in actuality, it represents only a single element of the overall projection that is necessary for an aircraft manufacturer to strategically plan for the future.

The market projection must also consider the size(s) of aircraft in terms of seat capacity and range that will be needed by the airlines and when the aircraft will need to be delivered. It is possible estimates could be developed based on the projected growth rate in air travel, but while the annual growth rate has generally increased it has not been consistent and, over the last several decades, the rate has varied depending on the region of the world (Boeing, 2010).

The Federal Aviation Administration (FAA) combines a similar methodology with economic projections to the develop its own industry forecasts, but goes a bit further and also attempts to identify forecast risks. In 2009, in its forecast for fiscal years 2009-2025, the FAA predicted the majority of the future growth in air travel would occur in the U.S. and China. While noting air travel demand had proven to be resilient over the years, the FAA acknowledged a greater degree of uncertainty surrounded its 2009 forecast than in past years. There had never been so many negative factors coming together at once. The FAA expressed concern about the condition of the economy. In 2001, the recession which was worsened by the events of 9/11 stalled economic growth resulting in a reduction in air travel demand. Although economic recovery was well underway by 2002, the demand for air travel did not rebound until 2004. In spite of that recovery period, in 2009, the FAA was

uncertain about how the downturn in the housing market and the financial sector and the resulting high unemployment would affect the demand for air travel. Furthermore, it was uncertain how long the demand for air travel would be affected or to what extent the turmoil in the financial sector would affect the airlines' ability to recover. The FAA considered its 2009 forecast at risk due to the uncertainties (FAA, 2009).

In 2010, the FAA began to express cautious optimism for the future of the commercial aerospace market. In its forecast for fiscal years 2010-2030, the FAA pointed to the upward trend in the deliveries of regional jet aircraft with seat capacities of 100 seats or less. However, there was one point of concern: In spite of the increase in air travel, how will the regional carriers manage the increased number of aircraft scheduled for delivery in the coming years if the major carriers such as American, Delta, United and U.S. Airways continue to acquire or merge with smaller carriers resulting in system consolidations? The FAA indicated there is a strong possibility that many regional carriers might lose portions of their "feeder" flights if the mergers continue. This could result in some of the regional carriers unable to sustain operations. Another factor which could affect the FAA forecast include the introduction of new and innovative technologies into the market since the acquisition of fuel-efficient and environmental-friendly aircraft will be a top priority for airlines in the future. This could result in more or less aircraft in the world fleet since improved products could increase performance and capacity of the airlines as well as accelerate retirement of older aircraft (FAA, 2010).

The impact of aircraft retirement on a fleet cannot be ignored. Aircraft retirement skews the correlation between air traffic growth and aircraft orders. Although the upward trend in orders may appear to indicate an increased market demand for regional aircraft, the Centre for Asia Pacific Aviation projects the overall number of regional aircraft in the world fleet will decrease over the next 10 years from 2,016 in 2011 to 1,166 in 2020 as a result of aircraft retirements (Centre for Asia Pacific Aviation, 2010).

It is simple to see that long-range planning, while complex, is critical to aircraft manufacturers, but one may ask, what benefit can be gained by employing business intelligence in this effort? In order to understand how the application of business intelligence enhances strategic planning within the commercial aerospace industry, one needs to review a basic objective of business intelligence. One element of business intelligence which is employed in this type of forecasting is referred to as "predictive analytics". *Infohatch for Professional Managers* hosts a website on which information for use by professional managers is compiled. According to Infohatch.com, management's utilization of predictive analysis is greatly increasing to improve decision-making. Infohatch.com defines predictive analysis as:

the process of studying and learning from data and discovering all sorts of visible and hidden patterns and relationships within data and applying that knowledge to predict future events (Infohatch, 2010).

After a data query and subsequent analysis, predictive analytics is the final phase of formulating a future projection. Figure 1 illustrates how these elements relate to each other as data is analyzed to predict a future event or occurrence in a typical application.

It has been illustrated that an aircraft manufacturer's task of forecasting future market demand involves much more than simply looking at the number of aircraft in the world fleet on a year-to-year basis. For each year along a historical time-line, commercial air transport data for the world market must be analyzed with particular attention given to variables such as: number of aircraft in the total fleet, number of scheduled commercial flights, load factors, economic conditions, major world events such as military conflicts or natural disasters, and what correlation, if any, exists between these variables and passenger volume? (Boeing, 2009).

One correlation which needs to be considered when attempting to forecast air travel demand is income per capita. Income appears to be closely related to long-haul flights. Individuals with more income tend to fly longer distances on larger aircraft while lower-income individuals tend to fly shorter distances on smaller aircraft (Love, Goth, Budde, Schilling, & Woffenden, 2006).

Airfares also affect air travel demand. The 2009 analysis by Airbus indicated a very close relationship between level of demand and airfares. Considering more fuel-efficient aircraft will result in lower airfares, it is likely the introduction of these new products will also increase air travel demand. So while increased fuel efficiency may increase range and reduce the number of aircraft an airline needs based on current conditions, the resulting increase in air travel will tend to have an opposite effect, necessitating an increase in the size of the world fleet (Airbus, 2009).

Figure 1. Data warehouse (adapted from http://www.infohatch.com/predictiveanalytics.htm)

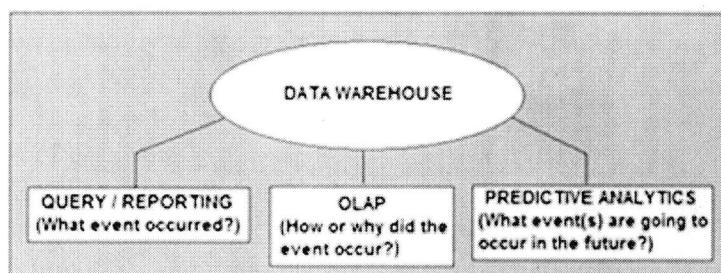

Air travel demand is also impacted by economical conditions. The economic measure most commonly used for analysis is the *gross domestic product* or GDP. The GDP refers to the total value of services and products output by a particular country or region. Aerospace manufacturers and the FAA agree that air travel demand is affected by the economy and the correlation is considered in forecasting.

Although air travel demand has historically exceeded economic growth, The Intergovernmental Panel on Climate Change (IPCC) reported in 2001 that there is a high correlation between the two and the aerospace industry does use economic growth as a primary predictor of air travel demand. Statistical analyses have proven the GDP accounts for 66% of the air travel growth. Figure 2 shows the relationship between the GDP and air travel (tonne-km) and the fluctuations in the growth of each from 1960 to 1995 based on the IPCC analysis. The effects of the economic recessions in 1974-75 and 1979-82 and the Gulf War in 1990-91 are clearly indicated by valleys on the plot (IPCC, 2001).

The econometric modeling of Airbus used to conduct sensitivity analysis around its baseline forecast revealed a similar relationship (Figure 3). More years are reflected, but similar valleys indicating the 1974-75 and 1979-82 recessions and the 1990-91 Gulf War are shown on the plot. The results of the 9/11 terror attacks and the economic downturn of 2009 are also evident by valleys (Airbus, 2009).

At this point, it should be noted there are some differences of opinion within the industry, particularly among certain analytical circles, regarding how and to what extent economic conditions affect the demand for air travel. The Boston Consulting Group (BCG) cites a rule of thumb that is often expressed in the airline industry that "Demand for air travel grows twice as fast as gross domestic product and airline yields always drop over time". While BCG is in at least partial agreement with this statement, they contend that there are actually two different types of growth that must be considered when analyzing air travel demand: underlying and induced (Love et al., 2006).

Figure 2. Relationship between the GDP and Air Travel (IPCC, 2001)

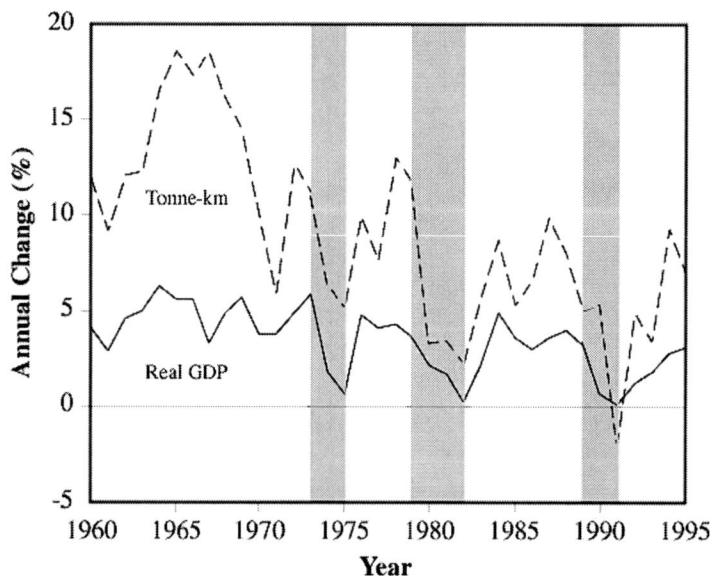

Figure 3. Sensitivity Analysis (Airbus, 2009)

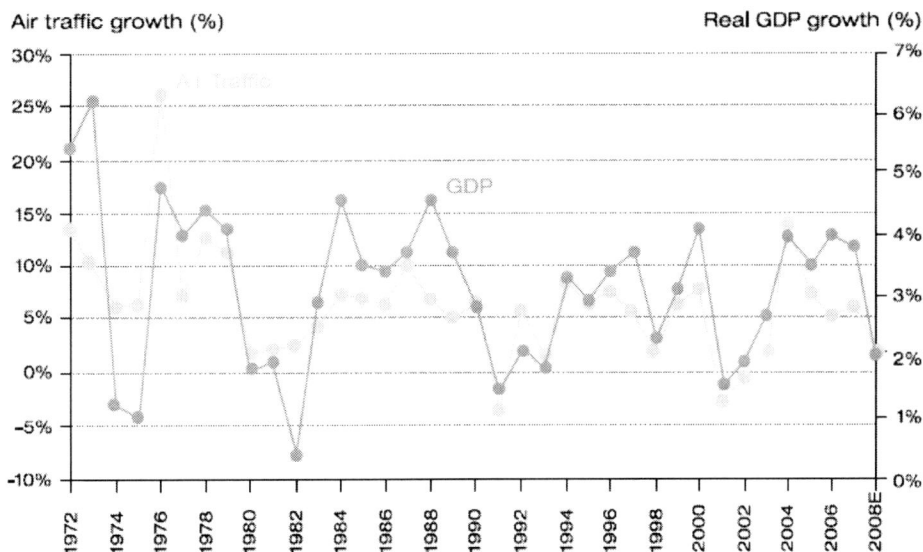

According to BCG, the historical growth rates in air travel demand do appear to grow at a multiple of GDP growth with a demand growth of 1.5 to 2 times the GDP growth being the norm, but problems occur when the demand growth rate is used to project future demand. The historical growth rate is a sum of underlying and induced growth. Underlying growth is that which occurs naturally over time and driven by factors outside the industry such as increases in population, income, trade and economic conditions while induced growth occurs as a result of decisions and actions taken within the industry. An example of induced growth would be an increase in demand for air travel due to a fare reduction implemented by airlines to fill empty seats on particular flights. Projecting future demand based on historical underlying growth makes sense while projections based on historical induced growth set the stage for an industry to repeat past mistakes in the future and possibly in greater magnitude. The latter introduces potential risks into the forecasting (Love et al., 2006).

Although forecasting is considered a science, the activity may not yield optimal accuracy if the appropriate factors are not considered. In the last 40 years, there have been several egregious miscalculations from forecasters within the aerospace industry with severe consequences. One such occurrence was during the aviation recession of 1989-1993 which resulted in a wide-spread imbalance in the supply and demand for commercial aircraft. The imbalance was so severe that it distressed three major industrial sectors to near-disastrous levels. The commercial airline sector in the United States had losses exceeding its cumulative profits from the previous 30 years resulting in a precipitous drop in orders for new aircraft. The aircraft manufacturing sector, including companies such as Boeing and Airbus, saw revenues drop by as much as 30%. Production rates were reduced and thousands of workers were laid off. The industry capital sector, including banks, stockholders, and aircraft lessors suffered straight financial losses in liquidity and investments. The financial losses such as those of the airlines can be quantified easily since they are reporting events, but the investment losses are more difficult to quantify and the long-term impacts to the sector including the cost of financial risk and loss of investor confidence are almost impossible to assess. While many of the losses were sustained in the U.S., with commercial aerospace being a global industry, the resulting consequences impacted investors and manufacturers around the globe. Although a single cause of this recession may never be known, it is certain that a number of economic factors combined to fuel the downturn, including the Gulf War, a spike in oil prices, an economic recession in the U.S. as well as similar economic conditions in Japan, Latin America and Europe, and global volatility in interest rates, currency and commodity prices. One may be able to understand how economic downturns such as the 1989 event simply cannot be predicted and wars and military conflicts are simply forecasters' worst nightmares, but the upward trends projected at the time for air travel demand, aircraft orders, and industry revenue, by many accounts, were overly optimistic and unsustainable as the 1980's came to an end. So while poor forecasting may have had little to do with the economic downturn itself, the consequences felt around the globe resulting from the imbalance in supply and demand probably was exacerbated by poor industry forecasting (Gallagher, 1998).

Another forecast blunder involved Airbus' A380. In spite of the similarity between the 20 Year Market Outlooks of Boeing and Airbus mentioned earlier, the industry behemoths have not always shared the same view of the commercial aerospace industry's future. The most recent divide between the companies' forecasts involved the feasibility of a new super-jumbo aircraft with a capacity of 600-700 seats. Beginning in 1993, the companies had several top-secret meetings in Seattle, Washington and Toulouse, France to discuss the aircraft potential and the possibility of undertaking its development as a joint venture to share the cost as well as the risk. Within a few years, Boeing grew more wary of the plan. Its forecast simply did not reflect a demand for such a large aircraft. In fact, Boeing's model indicated airlines in the future would use smaller aircraft to fly shorter routes point to point than large, jumbo aircraft flying longer routes between huge hubs.

For this reason, in 1995, Boeing walked out of a two-day meeting in Munich, Germany ending the discussions with Airbus. Afterwards, the companies continued their feasibility studies on their own. Airbus, confident of its forecast that indicated there would be strong market demand for a new super-jumbo aircraft, launched its A380 program with an estimated cost of $12 billion USD. In 2000, the Airbus Chief Executive of Sales, John Leahy, said, "Either this is going to be the flagship of the 21st century or it's going to be a disaster" (Wallace, 2007).

Realizing that there would be demand for *some* larger, long-range aircraft in the future, Boeing eventually decided on a much more economical approach and, almost simultaneously with its new 787 program, launched a *derivative* program to stretch the upper deck of its existing 747-400 jumbo jet and equip the resulting 747-8 with re-designed wings and engines to increase range and fuel efficiency.

After many production delays, Airbus finally delivered its first A380 in 2007. When the program was launched, Airbus had estimated nearly 1000 units of the new aircraft would be produced with profitability being recognized after the 250th delivery. After approximately $8 billion USD in overruns, numerous compatibility problems with airports such as taxiway widths, gates, etc., and the departure of two company executives, the estimated number of A380's to be produced was revised to 750 with the break-even point to be recognized after the 470th delivery. Critics now say Airbus made the wrong bet on the A380. "The A380 was a big mistake then and it is a big mistake now," said Richard Aboulafia of the Teal Group, an industry consulting firm (Wallace, 2007).

Commercial Aviation Report has also been critical of Airbus and the A380, stating,

It's reminiscent of the story of the Titanic when the captain said full-speed ahead even though the waters were iceberg infested (Commercial Aviation Report, 2007).

The verdict is still out on the 747-8 since Boeing will not deliver its first unit until 2011 after experiencing delays of its own in the derivative development, but based on sales figures, the future of the 747-8 is brighter than that of the A380. Although Airbus advanced their market share from 20% in 1990 to 50% in 1997, the setbacks associated with the A380 debacle and the ramifications of what appears to be a case of inaccurate market forecasting may require decades to overcome (Wallace, 2007).

The reports and other information discussed thus far illustrate how inaccurate forecasts can have disastrous repercussions and how the variables affecting the growth of air travel demand, particularly the underlying variables outside the industry, can make the task of developing a forecast in the commercial aerospace industry extremely complex. This is an area in which an aircraft manufacturer can benefit greatly from the employment of business intelligence tools.

2. ANALYSIS

In order to illustrate how business intelligence enhances an aircraft manufacturer's ability to prepare forecasting for strategic planning, current and past market conditions must be reviewed as well as underlying variables that may significantly impact those conditions. One source for accurate air carrier statistics is the Research and Innovative Technology Administration (RITA), U.S. Department of Transportation (U.S. DOT). RITA currently offers air travel statistics compiled from January, 1996 through August, 2010. The data can be sorted by region or globally (Bureau of Transportation Statistics, 2010).

Specific information relative to aircraft types and delivery rates is available in manufacturers' market reports. The reports also commonly include economic data, specifically, GDP growth rates. Boeing's 2010 Market Outlook Report was reviewed in conjunction with RITA's database to extract the data necessary to illustrate how business intelligence methodologies can be beneficial in the development of a forecast. For this study, Microsoft Excel was employed to illustrate the use of regression and correlation analysis tools in the development of a 20-year forecast such as that contained in the Boeing report.

The most important statistic in determining future air travel demand is how many people have been travelling in the past. Figure 4 shows the annual number of domestic and international passengers for 2000-2009. Notice the domestic line has a noticeable drop in 2002 indicating reduced travel after the events of 9/11 in 2001. Likewise, the downward slope of the line in 2009 is indicative of the current economic downturn. However, these events appear to have had less effect on the international volume as indicated by the somewhat flat line.

Figure 4. Passenger volume

Passengers (All Carriers - All Airports)

Year	DOMESTIC	INTERNATIONAL	TOTAL
2000	599,563,678	134,287,145	733,850,823
2001	559,618,055	122,907,077	682,525,132
2002	551,960,680	118,718,997	670,679,677
2003	583,293,766	117,569,855	700,863,621
2004	629,769,620	133,940,071	763,709,691
2005	657,261,487	143,588,422	800,849,909
2006	658,362,620	149,724,787	808,087,407
2007	679,185,450	156,250,990	835,436,440
2008	651,703,487	157,722,817	809,426,304
2009	617,977,711	149,179,400	767,157,111

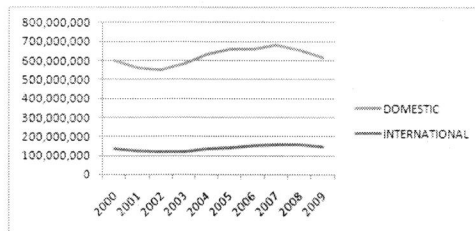

Note: All numbers are for scheduled services.
SOURCE: Bureau of Transportation Statistics T-100 Market data.

But, how many people will be traveling in the future? One method that can be used to project the domestic and international volume is a statistical tool referred to as linear regression. Linear regression uses the "least squares" method to fit a line through a set of observations. In this case, the domestic and international volumes for each year will each have a fitted line generated. Then each line is extended 20 years (the forecast period) into the future. The assumption is that future values will tend to increase or decrease in a linear manner falling along the projected lines. Figure 5 shows the revised plot projecting passenger volumes through the year 2029.

Figure 5 indicates the annual volume of domestic air travel, or travel within the U.S., is projected to reach approximately 880,000,000 in 2029. Based on this number, the projected annual rate of growth of domestic travel over the 20 year forecast period is about 1.75%. The same

process is followed to calculate the growth of travel from the U.S. to international destinations. The international volume in 2029 is expected to reach 209,000,000 which equates to a forecasted annual growth rate of 1.65%. The overall annual growth rate for passenger volume in the U.S. is the sum of the domestic and international growth rates, or 3.4%.

Although Boeing used Revenue Passenger Kilometers (RPK) in lieu of passenger volume to calculate traffic growth, the calculated rate above appears to be validated since Boeing's report also reflects an air traffic growth of 3.4% (Figure 6).

This 3.4% growth rate is only a baseline projection. As mentioned earlier, economic conditions, specifically the GDP, have been found to account for as much as 66% of the traffic growth, and the traffic growth rate may need to be adjusted accordingly. However, using the Boeing report and RITA statistics, an analysis of the cor-

Figure 5. Projected passenger volume

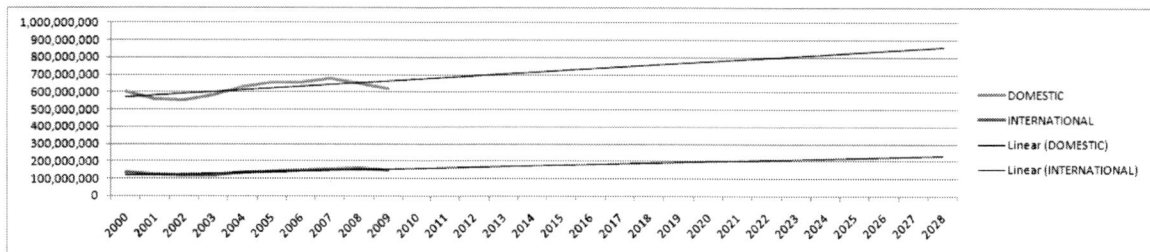

Figure 6. North America growths (adapted from Boeing, 2010)

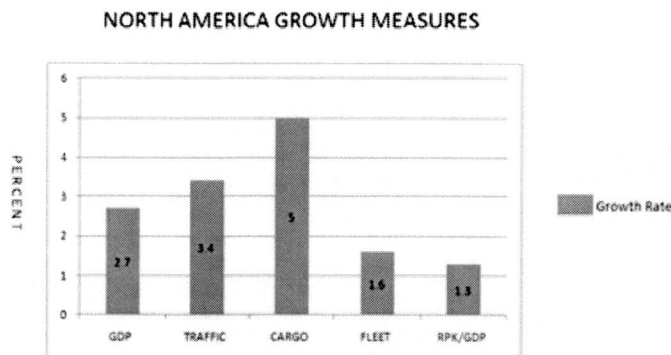

NORTH AMERICA GROWTH MEASURES

relation between the overall traffic growth rate and GDP of the U.S. for the years 2000-2009 produced an unexpected finding.

When performing a correlation analysis between two known variables, the resulting coefficient between the two range from -1 (no correlation at all) to 1 (directly correlated). The IPCC analysis discussed in Section 2 (Figure 2) reflected a close correlation between traffic growth and GDP between 1960 and 1995. However, the 2000-2009 analysis did not yield a similar correlation. In fact, as shown in Figure 7, the correlation coefficient between the two for the years 2000-2009 was found to be -.174 indicating much less correlation. The only plausible explanation for the difference is the large number of other factors coming together all at once since 2000, including the events of 9/11, the military conflicts in Iraq and Afghanistan, and the current economic downturn involving the housing, financial and industrial sectors and the resulting high unemployment. Based on a comparison between these findings and the ICCP analysis, it seems logical to conclude the correlation between air traffic growth and GDP, although present, is higher in a stable economy. As economic conditions become more unstable, the amount of correlation between air traffic growth and GDP decreases and the impact of GDP on air traffic growth becomes less predictable. This would also help explain the FAA's concern for its 2009 forecast discussed in Section 2. Consequently, in this case, the 3.4% baseline air traffic growth rate can be used without adjustment.

This type of correlation analysis used to assess the impact of the GDP can also be used to assess the impact significance of a wide range of other variables mentioned in this paper, including income per capita, number of flights, load factors, etc.

The traffic growth rates can also provide preliminary insight into aircraft sizes needed in the future. Although it is impossible to rely on the projected passenger volumes to determine the need for a particular sized aircraft, the fact the projected growth of the domestic volume (1.75%) exceeds the growth of international volume (1.65%) appears to indicate that small aircraft production will need to increase at a higher rate than large aircraft production since the larger aircraft are typically used for international traffic which, based on the analysis, is expected to experience less growth.

This assumption seems to be substantiated by the Boeing report which indicates 72% of all aircraft delivered in North America through 2029 is expected to be smaller (single-aisle) aircraft. In contrast, large aircraft such as the Boeing 747 series (and Airbus A380) are expected to account for only 1% of the North American deliveries. The remaining 27% of deliveries is expected to be twin-aisle and regional aircraft (Figure 8).

In conclusion, the number of aircraft scheduled to be removed from commercial service can also be calculated using information in Figure 8 by adding the new deliveries to the 2009 Fleet Size and then subtracting the 2029 Fleet Size. A total of 4,790 aircraft is scheduled to be retired or converted to freighters between 2009 and 2029. One can also see that in spite of the 800 new regional aircraft estimated to be delivered in the next 20 years, the regional fleet size will decrease

Figure 7. Total traffic vs. GDP correlation

	TOTAL AIR TRAFFIC	GDP
TOTAL AIR TR	1	
GDP	-0.174	1

Figure 8. North American fleet development (adapted from Boeing, 2010)

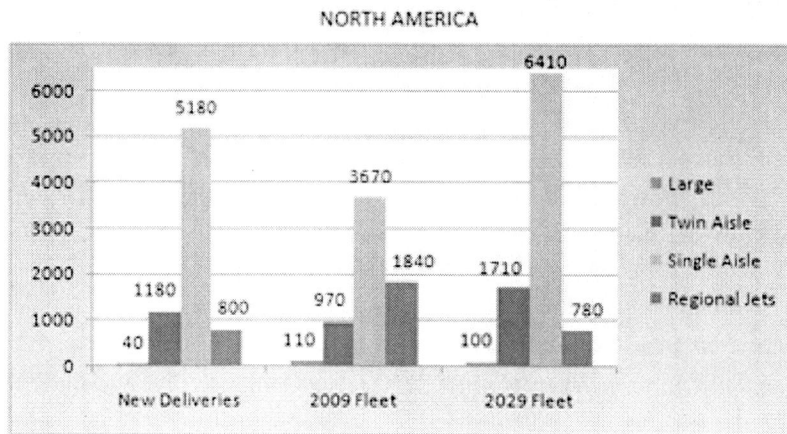

from 1,840 in 2009 to 780 in 2029 after 1,860 aircraft are retired from service. A reduction in fleet size by 2029 is also projected for large aircraft (Boeing, 2010).

3. SUMMARY

Forecasting future market conditions in the commercial aerospace industry has been illustrated to be a complex undertaking that demands the consideration of many underlying variables, or factors impacting the market conditions from outside the industry.

Although it varies greatly for each region of the world, air traffic growth was found to be the primary focus of aircraft manufacturers when projecting future market conditions. In most cases, air traffic growth is assumed to increase or decrease in a linear manner. Consequently, one of the most commonly used predictive analytic methodologies for projecting future growth is linear regression. Regression allows for an accurate prediction of future values based on a known set of values from the past. In commercial aerospace forecasting, the projected rate of air traffic growth forms a baseline upon which a complete forecast can be

developed. The baseline is adjusted as necessary to compensate for the impact of underlying variables.

One of the most prominent underlying variables affecting air traffic growth is the economy, specifically the GDP. While economic conditions are considered by the FAA and many of the commercial aircraft manufacturers when developing projections, there is clearly a lack of industry consensus relative to how the correlation between the economy and air traffic growth is analyzed, but most manufacturers use the results to adjust baseline projections with econometric modeling. There appears to be even more disagreement on the issue of impact significance, or the magnitude to which economic conditions affect air travel, with some entities claiming air traffic growth averages 1-2 times the GDP while others contend the GDP accounts for no more than 66% of air traffic growth. The analysis performed for this thesis did not substantiate either of these positions. The correlation was found to increase or decrease somewhat proportionately with economic stability. Events occurring in a short period of time such as the 9/11 attacks and the conflicts in Iraq and Afghanistan were found to diminish the correlation. Nonetheless, correlation analysis is a powerful business intelligence methodology that has been shown to be an excellent tool for assessing the significance of variables' impact on a given set of data.

The manner in which aircraft retirements and freighter conversions affect future fleet size has also been illustrated. Aircraft being removed from commercial service has to be considered in conjunction with expected future demand to develop accurate forecasting.

Due to the complexity of the required data analysis for forecasting, the utilization of business intelligence methodologies such as regression and correlation analysis greatly enhance long-range, strategic planning in the commercial aerospace industry.

One final note, in addition to traffic growth and aircraft quantity, aircraft manufacturers' market forecasting must also include aircraft sizes. In addition to aircraft retirements and freighter conversions, this element also requires a detailed analysis of airline routes combined with passenger volume and load factors which were not addressed in this thesis.

REFERENCES

Airbus. (2009). *Global market forecast 2009-2028*. Retrieved from http://www.airbus.com/en/corporate/gmf2009/

Boeing. (2010). *Long term market*. Retrieved from http://www.boeing.com/commercial/cmo/forecast_summary.html

Bureau of Transportation Statistics. (2010). *Research and innovative technology administration*. Retrieved from http://www.bts.gov/xml/air_traffic/src/index.xml#CustomizeTable

Centre for Asia Pacific Aviation. (2010). *Centre for Asia Pacific aviation*. Retrieved from http://www.centreforaviation.com/news/2010/11/05/global-fleet-drivers-changing-key-metric-is-flexibility/page1

Economics, T. (2010). *United States GDP growth rate*. Retrieved from http://tradingeconomics.com/Economics/GDP-Growth.aspx?Symbol=USD

FAA. (2009). *FAA aerospace forecast fiscal years 2009-2029*. Retrieved from http://www.docstoc.com/docs/840343/Risks-to-the-Forecast

FAA. (2010). *FAA aerospace forecast fiscal years 2010-2030*. Retrieved http://www.faa.gov/data_research/aviation/aerospace_forecasts/2010-2030/media/Risks%20to%20the%20Forecast.pdf

Gallagher, T. J. (1998). *Forecasting aviation markets*. Retrieved from http://aviation.se.edu/salluisi/avia2113/forecasting.pdf

Greer, W. R., & Liao, S. S. (1986). Forecasting capacity and capacity utilization in the U.S. aerospace industry. *Journal of Forecasting*, 57–67. doi:10.1002/for.3980050106

Infohatch. (2010). *Predictive analytics*. Retrieved from http://www.infohatch.com/predictiveanalytics.htm

Intergovernmental Panel on Climate Change (IPCC). (2001). *Aviation and the global atmosphere*. Arendal, Norway: GRID-Arendal.

Love, R., Goth, J., Budde, F., Schilling, D., & Woffenden, B. (2006). *Understanding the demand for air travel: How to compete more effectively*. Boston, MA: Boston Consulting Group.

Commercial Aviation Report. (2007). Noel Forgeard and the A380. *Commercial Aviation Report*, 10-11.

Wallace, J. (2007). *Seattle PI business*. Retrieved from http://www.seattlepi.com/business/

Chapter 9

Performance Management through Societal Performance Indicators

Joe White
Technical Consultant, USA

ABSTRACT

Performance management is tied to external forces and stakeholders whose assessment of performance is more focused on societal outcomes than purely financial outcomes. Government, corporate, and even personal performance measurement should take into account societal indicators that link these disparate yet intertwined spheres of influence. New initiatives in both government and commercial sectors are bringing greater understanding of how societal indicators can measure performance. This paper highlights how societal indicators are used to measure performance in corporate and government sectors. Corporate societal indicators are explored primarily though literary research. Government societal indicators are explored through an examination of the EPA and Superfund program. The paper demonstrates that there is synergy between corporate, government, and personal government performance measures and how business intelligence tools are making these relationships more transparent.

INTRODUCTION

The balanced scorecard put forth by Kaplan and Norton called for using financial, customer, internal, and growth perspectives to measure corporate performance. These perspectives are used for internal reporting of performance along strategic lines. Scorecards are used primarily with customers rather than with investors, according to Kaplan and Norton, because the scorecard does not translate to external audiences (Kaplan & Norton, 1993).

DOI: 10.4018/978-1-4666-2650-8.ch009

But external audiences and external factors cannot be separated from performance. As seen with the collapse of the financial, automobile, and housing markets in 2008 and the subsequent support from the Troubled Asset Relief Program (TARP), the relationships between economic sectors, the government, and consumers is intricate. Short-term gains (e.g., from questionable lending practices) have long-term consequences that impact all of society.

Something, therefore, is missing in how society views performance. Societal indicators need to be identified that measure the impact of economic sectors on social well-being. Short-term decisions need to be understood in context of their long-term impact. Making societal indicators a part of corporate, federal, or even personal performance management will support understanding these relationships.

This paper submits that sustainability measures should be incorporated into all strata of society. Corporations are increasingly finding that their reputation and compliance with regulations affects their performance. Governments are subject to constant scrutiny from a socially active population that wants constant justification of the cost of programs to their outcome. Sustainability within the governmental and corporate sectors, however, cannot be achieved without making better personal choices that show a clear understanding about how our individual choices impact the global community.

RESEARCH

Methodology

This paper will rely on evidence from literature, web research, and some anecdotal experience to demonstrate the value of performance measurement across public, private, and individual sectors. There is ample evidence of the importance of measuring performance. The balanced scorecard provided a framework for measuring performance that relates to internal stakeholders and has been adopted by numerous corporations. A similar framework for managing performance in the governmental sector has not been found that can express mission performance across the government functions. Likewise, personal performance management is challenging because it is difficult to associate an individual action with global impact. There is little statistical significance of individual data points until they are aggregated across society.

Emphasis in this paper is placed on illustrating the use of business intelligence tools in demonstrating government performance. There have been significant improvements in the past decade in both the quantity and quality of data provided to the public consumer by the federal government. Some of the major innovators in using business intelligence tools will be highlighted as these new sources of data provide a context and even a source of data that is most closely related to societal indicators.

Societal Indicators

Using societal indicators is challenging because of the complex relationships between society and its economic, governmental, and social forces. There are a lot of data sources that highlight performance of individual companies and individual government programs, but determining how this performance translates into general social improvements is extremely complex. Perspective on government performance is driven by external forces that cannot be completely accounted for using statistical models that do not operate on a geological scale. Natural disasters, weather, war, and outbreaks of disease may influence a government's performance. Much of the analysis of government performance is therefore subjective.

Societal indicators provide a better, albeit more complex, measure of outcome-oriented performance measurement. Societal indicators require supplementing internally driven performance metrics with externally focused metrics that emphasize attributes including quality of life, environmental health, and public safety (Kloby & Callahan, 2009). Societal indicators require more data aggregation and longer reporting periods than typical performance metrics. Kloby and Callahan illustrate the some important differences between performance measures and societal indicators in Table 1.

Corporate Societal Indicators

Corporate societal indicators measure the efficacy of a company in context of its relationship with external stakeholders. They measure how well the company performs in terms of resource consumption and carrying capacity. Natural resource consumption is measured in terms of raw materials consumed, utility costs, pollution, waste output, etc. Human resource consumption measures how a company may impact its workers and community. Societal indicators may be broad and require a long-term vision to see their benefits. Increasingly

companies are considering externally driven factors like corporate reputation and sustainability to craft their internal strategic decisions.

There is a link between social performance and financial performance. Corporate social performance (CSP) is positively correlated with both past and future financial performance (Waddock & Graves, 1997). This correlation may indicate that financially strong companies have more money to invest in "discretionary investments in traditional CSP activities such as philanthropy" that promote long-term strategy involving many different stakeholder groups. Companies that invest in education, healthcare, environmental protection, and resource conservation benefit in the long-term through improved corporate image and community relations. These benefits may be realized with growth in market share, customer numbers, or reductions in litigation costs. Financially strapped companies, however, may be punished with fines or litigation if they cannot afford to be proactive and make strategic investments towards societal performance.

Table 1. Comparison of performance measures and societal indicators (adapted from Kloby & Callahan, 2009)

Key Factors	Performance Measures	Societal Indicators
Who are the designers?	Public managers, agency personnel, and technical experts	The broader community: ranging from government personnel to citizens
What is the measurement focus?	Internal: agency or program specific performance	External: indicators of community conditions and quality of life
How are comparisons made?	The emphasis is on comparing current results to past agency or program performance	Comparisons of community conditions to the region and/or other jurisdictions
What is the focus of measurement?	Narrowly focused on the delivery of specific services provided by government	Focus on high-level community conditions that contribute overall quality of life, community health, community well-being, or community sustainability
What is the purpose of measurement?	Measures are usually intended to help manage government services	Indicators show trends in community conditions to alert people to when and where there is a need to improve conditions
Who is responsible for the results?	Agency personnel	Nonprofits, community groups, government, citizens
How often is data reported?	Quarterly, monthly, bi-weekly, or weekly	Annually or biennially
Who are the primary users?	Elected officials, public managers, agency personnel, and the public	The public, community leaders, and government

There have been attempts at determining explicit environmental performance indicators as one aspect of a societal indicator. Ilinitch, Soderstrom, and Thomas (1998, p. 403) analyzed common, publicly available environmental performance metrics with principle components analysis and demonstrated that "organizational systems, stakeholder relations, regulatory compliance, and environmental impacts" were most significant. Environmental impacts showed a high degree of variability which Ilinitch speculates is due to the influence of factors like reputation, managerial attitudes, and a litany of ecological indicators (habitat loss, resource degradation, etc.) whose data is not widely available (Ilinitch, Soderstrom, & Thomas, 1998).

Exploring the measurement of corporate social reputation reveals that it is very difficult to separate the reputation of one company from that of its peers (Bertels & Peloza, 2008). Another challenge is the lack of objective measurement criteria that can determine relative corporate social responsibility (CSR) across regions, industries, product types, and other factors. "Reputational spillover" can occur when an event that damages corporate reputation in one company affects the stock prices of other companies (Yu & Lester, 2008). Instead of benefiting from a rival's weakness the competitor suffers just by virtue of being in the same industry. In this situation the reputation of the worst becomes the reputation of all.

CSR's influences from external sources make it problematic as a potential performance indicator. It can be impaired, despite superior performance, by a competitor that may not be performing well. This is counter to a purely competitive model – one would expect a company to benefit from its rivals inferior performance. Reputation is therefore best compared across groups of companies with similar products, services, and sizes. An individual company cannot realistically use reputation to measure its own performance against societal indicators without this context.

Corporate sustainability provides a better measure of how well the company contributes to the continual satisfaction of human needs (Dyllick & Thomas, 2002). The emphasis on continual satisfaction speaks to the inclusion of both present and future stakeholders. These stakeholders may include customers, local communities, shareholders, employees, and the government and integrates both short-term and long-term aspects (Dyllick & Hockerts, 2002).

Sustainability requires the consideration of complex definitions of capital. Corporate sustainability must consider economic, social, and natural capital. A definition of economic capital in the context of sustainability guarantees sufficient cash flow to "ensure liquidity while producing a persistent above average return" to shareholders (Dyllick & Hockerts, 2002, p. 133). Sustainable natural capital consumption would only consume at a rate below the "natural reproduction or at a rate below the development of substitutes" (Dyllick & Hockerts, 2002, p. 133). Social capital in a sustainable company is expressed as the company's ability to bring value to individual partners (e.g., employees) and society while managing in a way that lends transparency to their motivations and understanding of the company's value system (Dyllick & Hockerts, 2002, p. 134).

Government Societal Performance Indicators

Measuring government performance is highly subjective. Government performance is not tied to supply and demand or inputs and outputs like a corporate model would be. Government performance is tied to external forces that encompass economic and social decision making at all levels of its society. One definition of government performance could be expressed as how well it protects its people, their property, and its sovereignty.

Modern government performance management was first institutionalized with the passage of the Government Performance and Results Act

(GPRA) of 2003. This bill called for a shift away from measuring performance by looking at purely financial considerations like grants, contracts, and expenditures. Instead, the bill shifted performance management towards the result that government work produced. Despite widespread optimism and support for the bill, the first results were received with skepticism (Radin, 1998).

Despite its imperfections, GPRA lead to an evolution in government management that has increased both the amount and quality of business data available to the public. Business intelligence tools, web-based delivery, and Open Government mandates are making these tools more accessible than ever. Providing access to this data has increased the scrutiny on government management. Transparency has also increased discussion as to whether government spending correlates to socio-economic improvements.

This paper submits that it is not possible to only look at GPRA metrics and socio-economic indicators to make a correlation between better government management and the state of the nation. The state of the nation is shaped by forces beyond the control of the government. These forces include the decisions and strategies of the business sectors, as well as the multiplication of individual decisions made by the members of a society. Responsibility is shared across all strata and dimensions of society.

The relationship between contractors and the government is an example of how the same performance measures may impact a company, citizens, and the Federal government in complex ways. The local economies tied closely to federal contracting dollars may behave differently than economies not as directly tied to governmental contracts. This is especially true in the "edge-cities" that surround Washington, D.C., where so much of the economy is driven by contracts with the Federal government (Stough, Haynes, & Campbell, 1998) yet takes place outside of the capital itself.

Government performance is thus best viewed in context of other sectors, environment factors, and social changes. It must be viewed at a scale that does not lend itself to quarterly or annual reporting. GPRA and the Program Assessment and Results Tool (PART), for all of their simplicity, have taken 17 years to begin to produce meaningful results and its focus was primarily on ensuring that money was spent effectively.

Government programs intended to produce long-lasting socio-economic benefits should be measured on a scale commensurate with their goals. Measuring the outcomes associated with these programs may take decades or generations. Government executives must realize that their responsibility is to take measurable action toward achieving these goals while "realizing that they are not fully responsible for realizing their outcome" (Kloby & Callahan, 2009, p. 20). This requires a long-term vision that extends beyond government executives individual tenures and well beyond the patience of voters.

To explore the complexity of government performance, this paper will use the Environmental Protection Agency (EPA) as a case study. It will examine the GPRA measures from the Superfund program and how this program could be viewed in context of societal indicators. It will also leverage the Federal IT Dashboard to assess the measurement of EPA IT investments to compare the efficacy of GPRA mandated performance metrics with new measures required by the OMB.

GPRA enjoyed broad bi-partisan support, having been introduced by Republican Senator William Roth in 1990 and signed into law by President Clinton in 2003 after three years of revision and deliberation in the Senate and House (Radin, 1998). All executive agencies were required to submit a five year strategic plan to the Office of Management and Budget and Congress by September 30, 1997 (except the Central Intelligence Agency, General Accounting Office, Panama Canal Commission, Postal Service, and Postal

Rate Commission which were exempted from the bill's provisions) (Roberts, 2000).

Data issues and challenges defining strategic objectives were frequent criticisms. Simultaneously while agencies were working to meet GPRA reporting standards they were simultaneously trying to meet other Congressional and Executive Order mandates that were part of President Clinton's National Performance Review. A few of these initiatives included:

- Federal Managers Financial Integrity Act of 1982,
- Chief Financial Officers Act of 1990,
- Government Management Reform Act of 1994,
- Information Technology Reform Act of 1996,
- Paperwork Reduction Act of 1995,
- Federal Financial Management Improvement Act of 1996,
- Customer Service Executive Order of 1993,
- REGO III of the National Performance Review, 1996,
- Reinvention Impact Center Initiative of the National Performance Review, 1997 (Radin, 1998).

Each of these initiatives required reports to Congress and or to the President and the focus of senior executives. With so many competing initiatives, it was difficult to effectively identify performance metrics that aligned with strategic objectives while not competing with other objectives' measurements.

In large part, though, GPRA was not successful because it attempted to manage a government like it was a corporation (Radin, 1998) and was implemented in what has been called a "synoptic approach to strategic planning" (Roberts, 2000, p. 299). This top-down approach to management and its application across Federal agencies assumes that it is uniformly applicable. In reality,

the disparate missions and constant change of leadership within democratic governments make this approach problematic (Roberts, 2000).

To better support GPRA, the Office of Management and Budget (OMB) under the second Bush administration created the Program Assessment Rating Tool (PART) to create performance metrics across governments (Newell, 2009). PART at that time was the most comprehensive government performance assessment ever conducted but was flawed in its implementation (Newell, 2009). It has been continuously improved, most recently under President Obama's administration, to encourage the use of metrics that measure outcomes instead of activities.

Under President Obama, OMB leadership has defined four priorities for improving government management through outcome-based metrics. Bruel (2010) identifies the following priorities:

1. "Eliminate waste by requiring each agency to appoint an official responsible for improper payments, provide targeted error measures to understand root cause, and provide incentives to all acquisition stakeholders to improve their processes for spending government dollars" (p. 57);
2. "Improve management of real property" (p. 57);
3. "Manage financial system modernization projects to bring them closer to their expected budgets and schedules" (p. 57);
4. "Increase transparency of financial information by providing timely and reliable data to public consumers through the spending. gov and recovery.gov web sites" (p. 57).

Specifically targeting the long-standing weakness of government information technology systems, OMB launched the Federal IT Dashboard at http://it.usaspending.gov in 2009 to publish performance metrics on IT projects across agencies and foster accountability. According to Breul, accountability has been a problem as responsibility for managing IT and performing some inherently governmental functions (e.g., measuring the performance of IT projects) has shifted to contractors as a cost saving measure (Breul, 2010).

IT systems and their management are poor examples of outcome-based measurements. The reason for investing in information technology is to improve a process or an output by saving time and or money. Information technology tools provide greater efficiency but do not necessarily mean that the governmental mission will be done any better after the tool's adoption. These measures are inherently input and output driven instead of satisfying the OMB's goal of improving the outcome of government programs.

The ability for the Federal government to publish data to the public consumers has increased dramatically over the last decade. While performance measures may not be perfect, the data is increasingly consumable in its raw form. The format of report distribution has shifted from reams of paper and enormous binders to interactive web sites. The site www.recovery.gov shows where the money from Total Asset and Recovery Program (TARP) was spent, how many jobs were created, and who is complying with reporting standards (The Recovery Accountability and Transparency Board, 2011). The sites www.usaspending.gov and www.fdps.gov track contracts and government spending across the entire Federal government.

These sites provide transparency and unfiltered data. Public data consumers can rely on the published reports and charts or they can perform their own analysis using the raw data sources. Interpretation of this data is driven by perception more than statistics. The data may be incomplete and can certainly be subject to manipulation. Putting out more data does not inherently make a country more transparent. Despite these improvements, the 2010 Transparency International Corruptions Perceptions Index ranks the United States 22nd of 178 countries (Transparency International, 2010).

One criticism of Government data sources and their dashboards is that performance has not shifted to outcomes instead of inputs and outputs. The Troubled Asset Relief Program (TARP) has been proclaimed the most "comprehensive, transparent assessment of program performance the federal government ever conducted" (Newell, 2009, p. 18). OMB leadership has acknowledged the improvements TARP has brought but is refocusing government executives on establishing outcome-based metrics to measure performance (Newell, 2009).

The Mercatus Center at George Mason University has evaluated GPRA reports every year since 1993. Their scoring process includes measures across transparency, public benefit, and forward leadership as seen in Table 2. Mercatus's finding show that agencies producing GPRA reports have about "10% more managers reporting that they have outcome, output, or efficiency measures" (Ellig, 2009, p. 11). Mercatus's study also shows that there is a correlation between a higher Mercatus score and reporters answering strongly in the affirmative that their leadership values results. Clearly performance improvement can only come when leadership values performance and knows that measuring performance is a precursor to improving performance.

Table 2. Mercatus center GPRA report performance measures (adapted from Ellig, 2009)

Transparency	Public Benefit	Forward Looking Leadership
Accessibility	Outcome-oriented goals	Vision
Readability	Outcome measures	Explanation of failures
Verification and validation	Agency affected outcomes	Major management challenges
Baseline and trend data	Results linked to costs	Improvement plans

Personal Performance Societal Indicators

There is much less data on personal performance available through literature searches than there is on measuring the performance of government or corporations. Perhaps this is because it is far more rewarding to judge someone else's performance than to examine our own. Or perhaps this is because each person has their own value system that may not translate into a universal set of balanced perspectives.

There are a few measures that could be submitted as personal performance measures. Smart cars now offer the ability to track fuel consumption rates and how individual driving choices (e.g., not using the air conditioner, driving at slower speeds, etc.) affect driving costs. Performance measures are reported in real-time through the dashboard (literally) and could be aggregated to show personal performance improvements overtime in context of natural resource consumption. Similarly, smart homes allow better monitoring of fuel consumption. Improving how homes connect to the power grid will provide better metrics on how personal fuel consumption choices affect local supply.

Other personal financial performance indicators could include debt to income ratios and credit scores. Little research was found to support a claim that there is a correlation between either of these factors and socio-economic health. Logically, however, if individuals were more conscious of their performance measures they may make different choices as they buy major purchases or take out mortgages. More people making more conscientious choices should make socio-economic conditions better, or so it would seem.

ANALYSIS

Case Study Background Information

EPA's mission objective is to "protect human health and the environment." Its strategic plan for 2011-2015 includes five goals, one of which is "Cleaning Up Communities and Advancing Sustainable Development" (US EPA, 2011). It has been pursuing these goals through the SUPERFUND program since 1980 and the passage of the Comprehensive Environmental Response, Compensation and Liability Act (CERCLA). CERCLA established the National Priorities List (NPL) of most contaminated sites and a trust fund to provide funding for their remediation. CERCLA provided the EPA authority to clean up these sites and enforce that the work is either executed or paid for by the responsible party. CERCLA was amended in 1986 with the Superfund Amendments and Reauthorization Act (SARA) which included additional enforcement provisions and strengthened local, state, and tribal partnerships with the EPA.

EPA was chosen as a case study as it had an overall IT Investment rating fairly close to the mean for the whole government (US Office of Management and Budget, 2010), publishes data that is easily understandable by a public consumer, and is represented on the Federal IT Dashboard. Its mission is also easily translated into societal indicators because of the emphasis on protecting human health.

GPRA Performance Metrics and their Usefulness in Assessing EPA Efficiency

EPA set the following metrics associated the Superfund program in response to the GPRA:

1. **"Sitewide Ready for Anticipated Use (SWRAU):** This measure tracks sites on the NPL where: (1) construction of the

remedy is completed, (2) all cleanup goals have been achieved to reduce unacceptable risk that could affect current and reasonably anticipated future land uses of the site, and (3) all institutional controls have been implemented." (US EPA, 2011)

2. **"Human Exposure Under Control (HEUC):** This measure tracks sites on the NPL where all identified unacceptable human exposures from site contamination for current land and/or ground water use conditions have been controlled." (US EPA, 2011)

3. **"Groundwater Migration Under Control (GMUC):** This measure tracks sites on the NPL where either: 1) contamination is below protective, risk-based levels or, if not, 2) where the migration of contaminated ground water is stabilized, there is no unacceptable discharge to surface water, and monitoring will be conducted to confirm that affected ground water remains in the original area of contamination." (US EPA, 2011)

4. **"Final Assessment Decision (FAD)**: This measure tracks sites at which remedial site assessment work under the Federal Superfund program has been completed, and available information indicates either: 1) no further work is necessary under the Federal Superfund Program; or 2) cleanup attention is needed under Superfund or another Federal, state or tribal environmental cleanup program." (US EPA, 2011)

5. **"Construction Completed (CC):** This measure tracks sites on the NPL where construction of the remedy is completed" (US EPA, 2011).

These metrics are important aspects of determining the health of a SUPERFUND site, but won't realistically be useful for performance measurement GPRA for a number of reasons. They involve natural processes for site recovery that may require years of natural recovery that cannot be hastened through application of more

resources (inputs). Congress and subsequently the public expect a success story before success can realistically be achieved.

All of these metrics are evaluated based on the number of sites that match the given criteria as if they were an input to EPA's process and their remediation was an output which would lead to an outcome of greater protection of human health and the environment. Corporate production models can gain efficiency by finding ways to use fewer inputs. That does not apply to this case, however, because the EPA has to react to the sites to the sites based on their entry on the NPL. The ultimate goal is to reduce demand by having fewer contaminated sites. Applying corporate performance measures associated with inputs and outputs to this scenario is counter-intuitive.

It is tempting to attempt to measure EPA's success by quantifying the reduction in a human health problem that could be attributed to reducing the amounts of known pollutants through SUPERFUND sites remediation. This is impossible because of the difficulty in establishing statistically relevant causal relationships between a disease and a specific pollutant from a specific location.

Superfund is unique in that there are clear relationships between the program and societal indicators. Proximity to Superfund sites has been shown to reduce property values and the threat of listing on the NPL does encourage local communities to pay for the remediation in advance of the Remedial Investigation (Gayer, Hamilton, & Viscusi, 2000). Once listed on the NPL, however, there is less incentive for the local community to clean up the site themselves, arguably because the Remedial Investigation provides a statistical assessment of risk that is much lower than the anecdotal assessment of residents (Gayer, Hamilton, & Viscusi, 2000).

Measuring Superfund performance based on cancer cases averted is also problematic. According to Hamilton and Viscusi:

The median number of expected cancer cases per site over 30 years is less than 0.1 expected cancer cases. Costs per cancer case averted are very high at most of these sites, with only 44 out of 145 sites having a cost per cancer case averted less than $100 million (Hamilton & Viscusi, 1999)

Spending $100 million and reporting that the community averted less than 1 cancer case in the next 30 years would likely not be well received by the populace. It does illustrate Superfund's relationship between program performance metrics (cost of the program) and societal indicators (human health). The cumulative effect of high remediation costs, reduced property values, and the threat of cancer, however, may cause communities to be proactive in mitigating environmental risks before the impact is felt.

For the EPA, the performance metrics required by GPRA are far from perfect but are still a valuable source of information. The location of Superfund sites is freely available and has been incorporated into numerous data "mash-ups" using geographic information systems (GIS). One

example of this is seen in Figure 1 which overlays Superfund sites over GIS maps. In this case the map shows relative rates of cancer related deaths (more specifically female deaths from malignant cancer in the counties surrounding Philadelphia, Pennsylvania). As discussed previously, the intent is not to imply a statistical relevance between the cancer rate and a single Superfund site. The relevance of this relationship is anecdotal from a mathematical standpoint but meaningful when expressed in terms of societal indicators.

Community leaders and special interest groups use this type of anecdotal evidence to sway political influence. As Gayer, Hamilton, and Viscussi point out, it is the anecdotal evidence that launches the Remedial Investigation which could lead to the sites placement on the Superfund site that launches communities to take direct action to clean up a site. Communities are less inclined to clean up a site after the Remedial Investigation is completed and expresses the risk in statistical terms that do lead to its inclusion on the NPL (Gayer, Hamilton, & Viscusi, 2000). The deterrent nature of the threat of a site being listed on the

Figure 1. Example superfund and NIH data mashup (US National Library of Medicine, 2010)

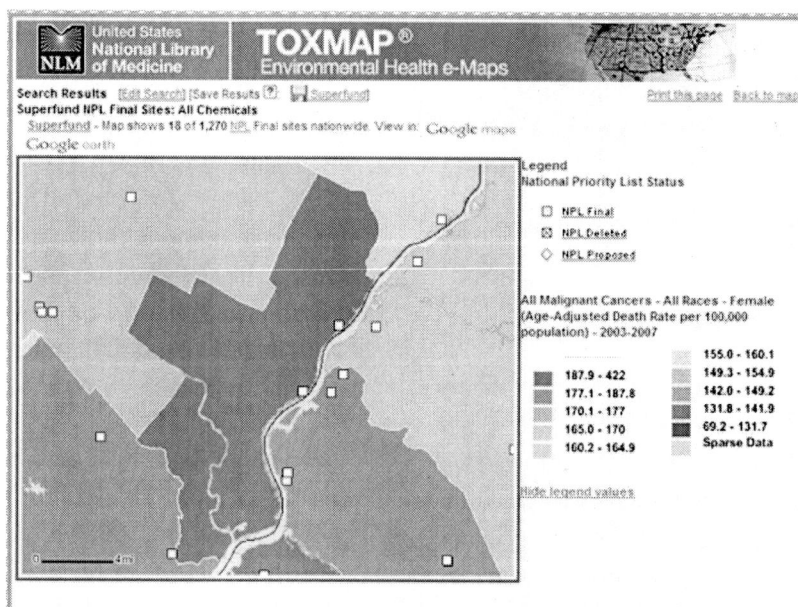

NPL may therefore be more valuable to a community than cleaning up the site after it has already been listed.

Possible Community Outcome Measurements from the Superfund Data Sources

Superfund requires responsible parties to pay or perform the remediation necessary at the site. There is a real and significant dollar value associated with the cost of cleanup and possible litigation against the potentially responsible party. The remediation costs could, therefore, be considered a performance metric for both the EPA and business entities whose waste products are found in Superfund sites. EPA's performance could be measured in terms of their effectiveness at collecting remediation costs and maintaining the Superfund trust. Businesses could consider maintaining low litigation and remediation costs at low levels to be performance indicators.

Communities could consider the number and scope of Superfund sites in their communities to be a performance indicator. Communities and corporations are more proactive in encouraging or even executing the cleanup independently when the threat of NPL site listing looms on the horizon (Gayer, Hamilton, & Viscusi, 2000). The real difference appears when communities and corporations work together proactively to stop sites from becoming contaminated in the first place.

RESULTS

OMB sets the overall government performance measures based on their concerns as well as those of citizen and Congressional stakeholders. To improve some aspect of their performance, a government agency may acquire a product or service from a contractor. The performance of the contractor in execution of the government agency's program is reflected in their award fee and opportunities for corporate growth. The contractor's performance and growth impacts the local economy and improves the quality of life for individuals within the region. Citizens are impacted as either a direct or indirect stakeholder of the service provided by the contractor that implemented the solution to the requirement.

The example above illustrates a top-down flow of performance improvement. In reality though, socio-economic performance improvements that lead to political stability and national prosperity must come from multiple sources as seen in Figure 2. The government alone cannot achieve lasting results without businesses and individuals also working toward shared national interests (Roberts, 2000).

Each of these performance areas can be defined using a balanced score-card approach. The perspectives chosen, however, cannot be lifted directly from the corporate model that earned the balanced scorecard its fame. The balanced score card does not work as well when including external factors (Kaplan & Norton, 1993). Instead an alternate balanced score card may look something like Figure 3.

GPRA measurements are still focusing on the performance measures and leaving the societal indicators open to interpretation. President Obama's initiatives to share this performance data has allowed broader analysis but economists warn that it is impossible to determine whether a single policy can take credit for an improvement in a societal indicator like job creation (McTague, 2009).

At present, with only a few years worth of data accumulated, it is not possible to clearly establish relationships between current government programs and many societal indicators. Over time, however, relationships between coordinated government programs for sustainable growth and environmental protection may become clearer. Continual improvement in the data captured will allow trends and analysis of these possible relationships. In 2110, providing data collection efforts

Figure 2. Federal, corporate, and personal synergy

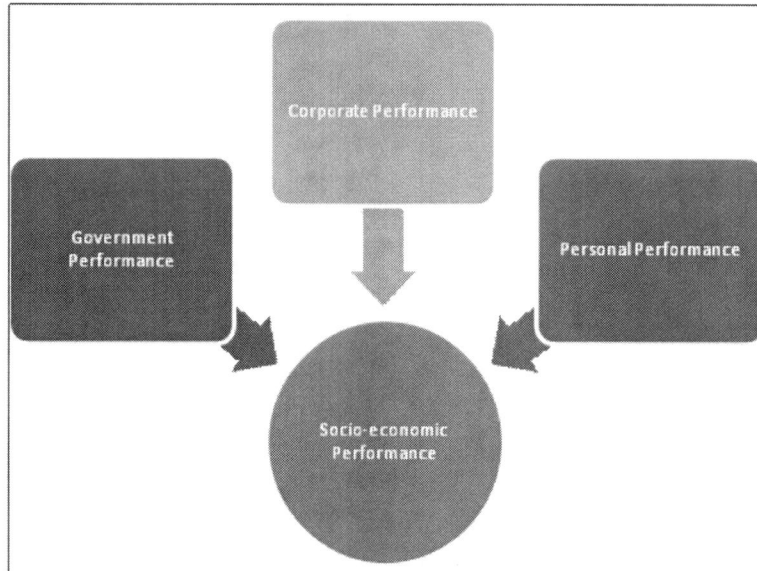

Figure 3. Example holistic performance metrics and relationships

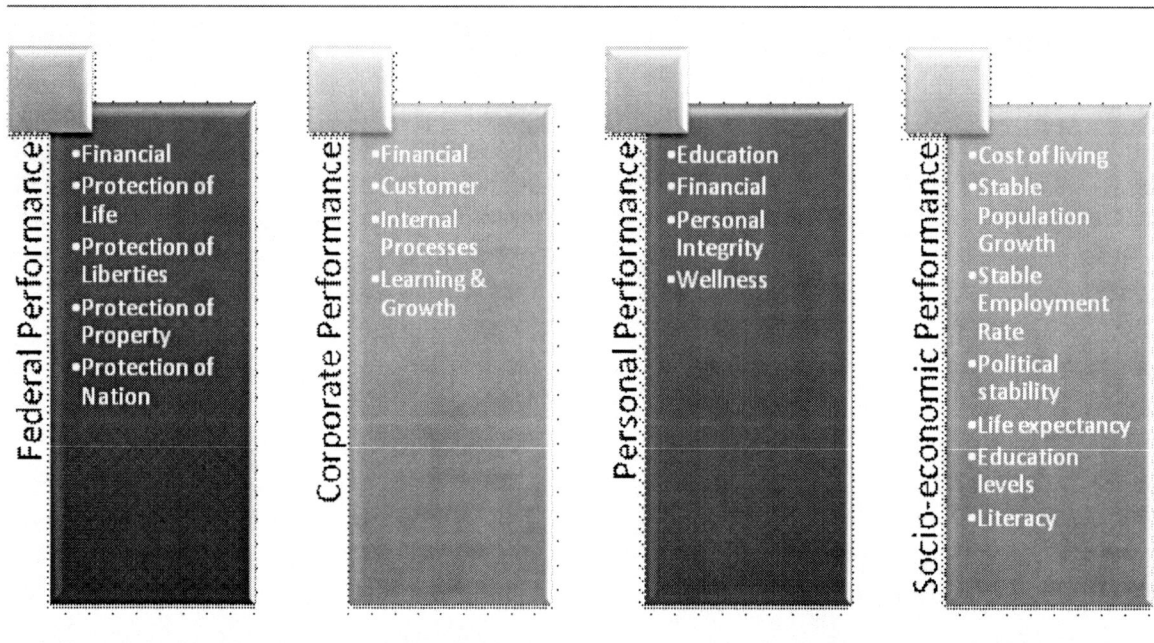

continue, it may be possible to look back at the past century and see what activities best spurred the economy or improved the quality of life.

The emergence of business intelligence tools like those used by the U.S. federal government and throughout corporations are making performance measurement easier than ever. Relationships are easier to identify and model as visualization software becomes more sophisticated. Social networking tools and distribution through the internet make dissemination of these complex performance measures cheaper and easier. Some countries are obviously more transparent than others and social performance management has not spread uniformly throughout the global society.

What can be done today, however, is to begin incorporating performance measurement into personal lives. Making better choices personally will positively affect production and over time lead to a more sustainable society with a strong government and vibrant economy. The relationships between personal choices may never be statistically relevant because in social experiments there are no real control groups to compare against. With the passage of enough time and accumulation of enough data points it is logical to conclude that socio-economic standing can only improve when every individual, business, and government component is working to continual improvement.

REFERENCES

Bertels, S., & Peloza, J. (2008). Running just to stand still? Managing CSR Reputation in an Era of Ratcheting Expectations. *Corporate Reputation Review, 11*(1), 56–72. doi:10.1057/crr.2008.1

Breul, J. (2010). Strategies to improve government performance. *Public Management, 39*(2), 56.

Dyllick, T., & Hockerts, K. (2002). Beyond the business case for corporate sustainability. *Business Strategy and the Environment, 11*, 130–141. doi:10.1002/bse.323

Ellig, J. (2009, Summer). Federal performance reporting: what a difference ten years makes! *The Public Manager*, pp. 5-12.

Gayer, T., Hamilton, J. T., & Viscusi, W. K. (2000). Private values of risk tradeoffs at SUPERFUND sites: housing market evidence on learning about risk. *The Review of Economics and Statistics, 82*(3), 439–451. doi:10.1162/003465300558939

Hamilton, J. T., & Viscusi, V. K. (1999). How costly is "clean"? An analysis of the benefits and costs of superfund site remediations. *Journal of Policy Analysis and Management, 18*(1), 2–28. doi:10.1002/(SICI)1520-6688(199924)18:1<2::AID-PAM2>3.0.CO;2-2

Ilinitch, A. Y., Soderstrom, N. S., & Thomas, T. E. (1998). Measuring corporate environmental performance. *Journal of Accounting and Public Policy, 17*, 383–408. doi:10.1016/S0278-4254(98)10012-1

Kaplan, R. S., & Norton, D. P. (1993, September). Putting the balanced scorecard to work. *Harvard Business Review*, (n.d.), 54–69.

Kloby, K., & Callahan, K. (2009). Aligning government performance and community outcome measurement. *The Public Manager*, 19-26.

McTague, J. M. (2009). Overly Stimulating. *Barron's National Business and Financial Weekly, 89*(46), 36.

Newell, E. (2009). For good measure. *Government Executive, 41*(8), 18–19.

Radin, B. A. (1998). The Government Performance and Results Act (GPRA): Hydra-heade monster or flexible management tool? *Public Administration Review*, (n.d.), 307–316. doi:10.2307/977560

Roberts, N. (2000). The synoptic model of strategic planning and the GPRA: lacking a good fit with the political context. *Public Productivity & Management Review*, 23(3), 297–311. doi:10.2307/3380721

Stough, R. R., Haynes, K. E., & Campbell, J. H. (1998). Small business entrepreneurship in the high technology services sector: an assessment for the edge cities of the U.S. national capital region. *Small Business Economics*, 10, 61–74. doi:10.1023/A:1007930720118

The Recovery Accountability and Transparency Board. (2011). *Recovery.gov Track the Money*. Retrieved March 15, 2011, from http://www.recovery.gov

Transparency International. (2010). *2010 Transparency International Corruption Perception Index*. Retrieved February 28, 2011, from Transparency International: http://www.transparency.org/policy_research/surveys_indices/cpi/2010/results

US EPA. (2011). *Accomplishments and Performance Measures | Superfund | US EPA*. Retrieved from Accomplishments and Performance Measures | Superfund | US EPA: http://www.epa.gov/superfund/accomplishments.htm

US National Library of Medicine. (2010). Retrieved March 15, 2011, from TOXMAP - TRI and Superfund Environmental Maps: http://toxmap.nlm.nih.gov

US Office of Management and Budget. (2010). *All Agencies | Federal IT Dashboard*. Retrieved March 6, 2011, from http://it.usaspending.gov/?q=portfolios

Waddock, S. A., & Graves, S. B. (1997). The Corporate Social Performance & Financial Performance Link. *Strategic Management Journal*, 18, 303–319. doi:10.1002/(SICI)1097-0266(199704)18:4<303::AID-SMJ869>3.0.CO;2-G

Yu, T., & Lester, R. (2008). Moving beyond firm boundaries: a social network perspective on reputation spill over. *Corporate Reputation Review*, 11(1), 94–108. doi:10.1057/crr.2008.6

This work was previously published in the International Journal of Business Intelligence Research, Volume 2, Issue 4, edited by Richard Herschel, pp. 29-41, copyright 2011 by IGI Publishing (an imprint of IGI Global).

Chapter 10
Business Intelligence Should be Centralized

Brian Johnson
Himalayan International Institute, USA

ABSTRACT

The implementation of BI into the business strategy and culture is laden with many potential points that could result in failure of the initiative, leaving BI to be underdeveloped and a source of wasted resources for the company. Due to the unique nature of BI in the business space, properly setting up BI within the organizational structure from the onset of integration minimizes the impact of the most common hurdles to BI implementation. Many companies choose to mitigate these problems by using a centralized approach by building a Center of Excellence, but their place in the company's organizational structure needs to be well-defined and properly empowered to be effective. This paper also reviews how the concept of centralization is defined, how it relates to the implementation of BI, and how it can effectively in overcome the common implementation hurdles.

INTRODUCTION

As business intelligence becomes more pervasive in businesses of all sizes and industries, a large problem many business leaders experience is exactly how to organize the company to best leverage the implementation of BI enterprise-wide. With

BI still in its adolescent phase of development, commonly accepted best practices are still few and far between. Many companies struggle to find the optimum solution that is applicable to their industry, size, culture, and organizational structure. Many approaches toward business organization have been tried with many successes, many failures, but mostly a mix of both.

DOI: 10.4018/978-1-4666-2650-8.ch010

This paper investigates the best approach toward organizing an enterprise for widespread adaptation of BI methodologies. Setting the proper organization structure and allocating the resources appropriately within an organization from the start can limit the chances of a poor acceptance of BI into the enterprise, reduce unnecessary structuring expenses, and allow the business to leverage the advantages of BI as quickly as possible.

In the ensuing Research section of this paper, the current state of BI implementation practices will be examined. The examination is of the typical lifecycle of BI implementation, including an overview of organizational structures and a focus on the Center of Excellence, followed by a review of the common hurdles to BI acceptance. An Analysis section will provide a review and critique of the concept of centralization and apply the benefits and strengths of both a centralized and a decentralized approach to the hurdles laid out in the research section, to determine the extent to which BI should be centralized.

RESEARCH

The new competitive edge in business is quickly forming to be the adaptation of business intelligence into every facet of decision making within an organization. Fully integrated BI companies like Harrah's and Amazon have pushed their competitive advantage to become leaders in their industries.

Even in companies that don't push BI as a competitive advantage, the importance of information is no longer a question in the minds of most business executives. Companies can no longer compete well without leveraging their information in some capacity. In fact, 95% of organizations in a Forbes survey recognize that information management is critical to business success (Forbes, 2010).

So the real challenge businesses have to deal with is how to organize their resources to best enable intelligence use to reach its full potential. BI sits on a technical infrastructure, and relies on it exclusively to deliver the information, but the technology is, for the most part, mature to the point where it is not an impediment to the implementation of BI. Instead, as Gerry Lee from Aviva states, "Business intelligence isn't a technology issue, it's a business issue." It's no longer whether you can do a particular task or project, but how, and who's responsible (Whiting, 2004).

Implementations of BI

As a company makes the move in their business to integrate data into decision making, it typically won't occur in one short project cycle. The path to a fully mature BI-centric enterprise takes years to accomplish, and the business will experience many different forms of organizational structure as BI becomes more pervasive. There is not a consensus as to what structure is the most optimal for a BI rollout, even within the same business. Businesses tend to cycle through different structures as they mature. There is a spectrum of organizational structure that could manifest, with a consolidated view on one end, and a decentralized embedded individualistic view on the other.

Organizational Structure

Centralization

A centralized BI unit houses all the technical, managerial, and technical expertise needed to perform all BI functions within the enterprise. Business units become the BI unit's clients, and the BI unit becomes the central hub for all intelligence activity.

The idea of centralizing a function in an organization usually centers around a focus on coordination, standardization and consolidation of equipment, processes, technology, and customer and vendor management. It enables a shared vision and reduces redundancies found in individual business units (Ulrich, 2009).

Standardization especially is an important function that a centralized BI unit can provide. "Without standards, you'll require more training, it limits collaboration, it increases software licensing costs and it may also require redundant capabilities if the technologies aren't compatible" (Henschen, 2008). With a primary purpose for enterprise BI is to establish the standards of enterprise BI, the drawbacks to not being standardized are significant. It is very difficult to create and enforce standards without a centralized body to govern them.

As an example, at Aviva, an Information Management Services department was established to develop a common business intelligence strategy. As the company continued to expand, they found that the centralization was critical to allow them to enter into a CRM initiative, something impossible to do until they had solid data management and BI capabilities (Whiting, 2004).

Decentralization

Diffusing the function across the business units in a decentralized manner also has benefits. It allows those units to make decisions that have their best interests in mind, and allows them to pursue their goals in an expedited and optimal manner. Those that are developing the BI solutions are those that work with the business units and have the knowledge of the processes they intended to analyze. The developers and consumers have the same unit culture, reporting structure, and same end goals in mind (Eckerson, 2010).

Decentralization is especially suited for functions that are specific to a particular location or process, processes that require a very short response time, or functions that require business expertise at the unit level (Brandel, 2010).

Hybrid BI Structure

In most cases, the line between having a pure centralized or purely decentralized approach to BI will typically fall between these two approaches. The BI maturization cycle generally will not allow either approach to be taken into its pure form unless the organization has reached certain points in the process.

Ulrich explains the state of IT in general is often in a state of constant shifting between being centralized and decentralized. BI follows that same pattern, known as the "reorganization yoyo" (Ulrich, 2009).

Often it starts as a decentralized approach as individual departments take up initiatives to help their lines of business. As more lines of business take up the practice of BI, the enterprise begins to centralize its efforts into a CoE and/or a full BI department. If the centralized group cannot keep up with the demands of the individual departments as the volume of data grows and BI permeates the business, BI decentralizes itself to an extent to fill the void. This constant bounce back and forth will continue to happen as the organization changes and adapts to new situations.

To illustrate the hybrid approach, ING Americas implemented an Information Competency Center that focuses on data management exclusively, but leaves the individual report writing to the business units. This allows the Center to focus on the enterprise wide issues of governance, standardization, and infrastructure, keeping the staff it uses low, but still allowing business units to get the information they need in the way they need it (Whiting, 2004).

Development Cycle

Businesses rarely are able to implement a data-driven philosophy of working, both in culture and in infrastructure in one full process. Most often, BI initiatives start small in scope, usually limited to a local unit that uses BI to perform some specific analytical tasks. Higher level managerial support generally doesn't exist, and the role of BI is generally to look backward into history and justify decisions that have already been made.

As more and more units begin to use data to guide their processes and decisions and the interaction of the activities between units becomes more integrated, the next phase is a more business-focused one, where support comes from a few members of executive management. In this stage, the business becomes aware of the necessities of having standardized data and processes to perform the analytical functions. Often times, a centralized task force is formed specifically dedicated to providing common data infrastructure, guidelines for data and process standards, analytical training, as well as providing project management for BI development. The idea of "single version of the truth" that BI strives for becomes a priority for this task force.

Both during and after BI becomes more enterprise-centric, the units that adopt BI processes into their everyday functions come as the implementation matures. BI usage usually starts in the core units of finance, operations, and sales and marketing. As these units start rooting themselves in information processes, other units begin to adopt BI in order to better integrate with projects that started with the core units. Strategy, business development, customer service, and R&D become the next units to become "intelligent". Finally, the remaining units like risk management, HR, and brand management fall into the fold of full BI pervasiveness (Lavalle, Hopkins, Lesser, Shockley, & Kruschwitz, 2010).

After this phase, processes begin to become infused with intelligence, all the way down to operational levels. As this phase, companies can take many directions in how to further enable their analytical proficiency. A fully sponsored analytical unit can be formed to handle most analytical functions, and services the individual business units as customers. Alternatively, the analytical

functions can end up diffusing back into the individual units where the business knowledge of the unit's functions is strongest.

This centralization process of BI has been the de facto process for most companies as they dealt with the transition to an analytical strategy. However, the same usage rules that applied to BI in the past, even as recently as 3-4 years ago, are not necessarily applicable today. The field of BI is maturing very quickly as businesses find new ways to apply strategies and tools to the data that they have. These applications are not necessarily good to use as best practices for all companies, but are worth noting as general trends in the BI space.

Data has become more accessible to all levels of workers, and the benefits of analytics are being applied to even the operational level of the enterprise. Almost half of companies have their operational staff making decisions, and have BI applications to support them. These tools are becoming more widespread throughout companies (Daniel, 2007).

As BI becomes more pervasive in the enterprise, business units are seeking their own solutions to solve the problems unique to themselves that are not fulfilled by the enterprise provided solutions. The technology surrounding the BI space has expanded in recent years to allow the creation of temporary, or virtualized, datamarts for use with experiments and exploratory analysis. These data sandboxes allow localized analysts to support their own department's needs quickly and without disrupting the global datastore and standards.

Some businesses run into some drawbacks as they progress further down the BI maturity cycle. Many of these drawbacks cannot be easily addressed with many of the current implementations of enterprise BI, leaving the business to become flexible when working with their setup. Having to deal with ever-changing business requirements, analysts' need for exploratory analysis, undefined requests for information from operational employees, incomplete and/or isolated BI solutions, as well as unaddressable data "black holes"—the "I don't know what I don't know" quandary—are becoming more of a common problem among maturing organizations (Forrester Consulting, 2009).

Center of Excellence

In response to the growing usage of BI throughout the enterprise, many companies shift to the next step in strategy by forming a central group of expertise. These groups are typically termed as a Center of Excellence (CoE) or a Business Intelligence Competency Center (BICC). This paper will be referring to all of these groups as "CoE".

The CoE's purpose, in relation to implementing BI in an organization, is to make BI strategic and repeatable (Henschen, 2008). It serves as a center point through which all standard processes and tools pass on their way to the enterprise usage, whether that is in the centralized BI unit, or out to individual business units.

As an organizational structure, most successful CoEs are created as an independent unit outside of IT. Since the practice of BI is the application of information to make decisions, it spans through both the technical unit as well as the business units that analyze and consume the same information.

The perception of the staff that provides business services to the greater enterprise will often change when a unit seen as an IT service. The Business vs. IT paradigm mentioned previously can rear its head. To avoid this, the CoE should be funded independently to avoid other units balking at making the necessary purchasing for a successful BI group (Henschen, 2008).

In practice, the CoE doesn't operate like many departments, in that it is project based, albeit with no real end date. Projects are constantly being introduced and completed, and staffing and activity levels will change depending on the project volume (Henschen, 2008). As a result, CoE staffing usually is reminiscent of a project,

spanning many skills and departments within the company, but in a permanent faculty, resulting in a department that is very fluid in nature and composition (Heizenberg, 2008).

Another way to view the CoE is as an internal consulting group. It interacts with IT to ensure technology availability, and interacts with business unit liaisons, and facilitates collaboration by assigning individuals from business units to float between their business unit tasks and the CoE (IDC, 2008).

The CoE staffing does not necessarily need to be static, however. When specific projects within the CoE ramp up, specialized staffing can rotate into the CoE to complete specific projects, then rotate back out. Alternatively, companies can regularly rotate analysts from business units, those that have the most complete knowledge of their respective operations, into the CoE to partner with the CoE enterprise-centric analysts for cross training, ensuring that both the CoE analysts and the line-of-business analysts are best trained and up to date on the processes relating to information analysis. Business units gain the ability to create consistency and rigor in analysis and facilitate sharing, while the CoE staff remains relevant and are able to better react to changes that occur at the line of business (Lavalle, Hopkins, Lesser, Shockley, & Kruschwitz, 2010).

CoE in Practice

The implementation of a CoE as part of an enterprise-wide BI initiative is considered an industry standard. The degree to which the CoE is staffed and the mandates it is tasked with may vary among organizations, but having a specialized team of people dedicated to the enterprise view of information management is consistently present.

This team of patchwork skills and departments that makes up a CoE must have a holistic business view and teach the concept of information based decision-making. With this, their focus should be

- **Knowledge Driven:** Taking information from one system and apply its analysis to other business domains
- **Business-Driven through Leading Practices:** A CoE will need to be able to "understand the essential trade-off between risk and profit for any management process"
- **Information Architecture:** Ensuring that the company has the right technology, architecture, and applications
- **Framework for Continuous Improvement:** The group must find ways to use information to quickly analyze new business initiatives and improve them (TNCR, 2008)

Enterprise-Centric

Given where the CoE stands within the organization structure as the hub of all main aspects that touch BI processes, it is impossible for a CoE to have anything other than an enterprise-centric focus in its activities and still be successful. In many ways, the CoE is one of the few departments outside of finance and IT that have a full, enterprise wide view of the organization.

With the onslaught of the voluminous amounts of information that organizations are collecting, standards need to be set up for practices and tools for business units to be able to handle this data. The CoE should be responsible for setting the "information agenda" for the rest of the organization. The information agenda "identifies foundational information practices and tools while aligning IT and business goals through enterprise information plans and financially justified deployment road maps" (Lavalle, Hopkins, Lesser, Shockley, & Kruschwitz, 2010). This provides the overlapping roadmap for the enterprise to engage in, and leads to the development of data collection, development of analytical models, and guidelines for data governance.

Once the information agenda is established, the unit provides enterprise-centric models and governance by:

- Advancing standard methods for identifying business problems to be solved with analytics;
- Facilitating identification of analytic business needs while driving rigor into methods for embedding insights into end-to-end processes;
- Promoting enterprise-level governance on prioritization, master data sources and re-use to capture enterprise efficiencies;
- Standardizing tools and analytic platforms to enable resource sharing, streamline maintenance and reduce licensing expenses (Lavalle, Hopkins, Lesser, Shockley, & Kruschwitz, 2010).

From its umbrella-like position over all business units, the CoE isn't only limited to the stewardship and consolidation of data, but also becomes involved in working with the businesses processes. The CoE gains the responsibility for managing processes (including standardization), reviewing processes that can be consolidated, cutting activities that add no value to a process, and determining if a process should be outsourced (TNCR, 2008).

Consistency and Standardization

One of the major mandates of a CoE is defining and maintaining data standardization processes and guidelines for the entire BI solution. With data quality and governance being one of the core needs for organizations to fill it ensure proper analytical results, the CoE's independent placement in the organizational structure and assertive mandate allows it to work with all business units to ensure understanding as to the standards, and the clout to ensure compliance.

Consistency between BI projects becomes easier to accomplish with the same team of people working on each project. Solutions, tools, and techniques learned and applied from one project can save resources when applied to future projects (Farris, 2006). This makes the CoE the ideal place to concentrate the assignment of BI tasks, with the expertise housed in the same location, instead of individual business units.

Furthermore, the CoE advances standard methods for identifying business problems to be solved with analytics, then using the tools and models that have already been adopted working with the business units to solve those problems. Or, where appropriate, creating new or adapting current models to address these problems (Lavalle, Hopkins, Lesser, Shockley, & Kruschwitz, 2010).

Analytical models can be pertinent to only a single business unit, but in many cases the same models can be repeatable throughout the enterprise as a way to see the single version of the truth. As with providing the standards for analytical models, the CoE is on the forefront for developing and applying these models. For instance, a model developed for a call center can also be applied to customer retention, or to new customer acquisition efforts. This allows resource sharing, streamlining maintenance and reducing licensing expenses (Henschen, 2008).

Quality and Governance

The IDC survey found that a very effective means to increasing the BI solution design quality, as well as the resulting data quality, is to set up a CoE. This is mostly the case for businesses that are mid or large sized where they have the resources available to dedicate specifically to a BI initiative, and tend to be more hierarchical in structure (2008).

Working with the goal of data quality, business must pay attention to the role of data governance and ownership. The CoE should be the principle designer of the organization's governance model. Information requires a high level of standardiza-tion so that it can be used across the organization. With standardization, this information becomes sharable throughout the organization, and should be freely used as an asset to each of the business units (Heizenberg, 2008).

Key Points to Successful CoE

With any project or initiative within an enterprise, even the most theoretically flawless venture can be subject to key points in implementation that can affect the resulting impact that the project can have on the enterprise. A CoE is no different, with a large number of factors that are key to a successful creation of a CoE. The main factors are executive support, organizational structure, proper staffing, and the unit focus of the CoE.

Executive Support

The building of a CoE starts at the top, with the need for high level management support. In order for a CoE to execute its mandates, it needs to have the authority and the backing of influential members of management to succeed. Without that backing, the CoE simply won't have an impact. To make sure it has the proper authority, the CoE is often placed directly under a C-level executive, with the ideal choice being COO to ensure cross-department support. The CIO is most common in organizations, but can suffer from having the CoE being identified as an IT operation, affecting how it is viewed by business units (Henschen, 2008).

Organizational Structure

Very often, this distinct nature of a CoE can cause barriers to its adaptation in the organization. CoEs "...are hard to sell within many organizations because they do not fit into the standard organization chart. If a CoE is a business department that reports into certain business domains, the other business domains might not receive the same level of support. If the CoE is part of IT, it usually is isolated within IT while having too much of a technology focus. If the CoE is seen as a virtual structure spanning multiple business domains, [it] often lacks a clear mandate" (Heizenberg, 2008).

Proper Staffing

The composition of the CoE team is also important. Since the CoE is the center point around which data operations proceed, the team must have a "holistic business view to drive efficiency across the enterprise and to teach effective decision-making based on information" (TNCR, 2008).

The CoE is responsible for most end-to-end solutions involving information management, and these solutions will often bridge across most, if not all, of the enterprise. As such, the team should consist of people can plan, architect, design, develop, and support the solutions. This includes project managers, analysts, developers, infrastructure specialists, and subject matter experts from stakeholder departments.

Hurdles in Enterprise BI

Any number of problems can cause problems for a company as it tries to roll out enterprise-wide business intelligence. In reviewing surveys taken from hundreds of companies that are engaging in this initiative, there are several common problems that tend cause problems in the process of adopting BI. The effect of running into these hurdles can be large sunk costs, long delays in the adoption of BI practices, or even down right abandonment of the initiative on the enterprise-wise basis. Most commonly, the hurdles that appear the most are lack of data quality, undefined or misunderstood data governance, incompatible corporate culture, and insufficient usage of BI tools and processes by the user base. Each of these hurdles will be discussed in more depth.

Poor Data Quality

The old saying "garbage in, garbage out" is most applicable to making decisions based on data. It is impossible to make good decisions if the information provided to make those decisions is inaccurate or incomplete. The entire analytical process starts with having sound, relevant data to work with. With companies awash in more data than they can handle, good data quality processes are essential for a BI initiative to succeed.

Poor data quality is one of the largest problems with BI implementations, because hits businesses directly on the balance sheet as the costs of making incorrect decisions based off bad data begins to accumulate. Beyond this, users begin to lose trust in the information they use to make decisions, don't rely on the data as much as they should, and end up exposing the business to risks that wouldn't have existed if the data was correct (Forbes, 2010).

In order to correct the quality issue, businesses need to be able to pin down the source. However, there is disagreement between business managers and IT managers over the quality of data that an enterprise has, making it difficult to find the actual sources when there is no agreement over the degree of the problem. According to the Forbes survey, when asked how good their data is, 64% of respondents from IT thought their data quality was high, compared to only 45% of all business line respondents. Moreover, the top problems in data quality also differed between the two groups, with IT citing duplicate data as the top problem, and business managers citing inconsistent data (Forbes, 2010).

But the more deep seated core as to the cause of some of the data quality problems can go deeper into how the organization approaches data and information management initiatives. In order to ensure the best success in an information management program in terms of data quality is to have deep collaboration between IT and line-of-business managers. Often times, business executives are not aware of many of the information management programs within their organization. Lack of communication between IT and business managers about data quality programs when the specific lines of business are not involved in the solutions (Forbes, 2010).

Undefined or Unclear Data Governance

Once an organization begins to pool its information, it becomes imperative that the data is defined, managed, and understood across business units. Data governance has a large role in ensuring that enterprise data is accessible and usable to all relevant business units in the organization through a set of standard processes, and declares ownership of data, to show were accountability for that data lies. The pursuit of the "single version of the truth" starts with a good data governance structure.

The IDC survey found that data governance was found to be the largest challenge in working with BI projects. Proper data governance requires a large amount of time, effort and resources. In larger organizations, data silos are prominent, as well as process silos, as no single unit is responsible for the entire process (IDC, 2008). This creates fragmentation in ownership, or uncertain ownership of the data, leaving no one accountable for its quality and maintenance.

The fragmentation of data ownership is the biggest roadblock to a successful enterprise information management program. One prime cause to the fragmentation of ownership is that there is a disagreement between the units that produce the data, and IT as to who owns and is accountable for the data produced (Forbes, 2010). This can create difficulties when the organization tries to improve data quality and the value of information.

IDC's survey supports the concept that the best data governance structure is that of a "virtual entity" that is made up members that have decision making authority. They draw support from the CoE to bring agreement common goals that are in the best interest to the enterprise. The leadership holders of this body are important to be able to resolve conflicts that arrive in the body's pursuit of its charter (IDC, 2008).

Unlike many hurdles to BI, the need to have a strong data governance unit in place to enforce stronger data standards and consistency and integration is not lost on many organizations. Better defining consistency and standardization is a priority for 39% of organizations (Lavalle, Hopkins, Lesser, Shockley, & Kruschwitz, 2010). It is a long, ongoing process for most organizations, making it difficult for some to commit resources and political will to the effort of a seemingly unreachable goal of perfect consistency and standardization.

Incompatible Culture

A successful competitive intelligence process requires attention to cultural issues, facilitated by technology to ease knowledge sharing (April & Bessa, 2006, p. 86).

If the culture of the organization does not conducive to rolling out an information management initiative, many other successes can be overshadowed. As with most enterprise-wide initiatives, if the project implements a change in the organization mindset that is counter to the way it currently works, a large amount of management will needs to be applied to provide the shift to a new way of working and thinking. In most cases of BI, "the adoption barriers organizations face most are related to management and culture rather than being related to data and technology" (Lavalle, Hopkins, Lesser, Shockley, & Kruschwitz, 2010).

With BI being comprised of business knowledge of processes and data and being enabled by IT functions and infrastructure, it is almost inevitable that the age old conflict and misunderstanding between business and IT should rear its head.

Business is tasked with reacting to events and adapting to new requirements, while IT is tasked with planning for controlled, standardized, secure, and optimized infrastructure and applications.

This struggle between maintaining flexibility and reaction time and maintaining standards and compliance "are creating a rift in what otherwise could be smoothly flowing BI processes" (Forrester Consulting, 2009). Business sees IT as an inhibitor to business innovation, while IT sees business as attempting to run amuck without looking at the larger, more standardized picture.

When awash with data, it is easy to get lost in attempting to gather all relevant data before understanding what the analysis should be about. Asking the right questions and starting with the right insights becomes an afterthought in the all-consuming desire to consolidate all available information. Decision makers need to be ingrained with the idea that they need to learn to ask the right questions first, before even looking at the data to make sure that they get the right insights and analysis that they seek. If they don't, they will often end up with unintended consequences that cause analysis rework or create new, unforeseen problems (Lavalle, Hopkins, Lesser, Shockley, & Kruschwitz, 2010). The idea of asking the right questions needs to permeate into the culture of the organization, from management on down to the front line workers.

Lack of Usage

The greatest of projects can be rolled out, but cannot be taken full advantage of if the resulting benefits are not used. Even with the strongest support of the executive team, BI usage is often not common enough to make a large impact on business. Lack of adaptation can become from many sources: lack of training, lack of resources, cost, or even a simple lack of will from the lower levels of business.

Any BI program that is implemented becomes a source of wasted time and expense if it doesn't get used. Providing proper tools for data analysis

can have all the intention of infusing the idea of intelligence into the organization, but regular use of these tools by organizations that have them has been found to be extremely low, around 11% (Finucane, 2010).

One often overlooked problem with providing a BI solution is making information that analysts and end users need easily accessible and organized. Reports, data marts, and other stores of information can be created, but workers still spend a large amount of time searching for the right data and information to use, rather than actually analyzing and reported on it. Inaccessible data is worthless to an organization that is driven by data-driven decisions (Forrester Consulting, 2009).

Another usage limitation that organizations are running into is not the actual use of the tools themselves, but rather the ability to process all the data they gather with the intent of adding to the information pool. Their ability to gather has far exceeded their ability to process, organize, and maintain the all the incoming flows of data from business units, external sources, and even existing data that is already in house, but needs to be further processed for new uses. This perception exists for about 75% of organizations, with 40% feeling severely overloaded with data (Daniel, 2007).

ANALYSIS

After reviewing the current state of how business intelligence is implemented in the enterprise environment, the question of whether BI should be centralized can be answered.

In finding the best way to organize BI activities within the organization, its best to examine the hurdles that business are currently running into in their attempt to have BI become pervasive enterprise-wide. These hurdles will be examined through the context of centralizing or decentralizing the BI functions to find the best possible solution.

Firstly, a key aspect in the analysis of whether BI operations should be centralized or not really depends on defining what centralized BI really would be when put in practice both now and in the future as a response of the growing trend toward operational use of BI analysis.

In the context of business organization, often times the idea of a unit being centralized is when the function is self contained, with end-to-end processes all happening within the unit. Classic business units of marketing or finance are generally self contained, and perform their functions independently of each other.

The opposite concept of being decentralized lends itself to the idea that the function of the unit in question is diffused between all the other departments of the business. A decentralized marketing process allows each line of business to perform its own marketing functions independently of other units.

The reality is that "centralized" really cannot mean "all in one place" when relating to BI. Such was the case 5 years ago, as companies were still developing strategies that relied more around information. The technology and awareness to bring intelligence functions down to the operational level was too expensive, and required too much technical training to become a feasible option. Technology vendors also contributed to this idea by developing and targeting their products toward the centralized business unit.

However, this will no longer be the case going forward, as the expense of providing BI functions to more users across an organization comes down, and BI tools become easier to use. Analytics is being performed at the operational level in many BI-mature organizations, removing the necessity of having a central analytics unit perform the same function.

This does not mean that decentralization will end up being the end result. Rather, centralization really means having a center point around which all functions relating to BI revolve, even if it ends up that the actual consuming of BI processes could end up being in the individual business units. The centralization is more along the lines of where in the organizational structure the core of BI functions (the CoE, for example) reside—outside of any business unit and IT. The core responsibilities of the CoE like data governance, standards development, collaboration, and a focus for cross training between analysts will be the primary responsibility of the centralized unit. These are the functions that are more difficult to leverage properly in an organization if they are not performed by a single body.

This is much like how IT has gone through its development as it became prevalent in business. In the beginning, there was limited access to computational services, so there were a core number of people or business units that had access to it, but as the cost and efficiency of IT came down, it became more and more available to more workers within business. Now many of IT functions are available to every worker in a company, and are consumed on the user level. However, IT functions of purchasing, standardization, and process improvement are still housed in a central, undiffused department of specialty. BI is following the same pattern, with more workers gaining access to BI functionality, but the core functions still must be handled by an independent specialized unit.

Using Organizational Structure to Overcome Hurdles

With the four main hurdles to BI implementation identified as well as the effects of the various organizational structures on the implementation in general, next is the review of these organizational structures to the hurdles of poor data quality, undefined or unclear data governance, incompatible culture to best identify the proper structure to mitigate these problems and allow for a successful rollout.

Poor Data Quality

Lack of communication and unclear accountability are common problems concerning the correction of poor data quality. It's difficult to correct a problem in process or function when there is no communication or agreement as to the extent, cause, or even existence of the problem itself. Coordination between the data generating business units and IT is imperative to creating processes to improve data quality by reducing duplicate data and aligning inconsistent data.

A centralized focus on data and BI functions allows a center point for which all communication and collaboration to revolve around. A centralized structure is more apt to address problems with data quality, since duplicate and inconsistent data most commonly is detected and can be reacted to when reviewed at the enterprise level, as opposed to individual business units. A properly empowered CoE, being involved in all aspects of BI, can investigate interdepartmental data incompatibilities and set standards for data processes and formats. In a decentralized structure with a weak or non-existent CoE, the burden of standards and communication is on the individual business units, providing less incentive to focus on the interoperability of data and the "single version of the truth".

Undefined or Unclear Data Governance

Data governance lends itself to a more centralized structure, or at least a strong central unit. Data governance, with its data and process standards, and providing accessibility to all departments requires a top-down, all encompassing view of BI functions. Governance does not necessarily need to be performed by an official dedicated BI unit, but it does require stakeholders from across the enterprise to ensure that data governance is properly handled in a way that is most efficient for the entire organization. This virtual group still represents a centralized effort, and is aided greatly by a centralized BI unit that can enforce governance policies. A decentralized BI structure would cause individual units to lose the ability to effectively share consistent information between units.

The siloing effect often found in a decentralized organization is a serious impediment to BI's goal of providing enterprise information sharing and the single version of the truth. Bob Tingstrom, enterprise reporting manager for Bio-Rad Laboratories found that the decentralized structure of his organization has "made it difficult to get a complete, consistent representation of data consolidated in a way suitable to analyze business performance" (Forbes, 2010).

Incompatible Culture

The inherent culture of the organization is the most difficult hurdle to overcome just through organizational structure. It is ingrained in the attitudes and politics of the organization and requires time and effort from management to shift the mindsets of the organization. Since changing the culture of an organization is a slow process at best, it is much more effective to adapt the implementation of BI to the extent that the culture will allow.

Forcing a centralized structure onto an organization that is culturally and functionally a decentralized in nature will not be effective, since the more independent nature of business units in a decentralized structure would have to make an adjustment in their processes to adapt to the new strategy. The opposite is also true.

In the case of culture, there is no necessarily ideal structure to instill to enable a more successful BI implementation, other than working within the current culture with an edge toward decentralizing functions where possible. Companies should "[a]lign their BI architectures with their company's organizational structure, distributing as much as is culturally acceptable" (Eckerson, 2010).

Lack of Usage

Once the BI strategy has been implemented, ensuring that it becomes more pervasive throughout the organization can be a rather difficult proposition. Users need to be able to find the right information with minimal effort so they can consume the information, rather than search for it. A centralized structure will allow a more common infrastructure and interface to the enterprise's information. Central repositories force the adherence to pooling all as much information available to all business units as possible.

CONCLUSION

BI progression within an organization can encounter a great many hurdles on the way to full integration. The organizational hurdles centered on how to structure the BI functions remains somewhat fluid when attempting to place the solution into the dichotomy of centralized/decentralized. In most cases, some centralization is necessary to ensure proper data quality, governance, and help ensure proper usage. The Center of Excellence is built to accomplish these tasks. However, the company's culture can sometimes be strong enough toward a decentralized nature that attempts to centralize BI functions would be a hurdle in itself.

Should BI be centralized? Yes, to an extent. Core functions must be centralized, but consumerist functions like analytical processing can be farmed out to business units, or be housed in a central analytical unit as works best with the company's culture. Wayne Eckerson sums it up well by suggesting decentralizing where you can, but remembering that "… distributing BI capabilities effectively requires a strong center to hold it together" (Eckerson, 2010).

REFERENCES

April, K., & Bessa, J. (2006, April). A critique of the strategic competitive intelligence process within a global energy multinational. *Problems and Perspectives in Management*, 86-99.

Brandel, M. (2010, March 8). *IT centralization is back in fashion.* Retrieved from http://www.reuters.com/article/idUS302398385920100309

Daniel, D. (2007, November 9). *Need for business intelligence grows: Too much information, not enough insight.* Retrieved from http://www.cio.com/article/153500/Need_for_Business_Intelligence_Grows_Too_Much_Information_Not_Enough_Insight

Eckerson, W. (2010, November 1). *Hybrid business intelligence organizations: Managing the trade-offs between central and distributed development.* Retrieved from http://tdwi.org/articles/2010/11/01/hybrid-bi-organizations-managing-the-trade-offs-between-central-and-distributed-development.aspx

Farris, R. (2006, October 12). *Organizing for an enterprise-wide BI and DW capability.* Retrieved from http://www.information-management.com/news/1064959-1.html

Finucane, B. (2010, November 3). *Business intelligence for the masses.* Retrieved from http://www.b-eye-network.com/view/14575

Forbes. (2010). *Managing information in the enterprise: Perspectives for business leaders.* New York, NY: Forbes.

Forrester Consulting. (2009, October 2). *Lean business intelligence - Why and how enterprises are moving to self-service business intelligence.* Retrieved from http://www.cfoinnovation.com/system/files/Lean_Business_Intelligence_Self-Service_BI_SAP.pdf

Heizenberg, J. (2008). Beyond the center of excellence. *Journal of Management Excellence, 3,* 19–23.

Henschen, D. (2008, August). *Seven steps to successful BI competency center.* Retrieved from http://intelligent-enterprise.informationweek. com/showArticle.jhtml?articleID=210200396

IDC. (2008). *Pervasive business intelligence.* Framingham, MA: IDC.

Lavalle, S., Hopkins, M., Lesser, E., Shockley, R., & Kruschwitz, N. (2010). *Analytics: The new path to value.* MIT Sloan Management Review.

TNCR. (2008). People, process, and technology. *Journal of Management Excellence,* 4-5.

Ulrich, W. (2009, February 25). *IT centralization versus decentralization: The trend towards collaborative governance.* Retrieved from http://www.cutter.com/content/trends/fulltext/ updates/2000/09/bttu000901.html

Whiting, R. (2004, April 19). *Centralized intelligence at work.* Retrieved from http://www. informationweek.com/news/software/integration/ showArticle.jhtml?articleID=18901738

This work was previously published in the International Journal of Business Intelligence Research, Volume 2, Issue 4, edited by Richard Herschel, pp. 42-54, copyright 2011 by IGI Publishing (an imprint of IGI Global).

Chapter 11

The Future Talent Shortage Will Force Global Companies to use HR Analytics to Help Manage and Predict Future Human Capital Needs

Carey W. Worth
Consultant, USA

ABSTRACT

During the recent recession the number of jobs lost has been widely publicized. However, lurking among this obvious and simple metric of how human capital is involved in the workforce, there is the need to analyze and predict future talent. As economic conditions are slow to improve, decisions to simply cut the traditional costs, benefits, compensation and headcount are no longer enough. Companies have already started using business intelligence (BI) to transform and maximize the potential of their human capital. The use of human capital based business intelligence (BI) has increasingly become one of the vital strategic components for world-class companies. This paper will focus on why companies should use analytics (a subset of Business Intelligence (BI)) to transform and maximize the potential of their human capital.

INTRODUCTION

Companies should use business intelligence (BI) to transform and maximize the potential of their human capital. The use of human capital based business intelligence (BI) has increasingly become one of the vital strategic components for world class companies. As competition for talented re-

sources intensifies, many senior managers have turned to BI to monitor staffing levels, predict turnover and retain top talent. In the past most software projects focused on automation and other operational efficiencies ahead of BI. Automation projects dealt with process inefficiencies. The key ingredients for human resources based business intelligence have been available for some time

DOI: 10.4018/978-1-4666-2650-8.ch011

now. With the emergence of easy-to-use tools, dashboards, scorecards and web portals BI is starting to offer a host of services. But is that enough? Other key components of an effective human resource based BI platform are a well-defined data management strategy, highly trained business analysts and a single repository for all human resource (HR) data.

Human capital is an important company asset. Senior managers who struggle to get accurate information regarding their associates within a timely manner may miss strategic opportunities. BI allows managers to turn strategy into execution by focusing on elements of workforce success. The four key categories of a successful Human Resource Strategy are Workforce success, Workforce mind-set and culture, Workforce competencies and workforce behaviors (Huselid, Becker, & Beatty, 2005).

Challenges Facing Human Resources

Most if not all managers would agree that "people are our most important asset." But even with this often used proclamation companies still struggle to connect workforce success with its strategic initiative. The current business environments are driven by increased competition and global expansion. A firm's competitive advantage and growth is increasingly being driven by intangible assets such as workforce success not just missed opportunities. Edward Gordon, president of Imperial Consulting Corp. and author of "Winning the Global Talent Showdown", predicts that by 2010 the U.S. labor market will be significantly out of balance with high-paid/high skill jobs accounting for 74% of the U.S. labor market and low-pay/low-skill jobs will account for 26% of the total available jobs. Mr. Gordon believes there will be 123 million people needed for the high-pay/high-skill job but only 50 million people will qualify. He also believes that 44 million people will be needed for low-pay/low skill job and 150 million

people will be available (Gordon, 2009). The inability to recognize the above trends or capitalize on workforce success is in many cases a direct threat to the very existence of an organization.

Three of the most common challenges for managing human resources are:

- **Perspective:** Do all managers understand how human resource capabilities and behaviors drive strategy execution?
- **Metrics:** Have we identified and collected the right measures for human resource success, leadership and workforce behaviors; workforce competencies; and workforce culture and mind-set? (Huselid, Becker, & Beatty, 2005)
- **Execution:** Do our managers have access, capability, and motivation to use data to communicate strategic intent and monitor progress towards strategy execution?

The perspective challenge for human resources deals with management's ability to adopt ideas on how the workforce can be a source of strategic value to the organization. Historically HR managers have put most of their focus on controlling labor cost. With payroll expenses representing 67.30% (Huselid, Becker, & Beatty, 2005) of operating expense, it is easy to understand why companies focus so much on controlling labor cost. Senior managers need to ask a different set of questions to help align human resource performance to the execution of the firm's strategy. The fundamental distinction here is the ability to develop and understand how the workforce contributes versus concentrating on the cost of the workforce. Meeting this challenge would require a firm to think different and to move away from a "one size fits all" workforce strategy. In the same way marketing strategies have segments, HR and workforce management systems are able to differentiate by position and the people who provide a contribution and workforce performance must distinguish between "A" performers and "C" performers.

The metric challenge deals with valuing and measuring an intangible asset referred to as the workforce. For this discussion we are considering intangible assets to be employee skills. We also know that intangible assets are claims to future benefits that do not have a physical or financial embodiment. Developing workforce measures with strategic value is not easy. When most managers think of value or performance, they often look at financial metrics such as ROI or labor cost to sales or training cost as a percentage of operating cost. Financial metrics fall short of providing insight into how the workforce is contributing to the overall strategy. Workforce metrics that measure such workforce attributes as speed, talent, learning, innovation, shared mind-set and accountability are also important to performance against strategic plans. Simply put, intangible assets would allow the firm to have a gr eater level of success executing on strategic initiatives. Firms that place measures on intangible assets have a higher level of strategic capabilities and perform consistently better than those who don't.

Benefits of Business and IT Partnership

The degree to which business and IT can partner together is considered one of the most important aspects of a successful business intelligence implementation. According to a successful BI survey conducted by Howson (2008) (industry analyst and BI consultant), BI Scorecard, 55% identified the business-IT partnership as essential while 53% believe executive level support to be as important (Howson, 2008). These numbers clearly indicate that a lack of partnership has a profound effect on the success of BI projects.

Achieving a great business-IT partnership is not as simple as a parent instructing two siblings, "You will learn to like each other or else". It often requires an understanding of how business and IT professionals are different and what motivates them both. Studies suggest that business profes-

sionals are extroverts while IT professionals are introverts (Huselid, Becker, & Beatty, 2005). These personality traits also suggest that an IT professional approaches decisions from a more logical and in some cases clinical point of view. Business professional however consider more the people impact of their decisions. This does not mean that both business and IT professional are not thinkers. Despite the differences in personalities, one difference that cannot be debated is what motivates both business and IT professionals. Business professionals are motivated and rewarded by behavior that impact increased revenue, return on capital and market share. While IT professional are motivated by behavior that cut cost, increase proficiencies, reduce risk and provides system stability. So how can we bridge the gap between these two personalities?

One way to bridge the gap between business and IT professionals is by cultivating hybrid business-IT people (Howson, 2008). The BI hybrid as we would call it are individuals who have gained proficiencies in both technology and business skills. One of the more recent trends and outcomes of outsourcing IT jobs was that many of the displaced IT professional landed jobs within business units. This did not in itself create the BI hybrid. Business leaders began to recognize the value of having such skilled individuals on their team. One of the major traits of the BI hybrid is that they tend to look for ways to use information technologies as a business enabler. Some companies in addition to a business analyst (BA) role have created a technical analyst (TA) role. While BA role focuses on business requirements, the TA role focuses more on translating business requirements into actionable and proven technology solutions.

In order for BI projects to succeed you must build a solid business-IT partnership. Business intelligence is a combination of people, process, technology and most importantly information. Business-IT can partner in the following three ways:

1. Develop a better understanding of each other. The business should know that IT itself operates like an internal consulting company and that they are both tasked with delivering a common solution at a low cost.
2. IT must become more agile by understanding from a business perspective the short windows of opportunities.
3. Recruit the BI hybrid. By having someone who can speak "techno geeko" and who has strong business acumen will foster a greater business-IT partnership.

Data Collection

Data is the foundation for a good business intelligence platform. One of the key components of a business intelligence application is a data warehouse. Data warehouses are used within the largest and most complex businesses throughout the world. Good decisions are made when all the relevant data is available and easily accessible in one place. The concept of a data warehouse is simple. Data is extracted periodically from transactional systems, also known as source systems. These source systems support the most widely used business processes such as staffing, compensation, learning and other HR functions. The data is collected from the source system on a periodic basic which is usually daily, weekly or monthly. The process of collecting the data is referred to as (ETL) Extract, Transform and Load. Aside from sampling loading data from the source system into the warehouse the process also validates, reformats, reorganizes, summarizes, restructures and supplements with data from other sources.

Many organizations believe that a data warehouse is synonymous with business intelligence. They also believe that if they purchase a sexy BI tool with cool graphs and flashy gadgets that they have the makings of a world class business intelligence environment. Successful business intelligence is influenced by data quality, people, business processes and information analytics. We'll now focus on the importance of data quality.

According to Howson data quality is rated as the most essential item for a successful BI deployment (Howson, 2008). Forty-six percent of respondents of a survey conducted by Howson shows data quality is so important that it often creates a stalemate between IT and the business. IT often insists that data quality issues be resolved within the sources system. Business users believe that data issues lead to a lack of trust and faith in reporting. For example, many of today's companies have grown through mergers and acquisitions. Often times the two newly married companies have different ways on how data is entered into the source system. One system may require that an officer code be entered as part of the associate profile whereas the other system did not have such a mandate. When the ETL team loads the data from the source, null values (or blanks) will be inserted into the database. In this example the officer code is often used to lookup the officer description with the officer master table. Since the code does not exist, the relationship is broken. The reports will now display bad or missing data. The IT department will insist that the reports are displaying correctly because the data is missing from the sources system. In some cases the IT department will enforce a policy requiring all null values be defaulted to some meaningless value. In this case, the null value could be transform to -999 during the ETL process. The master table would be inserted with -999 for the officer code and an officer description such as "No officer Title". There is often a great debate about this technique with the database right wing staffers arguing that the data should be fixed at the source. However, since data quality can destroy a user's confidences within the BI platform, this technique has it merits. Defaulting null values ensures that all underlining database tables maintain their one-to-one relationship. This is important to aggregation operations such as summing and counting. This allows reports to display an accurate count. One other benefit is that this technique supports data validation and cleansing. A business user can run a report for all -999 values to determine how many missing values officer codes require scrubbing. This in itself supports the right wing argument to clean the data at the source.

Global Human Resource Analytics

Today companies are beginning to shift their attention and focus on how to better manage human capital. This is due largely to the belief of a pending human resource talent shortage. Historically HR departments were seen only as a cost center. For example, a recent survey indicates that only 22% of respondents claim that HR is a full partner in developing and implementing business strategy. Less than half (47%) claim that HR does more than simply help implement business strategy once it has been developed (Fitz-enz, 2010). According to the 2010 McKinsey Global Survey, executives worldwide believe that the most important global development within the next five years is the shift of the global economic activity from developed economies to developing economies with the growing number of consumers in emerging markets. Corporate challenges centers on being able to find the right talent to meet the company's strategic goals, particularly because of low birth rates and the aging workforce in many developed countries. The survey found that less than 40% of executives were confident about having the talent needed in the next five years to meet strategic goals. Many are looking for talent in three areas: emerging markets (44%), new talent entering developed labor markets (41%) and talent from developing markets moving to emerging markets (35%) (McKinsey & Company, 2010).

Recently HR managers have turned to the bias free perspective of statistics to help articulate the value of the HR function. With annual spending on learning and development alone estimated to be as high as $100 billion in the United States (Fitz-enz, 2010), human capital analytics as a subset of business analytics has a strong potential for uncovering untapped opportunities for improvements in human performance with

better decisions about future required resources, plans, policies, costs and talent needs. Managers are using business intelligence concepts such as analytics and predictive analysis to change HR service delivery into a value-generating process. This new proposition of value is an example of HR analytics.

Unlike traditional reporting which focuses on the past, HR Analytics is an evolution of metrics that leads to business intelligence and predictability. A simple definition of analytics is "the science of analysis". A practical definition, however, would be that analytics is the process of obtaining an optimal or realistic decision based on existing data (Analytics). Common applications of analytics include the study of business data using statistical analysis in order to discover and understand historical patterns with an eye to predicting and improving business performance in the future. Also, some people use the term to denote the use of mathematics in business. Others agree that analytics includes the use of Operations Research, Statistics and Probability. However, it would be erroneous to limit the field of analytics to only statistics and mathematics (Analytics).

So what is the value of analysis? The power of analysis is in the patterns of data that it uncovers. Patterns are not readily apparent in standard reviews and reports. Analytics is more about structure and logic than about statistical procedures. Large organizations are so complex and their operations so huge that it is virtually impossible for management to see some of the vital connections and influences. By using computing power and analytic tools to mine the data companies can yield vast and varied phenomena. Most managers are reluctant to accept statistical methods and are more comfortable relying on their own judgment. Yet, the experience of managers is contaminated by common human traits of bias, misperception, and faulty memory. In 136 studies of the judgment accuracy of experienced managers, only 8 studies showed that manager predictions were more accurate than simple regression equations applied to the same problems. In a post-study review, the analysts believed that random-sampling errors accounted for the mistakes in the predictive power of statistics and that actually regression beat manager memory every time (Fitz-enz, 2010).

Cost, time, quantity, quality, and human reaction are the five ways to measure business. There are also five steps for analytics. Step one: involves recording the work or business process. For human resource processes this includes staffing, compensation, talent management and training and development. HR services can add value by providing metrics such as associate turnover, speed of onboarding and the correlation between associate satisfaction and customer retention. Step two: deals with organizational goals such as product quality, innovation, productivity and customer service. HR services can add value by providing metrics and analytics that sets and predict targets using internal data. Step three: compares our results to other competitors also known as benchmarking. During this step we compare our metrics with those of our peers. Step four: tries to understand past behavior and outcomes also known as descriptive analytics. This step is the first level of true analysis. Here we begin to see from the trends from the past. Step five: predicts future likelihood also known as predictive analytics. This form of analysis compares what happened yesterday to what will probably happen in the future. Human resources can apply it to decisions about the expected return on human capital investments in hiring, training, and planning.

It is not uncommon for capital-intensive companies to use statistical analysis. They know that their cost structure can be improved by using predictive analytics. Predictive analytics expresses the future in terms of probabilities. With human capital expenses representing as much as 30% of operating cost, unfortunately predictive analysis is hardly used. Companies need to move away from metrics and simple statistical analysis (sum, average and etc.) and shift towards predictions and optimization. Fitz-enz (2010) shows the progres-

sion from basic reporting to predictability and optimization. Simple metrics alone do little to help managers make effective decisions. Even with data warehouses collecting information from enterprise resource planning (ERP) and HR transactional systems and with complex integration, query and reporting tools, most companies are still limited with hindsight reporting. The more competitive and global business becomes the more you need forecasting, predictability and advanced modeling.

Correlation and causation are the two terms that companies need to understand when using predictive analysis. Correlation is when two events move in the same direction concurrently. An upward movement is viewed as a positive relationship and a downward movement is considered a negative relationship. Causation uses a number of independent variables to determine if the interrelationship of all variables can predict a likely outcome. For example, within a HR service like staffing, there are multiple inputs such as applicant sources, background, education and prior employment data to predict the quality of the new hire. How important would it be if you can hire the best talent on the market when you need them, pay them at market levels, build their skills to suit your needs and then retain talent them. Would it be useful to truly know what is likely to happen when you make investment decisions?

UnitedHealth Group (UHG) a leading health-care organization began using predictive analytics to improve care and HR concerns in an increasingly challenging environment. UHG is one of the largest health-care operators in the United States, with access to more than 340,000 physicians and 3,200 hospitals, and whose policyholders submit tens of thousands of health claims and related documents daily. UHG's mission is to explore innovations in health care that help people live healthier lives. The company consists of five distinct business segments and offers services ranging from network-based health-care coverage for small, medium, and large companies; to global drug development and marketing services for the pharmaceutical and biotech industries; to investment capital for start-up and early stage companies that operate in the areas of health and well-being.

Michelle Fernando, Manager, International Recruitment Operations, states that UHG faces human capital management challenges that includes, improving the quality of care and patient satisfaction while decreasing costs in an environment where hiring is an ongoing concern (Fitz-enz, 2010).

In the health-care industry, human resources (HR) challenges can be very complex. The issue of hiring and retention in the health-care industry is a major concern because of a shortage of qualified medical personnel such as nurses. In addition, the 24/7, year-round nature of the industry creates unique full-time and part-time employment problems that need to be solved. Workforce performance management systems for recruiting, hiring and retaining top talent can help the financial and operational performance. UHG decided that it needed to migrate to a talent management solution developed by Taleo. This software leveraged predictive metrics for hiring and retention. One area the company needed to focus was on its international hires, especially within its India offices. "The recruiting culture in India is very volatile; career opportunities and turnover rates are very high in a highly specialized health-care industry. It's a unique business with specific skill sets. It was a challenge for us to engage the employees, keep them happy, and give them reasons to stay," says Fernando. "In these offices in particular, we were looking for innovative ways to boost internal hiring percentages to improve overall staff retention. Using analytics helped us get a handle on the issues and gave us clear ways to measure and improve our processes" (Fitz-enz, 2010).

Using the Taleo platform to develop its International Recruitment Operations Dashboard, a self-service interactive web base portal that allowed employees to easily view and download relevant HR information. This system allowed the recruiting staff to analysis data to insure the right resources and skills are available to execute a successful hiring and retention strategy, to ensure the system helped capture the desired job knowledge metrics and requirements and the ability match them to the skills, competencies, and knowledge of the candidates within the HRIS data warehouse. UHG uses four metrics or measurements: quality of hire, source of hire, percentage of internal hires, and system utilization. These metrics enable them to ensure competent, qualified staff and high staff-retention rates. For example, the "quality of hire" measurement is crucial for the company to determine that the employees hired are the right people and a good fit from a cultural, productivity, and experience perspective. This system also helps the company improve employee retention and reduce the number of short-team hires. UHG has seen a reduction in first-year attrition rates. In terms of "source of hire," having an enterprise data warehouse allowed the company to easily streamline its global hiring practices by being able to trace back to the original source to weed out poor recruitment practices and firms. For example, the system now allows the organization to track and monitor data such as the specific career fairs or organizations that have provided a successful candidate in the past. "Using a predictive analytical model, we can better analyze the employers that people came from and the sources we hired from. As a result, we can determine if there's a specific company that has a high percentage of quality of hires and we then know that that's a company we may want to target. In terms of sourcing and recruitment, this is useful information for us, as it may lead to better hires in the future," says Fernando (Fitz-enz, 2010).

Effective Use of Enterprise Level Dashboards

Performance dashboards have become the preferred way for senior business executives, managers and staff to effectively monitor key business metrics quickly by providing actionable information at a glance. A performance dashboard is a layered information delivery system that parcels out information, insights and alerts to users on demand so they can measure, monitor, and manage business performance more effectively (Eckerson, 2011). A performance dashboard is made up of the following three separate applications: monitoring, analysis and management. The monitoring application allows an organization to view performance against key business processes and metrics that align to a business strategy. The analysis application enables companies to explore data across many dimensions allowing them to determine root cause, discover trends and predict future outcomes. The manage application supports a variety of features that foster collaboration and decision making. In addition to the three applications, performance dashboards also consist of three layers of information. Each successive layer provides additional details, views, and perspectives that enable users to understand a problem better and identify the steps they need to take to address it. This layered approach (known as the MAD framework) gives users self-service access to information and conforms to the natural sequence in which users want to handle that information: monitor, analyze and drill to detail. The layered approach helps users more easily get to the root cause of issues quicker. It also helps IT systems deliver information quickly by providing successive drill down path that reduces query row counts. For example, instead of allowing users to download large volumes of data that must be reconstructed for analysis this framework provides summary information with the ability to drill to the needed detail data. There are three types of performance dashboards: operational, tactical and strategic.

Operational dashboards provide detail data to front-line workers for managing and controlling operational processes. Tactical dashboards enable executives to monitor and manage operational processes across peer groups within the company. Strategic dashboards (also known as balance scorecards) monitor the execution of strategic initiatives. Table 1 displays each type of performance dashboard emphasize the three layers and applications described above to different degrees.

The benefits of performance dashboards within the HR service function are:

- **Communicating Strategy:** HR system for measuring and tracking pay for performance initiatives often use a 9 box grid ranking associates based on what they have achieved and how they achieved it.
- **Increase Motivation:** The HR function is often responsible for conducting associate satisfaction surveys with monitoring metrics such as associate engagement. These metrics are used as a benchmark to compare how satisfied a company's associates are compared to other companies.
- **Consistent View of the Firm Workforce:** HR often provides metrics such headcount, number of FTEs, turnover as well as di-

Table 1. Performance dashboard with the three layers and applications (adapted from Eckerson, 2011)

	Operational	Tactical	Strategic
Purpose	Monitor operations	Measure progress	Execute strategy
Users	Supervisors, specialists	Managers, analysts	Executives, managers, staff
Scope	Operational	Departmental	Enterprise
Information	Detailed	Detailed/summary	Detailed/summary
Updates	Intra-day	Daily/weekly	Monthly/quarterly
Emphasis	Monitoring	Analysis	Management

versity. These metrics allow managers to quickly perform trend analysis regarding their workforce and take action to reduce workforce risk.

The Business Need for HR Analytics

The current recession has made it even more critical for companies large and small to make employee retention and development a major business focus to ensure that valuable employees are not lost as the labor markets begins to improve. As firms begin the transition from retrenchment to growth they have an opportunity to excel (not just survive) and be even more competitive in the marketplace. During past economic downturns, firm focus only on cutting costs such as training, benefits, compensation and workforce headcount. While firms have continued this trend during this recession, they have also begun to use internal data to perform analysis to determine which employees are achieving their performance goals and to see which employees have the core competencies to help the firm build future competitive advance.

The CedarCrestone 2010-2011 Workforce Technologies Survey, for the first time introduced a new category referred to as workforce optimization. The applications in this category include: workforce planning, workforce analytics,

predictive analytics, labor budgeting, and mobile analytics. These applications are not widely adopted across all organizations (17% average), but large organizations with over 10,000 employees are the strongest adopters (22%) (Martin, 2010).

Workforce optimization (Figure 1) is a category of technologies and associated practices that will enable companies to determine and execute the best course of action for new or predicted workforce challenges to strategies and goals that impact an organization's business strategy. The CedarCrestone survey shows that workforce management adoption is positively correlated with net income growth. Those at the highest level of workforce management adoption including time and attendance, absence management, labor scheduling and labor budgeting have 38% net income growth compared to those without that high level of adoption and associated practices (21%). In addition, those organizations with greater than average talent management applications more frequently have career development, learning management, recruiting and compensation management applications also have higher sales per employee (Martin, 2010).

A new term within HR talent analytics called leading practices has emerged. The definition of the leading practice of talent analytics includes:

Figure 1. Workforce optimization usage

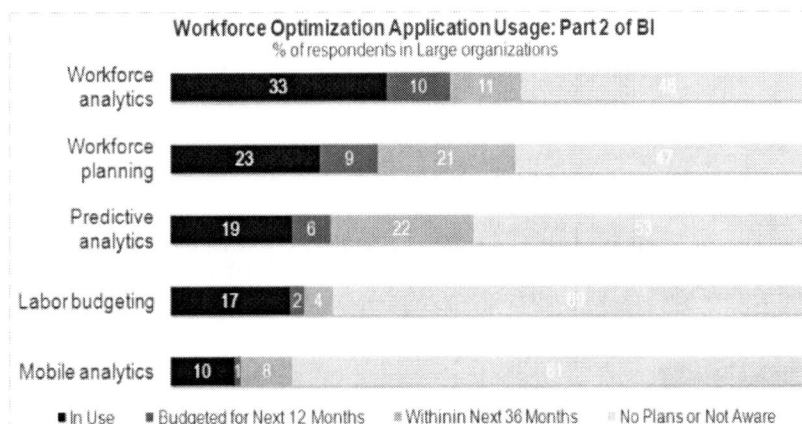

- Employees and managers are supported with automated tools to manage their competencies.
- Competencies are used in planning, recruiting, development and compensation activities.
- Reporting and analysis tools to support analyzing talent management processes are available and ideally used directly by line managers who are also able to analyze worker performance with data integrated from other sources.
- The organization is able to measure ROI based on the impact on the organization, not just HR, in all areas of talent management through an integrated view of the various talent management processes (Martin, 2010).

Leading practices for workforce optimization indicates on a scale from 1 to 15, large companies are 6.5 more likely to use business intelligence applications. 47% of large companies use workforce analytics and 29% have predictive analytics (Martin, 2010). 31% of managers within large organizations have access to business intelligence applications such as Oracle E-Business Suite or PeopleSoft HCM.

Do not forget the causal links between associate satisfaction, customer satisfaction and profits by analyzing associate engagement (also known as associate satisfaction). Companies identified as having enthusiastic employees out-performed average companies in the stock market by more than two and a half times, and blazed ahead of companies with unenthusiastic employees by more than five times (Sirota, 2005). The Gallup organization conducted research on the value of employee engagement with the following findings:

- Engaged employees average 27% less absenteeism than those who are actively disengaged.

- Organizations with a surplus of disengaged employees suffer 31% more turnover than those with a critical mass of engaged associates. This alone could lead to higher cost of employee acquisition.
- Workgroups with high disengagement lose 51% more inventory to shrink than those with high engagement.
- The chance of a disengaged worker having an accident on a given day are substantially higher than those of his engaged colleagues. The workgroups whose engagement puts them in the bottom quartile of the Gallup database average 62% more accidents than the workgroups in the top quartile (Harter, 2006).

Integrating Business Intelligence with HR Analytics

Vendors such as Oracle and SAP have begun to integrate their business intelligence platform with other key analytical applications. Oracle HR Analytics with its tight integration between Oracle's business intelligence enterprise edition (OBIEE) and the transaction system enables organizations to close the loop on HR issues such as turnover, headcount and talent management. Oracle's HR analytics has analytical workflows and embedded decision support as a key part of its user interface (Oracle Corporation, 2009). The analytical workflow that comes pre-built with the Oracle HR Analytics product addresses the objective of ensuring that Human Capital is leveraged properly, guiding the user from the summary level to detail stored in the Human Resources transactional system. It helps HR managers and executives answer questions about turnover, learning, compensation and staffing. It starts at the highest level – the Business Objective/Issue level and then guides users to explore the issue by enabling them to drill down from that high level to see the turnover data underneath. The KPI dashboard is created based on the companies threshold limits for turnover. A user can easily see that turnover is trending negative by the red highlighted alert. The user can drill into details to determine why turnover is increasing.

Oracle Human Resources Analytics offers the following seven subject areas: absence, compensation, HR performance, learning enrollment and completion, recruiting, US statutory compliance and workforce performance. It also includes nine dashboards, over 200 reports, over 300 metrics and more than 600 dimensional attributes (Oracle Corporation, 2009).

CONCLUSION

Global competition, market volatility and declining labor pools make investing in people a high risk gamble. Still, future success is dependent primarily on your company's ability to attract, retain and productively manage a shrinking pool of talented, motivated people.

By using HR analytics, organizations become more effective in managing and improving the performance of human capital and in the process become more competitive and profitable. HR analytics helps an organization improve its profitability through more effective workforce cost control, balancing the lowest effective headcount while ensuring satisfactory service delivery. This is very appealing to managers at all levels. Managers can now analyze top and bottom-performing employees to better develop and retain key talent pools addressing any retention trouble spots or looming gaps in needed competencies. Both executives and managers alike can better understand the causal effect of workforce investment on operational results. For example, balancing contact center performance such as average cost per call and abandonment rates with and without additional training to customer satisfaction levels and service delivery costs.

As global economic conditions are slow to improve, decisions to simply cut the traditional costs, benefits, compensation and headcount are not enough. To state it plainly, the forces driving economic growth still exist. From government interventions to newly discovered ideas and innovations major economic growth will happen again. Leading the way will be talented human capital. The inability to measure human capital and predict key metrics will become a competitive disadvantage.

REFERENCES

Eckerson, W. (2011). *Performance dashboards* (pp. 101–105). New York, NY: John Wiley & Sons.

Fitz-enz, J. (2010). *The new HR analytics: Predicting the economic value of your company's human capital investments* (p. 230). New York, NY: AMACOM.

Gordon, E. (2009). *Winning the global talent showdown*. Retrieved from http://www.shrm.org/Research/FutureWorkplaceTrends/Pages/WinningGlobalTalentShowdown.aspx

Harris, T. H., & Davenport, J. G. (2007). *Competing on analytics*. Boston, MA: Harvard Business School Publishing.

Harter, R., & Wagner, J. K. (2006). *The elements of great managing*. Washington, DC: Gallup Press.

Howson, C. (2010). *Successful business intelligence: Secrets to making a BI a killer app* (pp. 115–119). New York, NY: McGraw-Hill.

Huselid, M. A., Becker, B. E., & Beatty, R. W. (2008). *The workforce scorecard*. Boston, MA: Harvard Business School Publishing.

Martin, L. (2010). *Director research and analytics: Organizations adopting workforce optimization technologies deliver strong results.* Alpharetta, GA: CedarCrestone.

McKinsey & Company. (2010). Five forces re-shaping the global company. *McKinsey Quarterly.*

Oracle Corporation. (2009). *HR analytics: Driving return on human capital investment.* Retrieved from http://www.oracle.com/us/products/applications/045039.pdf

Sirota, D., Mischkind, L. A., & Meltzer, M. I. (2005). *The enthusiastic employee: How companies profit by giving workers what they want.* Philadelphia, PA: Wharton School Publishing.

This work was previously published in the International Journal of Business Intelligence Research, Volume 2, Issue 4, edited by Richard Herschel, pp. 55-65, copyright 2011 by IGI Publishing (an imprint of IGI Global).

Section 2
Analytic Issues

Chapter 12
Intelligent Analytics:
Integrating Business Intelligence and Web Analytics

Lakshmi S. Iyer
The University of North Carolina at Greensboro, USA

Rajeshwari M. Raman
Market America, USA

ABSTRACT

Organizations use web analytic tools and technologies to measure, collect, analyze, and report web usage data to help optimize websites. Traditionally, most of this data tends to be non-transactional and non-identifiable. In this regard, there has not been much integration with transactional data that is collected, stored, analyzed, and reported through Business Intelligence (BI). Emerging trends in web analytics provide organizations the ability to aggregate and analyze web analytics data with transactional data to provide valuable insights for building better customer relationship strategies. In this paper, the authors give an overview of web analytics tools, key players, new technology trends and capabilities to integrate web analytics with BI so organizations can leverage intelligent analytics for new marketing initiatives. While the benefits are significant, there are some challenges associated with the integration and a few possible solutions to address.

INTRODUCTION

To thrive in the competitive market place, it is important for organizations to device strategies to stay ahead of the competition (Fleisher & Bensoussan, 2003). In order to do so, it is important that decisions made by businesses are sound and based on reliable and accurate data (Davenport, 2010). Business Intelligence (BI), a broad set of technology, applications and processes that help gather, store, access, and analyze data assist organizations make better business decisions (Gartner, 2009). Through quality decision making, the goal of BI is to help improve a company's performance and promote its competitive advantage in the marketplace (Wixom & Watson, 2010).

DOI: 10.4018/978-1-4666-2650-8.ch012

In the past fifteen years, the emergence of Internet based technologies has expanded the way in which companies gather data and make business decisions. With every instance of consumer's web use, companies gather tremendous amounts of consumer behavior data based on site visits, purchases, and user experience feedback. While applications that provide decision support are generally defined as analytics, (Davenport, 2006), the Web Analytics Association defines web analytics as "the measurement, collection, analysis and reporting of Internet data for the purposes of understanding and optimizing Web usage" (www.waa.org). Organizations that gain competitive edge in the current market place successfully integrate online channel with all aspects of its business processes. While web analytics originally focused on measuring website traffic and optimizing web pages, current trends focus on using and analyzing the data for business and market research (Bhatnagar, 2009). Hamel (2009) provides a broader definition of web analytics as "extensive use of quantitative and qualitative data (primarily, but not limited to online data), statistical analysis, explanatory (e.g., multivariate testing) and predictive models (e.g., behavioral targeting), business process analysis and fact-based management to drive a continuous improvement of online activities; resulting in higher ROI." (p. 2). Web analytics, thus, is an emerging discipline that is changing rapidly as technologies and methodologies evolve to capture even more detailed, revealing data about how customers interact with a site's web content (Halvorson, 2009). As we progress through this emerging transformation, it is important to understand the similarities and differences between web analytics and BI and see where the synergies lie between the two that an organization can capitalize on for competitive advantage.

Web analytics and traditional BI tend to differ slightly in their goals. Web analytics aims to measure non-transactional and non-personally identifiable activities, BI relies heavily on historical transactional data where customers are identified. Use of web logs as traditional means of gathering data for web analytics is changing with the introduction of page tagging that can help distinguish between automated, masked, and actual users that visit a site and gather data on page views. Tagging techniques can be done such that it will not break the user experience and hence the business data. To gain the competitive edge in the market place, organizations should explore ways to empower marketing and IT to integrate BI and web analytics to identify potential opportunities for growth. The market for web analytics has grown significantly over the past few years and B2B magazine reports that by 2014 it is expected to grow to US$953 million from US$252 million in 2004 (Nakano 2009; Chatham, Tempkin, & Backer, 2004). One aspect of this growing trend is connected and integrated analytics: Connected analytics means that a website's content management system (CMS) and other applications are linked via page tags through third party solutions. Integrated analytics on the other hand focus on applications that include metric tools to automate communication between website and analytics software (Nakano, 2009). Using appropriate tools and strategies to integrate and mine both historic transaction data and current web usage data can provide actionable insights to organizations. The synergy between BI and Web Analytics should result in facilitating intelligent analytics that can give a leading edge to organizations proactive in doing so.

In this article, we first present an overview of web analytics including the methods, tools, and key players in the area. We follow that with a brief coverage of traditional BI and show were some of the gaps and opportunities lie for integration. Trends and capabilities for integration of web analytics and BI are then presented. We conclude with benefits and challenges of intelligent analytics.

WEB ANALYTICS: AN OVERVIEW

To do business effectively online, both, hybrid organizations and pure digital, need to continually refine and optimize their web-based marketing strategy, site navigation, and content. In order to optimize online strategies and remain competitive, organizations must be able to understand what aspects of the website are functioning well and what is below expectations. Web Analytics help organizations gather both offsite and onsite analytics data (Clifton, 2010a) and provide the tools to benchmark the effects. In this section, we first discuss how web analytics work, the current state of the art and key players. For a detailed discussion on web analytics please refer Kaushik (2007).

How it Works?

Web Analytics is used to measure user Internet activity to allow companies to more effectively design their content and maintain a competitive advantage (Rizzotto, 2007). Web analytic tools generally fall into two categories: offsite and onsite tools (Clifton, 2010a). Offsite web analytic tools help measure the potential website audience and hence the opportunity for an organization to grow. Onsite web analytic tools complement those metrics by helping measure the actual visitor traffic on the site and the website's performance. Figure 1 show how offsite and onsite tools work in tandem to gather information about a website's performance and benchmark its efforts.

Offsite web analytic tools include the resources available on the Internet, either free or paid, that help to determine the size of the potential audience, performance of competitors and users' sentiments regarding the firm's website and products that can help provide competitive advantage to the firm. These include tools like Nielson ratings, websites like Quantcast.com and Compete.com that provide comparative analysis of different websites, different Web 2.0 technologies like social media that provide invaluable information about the buzz surrounding the website.

Figure 1. Offsite and onsite web analytics

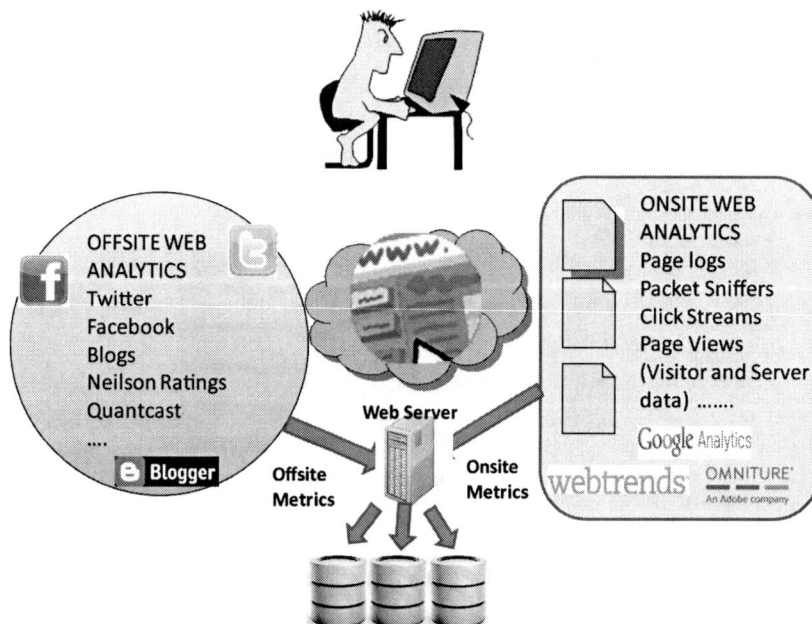

On the other hand, onsite web analytics help to track a user's behavior once they get on the website including the primary drivers of conversion. Primary onsite web analytic methods include log file analysis, page tagging, click analytics, packet sniffing and some hybrid methods.

Log File Analysis: Interprets data from a web server to measure the amount of unique users visiting a site and the specific areas of the site visited. Thus a web log analyzer could interpret how many visits and page views were made on a particular site. This is an inexpensive way for a company to perform an analysis of its content effectiveness because the data exists on its web server (Clifton, 2010b). Though third party services exist to perform this measure, free software allows companies with IT departments to perform this in house. Several factors make the accuracy of this form questionable. First, the invention of search engine spiders for web browser optimization and the lack of unique IP addresses make it difficult for log file analysis to distinguish actual users (IPInfoDB, 2009). In addition, web caches, local data utilized to speed up browsing, may prevent a browser from accessing content again. Jansen (2006) presents the strengths and limitations of transaction log analysis as a research method.

Page Tagging: A form of web analytics where JavaScript tags are written into a web page, cueing a browser to download a unique identifier called a cookie. This would allow the server to distinguish between automated, masked, and actual users that visit a site and gather data on page views. In addition, the server is also able to gain detailed information about the user and the pages they have visited and accessed (Clifton, 2010b). This is the information that allows savvy web designers to better market to users by banners and site suggestions based upon browser history. Most forms of page tagging are done by third party vendors though emergent technology and increased competition has greatly decreased the cost of implementing this form of analytics. New browser technology that blocks cookies and allows for private browsing has made this a less accurate form; therefore more creative ways of page tagging are being developed.

Hybrid Methods: Collect data using both log file analysis and page tagging. These methods are usually more accurate than either of the above methods on its own.

Packet Sniffing: Another sophisticated onsite web analytic tool, packet sniffing, is a network based data collection method where there are no logs or tags to monitor. Both software or a hardware, or combination of both, is used over the data layer in the web server and all traffic to the server is routed via this layer. When a user enters a URL in the browser, the request passes through the packet sniffer layer which collects additional information about the user such as attributes of the request and in addition, stores information transmitted back to the user. Ganguly (2010) provides a good overview of benefits and limitations of packet sniffing. The biggest limitation is doing a thorough review of the data collected against the privacy policy to ensure guidelines are met.

Click Analytics: A special type of web analytics that give special attention to clicks either on banners or on content itself. These clicks can be gathered in two ways; a click can be logged when it occurs and this information can be captured by the system or all pageviews can be considered to be results of clicks and hence the page views are logged. This is used in conjunction with log file analysis. Analysis of click stream data has inherent problems associated with data quality, size of data, and choice of metrics (Sen, Dattis, & Pattichis, 2006).

Tools for Web Analytics

Most companies use tools from Google Analytics, Omniture Site Catalyst, Webtrends, Clicktracks, or Xiti that primarily use data collected by a hybrid of web logs and JavaScript tags to understand what is happening on their websites.

In the past, only large companies could afford Web analytics tools. A few free web log–based solutions existed, but they were hard to implement and needed a good deal of IT caring and feeding; thus presenting a high barrier to entry for most businesses. In the recent years, the introduction of free Google Analytics tools was one of the biggest changes in this emergent technology arena. Google Analytics promoted a massive data democracy in a way that anybody could quickly add a few lines of JavaScript code to the footer file on their website and possess an easy-to-use reporting tool. Since then the number of people focusing on web analytics in the world grew exponentially from a few thousand to hundreds of thousands very quickly; and the field has still a lot of room to grow.

In 2008, Yahoo! acquired IndexTools, contributing to the growth of this technology. Yahoo! took a commercial enterprise web analytics tool, cleverly rebranded it as Yahoo! Web Analytics and provided it free to their current customers. Many more free tools became available, including small innovators such as Crazy Egg, free open source tools such as Piwik and open web analytics or niche tools such as MochiBot to track flash files. Some very affordable tools also entered the market, such as Mint, which costs just $30 and uses web logs to report data.

A search on Google today for free web analytics tools results in 49 million results, a testament to the popularity of all these types of tools (Kaushik, 2009). The free tools have put pressure on the commercial web analytics vendors to become better and more innovative. The competitive pressures resulted in some vendors struggling to keep up, and while a few have gone under, the ones that remain today have become more sophisticated and offer a multitude of associative solutions.

Nowadays, it is possible to not only measure the outcomes from web analytics tools, but also more robust outcomes from social media efforts such as blogs and twitter. Inexpensive online tools allow users to do card sorts, an expensive option

offline, to get rapid customer input into redesigns on websites' information architecture made effective by a huge number of free survey tools that are now available. The world of competitive intelligence has had a massive explosion in the past four years with tools that can transform businesses, such as Compete, as well as Google's Ad Planner and insights for search and Quantcast. Next, we discuss the key players in the web analytics area.

Key Players

The web analytics industry is considered to be in the growth phase. Currently, 78% of the market share in the industry is dominated by free tools. When businesses do pay for analytics, up to 37% of them do so as part of a free offering. Thus, the industry is considered highly competitive with relatively low profit margins. The industry is currently estimated to be worth $363 million with compounded annual growth over the next five years expected at 17.5% reaching a value of approximately $953 million by 2014 (Lager, 2009). An overview of the industries current major players is presented below:

Omniture is a leading Web Analytics Company based in Orem, Utah with revenues of $296 million dollars in 2008. While this was an increase of 106% from 2007 revenue, the company still posted a net operating loss of $43.1 million. Employing 1,189 people Omniture operates in North America, Europe, Asia and Australia providing online business optimization through its Sitecatalyst, Omniture DataWarehouse, Omniture discover, and Omniture Searchcenter software. Omniture began as SuperStats.com in 1998 and shortly thereafter changed its name to MyComputer.com. Later the company changed its name to Omniture and formed a strategic reseller partnership with Saxotech to integrate Omniture's web analytics software with Saxotech's online publishing platform. From 2006-2007 Omniture focused on strengthening its portfolio by purchasing several web analytics patents from IBM, forming several strategic partnerships, and acquiring Touch Clarity Limited and Visual Sciences (DataMonitor, 2009). Today, the company is owned by Adobe.

TeaLeaf is also a player in the web analytics market. A spin off from SAP, TeaLeaf differentiates itself from its competitors by offering the ability to capture session data in a searchable and re-playable format. This allows site owners to view the steps users made through their site in a movie like form. The majority of tools on the market focus on group behavior and visitor trends while TeaLeaf, thorough its TeaLeaf CX software, allows companies to simplify the complex interactions users face. The software, which retails for around $80,000, was developed as part of SAP AGs skunk works program. In its largest spin off at the time, SAP spun TeaLeaf off in 1999 only to see the company fall into near obscurity after the dot.com collapse (CBR, 2006). Today the company is privately held by a consortium of private equity firms and counts Wells Fargo, US Airways, Abercrombie and Fitch, Geico, and Comcast amongst its customers. The most recent versions of its software offers advanced segmentation tools, drag and drop reporting, and the ability to identify real-time patterns of behaviors that signify customer struggles (TeaLeaf, n.d.).

Unica, a Massachusetts based company founded in 1992, focuses exclusively on the needs of marketers. The company seeks to streamline the marketing processes of relationship marketing, online marketing and marketing operations through a comprehensive enterprise marketing management or EMM suite. Unica's EMM offers marketers the capability to capture, record, and manage customer and site data while managing the complexities and processes of marketing through a single platform. The EMM incorporates self-service analytics allowing for rapid testing of campaigns as well as behavioral data to uncover unspoken customer intentions. The company recorded revenue of $101 million in 2009 and net income of negative $22 million (Unica Corporation, 2009).

Webtrends is also considered to be a major player in the web analytics field. By demanding greater security and different metrics, Webtrends has differentiated itself from consumer web analytics offerings. The newest version of its software, Webtrends 9, offers the ability to transform analytic reports into narratives for use in reports and presentations (Walling, 2009). In addition, the company offers the ability to analyze trends across mobile applications and Facebook (Webtrends, n.d.).

In 2005 Google acquired Urchin Software Corporation creating what is now known as Google Analytics. Offering the ability to integrate its analytics software with its portfolio of other web products including; AdWords, AdSense, Website Optimizer, and Webmaster tools provides Google with a strong share of the analytics market. Their tools offer the ability to compare multiple forms of media across channels including flash, video, and social networking sites. Additionally, Google analytics offers a colorful and highly customizable dashboard and various visualization tools (Google, 2010).

TRADITIONAL BI: A SILO VIEW

There is no doubt about the importance of BI to firms. Every year, Gartner surveys top CIOs about their most important technology initiatives and every year from 2007 -2009, BI has been at the top (Gartner, 2009). Watson (2009) defines BI as "a broad category of applications, technologies, and processes for gathering, storing, accessing, and analyzing data to help business users make better decisions." (p. 487). Traditional BI systems provide organizations with insights for competitive action in the form of improved business processes or better pricing decisions based on historic, transactional data (Barone, Myopoulus, Jiamg, & Amyot, 2010).

Most BI environments consist of a source system (ERP, web data, customer data) that provides transactional data to the data repository (data warehouses, data marts) (Yermish, Miori, Yi, Malhorta, & Klimberg, 2010). This data is extracted, cleaned and loaded into the data repository systems using data integration technologies. This data would be made accessible to the end user using data access technologies like SQL queries, dashboards and Excel who can then use it to make business decisions.

Like most of IT, Business Intelligence is a changing technology that is driven by changes in technology, business needs and business processes. Watson (2009), in his tutorial on "BI: Past, present and future," indentifies the following as the most popular new trends in BI:

- **Pervasive BI:** When more and more users within a firm are enabled to use a BI system.
- **Operational BI:** This is the use of real time data rather than historic data in BI systems which makes it possible to make operational decisions in real time and which can also be used in interactive customer relationship management (CRM). This is one of the biggest trends and can be considered to be a paradigm shift in Business Intelligence.
- **The Bi-Based Organization:** For many firms, BI has gone from an optional technology to a requirement for them to function in the competitive landscape. For these firms like Harrah's Entertainment and Continental Airlines, BI plays a very significant role in their day to day operations and is a crucial contributing factor to their success (Wixom & Watson, 2010).
- **Scalability:** This is a BI system's ability to handle more data, more users and larger, more complex queries without a degradation of performance.

Even though the new trends in BI have it possible to use real time rather than historic data, it is still all transactional data (Beasty, 2006; Leon, 2001; Truviso, 2010) whereas Web Analytics typically capture only non- transactional, non- personally identifiable data. Organizations still have a silo view of analyzing transactional data and even in recent discussions; there is little evidence of looking at an integrated view of data analytics (Coghlan, Diehl, Karson, Liberatore, Luo, Nydick, Pollack-Johnson, & Wagner, 2010). Although, the executives interviewed in their study do recognize the importance of web analytics to organizations and have a "strong need for people who knew Web Analytics," (Coghlan et al., 2010, p. 7) New trends in Web Analytics have the ability to integrate non- transactional data with the transactional data of BI (Truviso, 2010) thus leading to "Intelligent Analytics". We discuss such trends and capabilities next.

INTELLIGENT ANALYTICS: TRENDS AND CAPABILITIES

Existing web analytics can be integrated with traditional BI with several upcoming new trends and technological developments such as multivariate testing, ability to integrate with social media, ad provider and email campaigns. The technological developments are described below and Figure 2 shows a schematic for the potential for intelligent analytics.

Technological Developments to Enable Intelligent Analytics

Integration with Social Media to Track the Performance of the Brand Across all Social Media: Social media channels are increasingly utilized by their customers and target audiences, but companies have typically struggled to measure and understand the importance and impact of these channels, such as popular social networking

Figure 2. A schematic representation that shows potential for intelligent analytics

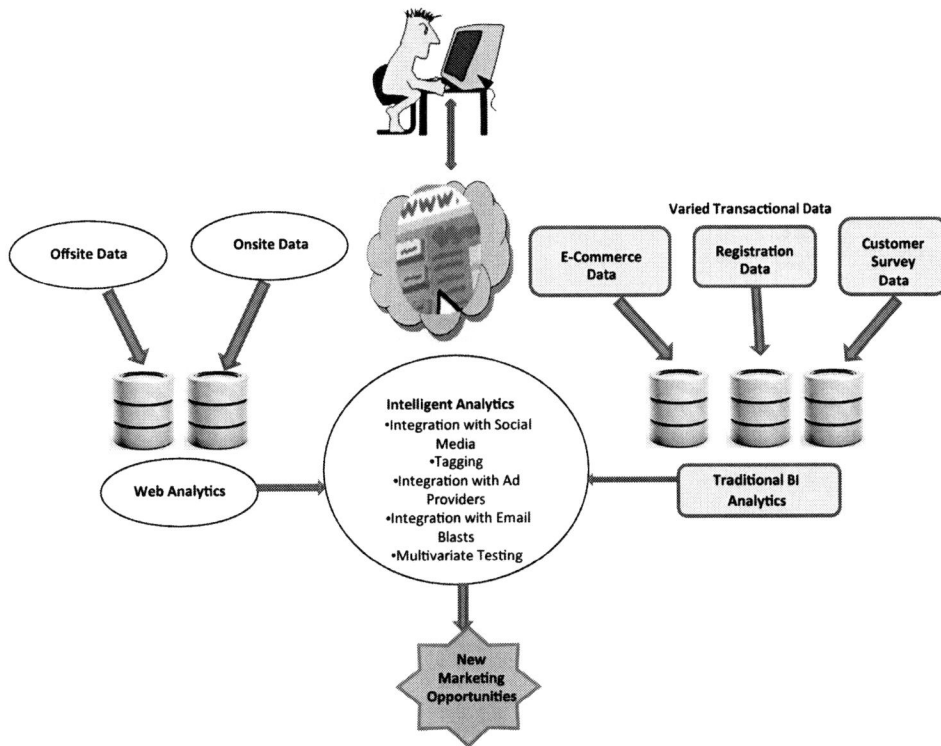

sites like Facebook and MySpace or social news aggregations services such as Digg, on brand awareness, marketing initiatives and business performance. But now, using web analytics, they can leverage the social media measurement and analytics capabilities of different analytics tools and deliver more actionable insight into social media activity, performance and impact (Truviso, 2010). This can work on two separate levels. On the one hand, the firm can track the performance of its fan pages, apps, etc by integrating its web analytics application with social media. This can be used for brand monitoring, to measure the efficacy of FaceBook apps and measure the popularity of fan pages, etc. On the other hand, this can be used to provide an electronic footprint of the customers and extract valuable information on how the firm's customers interact with different social networks. Managers can determine what the typical social networking websites frequented by their target

audience are, who among their segmented users are "influencers", who has the most friends or connections so that they can create their social media campaigns around this information.

Integration with Different Advertisement Providers such as DoubleClick and 24/7 Media: One of the latest trends is the integration of web analytics software with ad management platforms like DoubleClick and Open Ad Stream in order to combine the technology and business intelligence to optimally monetize ad inventory and thus lower operational costs while serving targeted campaigns to a segmented population. This integration can help leverage the analytics data to create behavioral and demographic segments and then create targeted banners and serve them to the relevant segments. Geo-targeting (serving local ads based on the user's location) is an example of how this integration can be used (Omniture, 2010).

Integration with Email Blast Systems to Measure the Performance of Email Campaigns: Web analytics can be used in conjunction with email marketing systems to track the performance of email blasts. By integrating email marketing with web analytics, we can estimate the actual value of the email campaign (by tracking the users' actions after the clicked through the email and landed on the website) rather than just immediate conversions and can use this information to develop future campaigns.

Multivariate Testing: In the context of Internet marketing, multivariate testing is a process "by which more than one component of a website may be tested in a live environment," (Wikipedia, 2010). This is usually employed to try different initiatives on a web site simultaneously and to see which one has the best conversion rate. Web analytics software can be used to determine which of the different variations was the most popular and thus help the decision makers in determining the ideal content and look and feel of the website. One example of such a tool is Test&Target from Omniture (www.omniture.com).

Essential Capabilities

While the following may not be an exhaustive list of capabilities, they are at least essential ones for the next level of analytics, i.e. intelligent analytics, integrating traditional BI with web analytics:

- **Auto Page Tagging:** Automatically implement coded tags to monitor web pages. As explained before, this enables the organization to obtained detailed information about the user and the pages they have visited and accessed. This can provide innovative marketing strategies based on user behavior and browsing history.
- **Track Conversion Rates:** According to Web Analytics Association (WAA) standard definition, a conversion is a visitor completing a target action. Conversion rate is also defined as the percentage of visitors to a website that go on to purchase, register etc depending upon the site's purpose (Child, 2006).
- **Track Abandonment Rate:** Abandonment Rate is a metric of the number of people who intended to buy, by clicking on the "add to cart" button, to those who actually made it out at the other end, by clicking "submit order". If people purchase multiple items in the same session on a website, that behavior will also be accounted for.
- **Data Mining:** Allows the ability to store performance of complex data mining queries on historical click-stream data and integrate detailed click-stream data feeds with internal data systems.
- **Analyze Key Metrics to Improve Return on Investment (ROI):** Making informed business decisions about which marketing campaigns to invest in requires real-time insight into what actions visitors might take – buy or not-buy.
- **Prevent Click Fraud:** Identify search marketing advertisements that are not delivering expected results.
- **Audience Segmentation:** A tool that enables users to isolate individuals and their behavior before pushing them into their action system of choice (CRM, e-mail, a data warehouse, applications, etc.).
- **Track Email Performance:** Web analytics can be used in conjunction with email marketing systems to track the performance of email blasts.
- **Track Visitor Behavior:** Web analytics tools enable the users to view detailed website visitor demographics and traffic patterns; differentiate between new visitors, returning visitors and unique visitors; and gain insight into website visitor activity and behavior.

- **Data Visualization:** Provision of data visualization capabilities will help view the analytics information at a glance to make key decisions.

BENEFITS AND CHALLENGES OF INTELLIGENT ANALYTICS

Having a unified view of customer data helps organizations build unique relationship strategies with them and look for retention and growth opportunities (Chan, 2005). Organizations that can successfully find ways to integrate BI and web analytics can realize the following potential benefits:

- **User Behavior Analysis:** A very important use of web analytics software is to analyze the behavior of the website's users. For example, using the software, managers will be able to know which sections of a website people visit the most, the typical paths taken by a user, what they search for on the website (search analytics), etc. This information is very useful when redesigning the website to better meet user needs.
- **Increased Revenue from Advertising:** By tracking the exact number of unique visitors on a monthly basis, it is possible to show these numbers to advertisers to start advertising on your website. Also, by monitoring the performance of campaigns, it is possible to get additional advertising revenue from advertisers if it is proven that the campaigns performed well.
- **Improve Channel Monetization:** By determining which campaigns (banners, emails, social media, etc) perform the best, managers can decide which channels to focus on. Conversion Rates and Abandonment Rate are also two other metrics used by managers to determine how effective their marketing campaigns are.

- **Brand Monitoring:** By using analytics for social media, managers can keep track of how many times their brand names are mentioned across these networks and in what context. Thus, they can monitor if any negative mention is made of their brand and take corrective action. For example, if Amazon sets up brand monitoring in Twitter with a web analytics software like Omniture, any time any user in Twitter talks about Amazon, it gets recorded and their managers can analyze the data and determine if there were negative comments and take proper corrective actions if necessary. This can also be used to reduce customer service costs if these issues are fixed at an early stage. Another potential use for this is to Measure awareness and impact of brands, products and services with consumers.

Challenges

As with any information technology (IT), there are both technological and non-technological challenges associated with integration of BI and web analytics. We list those challenges below and identify possible solutions that might exist to address the challenges.

Technological Challenges

Data Linkages: The biggest challenge in the integration of BI with web analytics is linking transactional data with non-identifiable web usage data. Visitor Insight & Anlalytics (VIA) by Truviso (2010) provides a context for site visitors based on "advanced web analytics and data integration solution designed to analyze multiple combined data sources," (p. 6). However, by applying data mining and BI to web analytics, patterns in usage behavior can be first determined and then linked with existing CRM data to see if new insights can be derived for new marketing initiatives.

Lack of Standards: The web analytics industry does not have any real standards. Definitions, tagging, metrics, vary from tool to tool. Web analytics is only one part of the bigger business analytics systems of the firm like a data warehouse, but because of the lack of standardization, integrating this information with data warehouses is very difficult. This presents a huge area for improvement in the future (Thayer, 2010).

Vertical Analysis: One of the biggest gaps is the lack of vertical web analysis. As more and more businesses are having a web presence, there will be more websites with unique business rules and processes and a generic solution may not work very well. For example, the analytics involved for the music industry may be very different for a medical portal and a potential growth opportunity for the analytics industry could be having analytics tools with specific knowledge of the business too (Page, 2009).

Storage and Scalability: Knau (2009) stated that data created and stored in organizations in the past three years is more than that created in past 40,000 years. According to IDC research, there was about a 62% growth in digital data worldwide between 2008 and 2009 to about 800,000 petabytes and is projected to grow to 1.2 zettabyes in 2010 and 35 zettabytes by 2020 (Erickson, 2010). This poses storage and scalability challenges issues to organizations. Cloud computing is a solution to managing storage needs and scalability. Organizations must have a strategy to deal with these challenges and find appropriate solution methods to ensure there is no degradation of performance.

Tracking across Affiliate Sites: Most web analytics tools do a great job of tracking information in one website but when there is a portal which links off to different shopping websites through affiliates like Commission Junction, it is not possible currently to track the exact revenue and click-throughs that occur through these affiliates. For example, if a user logs into shop.com and clicks on one of their featured brand, for example KitchenAid, he or she is directed to Macys.com. For all purchases made on Macys.com, shop.com will receive a commission through an affiliate. Any web analytics software will be able to track their visit until they click on Kitchenaid, but once they leave shop.com and go to Macys.com, that user cannot be tracked. Ergo, it is very challenging for the managers at shop.com to know exactly which user bought what specific item at Macys.com.

Mobile Applications: Emergence of mobile devices, mobile browsers and mobile users add another dimension to web analytics challenges. While the technology can help identify the device, many devices many not have or support Java script thus, making it hard to attach a marketing campaign's information to the URL and hence track its effectiveness (Beal, 2008).

Non-Technological Challenges

The main value of the web analytics is in the information it provides to the firm. However, for the different stakeholders involved, the control of this information is crucial in several areas.

Privacy: Internet privacy can be defined as the ability to control what information one reveals about oneself over the Internet, and to control who can access that information. Privacy is arguably the biggest concern that users have with visiting websites and especially making Internet purchases. By gathering statistics about users, web analytics software poses a potential threat to users' privacy depending on the level of information that is collected. One way to alleviate this problem is for organizations to have clear privacy policies that explain to the user what information is collected and for what purposes the collected information will be used for.

The web analytics association has link to drafts of legislative policies that address the issue of Internet privacy (WAA, 2010a). The privacy House Bill states, "To require notice to and consent of an individual prior to the collection and disclosure of certain personal information relating to that individual," (WAA, 2010b). There is extant detail on the different types of personal information that fall under the bill in the above referenced document.

Accuracy: Reports are only as good as the underlying data. Thus, impact of wrong data in making business decisions can be catastrophic. Some root causes of wrong data could be the lack of standardization discussed above or the users deleting their cookies (which can cause the number of visitors tracked to change). Another concern is that raw data is vulnerable to manipulation by unscrupulous vendors. For example, if a significant amount of revenue for a website is from advertisements, there is enormous financial incentive for the publisher to overinflate click-through data. This can be prevented by using some forms of secure accounting (Naor & Pinkas, 2010).

Data Ownership and Sharing: The vast amount of user specific data collected by websites has lead to increased concerns as to who in fact owns the data collected (Byrne & Kemelor, 2009). A related concern is who else the company will share their data with. If organizations use third-party organizations for BI purposes and efforts are not taken to de-identify customer data then it can lead to unintended consequences. This could be a potential problem for users of websites. Again, having a clear privacy policy could help mitigate some of these fears for Internet users.

Executive Support: Akin to several key IT initiatives, commitment and support of executives is critical to starting and sustaining an intelligent analytics strategy. This will require some culture shift in organizations as it is hard to get executives who are already grappling with challenges in each of the areas, BI and Web analytics, to move beyond.

SUMMARY

Web analytics is an evolving area which presents companies with myriad opportunities to enhance their online presence. In this paper, we make a case for organizations to find ways to integrate web analytics with traditional BI to be proactive in the competitive market place by exploring new growth strategies. We first indentified growing trends in web analytics that pave the way for integration and we discussed the capabilities that organization must consider in looking at possible solutions to adopt. If organizations find possible ways to accomplish the integration, the ability to track and market to existing or new consumer needs can give a firm a sizable competitive advantage. The challenge though is the constant innovation of online technologies to track user behavior. It is therefore important that as the field grows, structure and standards be implemented to balance stakeholders' concerns such as data rights management, accuracy, and privacy. Some possible research in the area include, but not limited to, developing standards for data representation, development of methods to analyze complex data such as audio or video, identifying appropriate metrics for measurement, organizations and governance issues, and text analysis of social media data.

ACKNOWLEDGMENT

The authors would like to acknowledge Zachary Engle, Karen Narita, and Joshua Watts who contributed to the research on some parts of the web analytics discussion.

REFERENCES

Barone, D., Myopoulos, J., Jiang, L., & Amyot, D. (2010, April 14). *The Business Intelligence Model: Strategic Modelling*. Retrieved June 11, 2010, from ftp://ftp.db.toronto.edu/pub/reports/csrg/607/BIM-TechReport.pdf

Beal, B. (2008, September). *Gartner: Evaluating Web analytics faces new challenges*. Retrieved May 25, 2010, from http://searchcrm.techtarget.com/news/1329232/Gartner-Evaluating-Web-analytics-faces-new-challenges

Beasty, C. (2006, December). *Analytics Brought to Bear*. Retrieved June 11, 2010, from http://www.destinationcrm.com/Articles/ReadArticle.aspx?ArticleID=42295

Bhatnagar, A. (2009, November/December). *Web Analytics for Business Intelligence*. Retrieved June 11, 2010, from http://pqasb.pqarchiver.com/infotoday/access/1895898461.html?dids=1895898461:1895898461:1895898461&FMT=ABS&FMTS=ABS:FT:PAGE&type=current&date=Nov%2FDec+2009&author=Alka+Bhatnagar&pub=Online&edition=&startpage=32&desc=Web+Analytics+for+Business+Intelligenc

Byrne, T., & Kemelor, P. (2009, March 16). *Do You Really Own Your Web Analytics Data*. Retrieved May 29, 2010, from http://www.cmswatch.com/Feature/191-Data-Ownership

CBR. (2006, June 5). *TeaLeaf Updates Web Analytics Platform*. Retrieved April 2010, from http://www.cbronline.com/news/tealeaf_updates_web_analytics_platform

Chan, J. O. (2005). Toward a Unified View of Customer Relationship Management. *Journal of American Academy of Business*, 6(1), 32–38.

Chatham, B., Tempkin, B. D., & Backer, E. (2004). Web Analytics Market: Continued [Forrester.]. *Growth*, 2005.

Child, D. (2006). *Ten Ways To Improve Your Website Conversion Rate*. Retrieved May 21, 2010, from http://www.addedbytes.com/online-marketing/ten-ways-to-improve-your-website-conversion-rate/

Clifton, B. (2010a). *Advanced Web Metrics with Google Analytics* (2nd ed.). New York: Wiley Publishing Inc.

Clifton, B. (2010b, April). *Understanding Web Analytics Accuracy*. Retrieved May 22, 2010, from http://www.advanced-web-metrics.com/docs/accuracy-whitepaper.pdf

Coghlan, T., Diehl, G., Karson, E., Liberatore, M., Luo, W., & Nydick, R. (2010). The Current State of Analytics in the Corporation: The View from Industry Leaders. *International Journal of Business Intelligence Research*, 1(2), 1–8.

DataMonitor. (2009). *Omniture Inc.: Company Profile*. DataMonitor.

Davenport, T. (2006). Competing on Analytics. *Harvard Business Review*, 2–10.

Davenport, T. (2010). Business intelligence and. *International Journal of Business Intelligence Research*, 1(1), 1–12.

Erickson, T. (2010, May 3). *Digital Data created in 2020 forecasted at 35 zettabytes; cloud computing will manage data growth*. Retrieved May 28, 2010, from http://searchstorage.techtarget.com/news/article/0,289142,sid5_gci1511342,00.html

Fleisher, C. S., & Bensoussan, B. E. (2003). *Strategic and Competitive Analysis: Methods and Techniques for Analyzing Business Competition*. Upper Saddle River, NJ: Prentice Hall.

Ganguly, S. (2010). *Collecting Data using Packet Sniffing*. Retrieved May 25, 2010, from http://ezinearticles.com/?Collecting-Data-Using-Packet-Sniffing&id=1834436

Gartner. (2009). *Howard Dresner*. Retrieved May 20, 2009, from http://www.gartner.com/research/fellows/asset_79427_1175.jsp

Google. (2010). *Google Analytics*. Retrieved April 23, 2010, from http://www.google.com/analytics/product.html

Halvorson, K. (2009). *Content Strategy for the web*. New Riders.

Hamel, S. (2009). *THE WEB ANALYTICS MATURITY MODEL: A strategic approach based on business maturity and critical success factors*. Retrieved from http://immeria.net/oamm/WAMM_ShortPaper_091017.pdf

IPInfoDB. (2009). *IPInfoDB*. Retrieved June 12, 2010, from http://ipinfodb.com/ip_database.php

Jansen, B. (2006). Search Log Analysis: What it is, what's been done, how to do it. *Library & Information Science Research, 28*(3), 407–432. doi:10.1016/j.lisr.2006.06.005

Kaushik, A. (2007). *Web Analytics, An Hour a Day*. New York: Wiley Publishing.

Kaushik, A. (2009). *Web Analytics 2.0: The Art of Online Accountability and Science of Customer Centricity*. Sybex.

Lager, W. (2009, May 26). *Web Analytics market to Hit the Billion-Dollar Mark by 2014*. Retrieved April 23, 2010, from http://www.destinationcrm.com/Articles/CRM-News/Daily-News/Web-Analytics-Market-to-Hit-the-Billion-Dollar-Mark-by-2014-53957.aspx

Leon, M. (2001, December 17). Merging Analytics and Intelligence. *InfoWorld*, 34–35.

Mason, R. (1986). Four Ethical Issues of the Information Age. *Management Information Systems Quarterly, 10*(1), 5–12. doi:10.2307/248873

Nakano, C. (2009, December 17). *How Integrated is Your Web Analytics Package and is That a Good Thing?* Retrieved from http://www.cmswire.com/cms/web-cms/how-integrated-is-your-web-analytics-package-and-is-that-a-good-thing-005763.php

Naor, M., & Pinkas, B. (2010). *Secure Accounting and Auditing on the Web*. Retrieved May 20, 2010, from http://www.pinkas.net/PAPERS/www7paper/p336.htm

Omniture. (2010). *Omniture Genesis*. Retrieved May 20, 2009, from http://www.omniture.com/da/products/marketing_integration/genesis

Page, B. (2009). *Is This the Future of Web Analytics?* Retrieved April 22, 2010, from http://bobpage.net/2009/01/11/is-this-the-future-of-web-analytics/

Rizzotto, R. (2007, June). *Adding Intelligence to Web Analytics*. Retrieved from http://www.domo-domain.com/press/IDC_WHITEPAPER.pdf

Sen, A., Dacin, P. A., & Pattichis, C. (2006)... *Communications of the ACM, 49*(11), 85–91. doi:10.1145/1167838.1167842

TeaLeaf. (n.d.). *TeaLeaf*. Retrieved April 22, 2010, from http://www.tealeaf.com

Thayer, S. (2010). *Web Analytics limitations... and a Bright Future*. Retrieved April 22, 2010, from http://www.trendingupward.net/2010/01/web-analytics-limitations-bright-future/

Truviso. (2010). *Visitor-Centric Web Analytics Build Better Relationships with Visitors to Improve Engagement, Optimize Conversion, and Increase Revenue*. Retrieved from http://www.truviso.com/docs/Truviso_Visitor_Analytics_whitepaper_201004.pdf

Unica Corporation. (2009). *Unica Corp Form 10-K*. Waltham, MA: Unica Corporation.

WAA. (2010b). *Privacy House Bill Draft 5-1.* Retrieved May 25, 2010, from http://www. webanalyticsassociation.org/resource/resmgr/ PDF_static/Privacy_House_Bill_Draft_5-1.pdf

WAA. (2010a). Retrieved May 25, 2010, from http://www.webanalyticsassociation. org/?page=privacy

Walling, S. (2009, August 4). *Webtrends 9: Google Analytics Eat Your Heart Out.* Retrieved April 22, 2010, from http://www.readwriteweb.com/enter-prise/2009/08/webtrends-9-google-analytics-eat-your-heart-out.php

Watson, H. (2009). Tutorial: Business Intelligence – Past, Present, and Future. *Communications of the Association for Information Systems, 25*(39), 487–510.

Webtrends. (n.d.). *Webtrends.* Retrieved April 22, 2010, from http://www.webtrends.com

Wikipedia. (2010). *Multivariate Testing.* Retrieved April 20, 2010, from http://en.wikipedia.org/wiki/ Multivariate_testing

Wixom, B., & Watson, H. (2010). The Bi-Based Organization. *International Journal of Business Intelligence Research, 1*(1), 13–28.

Yermish, I., Miori, V., Yi, J., Malhorta, R., & Klimberg, R. (2010). Business Plus Intelligence Plus Technology Equals Business Intelligence. *International Journal of Business Intelligence Research,* 48–63.

This work was previously published in the International Journal of Business Intelligence Research, Volume 2, Issue 1, edited by Richard Herschel, pp. 31-45, copyright 2011 by IGI Publishing (an imprint of IGI Global).

Chapter 13
Strategies for Improving the Efficacy of Fusion Question Answering Systems

José Antonio Robles-Flores
ESAN University, Peru

Gregory Schymik
Arizona State University, USA

Julie Smith-David
Arizona State University, USA

Robert St. Louis
Arizona State University, USA

ABSTRACT

Web search engines typically retrieve a large number of web pages and overload business analysts with irrelevant information. One approach that has been proposed for overcoming some of these problems is automated Question Answering (QA). This paper describes a case study that was designed to determine the efficacy of QA systems for generating answers to original, fusion, list questions (questions that have not previously been asked and answered, questions for which the answer cannot be found on a single web site, and questions for which the answer is a list of items). Results indicate that QA algorithms are not very good at producing complete answer lists and that searchers are not very good at constructing answer lists from snippets. These findings indicate a need for QA research to focus on crowd sourcing answer lists and improving output format.

DOI: 10.4018/978-1-4666-2650-8.ch013

INTRODUCTION

To succeed in today's business environment, every enterprise must be able to efficiently find information on the web. Although the web is a rich source of information, there are many challenges associated with finding the right information in a timely manner. Web search engines typically retrieve a large number of web pages and overload business analysts with irrelevant information (Chung, Chen, & Nunamaker Jr., 2005).

Ultraseek reported that the average employee spends 3.5 hours a week on unsuccessful searches (Ultraseek, 2006). KMWorld reported that middle managers spend approximately 25% of their time searching for information that is required for the successful completion of their jobs, that the information they find often is wrong, and that 86% of enterprise searchers are dissatisfied with their firms' search capabilities (KMWorld, 2008). More fine-grained technologies capable of understanding Business Intelligence tasks and representing their results in comprehensible formats are required.

One approach that has been proposed for overcoming some of these challenges is automated Question Answering (QA). The objective of a QA system is to locate, extract, and present the answer to a specific user question that has been expressed in natural language (Roussinov, Fan, & Robles-Flores, 2008). QA systems enable the searcher to pose queries as questions using natural language, and enable the computer to retrieve answers to questions that require the fusion of information from multiple sources. The ability to fuse information from multiple sources allows QA systems to take as input a question like "What are the countries in Central America?" and produce as output a list such as "Guatemala, Belize, El Salvador, Honduras, Nicaragua, Costa Rica, and Panama are countries in Central America." This is an example of a list question, so called because the answer is a list of items of information.

When dealing with list questions, it is important to differentiate between questions where constructing the answer list requires the fusion of information from multiple web sites (fusion questions), and questions where the answer list can be found on a single web page (non-fusion questions). An example of a non-fusion question is "What are the names of all the teams in the National Football League?" The complete answer to this question is available in many locations, and simply entering "names of all NFL teams" in the Google search bar will provide links to several sites that contain the desired list.

An example of a fusion question is "Which companies manufacture home appliances in the U.S.?" Entering "names of home appliance manufacturers located in the U.S." in the Google search bar will not and cannot provide links to a single site that contains the desired list, because there is no single site that contains the desired list. Answers to fusion questions require a search engine or service that can query the web for information, parse the returned web pages for the relevant information, and fuse the relevant information into an aggregated answer list. Fusion questions are very common in the business intelligence arena.

Search engines, like Google, Yahoo, and MSN, use many tools to identify relevant snippets for keyword searches; including page rank, term frequency, term proximity, and inverse document frequency. However, these tools are not designed to handle fusion list questions. They treat questions as a "bag of words". Entering "Who is the largest producer of software?" in the Google search bar, for example, will yield nearly the same results as entering "largest producer software"; and both of these produce unexpected snippets that identify the largest producers of carbon steel, pork, ethanol, and sugar; but do not identify Microsoft, which is the answer the user would expect (see Figure 1). Moreover, even if the correct answer is among the search results, the user still needs to review the snippets in order to locate it.

Figure 1. Results for question: "Who is the largest producer of software?"

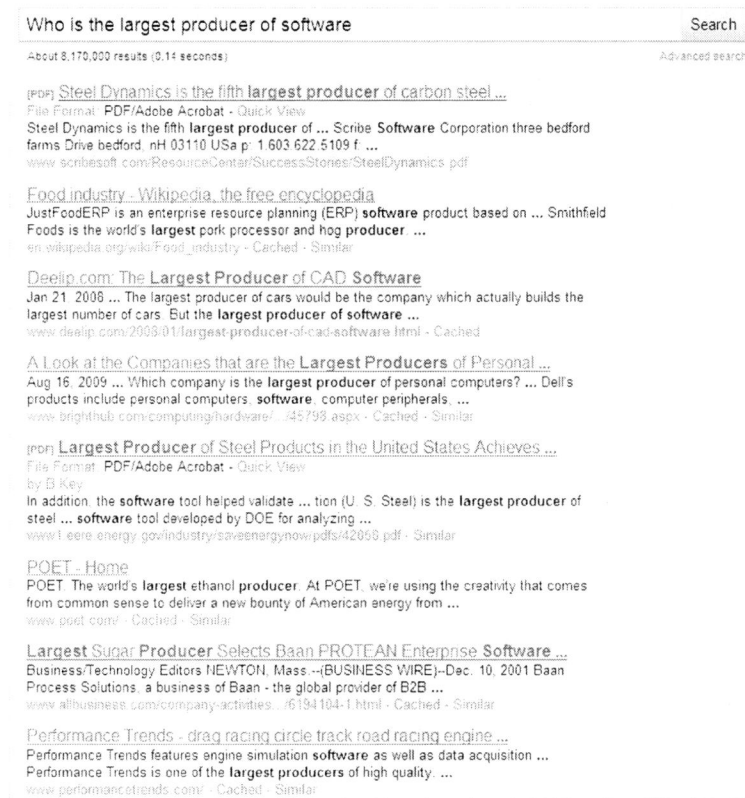

Prior research shows that Web users frequently have questions in mind even if they use keyword based search engines (Radev, Qi, Zheng, Blair-Goldensohn, Zhang, Fan, & Prager, 2001). Asking questions and finding the corresponding answers is an essential activity for learning (Bruner, 1960; Pask, 1975). This is why QA systems are gaining popularity, and are expected to play a more important role in the ubiquitous computing arena. Typing a question, such as "Who wrote King Lear?" is much more natural than typing a query such as "wrote OR written OR author AND King Lear".

When developing QA systems, it is important to note that the answers to some questions change over time. As new and taller buildings are constructed, for example, the name of the tallest building in the world changes. List questions are especially likely to have answers that change over time. The names of the teams in the National Football League changed substantially when leagues merged and new teams were created. Similarly, the names of home appliance manufacturers located in the United States changed substantially when companies merged, went out of business, or moved into new areas.

Thus far, researchers have assumed it currently is possible to design a QA system that can dynamically determine the answers for list questions. This paper describes a case study that was designed to determine whether it is possible to generate answers to list questions in real time. The results indicate that QA algorithms are not very good at producing answer lists to new fusion questions in real time; and that searchers are not very good at processing the information that is contained in the output of QA algorithms. Our results also indicate that co-production of the answer lists is essential, and that the output must be presented in an unambiguous format. These findings indicate a need for QA research to focus on incorporating user feedback and improving output format.

The remainder of this paper is organized as follows. First we review the literature on the technology that is used to support QA Systems. We then describe the experiment that we conducted to determine whether it is possible to dynamically determine the answers to list questions, and present the results of that experiment. We conclude by discussing the implications of our results for developing QA systems.

QA ALGORITHMS

The Text Retrieval Conference (TREC), sponsored by the National Institute of Standards and Technology (NIST) has been a major contributor to advances in QA systems. Its Question Answering Track has run a competition-like event every year since 1999. At TREC and elsewhere, most of the research on automated question answering systems has focused on the algorithms. The results from TREC annual evaluations demonstrate that state of the art QA systems are capable of delivering answers that are more precise and reliable than those provided by keyword searches (Voorhees & Buckland, 2005). However, the tests have been performed in "batch" mode only, leaving the interaction between the user and the system completely out of the picture.

Within the information retrieval community, many researchers and practitioners debate the superiority claims of QA technology. They argue that one can simply enter the question verbatim, or keywords from the question, into the search engine (e.g., Google) and visually scan for the answer in the top snippets. For this reason, they

doubt whether QA technology will ever be a superior technology. More formal evaluations (Roussinov et al., 2008) show that a correct answer to a question submitted verbatim as a query frequently occurs within the top snippets returned by the Web search engines, even if the systems are not designed to take natural language questions as input and instead treat the user queries as "bags of words." Most of the snippets returned by Google for the question "On which continent is Argentina located?" include the words "South America"; because that phrase frequently occurs around the word "Argentina," even though Google is not looking specifically for a continent as an answer. Even if the Google query includes only "Argentina" as the keyword, a similar output is obtained.

Entering fusion list questions into a keyword search engine, however, almost never provides the desired answer in a single top snippet. Figure 2 illustrates this for the question "What countries have been visited by Pope Benedict? It may be possible to derive the answer from the links provided in the snippets, but it is unlikely that the answer will be provided in a single web page. Moreover, it is at best time consuming to derive the answer from the set of referenced web pages, and at worst impossible to derive the answer from the referenced set of web pages.

Fully automatic QA systems are under development. These systems take questions as input and process them using algorithms that "understand" the semantics of the question. They then use this understanding to see if answers are available somewhere on the Web. The goal of these types of systems is to accept any question from any user, and apply their algorithms to search the web and identify the answer – even if the question has never been asked before.

Unlike keyword search algorithms, QA algorithms use all of the words entered in the question. Patterns are used to recognize the question and to identify possible answers. Typical QA algorithms parse the submitted natural language question

Figure 2. Results for question: "What countries have been visited by Pope Benedict?"

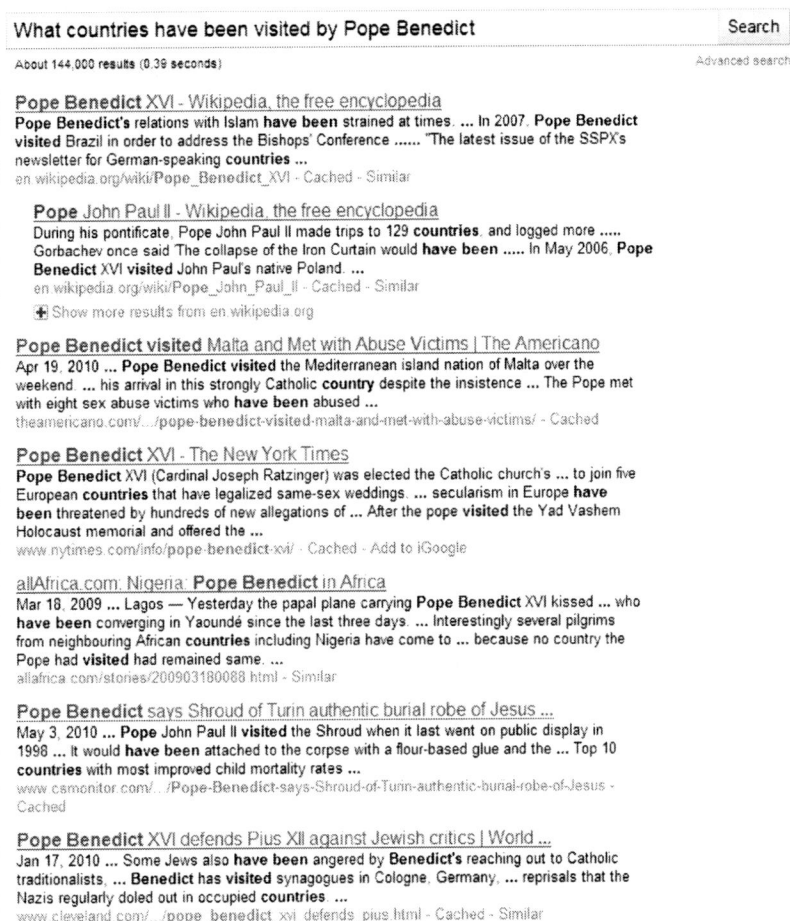

to identify the grammatical constructs used to form the question. Examples of such constructs include "what is", "who is", and "where was." QA algorithms also must identify the semantic category of the answer. The semantic category would be "city" in the case of the question "What is the capital of Peru?" Using the constructs of the question and the category of the answer, the algorithms can create multiple keyword queries in order to search for the answer.

For the question "What is the capital of Peru?" the algorithm will match that question with answer-patterns like "The capital of Peru is CITY", "Peru's capital, CITY,", or "CITY is the capital of Peru". Based on those patterns, the tool will build search queries like "The capital of Peru is", "Peru's capital", and "is the capital of Peru". These queries will be sent to a keyword search engine. The snippets that come back from the keyword search engine will be parsed to look for the target CITY. In the case of list questions, a similar mechanism is used but the algorithm searches for multiple "answers" which are treated as possible items of the answer-list. The next step is to confirm the possible answers.

Triangulation is a simple mechanism that can be used to estimate the likelihood that a possible answer belongs on the answer-list. This mechanism compares a possible answer found in one web page with possible answers found in other web pages. If a possible answer is found in multiple web pages containing the target patterns, then there is a high probability the possible answer is an actual answer and belongs on the answer-list. These two mechanisms (pattern matching and triangulation) are the core concepts underlying QA algorithms. Additional details about QA algorithms can be found in published articles in the IS literature (Roussinov et al., 2008; Roussinov & Robles-Flores, 2004a; Roussinov & Robles-Flores, 2004b; Roussinov & Robles-Flores, 2007; Roussinov, Robles-Flores, & Ding, 2004).

Current systems based on QA algorithms include:

- WikiAnswers (http://wiki.answers.com/);
- Language Computer Corporation (http://www.languagecomputer.com/);
- AnswerBus (http://www.answerbus.com/index.shtml);
- NSIR (http://tangra.si.umich.edu/clair/NSIR/html/nsir.cgi);
- Ask (http://www.ask.com/).

Although these systems are very useful, they do not achieve the goal set for fusion QA systems. In particular, unless a fusion list question has previously been asked and answered, the systems do not provide the answer in a single compiled list. Instead they provide snippets with links to pages that may contain the answer. The snippets, however, are different than the snippets that would be returned by keyword search. Keyword search algorithms look for matching keywords and assign ranks based on a combination of match and page popularity. This makes it highly likely that the same item of an answer list will be repeated several times in the top snippets. In contrast, QA algorithms try to build the result set with snippets that contain different items from the target answer-list. This should both reduce repetition and increase the number of relevant answers that appear in the most highly ranked snippets.

EXPERIMENT

To determine whether snippets returned by QA algorithms actually reduce repetition and increase the number of relevant answers that appear in the most highly ranked snippets, an experiment was conducted. This question can be broken into three sub questions: (1) Are more items that belong on the answer list to fusion list questions contained in the top ranked snippets that are returned by QA algorithms or in the top ranked snippets that are returned by KW algorithms?; (2) Do users find more items that belong on the answer list to fusion list questions in the top ranked snippets that are returned by QA algorithms or in the top ranked snippets that are returned by KW algorithms?; and (3) Do the top ranked snippets that are returned by either QA or KW algorithms contain a high percentage of the items that belong on the answer lists to fusion list questions? To answer these questions, it is necessary to select a sample of fusion list questions, determine the number of snippets to classify as top ranked for each selected question, and get a large number of persons to search for the answers to the selected questions using both QA and KW algorithms. To the researcher's knowledge, this is the first study to compare the results of participants that used both QA and KW algorithms. The experiment is described in depth in Robles-Flores (Robles-Flores, 2009).

Questions

To avoid researcher bias, a group of individuals were recruited to create the list questions. The instructions given to the individuals for creating the list questions are contained in Table 1, and the tool for self-checking the created questions is contained in Table 2. The persons recruited to create questions were all masters or doctoral students, or recent graduates with those degrees. People with varying fields of expertise were intentionally included in order to have questions from different knowledge domains: urban planning, social justice, information systems, management, biology, engineering, computer science, and psychology. The request to participate was sent to 42 individuals and 19 responded with questions (a 45.2% response rate). A total of 179 questions were collected.

After the questions were collected, they were evaluated by the researchers to insure they met the task characteristics. The researchers used the following guidelines to check each of the 179 question created by the participants.

1. Check that the answer list is not available in a single page on the web. In order to have a high degree of confidence that the answer list is not available on a single page, the following steps were performed:

a. A Yahoo! search that included the whole question verbatim.

b. A Yahoo! search of the target subject (the main subject or theme of the question). The keywords representing the target subject were searched.

c. A Wikipedia search of the target subject.

d. A "wiki" search (this means a search of the target subject adding the keyword "wiki" in the search query)

Table 1. Instructions for creating list questions

OBJECTIVE: Generate a set of list questions for which there is no single Web page containing all the possible answers. (Detailed Instructions Follow.)
DEFINITIONS: List Question: a question for which the answer is a list of items (a list-answer). The items are proper nouns, dates or numbers. (See the definitions below.)   List-answer: A list of items (proper nouns, dates, numbers) that is the answer to a list-question.   Proper nouns: (also called proper names) are nouns representing unique entries such as London or John, as distinguished from common nouns which describe a class of entities such as city or person   Date: A particular month, day, and year at which some event happened or will happen. Examples: July 4th, 176, Fourth of July, July 4th, July, 1776, 7/4/1776, 7-4-1776, 1776, Seventeen seventy six.   Number: A quantity expressed in numerals (digits) or in words. Examples: 25, Twenty-five, 2007, Two thousand seven".
INSTRUCTIONS: Using your intuition, please think of 10 list-questions for which the list-answer contains proper nouns, dates, or numbers. Please consider the following five(5) criteria and use your judgment as to whether the questions meet these criteria: 1) The question does not have more than 30 items in the list-answer, unlike the following examples: "Which cities are close to a river?" Most cities in the World are close to rivers.   "Which countries are considered developing countries?" Most countries fall under this classification.   2) The question should not have a controversial or ambiguous list-answer, unlike the following examples: "Which are the best restaurants in New York?" Different persons rate restaurants differently.   "What are the most beautiful mountains?" This is largely a matter of opinion.   3) The complete list-answer is not likely to be found in a single page on the web, such as popular sources like "Wikipedia" (www.wikipedia.com), "Britannica On Line" (www.britannica.com), or "Internet Movie Database" (www.imdb.com).   Examples of questions that do not follow the criterion: The cast of characters for a movie can be found on a single page on the Internet Movie Database.   Who commanded the 82nd Airborne Division" (http://en.wikipedia.org/wiki/82nd_Airborne_Division)   Who married Hedy Lamarr? (http://www.east-buc.k12.ia.us/99_00/PK/hl.htm)   4) The question should not contain negation, conjunction, or disjunction (use words like AND, OR, NOT), unlike the following examples: Which US companies in the S&P 500 also list their stocks outside the US?   Which countries are not members of the UN?   Who was president of the US and was not elected for congress?   Which European Union countries originally did not adopt the Euro?   What companies produce margarine or butter?   5) Avoid questions longer than than 20 words.
If you feel it is necessary, you can do search or browsing on the web to verify those conditions but please do not spend more time than 3 minutes for each question. You do not need to know, nor provide, the list-answers for your questions.
Use the table on the last page to write your questions on the left side only.

Table 2. Self-check tool for question creation

List-question: the answer is a list of items (items can be proper nouns, dates or numbers) and should follow the guidelines on the right →	No more than 30 items in answer list	No controversial or ambiguous answer-list web pages	List-answer not likely in a single web page	No negation, conjunction, or disjunction	No more than 20 words in the question
Your list-questions	Check 1	Check 2	Check 3	Check 4	Check 5
1)					
2)					
3)					
4)					
5)					
6)					
7)					
8)					
9)					
10)					

using Yahoo! This ensured that all public wikis were searched, including Wikipedia.

    e.   When the snippets from steps a through d indicated that the linked document may contain the answer list, the links in the snippets were followed to go to the web page. Only the first 10 snippets were reviewed because, based on our explorations, the chances of finding the answer on a single page are very low after the first 10 snippets.

    f.   For questions related to the movie or TV industry, the Internet Movie Database (www.imdb.com) was searched.

    g.   If a question referred to a particular company or institution, that company's web site was searched.

    h.   When the list-answer was found on a single web page, the URL was recorded in order to document the elimination of the candidate question.

2.   Check that the question refers to lists of cities, countries, names of persons, numbers, dates or other proper nouns.

3.   Check that there are no more than 20 words in the question.

4.   Check that the question does not contain negation, conjunction or disjunction (words like AND, OR, or NOT)

5.   Check that the question does not lead to a list-answer that may include controversial language (i.e., obscene language)

6.   Check that the question does not lead to an ambiguous list-answer (the meaning of the questions could be interpreted in more than one way).

7.   Check that the list-answer does not contain more than 30 items.

8.   Use common sense to verify that the question is suitable in a general setting.

After the verification process, 36 questions remained as candidates for the experiment.

For the experiment, 28 questions were selected based on the expected voluntary enrollment of participants, and the number of questions that could be assigned to each participant. This number of questions allowed for 4 groups of 7 questions (3 questions for the QA algorithm, 3 questions for the KW algorithm, and one choice question which was not analyzed as part of this paper). To avoid introducing a researcher bias, the final set of 28 questions was selected randomly from the 36 candidate questions. The list of questions used in the experiment is shown in Table 3.

Participants

The participants were recruited at a major research university. To guarantee a minimum level of ex-perience in the use of computers, only Business School students at the junior or senior level were invited to volunteer. All of the participants were taking a course on web design and development. This course includes information seeking on the web as a subject. Therefore, the participants were familiar with the type of tasks performed in the experiment, which increases the likelihood that the results are generalizable to all persons who search for answers to list questions.

Table 3. Final list of questions

201	Which countries has Governor Janet Napolitano visited?
202	What companies control low earth orbit satellites?
203	What are the locations of the manned lunar landings?
204	What fresh food products are exported from the Chilean Los Lagos region?
205	What types of chickens are raised in the United Kingdom?
206	Who were the contemporary composers of the medieval composer Moniot d'Arras?
207	Which towns in Germany were bombed in World War II?
208	Which baseball stadiums offer tacos?
209	What Latin America presidents were prosecuted for corruption?
210	Which cities have St. John Boutique outlets?
211	Which countries withdrew from OPEC?
212	What techniques exist to measure Fe isotopes?
213	What countries were members of the original League of Nations?
214	Which actors are also authors?
215	Who are the first ladies of South America countries?
216	Which Nobel Prize winners were born in Latin America?
217	What types of reptiles are confiscated annually at major airports?
218	Which actors were taller than Leonardo DiCaprio in Titanic?
219	Which Countries have launched military satellites?
220	With which African institutions has Arizona State University established agreements in the area of political sciences?
221	What unique minerals were found in underground crystal mines during the past 20 years?
222	Which Florida cities have opera houses?
223	Which public companies in the U.S have existed for more than 150 years?
224	What countries have Precambrian outcrops?
225	Which biographers wrote biographies of Che Guevara?
226	Which soccer players scored more than 500 goals?
227	What Klingon vessels did Captain Kirk order the Enterprise to attack?
228	Which countries have capitol cities that were founded before Christ?

Those who volunteered as participants in the experiment were promised and awarded additional credit in the course. All participants were informed in advanced that the experiment would take approximately 55 minutes, and that the extra credit would be awarded only to those students who completed all of the tasks. To motivate each student to perform her or his best, all participants were informed that there would be four prizes for those who provided the best and most complete answers to the list questions presented as tasks. Each prize was a $50 gift card.

The experiment was conducted in three sessions to accommodate all of the students who volunteered. They were offered three different dates and times to participate. The total number of participants from all three sessions was 142. The following information was collected about the participants through an exit questionnaire:

- 84 were male and 55 were female (3 did not respond)
- On average, they had 2.13 years of college (54 had one year of college, 44 had two years, 27 had three years and 14 reported more than three years of college)
- 134 participants reported their age between 18 and 30, while one reported below 18, and 6 reported between 31 and 50 (one participant did not respond to this question)
- 123 reported being English-language native speakers, and 16 listed another language as their native language (one left the question blank)
- 113 participants reported daily use of search tools, 24 reported using them several times per week, and 4 participants said they use them once per week or less (1 participant did not respond).
- On an "expertise" scale from 1 to 5 (1 = expert and 5 = inexperienced), 26 participants considered themselves in level 1, 80 in level 2, 33 in level 3, and only 2 in levels 4 or 5 (one participant did not respond the question).

- 130 participants responded that they use e-mail every day, 9 reported using it several times per week, and 2 reported using it once per week (one participant did not respond)
- 131 of the participants reported they use the world-wide-web daily, 9 reported several times per week, and 2 reported they use it once per week (1 did not respond).

These characteristics are typical of a large number of persons that conduct searches on the web.

Operationalization

Operationalization was accomplished by assigning specific tools and questions to the subjects. Two types of tools were used: one that used KW algorithms and one that used QA algorithms. The KW tool was derived from Google. Google was chosen because it is a widely available tool on the internet with free access, and therefore can be used to replicate the study. The KW tool was simply an interface that shows only the search box from Google. All other features were removed in order to have participants in the experiment focus on the keyword search. This was important because there was limited time. The interface sends the query directly to Google and presents the snippets returned from Google while isolating the non-relevant features of a regular Google output screen.

The QA tool was derived from ASUWebQA. ASUWebQA was chosen because it is based on algorithms that are publicly available and that provide performance comparable to other state of the art Web-based QA systems (Roussinov et al., 2008; Roussinov et al., 2007). It also is available for free and allows for replication of the study and independent testing by other researchers.

In order to avoid bias due to the interface, both the KW and the QA tools were "reduced" to the same interface. For the KW tool, the advertisement and the links to other Google tools (News, Email, Blogs, Images, Docs, etc.) were masked and hidden from the experimental interface. Overall, the two tools are comparable in every non-essential aspect. Figure 3 shows what the user sees when the keyword search tool is used. Figure 4 shows what the user sees when the WebQA tool is used. Both tools present a list of snippets as output.

Because the QA tool is only a prototype, a simulation of the search results was presented to the subjects. The primary reason to use simulated search results for the QA tool was the lack of resources to develop a full online system with response speed comparable to the keyword search tool (based on Google). The simulated results were generated by a prototype system that lacked a user-friendly interface. Because the results were simulated, it did not matter what the participant actually typed as input. That is, the output was

always presented as if the user had correctly typed as input the question that was assigned to her/ him. In order to reduce the effect of this design issue, the instructions led participants to believe they had to correctly and completely type their assigned questions as input. Random observation of the participants' work during the experiment confirmed they did not notice that the question did not have to be inputted either correctly or completely. In addition, because the ASU WebQA tool is a simulation, a one-second delay was added to its output to make it comparable to the Google interface used. The objective of this artificial delay is to control for response speed variances that could influence the subjects' perspectives of the tools.

Figure 3. The interface for the keyword search tool

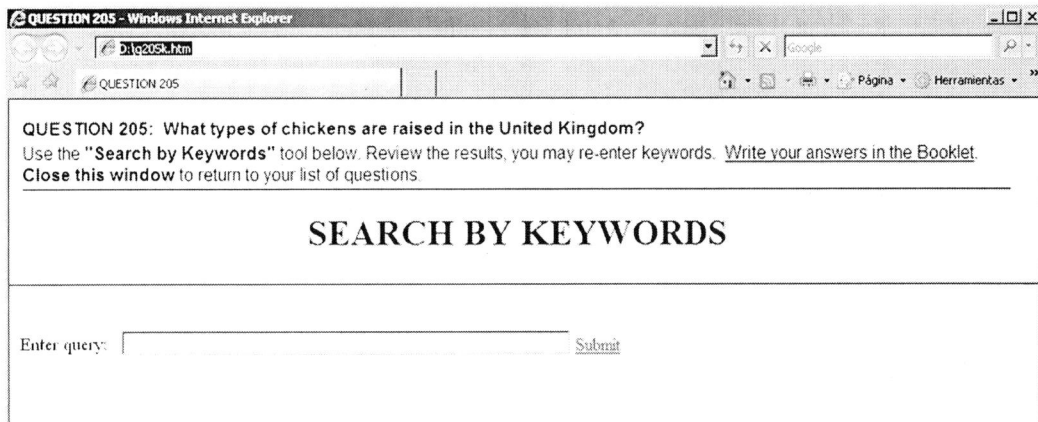

QUESTION 205: What types of chickens are raised in the United Kingdom?
Use the "Search by Keywords" tool below. Review the results, you may re-enter keywords. Write your answers in the Booklet.
Close this window to return to your list of questions.

SEARCH BY KEYWORDS

Enter query: [ ]   Submit

Figure 4. The interface for the WebQA tool

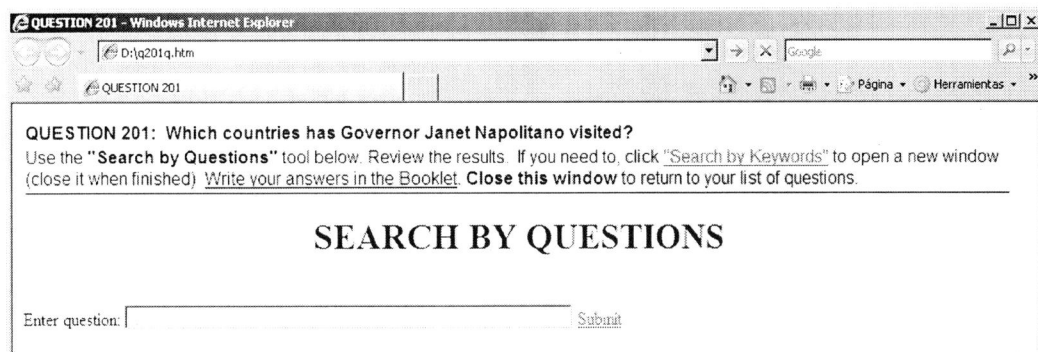

QUESTION 201: Which countries has Governor Janet Napolitano visited?
Use the "Search by Questions" tool below. Review the results. If you need to, click "Search by Keywords" to open a new window (close it when finished) Write your answers in the Booklet. Close this window to return to your list of questions.

SEARCH BY QUESTIONS

Enter question: [ ]   Submit

When using the QA tool, subjects were allowed to follow up with multiple uses of the KW tool if they did not believe the snippets (and associated web pages) returned by the QA tool included all of the items that belonged on the answer list. When using the KW tool, subjects were allowed to perform as many searches as they wanted, but they were not allowed to follow up with the QA tool. The reason for this is that we wanted to see if the QA tool results could be improved by following up with a KW search.

Each subject was required to complete six tasks, alternating between using the KW tool and the QA tool. To control for order effects (Neter et al., 1996), half of the participants started the first task using the QA tool and the other half started the first task using the KW tool. Participants were assigned the initial tool randomly. For each of the subsequent tasks, the tools were alternated, resulting in every participant performing three tasks with the QA tool and three tasks with the KW tool. Within each block, the questions were balanced to appear the same number of times in each position.

A paper-based booklet containing instructions, space to write down answers, and exit questions was prepared to provide step-by-step guidance to subjects. To validate the instrument, the instructions and sample tasks were sent to five of the individuals who created questions and agreed to pilot test the booklet. For this pilot test, the individuals were sent a booklet and they were asked to find answers using KW and QA tools. All five individuals returned their booklets by email. Interviews with the five reviewers of the booklet led to only minor adjustments. During the experiment, no major issues were observed regarding a lack of understanding of instructions.

Measurement

For this experiment, we want to know how many of the items that should be on the answer were contained in the snippets returned by the QA and KW tools; and how many of the item contained in the snippets were found by the subjects. To determine this, we have to know what items should have been included on the answer list. Constructing the answer list was more difficult than one might think. This is the case because the questions used in this experiment were questions for which no one, including the creators of the questions, knew the answer.

The following process was used to specify what we termed the "gold standard" answer list for each question. First, we took all the answer lists from all the participants who responded to a given question. Every item in the aggregated answer list was then checked to determine if it belonged in the answer list. For example, for the question "Which countries withdrew from OPEC?" the answer lists may have been: Subject #1 -- Indonesia, Venezuela, Russia; Subject #2 -- Gabon, Dubai, United Arab Emirates; and Subject #3 -- Indonesia, Mexico, Brazil. By checking each item in the three answer lists, we would have built the following Gold Standard: Gabon, Indonesia.

In order to check every item, we searched the Web. If we could not verify an item, we went to the logs to see all the snippets generated by the keyword searches done by the subject for that particular question. If the item was not verifiable in the logs, then it was considered wrong. All the items checked as correct were added to the gold standard. Although there is no guarantee that all of the items that should be included in the answer list are included in the gold standard, this is the best that can be done, and follows the methodology used in previous research in the information retrieval literature in order to find a measure of recall (Sparck Jones & van Rijsbergen, 1975).

RESULTS

The results from the experiment are summarized in Table 4. Despite our efforts to ensure that all 27 of the questions selected for the experiment were suitable for the experiment, four questions had to be dropped.

Table 4. Results from experiment

Question Number	Gold Standard	QA	KW	Avg Correct	
				QA	KW
201	9	3	0	1.3	1.9
202	16	8	6	1	1.7
203	9	0	3	1.5	0.7
205	21	3	3	0.1	1.7
206	15	6	1	0.7	0.6
207	31	2	3	1.8	3.2
208	8	5	3	1	1.3
209	30	1	3	1.4	1.6
210	22	7	4	2.5	3.5
211	2	2	2	1.9	1.4
212	14	7	2	0.5	0.9
213	33	5	8	3	5.1
214	68	7	3	2.8	4.9
215	7	1	1	1.4	1.5
216	15	6	4	2.7	2.9
218	2	0	0	0.2	0.2
219	15	12	9	5.5	5.3
222	9	1	3	1.5	2.7
223	35	11	1	1.6	1.5
224	28	8	6	2.8	1.9
225	22	3	3	2.3	1.9
226	4	3	0	0.1	0.7
227	5	0	0	0	0.4
228	49	3	3	1.8	2.5

- **Question 204:** What fresh food products are exported from the Chilean Los Lagos region? Originally, it was believed that the products would contain proper nouns such as the scientific names of fruits and vegetables. However, when evaluated, some of the items included common nouns like "grapes" and "apples". Therefore, the question failed to meet the requirement of proper nouns.
- **Question 217:** What types of reptiles are confiscated annually at major airports? It was thought that the valid answers would contain only the names of species. However, after reviewing the answers, it was clear that common nouns like "lizard" and "snake" were correct answers.
- **Question 220:** With which African institutions has Arizona State University established agreements in the area of political sciences? The participants did not find any answers.
- **Question 221:** What unique minerals were found in underground crystal mines in the past 20 years? This question failed to meet the requirement of proper nouns.

Originally, it was thought that the valid answers would contain only names of minerals. However, after reviewing the answers, it was clear that nouns like "gem" were correct answers. In addition, the question asks for "unique" minerals and, after reviewing the answers, it could not be determined what would be unique and what would not.

No data related to these questions was used for the analysis.

In Table 4, the column labeled Gold Standard records the number of items that should be on the answer-list for each question. How these items were found is explained above in the subsection titled Measurement. To compare how well the search tools performed compared to the gold standard, the researchers entered each question verbatim into the the QA and KW tools. The top 40 snippets were reviewed to determine if they included the answers from the Gold Standard. The QA column records the number of items that should be on the answer list and appeared in the snippets returned by the QA tool. The KW column records the number of items that should be on the answer list and appeared in the snippets returned by the KW tool. The Average Correct columns record the average number of items that should be on the answer list and were found by subjects that used the QA and KW tools.

Note that it is not possible to tell exactly what snippets were read by the subjects that used the QA and KW tools. We know how many snippets were presented to subjects by the QA tool. That number was 40. Research has shown that searchers rarely look beyond the first 20 snippets that are presented by a search tool (Jansen & Spink, 2006). We also found that new items for list questions rarely are found after the first 20 snippets. To be safe we doubled the number of snippets returned by our QA tool. However, individual subjects using the QA tool could have looked at more or less than 20 snippets. This is the case because subjects did not have to look at all 40 of the snippets that were presented by the QA tool, and because subjects were allowed to use the KW tool if they were not confident that all of the items that belong on the answer list appeared in the snippets that were returned by the QA tool. The QA column in Table 3 records the number of items that should be on the answer list and appeared in the 40 snippets returned by the QA tool. We ignored any snippets that may have been returned by the KW tool when used after the QA tool.

It is even more difficult to determine how many snippets were presented to subjects by the KW tool. Subjects could use the KW tool to do as many searches as they wanted within the five minute time period. To get a relevant comparison with the QA tool, we looked only at the first 40 snippets that were returned when the question was typed verbatim into the search box for the KW tool. The KW column in Table 3 records the number of items that should be on the answer list and appeared in those first 40 snippets.

An obvious question with respect to Table 3 is: "How can the number of items in the Gold Standard column be greater than the sum of the number of items in the QA and KW columns?" Because there likely is some duplication between the items in the QA and KW columns, it would seem like the number of items in the Gold Standard column would have to be less than the sum of the QA and KW columns. The explanation is that we searched only the snippets when counting items for the QA and KW columns. Subjects were free to follow the links in the snippets to search for answers. Thus many of the items that belong on the answer lists must have been found in the web pages rather than the snippets.

The results presented in Table 3 are very surprising. First, note that neither the QA tool nor the KW tool did a very good job of identifying all of the items that should be included on the answer list. The snippets from the QA tool included only 22% of the items that belonged on the answer list, and the snippets from the KW tool included only

15% of the items that belonged on the answer list. Second, note that subjects did not find all of the answers that were included in the snippets. When using the QA tool, subjects found only 27% of the answers that were contained in snippets that were presented. When using the KW tool, it appears that subjects found 70% of the answers that were contained in the snippets that were presented, but this probably is a biased estimate. It is likely that subjects performed more than one KW search, and thus it is likely that KW column understates the number of answers that were contained in the presented snippets. The implications of these results are discussed in the next section.

IMPLICATIONS

Our results strongly suggest that pattern matching and triangulation may not be powerful enough tools to find all of the items that belong on the answer list for many types of list questions. The snippets from our QA tool included only 22% of the items that belonged on the answer list. Although this was better than the 15% found by the KW tool, it leaves much room for improvement. These results caused us to question whether it is possible to generate the answers to new fusion list questions in real time using a QA algorithm.

Moreover, after all of the unique answers were aggregated into one list for each question, the person who created the question was asked to grade the aggregated answer list. From this exercise, we discovered that not only were the creators of the questions generally unable to specify in advance all of the items that should be included in the answer lists, but without doing additional research they often were unable to determine whether an answer on the aggregated list belonged on the answer list. This situation occurred primarily when the question was looking for very specific knowledge.

The implication of these results is that crowd sourcing may be the only way to generate answers for list questions. James Surowiecki (2005) iden-

tifies diversity, independence, decentralization, and aggregation as necessary conditions for wise crowds. Those conditions generally are met when persons are seeking the answers to list questions. Some QA systems do try to take advantage of the possibilities for co-creation of the answers to submitted questions. WikiAnswers, for example, presents the answers to list questions that previously have been asked and answered in a table or list format. If the question has not previously been asked and answered, it gives the searcher the opportunity to post her/his question to the community, and provides a list of related answers or links that might be helpful. It also gives the searcher the opportunity to submit an answer to an unanswered question, or to update the answer to an answered question. Our results suggest that this is the only way to generate complete answer lists for many types of fusion questions.

Our results also suggest that searchers are not very good at using snippets to identify items that should be included in the answer list. On average, our subjects found only 27% of the answers that were contained in the snippets returned by the QA tool. Two likely explanations for this are: (1) time constraints prevent searchers from closely reading the snippets that are returned, or examining the web page to which the snippet is linked; and (2) because they are not domain experts, searchers do not recognize the answer when they see it. If researchers have neither the time to find nor the expertise to identify correct answers, presenting the answer in an unambiguous format becomes very important.

Many question answering systems, including our own, do not present their results in a manner that is consistent with our findings. WikiAnswer provides the answer in a clear table format when the submitted question is one that previously has been asked and answered. Otherwise, it provides only related questions that have been answered and snippets with links that might be helpful. When it is a question that previously has been asked and answered, AnswerBus provides the answer in snippets, with links to the sources for the answer. Otherwise, it provides what it labels as possible answers (in linked snippet format) or simply says it doesn't know the answer. Ask provides both the answer list and links for additional information when it is a question that previously has been asked and answered. When the answer is not on file, it provides only linked snippets. Our results strongly suggest this is not the best format.

Because searchers will not or cannot process the snippets, we suggest that the answer list for list questions always be put in a table. This is simple to do if the question is one which does not change over time, and one for which an answer is on file. If the question is one that can change over time, or one for which the answer is not on file, our research suggests a three part output. First, present a table that has answers that are known to belong on the answer list. Second, present a table that has items that the QA algorithm determines have a high likelihood of belonging on the answer list along with links to the pages that produced the likely answers. And finally present a list of snippets with links to pages that the QA algorithm determines have a high likelihood of providing items that belong on the answer list.

Our research also strongly suggests that the QA system provide an opportunity for co-production of the result. Our QA tool was not very successful at finding all of the items that belonged on the answer lists. The only way we were able to get reasonably complete answer lists for our original (not previously asked or answered) questions was by aggregating and verifying the answers of our subjects. Until the precision and recall of QA algorithms is significantly improved, this is likely to remain the most viable way to develop answer lists. Answers to list questions useful to those doing BI research are very likely to change as economies, industries, markets, and consumer tastes evolve. Crowd sourcing appears to be the most effective way to develop and maintain the answers.

CONCLUSION AND FUTURE WORK

Our results strongly suggest that answers to list questions must be provided in a table or list format, that co-creation of the answers is essential, and that some provision must be made to allow for the fact that the answers to many questions change over time. However, our experiment was only a first step. As such, it has several limitations. These include the following:

- We do not know what effect the five minute time limit had on our results. Although searchers generally are time constrained, they typically are not limited to only five minutes. This time limit could explain why our subjects did so poorly with respect to finding the answers that were in the snippets. Additional studies should be performed that give subjects more time to find the items that belong on the answer list.
- Although we made every effort to motivate our subjects to find the answers, their motivation very likely was not as strong as the motivation of persons searching for an answer in a work setting. It would be very helpful to replicate this study in a work setting.
- We do not know how accurate QA algorithms are at picking answers out of the snippets and their associated links. As far as we could tell, none of the publically available QA algorithms do this; so additional research is required to determine their accuracy.
- Although there is every reason to believe that the recall of our QA algorithm is on a par with that of the algorithms used by WikiAnswer, AnswerBus, and Ask, we did not verify that it is. Additional work should be performed to determine whether the snippets returned by these algorithms

return a higher percentage of the items that should be included in the answer lists.

- We attempted to develop a representative category of original, fusion, list questions (questions that have not previously been asked and for which the answer is not likely to be contained in one site). Toward this end, we were careful to include questions that covered multiple domains, and questions for which the answers were likely to be stable, slowing changing, and rapidly changing. More research needs to be conducted on the most relevant way to categorize original list questions, and the ability of QA algorithms to find the answers to those different types of questions.

- Our results strongly suggest that changes need to be made in how QA systems present the results of their algorithms. We suggested possible changes for the output format. Additional research needs to be conducted to determine the extent to which these changes will improve the recall and precision of search results for users of QA algorithms.

Precise, timely, and factual answers are especially important when communication channels are limited. A growing number of internet users rely on mobile devices such as internet-enabled cell phones, which do not have the luxury of a large screen space. Moreover, military personnel, first-responders, and security specialists frequently are under such tight time constraints that every additional second spent browsing through search results puts human lives at risk. A high priority for BI researchers should be additional research to determine the extent to which QA algorithms can get the right information to the right person at the right time and in the right format to make the right decision.

REFERENCES

Bruner, J. (1960). *The Process of Education Harvard University Press*. Cambridge, MA: Harvard.

Chung, W., Chen, H., & Nunamaker, J. F. Jr. (2005). A Visual Framework for Knowledge Discovery on the Web: An Empirical Study of Business Intelligence Exploration. *Journal of Management Information Systems*, *21*(4), 57–84.

Jansen, B. J., & Spink, A. (2006). How are we searching the world wide web? A comparison of nine search engine transaction logs. *Information Processing & Management*, *42*(1), 248–263.

KMWorld. (2008). *Developing a Universal Search Strategy (Hint: Start with Usability)*. Retrieved January 16, 2009, from http://www.kmworld.com/Webinars/90-Developing-a-Universal-Search-Strategy-(Hint-Start-with-Usability).htm

Neter, J., Kutner, M., Wasserman, W., & Nachtsheim, C. (1996). *Applied linear statistical models* (4th ed.). New York: McGraw Hill/Irwin.

Pask, G. (1975). *Conversation, Cognition, and Learning*. New York: Elsevier.

Radev, D. R., Qi, H., Zheng, Z., Blair-Goldensohn, S., Zhang, Z., Fan, W., & Prager, J. (2001). Mining the Web for Answers to Natural Language Questions. In *Proceedings of the Tenth International Conference on Information and Knowledge Management*, Atlanta, GA (pp. 143-150). New York: ACM.

Robles-Flores, J. (2009). *Web Question Answering Technology: An Empirical Test of the Task-Technology Fit Model.* Unpublished doctoral dissertation, Arizona State University, Tempe, AZ.

Roussinov, D., Fan, W., & Robles-Flores, J. (2008). Beyond Keywords: Automated Question Answering on the Web. *Communications of the ACM, 51*(9), 60–65.

Roussinov, D., & Robles-Flores, J. (2004a). Self-Learning Web Question Answering System. In *Proceedings of the 13th International World Wide Web Conference (WWW2004)*, New York.

Roussinov, D., & Robles-Flores, J. (2004b). Web Question Answering: Technology and Business Applications. In *Proceedings of the Tenth Americas Conference on Information Systems*, New York.

Roussinov, D., & Robles-Flores, J. (2007). Applying Question Answering Technology to Locating Malevolent Online Content. *Decision Support Systems, 43*(4).

Roussinov, D., Robles-Flores, J., & Ding, J. (2004). Experiments with Web QA System and TREC2004 Questions. In *Proceedings of the TREC 2004 Conference*, Gaithersburg, MD.

Sparck Jones, K., & van Rijsbergen, C. (1975). *Report on the need for and provision of an "Ideal" Information retrieval test collection (British Library Research and Development Rep. No. 5266)*. Cambridge, UK: Computer Laboratory, University of Cambridge.

Surowiecki, J. (2005). *The Wisdom of Crowds*. New York: Anchor Books.

Ultraseek. (2006). *Business Search vs. Consumer Search: Five Differences Your Company Can't Afford to Ignore*. Retrieved from http://publications. autonomy.com/pdfs/Ultraseek/White%20Papers/ mk0759_Business_v_Consumer_WP.pdf

Voorhees, E. M., & Buckland, L. P. (2005). *Proceedings of the Sixteenth Text REtrieval Conference (TREC 2005)*, Gaithersburg, MD.

This work was previously published in the International Journal of Business Intelligence Research, Volume 2, Issue 1, edited by Richard Herschel, pp. 46-63, copyright 2011 by IGI Publishing (an imprint of IGI Global).

Section 3
Technology Issues

Chapter 14
Test–Driven Development of Data Warehouses

Sam Schutte
Unstoppable Software, Inc., USA

Thilini Ariyachandra
Xavier University, USA

Mark Frolick
Xavier University, USA

ABSTRACT

Test-driven development is a software development methodology that has recently gained a great deal of traction in the software development community. It focuses on creating software-based test cases that define the business requirements of an application before beginning the coding of the application itself. This paper proposes that test-driven development could be a useful methodology for data warehouse projects, in that it could help team members avoid some of the major pitfalls of data warehousing, and result in a higher-quality end product.

INTRODUCTION

Over the course of the last decade, the business of software development has gone through rapid changes due to the introduction of new light-weight methodologies. These methodologies - such as Extreme Programming, Agile Development, and SCRUM - emphasize a focus on "frequent inspection and adaptation" (*Agile Software Development,* 2009) of business requirements and technical architectural structure, and introduce new programming methods such as peer programming and stand-up meetings that help reduce re-work and improve quality.

DOI: 10.4018/978-1-4666-2650-8.ch014

One of the newer methods used by Agile development teams is test-driven development, which is "a software development technique that uses short development iterations based on pre-written test cases that define desired improvements or new functions" (*Test-Driven Development*, 2009). The overall result of the introduction of these new methodologies has been a measurable improvement in the quality, time-to-market, and productivity of software development teams (Desmond, 2009).

At present, as organizations compete in a dynamic, hyper competitive business environment characterized by a massive influx of data, business intelligence (BI), is seen as the ultimate solution that will help organizations leverage information to make informed, intelligent business decisions. According to Gartner, the worldwide BI platform revenue is forecast to grow at a compound annual growth rate of 8.1 percent through 2012, reaching $7.7 billion in 2012 (Knight, 2008).

While BI and data warehousing is now a mature market, historically, failure rates have been high (Kelly, 1997). A more recent assessment of data warehouse failure in 2007 suggests data warehouse failure rates can be as high as 50 percent (Embarcadero, 2008). In addition, ensuring high data quality within the data warehousing environment still continues to be a major issue. Industry trends in data quality indicate that companies are looking for "pragmatic approaches" to managing data quality (English, 2007). Organizations are searching for practical ways to handle errors and inconsistencies within source systems to create effective data staging practices. Test-driven development offers a unique opportunity to enhance current data warehouse implementation practices; especially in the area of improving data quality.

The purpose of this paper is to discuss the background and benefits of test-driven development and explore the application of this effective software development methodology to data warehouse implementation projects.

STATUS OF TDD IN THE BI AND DATA WAREHOUSING SPACE

While the data warehouse and business intelligence industry has adopted a few of the methods from agile development, such as "bite size analysis" (Arnett, 2002) and improved coding practices, the methods of test-driven development are only starting to gain use. For instance, test-driven development has been proposed as a way to verify the validity of business intelligence reports such as Crystal Reports (Landes, 2005). In the specific area of data warehousing however, test-driven development does not appear to have made an impact.

If the principles of test-driven development were applied to a data warehousing project, the resulting data warehouse would likely be of high quality and its functionality would not exceed the scope of the original request. Additionally, it would be scientifically provable through the use of the software-based test cases that the data within a data warehouse was correct – even in the face of disbelieving executives who may question the accuracy of reports generated from the data warehouse.

To succeed in a test-driven environment, a data warehouse team would have to follow several guidelines. First, all functionality and data in the system must be specified by end-users, and then test cases must be created which specifically address each piece of data or data relationship. Second, as the system is developed, these test cases must be run against the data warehouse. When a test passes, that particular feature (e.g., database table or field, or ETL process) within the data warehousing environment is considered complete. In this way, the pending tasks in the project implantation plan simply become any tests that are currently failing.

BACKGROUND: WHAT IS TEST-DRIVEN DEVELOPMENT?

Test-driven development (TDD) was first introduced as a part of Extreme Programming (XP), which is a software development methodology created by Kent Beck in the early 1990s. Extreme programming focuses on four core values: "Communication, Simplicity, Feedback, and Courage" (Wells, 1999). These core values lead to a series of best practices for software development, which – when taken to the extreme – will help to guarantee the success of a software development project. The best practice that eventually evolved into test-driven development was known as "Code the Unit Test First", a practice that would make system requirements more accurate, provide immediate feedback to the developer as to the progress of his or her work, and improve the granularity of the overall system design (Wells, 2000). Since that time, test-driven development has grown into a methodology in its own right and has gained a great deal of acceptance from the developer community, being used not only for the development of new software applications, but also migration of legacy systems to new environments (*Test-Driven Development*, 2009; Corbett, 2009).

TDD FOR A SOFTWARE PROJECT

To use test-driven development for a software development project, the software development team must first identify the requirements of the application, and convert the English-language requirements into a series of automated test cases, which are bits of code that can be executed by a unit testing framework (such as NUnit, JUnit, Team Foundation Server, etc.). This process of breaking down the requirements into software tests is the first benefit of test-driven development, in that it helps developers create a better thought-out design (Wells, 2000). From that point, all development tasks must follow a three step process: write

a test case, write code that fulfills the test case, and run the test case to verify that it passes. If at any time the test fails, the development task associated with the test is by definition unfinished. When the test passes, the task is complete and the developer can move on to the next task. A visual of the test driven software development flow is presented in Figure 1.

While this may seem a fairly simple idea, it provides the benefit of preventing "gold plating" (i.e., unnecessary features added by developers) and controlling scope because no new functionality is ever written unless there is a corresponding failing test (Freeman & Pryce, 2009). Also, because of the increased focus on the design of the code, one study found that projects that used TDD had 40 to 90 percent fewer defects than projects developed using non-TDD methodologies (Sims, 2009).

THE "RIGHT" LEVEL OF TESTING

When breaking down business requirements into automated test cases, it is also important that the level and depth of the test cases are adequate. That is, it is not sufficient simply to test a particular program method by simply calling it and verifying that the method output is valid. While this is a perfectly acceptable test on its own, the fact that such a simple test passes or fails does not prove that a given business requirement is met. Therefore, tests must be designed so that they not only test individual units of code (Unit Testing), but also external systems that rely on the software (Integration Testing) and so that they verify the whole system is working end-to-end (Acceptance Testing) (Freeman & Pryce, 2009).

Following this cycle also provides the development team with an ever-growing base of system tests that can be used to prove that their software is working correctly at any point in time. Over time, as future enhancements to the codebase are made, this is perhaps the most valuable result of

Figure 1. Test driven software development flow

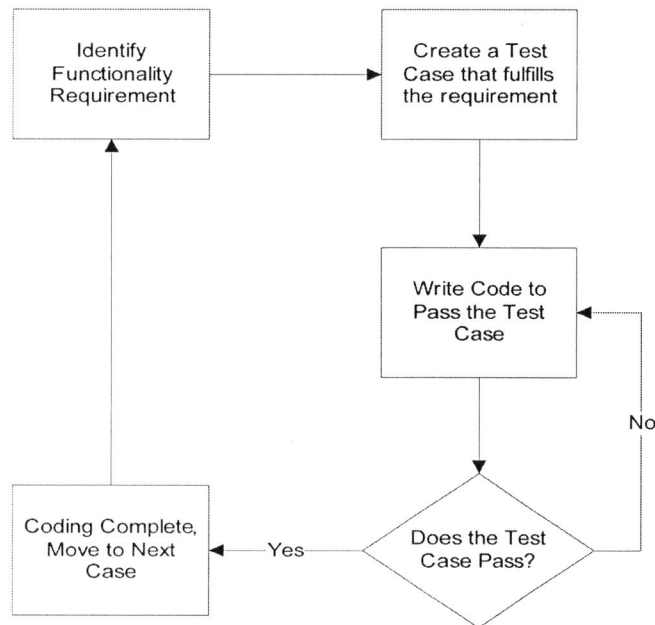

following a test-driven method. Instead of tending to grow frail and more bug-ridden as time passes, a test-driven software application will become more robust, and any future changes to the application that break existing functionality will immediately become apparent because existing test cases will begin to fail.

BUSINESS ENVIRONMENT CHALLENGES

In 2003, Gartner, Inc. reported that more than 50 percent of data warehouse projects fail, and the other 50 percent are either delivered late or over budget. This high rate of failure is often due to data integrity issues. In fact, in 2007, Gartner estimated that 50 percent of data warehouse projects would fail due to issues with data integrity (Embarcadero, 2008). While many of these data quality issues arise from the reliance on source data from legacy systems that may be of questionable accuracy, it is likely that data is-

sues also arise from simple human error during the development of the data warehouse, or from inadequate time devoted to testing. Unfortunately for data warehouse developers, data warehouse project managers are under increasing pressure to deliver business knowledge quickly, so the time consuming manual data integrity checks that have been relied on in the past are often skipped (Moss, 2009). Additionally, while much focus is placed on the quality of individual data elements, little focus is placed on testing the quality of the database schema and the connected application programs (Embarcadero, 2008).

FAILING TO MEET THE USER'S NEEDS

Aside from data issues, another leading cause of failure for data warehouse projects is a failure to adequately identify business requirements and translate them to the system (Watson et al., 2004). This is a problem common to all technology projects, however with data warehouses it is a particularly large problem because many businesses see the selection of a BI tool as the most important decision to be made for a data warehouse project. Once vendor selection is made, business stakeholders often assume that the development team has everything needed to make the data warehouse work, and may be resistant to dedicating the business resources necessary to fully document the requirements of the system (Wong, 2007).

Another key issue is data timeliness – that is, the data is not available when it is needed (*Data Warehouse Challenges*, 2009; Wixom & Watson, 2001). This can be due to performance issues caused by inadequate access to the database tables, because external feeder systems do not deliver the data as promised, or often because the manual processes that feed the data into the system are not carried out on schedule (*Data Quality Definition*, 2009).

While the issues contributing towards project failure discussed so far revolve around the data and functionality within the data warehouse, another key source of project failure has to do with integration with data feeder systems. This is principally done by creating extract, transform, and load (ETL) programs that interface with external systems to populate the data warehouse (Inmon, 2001). These programs can be either developed manually in code by developers, or as more often is the case, created in third party tools with a drag and drop interface (*Extract, Transform, Load,* 2009). Regardless of the environment they are created in, these programs are software, and as such will contain bugs, and therefore could benefit from automated testing.

Even when a data warehouse project succeeds, there are many risks to its stability and continued use in the future. This is because as changes are made to the system, it is very difficult to ensure that the changes will not "break" other items in the system. In any large data warehouse, there will be many dependencies on each data element, which may be difficult to document. Since not

all reports in any given BI system are run on a constant basis, it is possible that reports could be broken by changes in the system, but that the issue will not be discovered for quite some time.

APPLYING TDD TO A DW PROJECT

Fortunately for data warehouse developers, the damage caused by these issues can be lessened by the application of test-driven development practices. TDD practices can be applied to each of the major components within a data warehouse project.

At a conceptual level, the typical data warehouse involves the following major generic components: (1) data sources, (2) data staging, (3) data storage, and (4) end user access (Ariyachandra & Watson, 2010) (See Figure 2). The shaded region represents the typical data warehouse project scope at a conceptual level.

In data staging, first the data is extracted from various operational systems and external data sources and the data is transformed to a format that is suitable for data analysis. Overall, the data staging component provides an area where the data is cleaned, converted, and integrated to prepare it for storage and use in the data warehouse. The data is extracted, transformed, and loaded into the data warehouse. As a result of the ETL process, data in operational data sources are prepared for the warehouse.

The data storage for the data warehouse is a separate data repository composed of high quality data. Depending on the data warehouse architecture, the storage component may be composed of a centralized data store, data marts, or both (Hackney, 2000). Most data repositories employ relational database management systems while others use multidimensional database management systems (Watson et al., 2006).

Lastly, the data access component provides a set of data reporting and analysis capabilities developed to meet user data needs. These data

Figure 2. The main components of a data warehouse

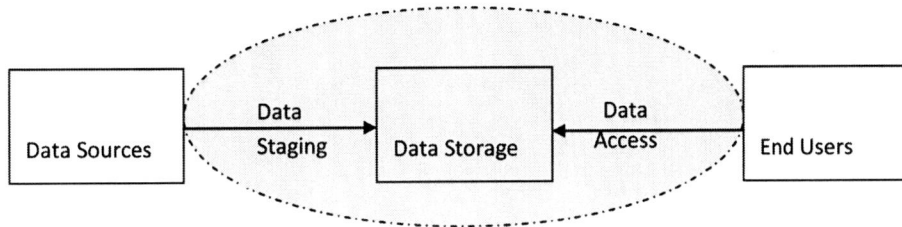

access tools enable end users to manipulate and retrieve data from the storage component. They vary in degrees of sophistication from canned standard reports, to ad hoc analysis, to real time dashboards and score cards (Frolick et al., 2006).

To apply test-driven development to each component within a data warehouse project, developers need to alter the way they think about test cases. Instead of testing a particular section of code in a program, test cases would instead focus more on testing specific aspects of the underlying warehouse database or system. Figure 3 presents a visual of a potential test case for a data warehouse project.

In addition, Table 1 provides a summary of some potential unit tests that could be created for each of the components of a data warehouse system. In general, data staging tests would verify that key statistics about the data matched the original source data, and that the data is properly cleaned and integrated as it should be at the end of the ETL process.

Tests for data storage verify not only that the data is in the proper relational format (database structure matches the architecture that was specified during the design process), but also that the data storage component is performing to expectations – for instance, if the system requirements specified that proper indexes on the relational data source should yield a 2 ms response time for the query "*select count(*) from customers*", a test that took 5 ms would fail. Lastly, tests

for the data access component would work much in the way that traditional User Interface Unit tests work. If the user interface in question was a data-driven dashboard, a test could be written that automatically clicked buttons on the dashboard interface (existing 3rd party tools can automate this kind of "clicking"), and checked the output to make sure that the values displayed were within valid ranges, and matched the data in the data store. This matching of expected values from the data store is particularly important, because the worst bugs in an end-user data access application are bugs where "the report is showing the wrong answer" (whereas the legacy mainframe that was the original source, for instance, displays the proper answer).

In order to gain all the benefits of test-driven development, data warehouse developers would need to carefully break down the business requirements into pieces that could be tested by automated tests before beginning any development. This process of both identifying all the business requirements and designing the system to be tested is likely to help greatly with one of the more difficult issues facing data warehouses – failure to capture business needs. Once the business needs are identified, developers should create a suite of tests for each feature, and then begin creating the data warehouse, all the while running the test suite until all tests pass. Once all tests pass, developers should consider that portion of the data warehouse complete, and move on to the next feature.

Figure 3. Potential DW test cases

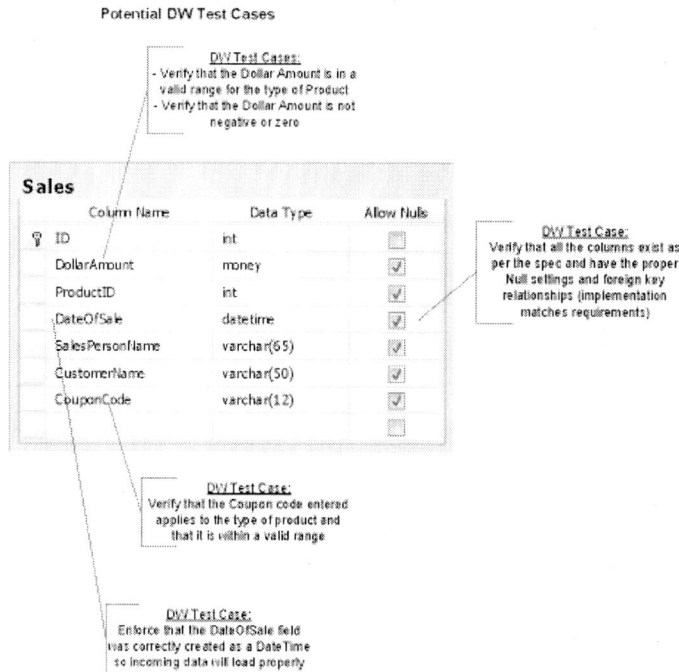

Table 1. TDD practices for DW components

Component	TDD Examples
Data Staging	All Data is in the proper format when matched against a regular expression (for instance, all Social Security Number fields are in the format ###-##-####) RowCount matches the row count from the original operational data source – if the number is different, not all data was successfully extracted "ModifiedDate" on the cleaned data is within an expected timeframe – data is properly refreshing in the expected time window For a given column "SalePrice", Mean, Mode, and Median of the cleaned data match those values for the operational data – should always match, or there may be a rounding issue, rows skipped, etc. Cleaned Rows are not missing any key fields that the unit tests require Values that are expected to be unique are in fact unique
Data Storage	Implementation of Table X matches the design specified for Table X (ColNames, keys, indexes) When data is refreshed from Data Staging process, any history tables, partitions, or backups that should be performed are being properly executed (e.g. check for existence of "DB_BackUp.bak" in a specified folder at a specific time Data Storage is performing as expected – query "*select count(*) from customers*" returns a value within 2 ms Lookup column values have a value that matches an available value in the lookup table Size of raw data on disk for the warehouse is not exceeding expectations – if this test fails, may need to add disk drives or move to another server Tests the validate the output of stored procedures housed within the data warehouse
Data Access	Tests that validate that "rolled up" values for "Quarterly Revenue" match true totals when report is "rolled up" to the city, state, and national level Expected wait time for report generation once a button is clicked is within set parameters User security is properly implemented – unit test can impersonate a user that does not have access to a certain report and verify that the system denies access Values for Averages, Totals, etc. match the values not only in the data storage layer, but the values in the original operational database system (all levels of the system should show the same value)

ADDRESSING DATA QUALITY

To help with data quality issues, test cases could be developed that check for missing values, test logic embedded in a value, ensure unique primary keys, and help enforce referential integrity (Moss, 2009). It order to cover all the possible data issues a system may have, it would be necessary to create tests for each data column in the system. Though this may at first seem like a daunting task, it is possible that a fair amount of the code behind these tests could be re-used, and the potential returns (being able to know immediately when bad data enters the system, or being able to prevent bad data outright) may justify the work.

Creating test cases that test the schema structure of the database will also add a great amount of value to the project, especially if developers establish a core set of schema "rules" that they wish to enforce (level of normalization required, maximum column count, etc.). Cases validating the schema also would be an excellent way to ensure that the design that is decided on by the team is the design that actually ends up in the system – and if the design needed to change along the way, it would merely mean that the test would need to be changed. In this instance, just having the test case around as a form of documentation for the team to share would be valuable.

To better ensure data timeliness, tests could be created that compare when the data is arriving from external systems versus when the business requirements state it is needed. These tests would likely fail up to the time the data warehouse is put into final testing and is receiving data from its external sources; however, since the task is not officially complete until this time, this is acceptable.

As mentioned, ETL processes that will be developed in a programming language can be developed following test-driven methods just like any other software. If ETL processes are to be developed in a third party system, the test-driven approach is still possible since regardless of the system used to develop them, ETL processes still have inputs and outputs. Therefore, it would just be necessary to develop a suite of tests for each ETL process to be created that validates the output from the process.

TEST CASES ENSURE SYSTEM ROBUSTNESS

Once tests have been created through the test-driven process for data warehouse components, the resulting warehouse also gains a great deal of resistance to the issue of future breaking changes. In the future, if a developer makes a change to a table that will negatively impact other aspects of the system, the suite of test cases would "see" this change, and the related tests would begin failing. This sort of on-going warehouse testability assumes that the tests are run on a timed basis (nightly, weekly, etc.), which is the standard for software development projects.

CONCLUSION

At the completion of a test-driven data warehouse project, the end result would be a provably-correct system. Additionally, any future changes to this system that "break" the rules of the requirements would quickly be visible because a test case would begin to fail. With the vast amount of data that resides in data warehouses, the only way to have such a provably-correct system is through the use of automated tests. By using test-driven development data warehouse implementation project teams can strive towards implementing a provably correct warehousing solution.

REFERENCES

Agile Software Development. (n.d.). Wikipedia. Retrieved March 8, 2009, from http://en.wikipedia.org/wiki/Agile_software_development

Ariyachandra, T., & Watson, H. (2010). Key Organizational Factors in Data Warehouse Architecture Selection. *Decision Support Systems, 49*, 200–212. doi:10.1016/j.dss.2010.02.006

Arnett, L. (2002). Architecting an Agile Data Warehouse. *Information and Management*. Retrieved March 8, 2009, from http://www.information-management.com/infodirect/20020927/5831-1.html

Corbett, N. (2009). *Test Driven Development, a Portable Methodology*. Retrieved April 16, 2009, from http://www.developer.com/design/article.php/3622546

Data Quality Definition – What is Data Quality? (n.d.). BiPM Institute. Retrieved April 19, 2009, from http://www.bipminstitute.com/data-quality/accuracy-consistency-audit.php

Data Warehouse Challenges and Issues. (n.d.). BiPM Institute. Retrieved April 19, 2009 from http://www.bipminstitute.com/data-warehouse/challenge-issues.php

Desmond, J. (2009). Agile Development Techniques Produce Record Results at BMC Software. *Software Magazine*. Retrieved November 5, 2009, from http://www.softwaremag.com/L.cfm?Doc=1198-3/2009

English, L. (2007). Data Quality in Plain English. *Information and Management*. Retrieved April 12, 2009, from http://www.information-management.com/issues/20070401/1079288-1.html

Extract, T. *Load*. (2009). Wikipedia. Retrieved April 20, 2009, from http://en.wikipedia.org/wiki/Extract,_transform,_load

Freeman, S., & Pryce, N. (2009). Growing Object-Oriented Software. *Guided by Tests*. Retrieved April 16, 2009, from http://www.mockobjects.com/book/tdd-introduction.html

Frolick, M., & Ariyachandra, T. (2006). Business Performance Management: The Real Truth. *Information Systems Management, 23*(1). doi:10.1201/1078.10580530/45769.23.1.20061201/91771.5

Hackney, D. (2000). Architecture anarchy and how to survive it: God save the queen. *Enterprise Systems Journal, 15*(4), 24–30.

Inmon, W., Imhoff, C., & Sousa, R. (2001). *Corporate Information Factory* (2nd ed.). New York: Wiley & sons.

Kelly, S. (1997). Data marts: The latest silver bullet. In *Data mart review* (pp. 12-16).

Knight, M. (2008). *BI Growth to Buck Economic Trends*. Retrieved from http://www.itpro.co.uk/183480/bi-growth-to-buck-economic-trends, retrieved 2/23/2010

Landes, E. (2005). *Test Driven Development for a Business Intelligence Projects with Crystal Reports*. Retrieved March 8, 2009, from http://aspalliance.com/712

Moss, L. (2009). Ten Mistakes to Avoid for Data Warehouse Project Managers. *Business Intelligence Journal*. Retrieved April 20, 2009, from http://www.tdwi.org/Publications/display.aspx?Id=7545#7

Sims, C. (2009). *Empirical Studies Show Test Driven Development Improves Quality, InfoQ*. Retrieved April 16, 2009, from http://www.infoq.com/news/2009/03/TDD-Improves-Quality

Technologies, E. (2008). *Why Data Warehouse Projects Fail*. Retrieved April 16, 2009, from http://www.embarcadero.com/resources/technical_papers/Why-Data-Warehouse-Projects-Fail.pdf

Test-Driven Development. (n.d.). Wikipedia. Retrieved March 8, 2009, from http://en.wikipedia.org/wiki/Test-driven_development

Watson, H., & Ariyachandra, T. (2006). Benchmarks for BI and Data Warehousing Success. *DM Review, 16*(1).

Watson, H., Ariyachandra, T., & Fuller, C. (2004). Data Warehousing Governance: Best Practices at Blue Cross Blue Shield of North Carolina. *Decision Support Systems, 38*(3). doi:10.1016/j.dss.2003.06.001

Wells, D. (1999). *The XP Philosophy*. Retrieved April 12, 2009, from http://www.extremeprogramming.org/Kent.html

Wells, D. (2000). *Code the Unit Test First*. Retrieved April 12, 2009, from http://www.extremeprogramming.org/rules/testfirst.html

Wixom, B. H., & Watson, H. J. (2001). An empirical investigation of the factors affecting data warehousing success. *Management Information Systems Quarterly, 25*(1), 17. doi:10.2307/3250957

Wong, J. (2007). *Problems in Building a Data Warehouse, SQLServerCentral.com*. Retrieved April 20, 2009, from http://www.sqlservercentral.com/articles/Design/2832/

This work was previously published in the International Journal of Business Intelligence Research, Volume 2, Issue 1, edited by Richard Herschel, pp. 64-73, copyright 2011 by IGI Publishing (an imprint of IGI Global).

Chapter 15
Uncovering Actionable Knowledge in Corporate Data with Qualified Association Rules

Nenad Jukic
Loyola University Chicago, USA

Svetlozar Nestorov
University of Chicago, USA

Miguel Velasco
University of Minnesota, USA

Jami Eddington
Oklahoma State University, USA

ABSTRACT

Association rules mining is one of the most successfully applied data mining methods in today's business settings (e.g. Amazon or Netflix recommendations to customers). Qualified association rules mining is an extension of the association rules data mining method, that uncovers previously unknown correlations that only manifest themselves under certain circumstances (e.g. on a particular day of the week), with the goal of improving action results, e.g. turning an underperforming campaign (spread too thin over the entire audience) into a highly targeted campaign that delivers results. Such correlations have not been easily reachable using standard data mining tools so far. This paper describes the method for straightforward discovery of qualified association rules and demonstrates the use of qualified association rules mining on an actual corporate data set. The data set is a subset of a corporate data warehouse for Sam's Club, a division of Wal-Mart Stores, INC. The experiments described in this paper illustrate how qualified association rules supplement standard association rules data mining methods and provide additional information which can be used to better target corporate actions.

DOI: 10.4018/978-1-4666-2650-8.ch015

1. INTRODUCTION

Rapid increase in the magnitude of the available and affordable computing power, storage, and memory has enabled corporations and organization to sustain, and in many cases accelerate, the trend of storing and maintaining ever-increasing quantities of data. One of the main information management challenges faced by corporations today is how to get valuable and actionable information from the massive amounts of data that they own.

A typical organization maintains and uses a number of operational data sources. These operational data sources include databases and other data repositories, which are used to support the organization's day-to-day operations. A data warehouse is created within an organization as an additional separate data store whose primary purpose is data analysis for the support of management's decision-making processes. Often, the same fact can have both operational and analytical purposes. For example, data describing that customer A bought product B in store C can be stored in an operational data store for business-process support purposes, such as inventory monitoring or financial transaction record keeping. That same fact can also be stored in a data warehouse where, combined with vast numbers of similar facts accumulated over a time-period, it is used to analyze important trends, such as sales patterns or customer behavior. A typical data warehouse periodically retrieves selected analytically-useful data from the operational data sources (Jukic, 2006). For a more in depth look see Kimball, Ross, Thornthwaite, Mundy, and Becker (2007) or Inmon (2005).

Unfortunately, many organizations often underutilize their already constructed data warehouses (Glassey, 1998; Gorla, 2003). While some information and facts can be gleaned from the data warehouse directly, much more can remain hidden as implicit patterns and trends. On-line analytical processing (OLAP) tools, which are also known as business intelligence (BI) tools,

provide analytical users with a user friendly way of retrieving data from data warehouses. These tools perform their primary reporting function well when the criteria for aggregating and presenting data are specified explicitly and ahead of time. However, it is the discovery of information based on implicit and previously unknown patterns that often yields important insights into the business and its customers, and may lead to unlocking the hidden potential of already collected information. Such discoveries require utilization of data mining methods.

Data mining is defined as a process whose objective is to identify valid, novel, potentially useful, and understandable correlations and patterns in existing data using a broad spectrum of formalisms and techniques (Chung & Gray, 1999; Smyth, Pregibon, & Faloutsos, 2002). Even though mining operational databases containing data related to current day-to-day organizational activities can be of limited use in certain situations, the most appropriate and fertile source of data for meaningful and effective data mining is the corporate data warehouse.

One of the most important and successful data mining methods for finding new patterns and correlations is association-rule mining (also known as market-basket analysis). However, standard association-rule method is limited to mining only selected portions of the data warehouse. Seeking to eliminate this restriction, and by doing so significantly improve the insight and the actionability of the discovered knowledge, we developed the concept of *qualified association rules* which is capable of answering a variety of questions based on the entire set of data stored in the data warehouse. Formal definitions, algorithms, and other technical details that provided the theoretical foundation for qualified association rules method are described in our previous papers (Jukic & Nestorov, 2003; Jukic & Nestorov, 2006). In this paper we provide a clear illustration of how this method can enable organizations to get more value out the data they already own. We demonstrate the capabilities of qualified association rules method by applying it on a relevant set of actual corporate data. The data was provided by Wal-Mart Stores, Inc. The data set is a subset of a corporate data warehouse containing 55 million rows representing thirty days of sales transaction data for 18 Sam's Club stores. The Sam M. Walton College of Business at the University of Arkansas has been gifted with this large-scale, real-world datasets donated by Walmart, and made it available for the academic teaching and research projects via Teradata University Network (an organization that serves as a bridge between academia and the world of practice and has more than 800 participating universities world-wide).

The lessons and findings about the applicability of qualified association rules from this retail-related example are applicable on a wide variety of other industries. Before we demonstrate how qualified association rules increased the value of discovered knowledge within the Sam's Club data set, we give a brief overview of both standard and qualified association rules.

2. MARKET BASKET ANALYSIS AND QUALIFIED ASSOCIATION RULES - OVERVIEW

Standard association-rule mining (Agrawal, Imielinski, & Swami, 1993; Agrawal & Srikant, 1994) discovers correlations among items within transactions. The correlations are expressed in the following form:

Transactions that contain X are likely to contain Y as well

Noted as association rule X→Y, where X and Y represent sets of transaction items. The prototypical example of utilizing association-rule mining determines what products are found together in a basket at a checkout line at the supermarket. Hence

the often-used term "market basket analysis", where correlations are represented in form of a rule:

Customers buying X are likely to buy Y during the same purchase transaction

There are two important quantities measured for every association rule: support and confidence. The support for rule X→Y is the fraction of transactions that contain both Item X and Item Y, i.e. support = (number of transactions containing X and Y) / (number of all transactions). The confidence for rule X→Y is the fraction of transactions containing items X, which also contain items Y, i.e. confidence = (number of transactions containing X and Y) / (number of transactions containing X). Intuitively, the support measures the significance of the rule, so we are interested in rules with relatively high support. The confidence measures the strength of the correlation, so rules with low confidence are not meaningful, even if their support is high. A rule in this context is the relationship among transaction items with high enough support and confidence, where high enough thresholds are determined by the analyst.

Association-rule data mining has drawn a considerable amount of attention from practitioners and researchers in the last decade, and it has been used in a variety of industries for purposes such as analysis of retail purchases for the "recommendation" feature in e-commerce sites, analysis of telephone calling patterns to anticipate churning, and identification of fraudulent medical insurance claims. We developed the concept of qualified association rules as a way of extending the scope and capability of association rule mining. This approach is designed to provide a real addition to the value of collected organizational information and is applicable in a host of real world situations.

Dimensional modeling (Kimball, Reeves, Ross, & Thornthwhite, 1998) which is the most prevalent technique for modeling corporate data warehouses, organizes tables into fact tables –

tables containing basic quantitative measurements of an organizational activity under consideration, and dimension tables – tables providing descriptions of the facts being stored. Dimension tables and their attributes are chosen for their ability to contribute to the analysis of the facts being stored in the fact tables.

The data model that is produced by the dimensional modeling method is known as a star-schema. Figure 1 shows a simple star-schema model of a data warehouse for a retail company.

The fact table contains the sale figures for each sale transaction and it connects the five dimensions: Item, Customer, Store, Transaction Characteristics, and Calendar. A standard association-rule mining question for this environment would be:

What products are frequently bought together?

This question examines the fact table as it relates to the product dimension only. A typical data warehouse, however, has multiple dimensions which are ignored by the above single-dimension question, as illustrated by Figure 2.

While determining which products are frequently purchased together can be insightful, an analyst at the corporate headquarters may ask the following question:

What products are frequently bought together during a particular day of the week?

This question requires examination of multiple dimensions of the fact table. The standard association-rule mining approach would not find the answer to this question directly because it only explores the fact table with its relationship to the dimension table containing transaction-items (in this case Item), while the other dimension tables are not considered. In fact, by applying standard algorithms directly, we may not discover any association rules in situations when there are several meaningful associations involving multiple dimensions. The following example illustrates an extreme case scenario of such situation.

Example 1: A major retail chain sells hundreds of different products including Item A and Item B. Through the usage of a membership card, the retail chain keeps track of

Figure 1. Example retail company star-schema

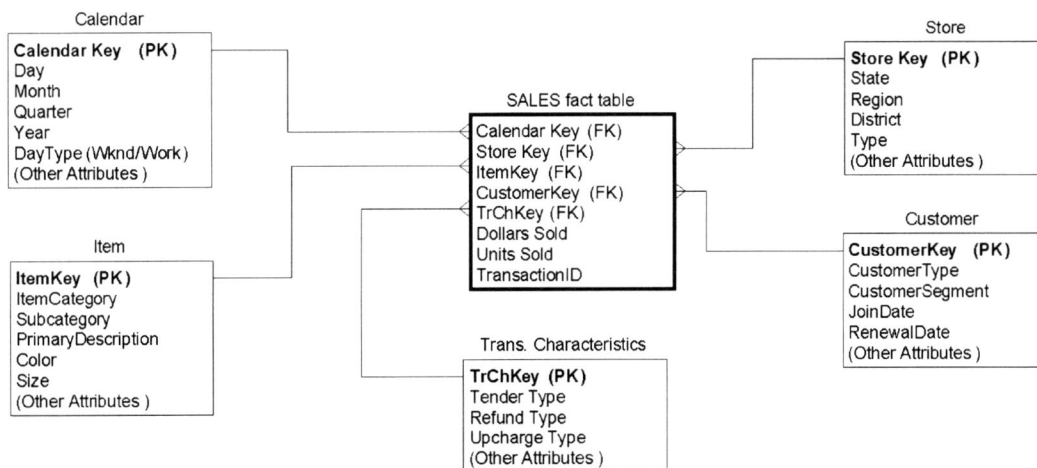

Figure 2. Association-rule data mining scope for the example retail company star schema

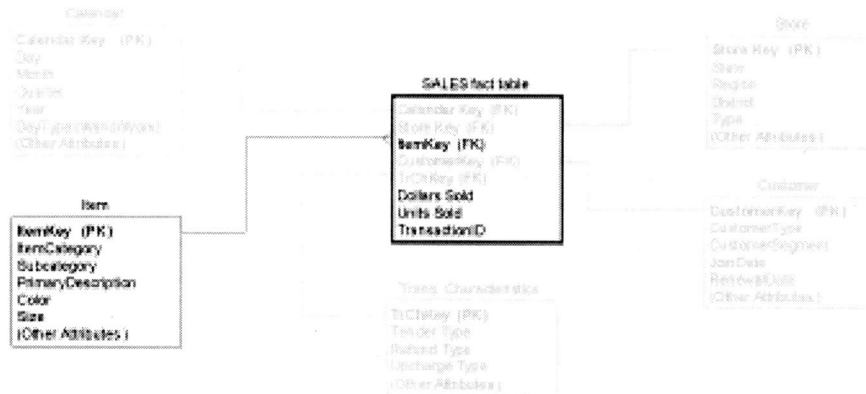

the customers involved in transactions. The retailer classifies customers as new (joined less than a year ago) or old (members for one year or longer).

Suppose we are looking for association rules with 0.5% support and 50% confidence (normally these thresholds are determined by the analyst and they can be revised in subsequent iterations of the data mining process). Let's first consider the transactions by all customers on all days. Table 1 shows the number of transactions involving Item A, Item B, or both Item A and Item B. There are 765 thousand total transactions and 11 thousand of them involve both Item A and Item B, so the support of the pair of items is 1.44% (support for A→B and for B→A is the same: 11/765 = 1.44%, support is always the same for both rules involving the same pair of items). There are 25 thousand transactions that involve item A and 30 thousand transactions that involve item B. Therefore the confidence of *Item A → Item B* is 44.00% and the confidence of *Item B → Item A* is 36.67% (confidence for A→B is 11/25 = 44% and for B→A is 11/30 = 36.67%, in both cases confidence is below 50%). Thus, no association rules involving Item A and Item B will be discovered.

Now, let's consider the transactions on workdays separately. Table 2 shows the number of transactions for each category of customers during a workday and during a weekend day, as well

Table 1. Transaction statics for example 1 (standard association rules)

Number of Transactions (x1000)	
	Total
Item A	*25*
Item B	*30*
Items A & B	*11*
All Items	*765*

as the number of transactions that involved the Item A, Item B, or both Item A and Item B. During all workdays Item A appears in 12 thousand transactions, Item B appears in 16 thousand transactions, and both Item A and Item B appear together in 5 thousand transactions. The support for both items is 0.65%, but the confidence for rules involving Item A and Item B are 41.67% and 31.25% (for workday transactions support for A→B and for B→A is 5/765 = 0.65%, confidence for A→B is 5/12 = 41.67% and for B→A is 5/16 = 31.25%. In both cases the confidence is below 50% - calculations equivalent to these are done for the rest of the examples.)

Thus, no association rule involving Item A and Item B will be discovered. Similarly, no rules involving both Item A and Item B will be discovered for the weekend days, and no associations will be discovered between Item A and Item B when we consider all the transactions by old and new customers separately.

However, if each combination of customer segment and day type were considered separately the following association rules would be discovered:

- Item A → Item B; new customers shopping during weekend days (sup=0.52%, conf=80.00%),
- Item B → Item A; new customers shopping during weekend days (sup=0.52%, conf=80.00%),

- Item A → Item B; old customers shopping during workdays (sup=0.52%, conf=66.67%).

When applied in a direct and straightforward fashion, the standard association rule mining would not discover these association rules because it does not account for non-item dimensions.

In addition to the possibility of suppressing some of the existing relevant rules (as illustrated by Example 1), another type of problem can arise when multiple dimensions are not considered: An overabundance of discovered rules may hide a smaller number of meaningful rules. Example 2 illustrates an extreme case scenario of this situation.

Example 2: The same retail chain considers transactions that involve the following three products: Item X, Item Y, and Item Z.

Table 3 shows the number of transactions for both customer segments on workdays and on weekend days. The table contains the number of transactions that involved Item X, Item Y, and Item Z; as well as the number of transactions that involved Item X and Item Y together, Item X and Item Z together, and Item Y and Item Z together.

Suppose we are looking for association rules with 0.50% support and 50% confidence. If we consider all of the transactions we will discover that every possible association rule involving two items satisfies the threshold, as shown below:

Table 2. Transaction statistics for example 1 (qualified association rules)

	Number of Transactions (x1000)				
	Old Customer		New Customer		
	Workday	Weekend	Workday	Weekend	*Total*
Item A	6	8	6	5	*25*
Item B	10	9	6	5	*30*
Items A & B	4	2	1	4	*11*
All Items	*400*	*170*	*90*	*105*	*765*

Table 3. Transaction statistics for example 2

	Number of Transactions (x1000)				
	Old Customer		New Customer		
	Workday	Weekend	Workday	Weekend	*Total*
Item X	7	6	4	4	21
Item Y	3	11	4	4	22
Item Z	3	10	5	4	22
Items X & Y	2	3	3	3	11
Items X & Z	2	3	3	3	11
Items Y & Z	2	5	3	3	13
All Items	400	170	90	105	765

- Item X → Item Y; (sup=1.44%, conf=52.38%)
- Item Y → Item X; (sup=1.44%, conf=50.00%)
- Item X → Item Z; (sup=1.44%, conf=52.38%)
- Item Z → Item X; (sup=1.44%, conf=50.00%)
- Item Y → Item Z; (sup=1.70%, conf=59.09%)
- Item Z → Item Y; (sup=1.70%, conf=59.09%)

In this example, any combination of two of the three products is correlated. Thus, it is difficult to make any conclusions, reach any decisions, or take any actions. This problem occurs when a mining process produces a very large number of rules, thus proving to be of little value to the user. However if we consider each customer segment and day type separately we will find only one rule within the given support and confidence limit:

- Item Z → Item Y; old customers shopping during weekend days (sup=0.65%, conf=50.00%)

Isolating this rule may provide valuable additional information to the corporation in question. The above two examples illustrate two types of situations in which association rules considering both the item-related dimension (e.g. Item) and non-item related dimensions (e.g. Customer Segment, Day Type) add new insight into the nature of data.

Standard association rules can express correlations between values of a single dimension of the star schema. However, as illustrated in Example 1, some associations become evident only when multiple dimensions are involved. In Example 1, Item A and Item B appear uncorrelated in the sales data as a whole, or even when the data is considered separately by customer segment or part of the week. Yet, several association rules are discovered if the focus is on the data for a particular customer segment during a particular part of the week. In Example 2 Items X, Y and Z all appear to be correlated within the threshold values when the sales data is considered as a whole. However, when the focus is put on the data for a particular customer segment during a particular part of the week, only one rule still holds.

The purpose of these examples was not to claim that qualified association rules are superior to standard association rules. Rather, the point is to illustrate that combining these two methods can result in better insights and therefore provide more value from the data.

3. APPLICATION OF QUALIFIED ASSOCIATION RULE DATA MINING METHOD ON A CORPORATE DATASET

In order to validate the potential and nature of qualified association rule mining, and to test the feasibility of the implementation of our approach in a working system (Section 5 of this paper contains a discussion on technical details of our system, including a comparison with a standard data mining tool), we created an analytical study of an actual corporate dataset. As stated, the dataset was provided by Wal-Mart Stores, Inc. The provided data set contains 55 million rows representing sales transaction data for 18 Sam's Club* stores in a 30 day cycle. The used dataset is a subset of a massive (terabytes of data) corporate data warehouse.

Sam's Club, a division of Wal-Mart Stores, Inc., is a warehouse club that specializes in selling to small businesses. A membership-based store, Sam's Club offers goods and services for consumers and business owners. The Sam's Club Database contains retail sales information gathered from sales at Sam's Club stores. The process used to gather this information begins with a Sam's Club member gathering all of the items they intend to purchase during the current visit to Sam's Club. The member then proceeds to a register to check out. A Sam's Club associate scans the member's Sam's Club card, at which point a transaction identifier is generated. The sales-associate proceeds by scanning each item with a barcode reader. When all of the items have been scanned, information about each individual type of product purchased during that visit is recorded. When payment is tendered for items purchased on that visit, summary information for the total order (transaction time and date, payment type, amount spent, number of unique items purchased, etc.) is recorded. This information, together with the data from tables that capture detailed information about stores, products, and members, is used to populate the repository equivalent to the schema shown in Figure 1. Although a portion of the data in this dataset has been scrubbed by Wal-Mart Stores, Inc. (e.g. some of the member information, product cost, etc.) the sales information is primarily intact.

Based on our experimental study, we conclude that qualified association rules provide significant new insights and valuable knowledge and improve dramatically the actionability of standard association rules. In particular, we identified three different ways (Table 4) in which qualified association rules approach elevates the quality of the discovered standard association rules.

In order to illustrate these factors we chose a query whose results are representative of our experiments in general. This query qualifies association rules by the day of the week:

What products are frequently bought together during a particular day of the week?

The qualified rules, discovered based on this query, have the following form:

$X \rightarrow Y (day\_of\_the\_week = Z)$

X and Y are items and Z is one of the seven days of the week (Monday - Sunday). For brevity, we omit the name of the dimension and simply write $X \rightarrow Y (Z)$. For example, *salsa → chips (Sunday)*.

Table 4. Insight factors

Insight Factor 1	Identifying qualified association rules whose transaction items are either more correlated or less correlated when compared to the equivalent discovered standard rules.
Insight Factor 2	Identifying qualified association rules which are partially-existent as compared to their equivalent discovered standard rules.
Insight Factor 3	Identifying qualified association rules whose equivalent standard rules are not discovered.

Insight Factor 1

For a concrete example, consider the rule *lowfat milk → eggs* with thresholds support 0.025% and confidence 25%. The support and confidence of this standard rule and its seven qualified versions (one for each day of the week) are shown in Table 5. The day names are represented by numbers (1=Monday, 2=Tuesday, ..., 7=Sunday). The support is measured in 1/100 of 1%, and the confidence is measured as standard percentage.

All eight rules meet the required support and confidence thresholds. However, the two qualified rules for Sunday and Monday have both significantly larger support and higher confidence than their other five counterparts. While the correlation between low fat milk and eggs is observed for every day of the week, analysis of all rules shown in Table 5 may reveal that marketing or sales campaign targeting this rule would be best directed towards Sunday and Monday shoppers. Without the additional information provided by the qualified rules, such campaign would require more resources (run throughout the week, instead of just two days) and likely be less effective (lower overall confidence).

Another example illustrating the same concept from our experiments is shown in Table 6: *peanut butter cups → snickers*. This rule is discovered by the standard association rule mining. The same rule is also discovered qualified for all days but

Sunday. However, its support and confidence are significantly larger on Tuesday.

Table 6(b) illustrates a way to quickly identify the rules exhibiting the significant effect of Insight Factor 1. In addition to showing values of Item A, Item B, and day, we show confidence and support values for both standard-regular (reg_conf, reg_sup) and qualified (qar_conf, qar_sup) association rules. We also show the column "improvement", identifying the factor by which the confidence of a particular qualified association rule increased from its equivalent standard version (e.g. in the first row of Table 6(b) - improvement 1.92 = 37.8/19.7, i.e. improvement = qar_conf/ reg_conf). This column is used to sort the table. Using this table we quickly discover that people who buy a box of Newport cigarettes are almost twice as likely to buy a 10-pack of Copenhagen chewing tobacco on Tuesday than on a random day of the week. Similarly people who buy milk on Thursday are 32% more likely to buy bananas than on a random day of the week. If the improvements in confidence are significant, this factor can be used, for example, to target promotions to specific time periods in order to maximize their effect.

Table 6(c) illustrates another way to identify the rules exhibiting strong effect of Insight Factor 1. In addition to showing values of Item A, Item B, and day, we again show confidence and support values for both standard and qualified association

Table 5. Rule lowfat milk → eggs

Item A	Item B	day	sup	conf
2% LOWFAT MILK, 1 GALLON	GRADE "A" LARGE EGGS, 18 COUNT	1	11.4	34.9
2% LOWFAT MILK, 1 GALLON	GRADE "A" LARGE EGGS, 18 COUNT	2	8	32.3
2% LOWFAT MILK, 1 GALLON	GRADE "A" LARGE EGGS, 18 COUNT	3	5.1	31.5
2% LOWFAT MILK, 1 GALLON	GRADE "A" LARGE EGGS, 18 COUNT	4	5.2	29.7
2% LOWFAT MILK, 1 GALLON	GRADE "A" LARGE EGGS, 18 COUNT	5	5.2	29.7
2% LOWFAT MILK, 1 GALLON	GRADE "A" LARGE EGGS, 18 COUNT	6	7.1	32.1
2% LOWFAT MILK, 1 GALLON	GRADE "A" LARGE EGGS, 18 COUNT	7	13.3	34.8
2% LOWFAT MILK, 1 GALLON	GRADE "A" LARGE EGGS, 18 COUNT	All	55.2	32.3

Table 6. Rules peanut butter cups → snickers

PEANUT BUTTER CUPS, *36 CT	SNICKERS, *48 CT	1	2.7	47.3
PEANUT BUTTER CUPS, *36 CT	SNICKERS, *48 CT	2	5	55.1
PEANUT BUTTER CUPS, *36 CT	SNICKERS, *48 CT	3	3.3	49.6
PEANUT BUTTER CUPS, *36 CT	SNICKERS, *48 CT	4	3.6	53.5
PEANUT BUTTER CUPS, *36 CT	SNICKERS, *48 CT	5	3.5	52
PEANUT BUTTER CUPS, *36 CT	SNICKERS, *48 CT	6	2.9	44.8
PEANUT BUTTER CUPS, *36 CT	SNICKERS, *48 CT	All	23.9	49.9
ENERGIZER AAA, 16PK, 4 RESALE, 4 PACKS	ENERGIZER AA-20PK,5 RESALE 4-PACKS	1	4.1	47.1
ENERGIZER AAA, 16PK, 4 RESALE, 4 PACKS	ENERGIZER AA-20PK,5 RESALE 4-PACKS	2	3.9	49.6
ENERGIZER AAA, 16PK, 4 RESALE, 4 PACKS	ENERGIZER AA-20PK,5 RESALE 4-PACKS	3	2.8	49.1
ENERGIZER AAA, 16PK, 4 RESALE, 4 PACKS	ENERGIZER AA-20PK,5 RESALE 4-PACKS	4	3.2	52.7
ENERGIZER AAA, 16PK, 4 RESALE, 4 PACKS	ENERGIZER AA-20PK,5 RESALE 4-PACKS	5	2.9	47.4
ENERGIZER AAA, 16PK, 4 RESALE, 4 PACKS	ENERGIZER AA-20PK,5 RESALE 4-PACKS	6	2.9	45.3
ENERGIZER AAA, 16PK, 4 RESALE, 4 PACKS	ENERGIZER AA-20PK,5 RESALE 4-PACKS	7	5.2	46.3
ENERGIZER AAA, 16PK, 4 RESALE, 4 PACKS	ENERGIZER AA-20PK,5 RESALE 4-PACKS	All	25	46.3

Table 6(b). Improvement

Item A		Item B		day	reg_conf	qar_conf	improvement	reg_sup	qar_sup
NEWPORT BX KG	LOR/NB	COPENHAGEN	10PK	2	19.7	37.8	1.92	3	1.2
MARLBORO LTS BX KING	PM/NB	COPENHAGEN	10PK	2	12.1	22.8	1.88	3.8	1.3
MARLBORO BX KING	PM/NB	COPENHAGEN	10PK	2	13.3	24.4	1.83	3.5	1.2
MARLBORO LTS BX 100	PM/NB	COPENHAGEN	10PK	2	15.7	28.3	1.8	3	1
MARLBORO ULT LTS BX	KING PM/NB	COPENHAGEN	10PK	2	19.5	34.5	1.77	2.8	1
COPENHAGEN	10PK	COPENHAGEN LONG CUT	5-CAN ROLL	2	32.1	44.3	1.38	4.8	2.6
2% LOWFAT MILK	1 GAL	BANANAS	3 LB	4	19.1	25.3	1.32	8.7	1.2
COPENHAGEN LONG CUT	5-CAN ROLL	COPENHAGEN	10PK	2	66.9	80.1	1.2	4.8	2.6
MARLBORO LTS BX 100	PM/NB	MARLBORO ULT LTS BX	KING PM/NB	3	32	38.1	1.19	6.1	1
RUSSET POTATOES	10 POUNDS	BANANAS	3 LB	4	23.9	28.4	1.19	12.9	1.6

Table 6(c). Concentration

Item A		Item B		day	reg_ conf	qar_ conf	concentration	reg_ sup	qar_ sup
COPENHAGEN	10PK	COPENHAGEN LONG CUT	5-CAN ROLL	2	32.1	44.3	0.54	4.8	2.6
COPENHAGEN LONG CUT	5-CAN ROLL	COPENHAGEN	10PK	2	66.9	80.1	0.54	4.8	2.6
COPENHAGEN	10PK	NEWPORT BX KG	LOR/NB	2	20.1	20.4	0.4	3	1.2
NEWPORT BX KG	LOR/NB	COPENHAGEN	10PK	2	19.7	37.8	0.4	3	1.2
MARLBORO ULT LTS BX	KING PM/ NB	COPENHAGEN	10PK	2	19.5	34.5	0.36	2.8	1
CHI CHI'S SALSA	64 OZ.	TOSTITOS TOR-TILLA	CHIPS 21.6 OZ	7	28.5	30.1	0.33	4.5	1.5
SPINACH & ARTICHOKE	CHEESE DIP	TOSTITOS TOR-TILLA	CHIPS 21.6 OZ	7	21.4	23.8	0.31	6.1	1.9
BEEF ROUND	LONDON BROIL	GROUND BEEF	MAXIMUM 10% FAT	7	20.1	22.7	0.31	3.9	1.2
BEEF ROUND TIP	ROAST CAP OFF	GROUND BEEF	MAXIMUM 10% FAT	7	20.2	21	0.31	3.9	1.2
TOSTITOS SALSA	69 OZ JUG	TOSTITOS TOR-TILLA	CHIPS 21.6 OZ	7	29.7	32.6	0.31	9.4	2.9

Table 7. Rule mustard → ketchup

Item A	Item B	day	sup	conf
FRENCH'S MUSTARD, 2-26 OZ.	SQUEEZE KETCHUP, 2PK-50 OZ BOTTLES	7	4.4	36.3
FRENCH'S MUSTARD, 2-26 OZ.	SQUEEZE KETCHUP, 2PK-50 OZ BOTTLES	All	16.9	35.9

rules. Note that this table is different than the previous table in that it includes the column "concentration" - which shows what fraction of the buying of certain parts of goods appears on a particular day of the week (e.g. in the first row of Table 6(c) - concentration 0.54 = 2.6/4.8, i.e. concentration = qar_sup/reg_sup). This column is used to sort the table. Analysis of records shown in Table 6(c) reveals new knowledge. For example, more than half of all purchases of the two Copenhagen products occur on Tuesday and there are a number of rules involving food for which more than 30% of all buying occurs on Sunday. Information of this kind could be of interest to supply managers as it could have an impact on stocking practices.

Insight Factor 2

The second way in which qualified rules expands the knowledge generated by standard association rules, arises from the fact that some standard rules are only discovered as qualified for a few values of the qualified dimension. For a concrete example, consider the rule *mustard → ketchup* with the following thresholds: support 0.025% and confidence 25%. This rule has the required confidence and support in the data set as whole, but is discovered as a qualified rule only on Sunday, as shown in Table 7.

This knowledge can be used, for example, to create a marketing campaign, based on this rule, targeted at Sunday shoppers, supplementing or

Table 8. Rules peanut butter cups → twix and green beans → kernel corn

Item A	Item B	day	sup	conf
PEANUT BUTTER CUPS, *36 CT	TWIX, * 36CT	2	3.4	36.9
PEANUT BUTTER CUPS, *36 CT	TWIX, * 36CT	4	2.6	39.6
PEANUT BUTTER CUPS, *36 CT	TWIX, * 36CT	All	16.3	34
CUT GREEN BEANS,8-14.5 OZ.	WHOLE KERNEL CORN, 8-15.25 OZ.	1	4.2	28.2
CUT GREEN BEANS,8-14.5 OZ.	WHOLE KERNEL CORN, 8-15.25 OZ.	7	6.3	28.6
CUT GREEN BEANS, 8-14.5 OZ.	WHOLE KERNEL CORN, 8-15.25 OZ.	All	23.2	27.3

Table 9. Unique rules

Item A	Item B	day	sup	conf
TOSTITOS SALSA, 69 OZ JUG	TOSTITOS TORTILLA, CHIPS 21.6 OZ	7	3.7	32.7
WHITE ENRICHED BREAD, 2 PACK-20 OZ	GRADE "A" LARGE EGGS, 18 COUNT	1	2.6	34.2
RED DELICIOUS APPLE, 8 LB	BANANAS, 3 LB	7	2.6	25.2

replacing an untargeted campaign lasting throughout the week. Under this scenario, the additional information in the form of qualified dimensions not only makes the rule more actionable, but also is critical to the success of any associated marketing campaign.

Two similar examples, both found as standard rules, from our experiments are: *peanut butter cups → twix*, discovered qualified only on Tuesday and Thursday, and *green beans → kernel corn*, discovered qualified only on Sunday and Monday (Table 8).

Since a large fraction of the targeted events occurs on a limited number of occasions, it is important to identify and distinguish these occasions. Taking action without such knowledge can result in substandard results and wasted resources. Insight Factor 2 can serve to provide the required knowledge for avoiding such inefficiencies.

Insight Factor 3

Finally, there are situations where qualified association rules simply do not appear as standard rules. Such rules can only be discovered with qualified dimensions. For a concrete example, consider the rule *salsa → chips (Sun)*. This rule appears only as qualified (Table 9) and would not be discovered by standard rule mining.

Thus, an important opportunity and valuable insights will be lost. Note that even though these chips are among the popular individual items (Table 10), they do not appear in any standard rule. Consequently, no campaign based on association rules can be designed for chips. On the other hand, the qualified rule *salsa → chips (Sun)* has excellent potential for a promotional campaign: The target audience is well defined (Sunday shoppers), and it involves a popular item (chips).

Two other examples from our experiments are *white bread → eggs (Mon)* and *apples → bananas (Sun)* (Table 9). Both of these rules are also not discovered by standard association rule mining.

Table 10. Top twelve most popular items

Item		tot # of Transactions
BONELESS SKINLESS	CHICKEN BREAST 6LB	231802
BOUNTY PAPER TOWELS	15 ROLL 64 SHT	210078
GRADE "A" LARGE EGGS	18 COUNT	190113
GROUND BEEF	MAXIMUM 10% FAT	170515
BANANAS	3 LB	164584
TOSTITOS TORTILLA	CHIPS 21.6 OZ	146832
BUTTER QUARTERS	4-1 LB	119567
BOUNCE SINGLES 160CT	FABRIC SOFTNER	115327
AMERICAN SINGLES	3 LB--72 CT	98997
GLAD TRASH BAG 13GAL	120CT .9ML DRWSTRING	95649
KLEENEX 8PK 95 SHTS	BOUTIQUE	93191
SQUEEZE KETCHUP	2PK-50 OZ BOTTLES	92098

4. STANDARD ASSOCIATION RULES VS. QUALIFIED ASSOCIATION RULES COMPARISON

In order to discuss the implication of adding the qualified association rule mining to the set of analytical methods used to drive corporate actions, we use the following two simple sets of results depicting general differences between standard association rules and qualified association rules. The chart in Figure 3 shows the number of discovered standard and qualified association rules within the Sam's Club data set for various support thresholds.

Note that when looking only at a certain number of rules, e.g. 1000, the support level for

Figure 3. Number of discovered standard and qualified association rules

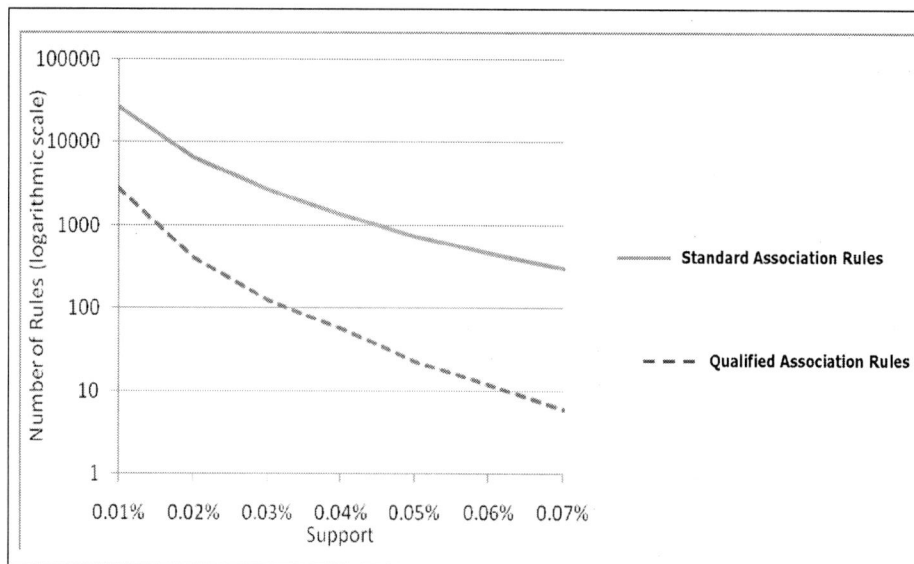

qualified and standard association rules is quite different. In order to find 1000 rules with standard association rules mining, the support threshold should be set to about 0.045%, while for qualified association rules the number is only 0.015%. Thus, the qualified rules will tend to be more "unexpected" or at a finer level of granularity. The standard rules on the other hand will tend to be more general and are more likely to already be noticed by implicit analysts such as observant store managers or supply specialists.

We can also phrase this observation in terms of the level of support that produces a feasible number of association rules. Note that setting support at 0.01% results in an extraordinary large number of standard associations (over 30,000), whereas there are only a few thousand qualified association rules with support of 0.01%. The qualified association rules are not only often more actionable individually, but also easier to handle as a whole and less likely to overwhelm a decision maker who is uncomfortable dealing with a very large number of possible targets.

Table 12 shows the distribution of qualified and equivalent standard association rules within the Sam's Club data set, across a broad spectrum of possible confidence and support thresholds.

The two parts of the tables show the distribution of the standard and qualified association rules (with any confidence and support >= 0.01%) in terms of the support and confidences levels. Of course, the total number of qualified rules at a given support level is significantly less that the number of standard rules, so we compare the fractions instead of the absolute number of rules.

The lower left corner cell where most the rules fall represents the lowest possible levels of support and confidence. Note that both types of association rules have roughly the same percentage shown in the lower left corner cell. However, the main difference in the two tables is that qualified association rules are more evenly spread out than

Table 11. Distribution of qualified and equivalent standard association rules

Qualified Association Rules (Percentages)							
Confidence	*84.8*	*10.9*	*2.5*	*1.2*	*0.6*	*0.0*	*0.0*	*TOTALS*
< 80% to = < 100%	0.7	0.2	0.0	0.2	0.1	0.0	0.0	**1.2**
< 60% to = < 80%	0.5	0.1	0.0	0.1	0.1	0.0	0.0	**0.8**
< 40% to = < 60%	4.0	0.8	0.2	0.2	0.0	0.0	0.0	**5.2**
< 20% to = < 40%	9.7	1.7	0.5	0.2	0.2	0.0	0.0	**12.3**
0% to =< 20%	69.9	8.1	1.8	0.5	0.2	0.0	0.0	**80.5**
Support	0.01% to =< 0.02%	0.02% to =< 0.03%	0.03% to =< 0.04%	0.04% to =< 0.05%	0.05% to =< 0.06%	0.06% to =< 0.07%	0.07% to ∞	
Standard Association Rules (Percentages)							
Confidence	*74.1*	*15.6*	*5.3*	*2.4*	*1*	*0.6*	*1*	*TOTALS*
< 80% to = < 100%	0.1	0.0	0.0	0.0	0.0	0.0	0.0	**0.1**
< 60% to = < 80%	0.1	0.0	0.0	0.0	0.0	0.0	0.0	**0.1**
< 40% to = < 60%	0.6	0.3	0.1	0.0	0.0	0.0	0.0	**1.0**
< 20% to = < 40%	2.4	0.6	0.3	0.2	0.1	0.1	0.1	**3.8**
0% to =< 20%	70.9	14.7	4.9	2.2	0.9	0.5	0.9	**95.0**
Support	0.01% to =< 0.02%	0.02% to =< 0.03%	0.03% to =< 0.04%	0.04% to =< 0.05%	0.05% to =< 0.06%	0.06% to =< 0.07%	0.07% to ∞	

Table 12. Data preparation for data mining tool

| | Item Columns | | | | | Non-Item Dimension Columns | | | | | | | |
| | Columns for all item's | | | | | Customer Segment Columns | | Day Type Columns | | Columns for other dimension's attributes (one column per each VALUE of the dimension's attribute) | | | |
RowID	Item A	Item B	(Columns for other items ...)			Old	New	Workday	Weekend	...	...	...	...
1	1	1	...	...	...	1	0	1	0	...	...	...	...
2	1	1	...	...	...	1	0	1	0	...	...	...	...
3	1	1	...	...	...	1	0	1	0	...	...	...	...
4	1	1	...	...	...	1	0	1	0	...	...	...	...
5	1	0	...	...	...	1	0	1	0	...	...	...	...
6	1	0	...	...	...	1	0	1	0	...	...	...	...
7	0	1	...	...	...	1	0	1	0	...	...	...	...
8	0	1	...	...	...	1	0	1	0	...	...	...	...
9	0	1	...	...	...	1	0	1	0	...	...	...	...
10	0	1	...	...	...	1	0	1	0	...	...	...	...
...	...	...	...	...	...	...	...	...	...	...	...	...	...

standard ones both in terms of confidence. When analyzing the right-most column notice that, for example, only 3.8% of all standard rules have confidence between 20 and 40 percent whereas 12.3% of all qualified have confidence in the same range. This indicates that, among all qualified rules, there are a greater percentage of strongly correlated rules, as compared to the equivalent percentage in standard rules. In other words, even though the quantity of qualified association rules is smaller (when compared to the number of standard association rules), a larger percentage of them depict more meaningful correlations.

When analyzing the comparison along the support levels, at the first glance the standard association rules appear to be more evenly distributed. This is mostly because standard association rules have (naturally) much higher support. The max support for standard rules is higher than max support for a qualified rule (which in this case is < 0.06%, demonstrated by the fact that 6th and 7th column in Qualified Association Rules portion of Table 11 are filled with zeros). However, if we partition the ranges of support proportionally (i.e. same number of columns for support values from 0.01% to max support) we actually observe more even distribution for qualified rules than for standard ones.

5. TECHNICAL AND IMPLEMENTATION ISSUES OF THE WORKING SYSTEM

Can qualified association rules be discovered directly from data warehouses by applying standard association rules mining methods? To answer this question, let us examine first if there is a feasible way to find qualified association rules in data warehouses by using the standard association rules mining methods included with the standard mining tools. Standard data mining tools (such as IBM SPSS Modeler – formerly SPSS Clementine) are actually able to find qualified association rules using standard methods. However, due to the substantial amount of pre-preprocessing of

Figure 4. Qualified association rules (example 1) in IBM SPSS modeler data mining tool

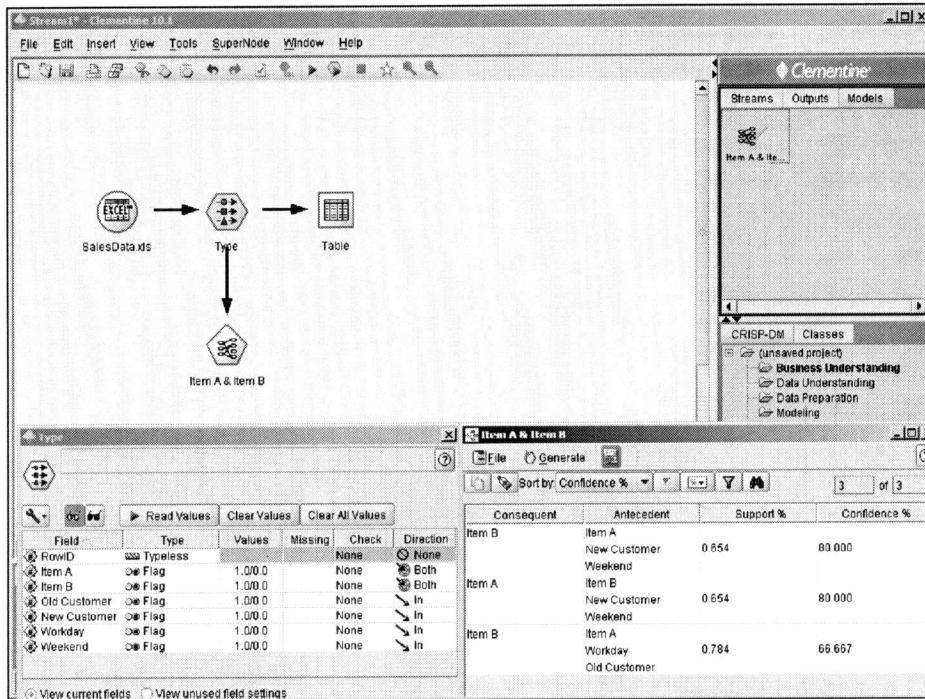

the data required by the data mining tools, this is feasible only on simple data sets with relatively few dimensional attributes. To illustrate let us observe how the qualified association rules mining process presented in Example 1 would be handled using IBM SPSS Modeler. First a table containing a column for each possible item would have to be created. In addition, this table would also have to contain a set of columns for each of the dimension's attributes. Each possible value of the dimension attribute would require a separate column. Table 12 illustrates this situation.

Figure 4 shows that it is possible to set up qualified association rules mining process with a standard data mining tool (e.g. IBM SPSS Modeler). Dimension's attributes are set as "In" only, which ensures that they will not appear on both sides of the rule. This is consistent with the fact that condition R in expression $P \rightarrow Q\ (R)$ appears only on one side of the rule.

In this dataset, the same qualified association rules that were outlined in Example 1 are actually found (see "Item A & Item B" box in Figure 3). For example, the rule from Example 1:

- Item A → Item B; new customers shopping during weekend days (sup=0.52[1], conf=80.00%)

Represented by the first row in the "Item A & Item B" box in Figure 3. The interpretation of the rule is as follows: *during the weekend days new customers who buy Item A are likely to buy Item B.*

As illustrated, a standard data mining tool is able to find qualified association rules in a small and simple dataset. However, in cases when data set contains large number of transactions that can include numerous items (for example, there are 432,233 different items in the Sam's Club dataset) preparing data as illustrated by Table 3 becomes prohibitively long and impractical, if not impossible. That is why most data mining tools, when dealing with actual transaction level corporate data, are limited to association rules mining only on aggregated item-related data (e.g. item category). Adding dimension-related data, as required by the qualified association rules mining process, would put exorbitant data preparation strain on the standard data mining tools approach. A typical corporate data set has multiple dimensions, each of whom has a number of attributes with multiple possible values for them. Each possible value for each column of each dimension would require a separate column. The data preparation process, already cumbersome due to the columns required by items, would require further effort for creation of columns for each individual value of the dimensions' attributes.

Our approach eliminates these burdens and does not require taking into account the values of the dimensions' attributes prior to the data mining process. The basic architecture of our system is shown in Figure 5.

The most notable feature of the system architecture is the tightly coupled integration with the

Figure 5. System architecture for the ad-hoc data mining system

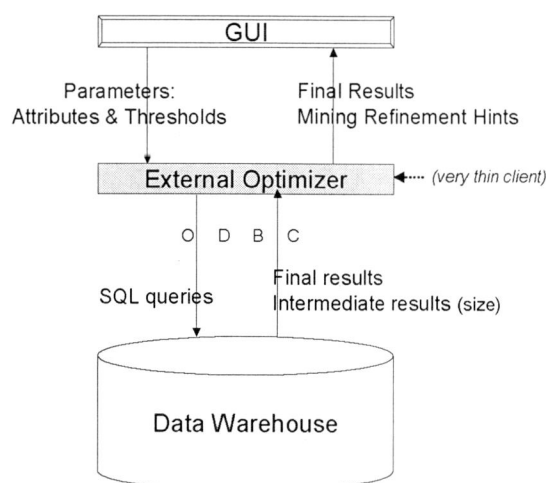

relational database that powers the data warehouse. The benefits of this integration are:

- No data leaves the data warehouse, reducing the redundancy and avoiding any privacy, security, and confidentiality issues related to data movement.
- There is no data preparation (restructuring) process. The data remains in original tables within the data warehouse, which do not have to be restructured and/or replicated (i.e. no creation of separate tables with large amount of columns).
- The relational database does all query processing, leveraging the computational and storage resources of the data warehouse.
- Qualified association rules can be mined from any set of tables within the relational database that is storing the data warehouse, so we enable wide-range ad-hoc mining.

The mining process starts with the user defining the extended association rule by choosing the non-item attributes to be involved (if a user chooses zero non-item attributes, standard association-rule mining will be performed). The choice can be made through a simple interface with pull down menus for each dimension. Finally, the user also specifies the support threshold. However, our choice of architecture allows certain flexibility about choosing thresholds. Later, we show how the threshold can be changed midstream. Once all parameters are chosen, the next step of the mining process is the creation of a sequence of SQL queries that implements the extended association rule specified by the user's choice of parameter values. There are many different SQL sequences that can implement the same rule, so the choice of the sequence is made according to an optimization algorithm.

Once the optimal sequence is selected, the relational database starts to execute its SQL queries one by one. The results of each query remain in the data warehouse in temporary tables. Only the sizes of the intermediate results are sent to the external optimizer (Figure 4). Herein lays an opportunity to make the mining process interactive. If the size of certain intermediate results is too large then we can expect that the complete mining process will take a long time and possibly generate too many rules. In this case, the system can alert the user and suggest revising the support threshold upwards. Similarly, if the size of certain intermediate results is too small and we expect that the number of mined rules is going to be very small, the system can advise the user to decrease the support threshold. The last query of the sequence computes the discovered rules. The rules are sent to the external optimizer, which displays them for the user.

Extensions of association-rule data mining have drawn a considerable amount of attention from researchers, over the last 15 years. Much of the published work focuses on expanding the extent of association-rule mining, such as mining generalized rules (i.e. when transaction items belong to certain types or groups, generalized rules find associations among such types or groups) (Han & Fu, 1995; Srikant & Agrawal, 1996); mining correlations and casual structures, which finds generalized rules based on implicit correlations among items, while taking into consideration both the presence and the absence of an item in a transaction (Silverstein, Brin, Motwani, & Ullman, 1998; Brin, Motwani, & Silverstein, 1997); finding association rules for numeric attributes, where association rules, in addition to Boolean conditions (i.e. item present in the transactions), may consider a numeric condition (e.g. an item that has a numeric value, must have a value within a certain range) (Fukuda, Morimoto, Morishita, & Tokuyama, 1996; Fukuda et al., 2001); finding associations among items occurring in separate transactions (Lu, Feng, & Han, 2000; Pei, Han, & Wang, 2002; Tung, Han, Lu, & Feng, 2003).

Qualified association rules extends the scope of association rule mining to include multiple database relations (tables), in a way that was not previously feasible. This approach is designed to provide a real addition to the value of collected organizational information and is applicable in a host of real world situations, as we illustrated throughout this paper. Many of the previously proposed association-rule extensions are either applicable to a relatively narrow set of problems, or represent a purely theoretical advance. In addition, they also often require computational resources that may be unrealistic for most of the potential organizational users. In contrast, our proposed method is both broadly applicable and highly practical from the implementation and utilization points of view.

6. CONCLUSION

Qualified association-rule mining discovers rules standard association-rule analysis overlooks. Additionally, qualified association-rule mining can provide new insights by breaking down standard association rules into qualified rules containing additional knowledge.

Our experiments on a substantial real-world data set provided by Sam's Club showed that qualified association rules, compared to standard association rules, provide additional information which can be used to better target actions based on existing rules. As we have emphasized throughout this paper, qualified association rules provide another method for mining data in addition to standard association rules and are not meant to supersede them.

Qualified association rules can dramatically improve the action results, e.g. turn an underperforming campaign (spread too thin over the entire audience) into a highly targeted campaign that delivers results. This approach can uncover previously unknown correlations that only manifest themselves under certain circumstances (e.g. on Tuesday). Such correlations do not exist in the data as a whole and so far have been out of reach of professionals using standard data mining tools.

By utilizing qualified association rules, organizations can add an inexpensive, and yet very practical and fruitful method of analyzing data that can quickly discover a layer of knowledge that was previously unknown (or very difficult to obtain, as we showed in Section 5 in the discussion on is it possible to find qualified association rules using standard association rules methods). As we demonstrated with our experiments, once this additional knowledge is discovered, its potential to affect and improve corporate performance is immediately apparent.

REFERENCES

Agrawal, R., Imielinski, T., & Swami, A. (1993). Mining association rules between sets of items in large databases. In *Proceedings of the ACM SIGMOD International Conference* (pp. 207-216). New York, NY: ACM Press.

Agrawal, R., & Srikant, R. (1994). Fast algorithms for mining association rules. In *Proceedings of the 20th International Conference on Very Large Databases* (pp. 487-499).

Brin, S., Motwani, R., & Silverstein, C. (1997). Beyond market baskets: Generalizing association rules to correlations. In *Proceedings of the ACM SIGMOD International Conference*, Tucson, AZ (pp. 265-276). New York, NY: ACM Press.

Chung, H. M., & Gray, P. (1999). Special section: Data mining. *Journal of Management Information Systems, 16*(1), 11–16.

Fukuda, T., Morimoto, Y., Morishita, S., & Tokuyama, T. (1996). Mining optimized association rules for numeric attributes. In *Proceedings of the ACM SIGACT-SIGMOD-SIGART Symposium on Principles of Database Systems*, Montreal, QC, Canada (pp. 182-191). New York, NY: ACM Press.

Fukuda, T., Morimoto, Y., Morishita, S., & Tokuyama, T. (2001). Data mining with optimized two dimensional association rules. *ACM Transactions on Database Systems, 26*(2), 179–213. doi:10.1145/383891.383893

Glassey, K. (1998). Seducing the end user. *Communications of the ACM, 41*(9), 52–60. doi:10.1145/285070.285083

Gorla, N. (2003). Features to consider in a data warehousing system. *Communications of the ACM, 46*(11), 111–115. doi:10.1145/948383.948389

Han, J., & Fu, Y. (1995). Discovery of multiple-level association rules from large databases. In *Proceedings of the International Conference on Very Large Databases*, Zurich, Switzerland (pp. 420-431).

Inmon, W. (2005). *Building the data warehouse* (4th ed.). New York, NY: John Wiley & Sons.

Jukic, J., & Nestorov, S. (2006). Comprehensive data warehouse exploration with qualified association-rule mining. *Decision Support Systems, 42*(2), 859–878. doi:10.1016/j.dss.2005.07.009

Jukic, N. (2006). Data modeling strategies and alternatives for data warehousing projects. *Communications of the ACM, 49*(4), 83–88. doi:10.1145/1121949.1121952

Jukic, N., & Nestorov, S. (2003). Ad-hoc association-rule mining within the data warehouse. In *Proceedings of the 36th Annual Hawaii International Conference on System Sciences* (p. 10). Washington, DC: IEEE Computer Society.

Kimball, R., Reeves, L., Ross, M., & Thornthwite, W. (1998). *The data warehouse lifecycle toolkit* (1st ed.). New York, NY: John Wiley & Sons.

Kimball, R., & Ross, M. Thornthwaite, W., Mundy, J., & Becker, B. (2007). *The data warehouse lifecycle toolkit* (2nd ed.). New York, NY: John Wiley & Sons.

Lu, H., Feng, L., & Han, J. (2000). Beyond intratransaction association analysis: Mining multidimensional intertransaction association rules. *ACM Transactions on Information Systems, 18*(4), 423–454. doi:10.1145/358108.358114

Pei, J., Han, J., & Wang, W. (2002). Mining sequential patterns with constraints in large databases. In *Proceedings of the 11th ACM Conference on Information and Knowledge Management*, McLean, VA (pp. 18-25). New York, NY: ACM Press.

Silverstein, C., Brin, S., Motwani, R., & Ullman, J. (1998). Scalable techniques for mining causal structures. In *Proceedings of the International Conference on Very Large Databases*, New York, NY (pp. 594-605). San Francisco, CA: Morgan Kaufmann.

Smyth, P., Pregibon, D., & Faloutsos, C. (2002). Data-driven evolution of data mining algorithms. *Communications of the ACM, 45*(8), 33–37. doi:10.1145/545151.545175

Srikant, R., & Agrawal, R. (1996). Mining quantitative association rules in large relational tables. In *Proceedings of the ACM SIGMOD International Conference on Management of Data*, Montreal, QC, Canada (pp. 1-12). New York, NY: ACM Press.

Tung, A. K. H., Han, J., Lu, H., & Feng, L. (2003). Efficient mining of intertransaction association rules. *IEEE Transactions on Knowledge and Data Engineering, 15*(1), 43–56. doi:10.1109/TKDE.2003.1161581

ENDNOTES

[1]   The reason behind different support values for rules calculated in Example 1 and the IBM SPSS Modeler version of the same rules is that the IBM SPSS Modeler default support for $X \rightarrow Y$ rules is support(X), instead of support ($X \rightarrow Y$).

This work was previously published in the International Journal of Business Intelligence Research, Volume 2, Issue 2, edited by Richard Herschel, pp. 1-21, copyright 2011 by IGI Publishing (an imprint of IGI Global).

Chapter 16
10 Principles to Ensure Your Data Warehouse Implementation is a Failure

Adam Hill
The Nielsen Company, USA

Thilini Ariyachandra
Xavier University, USA

Mark Frolick
Xavier University, USA

ABSTRACT

Demand for business intelligence solutions continues to grow in the industry at record rates to combat competitive pressures and to attain business agility. Still organizations continue to struggle on how to implement successful business intelligence solutions. Despite its growing popularity and maturity as a field, it appears that organizations follow key guidelines that ensure the failure of their business intelligence implementation. This paper highlights ten major principles that organizations follow to ensure the failure of their BI solution and in so doing describes how to avoid BI failure in terms of strategy and design, implementation management and communication, and technology and resource investment for BI solutions.

INTRODUCTION

At present, organizations compete in a dynamic, hyper competitive business environment characterized by a massive influx of data. Business intelligence (BI) is seen as the ultimate solution that will help organizations leverage information to make informed, intelligent business decisions (Turban et al., 2008). Consequently, the demand and interest in BI as a critical solution for organizations continues to grow. According to Gartner, the worldwide BI platform revenue is forecast

DOI: 10.4018/978-1-4666-2650-8.ch016

to grow at a compound annual growth rate of 8.1 percent through 2012, reaching $7.7 billion in 2012 (Knight, 2008). An IBM global survey of over 2500 CIOs revealed that *business intelligence is* the top visionary plan for enhancing their enterprises' competitiveness (IBM, n. d.).

Thus, as companies grow over time and acquire increasing masses of information, having a solid BI foundation in place becomes an essential means to organize the large quantities of data in a way that fits with the company's specific business needs. The data warehouse, the core component of a BI infrastructure foundation, is a copy of transaction data specifically structured for querying and reporting. Using a data warehouse an organization can extract the key insights that will help shape their strategic and tactical business decisions more easily (Watson, 2009). Data warehouses are also critical enablers of current strategic initiatives such as customer relationship management (CRM), business performance management (BPM) (Frolick & Ariyachandra, 2006), and supply chain management and a must have in almost every industry in business (Watson et al., 2004)

Several past research have investigated the critical success factors involved in the creation of a data warehouse (Wixom & Watson, 2001; Ariyachandra & Watson, 2010) to gain key insights to successfully complete in various business industries. Less exists on what not to do. While data warehousing is now a mature market (Ariyachandra & Frolick, 2008), historically, failure rates have been high (Kelly, 1997). A more recent assessment of data warehouse failure in 2007 suggests data warehouse failure rates can be as high as 50 percent (Embarcadero, 2008). With such high failure rates, there is ample opportunity for mishaps. According to data-quality software company Trillium, "60% of data-integration and data-warehouse projects get delayed, exceed budget or fail because of poor quality" (Fest, 2005).

Since numerous types of data warehouse failure are possible and definitions of such failure vary from one study to the next. This paper will adopt the definition proposed by Lindsey and Frolick (2003, p. 49.) as "the formal or informal cancellation of a data warehouse project, or the condition where a completed project's performance falls significantly short of the business need." Using this definition, this paper aims to provide ten principles a company should follow if it would like its data warehouse implementation to join the ranks of such failures by running over time, exceeding budget expectations, and underwhelming all parties involved.

Key steps to having one's project canceled or performing short of the company's business need will include a fuzzy focus on the goals of the data warehouse in initiating the project and planning its design, followed by a lack of communication and benchmarking, and finally a laissez-faire attitude toward resource investment. Following each principle is an explanation of what a company should do in order to beat the odds and successfully implement a data warehouse. Thus, the paper outlines principles to ensure the project's demise as well as the success measures to be adopted as an alternative.

DATA WAREHOUSE IMPLEMENTATION FAILURE

Based on past academic and practitioner literature on factors leading to data warehouse success and failure, ten principles emerge as being key factors that lead to data warehousing failure. These principles are organized according to the following three key aspects of the data warehousing project: strategy and design, implementation management and communication, and technology and resource investment.

STRATEGY AND DESIGN

In researching both data warehouse implementations that failed and succeeded, it became evident that one key differentiating factor was the level to which due diligence had been performed at the onset of the project concept. A successful implementation required a premeditated strategy and design phase, which included identifying the key goals of the data warehouse and testing pilot a portion of the project. The following four failure principles provide direction as to how one might butcher this key phase, followed by more sound advice on how to create a more reliable strategy and design.

Failure Principle 1: Create Now, Strategize Later

Before creating a data warehouse, it is essential to consider the corporate vision and mission associated with the project. This includes identification of short and long term objectives that the company wishes to achieve. A strategic plan is needed to map out how these objectives will be met. Key performance indicators should be used to measure performance toward these objectives. Potential hurdles that could hinder progress toward objectives should be identified.

Another key success element is the support of top management. As enterprise architect Michelle Poolet (2009, p. 30) articulates, "because a data warehouse combines the best of business practices and information systems technology, it requires the cooperation of both business and IT decision makers, continuously coordinating to align all the needs, requirements, tasks, and deliverables of a successful data warehouse implementation." Field experts generally suggest intervening right away if such support is not available. Likewise, user support is critical to the project's success. Development should not take place until both of these groups of stakeholders—key decision makers and end users—are aligned.

Failure Principle 2: Build the Data Warehouse as a Solution to a Specific BI Project/Need

In building a data warehouse structure, it is imperative that stakeholders focus on the bigger picture and the long-term business value that will be added for the future users and by the users of the data warehouse. Shaping the design of the DW around a specific, shorter-term business objective may greatly reduce the long-term return on this sizable business intelligence investment.

However, managers will often become impatient with the time it takes to properly implement the creation of a data warehouse. They will be tempted to pull or redirect funds that should be invested in this DW in favor of creating a side project to meet their current needs. This is inadvisable and it is best to ensure funding for the DW is decoupled from individual BI projects. One opportunity to incorporate a worthy current project would come in the pilot/proof of concept phase to be discussed next.

Failure Principle 3: Save Time and Money – Skip the Pilot/Proof of Concept

Investing the necessary time and resources to implement a pilot or proof of concept will often save much greater time and resource investments in the long run by identifying bugs or system design issues that may be resolved much earlier in the development process. In addition to the ability to work out the kinks, the pilot helps establish credibility and build momentum for the data warehouse project from the perspective of key stakeholders, including the company's leadership team.

An ideal proof of concept is completed in 1 to 2 months and includes a scaled-down deployment of the data warehouse architecture that uses the processes designed for data extraction, verification, cleansing, organization, and delivery. One of the components this deployment should leverage is the extract, transform, and load (ETL) software, to be discussed later in greater detail. The pilot should also include a small-scale execution of data acquisition from 1 to 2 of the source systems and a scaled-down delivery execution for one of the more high-profile, value-add business subject areas. Finally, the proof of concept should include a smaller-scale implementation of the strategies surrounding software qualification, training and support, and ongoing maintenance (Furey, 2005).

The project management team should meet with key stakeholders after the proof of concept deployment to assess the system's performance, discuss lessons learned, and create a detailed, action-oriented list of tasks that will be completed to ensure the first delivery and overall data warehouse implementation is a success.

Failure Principle 4: Assume Users Will Patiently Wait for the Release

Just as funding provides a potential conflict of interest between long-term data warehousing solutions and shorter-term business needs—illustrated by Principles 2 and 3—so does the DW organiza-tion's ability to follow the pace of changes in the business. Rather than having managers creating independent side projects, it is best to have a dual processing model, where the legacy system runs parallel to the one being created. Though this is a more costly approach, it is pivotal to providing a balance between meeting current business needs and providing an enhanced platform for meeting future ones.

Furthermore, it is essential to create and imple-ment a logistics process to ensure that the right information from source systems can be leveraged as meaningful information in a number of target systems, i.e. from source to extraction to DW to end users via data marts. Ad Stam (2007) provides a conceptual information logistic model (Figure 1) to depict an ideal process flow.

In order to facilitate the best flow of informa-tion, the process should leverage generic or standard models and be reusable, decoupled and federated. A data warehouse is essentially a col-lection of relational tables based off an informa-tional model that represents how a company views the world. Since this view is ever-changing and to add or change dimensions requires a high

Figure 1. Conceptual logistic model based on Stam (2007)

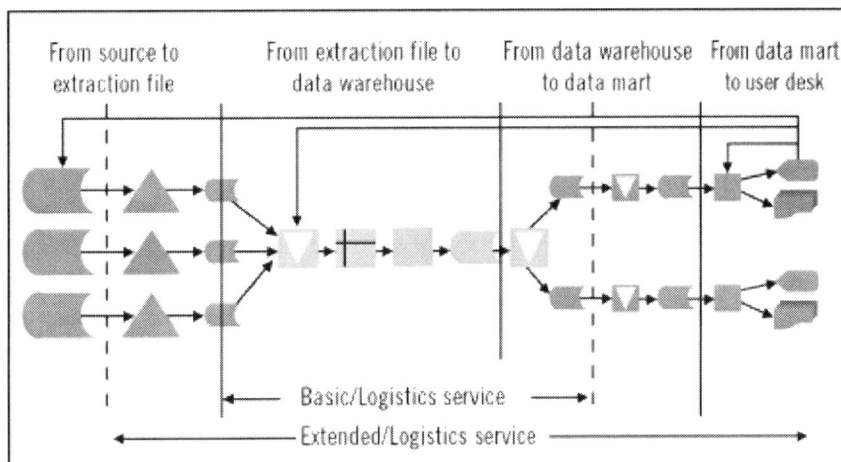

level of maintenance, company's often use generic industry sector model or data warehouse models into which standard content forming the enterprise resource planning (ERP) system may be fed. However, a great deal of adaptation is required to make industry sector models fit for the specific company and ERP systems are not the only source system, so changes must be applied to other systems as well. Stam (2007) cites there are alternative solutions that help circumvent some of these shortfalls. One such product is Kalido, inspired by a generic model, which enables information model changes to be addressed by changing or adding new rows to only the generic logical and physical models.

Where possible, it is best to use reusable, standardized components of processes in order to scale their use among other processes. As straightforward a concept as this is, it is oft overlooked in the mad dash to complete the initial phases of the system implementation. Decoupling rather than integrating logistic functions allows for changes to be required among an isolated number of functions, without affecting all others. Experts suggest, "next to decoupling, the more the design of individual functions is as generic or reusable as possible, the easier it is to isolate the impact of changes and minimize the throughput time of applying these changes" (Stam, 2007, p. 1).

Though data warehouses often use a central implementation, a federated model is often more appropriate. Federated models divide the data warehouse into a number of smaller, well organized partial implementations. This gives each region or operating function the autonomy needed to ensure the implementation for its division will best fit the changing business model under which it operates. With the shared part being owned at a higher level, consensus is only needed on matters that affect all divisions—those regarding the shared part of the model.

IMPLEMENTATION MANAGEMENT AND COMMUNICATION

Once the strategy and design have been established, meticulous implementation management is crucial to staying on time and on budget. Benchmarking against others, pausing to evaluate progress at key checkpoints, and perhaps most importantly, communication, are factors vital to strong implementation management. What follows are three failure principles and advice on how to manage around these.

Failure Principle 5: With Project Management Communication, Less Is More

Another key component to the planning process is project management communication. Project managers should communicate the project's scope, plan, and success criteria to all stakeholders. The project plan is the vehicle for conveying goals, timing, roles and responsibilities, and any additional relevant information to all involved in the project. Project managers should communicate the procedures for issue, risk, and change management. Plans for project management monitoring and communication and quality assurance should be shared. Strategies for stakeholder training, support, user acceptance, and marketing as well as necessary data logistics strategies—document management, backup and recovery, validation, and ongoing operation and maintenance—must be fleshed out and communicated.

As with all good communication, the process goes both ways, as key stakeholders serve as a valuable and necessary source of feedback on how the implementation is progressing. Project team members should provide weekly status updates and help track and communicate any variances on costs, tasks completed and milestones reached, software errors, and schedule deviations.

Failure Principle 6: Don't Worry About What Everyone Else Is Doing

Benchmarking is an essential factor in creating a successful data warehouse. Benchmarks should be used to measure both the product quality and its development. The accuracy and completeness of the information used and flexibility and scalability of the system are key components of the product quality measurement. Furthermore, even if system flexibility is not an immediate concern, the company should consider its role in the long-term effectiveness of the system.

In addition, the data system is of little value if the users cannot quickly and easily retrieve, comprehend, and leverage the data to make better business decisions. Likewise, organizational benefits such as support of the company's overall strategy, a measurable ROI, potential to better business processes, and improved integration of business units are fundamental. Finally, benchmarking end user and organizational impact allows a project manager to ensure the system's implementation is on track to serve the corporate vision and data warehousing mission identified at the outset.

Primary development benchmarks include the cost of creating and maintaining the data warehouse and the timing required to create the pilot version. For example, a recent study of 348 firms (Watson et al., 2006) resulted in a benchmark cost of $1.4 million for systems using a bus architecture, $1.5 million for those using a centralized architecture, and $2.4 million for hub-and-spoke architecture systems. Based on 424 firms, the development time benchmarks for these three system structures were 8.9 months, 8.8 months, and 11.4 months, respectively.

Failure Principle 7: Run the Red Lights (Or Do Not Stop At Checkpoints)

In addition to benchmarking against competition, a company should establish intervention checkpoints to guide the design and implementation process. As mentioned earlier, top management support and user support are factors crucial to a data warehouse implementation. For this reason, these two elements provide the first and second logical checkpoints. If neither top management nor users are supportive, the project will not succeed and should be halted. However, if just top management is on board, they may need to offer additional training or incentives to alter users' attitudes. Conversely, if users identify a strong enough business value, they may champion the warehouse, driving support up the ladder to top management. A greater degree of structure around the technology will lead to a greater level of comfort and acceptance among both parties. Once both groups are aligned to the technology's value, the organization may proceed to the next checkpoint—determining if users require access to a broad range of data.

If users do require a broader scope of data, the company should proceed with the creation of a single repository. For users equipped with the technical knowledge necessary to navigate such a data system, this approach offers the widest scope of data and allows for the application of characteristics across the entire data set. On the other hand, users often work within more specific sets of the data, and pulling from a single, large repository can be complex and confusing. If users need only to pull data against a specific partition of the data, the organization should create data marts—smaller databases specific to each business unit's needs. These help narrow the scope of the data set to just that which is of interest to the business unit, reducing the difficulty of digging through the entire set of data.

Similar to decisions regarding the range of data desired, the company must determine the range of analysis tools desired. This decision is often related to the previous checkpoint. Typically, data repository users have a higher level of technical proficiency and will desire unlimited access to data and analysis tools. In contrast, data mart users will want restrictive tools that help simplify the complex, ambiguous nature of the data set.

Following the decisions regarding the scope of data and analysis tools to be used, the organization must verify the users understanding of the fit between the data warehouse and business issues to be addressed using the unit. Business units leveraging data marts typically showed a stronger understanding of this fit because of the inherently focused nature of their data set, while this understanding may be harder to reach with the potentially overwhelming amount of data stored in a single repository model. In either case, if the task fit understanding is not clear, this is the opportunity in the process to provide further training and education on how the data system applies to their business needs.

While understanding the data warehouse task fit is crucial to its success, this and other key elements can be undermined by a lack of the technical knowledge necessary to maneuver the data system. Thus, the next checkpoint involves a gauge of the users' perception of IT as supportive. Those business units with a stronger working relationship with the data warehouse development team were more likely to reach out for help with their questions and concerns about their applications. Those users without this closer relationship often deemed the development team as being unsupportive to their needs. In this scenario, the company must work to foster a cooperative environment between users and the development team to ensure that users understand both the objective of the warehouse and also how to best use it.

An additional source for disbursing this valuable and requisite knowledge is through the identification and/or creation of power users. These super users are well aware of the purpose of the data warehouse as well as how to mine meaningful data from it. If such users do not exist naturally, it is up to management to provide the resources needed to create this key group of users.

TECHNOLOGY AND RESOURCE INVESTMENT

A final make-or-break aspect of data warehouse implementation is investment in resources, especially the project's technology ones. Project management must be involved in decisions regarding technology and vendor selection to ensure that the resources chosen are capable of fulfilling the project's main business objectives. The final three failure principles indicate how this should not be done, followed by suggestions on how to most effectively engage in technology and resource investment.

Failure Principle 8: Delegate All Technology Decisions to IT

It is crucial for a project manager and key stakeholders to be aligned on the technology to be leveraged in the data warehouse. Current resources should be thoroughly evaluated to determine if they may be leveraged to meet changing business needs before an investment in new technology is considered. The project team might also seek opportunities to collaborate or outsource implementation phases through experienced vendors if appropriate for the company. While an IT manager may be intimately familiar with the company's technological resources, his/her role is to provide the best quality technical systems possible and if left to make the decision alone, that might result in unnecessary investment that drives up the data warehouse's development costs.

Furthermore, the project team is responsible for ensuring that technology decisions most appropriately serve the business objectives of the data warehouse and match the social systems in place. Using the adaptive structuration theory that evolved in the 1990s to understand inconsistent results in group decision support systems, it is believed "the interaction of the context [or social systems] with the technology is the key to understanding data warehouse success" (Chenowith et al., 2006).

Failure Principle 9: There's No Need to get Into the Weeds with Something like ETL Development

Jim Keene, enterprise data warehouse senior project manager at Harley-Davidson, Inc. conveys its significance to the company's business: "We see ETL as perhaps the most critical component in the data warehouse because it includes data integration and cleansing and acquisition—the hard parts of the project" (Mrazek, 2003).

With impressive CRM solutions and higher-level talk of meeting business objectives and ROI, though, the less sexy subject of Extract, Transform, and Load processes is often given little thought or discussion. However, ETL design and development comprise over half of all development dollars spent on a data warehousing project. For data mining applications, this number rises to 80 percent (Mrazek, 2003).

The repercussions of a hasty ETL design include costly maintenance, modification, and updates. Worse yet, a slower, poorly-designed system could lead to an inability to make any further additions to the system. According to Mrazek (2003) smartly designed multilayered ETL can "substantially reduce development costs and improve maintainability and information quality," bringing annual savings of hundreds of thousands to millions of dollars.

Costly rework is too often the result of inadequate ETL planning. Earls (2003) describes provides an example of bad ETL planning at Premier Healthcare. The senior director of IT at Premier Healthcare Inc. Gary Feierstein wished his company had learned the ETL lesson earlier. The organization had set up its first data warehouse using proprietary tools. Over the years, the task of modifying these tools to fit the changing needs of the business and of its new customers required more and more resources. Eventually, costs escalated to the point that Feierstein was tasked with re-engineering the ETL process to improve its cost-efficiency and scalability. Feierstein was satisfied with the Ab Initio software he chose because of its abilities to function across disparate platforms as well as incorporate new hardware. He warns that "the key to any new ETL development is the learning curve" and suggests that key areas of focus include solid quality assurance processes and the capability to function across multiple platforms (Earls, 2003).

In order for ETL to work for the company and help achieve the business objectives and ROI that are usually the focus of data warehousing planning talks, it is crucial that IT managers ask the right questions. For example, Argosy wanted to integrate all customer data to improve management's operational oversight and build stronger customer relationships. A data-warehousing analyst hired to assist with Argosy's plan discovered that the varying and incompatible profiles of customers and operational practices among their riverboat casinos had resulted in differing definitions of a broad array of data types that lead to greater problems when the data was aggregated. Such ETL issues are not uncommon due to the innate complexity and business requirements, including a clear grasp of the company's desired objectives.

Success factors beyond this preparation and the quality assurance and scalability Feierstein recommended are a centralized system, real-time response, and metadata. According to Giga analyst Philip Russom, "Centralized ETL is generally preferable to distributed ETL because it is much simpler." Though ETL was once a batch process, more and more companies now desire real-time response from a data warehouse. ETL project managers should consider the ability of the tools they select to handle metadata so they are capable of monitoring this down the road. A final recommendation comes from Harley's Keene who emphasizes the importance of selecting a quality vendor with a top-notch suite of tools (Earls, 2003). This leads to the next failure objective.

Failure Principle 10: Choose a Low-Cost Consultant/Vendor

While cost should be a consideration, it must not be the sole basis of this decision, as it will greatly affect the outcome of an organization's data warehouse implementation. As field expert Larry Greenfield (2009) warns, "You will fail if you concentrate on resource optimization to the neglect of project, data, and customer management issues and an understanding of what adds value for the customer." The fit of the software and vendor with the needs of the company is an important consideration for the project's success.

For example, regardless of price, a company should avoid buying applications that are early in their product lifecycle, or Beta versions. This leads to the company discovering bugs and kinks in the tool, which is helpful to the vendor, but could potentially derail the implementation from its projected timeline (Agosta, 2005).

Other vendor watchouts include not hiring a doormat or divorcing a consultant too soon. It is vital that the consultant possess the knowledge and guts to challenge you when appropriate. Also, considering the size of the investment, the company should engage in active, ongoing feedback from the start of the project to guide the consultant regarding the company's expectations. This will help avoid miscommunication and frustration that could lead to a premature break (Jacobs, 1999).

The overall strategy and design of the data warehouse, the implementation process and communication that ensues and finally the resources and technology invested to the data warehousing project dictates the ten major principles that must be avoided when implementing a data warehousing project. Table 1 summarizes each of the ten principles within strategy and design, implementation management and communication and technology and resource investment.

Avoiding each of these principles would enable an organization to design and implement a successful data warehouse project. Looking at each project from the perspective of overall strategy, the implementation process and finally from a resource perspective would help identify the major pitfalls that a company should avoid when working on a data warehouse project. Sometimes, focusing on the critical success factors does not help an organization avoid failure as much as being mindful of the pitfalls (i.e., failure principles) to avoid.

Table 1. 10 Principles to ensure data warehouse implementation failure

10 Principles to Ensure Your Data Warehouse Implementation is a Failure
Strategy and Design
Failure Principle #1. Create now, strategize later.
Failure Principle #2. Build the data warehouse as a solution to a specific BI project/need.
Failure Principle #3. Save time and money – skip the pilot/proof of concept.
Failure Principle #4. Assume users will patiently wait for the release.
Implementation Management and Communication
Failure Principle #5. With project management communication, less is more.
Failure Principle #6. Don't worry about what everyone else is doing.
Failure Principle #7. Run the red lights (or do not stop at checkpoints)
Technology and Resource Investment
Failure Principle #8. Delegates all technology decisions to IT.
Failure Principle #9. There's no need to get into the weeds with something like ETL development.
Failure Principle #10. Choose a low-cost consultant/vendor.

CONCLUSION

With the amount of information data warehouses can store and organize for strategic querying and reporting, these information systems can serve as powerful business intelligence applications. This is manifest through the number of companies attempting to do so, despite discouragingly high failure rates. A company needs only to follow any combination of the ten principles above to cause their data warehousing project to run into overtime, exceed its budget, and disappoint users, with their experience, and managers, with the tools' ROI.

However, if the company is clear on what it intends to achieve with the project, allocates sufficient thought to design, ETL processes, and resource and technology investments, and benchmarks its progress, providing regular communication to all key stakeholders, it will have a much greater chance at achieving success in their data warehouse implementation.

REFERENCES

Agosta, L. (2005). Exploring the social life of the data warehouse. *DM Review*, 68-73.

Ariyachandra, T., & Frolick, M. (2008). Critical success factors in business performance management - striving for success. *Information Systems Management*, *25*(2). doi:10.1080/10580530801941504

Ariyachandra, T., & Watson, H. (2010). Selection of a data warehouse architecture: Key organizational factors. *Decision Support Systems*, *49*(2). doi:10.1016/j.dss.2010.02.006

Chenowith, T., Corral, K., & Demirkan, H. (2006). Seven key interventions for data warehouse success. *Communications of the ACM*, *49*(1), 115–119.

Earls, A. R. (2003). ETL: Preparation IS THE best bet. *Computerworld*, *37*(34), 25–26.

Embarcadero Technologies. (2008). *Why data warehouse projects fail.* Retrieved from http://etnaweb04.embarcadero.com/resources/technical_papers/Why-Data-Warehouse-Projects-Fail.pdf

Fest, G. (2005). Filling in the blanks. *U.S. Banker*, *115*(12), 20.

Frolick, M., & Ariyachandra, T. (2006). Business Performance Management: The Real Truth. *Information Systems Management*, *23*(1), doi:10.1201/1078.10580530/45769.23.1.20061201/91771.5

Furey, T. (2005). Data warehouse project management. *DM Review*, 70-73.

Greenfield, L. (2009). *A definition of data warehousing.* Retrieved from http://www.dwinfocenter.org/defined.html

IBM. (n. d.). *The new voice of the CIO.* Retrieved from http://www-935.ibm.com/services/us/cio/ciostudy/

Jacobs, P. (1999). Data mining: What general managers need to know. *Harvard Management Update*, 3-4.

Kelly, S. (1997). Data marts: The latest silver bullet. *Data Mart Review*, 12-16.

Knight, M. (2008). *BI growth to buck economic trends.* Retrieved from http://www.itpro.co.uk/183480/bi-growth-to-buck-economic-trends

Lindsey, K., & Frolick, M. N. (2003). Critical factors for data warehousing failures. *Journal of Data Warehousing*, *8*(1), 48–54.

Mrazek, J. (2003). ETL: The best-kept secret of success in data warehousing. *DM Review*, *13*(6), 44–45.

Poolet, M. A. (2009). 7 steps for successful data warehouse projects. *SQL Server Magazine*, 29-34.

Stam, A. (2007). *EDW: The four biggest reasons for failure*. Retrieved from http://license.icopyright.net/user/viewFreeUse.act?fuid=NTcwOTYzMA%3D%3D

Turban, E., Sharda, S., Aronson, J. E., & King, D. (2008). *Business intelligence: A managerial approach*. Upper Saddle River, NJ: Prentice Hall.

Watson, H. J. (2009). Tutorial: Business intelligence – past, present, and future. *Communications of the Association for Information Systems, 25*(39).

Watson, H. J., & Ariyachandra, T. (2006). Benchmarks for BI and data warehousing success. *DM Review, 24-25*, 34.

Watson, H. J., Ariyachandra, T., & Fuller, C. (2004). Data warehousing governance: Best practices at Blue Cross Blue Shield of North Carolina. *Decision Support Systems, 38*(3). doi:10.1016/j.dss.2003.06.001

Wixom, B., & Watson, H. J. (2001). Data warehouse critical success. *Management Information Systems Quarterly, 12*(24), 210–245.

This work was previously published in the International Journal of Business Intelligence Research, Volume 2, Issue 2, edited by Richard Herschel, pp. 37-47, copyright 2011 by IGI Publishing (an imprint of IGI Global).

Chapter 17
Business Intelligence Conceptual Model

Fletcher H. Glancy
Lindenwood University, USA

Surya B. Yadav
Texas Tech University, USA

ABSTRACT

A business intelligence conceptual model (BISCOM) is proposed as a process-focused design theory for developing, understanding, and evaluating business intelligence (BI) systems. Previous work has concentrated on subsets of the BI systems, use of BI tools, and specific business functional area requirements. BISCOM provides a unified and comprehensive design theory that integrates and synthesizes existing research. It extends existing research by proposing functionality that does not currently exist in BI systems. The BISCOM is validated through descriptive methods that demonstrate the model utility and through prototype creation to demonstrate the need for BISCOM.

1. INTRODUCTION

This paper proposes a design theory for developing business intelligence systems. Business intelligence systems are unlike other information systems such as management information systems (MIS), decision support systems (DSS), expert systems (ES), and executive information systems (EIS) (O'Brien & Marakas, 2007). MIS provide support to the business by automating

processes that were formerly performed manually. DSS provide specific techniques for analyzing information to evaluate potential decisions. ES provide specific high-level information as a subject area expert would. EIS condense and summarize internal business information for a business executive. Business intelligence (BI) systems provide relevant competitive intelligence, combine it with a business' internal information, provide expert information, incorporate advanced

DOI: 10.4018/978-1-4666-2650-8.ch017

analytical decision techniques, and are able to inform the executive of the relevance of the knowledge created from the system. We define competitive intelligence as relevant information about the competitive environment external to a business organization. Because a BI system needs to combine capabilities of several systems that currently exist independently with capabilities that do not currently exist, a BI system is unique and has unique characteristics. A BI system supports business needs that are data intensive, have cross-functional focus, require a process view, and require advanced analytical methods. These characteristics require a different architecture, one that is process-oriented instead of artifact-oriented. Extant system design theories do not cover such a business intelligence system, and a true BI system does not currently exist. We develop the design theory for business intelligence systems in the form of a conceptual model with clearly defined components, their interrelationships, and testable propositions.

Industry recognizes the importance of BI. Estimates of industry's annual investment in BI range from $7 to $52 billion. The size of the annual investment is a very difficult number to estimate, because there is not a commonly accepted definition of BI. One company, whose primary business is providing analytical tools for BI, reported record revenues of $2.26 billion in 2008 (SAS Institute, 2009). BI has been a very active area for research; the research has primarily concentrated on either developing analytical tools for BI (Clarabridge, 2006; de Ville, 2006; Watson, Wixom, Hoffer, Anderson-Lehman, & Reynolds 2006) or on business intelligence as it is applied in a specific business area (Fordham, Riordan, & Riordan, 2002) such as marketing. We develop an architectural model of BI that clarifies concepts and advances understanding (Young, 1995). We consider BI broader than the tools or the limited scope of current BI systems, and take a more comprehensive view. We develop a design theory (Baldwin & Yadav, 1995; Hevner, March, Park, &

Ram, 2004; Gregor & Jones, 2007) consisting of a conceptual architecture with a specific design specification.

Problem Statement

A BI system needs to support a BI process that creates relevant (Ackoff, 1967) actionable knowledge that credibly, transparently, and accurately reflects the internal and external environment. The BI process transforms relevant information into actionable knowledge. For this paper, we define a user as an executive decision maker who has the ability to act and direct the business. The BI system allows a user to see and evaluate the information and the transformation process. A unified articulation of such a BI system and the BI process are lacking in the current literature. We assert that:

1. A commonly accepted definition of BI or BI system does not exist.
2. BI has very little theoretical foundation.
3. BI lacks a common architecture.
4. BI is application dependent.

As with other emergent technologies (Markus, Majchrzak, & Gasser, 2002), most of the definitions of BI originate with system vendors, and define the system they are promoting (Clarabridge, 2006; Davenport, 2006; Gnatovich, 2007; 180 Systems, 2006). We do not find a generally accepted definition of the problem space addressed by BI systems (Newell and Simon, 1972). System vendors define the problem space to match their system. There is not a coordinated or unified model of a BI system. The attempts to define or create a BI model have been limited in scope. The extant BI models (Trim, 2004; Wright & Calof, 2006; Melo & Dumke de Medeiros, 2007; Green, 2007; Davenport & Harris, 2007) have contributed to research on BI systems. These models have taken a relatively narrow focus; few models have concentrated on the knowledge creation process

(Green, 2006). We believe that at a conceptual level the BI model should be a process-oriented model and not an artifact-oriented model. The process-oriented model focuses on the process view of BI driven by business needs. It is generalizable; the artifact-oriented model is system dependent and is difficult to generalize.

Research Issues

The unique characteristics of BI warrant a theoretical and conceptual model with a new set of features and capabilities to support the BI process. In this paper we focus on improving the quality of BI by combining the use of Porter's (1979) five forces model with Sun Tzu's (2005) Art of War and Gorry and Morton's (1971) explanation of strategic planning and unstructured decisions. We propose a prescriptive knowledge creation process model for BI that allows for user-defined domain and constraints. We consider the following issues to be critical to improving the quality of BI knowledge creation:

1. What business needs should the BI system address?
2. How do the user requirements drive the BI process?
3. What BI processes transform information into knowledge and how are they integrated into a BI system?
4. What conceptual methods and tools address knowledge creation in a BI system?

We answer these questions through a system architecture that conceptualizes and integrates the business needs, user-requirements, functions, and technology in a model that is process-oriented and without boundaries. The model is generalizable to any enterprise because the model is conceptual and not directly related to the technology.

We develop a BI architecture using the Unified Research Methodology (Baldwin & Yadav, 1995). The proposed BI architecture, the Business

Intelligence Conceptual Model (BISCOM), can be used for developing, assessing, and evaluating business intelligence systems, directing research, and assisting practitioners to understand the potential of a BI process. We use the Unified Research Methodology to validate BISCOM. The contribution of this research is a synthesis, integration, and extension of existing BI research in the form of a novel design theory of a BI system. For theory development, we follow the design theory guidance provided by Gregor and Jones (2007)

The paper is organized into the following five sections: In Section 2, we review the relevant literature; Section 3 describes the Unified Research Methodology and its relevance to model development. In Section 4, we develop the BISCOM model. In Section 5, we validate the BISCOM, Section 6 presents research contributions, and Section 7 presents conclusions and future work.

2. RELEVANT LITERATURE

The popularized term "business intelligence" is relatively recent; often, it is credited to Howard Dresner (Smalltree, 2006). BI systems are a relatively new development in MIS (Benbasat & Zmud, 2003; Berthon, Pitt, Ewing, & Carr., 2002). We believe that the issue of development of business intelligence systems is a major research area. It has been a major area of business expenditure in the quest for strategic advantage (Davenport, 2006).

Business Intelligence

The terms knowledge, information, and intelligence often are used interchangeably. For the purposes of this discussion, we consider intelligence and actionable knowledge interchangeable. Information is contextually supported data and the input to the BI process (Azvine, Cui, & Nauck, 2005). Information systems have expanded the ability to gather data, both structured and unstructured (Cody, Kreulen, Krishna, & Spangler, 2002).

Information is the process input, and descriptive knowledge is feedback to the BI process. Actionable knowledge is the output from the BI process, which includes intelligence focused within the business and external to the business. The concept of externally focused or environmental information gathering and subsequently transforming it into actionable knowledge predates use by the MIS discipline by centuries.

Externally Focused BI

From the advent of competition between organizations instead of between feudal states or war lords (Tzu, 2005), there has been a focus on intelligence that has attempted answering questions about the world external to the enterprise; questions that impact a business' profitability and impact its existence. The questions about the business environment such as what are our competitors doing? What is our market share? What are the customers buying and why? What governmental regulation will change our cost structure? What forces and events in other markets will have an effect on our business?

With the globalization of markets, the questions are relatively unchanged except in scope; the amount of information available and necessary to answer them has grown exponentially (Friedman, 2005). The amount of information available externally has increased dramatically over the last thirty years, as has the amount of internal information available. Open access to this information has also increased with the Internet, which is a great source of information as well as a major factor in globalization. In addition to external environmental information, a business possesses a wealth of information in its database; customer, supplier, service, and manufacturing information, both historical and current, are available to create knowledge.

Internally Focused BI

Organizations possess a large amount of information about their business and the external environment within the company databases. For example, customer information is in the customer feedback, returns, item sales volume, sales forecasts, the sales call reports, and supply chain management systems (Fordham et al., 2002; Martin, 2001). This information is only descriptive and looks backward in time; it only tells where the business has been, which is not necessarily where it is going. In order to create forecasts and develop predictive knowledge, it is necessary to transform the information through analysis. This transformation can be as simple as linear regression that creates trend data; it can be as complex as sophisticated data mining coupled with advanced statistical analysis.

Knowledge Creation

Knowledge is dual faceted; it is tacit or explicit (Polanyi, 1966). Tacit knowledge is internal to the individual; explicit knowledge is expressed and conveyed through documentation. The knowledge creation process is an iterative process alternating between tacit and explicit (Nonaka, 1994). Cook and Brown (1999) state that "for human groups, the source of new knowledge and knowing lies in the use of knowledge as a tool of knowing within situated interaction with the social and physical world" (p. 383). Knowledge creation is not automatic; it comes through human interaction with a BI System and informed use of BI tools. BI tools explore and mine the business and environmental information to create new knowledge.

Data mining has become the primary process for knowledge creation from the data warehouse (Whiting, 2006). The primary goal of BI knowledge creation is predictive. Data mining is only one tool and analytically oriented companies will have widespread use of predictive modeling and complex optimization techniques, not just descriptive statistics (Davenport, 2006). However many companies are not at this level of sophistication (Watson et al., 2006; Crounse, 2007; Ericson, 2006; 180 Systems, 2006)

Text is categorized as unstructured information (Cody et al., 2002). Text mining refers to a subset of data mining tools and techniques used to discover unknown information from natural language text (Hearst, 2003). Clarabridge (2006) makes the case that a common platform that can use unstructured data and match it to the appropriate structured data will provide the greatest results in business intelligence. The success of text mining is currently dependent on the expertise of the analyst.

Extant BI Research

Extant BI research has investigated several important factors for BI success. Trim (2004) concentrated on the organizational aspects of transformational marketing and corporate intelligence. Recognizing the need for senior management involvement in the BI process, he suggests that an advisory group of senior management is a way to ensure alignment between the staff groups. The need for senior management involvement is repeated and extended to the entire organization by several researchers (Green, 2006; Melo & Dumke de Medieros, 2007; Davenport & Harris, 2007).

Davenport and Harris (2007) describe several stages that companies go through as they develop an organizational culture that supports BI. The concepts of organizational process and structure, and culture, awareness and attitude are primary influences on the organizational development of a BI process (Wright & Calof, 2006); and the process model has four activities: planning and focus, collection, analysis, and communication. Davenport and Harris model the process as an integrated architecture that has metadata and operational processes underlying the BI activities. Mehra (2005) repeats that metadata is the primary integration that is necessary for real time enterprise BI.

Green (2006) describes the BI system as a knowledge valuation system driven by a framework of intangible valuation areas. The value drivers are the customer, competitor, employee, information, partner, process, product/service, and technology. She presents the system as ten constructs, but does not develop the constructs beyond a general definition. Melo and Dumke de Medieros (2006) develop a model of a system in the area of health insurers and demonstrate how it improves the competitive intelligence for the insurers. They limit the utility of the system to the insurers and do not attempt to create a generalizable system. All of the extant models make a contribution toward the development of a unified business intelligence model. Next, we give a brief explanation of the methodology used to create BISCOM.

3. RESEARCH METHODOLOGY

The Unified Research Methodology (Baldwin & Yadav, 1995) proposes multiple methods. This paper proposes a process-based model that is applicable across an entire organization and is not limited to one business function. The model is at the knowledge level; it describes and explains the interaction of knowledge components with the environment to produce new knowledge (Simon, 1981). We follow the concept of prototyping, inductively extrapolating from existing systems and conceptualizing potential uses of analytical tools, both existing tools and future tools. This extends the research to new areas and potential for application of BI.

We describe the BI System design theory in the form of an eight component-structure (Gregor & Jones, 2007) for specifying an information systems design theory The eight components of a design theory are (1) purpose and scope, (2) constructs, (3) principles of form and function, (4) artifact mutability, (5) testable propositions, (6) justificatory knowledge, (7) principles of implementation, and (8) expository instantiation. The BI system design theory is presented as part of the systematic discussion of the BISCOM development in the next section.

4. BISCOM DEVELOPMENT

In this section, we formulate the problem of improving the quality of actionable knowledge and develop a conceptual model as a solution to the problem. We assert that BI quality can be improved by integrating external and internal information, business needs, and the transformation process into a single system. We define a transformation process as the process of converting information into actionable knowledge. We now state the definitions and proposition that are the basis for the BISCOM model.

- **SubSys(InfQ):** Represents a system that knows about the external and internal environments, can provide quality information, and answer questions about the environment. *InfQ* stands for external and internal information quality. Quality information is accurate, complete, relevant, and timely with a reputable source.
- **SubSys(BN):** Represents a system that knows about the business needs and can use this knowledge to rate the importance of the information. *BN* stands for the business needs driving the BI system.
- **Subsys(TP):** Represents a system that knows the transformation processes available and can use that knowledge to select the most appropriate process(es). *TP* stands for transformation process. A transformation process uses information as input and acts on the information to transform it into knowledge.
- **Sys(BIQ):** Represents a system that knows about the quality of the BI and is able to evaluate and determine the overall qual-

ity of the BI. *BIQ* stands for business intelligence quality, which is measured by accuracy and predictive power. Using the above definitions, we state the following proposition:

Sys(BIQ) is effective in providing quality BI if

$$Sys(BIQ) = f(\textstyle\prod SubSys(InfQ) \bullet SubSys(BN) \bullet Subsys(TP))$$

Sys(BIQ) is a function of the product of *SubSys(InfQ)*, *SubSys(BN)*, and *Subsys(TP)*. *Sys(BIQ)* relies on these subsystems to provide and evaluate information with respect to the business needs and to appropriately transform the information into actionable knowledge. These subsystems are interrelated and integrated. The *SubSys(BN)* assists in information evaluation and in providing direction for appropriate transformation process selection. The conceptual process model that improves the *Sys(BIQ)* is the business intelligence conceptual model or BISCOM. A successful implementation of *Sys(BIQ)* assumes that:

1. The business understands its knowledge requirements and can clearly state these requirements in a manner the system can understand.
2. The system has access to all the information sources it requires.
3. All of the BI technology required is available to the system.

BISCOM starts with the definition of what makes a system a business intelligence system. We define a BI system as a collection of subsystems and components that are inter-related and work together to support a process that produces quality BI. The needs of the organization drive the user requirements; and they drive the BI process, which executes the necessary BI functions (task-performers) to provide relevant BI to the user. BI

Technology supports the BI functions with knowledge creation tools. This relationship is shown graphically in Figure 1. The process is iterative with multiple feedback loops. Iterations between the BI functions and the user requirements make the process dynamic. The BI process is longitudinal and builds on the prior knowledge to create new knowledge to meet changing requirements.

In the following subsections, we discuss each of these steps of the BI process.

Business Needs

We consider that there are four underlying business needs for intelligence (Herring, 1999; Negash & Gray, 2003). These are Profitability, Decision-making, Questioning, and Planning. The first need is profitability; the underlying reason a for-profit organization exists. There are forces outside the business as well as inside the business that effect profitability. The BI system's purpose is to identify and predict threats to profitability as well as the opportunities to increase profitability. Threats can come from a wide variety of external sources in addition to competitors; threats can come from increased regulation, de-regulation, financial markets, inflation or deflation, the weather, global warming, and cultural shifts. Internal threats can result from changing attitudes, failure of internal controls, loss of key personnel, and supply chain changes. The opportunities can lie in the response to the threats as well as in changing market conditions when viewed both locally and globally.

The second need for business intelligence is to support the decision making process by assisting in defining and evaluating potential responses to opportunities and threats. The BI System supports the decision making process by providing the appropriate amount of relevant information and communicating in an understandable manner to decision makers. The BI system supports evaluation of different actions based on possible outcomes to a decision. The system should assist in defining the correct questions and provide the knowledge base for decision-making. The BI system should be accessible to all appropriate levels of the organization to maximize its use and advantage (Davenport, 2006).

The third underlying need for the BI System is to answer why an unanticipated event occurred. The ideal BI System will not eliminate surprises, but it will decrease the occurrence and increase the speed of recognizing the event. The question "why" comes from areas that we know and think we understand, and from those areas outside our current perception. Evaluation needs include: Was this a single occurrence or was this a structural change in the environment?

Planning is required for all actions taken in response to the events identified by the BI System. Planning is an integral part of the BI process of creating actionable knowledge. The BI system assists in both strategic planning and in tactical planning to support the business strategy. The BI system is the provider of information and knowledge for strategy development and the information for the tactical implementation.

Each of these needs drive the BI process. They give direction and meaning to the BI process. These needs are the foundation of the user's BI requirements, and they require performance of specific tasks.

Figure 1. The BI Process relationship between business needs and BI functions

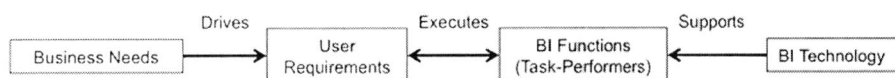

User Requirements

Using Juch's (1983) modes of learning in the process cycle (p. 20), the literature review, and our own introspection and experience, we propose the following list of tasks for which a manager might use a BI system. We do not propose this list to be all-inclusive or that a manager will use all of the proposed functions. We consider that the list is fairly comprehensive based on the learning process cycle. Employing the *Sys(BIQ)* proposition, a BI system should support the following user requirements:

1. Listening to the user-specific needs.
2. Analyzing the information required to meet the user-specific needs.
3. Prioritizing and scheduling resources to deliver timely knowledge.
4. Perceiving and searching all potential sources of relevant information.
5. Evaluating information sources.
6. Retrieving all pertinent information.
7. Combining and consolidating retrieved information.
8. Providing weighting of information based on quality, timeliness, and relevance.
9. Integrating all retrieved information with requirements.
10. Recording retrieved information in a manner that is transparent to the user.
11. Creating knowledge by transforming information
12. Trending information over time.
13. Utilizing past and current information to produce forecasts.
14. Proposing alternate solutions.
15. Making predictions based on information.
16. Giving decision support through evaluation of alternatives.
17. Giving a clear exposition of analysis results.
18. Scanning the environment.
19. Monitoring and providing feedback.

We use these user requirements to derive a set of conceptual architectural constructs. Following Yadav (2009), we use the term task-performer to objectify the function that performs tasks in BISCOM. We view these task-performers as knowledge level constructs (Newell, 1981; Newell, 1982). This is the most abstract level of system description and allows the greatest degree of generalization of a system's functionalities. We identify the necessary task-performers in the next section.

BI Functions

We conducted an analysis of user-oriented tasks and clustered them into groups as shown in Table 1. The user is the executive who has the ability to make strategic decisions for the business. These strategic decisions tend to be less structured and more complex than other decisions made in a business (Mintzberg et al., 1976). The proposed corresponding task-performers are also shown in Table 1. The concept of a task-performer is used to objectify the performance of the various task types in the BI knowledge creation process. We consider the term "task-performer" to be technology neutral; and therefore, it is available for generalization and operationalization using any technology. Each task performer construct knows how to do its task, has domain knowledge, understands the internal and external interactions required, and receives performance feedback. The four BI task-performers supporting the user requirements are: Prediction, Forecasting, Explaining, and Trending. The fifth task-performer is the User Information Handler, which provides an interface between the user and the four task-performers.

BISCOM - Conceptual Model

Conceptually, the task-performers are architectural constructs that support the business needs. They communicate with each other and have access to

Table 1. User oriented tasks and the corresponding architectural constructs

User Oriented Task to meet the user requirements	Conceptual Architectural Construct Task-performer to support the corresponding user requirements
• Listening to the user requirements. • Prioritizing and scheduling resources to deliver timely knowledge. • Give a clear exposition of analysis results. • Scan the environment. • Monitor and provide feedback.	User Information Handler
• Analyze the information required to meet the user requirements. • Perceiving and searching all potential sources of relevant information. • Evaluating information sources. • Retrieving all pertinent information. • Combining and consolidating retrieved information. • Providing weighting of information based on quality, timeliness, and relevance. • Integrating all retrieved information with requirements. • Recording retrieved information in a manner that is transparent to the user. • Perform knowledge creation transformation. • Propose alternate solutions. • Give decision support through evaluation of alternatives.	Explanation
• Analyze the information required to meet the user requirements. • Perceiving and searching all potential sources of relevant information. • Evaluating information sources. • Retrieving all pertinent information. • Combining and consolidating retrieved information. • Providing weighting of information based on quality, timeliness, and relevance. • Integrating all retrieved information with requirements. • Recording retrieved information in a manner that is transparent to the user. • Trending information over time.	Trending
• Analyze the information required to meet the user requirements. • Perceiving and searching all potential sources of relevant information. • Evaluating information sources. • Retrieving all pertinent information. • Combining and consolidating retrieved information. • Providing weighting of information based on quality, timeliness, and relevance. • Integrating all retrieved information with requirements. • Recording retrieved information in a manner that is transparent to the user. • Perform knowledge creation transformation. • Utilize past and current information to produce forecasts.	Forecasting
• Analyze the information required to meet the user requirements. • Perceiving and searching all potential sources of relevant information. • Evaluating information sources. • Retrieving all pertinent information. • Combining and consolidating retrieved information. • Providing weighting of information based on quality, timeliness, and relevance. • Integrating all retrieved information with requirements. • Recording retrieved information in a manner that is transparent to the user. • Perform knowledge creation transformation. • Make predictions based on information. • Propose alternate solutions. • Give decision support through evaluation of alternatives.	Prediction

the same tools. For the task-performers to interact with the user, another task-performer is required. The user interacts with the BISCOM through the user Information handler (UIH) task-performer. UIH evaluates the user's request, selects the appropriate task-performer to meet it, and communicates to the user the knowledge the task-performers create. The architecture of BISCOM is shown in Figure 2.

The UIH has responsibility for transmitting all routine scheduled reporting as well as maintaining all current trend reports. It is also responsible for all dashboard maintenance. It can access all stored query results and prior queries. The user creates a system request through the UIH. The UIH routes the request to the task-performer(s) that is best suited to meet the request. The UIH

has the responsibility for scheduling the task-performers as well as monitoring system performance; this requirement leads to the addition of another task-performer, the Performance Assessor.

The Performance Assessor monitors the output of the other task-performers and tracks the predictions, forecasts, trends, and explanations over time to determine the accuracy of the original output. The Performance Assessor calculates the variance from the original output and makes it available to both the task-performer and the UIH. This ensures the long-term accuracy of the knowledge created and the knowledge creation process. The BISCOM Performance Assessor allows the UIH to monitor variance and suggest possible re-evaluations when the variance is increasing compared to expected performance. The UIH makes this assessment

Figure 2. The Unified Architecture of Business Intelligence Conceptual Model (BISCOM)

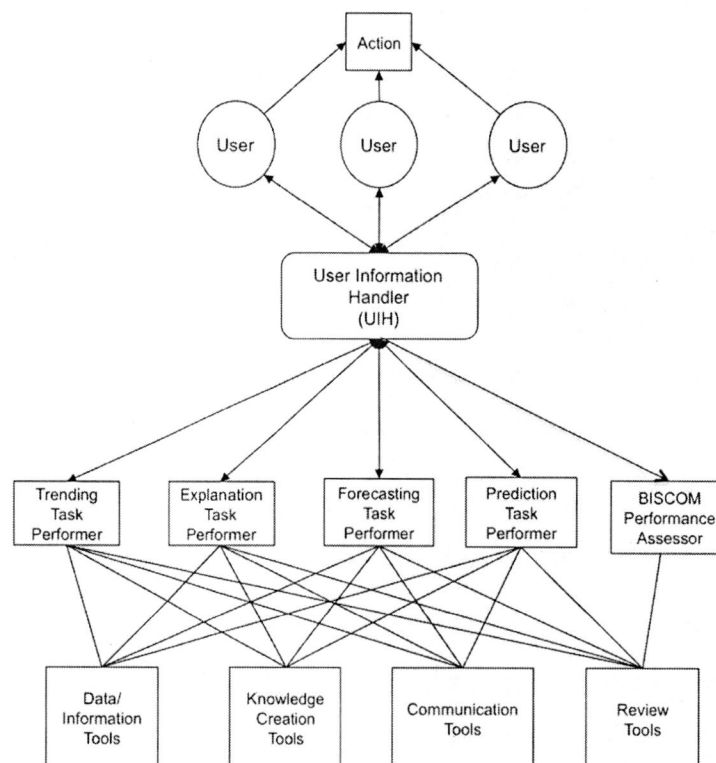

available to the users and to the task performers. The Performance Assessor provides a high level of system mutability. This allows the BISCOM to be independent of technology and to adapt to changing environmental conditions.

Each task-performer has access to all BISCOM technology that it needs to do its function. Conceptually, multiple task-performers can access the technology simultaneously, and each task-performer can handle simultaneous requests. In the same manner, all information is available to all task-performers. When new knowledge is created, it is added to the information base. All models created by the task-performers are available and can be accessed by each task performer. This allows use of predictive models by the trend task-performer for comparison and accuracy evaluation. The UIH can require predictive models be revised if the feedback indicates they accuracy is decreasing.

Prediction Task-Performer

Prediction is foretelling events based on a model and understanding the probability of an event happening, which is a measure of the models accuracy. The prediction task-performer calculates confidence intervals for the prediction and selects the model that provides the highest confidence level. It provides the user a clear understanding of the limitations and constraints of the prediction. The prediction task-performer is capable of responding to real world dynamic information and make corrections in the model based on current environmental feedback. The prediction task-performer is able to operate without user interaction or supervision for repetitive tasks. When the created knowledge is acted on, the prediction task performer updates the model based on the variance from the performance assessor.

Forecast Task-Performer

A forecast is an event planned in advanced. The event can be earnings, sales, etc. It is a planned

event. The difference between a forecast and a prediction is best shown by the example of an earnings forecast. "Total sales are expected to increase approximately 1 percent." (Lowe's, 2008) Note that there is no mention of a probability or confidence interval in the forecast. The forecast task-performer provides monitoring and communicates feedback to the user and to the prediction task-performer for model updating. The forecast task-performer also evaluates dynamic information flows for accuracy and quality utilizing the performance assessor. It is capable of having sensitivity levels integrated into its communication requirements. It will report variances based on user requirements or on internal defaults.

Explain Task-Performer

The function of the explain task-performer is to understand logically why an event took place. It creates a model that provides knowledge of the factors that created the event. It provides a model evaluation and explains the model constraints and confidence levels. It provides both input and feedback to the predictive task-performer to improve the predictive modeling. The explain task-performer is primarily a management tool for understanding unforeseen events. The performance assessor provides monitoring of the explanation variance and provides feedback when changes in the external and internal environments create other potential explanations.

Trend Task Performer

The trend task-performer tracks an event or events through time and supports the business with ongoing knowledge of current status. It can also provide knowledge of the effect of past actions on the current business status. Often multiple trends are tracked together because of a belief that they are significantly correlated with each other. The trend task-performer provides knowledge to the user and to the forecast and prediction task-performers. This provides additional feedback for refining models. Trending is the most frequently used task-performer because it is the easiest part of BISCOM to understand. It is the basis for most of the executive information systems that provide summary data on current status. With BISCOM, trending is integrated with the entire BI process and not simply a reporting system.

Performance Assessor

The performance assessor tracks the output from the other task performers and compares the prediction, trend, explanation, or forecast against actual events. It calculates variance and provides this information to the UIH for dissemination to the users and to the task-performers. It creates feedback for improvement of the task performer. By monitoring the actual results after the task-performer completes its task, the UIH allows for mutability of the BI and correction for new or previously unobserved information.

BISCOM–BI System Design Theory

BISCOM is proposed as a BI system design theory. BISCOM is defined in terms of all of the components of an information system design theory as suggested by Hevner et al. (2004) and as extended by Gregor and Jones (2007). The eight components of BISCOM and a summary description of the BISCOM components are given in Table 2.

In the BISCOM there are five technologies used by all task-performers within the BISCOM model. These technologies are Data/Information, Knowledge Creation, Communication, Action and Review/Feedback. They are task specific, inter-related, and generally dependent on each other. We discuss the BI technology in the next section.

BISCOM Technology

Figure 3 shows the relationship between the task-performers and the BI technology. The BISCOM system supports the following task-performers in

Table 2. BISCOM design theory components

Component	BISCOM Description
Purpose and Scope	The purpose is to improve the quality of actionable knowledge created by a BI system. The BISCOM is a design theory that provides a means and method for evaluating and improving BI systems.
Constructs	Task Performing Units: User Information Handler, Trending Task Performer, Explanation Task Performer, Forecasting Task Performer, Prediction Task Performer, BISCOM Performance Assessor.
Principles of Form and Function	BISCOM is a conceptual architectural model that shows the overall structure and form of a BI system. It shows the relationships between the task-performers, tools, and users.
Artifact Mutability	BISCOM is adaptive. BISCOM components can easily be extended to support new and changed business needs.
Testable Propositions	$Sys(BIQ)$ is effective in providing quality BI if $Sys(BIQ) = f(\prod SubSys(InfQ) \cdot SubSys(BN) \cdot Subsys(TP))$ Where BIQ is business information quality, InfQ is information quality, BN is business needs, and TP is the transformation process. The Sys(BIQ) and the subsystems are built upon BISCOM.
Justificatory Knowledge	The theoretical basis is Juch's learning spiral (Juch, 1983) that proposes how learning takes place. This is coupled with Porter's (1979) five forces model that describes the external forces driving business.
Principles of Implementation	BISCOM is implemented as a modular, component based system. It can be prototyped to implement the task-performers and tools necessary for information transformation.
Expository Instantiation	A prototype implementation is demonstrated using SAS Enterprise Miner technology.

Figure 3. A conceptual relationship between task-performers and BI technology

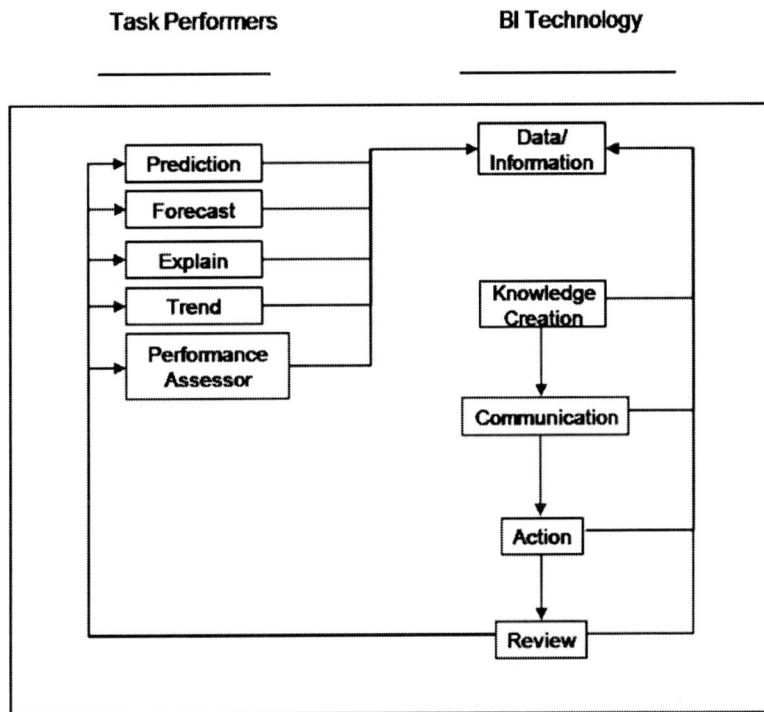

order to create knowledge. The task-performers all access the BI technology tools and the same data sources eliminating redundant data and operations.

Data/Information Technology

Data/information is where all data is accessed, retrieved, organized, cleaned, and validated. The data information technology is subdivided into five separate tools. The system must access the information in the repository. The access tool must be able to access both structured and unstructured information and to recognize relationships between the structured and unstructured.

The query tool creates a query to obtain relevant information. It needs operate compatibly with the repository system, regardless of syntax, language or format. It needs to take the BI System query and convert it to a repository query. The query tool

should be able to automatically generate multiple queries to ensure the retrieval of all relevant data.

The organize tool performs tasks of transforming retrieved information for use by the BI system to create a common syntax regardless of the information source. For each individual request, the data from all sources are compiled into a single data set, sorted, and sequenced.

The clean tool needs to be able to determine an appropriate method for the sorting and sequencing.

The de-clutter tool tests the information/data for relevance to the query parameters and segregates irrelevant information. This tool also removes duplicate records, reduces the amount of noise by replacing missing attributes or imputing their value based on an appropriate rule or algorithm.

The verify tool tests the data quality by looking for records that conflict with others, looking for multiple sources for the same information and comparing data with internal expert algorithms.

Knowledge Creation Technology

Knowledge creation is the heart of the BISCOM. Here the gathered information is mapped, analyzed, synthesized, transformed into knowledge and validated.

Mapping is the process of modeling using the data. The data is examined and appropriate models selected. Then the models are mapped to the data and the best model selected. Many types of models are available use.

In analysis, statistical tools are used to interpret the model and understand the significance of the results. Interpretation is necessary to understand the analysis results. Data and text mining commonly used to create knowledge through classification, decision trees, associations, dissociations, and exploratory methods.

Synthesis is the next step in knowledge creation. The result of the BI process is new knowledge. New knowledge is assimilated and integrated with the existing knowledge, creating a synthesis and extending the understanding.

The knowledge validation tool tests the new knowledge against information that was not used in the knowledge creation to validate that the new knowledge will accurately forecast, predict, explain or trend events. This testing gives a confidence level to the new knowledge using secondary information sources.

Communication Technology

The communication technology contains all of the tools necessary for exposition of the output of the BISCOM. These tools include report generation and recommendation. The reporting tools report the results, conclusions, methodology used, accuracy, risk or probability of error, assumptions, and constraints. The user-friendly reporting tool creates a report that is formatted in a manner

that is user defined and intuitive. Based on the parameters of the system request or query, the BISCOM recommends potential actions. The system is able to match the conclusions with user input strategic constraints.

Review Technology

The review technology maintains the history of system requests with all results and is available as a feedback mechanism or an updating mechanism. The review technology is used to calculate the variance between current information and expected information. While this technology is available to all task-performers, the performance assessor primarily uses it. This technology is the repository of frequent queries and their scheduling. A scheduled query would update the task-performer with a new query and provide that information to the data gathering process. This allows the use of Bayesian analytical methods. The new query replaces the old query results and archives the old results. Access to previous query results and access to current results for use of OLAP tools is through the review function of the Communications function.

5. EVALUATION OF BISCOM

Hevner et al. (2004) suggest several evaluation methods for design science. We use descriptive evaluation of the model utility and a descriptive prototype evaluation.

Descriptive Evaluation of BISCOM

In this section, we logically demonstrate that the proposed BISCOM model presents a synthesis and integration of the existing research, and extends it through a comprehensive and refined view of business intelligence systems. The model's utility is enhanced further by the high-level well-defined constructs that allow for future tool and method developments. Several studies have contributed to the design science development of business intelligence systems (Davenport & Harris, 2007; Green, 2006; Mehra, 2005; Melo & Dumke de Medeiros, 2007; Trim, 2004; Wright & Calof, 2006). Each has emphasized a specific aspect of BI.

Wright and Calof (2006) suggest that the critical elements of a BI system need to have process and structure as well as an enterprise culture, attitude, and awareness that support a BI system. They divided the BI system into four parts: planning and focus, data collection, analysis, and communication. They did not suggest a process or structure for the BI system. Trim (2004) developed a Strategic Corporate Intelligence and Transformational Marketing (Satellite) Model that is primarily concerned with the organizational structure that supports marketing intelligence. Trim's Satellite model assumes that the business has the ability to create BI; the primary concern is the organizational commitment to and ability to use the BI system output. Green (Green, 2006) agrees that an organizational commitment to BI is required. She describes the BI system as a knowledge valuation system (KVS). The ten characteristics of the KVS are concepts, structures, hypotheses, languages, logic, pattern recognition, representation, data retrieval, evidence, and contributions. The model Green proposes limits the BI system or concept to only three of these characteristics: structure, language, and data retrieval. The knowledge concept she proposes is the repository of the logic, pattern recognition, and representation characteristics. The BISCOM model proposes that the ten characteristics are integral to the BI process. Melo and Dumke de Medeiros (2007) add evaluation to the four phases of the continuous transformation process of BI proposed by Kahaner (1996). The four phases are planning, collection, analysis, and dissemination. Melo and Dumke de Medeiros discuss the importance of these phases; but they do it in a descriptive manner without indicating the structure for the BI process.

Unlike the existing models of BI, the BISCOM provides knowledge level constructs or task-performers that support the knowledge creation. Included are the functions that inform users and disseminate the BI. In addition, the process is iterative with multiple feedback loops that provide the process with a dynamic dimension that give longitudinal direction to the BI. The BISCOM model integrates the BI process across the enterprise. This ensures that the BI has a cross functionality, integration, and a higher degree of accuracy. Because the BISCOM is at the knowledge level, it can adapt to changing technologies and tools; it is platform independent. The performance assessor provides the BISCOM with the mutability necessary in the dynamic real-world environment.

Prototype Evaluation of the BISCOM Conceptual Model

We use SAS Enterprise BI Server® (BIServer) to create a prototype of the BISCOM at the current technology level and use this prototype to demonstrate how the BISCOM could be used to design enhancements to the BIServer. BIServer is advanced data mining and analytical software that has many of the tools discussed in BISCOM. In the interests of space, the prototype only looks at the predictive task-performer and the UIH. Figure 4 shows the prototype as a node diagram in the Enterprise Miner (EM) of the BIServer. The prototype retrieves information, explores the data, and imputes missing data or initiates additional information retrieval. It evaluates and weights the information, transforms variables as necessary, selects the relevant variables, and selects potentially relevant statistical analytical methods or models. It applies the selected models, compares and contrasts the model results (BI knowledge), and provides recommendations.

The prototype follows the BISCOM model and is read from left to right. In EM, the task-performer is a human analyst. The technology does not currently support task-performer. The

Figure 4. Prediction task-performer prototype

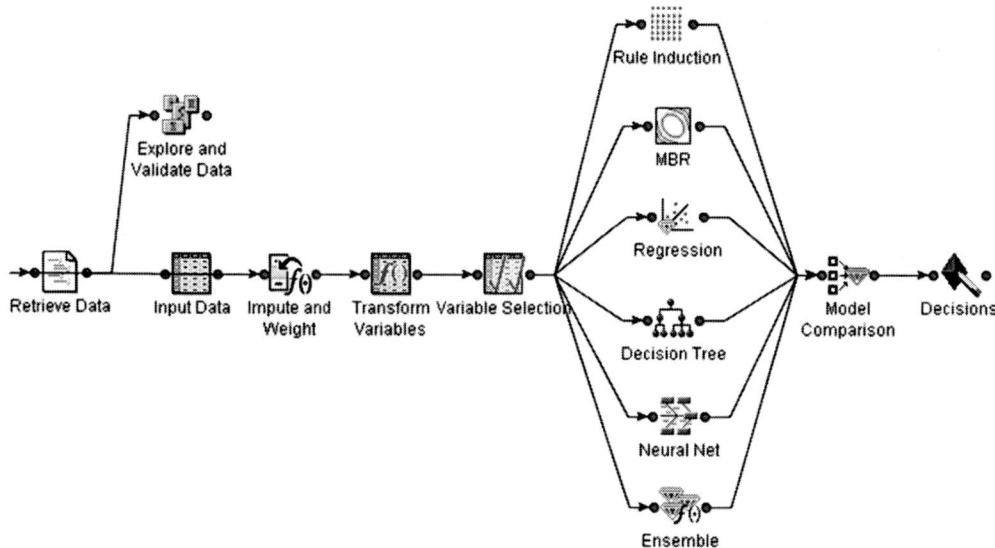

external information retrieval is by the analyst. It is possible to automate some retrieval tasks, but a program must be written for each task and source. The analyst can automate repetitive tasks, but the information tool envisioned in BISCOM is not currently in existence. The data cleaning is not yet automated. The variable imputing, weighting, transforming, and selecting are an analyst task. The tools assist in these tasks, but the analyst makes all decisions. The analyst also makes the choice of type of predictive tool, often using several and comparing models. The analyst also chooses the decision method. The communication tool for exposition of the BI created does not currently exist as envisioned by BISCOM. The analyst has the responsibility for exposition and the statement of assumptions and limitations.

Currently, the UIH has not been implemented in the SAS EM system. It is a human function to decide what type of BI is needed, prioritize the requests, and manage resources. Table 3 shows how the user-oriented tasks are accomplished today compared to the performance with the BISCOM task-performers for the prototype.

From this prototype, it can be seen that implementation of a BISCOM based system would meet the proposition for *Sys(BIQ)* discussed earlier. The prototype has the ability to obtain information, evaluate the quality of information, and evaluate information sources. It understands the business needs and can weight information based on those needs. It has the processes necessary to transform the information into knowledge and make predictions based on that knowledge, and it has the ability to create and evaluate alternate solutions based on the predictions.

6. RESEARCH CONTRIBUTIONS

BISCOM is a new and novel design theory for BI systems. It provides a basis for evaluating current BI systems, and it provides a theoretical basis for prototyping and developing new BI Systems. BISCOM is a unified and comprehensive BI

Table 3. UIH and prediction task-performer comparison with EM prototype

BISCOM Task-performer and User-oriented Task	Currently performed in EM in BIServer by:
User Information Handler • Listening to the user requirements. • Prioritizing and scheduling resources to deliver timely knowledge. • Give a clear exposition of analysis results. • Scan the environment. • Monitor and provide feedback.	Analyst or Manager
Prediction • Analyze the information required to meet the user requirements. • Perceiving and searching all potential sources of relevant information. • Evaluating information sources. • Retrieving all pertinent information. • Combining and consolidating retrieved information. • Providing weighting of information based on quality, timeliness, and relevance. • Integrating all retrieved information with requirements. • Recording retrieved information in a manner that is transparent to the user. • Perform knowledge creation transformation. • Make predictions based on information. • Propose alternate solutions. • Give decision support through evaluation of alternatives.	• Analyst • Analyst • Analyst • Analyst • Analyst and EM • EM as directed by Analyst • Analyst • Analyst • EM as directed by Analyst • EM as directed by Analyst • Analyst • Analyst

theory, because it integrates and synthesizes existing research into a single theory. BISCOM then extends it by proposing and modeling functionality that does not currently exist. It meets the all of the requirements of design science theory proposed by Hevner et al. (2004). BISCOM addresses the problem of lack of definition and scope for BI by providing both. It also meets the additional requirements of Gregor and Jones (2007) for design theory including an expository instantiation.

BISCOM addresses all of the research issues. It defines the needs that the BI system should address, addresses the how the need for intelligence drives the process through the user requirements that are met by the BI functions (task-performers), defines the task-performers that transform information into knowledge, defines the technology used by the task performers, and how they are integrated into the overall theory.

The introduction of the performance assessor is unique in the literature. The performance assessor is a key element for system mutability; and when instantiated, it will improve the BI system information quality.

BISCOM is the first theory to propose an artifact that can provide guidance for BI system evaluation and system development. It is a process-based theory that allows the researcher and practitioner to define the boundaries of the artifact. This is necessary as the boundaries are constantly changing with technology development and business needs, and it is possible because it is a process-based theory and not technology dependent. BISCOM provides direction for technology development in an area that is of high interest to practitioners.

7. CONCLUSION AND FUTURE WORK

The BISCOM is an integrated theory that can be used to prototype BI systems and provide a basis for evaluating commercial BI systems. At this stage in the development of BI systems, BISCOM provides guidance for comparing systems strengths and revealing their weaknesses. This will assist the practitioner in system evaluation and increase the probability of realizing a return on the investment. From the analytical evaluation, it is can be inferred that there is a tradeoff between BI ease of use and functionality. In BISCOM, we do not accept this as a necessary assumption. BI systems can increase ease of use and deliver high functionality.

In future research, we anticipate creating a more complete prototype and empirically testing it in a real world environment. It will more clearly indicate areas for future research that are attainable in the short term as well as longer term direction.

We propose to further develop the concept of the UIH and explore how it can be instantiated. The instantiation of the UIH is a key area for improving BI through communication of business needs and converting them into information requirements for knowledge creation. It provides mutability to the BISCOM through the Performance Assessor.

REFERENCES

Ackoff, R. L. (1967). Management misinformation systems. *Management Science*, *14*(4), 147–156. doi:10.1287/mnsc.14.4.B147

Azvine, B., Cui, Z., & Nauck, D. D. (2005). Towards real-time business intelligence. *BT Technology Journal*, *23*(3), 214–225. doi:10.1007/s10550-005-0043-0

Baldwin, D., & Yadav, S. B. (1995). The process of research investigaions in artificial intelligence - an unified view. *IEEE Transactions on Systems, Man, and Cybernetics*, *25*(5), 852–861. doi:10.1109/21.376497

Benbasat, I., & Zmud, R. W. (2003). The identity crisis within the IS discipline: Defining and communication the discipline's core properties. *Management Information Systems Quarterly*, *27*(2), 183–194.

Berthon, P., Pitt, L., Ewing, P., & Carr, C. L. (2002). Potential research space in MIS: A framework for envisioning and evaluating research replication, extension, and generation. *Information Systems Research*, *13*(4), 416–427. doi:10.1287/isre.13.4.416.71

Clarabridge, I. (2006). *Converging text and BI: The case for a content mining platform*. Retrieved from http://www.clarabridge.com/resources/downloads.php

Cody, W. F., Kreulen, J. T., Krishna, V., & Spangler, W. S. (2002). The integration of business intelligence and knowledge management. *IBM Systems Journal*, *41*(4), 697–714. doi:10.1147/sj.414.0697

Cook, S. D. N., & Brown, J. S. (1999). Bridging epistemologies: The generative dance between organizational knowledge and organizational knowing. *Organization Science*, *10*(4), 381–400. doi:10.1287/orsc.10.4.381

Crounse, B. (2007). *Business intelligence systems give meaning to mountains of healthcare data, 3*. Retrieved from http://www.microsoft.com/industry/healthcare/providers/businessvalue/housecalls/housecalls_patientbi.mspx

Davenport, T. H. (2006). Competing on analytics. *Harvard Business Review*, *84*(1), 99–107.

Davenport, T. H., & Harris, J. G. (2007). *Competing on analytics: The new sience of winning*. Boston, MA: Harvard Business School Press.

de Ville, B. (2006). *Decision trees for business intelligence and data mining: Using SAS enterprise miner* (1st ed.). Cary, NC: SAS Institute.

Ericson, J. (2006). Health care's knowledge quest: Data integration supports research at Children's Hospital, Boston. *Business Intelligence Review*, *2*(3), 12.

Fordham, D. R., Riordan, D. A., & Riordan, M. P. (2002). Business intelligence: How accountants bring value to the marketing function. *Strategic Finance*, *83*(11), 6.

Friedman, T. L. (2005). *The world is flat: A brief history of the twenty-first century* (1st ed.). New York, NY: Farrar, Straus and Giroux.

Gnatovich, R. (2007). Making a case for business analytics. *Strategic Finance, 88*(8), 46–52.

Gorry, G. A., & Morton, M. S. S. (1989). A framework for management information systems. [SMR Classic Reprint]. *Sloan Management Review*, 49–61.

Green, A. (2006). Building blocks to a knowledge valuation system (KVS). *The Journal of Information and Knowledge Management Systems, 36*(2), 146–154.

Green, A. (2007). Business information - a natural path to business intelligence: Knowing what to capture. *The Journal of Information and Knowledge Management Systems, 37*(1), 18–23.

Gregor, S., & Jones, D. (2007). The anatomy of a design theory. *Journal of the Association for Information Systems, 8*(5), 312–335.

Hearst, M. (2003). *What is text mining?* Retrieved from http://www.ischool.berkley.edu

Herring, J. P. (1999). Key intelligence topics: A process to identify and define intelligence needs. *Competitive Intelligence Review, 10*(2), 4–14. doi:10.1002/(SICI)1520-6386(199932)10:2<4::AID-CIR3>3.0.CO;2-C

Hevner, A. R., March, S. T., Park, J., & Ram, S. (2004). Design science in information systems research. *Management Information Systems Quarterly, 28*(1), 75–105.

Juch, B. (1983). *Personal development: Theory and practice in management training.* Chichester, UK: John Wiley & Sons.

Kahaner, L. (1996). *Competitive intelligence: From black ops to boardrooms - how businesses gather, analyze, and use information to succeed in the global marketplacy* (1st ed.). New York, NY: Simon & Schuster.

Markus, M. L., Majchrzak, A., & Gasser, L. (2002). A design theory for systems that support emergent knowledge processes. *Management Information Systems Quarterly, 26*(3), 179–212.

Martin, J. (2001). Alien intelligence. *The Journal of Business Strategy, 22*(2), 18–23. doi:10.1108/eb040153

Mehra, V. (2005). Building a metadata-driven enterprise: A holistic approach. *Business Intelligence Journal, 10*(3), 7–16.

Melo, M. A. N., & Dumke de Medeiros, D. (2007). A model for analyzing the competitive strategy of health plan insurers using a system of competitive intelligence. *The TQM Magazine, 19*(3), 206–216. doi:10.1108/09544780710745630

Mintzberg, H., Raisinghani, D., & Theoret, A. (1976). The structure of "unstructured" decision processes. *Administrative Science Quarterly, 21*(2), 246–275. doi:10.2307/2392045

Negash, S., & Gray, P. (2003). *Business intelligence.* Paper presented at the Ninth Americas Conference on Information Systems.

Newell, A. (1981). The knowledge level. *AI Magazine*, 1–19.

Newell, A. (1982). The knowledge level. *Artificial Intelligence, 18*(1), 87–127. doi:10.1016/0004-3702(82)90012-1

Newell, A., & Simon, H. A. (1972). *Human problem solving* (1st ed.). Upper Saddle River, NJ: Prentice Hall.

Nonaka, I. (1994). A dynamic theory of organizational knowledge creation. *Organization Science, 5*(1), 24. doi:10.1287/orsc.5.1.14

O'Brien, J. A., & Marakas, G. M. (2007). *Introduction to information systems* (13th ed.). New York, NY: McGrawHill.

Polanyi, M. (1966). *The tacit dimension.* Garden City, NY: Doubleday.

Porter, M. E. (1979). How competitive forces shape strategy. *Harvard Business Review, 57*(2), 137–145.

SAS Institute. (2009, February 4). *SAS Achieves Record Revenue: $2.26 Billion in 2008: SAS Institute Press Release.* Retrieved on from http://www.sas.com/news/prereleases/2008financials.html

Simon, H. A. (1981). *The sciences of the artificial.* Cambridge, MA: MIT Press.

Smalltree, H. (2006). *BI's founding father speaks: Q&A with Howard Dresner.* Retrieved from http://searchdatamanagement.techtarget.com/news/interview/0,289202,sid91_gci1174419,00.html.

180Systems. (2006). *BI comparisons 2006.* Retrieved from http://www.180systems.com/BIsystem-comparison.php

Trim, P. R. J. (2004). The strategic corporate intelligence and transformational marketing model. *Marketing Intelligence & Planning, 22*(2-3), 240–256. doi:10.1108/02634500410525896

Tzu, S. (2005). The art of war. In Clavell, J. (Ed.), *The art of war* (p. 82). Boston, MA: Shambhala Publications.

Watson, H. J., Wixom, B. H., Hoffer, J. A., Anderson-Lehman, R., & Reynolds, A. M. (2006). Real-time business intelligence: Best practices at continental airlines. *Information Systems Management, 23*(1), 12. doi:10.1201/1078.10580530/45769.23.1.20061201/91768.2

Whiting, R. (2006, May 29). Businesses mine data to predict what happens next. *Information Week*, p. 5.

Wright, S., & Calof, J. L. (2006). The quest for competitive, business and marketing intelligence: A country comparison of current practices. [Commentary]. *European Journal of Marketing, 40*(5-6), 453–465. doi:10.1108/03090560610657787

Yadav, S. B. (2009). A conceptual model for user-centered quality information retrieval on the world wide web. *Journal of Intelligent Information Systems, 35*(1), 91–121. doi:10.1007/s10844-009-0090-y

Young, R. M. (1995). Conceptual research. *Changes: An International Journal of Psychology and Psychotherapy, 13*, 145–148.

This work was previously published in the International Journal of Business Intelligence Research, Volume 2, Issue 2, edited by Richard Herschel, pp. 48-66, copyright 2011 by IGI Publishing (an imprint of IGI Global).

Chapter 18
Mitigating Risk:
Analysis of Security Information and Event Management

Ken Lozito
GSK, USA

ABSTRACT

Business Intelligence (BI) has often been described as the tools and systems that play an essential role in the strategic planning process of a corporation. The application of BI is most commonly associated with the analysis of sales and stock trends, pricing and customer behavior to inform business decision-making. There is a growing trend in utilizing the tools and processes used in the analysis of data and applying them to security event management. Security Information and Event Management (SIEM) has emerged within the last 10 years providing a centralized source to enable both real-time and deep level analysis of historical event data to drive security standards and align IT resources in a more efficient manner.

INTRODUCTION

Security event management and response is something that all IT organizations struggle with due to the multitude of events created by security technologies. Limited resources and tight budgets require organizations to strategically deal with

security event data to protect the enterprise's 'crown jewels'. Business Intelligence (BI) based technologies, applications, and processes utilized in various industries easily transfer into Security Information and Event Management (SIEM). It is important to first understand the threat landscape that led to the requirement to centralize security event analysis.

DOI: 10.4018/978-1-4666-2650-8.ch018

Over the past few years there has been a growing awareness of internet based threats that could have a significant negative impact to an organization. This increased visibility has been brought to the forefront through numerous embarrassing media stories where consumer data has been compromised and by regulatory mandates that have emerged in the face of major corporate scandals. Further compounding this problem is a steady increase in insider theft of valuable corporate information by unethical employees.

A Google search for 'consumer data theft' returns almost 7 million results. Among the top results is TJX consumer data theft which disclosed in January 2007 that at least 45.7 million credit and debit cards were stolen by hackers. TJX is the parent company of retailer T.J. Maxx. The theft actually occurred over a period of time from January 2003 – December 2006 and was able to occur due to glaring security holes in the computer systems that process and store payment information (Cheng, 2007). TJX is certainly not alone in this arena where data theft resulted in significant costs both in capital and consumer confidence.

Because the threat landscape for digital assets is constantly evolving and a multitude of security technologies are often deployed to mitigate these threats, a strategy for using the event data from all security technologies should be implemented that is equipped to perform event correlation and provide insight into the internal threat landscape down to the regional level. There is a growing struggle among enterprise IT organizations to manage security risks given the limited resources available. The ability to focus resources by utilizing existing log data to develop more effective endpoint protection policies to protect digital assets is extremely valuable. Most enterprise security technologies have the ability to process their own event logs and export them to an external system. In addition, most vendors of Security Incident and Event Management (SIEM) systems use agents that interface with the management consoles of security software to process the event data from the

source system to the SIEM system. It is important to first examine a bit of recent history of security technologies and the threat landscape.

SECURITY TECHNOLOGY-PAST 10 YEARS

Organizations have invested heavily in targeted security solutions including firewalls, VPNs, intrusion detection and prevention systems, and vulnerability scanners. Unfortunately these solutions alone have not been able to completely protect organizations from the evolving landscape of threats. Recently there has been a steady increase in the complexity of threats, including zero day attacks, worms and trojans that span many systems and are difficult to detect using existing security solutions (Q1Labs, 2009a). Many companies have implemented some or all of the following security technologies:

- Network Intrusion Detection and Prevention Systems
- Firewalls
  - ◦ Perimeter
  - ◦ Application
  - ◦ Endpoint
- Antivirus and AntiSpyware
- Host Intrusion Prevention – HIPS
- Behavioral Heuristic Detection
- Information/Data Leakage Protection.

Most of these systems were implemented separately utilizing different vendors with varying logging and reporting capabilities. The common limiting factor for all these solutions is the apparent lack of these technologies to effectively correlate their events with one another, which in turn limits one of Security's primary roles within an organization, to mitigate risk. Dan Borge states in his book, "The purpose of risk management is to improve the future, not to explain the past" (Borge, 2001). Security Metrics are used to justify and measure the effectiveness of a given security solution. If we don't measure, we don't know the value the technology or process offers.

Below are slides given during a Symantec Endpoint Protection workshop, which gives an excellent visual display of a computer's surface exposure when connected to the Internet. A computer without any client security is vulnerable to most internet based threats. The progression of the shrinking target allows one to see how implementing multiple security technologies allows for the mitigation of multiple types of threats. The same would also apply to an organization's perimeter.

The above visual depictions are good examples of how different security technologies can successfully mitigate threats, which are offered by multiple security software vendors. But even if a company successfully implements and actively manages its endpoint security, digital assets are still vulnerable to attack. At the network layer Firewalls, Intrusion Detection System (IDS), and Intrusion Prevention System (IPS) technologies have been deployed. In some scenarios platforms that run Firewalls can also run IPS (CheckPoint & Palto Alto), which allow for some event correlation to occur, but there are extreme limitations with this type of setup in comparison with a dedicated IPS. Some limitations include the following:

- Hardware limitation – more enabled IPS signatures negatively impact the performance on the device.
- Limited IPS signature offerings.

With the advent of dynamic threats, security companies like Sourcefire have created software that differs from standard security tools which are based mainly on static mechanisms. For example, a firewall blocks traffic on a particular TCP or UDP port. Intrusion detection systems use fixed signatures to identify malware. The original assumption for these static tools is that they would be used by knowledgeable human operators. Modern security analysts are normally pulled in many different directions, needing to maintain multiple network and host-based technologies in addition to monitoring their output. When crises occur the analyst must also be able to respond at any time, which results in a lack of time to monitor and update one tool closely.

Malware has evolved considerably in the last 10 to 15 years, where worms and viruses were once written by curious hobbyists, they are now developed by dedicated research labs funded by organized crime. These organizations are financially motivated to steal personal data and sell it to whomever will pay the most money for it. According to a 2009 Verizon Business study of almost 600 data breaches, which had taken place over five years, 71% of the breaches were not discovered by the organizations that had been breached but by a third party, confession of a perpetrator, or external audit (Sourcefire, 2009). It is essential that organizations understand the types of hosts on their network and the applications that those hosts are running. This intelligence provides the context needed to prioritize alerts and evaluate malicious intent.

Technologies have emerged to help reduce the number of alerts that a security analyst would normally be required to analyze should time permit. One example is Sourcefire RNA (Real-time Network Awareness), which is a passive sensing technology meant to assist intrusion analysis by monitoring network traffic in real time and tracks the configuration changes and network behavior of hosts. Data is gathered about the hosts on the network which becomes the basis of a network map of all hosts along with their operating systems, applications, and potential vulnerabilities. For example, IPS sees a packet in the network that exploits a vulnerability in Windows XP SP2, but since this packet is sent to a host that has been classified as a Linux host the event is rated as not vulnerable allowing the analyst to focus on vulnerable systems for these alerts (Sourcefire, 2009). This type of technology is a step in the right direction to help the security analyst focus on relevant threats by reducing and/or reprioritizing the thousands of alerts for maximum benefit. However, there are factors that limit its effectiveness. In the case of Sourcefire RNA it only works with Sourcefire products and cannot correlate data from other security devices and technologies. Therefore an organization could not leverage existing security technology to find threats that may be lost among the millions of log data generated daily.

MANAGING RISK AND THE CURRENT THREAT LANDSCAPE

Security professionals are anxiously aware of the growing risk of threats from both inside and outside an organization. Stories appear in the News about the complex and sophisticated crime operations that are behind some of the more significant breaches that have occurred. "It's official: Today's security managers are more worried about insiders leaking sensitive corporate data than they are about outsiders breaking in to steal it" (Wilson, 2009). The consequences of any network security breach to an organization are far-reaching and cleanup costs are significant (Q1Labs, 2009b).

Companies are flying blind in their ability to manage threats because of the lack of integrated visibility among security solutions that are in place. In the case of insider threats, companies lack the surveillance necessary to accurately pinpoint the actual individual or system that is responsible for the malicious behavior. A major challenge for organizations regardless of size is how to extract useful information from the flood of network and security events that are generated on the network daily. Many of today's threats attempt to compromise confidential information for illegal financial reward and to utilize computing resources to do harm to others. Emerging threats may not be known to existing security solutions

and go undetected resulting in indeterminable expense to the enterprise. There is the risk that when threats are detected by existing security solutions they may not be presented by the existing event monitoring and reporting solutions because events referencing the threat were not properly correlated and prioritized. Organizations are starting to accept that there is a need for centralized command and control that can more effectively manage the existing and emerging threats on their network that can be provided by an integrated network security management solution (Q1Labs, 2009a).

There is another layer to managing security events which focuses mainly on the large enterprises that have a portion of their security infrastructure outsourced to a managed security service provider (MSSPs). While some may agree that MSSPs serve a purpose, at the very least it adds complexity to any sophisticated security service. Managed security service providers (MSSPs) do make the promise of event correlation between firewall and intrusion detection sensors in an environment, but lack the internal insight of environment to effectively act upon these events. Also, companies are reluctant to spend the substantial and additional money to put more devices that would allow a managed security service providers (MSSPs) to gain insight into the internal network to allow for real-time analysis and response.

Most managed security service providers (MSSPs) have service offerings for security information management (SIM) in addition to their security event management (SEM) services. These services include the collection, analysis, reporting and storage of log data from servers, user directories, applications and databases. Security Information Management (SIM) services typically do without real-time monitoring and alerting, and concentrate on compliance-oriented reporting regarding exceptions, reviews and documentation, with the ability to store and archive logs for investigation at a later time (Gartner, 2010).

SECURITY INFORMATION AND EVENT MANAGEMENT - SIEM

Wikipedia defines Security Event Manager as "a computerized tool used on enterprise data networks to centralize the storage and interpretation of logs, or events, generated by other software running on the network." Security event managers or SEM were pioneered in 1999 by a small company called e-Security and have continued to evolve. SEM are also known as Security Information and Event Managers (SIEMs). A similar market exists for Log Management. The two fields are closely related, but Log Management typically focuses on collection and storage of data whereas SIEM focuses on the analysis of data. There are clear advantages to send all events to a centralized SIEM system:

- Access to all logs is provided consistently through a central interface.
- The SIEM can store logs securely and for greater periods of time than the sending system.
- Powerful data mining tools can be run on the SIEM to glean useful information and patterns.
- Events can be prioritized based upon significance and alerts; notifications can be immediately escalated to all pertinent parties.
- Events that occur on multiple systems can be pieced together to paint a more accurate picture of a malicious event.

SIEMs distinguish themselves by providing deeper level of event analysis and can also integrate with external remediation, ticketing, and workflow tools to assist with the process of incident resolution (Wikipedia, n. d.).

"The primary driver of the North American SIEM market continues to be regulatory compliance. More than 80% of SIEM deployment projects are funded to close a compliance gap.

European and Asia/Pacific SIEM deployments have been focused primarily on external threat monitoring, but compliance is also becoming a strong driver in these regions" (Gartner, 2010). The broad set of companies that have adopted SIEM technology have fostered a demand for products that provide predefined compliance reporting and security monitoring functions. Compliance for log management functions is an important customer requirement for the following reasons:

- PCI Data Security Standards requirement for log management.
- The usefulness of details and historical log data analysis for breach investigation and general analysis.
- Log management in front of a SIEM deployment enables more selective forwarding of events to correlation engines.

SIEM project funding normally derives from compliance requirements, but most organizations want to improve external and internal threat monitoring capabilities. There are requirements for monitoring user activity and resource access for host systems and applications, as well as requirements for real-time event management for network security. Application layer monitoring for fraud detection and internal threat management continues to evolve as a use case for SIEM technology. SIEM technology is being deployed alongside fraud detection and application monitoring point solutions to extend their scope (Gartner, 2010).

Corporations refer to Gartner's analysis of technology as a foundation to establishing an industry standard for various technologies including Security Information and Event Management. According to Gartner's 'Magic Quadrant for Security Information and Event Management', an optimal SIEM solution will:

- Support the real-time collection and analysis of log data from host systems, security devices and network devices.

- Support long-term storage and reporting.
- Not require extensive customization.
- Be easy to deploy and maintain.

Companies are included in this quadrant if they meet a specific set of inclusion criteria. A separate set of evaluation criteria is used to determine a company's placement in the quadrant. An organization would utilize this information to align a SIEM solution with its own requirements

Ten years ago security management was still mostly a manual set of processes and tasks. Large organizations were beginning to deploy firewalls, IDSs, and endpoint security software. In 2009 there was a radical change. The number of malware variants has increased from about 60,000 in 2000 to approximately 500,000 in 2008. Large organizations now believe that security management systems are mandatory. This change is illustrated in the Enterprise Strategy Group (ESG) survey of security professionals working at enterprise companies (i.e., 1,000 employees or more), 60% said that their organizations have security management technologies deployed while another 30% are planning to deploy (Oltsik, 2009).

Why did security management go from a non-entity to an essential part of defense?

- A drastic increase in fraud, malicious code threats, vulnerabilities, and cyber crime. In 2008 malware variants grew around 200%, while data theft Trojans increase by more than 1000% over 2007. Today's malware are far more sophisticated and virulent than earlier viruses. Half of all reported vulnerabilities were related to Web applications in 2008. Internal threat and fraud surpassed external threats and fraud during the first half of 2008. Security management is needed to address the growing threat across a broader portion of the IT infrastructure.
- Damages from publicly disclosed data breaches were estimated in the billions of dollars. A total of 615 publicly-disclosed

data breaches in 2008 exposing more than 83 million personal records (source data-lossdb.org). These breaches are caused by variety of events. About 21% of these incidents are the result of stolen or lost laptops, 17% are the results of "hacks," 14% are the results of attacks on Web applications, and 7% are the result of fraud.

Enterprise Strategy Group research shows how these and other factors have a significant influence on determining security requirements at large organizations (Oltsik, 2009).

The top drivers, protecting data and complying with government regulations appear to be primary focal points for organizations investing in security event management. While the remaining drivers are key benefits to a security organization, from a business perspective the top two drivers represent the key points for allocating capital in this area.

THE FUTURE OF SIEM

Traditional SIEM solutions have the ability to define rules that correlate specific pattern of events. When rules have been properly written and tuned, a SIEM solution can provide a valuable reduction in the number of items that are presented to a security analyst to investigate. Unfortunately, even with the reduction there is still an overwhelming set of information to investigate for many reasons including:

- No context about the reliability of the alerts or prioritization based on the value of the targets.
- The correlated results tell the security analyst that unusual activity is occurring, but lacks the ability to single out the root cause.
- Information being correlated is tainted with misleading information, including false positives that are common among existing security solutions.

• The SIEM solution lacks the ability to piece together information from all the relevant data sources available, resulting in an inability to detect threats because of the lack of insight of the overall network behavior.

There are many threats on the network that are not known to existing security applications and can impact an organization at any time. These exploits leverage existing vulnerabilities to propagate harmful code. These events are known as the zero-day-exploit which can be further described in the following scenario:

A user clicks on a link which takes them to a website. Embedded in this website is new malicious code that installs a backdoor onto the computer. The victim machine makes an IRC connection over a non-standard port in order to hide the connection from security devices. Once it connects to the IRC server it joins a channel and waits for a command to scan certain subnets for open mail servers (port 25) and return the results back to a chat room. Once the results have been returned, the attacker then sends a command to the back door telling it to send out mail to those hosts with open mail ports. (Q1Labs, 2009a)

The SillyFDC worm utilizes the AutoRun feature in Windows that allows an executable to run automatically to spread itself. SillyFDC would copy itself to mapped drives, removable drives, and then download other files or perform other malicious activities (Symantec, 2007). Data collected in the SIEM could be used to determine by location where the greatest number of infections occurred and how the worm spread itself. Normally this information would be available from endpoint protection software (Antivirus) provided that the current signatures detect the threat, Intrusion Detection Systems, and Firewall logs. The SIEM gives insight into which type of distribution the worm was most effective. The information could then be used justify a change to the environment. In the case of SillyFDC an enterprise could choose to do one or all of the following actions:

• Disable AutoRun feature in Windows.
• Implement device control to prevent or control the use of removable drives.
• Patch Systems against the vulnerability.

Correlation to tie these events together is required to get an accurate picture of what is occurring. Using tools such as SAS JMP or Enterprise Miner would be beneficial here. The firewall will log the accept for the connection to the website and possibly over port 25 for mail server. An IDS sensor may log a machine's access to an external IRC server and the instructions received from the malicious server outside the corporate network if the activity meets a signature's criteria for alert. A SIEM could be configured to put together all these events and essentially put up a red flag for the event for further analysis. Another way this event could go is if local client security software has mitigated the threat because of a behavioral analysis tool that scans local processes and logs a blocked event. If all these logging events are brought into the SIEM then a real time alert could be avoided and a security analyst's time could be better utilized managing a more prevalent threat.

Managing security incidents can be an exceptional challenge for organizations because of the dynamic nature of networked applications. Parts of the IT infrastructure which are in a continuous state of change are:

• Network addresses mapped to servers and hosts.
• Applications running on a specific server
• Network ports used for specific applications.
• Risk of servers known vulnerabilities.
• Business criticality of specific servers and applications.

- Ability of network and security systems to report security incidents accurately.

It is important for a network security management solution to record all changes in these areas to assess the importance and relevance of observed events collected by the system (Q1Labs, 2009a). Technology not unlike Sourcefire's Real Time Network Awareness has been incorporated into some SIEM solutions giving the SIEM the much needed insight into the internal network, which provides more intelligence to the event correlation.

ArcSight, which appears in the upper right most quadrant of Gartner's Magic Quadrant for SIEM qualifying this company as a top visionary, has a product called EnterpriseView. ArcSight EnterpriseView was created to help organizations gain a better understanding of who is on the network, data they are seeing, and which actions they are taking with that data. Many companies look to Security Information and Event Management (SIEM) technologies to correlate events and detect network threats. EnterpriseView applies real-time correlation and analysis and is made up of the following components and services (ArcSight, 2009):

- **User Model:** Allows for direct correlation of key attributes such as user role, department, etc.
- **IdentitySync Adapters:** Synchronizes the user's identity and role information by connecting to user identity stores, such as directories and identity management solutions.
- Built in Rules and Reporting for the following:
  - **Role Violation Monitoring:** Included with built-in rules and reports for detecting role violations.
  - **Unique ID Mapping:** Component for mapping multiple accounts to a single master ID. This information is then collects all activity across all of

the user's accounts and rolls the activity up to the user level.
  - Activity Profiling.
  - Data Leakage Protection and Fraud Detection Rules.
  - **Auto-Escalation Watchlists:** Based upon pre-built or customer-defined rules where users are ordered based upon risks to the business.

CONCLUSION – THE BOTTOM LINE

With all the security event logs pointing to a centralized source it then becomes possible to perform deeper analysis of past events to determine which corporate policies concerning security would be beneficial for the future. For example, determining a common infection source could give valuable insight into either expanding or tweaking the current security solutions in place. Initiatives necessary to fill the security gaps being exploited at the regional level will have cross platform data from multiple security technologies to provide the foundations to reach decisions. This is in essence evidence-based decision making to improve the resiliency of the IT infrastructure.

Business Intelligence is about putting data and analytics together to provide value into a system or process. With the emergence of SIEM solutions, which bridge the gaps between security technologies, an underlying deeper level of analysis is made possible by the advancement of BI based technologies in other industries. Insurance companies who invested heavily in systems and services for detecting fraud, banking and online vendors like Amazon invested in CRM technology to achieve specific goals which are all based upon analyzing behavior have all influenced the development of SIEM, which is used to evaluate the behavior of malicious activity. Different companies approach Security Incident and Event Management in different ways, but they all have similar foundations upon which to build a solution for an organization. They seek to reduce and mitigate risk by utilizing the technology to perform the first wave of analysis prior to the events requiring human analyst input and correlating the events into a meaningful report so that the analyst can action these events. There is the growing demand for SIEM to be able to action events in real-time and vendors have solutions to fulfill this need. Properly correlated events from silo'd security technologies allow for the SIEM to validate or refute the suspicious events.

SIEM is a solution that requires cooperation and planning from within an organization. The benefits of compliance and gaining a centralized view of a security infrastructure as a whole gives a distinct advantages over other organizations that do not implement this type of solution. Another key benefit of SIEM is the ability to perform deep threat analysis to drive security policy initiatives that will reduce the risk of exposure overall.

REFERENCES

Q1Labs. (2009a). *A proactive approach to battling today's complex network threats.* Retrieved from http://q1labs.com/resource-center/white-papers/details.aspx?id=29

Q1Labs. (2009b). *The business case for a next-generation SIEM.* Retrieved from http://q1labs.com/resource-center/white-papers/details.aspx?id=27

ArcSight. (2009). *ArcSight enterprise view - monitoring enterprise-wide business risk.* Retrieved from http://www.arcsight.com/library/download/WPArcSightEnterpriseView/

Borge, D. (2001). *The book of risk.* New York, NY: John Wiley & Sons.

Cheng, J. (2007). *TJX consumer data theft largest in history.* http://arstechnica.com/business/news/2007/03/tjx-consumer-data-theft-largest-in-history.ars

Gartner. (2010). *Magic quadrant for security information and event management.* Retrieved from http://www.gartner.com/it/products/mq/mq_ms.jsp-s

Oltsik, J. (2009). *Security management evolution.* http://q1labs.com/resource-center/analyst-reports/details.aspx?id=18

SourceFire. (2009). *Network awareness: Continuous network intelligence and network visibility.* Retrieved from http://www.sourcefire.com/products/3D/rna

Symantec. (2007). *W32. SillyFDC.* Retrieved from http://www.symantec.com/security_response/writeup.jsp?docid=2006-071111-0646-99

Symantec. (2010). *Symantec Endpoint Protection 11.0.6 Advanced Workshop.* Retrieved from http://www.symantec.com

Wikipedia. (n. d.). *Security event manager.* Retrieved from http://en.wikipedia.org/wiki/Security_event_manager

Wilson, T. (2009). *Reports: Security pros shift attention from external hacks to internal threats.* Retrieved from http://www.darkreading.com/insiderthreat/security/vulnerabilities/showArticle.jhtml?articleID=215801195

This work was previously published in the International Journal of Business Intelligence Research, Volume 2, Issue 2, edited by Richard Herschel, pp. 67-75, copyright 2011 by IGI Publishing (an imprint of IGI Global).

Chapter 19
IT and Business Can Succeed in BI by Embracing Agile Methodologies

Alex Gann
BAE Systems, USA

ABSTRACT

While the potential benefits from BI are vast, organizations have struggled to successfully deploy it. BI applies myriad advanced techniques, performed by the firm's Information Technology (IT) group, to fulfill the reporting, analysis, and decision-support needs of the Lines of Business. Two of the greatest challenges in BI are accurately and continuously communicating requirements from the business to IT and quickly yet affordably delivering the requested functionality from IT to the business. Companies can overcome these challenges by embracing a prescribed set of Agile development methodologies for BI. This paper examines the history of selected systems development approaches, weighs the advantages and disadvantages of prevailing practices, and ultimately recommends a path forward to succeeding in BI through the application of Agile methodologies.

INTRODUCTION

Business Intelligence (BI) is defined as "a set of methodologies, processes, architectures, and technologies that transform raw data into meaningful and useful information" (Evelson, 2008). Companies today generate and store vast amounts of raw data. What BI proposes is that any company that can effectively leverage this naturally-occurring business resource to measure performance, guide decisions, and implement strategies stands to create a sustainable competitive advantage out of these otherwise dormant stores of transactional, financial, and demographic records. Most companies have recognized the potential value of BI and have made various attempts to realize it; however, with only 21% of surveyed companies rating their BI deployment as "Very Successful" (Howson, 2009) it is clear that translating the vision into reality is much easier said than done.

DOI: 10.4018/978-1-4666-2650-8.ch019

What is reality for a twenty-first century company hoping to reap the benefits that BI presents? For many, budgets have been slashed, as a recent economic downturn and increased global market competition forces companies to "do more with less." Schedules are being crashed, with executive-level pressures pushing on management to sustain a dozen "top priority" initiatives at once, and flavor-of-the-week issues result in frequent "student body left" engagement tactics. With this environment, it is no wonder that teams are overwhelmed with their workloads while customers remain underwhelmed with the results.

What can be done to succeed in such an environment? Business Intelligence lies at the intersection of applied technical skillsets and business function understanding, so achieving it cannot be the singular responsibility of either IT or Business; it will always require a highly-coordinated effort between the two. Exploring the why, how, who, and where of bringing IT and Business together, and examining a history of software development approaches, will ultimately reveal a path forward for BI success through leveraging a selection of methodologies from the well-known "Agile" movement (most notably, Scrum).

This paper begins with a study of four research questions, the answers to which will guide the end analysis. The research questions explored are the following: Why do IT and Lines of Business have to effectively cooperate for BI to succeed? How did the relationship between IT and Business become so strained? Whom should the company look for when forming the BI team? Where should the members of the BI team be located? These questions are each thoroughly addressed in independent sections.

Having reviewed the findings for these four BI organizational questions, a brief timeline leading up to Agile methodologies is presented. The solutions to the potentially disparate issues examined have common themes that move throughout. These themes ultimately come together in the form of a single, comprehensive approach to BI, found under the umbrella of Agile methodologies. After providing a proper exposition for the recommended approach, this paper concludes with a more detailed prescription of Agile applied to Data Warehousing and Business Intelligence (DWBI), reviewing probable benefits and possible pitfalls.

Agile is defined as "a group of software development methodologies based on iterative and incremental development, where requirements and solutions evolve through collaboration between self-organizing, cross-functional teams" (Wikipedia, 2010). It is argued herein that IT and Business together can succeed by embracing Agile methodologies. An attempt to argue that IT and Business will succeed would be naïve. There is no "silver bullet" prescription to rescue an untalented or uncommitted team. For every glowing success story of effectively applied Scrum, XP, or other "Agile" methodology, one can find several documented failures. Opponents of Agile – perhaps justifiably wearied of wading through the immensely broad yet shallow pool of buzz-word-laden attention that the movement has garnered – may be quick to point to these failures in blatant FUD (fear, uncertainty, and doubt) tactics at the very mention of the term. However, thoughtful practitioners should remain ever mindful of the Ted Sturgeon's (1958) maxim:

I repeat Sturgeon's Revelation, which was wrung out of me after twenty years of wearying defense of science fiction against attacks of people who used the worst examples of the field for ammunition, and whose conclusion was that ninety percent of SF is crud. Using the same standards that categorize 90% of science fiction as trash, crud, or crap, it can be argued that 90% of film, literature, consumer goods, etc. are crap. In other words, the claim (or fact) that 90% of science fiction is crap is ultimately uninformative, because science fiction conforms to the same trends of quality as all other art forms (p. 66).

Neither Agile nor any other methodology will be able to refute this timeless observation which has far transcended its original scope due to its universal applicability. Yet, a team otherwise capable of succeeding in BI, but hindered by ubiquitous, exogenous impediments, can have their path made much clearer by applying the Agile frameworks.

Lastly, it is frequently observed that organizations that adopt [A]gile practices without embracing the values and principles often struggle (Collier, 2010). There is a gross difference between merely imitating and fully embodying something and the results that follow will differ just as widely. Though Agile aims to be lightweight, this does not mean that embracing and embodying its precepts will occur effortlessly. While detractors may liken Agile methodologies such as Scrum to an idiotic fad-diet of a marketing scam (Yegge, 2006) someone who goes about "setting out to 'prove' Scrum doesn't work is a bit like the person who starts a diet but never manages to change his eating or exercise habits and then claims he 'can't lose weight'" (Druckman, 2007). If the organization refuses to change its "unhealthy" habits, then its burdensome weight will never be shed.

RESEARCH QUESTIONS

Why Do IT and Lines of Business Have to Effectively Cooperate for BI to Succeed?

Business intelligence is one of the few areas in the IT sector to have remained buoyant during the economic downturn, as organizations use the technology to help them reduce costs and optimize operations (Binning, 2009). Conceding that BI technologies must be pursued, why should IT and Business have to effectively cooperate in order to succeed in BI? While to some this question may seem unnecessary or somewhat overt, there are several IT activities that do not require direct Busi-

ness participation, and certainly many Business functions that do not need direct IT involvement. BI is not one of these activities, as can be revealed by examining how IT and the Business attempt BI when they are kept apart.

On the IT side, a company may employ the most skillful team of ETL (Extract, Translate, Load) architects, data modelers, and systems analysts; however, this team is ultimately impotent without an intimate understanding of the functional processes and imperatives from the Business. By definition, BI is designed to allow "business users to make informed business decisions," (Evelson, 2008) yet this goal will not likely be met without heavy ownership and direct involvement by BI's key stakeholder and primary end user. While not unique to BI, in all ways and at all times IT should remain mindful that, in order to justify its existence, IT needs the Business.

Likewise, the Business could have the brightest subject matter experts (SMEs), surrounded by requirements and teeming with ideas to meet them. Detached from the technical team's offerings, however, these hard-working and well-intentioned employees are left faltering for an elegant and robust presentation of their functions' data, only to find themselves jailed behind endless spreadsheet grids. That is, while spreadsheet applications are quite proficient when it comes to quick, ad-hoc data manipulation and analysis, those particular operations are but a minor subset of the BI portfolio. Left with no other option, the inherent limitations of spreadsheets can leave analysts feeling trapped or cut off from the greater world of BI capabilities, often kept at the sole privilege and disposal of IT. Petermen (2010) notes that another common outcome is shadow IT where a business team starts to take on the technical role and you see a pocket of traditional IT skills popping up in business…that can be very distracting and just adds into the adversity and tension between business and IT. This extreme measure, where a business unit would hire and train its own mini-IT team, is a clear yet all-too-common pointer to the fact that the Business needs IT.

IT and Lines of Business depend on one another, and yet are so often kept apart, reporting to different sets of management, submitting to conflicting priorities, and stealing away time together strictly on an exceptions basis (without a signed and prioritized change request ticket, the two shall not interact). "In contrast, technical teams embedded in departments or lines of business often enjoy a much healthier relationship with their business counterparts than corporate IT. Why? Rather than existing in a technical subculture, these 'embedded' IT staff members sit side by side with the business people and function as a single team, with the same goals, bosses, and incentives" (Eckerson, 2006, p. 256). This observation by Wayne Eckerson, 8-year Director of Research for The Data Warehouse Institute, is not provided to dispute whether technical teams should be embedded in the business or vice-versa, but simply to further support the notion that placing IT staff members and Business people side by side adds value. Without both fuel and oxygen the combustion engine will stall; so it is with any BI initiative that lacks either of the primary inputs

– technical excellence from IT and functional comprehension from the Business.

How Did the Relationship Between IT and Business Become So Strained?

In the anonymously authored joke in Figure 1, IT is described by Business as being "technically correct," but misinterpreting their requests and adding little real value, while Business is explained by IT as being hopelessly lost and scapegoating their problems on IT. The tale, circulating for well over a decade, would not be funny if people were not near-universally able to relate to the relationship it details. Putting the humor aside, this strained relationship is a serious problem for companies today.

Michael Krigsman, CEO of Asuret, Inc, posed the question on focus.com (Bagdanov, Dix, Krigsman, & Natoli, 2010) – a site that channels the advice and opinion of thousands of industry experts on pointed questions for others to benefit – asking, "Why do IT and lines of business have so much tension?" The question received over 35 answers in the first 4 months, the highest rated of which explained, "A lot of the tension comes from each

Figure 1. The Balloonist and the Field Worker (Bagdanov, Dix, Krigsman, & Natoli, 2010)

A man is flying in a hot air balloon and realizes he is lost. He reduces height and spots another man down below.

He lowers the balloon further and shouts:

"Excuse me, can you tell me where I am?"

The man below says: "yes, you're in a hot air balloon, hovering 30 feet above this field."

"You must work in Information Technology" says the balloonist.

"I do" replies the man. "How did you know?"

"Well" says the balloonist, "everything you have told me is technically correct, but it's no use to anyone."

The man below says "you must work in Business."

"I do" replies the balloonist, "but how did you know?"

"Well", says the man, "you don't know where you are, or where you're going, but you expect me to be able to help.

You're in the same position you were in before we met, but now it's my fault."

side believing that the other does not understand its needs. The business side is frustrated because IT does not (typically) live in the world of the customer and does not focus on how to serve the customer with all of its energy…which is seen as is natural given that IT has different goals, different incentives, than does the business side (Bagdanov, Dix, Krigsman, & Natoli, 2010). To expand on the introductory analogy, the IT man down in the field is not nearly as exposed to the directing "winds" of customer requests and demands as the Business balloonist. Perhaps the IT man in the field has a job to get done, one that is very demanding, often tedious, and while it may indirectly sustain the Business balloonist, the specific goals and incentives differ greatly from those of the Business. Ultimately, the joke works because the two characters exist in entirely detached and unrelated environments. If the two men had any established relationship or common concerns, the frank disinterest and lack of understanding which makes the tale so funny, and so true, would not work.

The majority of the focus.com Q&A pointed to two common pain-points that need to be addressed: organizational structure and direct, proactive executive-level leadership. The organizational structure issue often boils down to a dichotomy of centralized versus decentralized IT. There are many attractive benefits to both models: "Arguments for centralization focus on coordination, standardization and consolidation of equipment, processes, technology, [and] customer and vendor management. Centralization also enables the creation and execution of a shared vision of how IT should support and drive market opportunities and growth. Centralization also provides significant economies of scale, reduction of redundancies and improved management efficiencies" (Ulrich, 2009). These real and demonstrable benefits are clearly the main appeal and thrust for why most companies today have centralized IT.

Advocates for decentralization claim a recognizable pattern of centralized IT's "inability to understand and fulfill business information requirements" (Ulrich, 2009). Though somewhat "softer" than the concrete benefits cited for centralized IT, the implications of this single complaint are vast – to the extent today that any company which fails to compete in Information Technology fails to compete at all. Many researchers and practitioners are now suggesting that the answer to this familiar conundrum is found through forming collaborative governance structures. This same answer for the overarching IT organization issue has found its way into BI-specific literature: "[the BI team] needs to recruit the business to run the BI program while it assumes a supportive role. The key indicator of the health of a BI program is the degree to which the business assumes responsibility for its long-term success. Such commitment is expressed in a formal BI governance program" (Eckerson, 2010c).

Eckerson goes on to explain that BI governance programs often take form as two separate steering committees: one, an executive level team of BI sponsors who prioritize major projects and secure funding for BI initiatives; the other, a working committee of business analysts and SMEs who suggest enhancements, select products, define data warehouse subject areas, and create the company's BI roadmap. In this vision of BI governance, the IT team trusts, supports, and takes direction from these steering committees, giving the Business a strong voice in BI without requiring an overhaul in established organizational structures.

Whom Should the Company Look for When Forming the BI Team?

When forming a BI team, the company has several obvious technical skillsets it will need to acquire: ETL (extract, translate, and load) specialists, data modelers, and database administrators, to name a few. As BI technologies matured, their vendors began consolidating disparate applications into large BI suites. IT responded to these "Big BI" packages by isolating the skillsets needed for "requirements, data modeling, ETL, database tuning, BI design, and administration. That really increased the technical mastery required to perform each step" (Peterman, 2010). The need for these key players seems to be well understood by IT groups today and is staffed for accordingly. Yet, as addressed above, if both IT and Business need to come together to succeed in BI, whom does the Business need to bring to the table?

First, the Business should be introduced to the notion of "purple people." Purple people are often rare but seldom non-existent employees "who can straddle the worlds of business and information technology (IT). These people are neither blue (i.e., business) nor red (i.e., IT) but a combination of both. These so-called purple people can speak both the language of business and data, making them perfect intermediaries between the two groups" (Eckerson, 2010c). To some extent, every primary business function (Finance, Supply Chain, Operations, Quality, Engineering, Marketing, etc) will have at least one of these extremely valuable individuals, whether formally declared or not. Officially bringing them into an understanding and accepted responsibility of the critical roles they can play for a company's BI initiatives is a significant step towards successful BI.

Second, the Business should consider hiring a dedicated BI Director. When IT collects and segregates the various technical players required to successfully develop, deploy, and maintain a DWBI platform, it more than likely also employs a manager for this team. While understandably necessary, this manager position in the IT organization is not effectively positioned to form and direct the strategy for a company's BI initiatives. As early as 2005, the growing importance of a Business-based BI director was being noted: "In most organizations, business intelligence (BI) has always played second fiddle to transaction applications. Organizations have traditionally lavished millions of dollars on projects to implement packaged operational applications and rewarded the IT managers who supervised these projects

with hefty salaries. In contrast, until recently, BI projects have always been an afterthought, viewed by executives as departmental systems or the responsibility of a few programmers who write custom reports" (Information Management Magazine, 2005). One with experience in large-scale ERP implementations will likely resonate with this observation that BI came about mostly as an afterthought. Since then, however, efficient operational systems have fully become a given in companies, and the next significant competitive advantage lies in Business Intelligence. BI has gone from being a niche "stepchild" of IT services to a "strategic resource" that guides organizations and supports effective decision making. If BI is meant to steer an organization, certainly there should be someone positioned to steer BI.

One can turn to the faithful "Google relevancy check" to get a sense of how necessary and prominent the BI Director position has become. As of the date of this report, a search for "Business Intelligence Director" yields just over 10 million results (Google, 2010a); the more familiar "Information Technology Director" yields 62 million (Google, 2010b). A simple deduction would suggest that 1 in 6 companies today recognize the need for, or have implemented, a BI Director position (a search using the abbreviated "BI Director" versus "IT Director" yields a more pronounced variance of 44M to 430M – approximately 1 in 10). Beyond this relevancy check, nearly every publication on Business Intelligence flatly assumes the existence of this critical position, detailing the roles and responsibilities this individual must fulfill, but seldom taking the time to explain the necessity of the role as a discrete topic.

Where Should the Members of the BI Team be Located?

The question, "where should the members of the BI team be located?" can be answered in a word: together. This does not mean simply co-locating the IT members of the BI team; in fact, if one had to choose between a fully segregated, centralized IT BI team and a functionally embedded, decentralized one, it is advisable to go with the latter (Eckerson, 2010a). What it does mean is co-locating both IT and Business (purple people) into a single BI block. While this prescription may seem quite simple at face value, the research behind is actually quite scientific. More than anything else, the decision to co-locate the team is based primarily on the dynamics of human communication.

Figure 2 plots the most common business communication mediums into quadrants. The horizontal axis spans from learned communications on the left to innate on the right. The vertical places asynchronous (i.e. transmission and reception happen at different times) communications at the bottom and synchronous at the top. This diagram was conceived by Kathy Sierra, author of the acclaimed Head First programming series, after attending several presentations by neuroscientist Dr. Thomas Lewis at the 2006 Conference on World Affairs. She took away the following: "One of the key points he made was that we are fooling ourselves into thinking that text is even half as effective as face-to-face at communicating

Figure 2. Humans require synchronous, innate communication (Sierra, 2006)

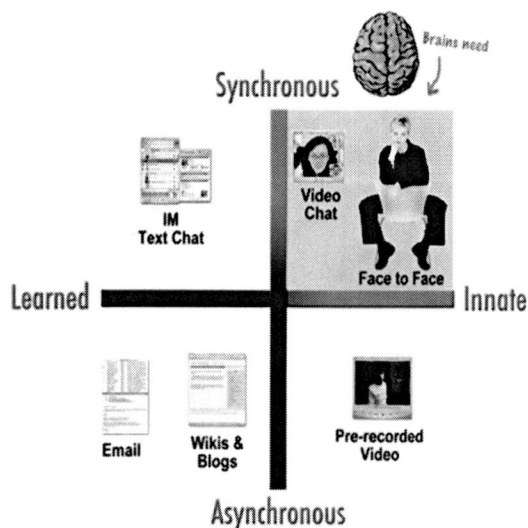

a message... We never had to learn to process body language, facial expressions, and tone of voice. We evolved this capability...it's innate. But we had to spend years learning to read and write with any level of sophistication. The brain needs and expects these other – more significant – channels of information, and when they don't come...the brain suffers (and so does the communication)" (Sierra, 2006). As addressed several times above, ineffective communication crops up time and again on the list of barriers between IT and Business, so any means available to improve communication between these two groups should be considered carefully.

Written, asynchronous communications have some very important qualities that verbal, synchronous communications lack. Unlike an informal conversation, "Writing provides evidence of reasoning and it documents a decision-making process...[serving] as an important means for creating, storing, and sharing knowledge across time and place" (Herschel, 2009). Beyond this, effectively managed email can double as a natural task-tracking system, a necessary functionality for many developers who can hardly address each issue to completion the moment it arises. Despite these particular benefits of written word, the incredible volume of rapid-fire knowledge discovery required between business analysts and data modelers when developing a new BI capability makes all other communication methods pale in comparison to on-demand, face-to-face interaction.

Wayne Eckerson (2010b) recently put down to writing his own excited discovery of this critical yet basic approach:

After 15 years in the business intelligence industry, I've hit the mother lode: I've discovered the true secret to BI success. It's really quite simple, and it's been staring at us for years. It's the principle of proximity. By proximity, I mean seating your BI developers next to your business experts. Not just in a joint application design session, a requirements interview, or scrum stand-up, but ALL THE TIME! Make them work side by side, elbow to elbow, nose to nose. It doesn't work to merely locate them on the same campus or in the same building. You need to put them in the same cubicle block, or better yet, in one big room with no walls so everyone can see, hear, smell, and touch everyone else all the time. And don't mistake me: I'm not talking about business requirements analysts – I'm talking about developers who write the code and design the models. Yes, make the developers get the requirements right from the horse's mouth. Don't force them to learn requirements second hand through a business requirements analyst. Trust me, something always gets lost in translation. To develop awesome BI applications, you have to function like a small start up where there are no departments or organizational boundaries, no separate jargon or incentives, no separate managers or objectives, and NO WALLS. Just one big, messy, energetic, on-the-same-wavelength family that gets things done. And fast (p. 1).

One of the best things about this approach is how affordably and immediately implementable it is. The recommendation does not add any new resource requirements (in fact, it subtly obviates the roll of the business requirements analyst).

However, it clearly presents some heavy political and organizational challenges by suggesting the imitation of an organization without separate departments and managers, where in almost all cases those elements will be forcibly present.

Figure 3, an original rendering for this report, presents a comparison of potential cubicle arrangements, with a more standardized workspace of the left, and a customized, collaborative design on the right. In many traditional companies, the business analysts would be located at disparate locations, grouped by function, and IT's BI team would be detached from all of the functions. Each individual team would likely be seated in a configuration similar to that presented on the left. An alternative layout, on the right, would permit a few chief business analysts (purple people) on one side, the primary BI development team in the open center space, and the key support IT functions (systems analysts, project management, database administrator) on the other side. The collaborative layout takes up no more space than the standard and simply replaces four corner-desk-pieces with a table and a large whiteboard; otherwise all materials are the same. Once the cross-functional team is situated in direct proximity to one another, what approaches might they follow to effectively organize their development activities?

Figure 3. Comparison of standard and collaborative office layouts

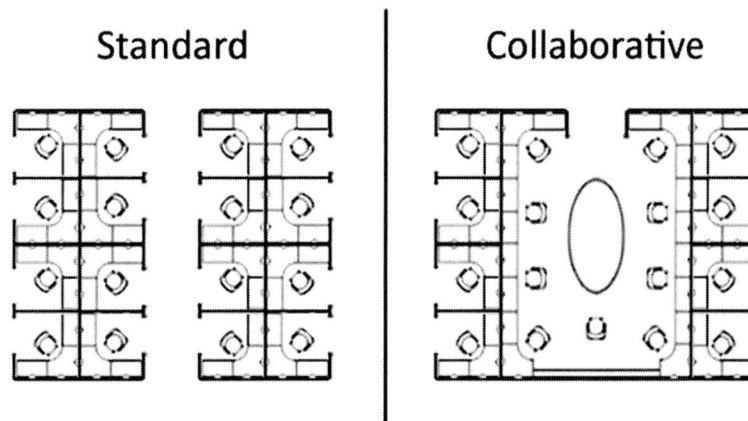

TIMELINE LEADING UP TO AGILE METHODOLOGIES

1970 – The Waterfall Model Defined

Dr. Winston W. Royce, director of the Lockheed Software Technology Center, presents an article entitled "Managing the Development of Large Software Systems" at the 1970 Western Electronic Show and Convention (WesCon). In his article, Royce describes the "essential steps common to all computer program developments, regardless of size or complexity" (Royce, 1970). Figure 4 is Royce's representation of these steps, and the apparent namesake of the method he describes.

It is critical to note that later in the same paper, Royce cautions that this simplified, single-pass development approach is "risky and invites failure" (Royce, 1970) and ultimately recommends several modifications to transform this basic "waterfall" model into an iterative, incremental approach which addresses its inherent shortcomings.

1985 – U.S. Department of Defense Requires Waterfall

In 1985, the U.S. Department of Defense releases specification DOD-STD-2167, "Defense System Software Development." The spec defines the necessary project documentation to be delivered when developing a computer software system for the U.S. Military – using the single-pass waterfall model (Figure 5). Note the resemblance to Royce's observed, but non-recommended, model in Figure 4.

This specification ultimately proves to be very influential and propagates into further standards both within the U.S. and abroad. Peeking ahead, "In 1994, DOD [replaces DOD]-STD-2167 with an [Iterative and Incremental Development]-promoting standard. Unfortunately, the other governments and standards bodies that based their methods on the earlier spec [do] not update their policies to match, so the single-pass waterfall approach sadly remains the basis of many methodological standards today" (Hughes, 2008, p.

Figure 4. Implementation steps to develop a large computer program for delivery to a customer (Royce, 1970)

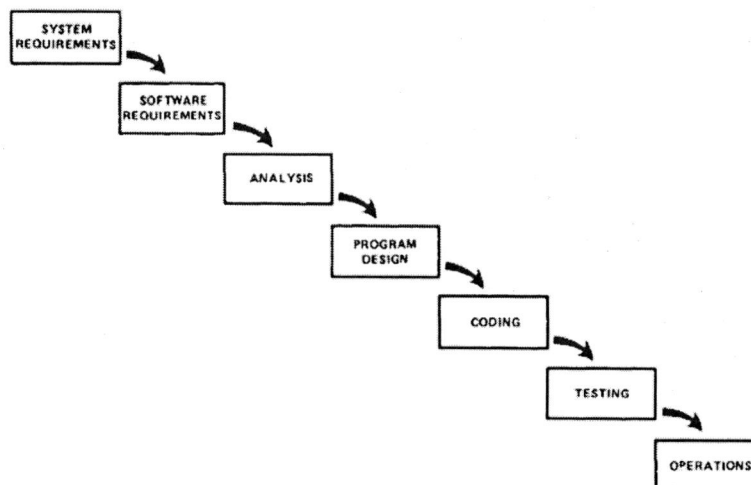

Figure 5. System development cycle within the system life cycle (U.S. Department of Defense, 1985)

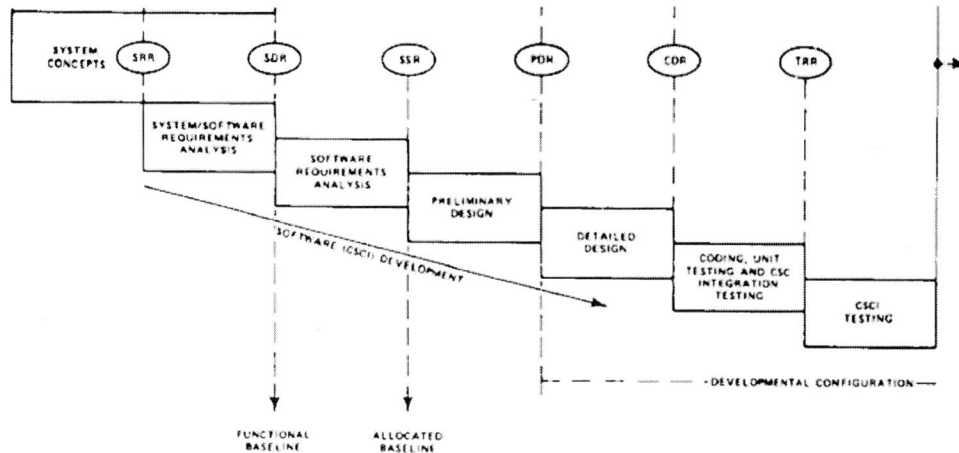

48). In 1996, Craig Larman interviews the principal author of DOD-STD-2167, who expresses regret for the propagation of the rigid single-pass waterfall standard (Larman, 2004).

1986 – Researchers in Japan First Present Iterative Development

Just one year later, Hirotaka Takeuchi and Ikujiro Nonaka, then professors at Hitotsubashi University in Japan, are researching new solutions to product development. They publish "The New New Product Development Game" for the Harvard Business Review. In their article, the professors use the game of rugby to form an analogy around a holistic approach for overlapping (vs. sequential) product development phases – "Moving the Scrum downfield" (Takeuchi & Nonaka, 1986). Figure 6 presents the simplistic, sequentially phased development process seen in the waterfall model, as well as two possible overlapping, iterative models as the authors envision them. The key here is the recognition that many development processes are not best executed sequentially, contrary to the waterfall model's implication.

Figure 6. Sequential (A) vs. overlapping (B and C) phases of development (Takeuchi & Nonaka, 1986)

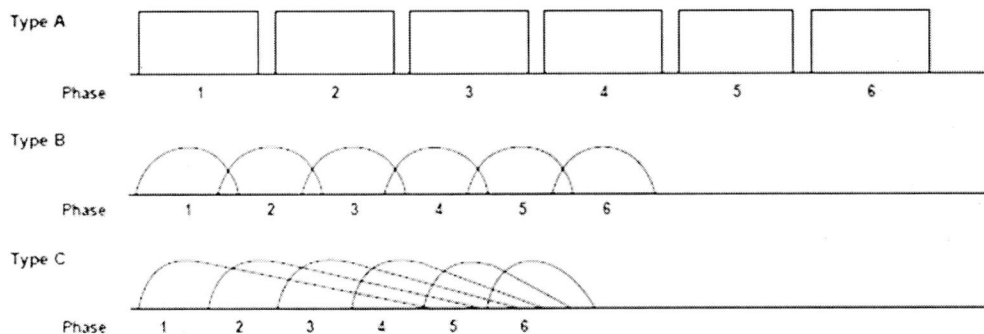

1995 – First Chaos Report Released

A decade after the release of DOD-STD-2167, the Standish Group, an IT consulting firm specializing in project value and performance evaluation, releases their sector-shaking Chaos report. The report presents the findings of their survey of 365 companies, with a total of 8,380 application development projects. Defining success as: costs at or under plan, schedule at or under plan, and functionality at or above plan, a shockingly low 16.2% of projects are found to be successful; 52.7% are challenged (the inverse of any or all of the above criteria); and 31.1% are impaired (i.e. cancelled) (The Standish Group, 1995). While Standish's "success" criteria is often disputed – what if only one of the criteria was not met, by how much, etc. (Eveleens & Verhoef, 2010) – the publication still manages to have a large and lasting impact on perceptions and understandings of the state of IT Project Management.

1995 – Scrum Software Development Process Defined

The same year that the catalytic Chaos report is published, a new approach to software development is presented at OOPSLA (Object-Oriented Programming, Systems, Languages & Applications) 1995. Dr. Jeff Sutherland and Ken Schwaber co-author the Scrum software development process, selecting its name from the research by Takeuchi and Nonaka published nearly a decade prior. Scrum is revealed as an iterative, incremental methodology for software development and project management, an alternative to the longstanding Waterfall methodology. Figure 7 provides a basic summary of the approach (detailed in the final section).

2001 – Manifesto for Agile Software Development

Several years after the introduction of Scrum, a half-dozen other waterfall-alternatives have been established. The chief representatives of these approaches meet to define a unifying thread between them, hoping the alliance would help solidify each of their relatively nascent techniques. What results is the Agile Manifesto (Beedle et al., 2001), which reads:

- Individuals and interactions over processes and tools
- Working software over comprehensive documentation
- Customer collaboration over contract negotiation
- Responding to change over following a plan

Figure 7. Graphical representation of the Scrum process (Mountain Goat Software, 2010)

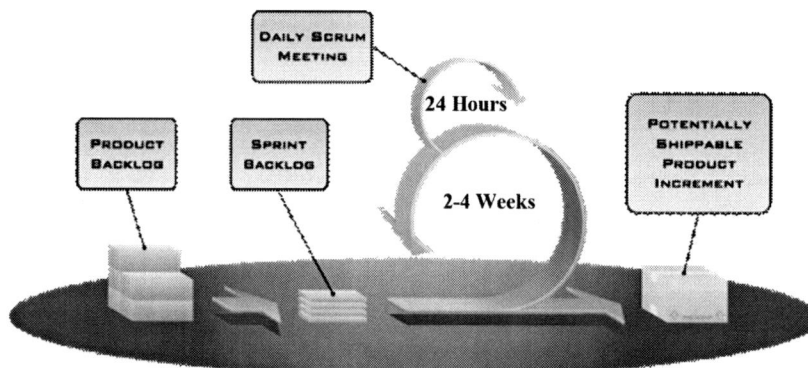

That is, while there is value in the items on the right, we value the items on the left more

Apparently the authors tapped into a critical pain-point in the industry; at present, nearly 10,000 independent signatories have pledged their allegiance to Agile's principles (Agile Alliance, 2010).

2008 – Agile Data Warehousing Published

Ralph Hughes, a DWBI consultant and data warehouse architect since 1982, publishes "Agile Data Warehousing: Delivering World-Class Business Intelligence Systems Using Scrum and XP." The approach documented therein handpicks best practices from leading Agile methodologies and applies them to Data Warehousing and Business Intelligence initiatives in ways heretofore undocumented. Having researched the major organizational questions for BI, inspecting Agile's appeal over misguided "traditional" methodologies, and looking out for well-researched detractors to the primary components of Agile approaches, it is found that this text presents, quite succinctly, a baseline prescription to BI success through Agile methodologies.

RECOMMENDATION – AGILE DATA WAREHOUSING (ADW)

Research Review and Concept Definition

Given a Business Intelligence environment of slashed budgets, crashed schedules, overwhelmed teams, and underwhelmed customers, IT and Business together can succeed by embracing Agile methodologies. Through the research performed, one can see that BI is a technology that only works when IT and Business work together. The relationship between these two groups is notoriously strained due to disparate organizational structures, lack of proactive executive-level leadership, and

broken lines of communication. One effective yet non-revolutionary way to bridge this chasm is co-locating both the IT team and Business stakeholders in an open, collaborative workspace. This common workspace is necessary to facilitate the high-bandwidth, real-time, face-to-face verbal communication that exceptionally speeds up nearly every aspect of BI delivery – requirements, planning, development, testing, deployment, and maintenance.

The prevailing Waterfall project management approach is based on an unfortunate mistake by the U.S. Department of Defense Standards group which, while later corrected, has entrenched itself so deep into organizations that moving on can seem like an impossibility. A multitude of reports, with Standish's Chaos report at the forefront, document the consequence of this mistake. Hughes (R. Hughes, personal communication, June 16, 2010) provides several detailed explanations on why "Waterfall BI" is not the best approach. He has several strong points: customers are increasingly impatient to get BI benefits; BI teams cannot avoid tackling the unknown, a critical fact which Waterfall's "big requirements up front" [BRUF] approach naively ignores; infrastructure problems as well as misunderstood business rules lie hidden until the very end of the project since implementation is held off until the final step; projects take fatal risks by demanding complete design and requirement specifications before development begins, yet when unexpected obstacles are encountered, these in-depth "to-be" documents quickly lose all relevance and must ultimately be reworked, along with any initial misguided development; project management itself consumes large portions of the budget, creating complex, elaborate plans which rarely perform well (Hughes, 2008, pp. 5-8).

As presented earlier, Agile methodologies were created with a common goal – to address the primary shortcomings present in Waterfall projects. Scrum, ADW's prescribed project management approach, can be explained rather quickly for the uninitiated: "Scrum is an Agile process for software development... [P]rojects progress via a series of iterations called sprints. Each sprint is typically 2-4 weeks long. Scrum is ideally suited for projects with rapidly changing or highly emergent requirements" (Mountain Goat Software, 2010). There are three primary players in Scrum: the Scrum team, the product owner, and the ScrumMaster. "[The S]crum team is typically made up of between five and nine people... work[ing] together to complete the set of work they have collectively committed to complete within a sprint... The product owner is the project's key stakeholder and represents users, customers and others in the process. The ScrumMaster is responsible for making sure the team is as productive as possible...by helping the team use the Scrum process, by removing impediments to progress, [and] protecting the team from outside, and so on" (Mountain Goat Software, 2010).

The work selected for any given sprint is picked from the product backlog: a continuously maintained set of desired features, listed in priority order as deemed by the product owner. This prioritization is performed in advance of the sprint planning meeting, which is held at the beginning of each sprint. At this meeting, "the [S]crum team selects the work they can complete during the coming sprint [which] is then moved from the product backlog to the sprint backlog... Each day during the sprint, a brief meeting called the daily scrum is conducted. This meeting helps set the context for each day's work and helps the team stay on track. All team members are required to attend the daily scrum" (Mountain Goat Software, 2010). The daily scrum is typically comprised of each team member preparedly answering three specific questions: What have you done since yesterday? What are you planning to do today? Do you have any problems preventing you from accomplishing your goal?

Each sprint ends with a user demonstration of the newly created, potentially shippable product.

The product owner operates the new functionality and then accepts or rejects each of the sprint's tasks. Immediately following the user demonstration, a sprint retrospective is conducted where each team member performs honest self and team-appraisals, and then takes notes on what went well and what could have gone better, ultimately taking on actions to implement the suggestions. In this way, Scrum naturally promotes continuous improvement (Hughes, 2008, p. 36).

Estimation and planning in Scrum, when done as prescribed, can quickly become exceedingly accurate compared to the BRUF (Big Requirements Up Front) estimates of Waterfall projects. The team achieves this accuracy by estimating each functionality request, called a "user story," using a relative unit of measure called "story points." Possible selection of story points generally follows the Fibonacci Sequence (1,2,3,5,8,13...), in order to reflect the "long tail" of software development (i.e. required effort tends to grow exponentially rather than linearly). Since these story points are estimated and validated every 2-4 weeks, the team continuously improves its estimating accuracy. The primary performance measure for Scrum, then, is the team's velocity, measured in story points completed per sprint. After several successive sprints with increasingly accurate estimates, this derived velocity can be applied to the remainder of the product backlog to produce plans and timelines that are rooted in demonstrated team output, rather than the sometimes-wild estimates produced ad-nauseam during a three-day Waterfall project planning lockdown (Hughes, 2008, p. 107).

Probable Benefits of Agile Data Warehousing

With the basic framework of Scrum now understood, one can turn back to Agile Data Warehousing to review an abstracted list of key benefits derived from this approach. Scrum avoids over-investment in fragile artifacts, such as to-be requirements and specification documents. It connects developers with real user requirements, straight from the full-time-embedded product owner – addressing Eckerson's concerns of requirements being lost in translation through mediating analysts. Scrum's lightweight approach has little trouble co-existing with most EIS "best-practices." It allows customers to change their minds (which they nearly always do), as each new sprint draws from the latest prioritized product backlog, rather than tightly following a 1,000 line project plan, painfully prognosticated months-to-years prior. The continuous release and integration of new "potentially shippable" product helps surface problems early on that would otherwise go undetected for months in a Waterfall BI project. Even more, Scrum directly addresses Customer fears. "Customers fear the big requirements specification process, knowing that a large development effort will be based upon this one snapshot of what they think they need. From their perspective, the large requirements document seems more like a contract, and one that will largely transfer to them the blame for any failure that occurs" (Hughes, 2008, pp. 49-55).

Possible Pitfalls of Agile Data Warehousing

James Shore reminds the prospective "Agilyte" that "There are a lot of teams right now failing with Agile. These teams are working in short cycles… They feel good, and they really are seeing more success than they were before. But they aren't working in shared workspaces or emphasizing high-bandwidth communication. [They] don't have on-site customers or work in cross-functional teams" (Shore, 2008). He observes that, due largely to Scrum's ease of understanding, many teams who claim to be Agile are simply imitating the most basic elements of a primarily open-ended framework. Shore (2008) concludes his reflection on Agile's perceived failings with the following thoughts:

Maybe we need to say, 'Agile is hard, and you can't master it by sitting through a two-day [Scrum Certification] course.' Maybe we need to be firm and say, 'Sorry, if you don't use [A]gile engineering practices, if you don't have high-bandwidth communication, and if you don't include a strong customer voice, you're not going to succeed. Try something else instead.' Scrum is popular because it's easy – and that's part of the problem (p. 1).

Beyond the pitfall of "faking" Agile implementation, Hughes provides a handful of potentially unforeseen ADW-specific adverse side effects. Since ADW's project forecasting relies almost exclusively on a velocity metric specific to a particular set of individuals on a team, Agile team members cannot be easily redeployed. Doing so not only causes setbacks in team cohesion and performance, but could potentially derail an otherwise exceptionally accurate plan. As mentioned earlier, as a tradeoff for increased planning accuracy, executive and director-level project sponsors must "float" a development effort for at least several weeks, if not a few months, before seeing complete budget and planning estimates. Lastly, for ADW to work, the Business must "give up" their best and brightest business analysts to become fully embedded into the BI team. Granted, working directly with IT's BI team will allow these analysts to deliver far greater, enduring value than could possibly be achieved if "left out" of the BI team. Yet, even if the Business – understanding the incredible benefits of effective BI that would be otherwise heavily delayed or missed altogether – commits a resource, the product owner will likely be drawn out by the same organizational duties from which she was notionally released (Hughes, 2008, pp. 267-268).

Weighing the probable benefits and possible pitfalls of an Agile approach to Business Intelligence against the observed and documented impediments to success found in traditional approaches, this study recommends that any organization struggling to turn BI promises into reality immediately bring key players from IT and Business together under the guidance of Agile methodologies. Following these methodologies will permit an otherwise stove-piped, uncoordinated organization to continuously and incrementally deliver maximum value through BI. Management's fretting over slashed budgets and crashed schedules can be replaced by complete team focus on generating new, relevant, desired functionality to the customer, piece-by-piece. Overwhelmed teams can be freed from quickly obviated up-front design specs and placed eye-to-eye with latest requirements and best-available business process knowledge from the product owner. They can rest assured that the project is planned based on their latest, consistently-demonstrated best efforts and thereby start feeling more in control and directly valuable to the company. Underwhelmed users currently wait months to receive a massive bulk of requested functionality. Once released, these requests invariably bounce back-and-forth between user test and development as misinterpreted business logic is found out and wait-and-see implementation reveals deep architectural issues. These same users, through Agile, can be quickly satisfied by the repeated delivery of incremental – fully functional – business requirements which reflect only the most relevant business needs and meet the exact real-time verbal specifications they communicated to the developer just days prior. Altogether, embracing Agile methodologies, while not an effortless task, can provide a path to BI success for the majority of companies who have yet to achieve it. Those who are willing to take the measured risk of change can reap the greater rewards of Business Intelligence; all others should only expect more of the same.

REFERENCES

Agile Alliance. (2010). *Independent signatories of the manifesto for agile software development.* Retrieved from http://agilemanifesto.org/sign/display.cgi?ms=all

Bagdanov, J., Dix, J., Krigsman, M., & Natoli, J. (2010). *Why do IT and lines of business have so much tension?* Retrieved from http://www.focus.com/questions/information-technology/why-do-it-and-lines-business-have-so-much-tension/?sort=rating#

Beedle, M., van Bennekum, A., Cockburn, A., Cunningham, W., Fowler, M., Highsmith, J. et al. (2001). *Principles behind the agile manifesto.* Retrieved from http://agilemanifesto.org/

Binning, D. (2009). *Using business intelligence to steer through the recession.* Retrieved from http://www.computerweekly.com/Articles/2009/07/30/237111/Using-business-intelligence-to-steer-through-the-recession.htm

Collier, K. (2010). *"Being" agile vs. "doing" agile.* Retrieved from http://tdwi.org/articles/2010/06/02/being-agile-vs-doing-agile.aspx

Druckman, A. (2007). *What scrum can and cannot fix.* Retrieved from http://www.scrumalliance.org/articles/68-what-scrum-can-and-cannot-fix

Eckerson, W. W. (2006). *Performance dashboards: Measuring, monitoring, and managing your business.* Hoboken, NJ: John Wiley & Sons.

Eckerson, W. W. (2010a). *How to organize business analysts.* Retrieved from http://tdwi.org/Blogs/Wayne-Eckerson/2010/05/Organizing-Analysts.aspx

Eckerson, W. W. (2010b). *Principle of proximity - the best practice in BI.* Retrieved from http://tdwi.org/Blogs/Wayne-Eckerson/2010/01/Principle-of-Proximity.aspx

Eckerson, W. W. (2010c,). *Strategies for creating a high-performance BI team.* Retrieved from http://tdwi.org/Blogs/Wayne-Eckerson/2010/03/High-Performance-Teams.aspx

Eveleens, J. L., & Verhoef, C. (2010). The rise and fall of the chaos report figures. *IEEE Software, 27*(1), 30–36. doi:10.1109/MS.2009.154

Evelson, B. (2008). *Topic overview: Business intelligence.* Retrieved from http://www.forrester.com/rb/Research/topic_overview_business_intelligence/q/id/39218/t/2

Google. (2010a). *Business intelligence director.* Retrieved from http://www.google.com/search?q=Business+Intelligence+Director

Google. (2010b). *Information technology director.* Retrieved from http://www.google.com/search?q=Information+Technology+Director

Herschel, R. T. (2009). *A business intelligence report is a "thesis" that requires effective writing.* Retrieved from http://www.b-eye-network.com/view/11857

Howson, C. (2009). *Successful BI survey: Best practices in business intelligence for greater business impact.* BI Scorecard.

Hughes, R. (2008). *Agile data warehousing - delivering world-class business intelligence systems using scrum and XP.* Bloomington, IN: iUniverse.

Information Management Magazine. (2005). *The dawn of the BI director.* Retrieved from http://www.information-management.com/issues/20050301/1021508-1.html

Larman, C. (2004). *Agile and iterative development: A manager's guide.* Upper Saddle River, NJ: Pearson Education.

Lewis, J., & Neher, K. (2007). Over the waterfall in a barrel - MSIT adventures in scrum. In *Proceedings of the AGILE Conference* (pp. 389-394). Washington, DC: IEEE Computer Society.

Mountain Goat Software. (2010). *An overview of scrum for agile software development.* Retrieved from http://www.mountaingoatsoftware.com/scrum/overview

Peterman, B. (2010). *Crossing the chasm between IT and business teams with new approaches to business intelligence.* Retrieved from http://www.b-eye-network.com/view/13980

Royce, W. W. (1970). Managing the development of large software systems. In *Proceedings of the 9th International Conference on Software Engineering* (pp. 328-338). Washington, DC: IEEE Computer Society.

Shore, J. (2008). *The decline and fall of agile.* Retrieved from http://jamesshore.com/Blog/The-Decline-and-Fall-of-Agile.html

Sierra, K. (2006). *Why face-to-face still matters!* Retrieved from http://headrush.typepad.com/creating_passionate_users/2006/04/why_face-toface_.html

Sturgeon, T. (1958). Sturgeon's revelation. *Venture Science Fiction, 2,* 66.

Takeuchi, H., & Nonaka, I. (1986). The new new product development game. *Harvard Business Review.*

The Standish Group. (1995). *Chaos.* Retrieved from http://www.projectsmart.co.uk/docs/chaos-report.pdf

Ulrich, W. M. (2009). *IT centralization versus decentralization: The trend towards collaborative governance.* Retrieved from http://www.system-transformation.com/Org_Transformation_Articles/org_decentralization.htm

U.S. Department of Defense. (1985). *DOD-STD-2167: Defense system software development.* Retrieved from http://www.everyspec.com/DoD/DoD-STD/DOD-STD-2167_278/

Yegge, S. (2006). *Good agile, bad agile.* Retrieved from http://steve-yegge.blogspot.com/2006/09/good-agile-bad-agile_27.html

This work was previously published in the International Journal of Business Intelligence Research, Volume 2, Issue 3, edited by Richard Herschel, pp. 36-51, copyright 2011 by IGI Publishing (an imprint of IGI Global).

Chapter 20
Agile Development in Data Warehousing

Nayem Rahman
Intel Corporation, USA

Dale Rutz
Intel Corporation, USA

Shameem Akhter
Western Oregon University, USA

ABSTRACT

Traditional data warehouse projects follow a waterfall development model in which the project goes through distinct phases such as requirements gathering, design, development, testing, deployment, and stabilization. However, both business requirements and technology are complex in nature and the waterfall model can take six to nine months to fully implement a solution; by then business as well as technology has often changed considerably. The result is disappointed stakeholders and frustrated development teams. Agile development implements projects in an iterative fashion. Also known as the sixty percent solution, the agile approach seeks to deliver more than half of the user requirements in the initial release, with refinements coming in a series of subsequent releases which are scheduled at regular intervals. An agile data warehousing approach greatly increases the likelihood of successful implementation on time and within budget. This article discusses agile development methodologies in data warehousing and business intelligence, implications of the agile methodology, managing changes in data warehouses given frequent change in business intelligence (BI) requirements, and demonstrates the impact of agility on the business.

DOI: 10.4018/978-1-4666-2650-8.ch020

1. INTRODUCTION

Traditional data warehouse projects often follow a typical waterfall development model in which rigorous serial efforts are made to collect complete requirements, design comprehensive architectures and data models, develop and populate reposi- tories, thoroughly test all functionality under a variety of scenarios, and, ultimately, deliver the analytical reports and artifacts that users require to run the business. In real world enterprise data warehouses (EDW) we have seen that the duration of these projects are often nine months to more than a year, with few lasting less than six months. These complex affairs involve various stakehold- ers often with conflicting priorities. The water-fall model often disappoints the business intelligence community. We attribute many of these unsuc- cessful outcomes to frequently changing business requirements coupled with the blazing speed of technology innovation. Business users are often unaware of advances in technology, and technolo- gists are frequently out of touch with the rapid changes occurring in the business environment. As a result, it is often not until the testing or even the deployment phase that significant learnings are achieved resulting in extensive redesign, redevelopment, and retesting. Thus slippage can be anticipated with the waterfall model. A solu- tion designed 9 months or a year ago is almost guaranteed to be obsolete on delivery.

Software projects are labor intensive, time consuming and expensive, hence, there is sig- nificant pressure to deliver on-time. Issues with resource assignment are encountered throughout the traditional development life cycle, as not all team members are equally engaged during differ- ent periods. While the analysts are busy describing business processes and requirements in natural language, the developers play a consultative role only. Later, the developers will be working night and day to meet the deadline while the analysts play a consultative role. Usually, at some point in

project's life cycle, it falls behind schedule raising concerns of stakeholders. To resource manpower in such lengthy projects under waterfall approach managers have to make extraordinary efforts to deal with schedule pressures and late software projects (Williams et al., 2004). Often they respond by adding more man power to stay on schedule. This method of addressing schedule slippage is often counterproductive. Through his law, "add- ing manpower to a late software project makes it later," Brooks (1995) asserts that the assimilation, training, and intercommunication costs of adding new team members outweigh the associated team productivity gain in the short term.

Agile development methodologies can help to overcome the manpower issues, schedule pressures, and late delivery of projects. These methodologies help the development team to work together, being more equally engaged throughout the process. Waterfall development life cycles consume large numbers of resources in data warehousing projects and often take longer than expected time to complete. Organizations have been working to remove redundancy and mini- mize project duration by eliminating idle time of project members during the project life cycle. It is critical to find ways to successfully implement software development projects on time, as nearly all of these initiatives contribute directly to an organization's bottom line.

An agile development approach is proving essential for effective project implementation for data warehousing (Brobst et al., 2008). Life cycle analysis (LCA) is useful to identify redundancy among systems analysts, data modelers, devel- opers and testers' idle time as well as time used by each stage of a project. Agile development methodologies can help to identify inefficiency in each part of a data warehousing task or each phase of a data warehousing project. Identifying various ways to reduce inefficiency, redundancy, wasted time is best serviced with the development of a system of metrics. These metrics can help to identify which resources are best used for what tasks and at what point in the projects life cycle. Additionally they can highlight idle periods and waste.

The major driving force for shifting to an agile development approach is the need to achieve competitiveness from data warehousing applications which is put at risk by late project implementation and cost overruns. A mix of measures including iterative releases, a switch from waterfall approach to agile development principles and frequent production releases (Khramov, 2006) are needed. Agile development is the study and practice of implementing software projects efficiently and within a short cycle time via iterative releases. It usually involves using more efficient and experienced developers, using automated tools, such as the one proposed by Rahman et al. (2010), that consume fewer resources and use less project time. Another key component is that the same resources remain engaged with the project for successive iterations. This is critical as relationships as well as partnerships grow stronger with each release. Business people become savvier about the technology at the same time the technologists are becoming more aware of the business processes they are trying to enhance. In data warehousing there is growing pressure to satisfy stakeholders' needs by using innovative development methodologies, delivering products more frequently and in modules with several iterations thereby minimizing product delivery time (Morien, 2005) and risk.

2. LITERATURE RESEARCH

Data warehousing is a critical layer in information technology (IT), as it lays the foundation for all data mining and business intelligence initiatives. Data warehousing and data management have been identified as one of the six physical capability clusters of IT-infrastructure services required for strategic agility (Weill et al., 2002). Significant research work has been done on different aspects

of data warehousing over the last one decade. Most previous work on data warehousing focused on design issues (Dey et al., 2006; Evermann, 2008; García-García & Ordonez, 2010; Storey & Goldstein, 1993), extract-transform-load (ETL) tools (Karakasidis et al., 2005; Simitsis, 2005; Rahman, 2010), data maintenance (Labio et al., 2000) strategies relating to view materialization (Agrawal et al., 1997; Lee et al., 2001; Mohania & Kambayashi, 2000), implementation issues (Widom, 1995; Schiesser, 2010; Rahman, 2007), and business intelligence (Davenport, 2010; Yermish et al., 2010; Wixom & Watson, 2010).

Research work has also been done on data warehouse load efficiency, structured query language (SQL) performance (Payton & Handfield, 2004; Lam & Lee, 2006), and maintaining a stable and healthy data warehousing environment. Many efforts have been undertaken in order to make the data environment efficient from a performance and resource consumption standpoint. Now research is shifting towards customer service, specifically looking for better ways of designing and building BI and data mining initiatives which access these data warehouses efficiently and effectively.

The important aspects of customer projects implementation in data warehouses are efficient development, effective solutions, fast deployment, and overall time to market. Data warehousing is becoming mature. Efforts are recognized as being highly successful when a high volume of different applications get implemented on schedule, within budget and without compromising with quality data. This leads to increasing adoption of an organization's enterprise data warehouse. In order to implement projects in data warehouses faster we propose agile development methodologies that allow data warehousing projects to stay within budget while meeting customer requirements as well as the implementation deadline. We have seen that agile development methodologies which go through multiple development iterations help save manpower resources, provide quality software, and deliver flawless data.

A data warehousing system is required to integrate data from all of the different aspects of the corporation. This data warehouse can then process complex repetitive queries as well as ad hoc queries which may require processing of millions of rows of data. In order to meet these needs, it is critical to ensure that processes in the data warehouse are optimized for performance. These processes must include load transformation logic, views, stored procedures, and macros. By optimizing to ensure that precompiled objects consume the least possible computing resources we leave every possible scrap of computing power available to the ad hoc queries. Agile development methodologies are very well suited to performance tuning and optimization because a few experienced developers will work on each project and that projects associated objects. Due to iterative nature of agile development approach, these same developers become more and more familiar with the objects and data structures within a given subject area. This allows developers to spend sufficient time analyzing and optimizing each code block so that they run most efficiently. It also allows some level of specialization so that developers know their data and how best to access it using various objects.

In this article we examine the essence of adopting agile development methodologies in data warehouse projects implementation. In our approach, most of the ETL development effort will be metadata driven (Rahman, 2010) and automated (Rahman et al., 2010). An ETL developer will do a significant amount development work through automated tools such as utility stored procedures and macros. This will allow developers to spend most of their time on other things such as optimizing ETL transformations, analyzing data quality and timeliness issues, and working more closely with report developers, testers, and customers to assist them and better understand their needs and objectives.

Many data warehousing projects do not follow best practices in software engineering (Eastwood, 2009) given the projects are implemented under traditional waterfall method. There are several drawbacks of the waterfall methodology which contribute to late implementation. Past studies suggest that many factors contribute to failing to deliver a useful information system (Parsons et al., 2007) under the waterfall lifecycle approach. A software development process should focus on managing and efficiently deploying human resources; collaboration and team work amongst the people involved in software development (Parsons et al., 2007). Even when implemented as per schedule, a software development project which uses the waterfall approach is implementing a solution designed approximately a year ago. In almost all cases the business use case as well as available technology options will have changed drastically in that time period. An agile development approach with its frequent iterations through all phases of the project life cycle overcomes many of the shortcomings of waterfall project lifecycle.

Agile Software development has been a research topic for last one decade. Most of the work has been done in software development projects. There is an opportunity to incorporate this approach in data warehousing projects as well given that the data warehouse refresh cycles as well as data retrieval cycles (via reporting tools) require use of complex transformation logic embedded in SQL using views, stored procedures, and macros. Additionally, today most data warehousing projects are laying foundations for BI or data mining applications. By using agile development approaches we have been able to meet our goals both in terms of time to market as well as continuing to serve evolving business needs.

3. WATERFALL VS. AGILE DEVELOPMENT METHODOLOGIES

The Waterfall development cycle follows a very structured methodology. There are distinct stage including requirements gathering, analysis, design, coding, and testing and deployment into production. Under this approach progress is usually measured in terms of completion of a stage, or percentage completion. No stage is begun until its preceding phase is deemed complete.

A common criticism of the waterfall model is that project scope and timelines are committed at the onset, often before sufficient analysis has been done. These rigid commitments make it difficult to react to changes in the business climate which almost always results in corresponding changes to project requirements as the project executes. The end result is that the waterfall model is unsuitable, and as requirements change in the course of the project the project team tries to recover by actually following an agile, iterative approach while being measured and tracked by waterfall methodology timelines. Management looks at results which seem to show all of the time being spent in development and testing because they cannot see that the other stages are revisited again and again. Thus the management will believe development teams are inefficient and ineffective rather than comprehend the true reasons for delays and budget overruns. The waterfall model should only be used when the requirements are well understood and unlikely to change radically during system development (Sommerville, 2004). One of the biggest drawbacks of waterfall model is implementation slippages and software quality issues resulting from too much design and re-engineering during development which in fact requires redesign and reimplementation to resolve user disappointment around broken features (Eastwood, 2009).

Agile software development methodologies refer to implementation of software projects based on iterative development, where requirements and solutions evolve through collaboration between developers, testers, customers, and other stakeholders. Agile processes build software by adding new features iteratively; building on those implemented in previous releases. Incremental change is the process of adding new functionality to existing code, and it is a basic component of all agile processes (Febbraro & Rajlich, 2007).

The agile approach differs significantly from the traditional waterfall model. There are rapid incremental design and development periods which precede frequent releases as opposed to one large unified release. There is a greater emphasis on progressive elaboration, just-in-time modeling techniques and on a metadata driven development approach (Patil, 2008). Agile methods generally promote a set of software engineering best practices that allow for rapid delivery of high-quality software, and which also aligns development with customer needs and business organization's objectives. This methodology allows a project to deliver to a moving target by refining requirements along with the software in each of the incremental releases. An agile development project allows for decoupling of various elements in the project, accommodating faster and even parallel development, and deployment in stages. It is not based on size or longer duration of the whole project as is characteristic in a waterfall model. A project is agile if it is able to execute its reorienting and action-taking cycle faster than the changes occurring in its environment (Adolph, 2006).

The manifesto for agile software development puts forth principles (Sommerville, 2004) of customer involvement, incremental delivery, people - not process, embracing change, and maintaining simplicity. The underlying philosophy that drives these values in data warehousing puts the highest priority on satisfying end-use requirements through early and continuous delivery of analytic capabilities (Brobst et al., 2008). Agile methodologies break tasks into logical units of work, usually four to five weeks in duration, with minimal planning as opposed to long-term planning. Iterations are short time frames that typically last from one to four weeks. Each of the iterations involves a full software development cycle including requirements analysis, data analysis, programming, unit testing, data validation, and acceptance testing. This helps improve the quality of software and also to minimize risks and customer dissatisfaction. It also allows for changes of direction which are a natural part of the business climate. The following sections describe pros and cons of waterfall model and agile development methodologies.

3.1. Understanding Requirements

In an agile data warehousing project the systems analysts will do requirement analysis with users, data analysts and other stakeholders on a rolling basis for each of the iterations of development throughout the project life. Discussions may include high level scope of future iterations, but details will be limited to the scope at hand for the current release. Under the waterfall method, all requirements will be gathered and analyzed early in the project life cycle, and not revisited. This not only takes a very long time, in most cases months, it also creates an environment in which people are very stressed to get all of the requirements complete and correct before they have achieved key learnings which occur during the design phase. Additionally, developers, testers, data modelers and others are underutilized during this phase. Later, when business needs change or design causes requirements to be revisited cross team friction can occur, with finger pointing and other counterproductive behaviors which undermine trust and teamwork. All of this causes inefficiencies, breakdowns in communications, and schedule misses.

The authors of this article have observed that prototypes are used extensively in the iterative approach as the primary vehicle for communication and collaboration between technical and non technical team members. Often as a result of experimentation with prototypes new ideas and opportunities emerge which are then incorporated into subsequent releases. This method of collaboration allows software projects to deliver more value in a much shorter period of time. It also allows for abandoning aspects of projects which turn out to add little value in favor of previously unnoticed avenues which will return far greater benefit. These determinations can be made much sooner

and with greater accuracy by using prototypes and the iterative approach. By contrast, under the waterfall model, no development is done until after the design is "set in stone." Much later in the process, usually during user acceptance testing, users will make the discoveries they would have made during prototyping and send the whole project back to requirements analysis and design under the heading of a software defect. In summary the agile approach allows early interaction between business people, engineers and software; greatly reducing later rework.

3.2. Designing Solutions

In the design phase the data analysts and developers work together to perform technical analysis of the business requirements and define deliverables. Deliverables include mapping documents for database tables and ETL development, report mockups, service level agreements, success criteria and basic test cases. A large project executing under the waterfall methodology can easily include hundreds of tables, dozens of reports, and a plethora of transformations. Capturing the details for all of these frequently requires months. During this period developers and testers are largely idle. In many cases initial design documents will require further refinement. This is often revealed during the development phase leaving team members with the painful choice of either revising design documents during development and absorbing the time or else failing to revise the design documents leaving them out of sync with what actually gets implemented. Dealing with such a large volume of tasks involves a considerable amount of ambiguity and as a result estimation of resources and time required is difficult to near impossible.

Agile development methodologies provide solutions for many of these challenges. The design will focus initially on core functionality. After the initial functionality is designed, built and implement then subsequent functionality will begin design phase. If during development or testing issues with the design are found, then design can be revisited on the subsequent iteration. The authors of this paper have observed that teamwork is enhanced considerably by the iterative approach for several reasons. First of all the ambiguity present when starting off a large project is less of a concern because pressure to get things perfect in the first iteration is eliminated. People are free to "try things out" knowing that not everything will work out in terms of performance and usability. Those parts of the application which are less than perfect will be revisited on subsequent iterations so there is no need to blame nor panic. After the first few iterations all team members become more familiar with business needs, technical constraints, data gaps, business process goals and also each other. The team becomes more like a well oiled machine, working together toward common goals.

3.3. Building Solutions

In the development phase the Developers write ETL utility scripts, stored procedures, and macros to load the data into the data warehouse. Views are created for users and reporting teams to retrieve data from the newly built tables. Report developers use these newly created objects to create their reports for the testers. Software development is laborious, complex and takes significant amounts of time. When following the waterfall methodology requirement analysis and data mapping can take longer than scheduled which ultimately impacts development by causing the development time window shrinks. Additionally rework of the design and accompanying documents is often required and needs to be absorbed into the shrinking development window. The authors of this article have observed that developers are often required to work extremely long hours during the development phase in an attempt to meet a deadline which was specified before analysis and design had even begun. The result can be suboptimal code which will require extensive rework during the testing phase. This makes fix-

ing bugs found during testing more difficult, and can result in more bugs being introduced as others are fixed. The end result is often compromised, as completing development work within a shorted window often causes software quality as well as data quality issues.

Quite often data quality issues do not appear until after the solution reaches the production environment. Because the cost to fix a bug increases exponentially with every phase, it is most expensive to fix defect in production. It is well established that the cost of fixing defects grows in geometrical progression depending on the stage where they have been discovered (Khramov, 2006). Boehm and Turner (2003) state that it costs 100 to 200 times more to fix a defect "in the fields" than it does to do so during the development process.

Under the waterfall model we have a huge amount of development to complete. The allocated time is often underestimated, and then further compromised with revisions to the design. The result of all this is a lack of overall data and software quality which in many cases impacts deliverables causing project timeline to get pushed out. In order to tackle rework and slippage the project managers often to assign additional developers in the middle of the development phase. Adding new people to the project is usually not a good choice as getting new developers up to the speed take longer than trying to do more work themselves for the experienced resources already on the project.

3.4. Managing Changes

A business organization normally holds more than one data warehousing environment including (at least) development, testing, and production. Migrating tables and code from development to test and then on to production and keeping them in sync across all environments is a huge task. A large project contains hundreds of objects including base tables, base views, reporting layer views, stored procedures, indexes and triggers.

Given that user acceptance testing is destined to be done in testing environment while unit testing is done by the developers in a development environment it is obvious that every time a table or view structure or transformation logic is changed it needs to be moved from the development to the testing environment. This needs to happen iteratively as issues are identified in test, resolved in development, and then once again migrated to test for retesting. This process is usually very hectic for developers as well as migration analysts as they must comprehend at all times what is changed and also the order of dependencies for all changed objects. Under the iterative approach, there are fewer objects involved in every release; hence object migration tasks are greatly simplified, reducing errors and rework. Given frequent and iterative migrations, we have found that an automated migration tool (Rahman et al., 2010), which automates software installation across all warehouses, can help eliminate error prone manual procedures, increase flawless object installation and reduce installation time.

3.5. Testing Solutions

The waterfall methodology weighs heavily on the testing phase and often bogs down there. The when large numbers of related objects are changed, more intersections exist, thus more possible points of failure exist. Before releasing an application to production all objects need to be tested thoroughly in multiple environments. First, developers unit test their individual components. After unit testing components are moved to a consolidated testing environment where a dedicated testing team executes predefined test cases against groups of changed objects. After both development teams and testing teams have approved the code then business users perform user acceptance testing. Validating data in terms of number of rows and individual column values and is a huge task. The more complex and varied the changes, the more complex scenarios which must be tested. Agile

methodologies bundle changes into manageable groups of related objects and thus testing is greatly simplified.

In an enterprise data warehouse data quality has been a research topic for decades. The testing needs to ensure not only that the code works correctly, but also that data quality is not compromised. Under the waterfall methodology, the magnitude of the change is very large. With such a large number of objects a solid testing plan is nearly impossible to design and execute. Additionally, managing this task is extremely complex. Without successful testing by developers, testers and end users the project cannot be released to production. Complications arise due to missed expectations, miscommunications, and changes in the business processes which occur during the projects life cycle. All of these issues often combine to send the project back to design and development rather than onward to production. An agile methodology can overcome these obstacles.

4. FITTING AGILE DEVELOPMENT METHODOLOGY IN DATA WAREHOUSING

Applying agile development methods to data warehousing projects is a new, emerging concept. The problems that agile development solves make it a natural evolution for data warehousing applications. Each iteration can bring one more logical unit of work into the data warehouse in the form of a subject area (Eastwood, 2009). A database schema, and associated processing and reporting functionality, can be developed in an iterative, incremental fashion, in accordance with an agile development approach (Morien, 2005), and any further adjustments/enhancements can be incorporated into subsequent iterations with a minimum amount of disruption to the project team.

Historically, data warehousing projects have been implemented with traditional waterfall development methodologies. Under this methodology the focus is on tracking large project phases such as analysis, design, development, testing and deployment (Patil, 2008). This kind of thinking leads management to believe that development and testing is running behind because this model does not comprehend that projects executing under the waterfall methodology routinely revisit analysis, design and development. The waterfall project is often forced to circle back and rapidly reanalyze and redesign during the development and testing phase. Under the agile development approach software development is expected to be done in iterative fashion. Each iteration will contain a logical unit of work. If a portion of work is found to be in need of rework adjustments can be made in a later iteration. Iterative development and delivery is fundamental to the agile approach (Brobst et al., 2008). In applying agile software development techniques to data warehousing the actual development is done in frequent cycles of small releases, each of which incrementally builds on the last (Patil, 2008).

Applying the agile development methodology to data warehousing greatly enables development work for data warehousing. Data warehouses are used for reporting purposes, as well as data mining. Applications in the data warehouse usually consist of reports which access views. Each report and its corresponding views use a small of set of tables in the data warehouse subject area to pull data from. So, by prioritizing groups of related reports for each particular release we can grow a subject area a few objects at a time. In other words; to fulfill the requirements of a particular group reports we need to build those required tables and columns that will be used by those reports. For a subsequent release we may add more new tables and can also add new columns to existing tables as needed to fulfill the additional requirements of new reports, or enhancements to previously release reports under the said release. By building fewer reports, tables, columns, views and other objects in a given cycle; everyone (analysts, data modelers, developers, testers and business super

users) are all able concentrate on the limited scope of work for each release. This tremendously helps everyone to perform the tasks flawlessly, teamwork is enhanced dramatically. This helps to ensure efficient coding, flawless delivery of ETL and reporting work, as well as excellent quality data. Overall, customer satisfaction is greatly enhanced by rapid, continuous delivery of useful and trustworthy software.

Agile principles state that working software is the principal measure of progress (Parsons et al., 2007) as opposed to anything else in the project implementation. Working software is defined as software which reliably produces the desired result with acceptable performance. Under agile data warehousing methodologies working software is delivered frequently, often monthly as opposed to annually as is often seen under the waterfall methodology. These frequent iterations allow for adjustment to design as the business changes over the life cycle of the software. The agile philosophy takes the position that if project goals are infeasible, it is better to know after one month than after 15 months (Brobst et al., 2008). Another aspect of agile methodology is that late changes in requirements are a natural part of project life and hence they are welcomed. Its emphasis on continuous feedback (before, during and after release), constant changes and frequent releases allows the business process to continue to evolve unencumbered and those changed are comprehended during the next development phase. Thus agile development serves changing business needs much better than any other methodology (Khramov, 2006).

The agile philosophy greatly emphasizes close, daily cooperation between business people and developers. There must be frequent communications (Keil & Carmel, 1995) between the developers, testers, customers, and other stakeholders which could be face-to-face, via instant messengers, emails, or over the phone. Core to the methodology is that not only is software being developed but also relationships. Business people become more familiar with technology even as technical people become more familiar with the business. This cross pollination results in better ideas which reach production faster and faster to the benefit of all parties involved. Agile projects rely heavily on experienced and motivated individuals who pay attention to details, technical excellence and good design. Trust becomes an integral part of the process as the team members grow and learn from each other.

Tables 1 and 2 show resources used in two real world projects. Under the waterfall model the project is undertaken with a huge scope and for the duration of 18 months. Under agile development approach the project is implemented over several iterations during an 18 month time period. Each of the iterations is implemented in production in about four to five weeks.

The difference between two approaches is obvious in terms of manpower utilization. The agile approach depends on experienced developers who are motivated and detail oriented. So, fewer individuals working in an iterative approach can do development work efficiently and flawlessly. Under the waterfall approach, a larger number of developers are involved. This means that relationships and deep understanding between analysts and developers and end users is more difficult to achieve. Because of the sheer numbers it is more likely that junior developers will be included in the scope as well. The result is that under the waterfall model development work takes longer and consumes more resources.

In any data warehousing project different sub teams and skill sets are required and there is a dependency of tasks between them. Under the waterfall model interaction among various players (analysts, developers, testers, and users) tends to be fairly rigid and structured. People work on their key tasks during a particular phase and their peers tend to be largely consultative. As a result some resources are underutilized while others are extremely overloaded throughout the project. Periods of inactivity cost money and at

Table 1. Manpower used in waterfall model

Waterfall Methods	Resources
Requirements Gathering	5
Data Analysis and Mapping	7
ETL Development	11
Report Development & Analysis	10

Table 2. Manpower used in agile development

Agile Method	Resources
Requirements Gathering	2
Data Analysis and Mapping	3
ETL Development	4
Report Development & Analysis	3

the same time it is difficult to gain assignment for the large number of resources in terms of persons for the project's life time. The intent of agile data warehousing is to build new analytic applications without the overhead of long project cycles and painful financial justifications (Brobst et al., 2008). The idea is that initial phases of the project will already be showing positive ROI (return on investment) as later phases enter development.

Tables 3 and 4 show project durations used in two real world projects. Under the waterfall model the whole project is completed with 18 months. Each stage of development is begun only after the previous phase is deemed complete for all of the project scope. Under the agile development approach the project is implemented via monthly iterations covering 18 months. Each of the iterations is implemented into production in about four to five weeks. Facilitating faster deployment of processes that promote informed decision making can bring competitive advantages to an enterprise (Brobst et al., 2008).

In agile data warehouse development we have both a smaller scope and a cohesiveness of work. During each iteration, each stage of work from

Table 3. Duration of stages under waterfall

Waterfall Method	Durations
Requirements Gathering and Analysis	16 weeks
Data Analysis and Mapping	16 weeks
ETL Development	12 weeks
Report Testing and Data Validation	28 weeks

Table 4. Duration of stages under agile model

Agile Method	Durations
Requirements Gathering and Analysis	2 weeks
Data Analysis and Mapping	2 weeks
ETL Development	2 weeks
Report Testing and Data Validation	2 weeks

requirements gathering to report testing and validation tasks are manageable within two to three weeks of time. In data warehousing, ETL development consists of work many tasks that are of the same nature and they can be automated or be made metadata driven. For our real word project implementation we have developed several utility stored procedures and macros that are driven by a database dictionary and metadata. These utility tools are used to generate views, and stored procedures that are used to load data warehouse tables. These utility objects not only help save development time but they also make ETL work more standardized and helps eliminate errors. No manual inspection is needed for this. We find that the use of these utility tools for generating data warehouse views and stored procedures is essential to rapid delivery. Testing and continuous integration is made much more efficient with metadata-driven approaches to design and deployment (Brobst et al., 2008). One of the key advantages of using agile methodology in data warehousing is that creation of multiple instances of a database is feasible. This allows for fa-

cilitating development and testing more than one iterations in parallel. For all of these reasons the agile development model is a perfect fit for data warehousing applications.

One of the greatest advantages of the agile approach is that a portion of the project deliverables is delivered at the end of each monthly-iteration. Achieving these monthly deliverables helps build confidence that the projects end goals are feasible. It validates key assumptions made during analysis. Teamwork is enhanced by the demonstrable value which is achieved and ROI is already occurring as subsequent iterations have begun. In terms of product delivery, this is one of the key differences between waterfall and agile models. The agile methodology allows for producing higher quality and more efficient and valuable products in less time (Melnik & Maurer, 2004).

Table 5 shows possible time savings (in months) for a project implemented in 18 iterations under agile methodology as opposed to a waterfall method with a project-duration of 18 months time. Under waterfall approach, the project consisting of 54 reports are delivered at the end of 18 months. Since we are holding up delivering any reports until the end of 18 months we are in fact using 18 (iterations) times 18 (months) which is equal to 324 project-months. Under the agile development approach the project is implemented via monthly iterations covering 18 months. Each of the iterations is implemented into production every four to five weeks – that is once a month. Under agile methodology, in this particular case, three analytical reports are delivered in each iteration. In the first iteration, three reports are delivered in one month. This means that a savings of 17 months are achieved since these three repots delivery are not hold up until the end of 18 months as opposed to waterfall method. The same way, another three repots are delivered at the end of two months (i.e., starting from the beginning of the project). This time a savings of 16 months are achieved. This way all 54 reports and all associated underlying database objects and

ETL developments are delivered in 18 iterations and a total of 163 project-months are saved (as shown in the third column in Table 5). So, we can see that the agile methodology saves about 50% of the time (163 project-months) compared to 324 project-months under waterfall approach. Agile methodology allows for delivering the same functionality about half of the time earlier than that of waterfall method.

Testing has a prominent role in agile projects. In our agile data warehousing projects we found that it was easy for developers to work with testers on a one-on-one basis given narrower scope and fewer developers and testers. Additionally, relationships and shared understanding are built up over the course of several iterations causing cohesiveness of the team. Under the waterfall

Table 5. Project-months saved under agile

No. of Iterations	Time (months) Spent Under Waterfall	Time (months) Saved Under Agile (compared to waterfall)
1	18	18 – 1 = 17
2	18	18 – 2 = 16
3	18	18 – 3 = 18
4	18	18 – 4 = 14
5	18	18 – 5 = 13
6	18	18 – 6 = 12
7	18	18 – 7 = 11
8	18	18 – 8 = 10
9	18	18 – 9 = 9
10	18	18 – 10 = 8
11	18	18 – 11 = 7
12	18	18 – 12 = 6
13	18	18 – 13 = 5
14	18	18 – 14 = 4
15	18	18 – 15 = 3
16	18	18 – 16 = 2
17	18	18 – 17 = 1
18	18	18 – 18 = 0
Total	324 Months	163 Months

model we have observed breakdowns in teamwork and finger pointing as projects entered the testing phase. This is in direct contrast to the agile approach where we observed teamwork and collaboration with the shared goal of delivering the given iteration and the knowledge that the same team players would begin the next iteration together as soon as the current phase was delivered. Using agile development we have found that testing was focused and data validation was perfect. We attribute these facts to a smaller number of analytical reports being tested within each iteration along with the teamwork, shared knowledge and understanding of all involved players.

5. CONCLUSION

Agile development methodologies greatly simplify the business case for including or excluding new data content into a warehouse without prolonged investment in front-loaded design and documentation tasks.

Facilitating faster deployment can bring competitive advantages to an enterprise. Agile data warehousing significantly increases an organization's ability to more quickly deliver great value from enterprise information using fewer resources. This is because of the iterative nature of agile solutions. By laying a foundation of related data objects and building on those the business can continue to evolve even as the data warehousing solution evolves without one hindering the others growth and execution. Agile development methodologies promise higher customer satisfaction, lower defect rates, faster development times and a solution to rapidly changing requirements (Boehm & Turner, 2003).

The measure of success in this methodology is the fact that trustworthy and useful information is made available to knowledge workers quickly through iterations. The agile approach reduces reliance on indirect links, substituting direct links (Keil & Carmel, 1995) between customers and developers where possible. Agile development methodologies promise higher customer satisfaction, lower defect rates, better governance, faster development times and a solution to rapidly changing requirements (Boehm & Turner, 2003).

ACKNOWLEDGMENT

We would like to thank Aroul Ramadoss and Andy Wong, Intel Corporation, for providing us real-world resource usage data and milestone document based on a project implemented under waterfall method. We are also grateful to Venice Tunnitisupawong, an ETL Application Developer at Intel, and the anonymous reviewers whose comments have improved the quality of the paper substantially.

REFERENCES

Adolph, S. (2006). What lessons can the agile community learn from a maverick fighter pilot? In *Proceedings of the Agile Conference* (pp. 94-99).

Agrawal, D., Abbadi, A., Singh, A., & Yurek, T. (1997). Efficient view maintenance at data warehouse. *SIGMOD Record*, *26*(2), 417–427. doi:10.1145/253262.253355

Boehm, B., & Turner, R. (2003). Observations on balancing discipline and agility. In *Proceedings of the Agile Development Conference* (pp. 32-39).

Brobst, S., McIntire, M., & Rado, E. (2008). Agile data warehousing with integrated sandboxing. *Business Intelligence Journal, 13*(1).

Brooks, F. P. (1995). *The mythical man-month: Essays on software engineering*. Reading, MA: Addison-Wesley.

Davenport, T. H. (2010). Business intelligence and organizational decisions. *International Journal of Business Intelligence Research, 1*(1). doi:10.4018/jbir.2010071701

Dey, D., Zhang, Z., & De, P. (2006). Optimal synchronization policies for data warehouse. *Information Journal on Computing, 18*(2), 229–242.

Eastwood, V. (2009). *Agile for data warehouse projects?* Retrieved from http://www.infobright.org/Blog/Entry/agile_for_data_warehouse_projects

Evermann, J. (2008). An exploratory study of database integration processes. *IEEE Transactions on Knowledge and Data Engineering, 20*(1). doi:10.1109/TKDE.2007.190675

Febbraro, N., & Rajlich, V. (2007). The role of incremental change in agile software processes. In *Proceedings of the Agile Conference* (pp. 92-103).

García-García, J., & Ordonez, C. (2010). Extended aggregations for databases with referential integrity issues. *Data & Knowledge Engineering, 69*, 73–95. doi:10.1016/j.datak.2009.08.008

Karakasidis, A., Vassiliadis, P., & Pitoura, E. (2005). ETL queues for active data warehousing. In *Proceedings of the 2nd International Workshop on Information Quality in Information Systems*, Baltimore, MD (pp. 28-39).

Keil, M., & Carmel, E. (1995). Customer-developer links in software development. *Communications of the ACM, 38*(5), 33–44. doi:10.1145/203356.203363

Khramov, Y. (2006). The cost of code quality. In *Proceedings of the Agile Conference* (pp. 119-125).

Labio, W., Yang, J., Cui, Y., Garcia-Molina, H., & Widom, J. (2000). Performance issues in incremental warehouse maintenance. In *Proceedings of the 26ᵗʰ International Conference on Very Large Data Bases*, Cairo, Egypt (pp. 461-472).

Lam, K., & Lee, V. C. S. (2006). On consistent reading of entire databases. *IEEE Transactions on Knowledge and Data Engineering, 18*(4).

Lee, K. Y., Son, J. H., & Kim, M. H. (2001). Efficient incremental view maintenance in data warehouses. In *Proceedings of the Tenth International Conference on Information and Knowledge Management*, Atlanta, GA (pp. 349-256).

Melnik, G., & Maurer, F. (2004). Direct verbal communication as a catalyst of agile knowledge sharing. In *Proceedings of the Agile Development Conference* (pp. 21-31).

Mohania, M., & Kambayashi, Y. (2000). Making aggregate views self-maintainable. *Journal of Data and Knowledge Engineering, 32*(1), 87–109. doi:10.1016/S0169-023X(99)00016-6

Morien, R. (2005). Agile development of the database: A focal entity prototyping approach. In *Proceedings of the Agile Conference* (pp. 103-110).

Parsons, D., Lal, R., Ryu, H., & Lange, M. (2007, December 5-7). Software development methodologies, agile development and usability engineering. In *Proceedings of the 18th Australasian Conference on Information Systems*, Toowoomba, Australia (pp. 172-178).

Patil, A. (2008). *Agile data warehousing - applying agile development methodology to DW development*. Retrieved from http://infonitive.com/?p=43

Payton, F., & Handfield, R. (2004). *Strategies for data warehousing*. MIT Sloan Management Review.

Rahman, N. (2007). Refreshing data warehouses with near real-time updates. *Journal of Computer Information Systems, 47*(3), 71–80.

Rahman, N. (2010). Incremental load in a data warehousing environment. *International Journal of Intelligent Information Technologies, 6*(3). doi:10.4018/jiit.2010070101

Rahman, N., Burkhardt, P. W., & Hibray, K. W. (2010). Object migration tool for data warehouses. *International Journal of Strategic Technology and Applications, 1*(4), 55–73. doi:10.4018/jsita.2010100104

Schiesser, R. (2010). *IT systems management* (2nd ed.). Upper Saddle River, NJ: Prentice Hall.

Simitsis, A., Vassiliadis, P., & Sellis, T. (2005). Optimizing ETL processes in data warehouses. In *Proceedings of the 21st International Conference on Data Engineering* (pp. 564-575).

Sommerville, I. (2010). *Software engineering* (9th ed.). Reading, MA: Addison-Wesley.

Storey, V. C., & Goldstein, R. C. (1993). Knowledge-based approaches to database design. *Management Information Systems Quarterly, 17*(1), 25–46. doi:10.2307/249508

Weill, W., Subramani, M., & Broadbent, M. (2002). *Building IT infrastructure for strategic agility*. MIT Sloan Management Review.

Widom, J. (1995). Research problems in data warehousing. In *Proceedings of the 4th International Conference on Information and Knowledge Management* (pp. 25-30).

Williams, L., Shukla, A., & Anton, A. I. (2004). An initial exploration of the relationship between pair programming and Brooks' Law. In *Proceedings of the Agile Development Conference* (pp. 11-20).

Wixom, B., & Watson, H. (2010). The bi-based organization. *International Journal of Business Intelligence Research, 1*(1). doi:10.4018/jbir.2010071702

Yermish, I., Miori, V., Yi, J., Malhotra, R., & Klimberg, R. (2010). Business plus intelligence plus technology equals business intelligence. *International Journal of Business Intelligence Research, 1*(1). doi:10.4018/jbir.2010071704

Compilation of References

180 Systems. (2006). *BI comparisons 2006.* Retrieved from http://www.180systems.com/BIsystem-comparison.php

Abbasi, A., Chen, H., & Salem, A. (2008). Sentiment analysis in multiple languages: Feature selection for opinion classification in web forums. *ACM Transactions on Information Systems, 26*(3).

Aberdeen Group. (2009). *The business value of pervasive BI.* Boston, MA: Aberdeen Group.

Ackoff, R. L. (1967). Management misinformation systems. *Management Science, 14*(4), 147–156. doi:10.1287/mnsc.14.4.B147

Adolph, S. (2006). What lessons can the agile community learn from a maverick fighter pilot? In *Proceedings of the Agile Conference* (pp. 94-99).

Agile Alliance. (2010). *Independent signatories of the manifesto for agile software development.* Retrieved from http://agilemanifesto.org/sign/display.cgi?ms=all

Agile Software Development. (n.d.). Wikipedia. Retrieved March 8, 2009, from http://en.wikipedia.org/wiki/Agile_software_development

Agosta, L. (2005). Exploring the social life of the data warehouse. *DM Review*, 68-73.

Agrawal, R., & Srikant, R. (1994). Fast algorithms for mining association rules. In *Proceedings of the 20ᵗʰ International Conference on Very Large Databases* (pp. 487-499).

Agrawal, R., Imielinski, T., & Swami, A. (1993). Mining association rules between sets of items in large databases. In *Proceedings of the ACM SIGMOD International Conference* (pp. 207-216). New York, NY: ACM Press.

Agrawal, D., Abbadi, A., Singh, A., & Yurek, T. (1997). Efficient view maintenance at data warehouse. *SIGMOD Record, 26*(2), 417–427. doi:10.1145/253262.253355

Airbus. (2009). *Global market forecast 2009-2028.* Retrieved from http://www.airbus.com/en/corporate/gmf2009/

Allen, J., & Robbins, S. B. (2008). Prediction of college major persistence based on vocational interests, academic preparation, and first-year academic performance. *Research in Higher Education, 49*(1), 62–79. doi:10.1007/s11162-007-9064-5

Andriessen, D. (2004). *Making sense of intellectual capital: Designing a method for the valuation of intangibles.* Maryland Heights, MO: Elsevier Butterworth-Heinemann.

Angelo, J. (2008). *Business intelligence: A new technology can analyze data at amazing speeds. So why is higher ed slow to adopt?* Retrieved from http://www.universitybusiness.com/viewarticle.aspx?articleid=659

Antons, C. M., & Maltz, E. N. (2006). Expanding the role of institutional research at small private universities: A case study in enrollment management using data mining. *New Directions for Institutional Research, 131*, 69–81. doi:10.1002/ir.188

April, K., & Bessa, J. (2006, April). A critique of the strategic competitive intelligence process within a global energy multinational. *Problems and Perspectives in Management*, 86-99.

ArcSight. (2009). *ArcSight enterprise view - monitoring enterprise-wide business risk.* Retrieved from http://www.arcsight.com/library/download/WPArcSightEnterpriseView/

Ariyachandra, T., & Frolick, M. (2008). Critical success factors in business performance management - striving for success. *Information Systems Management, 25*(2). doi:10.1080/10580530801941504

Ariyachandra, T., & Watson, H. (2010). Key Organizational Factors in Data Warehouse Architecture Selection. *Decision Support Systems, 49*, 200–212. doi:10.1016/j.dss.2010.02.006

Ariyachandra, T., & Watson, H. (2010). Selection of a data warehouse architecture: Key organizational factors. *Decision Support Systems, 49*(2). doi:10.1016/j.dss.2010.02.006

Arnett, L. (2002). Architecting an Agile Data Warehouse. *Information and Management*. Retrieved March 8, 2009, from http://www.information-management.com/infodirect/20020927/5831-1.html

Azvine, B., Cui, Z., & Nauck, D. D. (2005). Towards real-time business intelligence. *BT Technology Journal, 23*(3), 214–225. doi:10.1007/s10550-005-0043-0

Bagdanov, J., Dix, J., Krigsman, M., & Natoli, J. (2010). *Why do IT and lines of business have so much tension?* Retrieved from http://www.focus.com/questions/information-technology/why-do-it-and-lines-business-have-so-much-tension/?sort=rating#

Baker, S. L. (2000). *Economics interactive tutorial: Perils of the internal rate of return.* Retrieved from http://hadm.sph.sc.edu/courses/econ/invest/invest.html

Balahur, A., & Montoyo, A. (2008). A feature dependent method for opinion mining and classification. In *Proceedings of the International Conference on Natural Language Processing and Knowledge Engineering*.

Baldwin, D., & Yadav, S. B. (1995). The process of research investigaions in artificial intelligence - an unified view. *IEEE Transactions on Systems, Man, and Cybernetics, 25*(5), 852–861. doi:10.1109/21.376497

Bao, S., Li, R., Yu, Y., & Cao, Y. (2008). Competitor mining with the web. *IEEE Transactions on Knowledge and Data Engineering, 20*(10), 1297–1310. doi:10.1109/TKDE.2008.98

Barone, D., Myopoulos, J., Jiang, L., & Amyot, D. (2010, April 14). *The Business Intelligence Model: Strategic Modelling.* Retrieved June 11, 2010, from ftp://ftp.db.toronto.edu/pub/reports/csrg/607/BIM-TechReport.pdf

Beal, B. (2008, September). *Gartner: Evaluating Web analytics faces new challenges.* Retrieved May 25, 2010, from http://searchcrm.techtarget.com/news/1329232/Gartner-Evaluating-Web-analytics-faces-new-challenges

Beasty, C. (2006, December). *Analytics Brought to Bear.* Retrieved June 11, 2010, from http://www.destinationcrm.com/Articles/ReadArticle.aspx?ArticleID=42295

Benbasat, I., & Zmud, R. W. (2003). The identity crisis within the IS discipline: Defining and communication the discipline's core properties. *Management Information Systems Quarterly, 27*(2), 183–194.

Berry, M. J. A., & Linoff, G. S. (2004). *Data mining techniques* (2nd ed.). New York: Wiley.

Bertels, S., & Peloza, J. (2008). Running just to stand still? Managing CSR Reputation in an Era of Ratcheting Expectations. *Corporate Reputation Review, 11*(1), 56–72. doi:10.1057/crr.2008.1

Berthon, P., Pitt, L., Ewing, P., & Carr, C. L. (2002). Potential research space in MIS: A framework for envisioning and evaluating research replication, extension, and generation. *Information Systems Research, 13*(4), 416–427. doi:10.1287/isre.13.4.416.71

Bhatnagar, A. (2009, November/December). *Web Analytics for Business Intelligence.* Retrieved June 11, 2010, from http://pqasb.pqarchiver.com/infotoday/access/1895898461.html?dids=1895898461:1895898461:1895898461&FMT=ABS&FMTS=ABS:FT:PAGE&type=current&date=Nov%2FDec+2009&author=Alka+Bhatnagar&pub=Online&edition=&startpage=32&desc=Web+Analytics+for+Business+Intelligenc

Binning, D. (2009). *Using business intelligence to steer through the recession.* Retrieved from http://www.computerweekly.com/Articles/2009/07/30/237111/Using-business-intelligence-to-steer-through-the-recession.htm

Bitterer, A. (2010). *The BI(G) discrepancy: Theory and practice of business intelligence.* Stamford, CT: Gartner Research.

Boehm, B., & Turner, R. (2003). Observations on balancing discipline and agility. In *Proceedings of the Agile Development Conference* (pp. 32-39).

Boeing. (2010). *Long term market.* Retrieved from http://www.boeing.com/commercial/cmo/forecast_summary.html

Bolasco, S., Canzonetti, A., Capo, F. M., Ratta-Rinaldi, F., & Singh, B. K. (2005). Understanding text mining: A pragmatic approach. *Studies in Fuzziness and Soft Computing, 185*, 31–50. doi:10.1007/3-540-32394-5_4

Borge, D. (2001). *The book of risk.* New York, NY: John Wiley & Sons.

Bousquet, F. (2003). *Dealing with standardization: do you need a guru? Paradoxes and tricks of standardization management.* In T. Egyedi (Ed.), *The 3rd International Conference on Standardisation and Innovation in Information Technology (SIIT)*, Delft, The Netherlands (pp. 51-57).

Bousquet, F. (2003). *Role and best practices of "technical officers" in standards setting organizations.* Paper presented at the The European Academy for Standardization 9th EURAS Workshop on Standardization, Paris.

Brandel, M. (2010, March 8). *IT centralization is back in fashion.* Retrieved from http://www.reuters.com/article/idUS302398385920100309

Breul, J. (2010). Strategies to improve government performance. *Public Management, 39*(2), 56.

Brin, S., Motwani, R., & Silverstein, C. (1997). Beyond market baskets: Generalizing association rules to correlations. In *Proceedings of the ACM SIGMOD International Conference*, Tucson, AZ (pp. 265-276). New York, NY: ACM Press.

Brobst, S., McIntire, M., & Rado, E. (2008). Agile data warehousing with integrated sandboxing. *Business Intelligence Journal, 13*(1).

Brooks, F. P. (1995). *The mythical man-month: Essays on software engineering.* Reading, MA: Addison-Wesley.

Bruner, J. (1960). *The Process of Education Harvard University Press.* Cambridge, MA: Harvard.

Bureau of Transportation Statistics. (2010). *Research and innovative technology administration.* Retrieved from http://www.bts.gov/xml/air_traffic/src/index.xml#CustomizeTable

Business Objects. (n. d.). *Business intelligence standardization.* Retrieved from http://www.kleere.com/docs/white_paper_bi_standardization.pdf

Byrne, T., & Kemelor, P. (2009, March 16). *Do You Really Own Your Web Analytics Data.* Retrieved May 29, 2010, from http://www.cmswatch.com/Feature/191-Data-Ownership

Cabrera, C. (2009). *BI projects or BICC: Building the dream team.* Retrieved from http://www.element61.be/e/resourc-detail.asp?ResourceId=53

CBR. (2006, June 5). *TeaLeaf Updates Web Analytics Platform.* Retrieved April 2010, from http://www.cbronline.com/news/tealeaf_updates_web_analytics_platform

Centre for Asia Pacific Aviation. (2010). *Centre for Asia Pacific aviation.* Retrieved from http://www.centreforaviation.com/news/2010/11/05/global-fleet-drivers-changing-key-metric-is-flexibility/page1

Chang, L. (2006). Applying data mining to predict college admissions yield: A case study. *New Directions for Institutional Research, 131*, 53–68. doi:10.1002/ir.187

Chan, J. O. (2005). Toward a Unified View of Customer Relationship Management. *Journal of American Academy of Business, 6*(1), 32–38.

Chatham, B., Tempkin, B. D., & Backer, E. (2004). Web Analytics Market: Continued [Forrester.]. *Growth*, 2005.

Chen, C.-K. (2008). An integrated enrollment forecast model. *IR Applications, 15*, 1–17.

Cheng, J. (2007). *TJX consumer data theft largest in history.* http://arstechnica.com/business/news/2007/03/tjx-consumer-data-theft-largest-in-history.ars

Chen, H., Chau, M., & Zeng, D. (2002). CI Spider: a tool for competitive intelligence on the Web. *Decision Support Systems, 34*(1), 1–17. doi:10.1016/S0167-9236(02)00002-7

Chenowith, T., Corral, K., & Demirkan, H. (2006). Seven key interventions for data warehouse success. *Communications of the ACM, 49*(1), 115–119.

Chen, Y., & Xie, J. (2008). Online consumer review: Word-of-mouth as a new element of marketing communication mix. *Management Science, 54*, 477–491. doi:10.1287/mnsc.1070.0810

Chesbrough, H. W., & Appleyard, M. M. (2007). Open Innovation and Strategy. *California Management Review, 50*(1), 57–76.

Child, D. (2006). *Ten Ways To Improve Your Website Conversion Rate.* Retrieved May 21, 2010, from http://www.addedbytes.com/online-marketing/ten-ways-to-improve-your-website-conversion-rate/

Chung, H. M., & Gray, P. (1999). Special section: Data mining. *Journal of Management Information Systems, 16*(1), 11–16.

Chung, W., Chen, H., & Nunamaker, J. F. Jr. (2005). A Visual Framework for Knowledge Discovery on the Web: An Empirical Study of Business Intelligence Exploration. *Journal of Management Information Systems, 21*(4), 57–84.

Ciric, B. (2009). *Business intelligence competence center – the essential need of strategic deployment of BI.* Retrieved from http://www.globaldataconsulting.net/articles/best-practice/business-intelligence-competence-center-%E2%80%93-essential-need-strategic-deployment

Clarabridge, I. (2006). *Converging text and BI: The case for a content mining platform.* Retrieved from http://www.clarabridge.com/resources/downloads.php

Clifton, B. (2010b, April). *Understanding Web Analytics Accuracy.* Retrieved May 22, 2010, from http://www.advanced-web-metrics.com/docs/accuracy-whitepaper.pdf

Clifton, B. (2010). *Advanced Web Metrics with Google Analytics* (2nd ed.). New York: Wiley Publishing Inc.

Cody, W. F., Kreulen, J. T., Krishna, V., & Spangler, W. S. (2002). The integration of business intelligence and knowledge management. *IBM Systems Journal, 41*(4), 697–714. doi:10.1147/sj.414.0697

Coghlan, T., Diehl, G., Karson, E., Liberatore, M., Luo, W., & Nydick, R. (2010). The Current State of Analytics in the Corporation: The View from Industry Leaders. *International Journal of Business Intelligence Research, 1*(2), 1–8.

Cognos. (2008). *Customer success in the public sector.* Retrieved from http://public.dhe.ibm.com/software/data/sw-library/cognos/pdfs/casestudies/ss_bundle_customer_success_in_government.pdf

Collier, K. (2010). *"Being" agile vs. "doing" agile.* Retrieved from http://tdwi.org/articles/2010/06/02/being-agile-vs-doing-agile.aspx

Commercial Aviation Report. (2007). Noel Forgeard and the A380. *Commercial Aviation Report,* 10-11.

Conrad, J. G., & Schilde, F. (2007). Opinion mining in legal blogs. In *Proceedings of the International Conference on Artificial Intelligence and Law* (pp. 231-236).

Cook, S. D. N., & Brown, J. S. (1999). Bridging epistemologies: The generative dance between organizational knowledge and organizational knowing. *Organization Science, 10*(4), 381–400. doi:10.1287/orsc.10.4.381

Corbett, N. (2009). *Test Driven Development, a Portable Methodology.* Retrieved April 16, 2009, from http://www.developer.com/design/article.php/3622546

Crounse, B. (2007). *Business intelligence systems give meaning to mountains of healthcare data, 3.* Retrieved from http://www.microsoft.com/industry/healthcare/providers/businessvalue/housecalls/housecalls_patientbi.mspx

Cruickshank, B. (2010). *Making business intelligence work.* Retrieved from http://proquest.umi.com.argo.library.okstate.edu/pqdlink?did=2155971561&Fmt=3&clientld+4653&RQT+309&VName+PQD

Daniel, D. (2007, November 9). *Need for business intelligence grows: Too much information, not enough insight.* Retrieved from http://www.cio.com/article/153500/Need_for_Business_Intelligence_Grows_Too_Much_Information_Not_Enough_Insight

Das, S. R., & Chen, M. Y. (2007). Yahoo! for Amazon: Sentiment extraction from small talk on the web. *Management Science, 53*, 1375–1388. doi:10.1287/mnsc.1070.0704

Data Quality Definition – What is Data Quality? (n.d.). BiPM Institute. Retrieved April 19, 2009, from http://www.bipminstitute.com/data-quality/accuracy-consistency-audit.php

Data Warehouse Challenges and Issues. (n.d.). BiPM Institute. Retrieved April 19, 2009 from http://www.bipminstitute.com/data-warehouse/challenge-issues.php

DataMonitor. (2009). *Omniture Inc.: Company Profile.* DataMonitor.

Davenport, T. H. (2004). Competing on analytics. *Harvard Business Review.*

Davenport, T. H. (2010). Are you ready to reengineer your decision making? *MIT Sloan Management Review*, 2-7.

Davenport, T. H., & Harris, J. G. (2009). What people want (and how to predict it). *MIT Sloan Management Review*, 23-31.

Davenport, T. (2006). Competing on Analytics. *Harvard Business Review*, 2–10.

Davenport, T. (2010). Business intelligence and. *International Journal of Business Intelligence Research*, *1*(1), 1–12.

Davenport, T. H., & Harris, J. G. (2007). *Competing on analytics: The new sience of winning.* Boston, MA: Harvard Business School Press.

Davenport, T. H., Harris, J. G., & Morison, R. (2010). *Analytics at work.* Boston, MA: Harvard Business Press.

de Ville, B. (2006). *Decision trees for business intelligence and data mining: Using SAS enterprise miner* (1st ed.). Cary, NC: SAS Institute.

de Vries, H. (1999). *Standards for the Nation. Analysis of National Standardization Organizations.* Unpublished Doctoral Dissertation, Erasmus University Rotterdam, Rotterdam, The Netherlands.

Desmond, J. (2009). Agile Development Techniques Produce Record Results at BMC Software. *Software Magazine.* Retrieved November 5, 2009, from http://www.softwaremag.com/L.cfm?Doc=1198-3/2009

Dey, D., Zhang, Z., & De, P. (2006). Optimal synchronization policies for data warehouse. *Information Journal on Computing*, *18*(2), 229–242.

Dey, L., & Haque, M. (2009). Opinion mining from noisy text data. *International Journal of Document Analysis and Recognition*, *12*(3), 205–226. doi:10.1007/s10032-009-0090-z

Dhar, V., & Sundararajan, A. (2007). Information technologies in business: A blueprint for education and research. *Information Systems Research*, *18*(2). doi:10.1287/isre.1070.0126

Ding, X., & Liu, B. (2007). The utility of linguistic rules in opinion mining. In *Proceedings of the 30th Annual International ACM SIGIR Conference on Research and Development in Information Retrieval* (pp. 811-812).

Doran, G. T. (1981). There's a S.M.A.R.T. way to write management's goals and objectives. *Management Review*, *70*(11).

Druckman, A. (2007). *What scrum can and cannot fix.* Retrieved from http://www.scrumalliance.org/articles/68-what-scrum-can-and-cannot-fix

Du Toit, A. S. A. (2003). Competitive intelligence in the knowledge economy: what is in it for South African manufacturing enterprises? *International Journal of Information Management*, *23*(2), 111–120. doi:10.1016/S0268-4012(02)00103-2

Dyché, J. (2010). *How to make the case for a BI center of excellence.* Retrieved from http://www.information-management.com/issues/20_1/center_of_excellence_bi_business_intelligence-10016936-1.html

Dyllick, T., & Hockerts, K. (2002). Beyond the business case for corporate sustainability. *Business Strategy and the Environment*, *11*, 130–141. doi:10.1002/bse.323

Earls, A. R. (2003). ETL: Preparation IS THE best bet. *Computerworld*, *37*(34), 25–26.

Eastwood, V. (2009). *Agile for data warehouse projects?* Retrieved from http://www.infobright.org/Blog/Entry/agile_for_data_warehouse_projects

Eckerson, W. (2009). *One size does not fit all.* Retrieved from http://www.teradatamagazine.com/v09n04/Features/One-size-does-not-fit-all/

Eckerson, W. (2010, November 1). *Hybrid business intelligence organizations: Managing the trade-offs between central and distributed development*. Retrieved from http://tdwi.org/articles/2010/11/01/hybrid-bi-organizations-managing-the-trade-offs-between-central-and-distributed-development.aspx

Eckerson, W. W. (2007). *The myth of self-service BI*. Retrieved from http://tdwi.org/articles/2007/10/18/the-myth-of-selfservice-bi.aspx

Eckerson, W. W. (2010). *How to organize business analysts*. Retrieved from http://tdwi.org/Blogs/Wayne-Eckerson/2010/05/Organizing-Analysts.aspx

Eckerson, W. W. (2010). *Principle of proximity - the best practice in BI*. Retrieved from http://tdwi.org/Blogs/Wayne-Eckerson/2010/01/Principle-of-Proximity.aspx

Eckerson, W. W. (2010c,). *Strategies for creating a high-performance BI team*. Retrieved from http://tdwi.org/Blogs/Wayne-Eckerson/2010/03/High-Performance-Teams.aspx

Eckerson, W. (2011). *Performance dashboards* (pp. 101–105). New York, NY: John Wiley & Sons.

Eckerson, W. W. (2006). *Performance dashboards: Measuring, monitoring, and managing your business*. Hoboken, NJ: John Wiley & Sons.

Economics, T. (2010). *United States GDP growth rate*. Retrieved from http://tradingeconomics.com/Economics/GDP-Growth.aspx?Symbol=USD

Ellig, J. (2009, Summer). Federal performance reporting: what a difference ten years makes! *The Public Manager*, pp. 5-12.

Embarcadero Technologies. (2008). *Why data warehouse projects fail*. Retrieved from http://etnaweb04.embarcadero.com/resources/technical_papers/Why-Data-Warehouse-Projects-Fail.pdf

English, L. (2007). Data Quality in Plain English. *Information and Management*. Retrieved April 12, 2009, from http://www.information-management.com/issues/20070401/1079288-1.html

Erickson, T. (2010, May 3). *Digital Data created in 2020 forecasted at 35 zettabytes; cloud computing will manage data growth*. Retrieved May 28, 2010, from http://searchstorage.techtarget.com/news/article/0,289142,sid5_gci1511342,00.html

Ericson, J. (2006). Health care's knowledge quest: Data integration supports research at Children's Hospital, Boston. *Business Intelligence Review, 2*(3), 12.

Evans, P. (2010). *Business intelligence is a growing field*. Retrieved from http://www.databasejournal.com/sqletc/article.php/3878566/Business-Intelligence-is-a-Growing-Field.htm

Eveleens, J. L., & Verhoef, C. (2010). The rise and fall of the chaos report figures. *IEEE Software, 27*(1), 30–36. doi:10.1109/MS.2009.154

Evelson, B. (2008). *Topic overview: Business intelligence*. Retrieved from http://www.forrester.com/rb/Research/topic_overview_business_intelligence/q/id/39218/t/2

Evermann, J. (2008). An exploratory study of database integration processes. *IEEE Transactions on Knowledge and Data Engineering, 20*(1). doi:10.1109/TKDE.2007.190675

Extract, T. Load. (2009). Wikipedia. Retrieved April 20, 2009, from http://en.wikipedia.org/wiki/Extract,_transform,_load

FAA. (2009). *FAA aerospace forecast fiscal years 2009-2029*. Retrieved from http://www.docstoc.com/docs/840343/Risks-to-the-Forecast

FAA. (2010). *FAA aerospace forecast fiscal years 2010-2030*. Retrieved http://www.faa.gov/data_research/aviation/aerospace_forecasts/2010-2030/media/Risks%20to%20the%20Forecast.pdf

Farrell, J., & Saloner, G. (1985). Standardization, compatibility, and innovation. *The Rand Journal of Economics, 16*(1), 70–83. doi:10.2307/2555589

Farris, R. (2006, October 12). *Organizing for an enterprise-wide BI and DW capability*. Retrieved from http://www.information-management.com/news/1064959-1.html

Febbraro, N., & Rajlich, V. (2007). The role of incremental change in agile software processes. In *Proceedings of the Agile Conference* (pp. 92-103).

Feldman, R., & Sanger, J. (2007). *The text mining handbook advanced approaches in analyzing unstructured data.* Cambridge, UK: Cambridge University Press.

Fest, G. (2005). Filling in the blanks. *U.S. Banker, 115*(12), 20.

Few, S. (2006). *BizViz: The power of visual business intelligence.* Retrieved from http://www.perceptualedge.com/articles/b-eye/visual_business_intelligence.pdf

Few, S. (2010). *BI has hit the wall.* Retrieved from http://www.perceptualedge.com/blog/?p=820

Fielding, R. L. (n.d.). *The CEO's guide to the top 5 issues that misguide business intelligence decisions.* Retrieved from http://www.advancingwomen.com/mobile%20cell%20phone/the_ceos_guide_to_the_top_5_issues_that_misguide_business_intelligence_decisions.php

Financial Times. (2009, November 27). Digital digest managing intelligence: How to make sense of the pieces. *Financial Times.*

Finucane, B. (2010, November 3). *Business intelligence for the masses.* Retrieved from http://www.b-eye-network.com/view/14575

Fiske, E. B. (2008). How college admissions came to be hawked in the marketplace. *The Chronicle of Higher Education, 55*(5), A112.

Fitz-enz, J. (2010). *The new HR analytics: Predicting the economic value of your company's human capital investments* (p. 230). New York, NY: AMACOM.

Fleisher, C. S., & Bensoussan, B. E. (2003). *Strategic and Competitive Analysis: Methods and Techniques for Analyzing Business Competition.* Upper Saddle River, NJ: Prentice Hall.

Fomin, V. V., & Vries, H. J. d. (2009). *How balanced is balanced enough? Case studies of stakeholders' (under-) representation in standardization process.* In T. Morioka (Ed.), *Proceedings of the 6th biennial Standardisation and Innovation in Information Technology (SIIT) conference,* Kogakuin University, Tokyo, Japan (pp. 99-112).

Fomin, V. V., King, J. L., Lyytinen, K., & McGann, S. (2005). Diffusion and Impacts of E-Commerce In the United States of America: Results from an Industry Survey. [CAIS]. *Communications of the Association for Information Systems, 16*(31), 559–603.

Forbes. (2010). *Managing information in the enterprise: Perspectives for business leaders.* New York, NY: Forbes.

Fordham, D. R., Riordan, D. A., & Riordan, M. P. (2002). Business intelligence: How accountants bring value to the marketing function. *Strategic Finance, 83*(11), 6.

Forrester Consulting. (2009, October 2). *Lean business intelligence - Why and how enterprises are moving to self-service business intelligence.* Retrieved from http://www.cfoinnovation.com/system/files/Lean_Business_Intelligence_Self-Service_BI_SAP.pdf

Freeman, S., & Pryce, N. (2009). Growing Object-Oriented Software. *Guided by Tests.* Retrieved April 16, 2009, from http://www.mockobjects.com/book/tdd-introduction.html

Friedman, T. L. (2005). *The world is flat: A brief history of the twenty-first century* (1st ed.). New York, NY: Farrar, Straus and Giroux.

Froelich, J., Ananyan, S., & Olson, D. L. (2005). Business intelligence through text mining. *Business Intelligence Journal,* 43-50.

Frolick, M., & Ariyachandra, T. (2006). Business Performance Management: The Real Truth. *Information Systems Management, 23*(1), doi:10.1201/1078.10580530/45769.23.1.20061201/91771.5

Fukuda, T., Morimoto, Y., Morishita, S., & Tokuyama, T. (1996). Mining optimized association rules for numeric attributes. In *Proceedings of the ACM SIGACT-SIGMOD-SIGART Symposium on Principles of Database Systems,* Montreal, QC, Canada (pp.182-191). New York, NY: ACM Press.

Fukuda, T., Morimoto, Y., Morishita, S., & Tokuyama, T. (2001). Data mining with optimized two dimensional association rules. *ACM Transactions on Database Systems, 26*(2), 179–213. doi:10.1145/383891.383893

Funk, J. L. (2002). *Global Competition Between and Within Standards. The Case of Mobile Phones.* New York: Palgrave.

Furey, T. (2005). Data warehouse project management. *DM Review*, 70-73.

Gallagher, T. J. (1998). *Forecasting aviation markets.* Retrieved from http://aviation.se.edu/salluisi/avia2113/forecasting.pdf

Ganguly, S. (2010). *Collecting Data using Packet Sniffing.* Retrieved May 25, 2010, from http://ezinearticles.com/?Collecting-Data-Using-Packet-Sniffing&id=1834436

Gao, P. (2005). Using actor-network theory to analyse strategy formulation. *Information Systems Journal, 15*(3), 255–275. doi:10.1111/j.1365-2575.2005.00197.x

García-García, J., & Ordonez, C. (2010). Extended aggregations for databases with referential integrity issues. *Data & Knowledge Engineering, 69*, 73–95. doi:10.1016/j.datak.2009.08.008

Gartner. (2009). *Howard Dresner.* Retrieved May 20, 2009, from http://www.gartner.com/research/fellows/asset_79427_1175.jsp

Gartner. (2010). *Gartner EXP worldwide survey of nearly 1,600 CIOs shows IT budgets in 2010 to be at 2005 levels.* Retrieved from http://www.gartner.com/it/page.jsp?id=1283413

Gartner. (2010). *Magic quadrant for security information and event management.* Retrieved from http://www.gartner.com/it/products/mq/mq_ms.jsp-s

Gayer, T., Hamilton, J. T., & Viscusi, W. K. (2000). Private values of risk tradeoffs at SUPERFUND sites: housing market evidence on learning about risk. *The Review of Economics and Statistics, 82*(3), 439–451. doi:10.1162/003465300558939

Glassey, K. (1998). Seducing the end user. *Communications of the ACM, 41*(9), 52–60. doi:10.1145/285070.285083

Gnatovich, R. (2007). Making a case for business analytics. *Strategic Finance, 88*(8), 46–52.

Goenner, C. F., & Pauls, K. (2006). A predictive model of inquiry to enrollment. *Research in Higher Education, 47*(8), 935–956. doi:10.1007/s11162-006-9021-8

Google. (2010). *Google Analytics.* Retrieved April 23, 2010, from http://www.google.com/analytics/product.html

Google. (2010). *Business intelligence director.* Retrieved from http://www.google.com/search?q=Business+Intelligence+Director

Google. (2010). *Information technology director.* Retrieved from http://www.google.com/search?q=Information+Technology+Director

Gordon, E. (2009). *Winning the global talent showdown.* Retrieved from http://www.shrm.org/Research/FutureWorkplaceTrends/Pages/WinningGlobalTalentShowdown.aspx

Gorla, N. (2003). Features to consider in a data warehousing system. *Communications of the ACM, 46*(11), 111–115. doi:10.1145/948383.948389

Gorry, G. A., & Morton, M. S. S. (1989). A framework for management information systems. [SMR Classic Reprint]. *Sloan Management Review*, 49–61.

Green, A. (2006). Building blocks to a knowledge valuation system (KVS). *The Journal of Information and Knowledge Management Systems, 36*(2), 146–154.

Green, A. (2007). Business information - a natural path to business intelligence: Knowing what to capture. *The Journal of Information and Knowledge Management Systems, 37*(1), 18–23.

Greenfield, L. (2009). *A definition of data warehousing.* Retrieved from http://www.dwinfocenter.org/defined.html

Greer, W. R., & Liao, S. S. (1986). Forecasting capacity and capacity utilization in the U.S. aerospace industry. *Journal of Forecasting*, 57–67. doi:10.1002/for.3980050106

Gregor, S., & Jones, D. (2007). The anatomy of a design theory. *Journal of the Association for Information Systems, 8*(5), 312–335.

Hackney, D. (2000). Architecture anarchy and how to survive it: God save the queen. *Enterprise Systems Journal, 15*(4), 24–30.

Hall, M. (2010). *A solution for IT.* Retrieved from http://global.factiva.com.argo.library.okstate.edu/ga/default.aspx

Halvorson, K. (2009). *Content Strategy for the web.* New Riders.

Hamel, S. (2009). *THE WEB ANALYTICS MATURITY MODEL:A strategic approach based on business maturity and critical success factors.* Retrieved from http://immeria.net/oamm/WAMM_ShortPaper_091017.pdf

Hamilton, J. T., & Viscusi, V. K. (1999). How costly is "clean"? An analysis of the benefits and costs of superfund site remediations. *Journal of Policy Analysis and Management, 18*(1), 2–28. doi:10.1002/(SICI)1520-6688(199924)18:1<2::AID-PAM2>3.0.CO;2-2

Han, J., & Fu, Y. (1995). Discovery of multiple-level association rules from large databases. In *Proceedings of the International Conference on Very Large Databases,* Zurich, Switzerland (pp. 420-431).

Harris, L. (2008). *Delivering useful BI tools for the masses.* Retrieved from http://www.busmanagement.com/article/Delivering-Useful-BI-Tools-for-the-Masses/

Harris, T. H., & Davenport, J. G. (2007). *Competing on analytics.* Boston, MA: Harvard Business School Publishing.

Harter, R., & Wagner, J. K. (2006). *The elements of great managing.* Washington, DC: Gallup Press.

Hatch, D. (2008). *BI: Is one version of the truth still out there?* Retrieved from http://www.ecommercetimes.com/rssstory.65359.html?wlc-1288713846

Hearst, M. (2003). *What is text mining?* Retrieved from http://www.ischool.berkley.edu

Heizenberg, J. (2008). Beyond the center of excellence. *Journal of Management Excellence, 3,* 19–23.

Henschen, D. (2008). *Seven steps to successful BI competency centers.* Retrieved from http://intelligent-enterprise.informationweek.com/

Henschen, D. (2009). *4 technologies that are reshaping business intelligence.* Retrieved from http://www.informationweek.com/news/business_intelligence/analytics/showArticle.jhtml?articleID=219500363

Henschen, D. (2009). *Readers weigh in on biggest obstacles to business success.* Retrieved from http://www.informationweek.com/news/business_intelligence/analytics/showArticle.jhtml?articleID=215901169&queryText=BICC

Herring, J. P. (1999). Key intelligence topics: A process to identify and define intelligence needs. *Competitive Intelligence Review, 10*(2), 4–14. doi:10.1002/(SICI)1520-6386(199932)10:2<4::AID-CIR3>3.0.CO;2-C

Herschel, R. (2010). *Marketing business intelligence.* Retrieved from http://www.b-eye-network.com/print/12563

Herschel, R. (2010). *What is business intelligence?* Retrieved from http://www.b-eye-network.com/print/13768

Herschel, R. T. (2009). *A business intelligence report is a "thesis" that requires effective writing.* Retrieved from http://www.b-eye-network.com/view/11857

Hevner, A. R., March, S. T., Park, J., & Ram, S. (2004). Design science in information systems research. *Management Information Systems Quarterly, 28*(1), 75–105.

Hewlett Packard. (2009). *Building the business intelligence competency center: Business white paper.* Retrieved from http://h20195.www2.hp.com/v2/GetPDF.aspx/4AA2-7082ENW.pdf

Hoberman, S. (2006). *What is the enterprise data model ROI?* Retrieved from http://www.information-management.com/issues/20060501/1053415-1.html

Hostmann, B. (2007). *BI competency centers: Bringing intelligence to the business.* Retrieved from http://bpm-mag.net/mag/bi_competency_centers_intelligence_1107/index1.html

Hostmann, B. (2010). *Business intelligence competency center key initiative overview.* Stamford, CT: Gartner.

Howson, C. (2010). *Ease of use and interface appeal in business intelligence tools.* Retrieved from http://www.beyeresearch.com/study/13006

Howson, C. (2006). Seven pillars of BI success - BI tools are getting better, but technology is only part of the story. *Intelligent Enterprise, 9*(9), 33.

Howson, C. (2009). *Successful BI survey: Best practices in business intelligence for greater business impact*. BI Scorecard.

Howson, C. (2010). *Successful business intelligence: Secrets to making a BI a killer app* (pp. 115–119). New York, NY: McGraw-Hill.

Hughes, R. (2008). *Agile data warehousing - delivering world-class business intelligence systems using scrum and XP*. Bloomington, IN: iUniverse.

Huselid, M. A., Becker, B. E., & Beatty, R. W. (2008). *The workforce scorecard*. Boston, MA: Harvard Business School Publishing.

IBM. (2010). *The enterprise of the future*. Armonk, NY: IBM.

IBM. (n. d.). *The new voice of the CIO*. Retrieved from http://www-935.ibm.com/services/us/cio/ciostudy/

IDC. (2008). *Pervasive business intelligence*. Framingham, MA: IDC.

Ilinitch, A. Y., Soderstrom, N. S., & Thomas, T. E. (1998). Measuring corporate environmental performance. *Journal of Accounting and Public Policy*, *17*, 383–408. doi:10.1016/S0278-4254(98)10012-1

Infohatch. (2010). *Predictive analytics*. Retrieved from http://www.infohatch.com/predictiveanalytics.htm

Information Management Magazine. (2005). *The dawn of the BI director*. Retrieved from http://www.information-management.com/issues/20050301/1021508-1.html

Inmon, W. (2005). *Building the data warehouse* (4th ed.). New York, NY: John Wiley & Sons.

Inmon, W. H. (1996). *Building the data warehouse* (2nd ed.). Hoboken, NJ: John Wiley & Sons.

Inmon, W., Imhoff, C., & Sousa, R. (2001). *Corporate Information Factory* (2nd ed.). New York: Wiley & sons.

Intergovernmental Panel on Climate Change (IPCC). (2001). *Aviation and the global atmosphere*. Arendal, Norway: GRID-Arendal.

Investopedia. (n. d.). *Investopedia*. Retrieved from http://www.investopedia.com

IPInfoDB. (2009). *IPInfoDB*. Retrieved June 12, 2010, from http://ipinfodb.com/ip_database.php

Isaak, J. (2006). The Role of Individuals and Social Capital in POSIX Standardization. *International Journal of IT Standards and Standardization Research*, *4*(1), 1–23.

Isidore, C. (2008). *It's official: Recession since Dec. '07*. Retrieved from http://money.cnn.com/2008/12/01/news/economy/recession/index.htm

Jacobs, P. (1999). Data mining: What general managers need to know. *Harvard Management Update*, 3-4.

Jansen, B. (2006). Search Log Analysis: What it is, what's been done, how to do it. *Library & Information Science Research*, *28*(3), 407–432. doi:10.1016/j.lisr.2006.06.005

Jansen, B. J., & Spink, A. (2006). How are we searching the world wide web? A comparison of nine search engine transaction logs. *Information Processing & Management*, *42*(1), 248–263.

Jansen, B. J., Zhang, M., Sobel, K., & Chowdury, A. (2009). Twitter power: Tweets as electronic word of mouth. *Journal of the American Society for Information Science and Technology*, *60*(11), 2169–2188. doi:10.1002/asi.21149

Johnson, I. (2008). Enrollment, persistence and graduation rate of in-state students at a public research university: Does high school matter? *Research in Higher Education*, *49*(8), 776–793. doi:10.1007/s11162-008-9105-8

Jonas, J. (2006). *Enterprise intelligence – my presentation at the third annual Web 2.0 summit*. Retrieved from http://jeffjonas.typepad.com/jeff_jonas/2006/11/enterprise_inte.html

Juch, B. (1983). *Personal development: Theory and practice in management training*. Chichester, UK: John Wiley & Sons.

Jukic, N., & Nestorov, S. (2003). Ad-hoc association-rule mining within the data warehouse. In *Proceedings of the 36th Annual Hawaii International Conference on System Sciences* (p. 10). Washington, DC: IEEE Computer Society.

Jukic, J., & Nestorov, S. (2006). Comprehensive data warehouse exploration with qualified association-rule mining. *Decision Support Systems*, *42*(2), 859–878. doi:10.1016/j.dss.2005.07.009

Jukic, N. (2006). Data modeling strategies and alternatives for data warehousing projects. *Communications of the ACM, 49*(4), 83–88. doi:10.1145/1121949.1121952

Kahaner, L. (1996). *Competitive intelligence: From black ops to boardrooms - how businesses gather, analyze, and use information to succeed in the global marketplacy* (1st ed.). New York, NY: Simon & Schuster.

Kanaracus, C. (2010). *Professors cite challenges in teaching BI*. Retrieved from http://www.pcworld.com/businesscenter/article/192138/professors_cite_challenges_in_teaching_bi.html

Kao, A., & Poteet, S. (Eds.). (2007). *Natural language processing and text mining*. London, UK: Springer. doi:10.1007/978-1-84628-754-1

Kaplan, R. S., & Norton, D. P. (1993, September). Putting the balanced scorecard to work. *Harvard Business Review*, (n.d.), 54–69.

Karakasidis, A., Vassiliadis, P., & Pitoura, E. (2005). ETL queues for active data warehousing. In *Proceedings of the 2nd International Workshop on Information Quality in Information Systems*, Baltimore, MD (pp. 28-39).

Kaufnabb, M. (2007). *Common business intelligence (BI) mistakes*. Retrieved from http://searchbusinessanaltyics.techtarget.com/tip/Common-business-intelligence-BI-mistakes

Kaushik, A. (2007). *Web Analytics, An Hour a Day*. New York: Wiley Publishing.

Kaushik, A. (2009). *Web Analytics 2.0: The Art of Online Accountability and Science of Customer Centricity*. Sybex.

Keil, M., & Carmel, E. (1995). Customer-developer links in software development. *Communications of the ACM, 38*(5), 33–44. doi:10.1145/203356.203363

Keil, T. (2002). De-facto standardization through alliances - lessons from Bluetooth. *Telecommunications Policy, 26*(3-4), 205–220. doi:10.1016/S0308-5961(02)00010-1

Kelly, J. (2009). *Business intelligence not all it can be at most organizations, according to Gartner*. Retrieved from http://searchbusinessanalytics.techtarget.com/news/1507079/Business-intelligence-not-all-it-can-be-at-most-organizations-according-to-Gartner

Kelly, J. (2009). *School district overcomes 'catastrophic' business intelligence deployment failure*. Retrieved from http://searchbusinessanalytics.techtarget.com/news/1507086/School-district-overcomes-catastrophic-business-intelligence-deployment-failure

Kelly, S. (1997). Data marts: The latest silver bullet. *Data Mart Review*, 12-16.

Khramov, Y. (2006). The cost of code quality. In *Proceedings of the Agile Conference* (pp. 119-125).

Kimball, R., & Ross, M. Thornthwaite, W., Mundy, J., & Becker, B. (2007). *The data warehouse lifecycle toolkit* (2nd ed.). New York, NY: John Wiley & Sons.

Kimball, R., Reeves, L., Ross, M., & Thornthwhite, W. (1998). *The data warehouse lifecycle toolkit* (1st ed.). New York, NY: John Wiley & Sons.

King, J. L., Gurbaxani, V., Kraemer, K. L., McFarlan, F. W., Raman, K. S., & Yap, C. S. (1994). Institutional Factors in Information Technology Innovation. *Information Systems Research, 5*(2), 139–169. doi:10.1287/isre.5.2.139

Klimberg, R. K., & Miori, V. (2010). Back in business. *ORMS, 37*(5).

Kloby, K., & Callahan, K. (2009). Aligning government performance and community outcome measurement. *The Public Manager*, 19-26.

KMWorld. (2008). *Developing a Universal Search Strategy (Hint: Start with Usability)*. Retrieved January 16, 2009, from http://www.kmworld.com/Webinars/90-Developing-a-Universal-Search-Strategy-(Hint-Start-with-Usability).htm

Knight, M. (2008). *BI growth to buck economic trends*. Retrieved from http://www.itpro.co.uk/183480/bi-growth-to-buck-economic-trends

Kobayashi, N., Inui, K., & Matsumoto, Y. (2007). Opinion mining from web documents: extraction and structurization. *Information and Media Technologies, 2*(1), 326–337.

Kosambia, S., & Mandhana, S. (2008). *Enterprise intelligence everywhere*. BI Review Online.

Kotadia, M. (2006). *Business intelligence lies beyond IT: Dresner*. Retrieved from http://www.zdnet.com.au/business-intelligence-lies-beyond-it-dresner-139240318.htm

Ku, L. W., Huang, T. H., & Chen, H. H. (2009). Using morphological and syntactic structures for Chinese opinion analysis. In *Proceedings of the Conference on Empirical Methods in Natural Language Processing* (pp. 1260-1269).

Ku, L. W., & Chen, H. H. (2007). Mining opinions from the web: Beyond relevance retrieval. *Journal of the American Society for Information Science and Technology, 58*(12), 1838–1850. doi:10.1002/asi.20630

Labio, W., Yang, J., Cui, Y., Garcia-Molina, H., & Widom, J. (2000). Performance issues in incremental warehouse maintenance. In *Proceedings of the 26th International Conference on Very Large Data Bases*, Cairo, Egypt (pp. 461-472).

Lager, W. (2009, May 26). *Web Analytics market to Hit the Billion-Dollar Mark by 2014*. Retrieved April 23, 2010, from http://www.destinationcrm.com/Articles/CRM-News/Daily-News/Web-Analytics-Market-to-Hit-the-Billion-Dollar-Mark-by-2014-53957.aspx

Lam, K., & Lee, V. C. S. (2006). On consistent reading of entire databases. *IEEE Transactions on Knowledge and Data Engineering, 18*(4).

Landes, E. (2005). *Test Driven Development for a Business Intelligence Projects with Crystal Reports*. Retrieved March 8, 2009, from http://aspalliance.com/712

Larman, C. (2004). *Agile and iterative development: A manager's guide*. Upper Saddle River, NJ: Pearson Education.

Lavalle, S., Hopkins, M., Lesser, E., Shockley, R., & Kruschwitz, N. (2010). *Analytics: The new path to value*. MIT Sloan Management Review.

Lee, K. Y., Son, J. H., & Kim, M. H. (2001). Efficient incremental view maintenance in data warehouses. In *Proceedings of the Tenth International Conference on Information and Knowledge Management*, Atlanta, GA (pp. 349-256).

Leon, M. (2001, December 17). Merging Analytics and Intelligence. *InfoWorld*, 34–35.

Levy, E. (n. d.). *Ten mistakes to avoid when estimating ROI for business intelligence*. Retrieved from http://www.bi-bestpractices.com/view-articles/4781

Lewis, J., & Neher, K. (2007). Over the waterfall in a barrel - MSIT adventures in scrum. In *Proceedings of the AGILE Conference* (pp. 389-394). Washington, DC: IEEE Computer Society.

Lindsey, K., & Frolick, M. N. (2003). Critical factors for data warehousing failures. *Journal of Data Warehousing, 8*(1), 48–54.

Liu, B. (2010). Sentiment analysis and subjectivity. In Indurkhya, N., & Damerau, F. J. (Eds.), *Handbook of natural language processing* (2nd ed.). New York, NY: ACM Press.

Lovelock, C. H., & Yip, G. S. (1996). Developing global strategies for service businesses. *California Management Review, 38*(2), 64–86.

Love, R., Goth, J., Budde, F., Schilling, D., & Woffenden, B. (2006). *Understanding the demand for air travel: How to compete more effectively*. Boston, MA: Boston Consulting Group.

Lucker, J. (2010). *The BI and analytics treadmill*. Retrieved from http://techdecisions.com/Issues/2010/March/Pages/The-BI-and-Analytics-Treadmill.aspx

Lu, H., Feng, L., & Han, J. (2000). Beyond intratransaction association analysis: Mining multidimensional intertransaction association rules. *ACM Transactions on Information Systems, 18*(4), 423–454. doi:10.1145/358108.358114

Luhn, H. (1958). A business intelligence system. *IBM Journal of Research and Development, 2*(4), 314. doi:10.1147/rd.24.0314

Luhn, H. P. (1958). A business intelligence system. *IBM Journal of Research and Development, 2*(4), 314–319. doi:10.1147/rd.24.0314

Lyytinen, K. J., Keil, T., & Fomin, V. V. (2008). A framework to build process theories of anticipatory Information and Communication Technology (ICT) Standardizing. *International Journal of IT Standards and Standardization Research, 6*(1), 1–38.

Lyytinen, K., & King, J. L. (2002). Around the cradle of the wireless revolution: the emergece and evolution of cellular telephony. *Telecommunications Policy, 26*(3-4), 97–100. doi:10.1016/S0308-5961(02)00002-2

MacMillan, L. (2008). *Strategies for building a successful business intelligence competency center (BICC).* Retrieved from http://www.dbta.com/Articles/Editorial/Trends-and-Applications/Strategies-for-Building-a-Successful-Business-Intelligence-Competency-Center-%28BICC%29-52022.aspx

MacMillan, L. (2010). *The full promise of business intelligence.* Retrieved from http://www.information-management.com/newsletters/

Marion, L. (2010). *Business intelligence software: 10 common mistakes.* Retrieved from http://itmanagement.earthweb.com/entdev/article.php/3776376/Business-Intelligence-Software-10-Common-Mistakes.htm

Markus, M. L., Majchrzak, A., & Gasser, L. (2002). A design theory for systems that support emergent knowledge processes. *Management Information Systems Quarterly, 26*(3), 179–212.

Martens, C. (2006). *Business intelligence at age 17.* Retrieved from http://www.computerworld.com/s/article/266298/BI_at_age_17

Martin, J. (2001). Alien intelligence. *The Journal of Business Strategy, 22*(2), 18–23. doi:10.1108/eb040153

Martin, L. (2010). *Director research and analytics: Organizations adopting workforce optimization technologies deliver strong results.* Alpharetta, GA: CedarCrestone.

Mason, R. (1986). Four Ethical Issues of the Information Age. *Management Information Systems Quarterly, 10*(1), 5–12. doi:10.2307/248873

Matignon, R. (2007). *Data mining using SAS enterprise miner.* New York: Wiley. doi:10.1002/9780470171431

Mattli, W. (2001). The politics and economics of international institutional standards setting: an introduction. *Journal of European Public Policy, 8*(3), 328–344. doi:10.1080/13501760110056004

McKendrick, J. (2009). *Business intelligence comes to the masses.* Retrieved from http://www.dbta.com/Articles/Editorial/Trends-and-Applications/Business-Intelligence-Comes-to-the-Masses--54648.aspx

McKinsey & Company. (2010). Five forces reshaping the global company. *McKinsey Quarterly.*

McKnight, W. (2003). Business intelligence requirements analysis, part 1. *DM Review, 13*(11), 50.

McTague, J. M. (2009). Overly Stimulating. *Barron's National Business and Financial Weekly, 89*(46), 36.

Mehra, V. (2005). Building a metadata-driven enterprise: A holistic approach. *Business Intelligence Journal, 10*(3), 7–16.

Melnik, G., & Maurer, F. (2004). Direct verbal communication as a catalyst of agile knowledge sharing. In *Proceedings of the Agile Development Conference* (pp. 21-31).

Melo, M. A. N., & Dumke de Medeiros, D. (2007). A model for analyzing the competitive strategy of health plan insurers using a system of competitive intelligence. *The TQM Magazine, 19*(3), 206–216. doi:10.1108/09544780710745630

Merante, J. A. (2009). *The digital frontier: The implications of evolving technology on strategic enrollment management.* Retrieved March 30, 2010, from http://www.blackboard.com

Miller, G. J., Brautman, D., & Gerlach, S. (2006). *Business intelligence competency centers: A team approach to maximizing competitive advantage.* Hoboken, NJ: John Wiley & Sons.

Miller, G., Beckwith, R., Fellbaum, C., Gross, D., & Miler, K. (1990). Introduction to WordNet: An on-line lexical database. *International Journal of Lexicography, 3*(4), 235–312. doi:10.1093/ijl/3.4.235

Miller, T. (2005). *Data and text mining: A business applications approach.* Upper Saddle River, NJ: Pearson.

Mintzberg, H., Raisinghani, D., & Theoret, A. (1976). The structure of "unstructured" decision processes. *Administrative Science Quarterly, 21*(2), 246–275. doi:10.2307/2392045

Mohania, M., & Kambayashi, Y. (2000). Making aggregate views self-maintainable. *Journal of Data and Knowledge Engineering, 32*(1), 87–109. doi:10.1016/S0169-023X(99)00016-6

Morabito, J., & Singh, M. (1993). A new approach to object-oriented analysis and design. In *Proceedings of the 11ᵗʰ International Conference of Object-Oriented Languages and Systems*, Santa Barbara, CA (pp. 45-55).

Morabito, J., Sack, I., & Bhate, A. (1999). *Organization modeling: Innovative architectures for the 21ˢᵗ century.* Upper Saddle River, NJ: Prentice Hall.

Morabito, J., & Stohr, E. (2009). Online analytical processing. In Hossein, B. (Ed.), *The handbook of technology management.* New York, NY: John Wiley & Sons.

Morien, R. (2005). Agile development of the database: A focal entity prototyping approach. In *Proceedings of the Agile Conference* (pp. 103-110).

Moss, L. (2009). Ten Mistakes to Avoid for Data Warehouse Project Managers. *Business Intelligence Journal.* Retrieved April 20, 2009, from http://www.tdwi.org/Publications/display.aspx?Id=7545#7

Mountain Goat Software. (2010). *An overview of scrum for agile software development.* Retrieved from http://www.mountaingoatsoftware.com/scrum/overview

Mrazek, J. (2003). ETL: The best-kept secret of success in data warehousing. *DM Review, 13*(6), 44–45.

Murthy, G., & Bing, L. (2008). Mining opinions in comparative sentences. In *Proceedings of the 22nd International Conference on Computational Linguistics* (pp. 18-22).

Naik, B., & Ragothaman, S. (2004). Using neural networks to predict MBA student success. *College Student Journal, 38*(1), 143–149.

Nakano, C. (2009, December 17). *How Integrated is Your Web Analytics Package and is That a Good Thing?* Retrieved from http://www.cmswire.com/cms/web-cms/how-integrated-is-your-web-analytics-package-and-is-that-a-good-thing-005763.php

Naor, M., & Pinkas, B. (2010). *Secure Accounting and Auditing on the Web.* Retrieved May 20, 2010, from http://www.pinkas.net/PAPERS/www7paper/p336.htm

Nash, K. (2010). Analyzing the future: When business intelligence is used to inform business process changes, companies find new ways to save money and connect more closely with customers. *CIO, 23*(14).

Negash, S., & Gray, P. (2003). *Business intelligence.* Paper presented at the Ninth Americas Conference on Information Systems.

Neter, J., Kutner, M., Wasserman, W., & Nachtsheim, C. (1996). *Applied linear statistical models* (4th ed.). New York: McGraw Hill/Irwin.

Newell, A. (1981). The knowledge level. *AI Magazine,* 1–19.

Newell, A. (1982). The knowledge level. *Artificial Intelligence, 18*(1), 87–127. doi:10.1016/0004-3702(82)90012-1

Newell, A., & Simon, H. A. (1972). *Human problem solving* (1st ed.). Upper Saddle River, NJ: Prentice Hall.

Newell, E. (2009). For good measure. *Government Executive, 41*(8), 18–19.

Nonaka, I. (1994). A dynamic theory of organizational knowledge creation. *Organization Science, 5*(1), 24. doi:10.1287/orsc.5.1.14

Nonaka, I., & Takeuchi, H. (1995). *The knowledge-creating company.* New York, NY: Oxford University Press.

Nucleus Research Inc. (2004). *ROI Case Study: Teradata Harrah's Entertainment, E65.* Retrieved from http://nucleusresearch.com/research/roi-case-studies/roi-case-study-teradata-harrahs-entertainment/

Nucleus Research Inc. (2005). *ROI case study: Cognos United States Coast Guard, F66.* Retrieved from http://nucleusresearch.com/research/roi-case-studies/roi-case-study-cognos-united-states-coast-guard/

Nucleus Research Inc. (2008). *ROI Case Study: IBM Cognos TM1 Blue Mountain Resorts, 165.* Retrieved from http://nucleusresearch.com/research/roi-case-studies/roi-case-study-cognos-blue-mountain-resorts/

Nucleus Research Inc. (2009). ROI case study: IBM Cognos BI Competency Center Martin's Point. *Health Care, J40,* Retrieved from http://nucleusresearch.com/research/roi-case-studies/roi-case-study-ibm-cognos-bicc-martins-point-health-care/.

O'Brien, J. A., & Marakas, G. M. (2007). *Introduction to information systems* (13th ed.). New York, NY: McGrawHill.

Oltsik, J. (2009). *Security management evolution.* http://q1labs.com/resource-center/analyst-reports/details.aspx?id=18

Omniture. (2010). *Omniture Genesis.* Retrieved May 20, 2009, from http://www.omniture.com/da/products/marketing_integration/genesis

Oracle Corporation. (2009). *HR analytics: Driving return on human capital investment.* Retrieved from http://www.oracle.com/us/products/applications/045039.pdf

Page, B. (2009). *Is This the Future of Web Analytics?* Retrieved April 22, 2010, from http://bobpage.net/2009/01/11/is-this-the-future-of-web-analytics/

Pang, B., & Lee, L. (2008). *Opinion mining and sentiment analysis.* Boston, MA: Boston Publishers.

Parsons, D., Lal, R., Ryu, H., & Lange, M. (2007, December 5-7). Software development methodologies, agile development and usability engineering. In *Proceedings of the 18th Australasian Conference on Information Systems,* Toowoomba, Australia (pp. 172-178).

Pask, G. (1975). *Conversation, Cognition, and Learning.* New York: Elsevier.

Patil, A. (2008). *Agile data warehousing - applying agile development methodology to DW development.* Retrieved from http://infonitive.com/?p=43

Payton, F., & Handfield, R. (2004). *Strategies for data warehousing.* MIT Sloan Management Review.

Pedersen, M. K., Fomin, V. V., & Vries, H. J. d. (2009). The Open Standards and Government Policy. In Jakobs, K. (Ed.), *ICT Standardization for E-Business Sectors: Integrating Supply and Demand Factors* (pp. 188–199). Hershey, PA: IGI Global.

Pei, J., Han, J., & Wang, W. (2002). Mining sequential patterns with constraints in large databases. In *Proceedings of the 11th ACM Conference on Information and Knowledge Management,* McLean, VA (pp. 18-25). New York, NY: ACM Press.

Peterman, B. (2010). *Crossing the chasm between IT and business teams with new approaches to business intelligence.* Retrieved from http://www.b-eye-network.com/view/13980

Phillips, N. (2010). *Achieve business intelligence project success with executive sponsorship.* Retrieved from https://community.altiusconsulting.com/blogs/noelphillips/archive/2010/03/05/achieve-business-intelligence-project-success-with-executive-sponsorship.aspx

Polanyi, M. (1966). *The tacit dimension.* Garden City, NY: Doubleday.

Poolet, M. A. (2009). 7 steps for successful data warehouse projects. *SQL Server Magazine,* 29-34.

Porter, M. E. (1979). How competitive forces shape strategy. *Harvard Business Review, 57*(2), 137–145.

Porter, M. E. (1980). *Competitive strategy: techniques for analyzing industries and competitors.* Toronto: Maxwell Macmillan Canada.

Purcell, D. E. (2007). *Presentation on course for Strategic Standardization at the School of Engineering, Catholic University of America.* Delft, The Netherlands: Delft University of Technology.

Q1Labs. (2009). *A proactive approach to battling today's complex network threats.* Retrieved from http://q1labs.com/resource-center/white-papers/details.aspx?id=29

Q1Labs. (2009). *The business case for a next-generation SIEM.* Retrieved from http://q1labs.com/resource-center/white-papers/details.aspx?id=27

Quinn, K. R. (2007). *Worst practices in business intelligence: Why BI applications succeed where BI tools fail.* Retrieved from http://www.b-eye-network.com/files/2007%20Information%20Builders%20Worst%20Practices%20in%20BI%20WP.pdf

Radev, D. R., Qi, H., Zheng, Z., Blair-Goldensohn, S., Zhang, Z., Fan, W., & Prager, J. (2001). Mining the Web for Answers to Natural Language Questions. In *Proceedings of the Tenth International Conference on Information and Knowledge Management,* Atlanta, GA (pp. 143-150). New York: ACM.

Radin, B. A. (1998). The Government Performance and Results Act (GPRA): Hydra-heade monster or flexible management tool? *Public Administration Review,* (n.d.), 307–316. doi:10.2307/977560

Rahman, N. (2007). Refreshing data warehouses with near real-time updates. *Journal of Computer Information Systems, 47*(3), 71–80.

Rahman, N. (2010). Incremental load in a data warehousing environment. *International Journal of Intelligent Information Technologies, 6*(3). doi:10.4018/jiit.2010070101

Rahman, N., Burkhardt, P. W., & Hibray, K. W. (2010). Object migration tool for data warehouses. *International Journal of Strategic Technology and Applications, 1*(4), 55–73. doi:10.4018/jsita.2010100104

Ralph, K., & Ross, M. (2002). *The data warehouse toolkit: The complete guide to dimensional modeling* (2nd ed.). New York, NY: John Wiley & Sons.

Ranjan, J. (2008). Business justification with business intelligence. *Vine, 38*(4), 461–475. doi:10.1108/03055720810917714

Rizzotto, R. (2007, June). *Adding Intelligence to Web Analytics.* Retrieved from http://www.domodomain.com/press/IDC_WHITEPAPER.pdf

Robbins, S. P. (1990). *Organization theory: Structure, design, and applications.* Upper Saddle River, NJ: Prentice Hall.

Roberts, N. (2000). The synoptic model of strategic planning and the GPRA: lacking a good fit with the political context. *Public Productivity & Management Review, 23*(3), 297–311. doi:10.2307/3380721

Robles-Flores, J. (2009). *Web Question Answering Technology: An Empirical Test of the Task-Technology Fit Model.* Unpublished doctoral dissertation, Arizona State University, Tempe, AZ.

Rollings, M. (2010). *Too much automation, not enough insight -- the redefinition of BI.* Retrieved from http://blogs.computerworlduk.com/computerworld-archive/2010/03/too-much-automation-not-enough-insight--the-redefinition-of-bi/index.htm

Rouach, D., & Santi, P. (2001). Competitive intelligence adds value: five intelligence attitudes. *European Management Journal, 19*(5), 552–559. doi:10.1016/S0263-2373(01)00069-X

Roussinov, D., & Robles-Flores, J. (2004). Self-Learning Web Question Answering System. In *Proceedings of the 13th International World Wide Web Conference (WWW2004)*, New York.

Roussinov, D., & Robles-Flores, J. (2004). Web Question Answering: Technology and Business Applications. In *Proceedings of the Tenth Americas Conference on Information Systems*, New York.

Roussinov, D., Robles-Flores, J., & Ding, J. (2004). Experiments with Web QA System and TREC2004 Questions. In *Proceedings of the TREC 2004 Conference*, Gaithersburg, MD.

Roussinov, D., Fan, W., & Robles-Flores, J. (2008). Beyond Keywords: Automated Question Answering on the Web. *Communications of the ACM, 51*(9), 60–65.

Roussinov, D., & Robles-Flores, J. (2007). Applying Question Answering Technology to Locating Malevolent Online Content. *Decision Support Systems, 43*(4).

Royce, W. W. (1970). Managing the development of large software systems. In *Proceedings of the 9th International Conference on Software Engineering* (pp. 328-338). Washington, DC: IEEE Computer Society.

Sankaran, V. (2002). *Justifying your BI project in these times of need.* Retrieved from http://www.gantthead.com/article.cfm?ID=93697

SAS Institute. (2009, February 4). *SAS Achieves Record Revenue: $2.26 Billion in 2008: SAS Institute Press Release.* Retrieved on from http://www.sas.com/news/prereleases/2008financials.html

SAS. (2010). *Technologies/enterprise intelligence platforms.* Retrieved from http://findaccountingsoftware.com/directory/sas-institute/sas-financial-intelligence/sas-enterprise-intelligence-platform/

Schepel, H. (2005). The Constitution Of Private Governance: Product Standards. In *The Regulation Of Integrating Markets* (*Vol. 4*). Oxford, UK: Hart Publishing.

Schiesser, R. (2010). *IT systems management* (2nd ed.). Upper Saddle River, NJ: Prentice Hall.

Sen, A., Dacin, P. A., & Pattichis, C. (2006)... *Communications of the ACM, 49*(11), 85–91. doi:10.1145/167838.1167842

Sherman, R. (2010). *Business intelligence vendors, BI buyers could do more with less.* Retrieved from http://search-businessanalytics.techtarget.com/news/2240022985/Business-intelligence-vendors-BI-buyers-could-do-more-with-less

Shore, J. (2008). *The decline and fall of agile.* Retrieved from http://jamesshore.com/Blog/The-Decline-and-Fall-of-Agile.html

Sierra, K. (2006). *Why face-to-face still matters!* Retrieved from http://headrush.typepad.com/creating_passionate_users/2006/04/why_facetoface_.html

Silverstein, C., Brin, S., Motwani, R., & Ullman, J. (1998). Scalable techniques for mining causal structures. In *Proceedings of the International Conference on Very Large Databases,* New York, NY (pp. 594-605). San Francisco, CA: Morgan Kaufmann.

Simitsis, A., Vassiliadis, P., & Sellis, T. (2005). Optimizing ETL processes in data warehouses. In *Proceedings of the 21st International Conference on Data Engineering* (pp. 564-575).

Simon, H. A. (1973). The organization of complex systems. In Pattee, H. H. (Ed.), *Hierarchy theory: The challenge of complex systems.* New York, NY: George Braziller.

Simon, H. A. (1981). *The sciences of the artificial.* Cambridge, MA: MIT Press.

Sims, C. (2009). *Empirical Studies Show Test Driven Development Improves Quality, InfoQ.* Retrieved April 16, 2009, from http://www.infoq.com/news/2009/03/TDD-Improves-Quality

Sirota, D., Mischkind, L. A., & Meltzer, M. I. (2005). *The enthusiastic employee: How companies profit by giving workers what they want.* Philadelphia, PA: Wharton School Publishing.

Smalltree, H. (2006). *BI's founding father speaks: Q&A with Howard Dresner.* Retrieved from http://searchdatamanagement.techtarget.com/news/interview/0,289202,sid91_gci1174419,00.html.

Smyth, P., Pregibon, D., & Faloutsos, C. (2002). Data-driven evolution of data mining algorithms. *Communications of the ACM, 45*(8), 33–37. doi:10.1145/545151.545175

Sommerville, I. (2010). *Software engineering* (9th ed.). Reading, MA: Addison-Wesley.

SourceFire. (2009). *Network awareness: Continuous network intelligence and network visibility.* Retrieved from http://www.sourcefire.com/products/3D/rna

Sparck Jones, K., & van Rijsbergen, C. (1975). *Report on the need for and provision of an "Ideal" Information retrieval test collection (British Library Research and Development Rep. No. 5266).* Cambridge, UK: Computer Laboratory, University of Cambridge.

Srikant, R., & Agrawal, R. (1996). Mining quantitative association rules in large relational tables. In *Proceedings of the ACM SIGMOD International Conference on Management of Data,* Montreal, QC, Canada (pp. 1-12). New York, NY: ACM Press.

Stam, A. (2007). *EDW: The four biggest reasons for failure.* Retrieved from http://license.icopyright.net/user/viewFreeUse.act?fuid=NTcwOTYzMA%3D%3D

Stewart, G. (2004). Defining the enrollment manager: Visionary, facilitator, and collaborator. *Journal of College Admission, 183,* 21–25.

Stiens, K. P., & Turley, S. L. (2010). Uncontracting: The move back to performing in-house. *The Air Force Law Review, 65,* 145–186.

Stokes, D. E. (1997). *Pasteur's Quadrant: Basic Science and Technological Innovation.* Washington, DC: Brookings Institution Press.

Storey, V. C., & Goldstein, R. C. (1993). Knowledge-based approaches to database design. *Management Information Systems Quarterly, 17*(1), 25–46. doi:10.2307/249508

Stough, R. R., Haynes, K. E., & Campbell, J. H. (1998). Small business entrepreneurship in the high technology services sector: an assessment for the edge cities of the U.S. national capital region. *Small Business Economics, 10,* 61–74. doi:10.1023/A:1007930720118

Strong, D. M., Lee, Y. W., & Wang, R. Y. (1997). Data quality in context. *Communications of the ACM, 40*(5). doi:10.1145/253769.253804

Sturgeon, T. (1958). Sturgeon's revelation. *Venture Science Fiction, 2,* 66.

Su, Q., Xu, X., Guo, H., Guo, Z., Wu, X., Zhang, X., et al. (2008). Hidden sentiment association in Chinese web opinion mining. In *Proceedings of the International World Wide Web Conference* (pp. 959-968).

Subrahmanian, V. S. (2009). Mining online opinions. *Computer, 42*(7), 88–90. doi:10.1109/MC.2009.229

Sullivan, P. H. (1998). Basic definitions and concepts. In Sullivan, P. H. (Ed.), *Profiting from intellectual capital: Extracting value from innovation.* New York, NY: John Wiley & Sons.

Surowiecki, J. (2005). *The Wisdom of Crowds.* New York: Anchor Books.

Sutcliff, M. (2004). Beyond ROI: Justifying a business intelligence initiative. *DM Review, 14*(1), 44.

Sutton, P. (2007). A brief history of the enrollment management industry. *Innovation Ads*, 1-2.

Swaminathan, J. M. (2001). Enabling customization using standardized operations. *California Management Review, 43*(3), 125–135.

Swoyer, S. (2010). *Pervasive business intelligence: Still not a vision, not reality.* Retrieved from http://tdwi.org/articles/2010/01/20/pervasive-bi-still-a-vision-not-reality.aspx

Symantec. (2007). *W32. SillyFDC.* Retrieved from http://www.symantec.com/security_response/writeup.jsp?docid=2006-071111-0646-99

Symantec. (2010). *Symantec Endpoint Protection 11.0.6 Advanced Workshop.* Retrieved from http://www.symantec.com

Takeuchi, H., & Nonaka, I. (1986). The new new product development game. *Harvard Business Review.*

Tang, H., Tan, S., & Cheng, X. (2009). A survey on sentiment detection of reviews. *Expert Systems with Applications, 36*, 10760–10773. doi:10.1016/j.eswa.2009.02.063

TeaLeaf. (n.d.). *TeaLeaf.* Retrieved April 22, 2010, from http://www.tealeaf.com

Technologies, E. (2008). *Why Data Warehouse Projects Fail.* Retrieved April 16, 2009, from http://www.embarcadero.com/resources/technical_papers/Why-Data-Warehouse-Projects-Fail.pdf

Teradata. (2010). *Teradata professional services helps to establish business intelligence competency center.* Retrieved from http://www.rfpconnect.com/news/2010/9/8/teradata-professional-services-helps-to-establish-business-intelligence-competency-center

Test-Driven Development. (n.d.). Wikipedia. Retrieved March 8, 2009, from http://en.wikipedia.org/wiki/Test-driven_development

Thayer, S. (2010). *Web Analytics limitations...and a Bright Future.* Retrieved April 22, 2010, from http://www.trendingupward.net/2010/01/web-analytics-limitations-bright-future/

The Recovery Accountability and Transparency Board. (2011). *Recovery.gov Track the Money.* Retrieved March 15, 2011, from http://www.recovery.gov

The Standish Group. (1995). *Chaos.* Retrieved from http://www.projectsmart.co.uk/docs/chaos-report.pdf

Thelwall, M., Wilkinson, D., & Uppal, S. (2010). Data mining emotion in social network communication: Gender differences in MySpace. *Journal of the American Society for Information Science and Technology, 61*(1), 190–199.

TNCR. (2008). People, process, and technology. *Journal of Management Excellence*, 4-5.

Toth, R. B. (1997). *Profiles of National Standards-Related Activities.* NIST.

Transparency International. (2010). *2010 Transparency International Corruption Perception Index.* Retrieved February 28, 2011, from Transparency International: http://www.transparency.org/policy_research/surveys_indices/cpi/2010/results

Trim, P. R. J. (2004). The strategic corporate intelligence and transformational marketing model. *Marketing Intelligence & Planning, 22*(2-3), 240–256. doi:10.1108/02634500410525896

Truviso. (2010). *Visitor-Centric Web Analytics Build Better Relationships with Visitors to Improve Engagement, Optimize Conversion, and Increase Revenue.* Retrieved from http://www.truviso.com/docs/Truviso_Visitor_Analytics_whitepaper_201004.pdf

Tung, A. K. H., Han, J., Lu, H., & Feng, L. (2003). Efficient mining of intertransaction association rules. *IEEE Transactions on Knowledge and Data Engineering, 15*(1), 43–56. doi:10.1109/TKDE.2003.1161581

Turban, E., Sharda, S., Aronson, J. E., & King, D. (2008). *Business intelligence: A managerial approach.* Upper Saddle River, NJ: Prentice Hall.

Tzu, S. (2005). The art of war. In Clavell, J. (Ed.), *The art of war* (p. 82). Boston, MA: Shambhala Publications.

U.S. Department of Defense. (1985). *DOD-STD-2167: Defense system software development.* Retrieved from http://www.everyspec.com/DoD/DoD-STD/DOD-STD-2167_278/

Ulrich, W. (2009, February 25). *IT centralization versus decentralization: The trend towards collaborative governance.* Retrieved from http://www.cutter.com/content/trends/fulltext/updates/2000/09/bttu000901.html

Ulrich, W. M. (2009). *IT centralization versus decentralization: The trend towards collaborative governance.* Retrieved from http://www.systemtransformation.com/Org_Transformation_Articles/org_decentralization.htm

Ultraseek. (2006). *Business Search vs. Consumer Search: Five Differences Your Company Can't Afford to Ignore.* Retrieved from http://publications.autonomy.com/pdfs/Ultraseek/White%20Papers/mk0759_Business_v_Consumer_WP.pdf

Unica Corporation. (2009). *Unica Corp Form 10-K.* Waltham, MA: Unica Corporation.

US EPA. (2011). *Accomplishments and Performance Measures | Superfund | US EPA.* Retrieved from Accomplishments and Performance Measures | Superfund | US EPA: http://www.epa.gov/superfund/accomplishments.htm

US National Library of Medicine. (2010). Retrieved March 15, 2011, from TOXMAP - TRI and Superfund Environmental Maps: http://toxmap.nlm.nih.gov

US Office of Management and Budget. (2010). *All Agencies | Federal IT Dashboard.* Retrieved March 6, 2011, from http://it.usaspending.gov/?q=portfolios

Voorhees, E. M., & Buckland, L. P. (2005). *Proceedings of the Sixteenth Text REtrieval Conference (TREC 2005),* Gaithersburg, MD.

WAA. (2010). Retrieved May 25, 2010, from http://www.webanalyticsassociation.org/?page=privacy

WAA. (2010). *Privacy House Bill Draft 5-1.* Retrieved May 25, 2010, from http://www.webanalyticsassociation.org/resource/resmgr/PDF_static/Privacy_House_Bill_Draft_5-1.pdf

Waddock, S. A., & Graves, S. B. (1997). The Corporate Social Performance & Financial Performance Link. *Strategic Management Journal, 18,* 303–319. doi:10.1002/(SICI)1097-0266(199704)18:4<303::AID-SMJ869>3.0.CO;2-G

Wallace, J. (2007). *Seattle PI business.* Retrieved from http://www.seattlepi.com/business/

Walling, S. (2009, August 4). *Webtrends 9: Google Analytics Eat Your Heart Out.* Retrieved April 22, 2010, from http://www.readwriteweb.com/enterprise/2009/08/webtrends-9-google-analytics-eat-your-heart-out.php

Wang, W., & Zhou, Y. (2009). E-business websites evaluation based on opinion mining. In *Proceedings of the International Conference on Electronic Commerce and Business Intelligence* (pp. 87-90).

Wang, H., & Wang, S. (2008). A knowledge management approach to data mining process for business intelligence. *Industrial Management & Data Systems, 108*(5), 622–634. doi:10.1108/02635570810876750

Watson, H., & Ariyachandra, T. (2006). Benchmarks for BI and Data Warehousing Success. *DM Review, 16*(1).

Watson, H. (2009). Tutorial: Business Intelligence – Past, Present, and Future. *Communications of the Association for Information Systems, 25*(39), 487–510.

Watson, H. J., Ariyachandra, T., & Fuller, C. (2004). Data warehousing governance: Best practices at Blue Cross Blue Shield of North Carolina. *Decision Support Systems, 38*(3). doi:10.1016/j.dss.2003.06.001

Watson, H. J., Wixom, B. H., Hoffer, J. A., Anderson-Lehman, R., & Reynolds, A. M. (2006). Real-time business intelligence: Best practices at continental airlines. *Information Systems Management, 23*(1), 12. doi:10.1201/1078.10580530/45769.23.1.20061201/91768.2

Watson, H., Ariyachandra, T., & Fuller, C. (2004). Data Warehousing Governance: Best Practices at Blue Cross Blue Shield of North Carolina. *Decision Support Systems, 38*(3). doi:10.1016/j.dss.2003.06.001

Webtrends. (n.d.). *Webtrends*. Retrieved April 22, 2010, from http://www.webtrends.com

Weill, W., Subramani, M., & Broadbent, M. (2002). *Building IT infrastructure for strategic agility*. MIT Sloan Management Review.

Wells, D. (1999). *The XP Philosophy*. Retrieved April 12, 2009, from http://www.extremeprogramming.org/Kent.html

Wells, D. (2000). *Code the Unit Test First*. Retrieved April 12, 2009, from http://www.extremeprogramming.org/rules/testfirst.html

West, J. (2006). The Economic Realities of Open Standards: Black, White and Many shades of Gray. In Greenstein, S., & Stango, V. (Eds.), *Standards and Public Policy*. Cambridge, UK: Cambridge University Press. doi:10.1017/CBO9780511493249.004

Whiting, R. (2004, April 19). *Centralized intelligence at work*. Retrieved from http://www.informationweek.com/news/software/integration/showArticle.jhtml?articleID=18901738

Whiting, R. (2006, May 29). Businesses mine data to predict what happens next. *Information Week*, p. 5.

Whiting, R. (2004). *Centralized intelligence at work*. Information Week.

Widom, J. (1995). Research problems in data warehousing. In *Proceedings of the 4th International Conference on Information and Knowledge Management* (pp. 25-30).

Wikipedia. (2010). *Multivariate Testing*. Retrieved April 20, 2010, from http://en.wikipedia.org/wiki/Multivariate_testing

Wikipedia. (n. d.). *Rate of return*. Retrieved from http://en.wikipedia.org/wiki/Rate_of_return

Wikipedia. (n. d.). *Security event manager*. Retrieved from http://en.wikipedia.org/wiki/Security_event_manager

Williams, L., Shukla, A., & Anton, A. I. (2004). An initial exploration of the relationship between pair programming and Brooks' Law. In *Proceedings of the Agile Development Conference* (pp. 11-20).

Williams, S. (2008). *BeyeNETWORK: Business intelligence business requirements and the BI portfolio*. Retrieved from http://www.b-eye-network.com/view/6887

Wilson, T. (2009). *Reports: Security pros shift attention from external hacks to internal threats*. Retrieved from http://www.darkreading.com/insiderthreat/security/vulnerabilities/showArticle.jhtml?articleID=215801195

Wixom, B. H., & Watson, H. J. (2001). An empirical investigation of the factors affecting data warehousing success. *Management Information Systems Quarterly, 25*(1), 17. doi:10.2307/3250957

Wixom, B., & Watson, H. (2010). The bi-based organization. *International Journal of Business Intelligence Research, 1*(1). doi:10.4018/jbir.2010071702

Wixom, B., & Watson, H. J. (2001). Data warehouse critical success. *Management Information Systems Quarterly, 12*(24), 210–245.

Wong, J. (2007). *Problems in Building a Data Warehouse, SQLServerCentral.com*. Retrieved April 20, 2009, from http://www.sqlservercentral.com/articles/Design/2832/

Wright, S., & Calof, J. L. (2006). The quest for competitive, business and marketing intelligence: A country comparison of current practices. [Commentary]. *European Journal of Marketing, 40*(5-6), 453–465. doi:10.1108/03090560610657787

WTO. (2005). *World Trade Report 2005: Exploring the Links between Trade, Standards and the WTO*. Geneva, Switzerland: World Trade Organization (WTO).

Wu, J., & Weitzman, N. (2006). *Information management*. Retrieved from http://www.information-management.com/issues/20060801/1060142-1.html?pg=1

Xiaowen, D., Bing, L., & Lei, Z. (2009). Entity discovery and assignment for opinion mining applications. In *Proceedings of the ACM International Conference on Knowledge Discovery and Data Mining*, Paris, France.

Yadav, S. B. (2009). A conceptual model for user-centered quality information retrieval on the world wide web. *Journal of Intelligent Information Systems, 35*(1), 91–121. doi:10.1007/s10844-009-0090-y

Yegge, S. (2006). *Good agile, bad agile.* Retrieved from http://steve-yegge.blogspot.com/2006/09/good-agile-bad-agile_27.html

Yermish, I., Miori, V., Yi, J., Malhotra, R., & Klimberg, R. (2010). Business plus intelligence plus technology equals business intelligence. *International Journal of Business Intelligence Research, 1*(1). doi:10.4018/jbir.2010071704

Yin, R. K. (2003). *Case study research: Design and methods* (3rd ed., pp. 5–7). Thousand Oaks, CA: Sage.

Young, R. M. (1995). Conceptual research. *Changes: An International Journal of Psychology and Psychotherapy, 13*, 145–148.

Yu, L., Ma, J., Tsuchiya, S., & Ren, F. (2008). Opinion mining: A study on semantic orientation analysis for online document. In *Proceedings of the 7th World Congress on Intelligent Control and Automation.*

Yu, T., & Lester, R. (2008). Moving beyond firm boundaries: a social network perspective on reputation spill over. *Corporate Reputation Review, 11*(1), 94–108. doi:10.1057/crr.2008.6

Zeid, A. (2006). Your BI competency center: A blueprint for successful deployment. *Business Intelligence Journal, 11*(3), 14–20.

Zhao, L., & Li, C. (2009). Ontology based opinion mining for movie review. In D. Karagiannis & Z. Jin (Eds.), *Proceedings of the Third International Conference on Knowledge Science, Engineering, and Management* (LNCS 5914, pp. 204-214).

About the Contributors

Richard Herschel is Chair of the Department of Decision & System Sciences at Saint Joseph's University in Philadelphia. Before becoming an educator, he worked at Maryland National Bank, Schering-Plough Corporation, Johnson & Johnson, and Columbia Pictures as a systems analyst. He received his BA in journalism from Ohio Wesleyan University, his Master's in Administrative Sciences from Johns Hopkins University, and his Ph.D. from Indiana University in Management Information Systems. He holds the Certified Systems Professional designation. Dr. Herschel has written extensively about business intelligence, and he is the Editor of the *International Journal of Business Intelligence Research*.

* * *

W.O. Dale Amburgey is Director of Enrollment Analysis at Saint Joseph's University. His research interests are in enrollment forecasting models, employee motivation, financial aid leveraging, and enrollment operations analysis. Prior to his current position, Dr. Amburgey served as Associate Director of Data Management and Analysis at Drexel University and as Director of Operations for Undergraduate Admissions at Embry-Riddle Aeronautical University. Dr. Amburgey earned degrees from the University of Central Florida, University of Louisville, Saint Joseph's University, and Transylvania University.

Thilini Ariyachandra is an Assistant Professor of MIS in the Williams College of Business at Xavier University in Cincinnati. Her research is focused on the selection, design, and implementation of decision support systems in organizations. She has published in journals such as Information Systems Management, Business Intelligence Journal, Communications of the ACM and Decision Support Systems. She is also a board member of the Teradata University Network, a free portal for faculty who teach and research data warehousing, BI/DSS, and database.

Ranjit Bose is a regents' professor of management and is currently the associate dean of the Anderson School of Management at The University of New Mexico in Albuquerque. His current research interests include design and application of intelligent technologies in e-business environment, opinion mining of subjective web data, and green IT. He has published in several management information systems and computer science journals. Bose has a PhD in management information systems from the University of Texas at Austin.

Françoise Bousquet, senior consultant, started her carrier as a Teacher of Mathematics. She then joined Burroughs as a system analyst, became the IT department manager in the French subsidiary of ARBED. She worked with SITA (the worldwide network offering IT solutions for the airline industry) for ten years, then joined AFNOR (The French National Standardization Body) as Information Technology and Applications Standardization Manager. She has been Standardization and Regulation Manager at Digital Equipment France for several years before joining Akela S.A,. in charge of the Strategic Consultancy activity on Standardization. She then founded ZFIB Conseil, providing consulting to companies from the market knowledge acquisition to the first sales, providing help and coaching when deciding the necessary strategy in terms of standards, marketing and sales. Françoise Bousquet holds the Chair on Standardization in the Specialized Master of Competitive Intelligence in EISTI (Ecole Internationale des Sciences du Traitement de l' Information), France.

Julie Smith David is an Associate Professor in the W. P. Carey School of Business at Arizona State University and the Director of the Center for Advancing Business through IT (CABIT). She gained industry experience as an Andersen Consultant and then as the Director of IT for one of her clients. Since returning to academics, she has built upon those experiences by performing research focused on enterprise applications (both traditionally delivered and those offered as services), their design, and how they can provide value to companies adopting them. This work has been published in journals including *Management Science, Communications of the ACM,* and the *Journal of Information Systems.*

Dominique Drillon, Associate Professor, joined La Rochelle business school in France in 2010. Prior to La Rochelle, he was Associate Professor at GSC Montpellier Business School from 1999 to 2010 and at Rennes Business School from 1990 to 1999. In 1995 he obtained PhD in Human Sciences from the University of Paris X Nanterre, France. Prior to starting his academic career, he spent many years as a cardio engineer in heart surgery, taking positions in Switzerland and in CHU Rennes in France. He holds a Master in Clinical Psychology and Psychoanalyst degree and has worked as a psychologist, coach and consultant for companies, people and sportsmen. His current research interests are focused on management, human resources, learning with ICT, quality of life at work, social auditing, corporate social responsibility, and sustainable development. He is also founder and past president of the Institut Psychanalyse et Management and member of the GSCM Research center (CEROM), which he directed in 2003-2007.

Irina Dymarsky has a broad base of experiences in the field of Information Technology and applied Business Intelligence (BI). Irina graduated from Drexel University with a dual Bachelor/Masters Degree in Information Systems and Technology. Post graduation, she joined Johnson and Johnson as a member of the rotational Information Technology Leadership Development Program. Her rotations included positions supporting regulatory compliance, sales and marketing, and technology standards. Irina's experiences in the field of BI range from implementations of dashboard reporting solutions to data warehouse mart and application enhancements. Irina has a MS in Business Intelligence degree and she is currently employed by Purdue Pharma L.P. where she is responsible for IT planning, communications and reporting.

Jami Eddington is a doctoral student of Management Science and Information Systems at Spears School of Business, Oklahoma State University. Ms Eddington holds a B.S. degree in Information Systems and Economics from Loyola University of Chicago, School of Business Administration where she also worked as a teaching and research assistant in both the Information Systems and Operations Management Department and the Economics Department. During her professional career, prior to joining doctoral program at Oklahoma State University, Ms. Eddington worked in a number of capacities at The McTigue Financial Group, including the position of a software specialist in which she spear-headed the agency's CRM initiative. Ms. Eddington's research interests include data mining, data warehousing, business intelligence, information assurance, and information security.

David Ellis is a supplier quality specialist in the aerospace industry. For over 25 years, he has performed surveillance over quality management systems implemented and maintained by manufacturers in the commercial and military sectors of the aerospace industry. In 2007, Mr. Ellis achieved certification by the American Society for Quality as a Certified Quality Auditor (ASQ-CQA). Mr. Ellis completed his master of science in business intelligence degree in 2011 and is already applying the mastery of analytical tools and decision-making methodologies to his daily coaching and counseling of aerospace suppliers to drive performance improvement. In addition, he also routinely works with, and on behalf of, the Federal Aviation Administration (FAA) to perform Conformity Inspections and other activities. Mr. Ellis resides in Pennsylvania with his wife, Jana and they have 3 grown children.

Vladislav V. Fomin is a professor at the department of Applied Informatics at Vytautas Magnus University in Kaunas, Lithuania, and a principal research fellow at The School of Business Administration Turība in Riga, Latvia. Fomin holds Dipl.Eng.Oec and MSc.BA degrees from the University of Latvia (1995, 1997), Licenciate and PhD degrees from the University of Jyväskylä in Finland (2000, 2001), and has conferred a procedure for Habilitation Degree at the Vytautas Magnus University in Kaunas, Lithuania (2008). After earning his PhD degree in 2001, Vladislav V. Fomin held academic positions at the University of Michigan in Ann Arbor (2001-3), Copenhagen Business School (2004-6), Delft University of Technology (2006), Montpellier Business School (2007), and Rotterdam School of Management, Erasmus University (2008). Fomin's current research interests include studies of development of information and communication technologies (ICT) infrastructure, studies of design and implementation of Information Systems (IS) in organizations, standard making processes in the field of ICT, as well studies of technology innovation. Vladislav has over 60 scientific publications in journals, conferences, and as book chapters, including Journal of Strategic Information Systems, Communications of the Association for Information Systems, International Journal of IT Standards & Standardization Research, Telecommunications Policy, Knowledge, Technology & Policy. He is serving on the editorial board of the International Journal of IT Standards & Standardization Research (JITSR), is a member of European Academy of Standardization (EURAS) and The Association for Information Systems (AIS).

Mark N. Frolick is a Professor of MIS in the Williams College of Business at Xavier University and the holder of the Western & Southern Chair in Management Information Systems. Dr. Frolick was formerly Professor of MIS and Associate Director of the FedEx Center for Cycle Time Research at The University of Memphis. This research center, which he and Dr. James C. Wetherbe established, was the result of a strategic alliance between FedEx and The University of Memphis. The purpose of the center was to conduct research concerning ways to reduce the time it takes to complete organizational processes. Dr. Frolick is considered to be a leading authority on business intelligence. His specialties include business performance management, business intelligence, data warehousing, executive information systems, e-business, cycle time reduction, and the diffusion of information technology in organizations. Dr. Frolick has authored over 120 articles. His research has appeared in such prestigious journals as *MIS Quarterly, Decision Sciences, Journal of Management Information Systems, Decision Support Systems, and Information & Management*. He also worked with Dr. James Wetherbe on the book *Systems Analysis and Design: Best Practices* (West Publishing, 1994). This book was ranked by Computing Newsletter as the top textbook on the topic. Additionally, Dr. Frolick serves as a consulting editor for several publishing companies.

Alex Gann is a Senior Supply Chain Analyst for BAE Systems, U.S. Combat Systems (USCS). For the past 5 years he has continuously worked to introduce, promote, and expand Business Intelligence best practices both within the Supply Chain group and USCS at large. Alex formed and leads the 100-plus-member Data Warehousing and Business Intelligence (DWBI) working group for all of USCS. Beyond theoretical BI concepts, Alex directly performs critical reporting and analytics for the company using Oracle BI Suite, MS Office, and Open Source Data Mining applications. Outside of BI, he has over a decade of experience developing professional websites for small and mid-sized businesses.

Yegin Genc is a second year PhD student in Information Management at Stevens Institute of Technology. He received his M.S. in Information Technology from the University of Central Missouri. Before coming to Stevens, he was working as a Business Process Consultant overseeing Business Process Management system implementations. He holds a B.S. in Mechanical Engineering from Istanbul Technical University.

Fletcher H. Glancy is an Assistant Professor of MIS at the School of Business and Entrepreneurship, Lindenwood University. He received his Bachelors of Science degree in mechanical engineering from Missouri S & T in 1970, his MBA from Texas Tech University in 2006, and his Ph.D. from the Rawls College of Business, Texas Tech University in 2010. He has 35 years of industry experience. His areas of interest include: business intelligence, text and data mining, linguistics, theory development, and analytical methodology.

Adam Hill is a Market Research Analyst with The Nielsen Company, at which he has worked on the Procter & Gamble and Red Bull North America businesses. He studied Information Systems as part of his Masters of Business Administration in International Business at Xavier University. He received his Bachelors of Science in Business Administration with concentrations in Marketing and Spanish from Saint Louis University.

Lakshmi Iyer is an Associate Professor in the Information Systems and Operations Management Department at the University of North Carolina, Greensboro. She obtained her PhD from the University of Georgia, Athens. Her research interests are in the area of e-business/e-commerce, health IT, emerging technologies, business intelligence, decision support systems and Knowledge Management. Her research work has been published or accepted for publication in *Journal of Association for Information Systems, European Journal of Information Systems, Communications of the ACM, eService Journal, Journal* *of Electronic Commerce Research, Decision Support Systems, Information Systems Management,* and others. Dr. Iyer has served or is serving as a Guest Editor for *Communications of the ACM,* the *Journal of Electronic Commerce Research,* and the *International Journal of E-Politics.* She is a Board member of Teradata University Network.

Brian Johnson is a business intelligence analyst with the Himalayan International Institute. He holds a BS in computer science and an MS in business intelligence. His concentration of work centers on information visualization and reporting, performance management, business process improvement, data analysis, and the application of information and data for humanitarian causes.

Nenad Jukic is a Professor of Information Systems and the Director of Graduate Certificate Program in Data Warehousing and Business Intelligence at Loyola University Chicago School of Business Administration. Dr. Jukic conducts active research in various information technology related areas, including data warehousing/business intelligence, database management, e-business, IT strategy, and data mining. His work was published in a number of management information systems and computer science academic journals, conference publications, and books. In addition to his academic work, his engagements include providing expertise to a range of data management, data warehousing, and business intelligence projects for U.S. military and government agencies, as well as for corporations that vary from startups to Fortune 500 companies.

Ken Lozito is a Threat and Vulnerability analyst specializing in Endpoint Protection and Intrusion Detection at GSK a major pharmaceutical company. Prior to GSK he has worked as a systems analyst at Unisys doing software delivery and patch management and has held various roles within IT for past 13 years. Additional specialties include information security policies and frameworks, Six Sigma, metrics and information presentation. He holds a BA in English and an MS in Business Intelligence.

Olivera Marjanovic specialises in business process innovation. Her research seeks to link business processes and IT in business, government and non-profit organisations and to assist them in effectively managing IT-enabled organisational process innovations. Olivera works particularly in the design and improvement of technically enabled, knowledge intensive, business processes. Olivera is co-founder and co-leader of the Business Process Management Research Group (BPMRG), University of Sydney. In 2007, she founded the inaugural BPM Minitrack in the International HICSS Conference and is currently the Australia-Pacific editor for Teradata University Network - the leading world-wide community of industry practitioners, thought leaders, academics and their students in the area of Business Intelligence (BI). In this role, Olivera is actively engaged in research and teaching related activities designed to enhance collaboration among industry and academic partners and hence improve BI-related teaching and research as well as create new opportunities for future BI practitioners.

Joseph Morabito is Associate Graduate Professor and Program Director for Knowledge Management in the Howe School of Technology Management at the Stevens Institute of Technology. He is a coauthor of *Organization Modeling* and other publications on architecture, modeling, and business intelligence. Formerly, Vice President of Business Intelligence and Data Architecture at the Union Bank of

Switzerland (UBS), and prior to that, research leader at Bell Communications Research in the areas of enterprise meta-models and object-oriented modeling.

Svetlozar Nestorov is a Senior Research Associate at the Computation Institute at the University of Chicago. Dr. Nestorov's research is centered around the management and mining of large amounts of data. He serves as the data architect for a number of collaborative projects with academic researchers in bioinformatics, economics, marketing, and physics. Dr. Nestorov is also involved with several venture-funded web 2.0 startups as a co-founder and an advisor.

Dan O'Neill is currently a manager of Global Implementations within the Enterprise Information Delivery group at Avon Products Inc. in Rye, NY. In his current role, he is responsible for leading multinational implementations and enhancements for the Avon Leadership Manager application. Prior to joining Avon, Dan worked for Gartner Inc. in Connecticut. Dan spent 5 years as a Senior Business Intelligence Analyst. In the role of Senior Business Intelligence Analyst, Dan was responsible for working across Gartner's business units to develop and release the reporting components of their BI reporting platform. In 2009, Dan was awarded Gartner's CFO award for excellence for his work on this project. Dan has extensive experience working within a centralized BI model and a business intelligence competency center (BICC). Dan has assumed the roles of BI application administrator, business analyst, data modeler, data quality analyst as well as a dashboard designer.

Rajeshwari M. Raman is a web analyst with Market America and has over 12 years of experience working at Citigroup, Nortel Networks, Glaxo Smithkline, and The Center for Creative Leadership in the field of Information Technology and Business Intelligence. She has been heavily involved in efforts to improve channel monetization and the optimization of campaign portfolios using Web Analytics. She will be receiving her MBA from the University of North Carolina at Greensboro in December 2010. Raman's research interests include integration of web analytics with social media, analysis of user behavior online and the integration of web analytics data with the data in the data warehouse using an integration of both quantitative and qualitative methods like statistics and data mining.

José Antonio Robles-Flores is an assistant professor (research track) at Universidad ESAN in Lima, Perú. His research interests are in the areas of information retrieval and knowledge management. He has published in Communications of the ACM, Decision Support Systems and the International Journal on Internet and Enterprise Management. He received his PhD from the W.P. Carey School of Business at Arizona State University, an MBA from ESAN Univeristy, and a bachelor's degree in computer science from Universidad Francisco Marroquin.

Robert Sawyer is an active duty Marine with over 19 years of honorable service currently serving with the Marine Corps Recruiting Command in Atlanta as a recruiter for the Marine Officer Commissioning Programs. Robert routinely analyzes various data ranging from prospecting to demographical to identify trends and develop into actionable insights to evaluate and select strategies that will drive the greatest impact to achieve recruiting objectives. Robert's passion to transform the culture of military recruiting into a data decision driven environment by implementing various BI initiatives has led to numerous awards and is recognized among his peers as a subject matter expert on operational efficiency.

Gregory Schymik is a PhD student in the Information Systems Department at the W. P. Carey School of Business. He holds a BSE in Computer Engineering from The University of Michigan and a MSCIS from The University of Detroit-Mercy. His research interests are in the areas of Enterprise Search, Knowledge Management, and Services Science, Management, and Engineering. His work has been published in journals including Decision Analysis, The Business Intelligence Journal, and in the proceedings of the HICSS and AMCIS conferences.

Sam Schutte is an MBA student at Xavier University majoring in Business Intelligence, and is the President of Unstoppable Software, Inc. (http://www.unstoppablesoftware.com), an electronic document management and business intelligence solution provider. He holds a BS in Computer Science from the University of Pittsburgh, and has over 10 years of software development experience working with early stage and established commercial software companies, as well as large industrial and healthcare firms. He specializes in utilizing Agile development techniques to deliver comprehensive electronic document and BI solutions to corporations.

Robert D. St. Louis is a Professor in the Information Systems Department at the W. P. Carey School of Business. He received his AB degree from Rockhurst College, and his MS and Ph.D. degrees from Purdue University. His research and teaching interests are in the areas of forecasting, data mining, and decision support systems. His work has been published in a variety of journals, including the *Academy of Management Journal, Decision Support Systems, Journal of Econometrics, Communications in Statistics*, and *Communications of the ACM.*

Edward A. Stohr is Professor of Information Systems and Co-Director of the Center for Technology Management Research at Stevens Institute of Technology. He received his MBA and Ph.D. from the University of California, Berkeley. Prior to joining Stevens in 2001, Professor Stohr was a faculty member at NYU's Stern School of Business, where he served for over ten years as Chair of the Department of Information Systems. His research focuses on the problems of developing computer systems to support work and decision making in organizations. He has published in leading management and information systems journals and is the co-editor of three books in the field of information systems. In 1991, he was General Chair of the International Conference on Information Systems (ICIS). He serves, or has served, as Associate Editor for *Information Systems Research, Journal of Management Information Systems, Decision Support Systems* and *Information Systems Frontiers*, among others.

Miguel Velasco is a PhD candidate in Information and Decision Science at the Carlson School of Management, University of Minnesota. Mr. Velasco conducts active research in various information technology related areas, including data warehousing/business intelligence, prediction markets, e-business, and data mining. Besides his academic work, Mr. Velasco's professional career included a position as a quality director of a major investment firm in Spain (Grupo Fineco), as well as collaboration and participation in various information systems and information technology projects within the finance industry.

Joe White is a technical consultant supporting enterprise information systems for U.S. government agencies. Mr. White's experience ranges from software development, data analysis, project management, and enterprise information technology strategic planning.

Carey Worth is a senior service delivery manager for a large financial institution. He currently manages a global reporting team responsible for developing reporting solutions for a global human resource technology department. He is also responsible for developing BI delivery standards. He often provides advice to senior management and business leaders on how to implement Business Intelligence solutions. He has over 25 years of technology experience including almost 12 year of banking experience. Carey began his career as a database developer producing report solutions. He later became a senior developer on a major enterprise application responsible for customer data integrity. He currently lives in Waxhaw, North Carolina and is married with two daughters.

Surya B. Yadav is the James & Elizabeth Sowell Professor of Telecom Technology in Rawls College of Business, Texas Tech University, Lubbock, Texas. He received his Bachelors of Science degree in electrical engineering from Banaras University in 1972, the M.Tech. degree from IIT Kanpur, India in 1974, and the Ph.D. degree in business information systems from Georgia State University, Atlanta in 1981. He has published in several journals including Communications of the ACM, IEEE Transactions on Software Engineering, IEEE Transactions on Systems, Man, and Cybernetics, Journal of Management Information Systems, Decision Support Systems, and Journal of Intelligent Information Systems. His research areas include intelligent information retrieval systems, text mining, and system security.

John C. Yi is an Assistant Professor of Decision and System Sciences in the Haub School of Business, Saint Joseph's University. His research interests are in modeling complex business problems using integration of quantitative methods including operations research, data mining, and knowledge management. Prior to his academic position, Dr. Yi was managing analytical projects involving marketing resource optimization, new and in-line product forecasting, strategic decision planning, sales operations optimization, product portfolio optimization, and manufacturing process improvement at Sanofi-Aventis (2 years), Johnson & Johnson (8 years), and GEC (2 years). Dr. Yi earned degrees from University of Pennsylvania, University of California at Berkeley, and Rutgers University.

Index

U

Ultraseek 182, 198
Unica 171, 179
unique ID mapping 268
UnitedHealth Group (UHG) 158
unit testing 202, 290, 293
University of Illinois at Chicago (UIC) 6
U.S. Department of Transportation (U.S. DOT) 119
user Information handler (UIH) 250
user model 268

V

virtual entity 147

W

waterfall model 278-279, 286-287, 290-292, 295, 297
web analytics 166-179
Web Analytics Association (WAA) 174
web opinion mining 98-99, 101-102, 111
Webtrends 169, 171, 180
Western Electronic Show and Convention (WesCon) 278
WikiAnswers 186, 195
WordNet 102-103, 111
word of mouth 97, 110
Working Groups (WGs) 21
working software 280, 294
World Wide Web Consortium (W3C) 21

Y

yield rate 5

CPSIA information can be obtained at www.ICGtesting.com
Printed in the USA
BVOW020816311012

304082BV00006B/16/P